Building Structures

Understanding the Basics

Third Edition

Malcolm Millais

Routledge
Taylor & Francis Group

LONDON AND NEW YORK

Third edition published 2017
by Routledge
2 Park Square, Milton Park, Abingdon, Oxon OX14 4RN

and by Routledge
711 Third Avenue, New York, NY 10017

Routledge is an imprint of the Taylor & Francis Group, an informa business

© 2017 Malcolm Millais

First edition published by Spon Press 1997

Second edition published by Routledge 2005

British Library Cataloguing-in-Publication Data
A catalogue record for this book is available from the British Library

Library of Congress Cataloging-in-Publication Data
Names: Millais, Malcolm, author.
Title: Building structures : understanding the basics / Malcolm Millais.
Description: Third edition. | New York : Routledge, 2017. |
Includes bibliographical references and index.
Identifiers: LCCN 2016036628| ISBN 9781138119741 (hb : alk. paper) |
ISBN 9781138119758 (pb : alk. paper) | ISBN 9781315652139 (ebook)
Subjects: LCSH: Buildings. | Structural design. | Structural analysis
(Engineering)
Classification: LCC TH845 .M63 2017 | DDC 690—dc23
LC record available at https://lccn.loc.gov/2016036628

ISBN: 978-1-138-11974-1 (hbk)
ISBN: 978-1-138-11975-8 (pbk)
ISBN: 978-1-315-65213-9 (ebk)

Publisher's Note
This book has been prepared from camera-ready copy provided by
the author

Printed in the United Kingdom
by Henry Ling Limited

Contents

Preface to the third edition

It was only during the 19th century that the idea arose that the structure of a building could be seen as separate from the concept of the building itself. Nowadays, the division between the architectural design of a building and the structural design is almost complete and this has led to numerous problems both large and small. This third edition aims, in various ways, to narrow this division with a consequent reduction in problems. Ideally, everyone involved in the commissioning, design, construction, alteration and maintenance of buildings should have a mature understanding of the structural aspects; unfortunately, this is not the current situation.

The key to this is the conceptual understanding of structural behaviour. This is explained by a combination of diagrams and written descriptions and **without recourse to any mathematics**. The basic concepts are explained in the first seven chapters, and remain the core of the book, with further chapters showing how the basic concepts apply to real buildings structures. The chapters that were added for the 2nd edition are retained, though some of the new chapters are interspersed.

To enable readers to gain a wider understanding, new material six new chapters have been added to this Third Edition. These are chapters about *Below-ground structures*, *Structures in existing buildings*, *Dynamic behaviour*, *Progressive collapse and robustness*, *The basis for computer calculations* and *The successful structural project*. These cover many topics that are usually only found in more advanced texts; however, the approach of using a combination of diagrams and written description without recourse to mathematics is retained as far as possible.

It is a pleasure to thank the following people: Andrew MacKeith, Vera d'Almeida Ribeiro, Wanda Lewis, Lesley Paine, and Stana Zivanovic for all the help they gave me. I would especially like to thank Michael Bussell, whose support by commenting, checking, giving references and sending technical information was invaluable in the preparation of the six new chapters.

Fran Ford and Trudy Varcianna at Taylor & Francis Ltd. were continuously supportive. Book production was very effectively carried out by Susan Leaper of Florence Productions Ltd.

The book design and the diagrams were done by the author.

Malcolm Millais 2017

Introduction

People are surrounded by natural and designed structures. They live in them, travel in them, eat with them, sleep on them, they contribute to almost every aspect of our lives. Indeed, humans, animals and plants are themselves structures. But few people give much thought to structures until they fail. Forks bend, glasses break, cars are wrecked in crashes, less often buildings and bridges collapse. These structural failures always cause inconvenience that may be minor, such as a broken glass, or major, involving loss of life and large financial cost such as the collapse of a bridge.

The horror of the attack on the World Trade Center towers on 11th September 2001 was not only the initial deliberate collision of large, fuel laden, passenger aircraft with the buildings but the subsequent dramatic collapse of both these enormous towers. These collapses, seen globally on television, caused not only great loss of life and enormous disruption to a major city but had a dramatic effect on the world political situation. The original designers had taken into account the possibility of an aircraft collision but not ones of the magnitude that actually occurred. So clearly it is important to know if structures are: **strong enough** and **stiff enough**.

For the designers of any structure, whether a fork or a bridge, there has to exist sufficient knowledge for them to feel confident that the proposed structure will be both strong enough and stiff enough under all reasonably foreseeable uses. There are also ancillary, but important requirements, such as whether the proposed structure is affordable or sufficiently durable.

These requirements seem perfectly reasonable but to satisfy them is not always so simple. Through the ages people have adopted various strategies to try and ensure that the structures they use are as safe as possible.

0.1 Pre-historic design

In pre-historical time people lived in small, more or less, self-contained groups. These groups would live as hunter-gatherers or perhaps herd animals. They would construct artefacts and shelters using natural materials and their designs, which would be typical for each group – see **Figs. 0.1** and **0.2** – were repeated endlessly. How these designs evolved is not known, nor how they were modified.

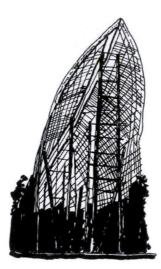

Fig. 0.1   Clubhouse structure in New Guinea

The origin of these designs is not known but they were built repetitively without any recorded form of instructions. Older members of the group would hand down their experience and often the construction process would be a group activity.

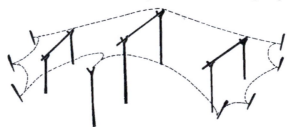

Fig. 0.2 Nomad tent structure

As the way of life of these groups was only changed temporarily by alterations in nature – such as droughts or storms – there was no need to make design changes, or to know how to make their structures stronger or stiffer.

0.2 Traditional design

With the discovery of agriculture in South West Asia in about 8000 BC the hunter-gatherers and nomads were gradually marginalised. The idea of cultivation meant that groups became geographically fixed; agricultural surpluses were produced needing storage and defence against other groups. The cultivators, due to the power they obtained from their productivity, became the dominant culture.

Fig. 0.3 Small granary in West Africa

This need for more permanent structures led to advances in building technology using mud, mud-dried bricks, and selected timber. But once cultivation became the way of life there was little further change for a long period. This meant that forms of building and the associated structures became fixed and thus traditional in each different area.

Fig. 0.4 Greek village

Traditional building was carried out by specially trained people who became craftsmen. With the rise of cities and powerful elites, new and different forms of building and structures were required. But as these new city buildings also developed over a long period, the result was again what became traditional building methods.

In terms of structures these traditional buildings could be of impressive dimensions – the seven-storey buildings in the Yemen or English barns for example. These buildings and structures were built by men without scientific knowledge or even the ability to read and write, yet they were practical, basing their work on experience. They left no evidence of what thought processes went into their designs and only (some of) the buildings remain. However as Bernard Rudofsky[1] has noted *"The beauty of this architecture has been dismissed as accidental but we should be able to recognise it is the result of rare good sense in the handling of practical problems".*

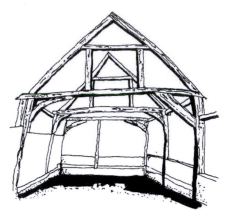

Fig. 0.5 Post and truss building circa 1400 AD

As these agrarian societies expanded and became richer, some villages grew into bigger centres that became towns and then cities.[2] The cities grew out of the Neolithic villages and by 3500 BC sizeable cities existed in Mesopotamia, the Indus valley and on the Yellow and Nile rivers.

0.3 The effect of civilisation

Cities were a manifestation of **civilisations**, which is an evolving rather than static culture, and included new specialised groups such as ruling and religious elites and specially trained warriors as well as new forms of administrations and the levying of taxes. These developments meant that new types of buildings were required: temples, storehouses, castles and so on. Many of these buildings are well known such as the pyramids in Egypt, the Parthenon in Greece and the Coliseum in Rome amongst many others.

As the traditional methods no longer applied, new technology and design processes were required. What these design processes were is not known with any certainty, but there is no evidence that any sort of theory about the behaviour of structures was used before 1742.[3] As stone structures were almost always used for these monumental constructions, the predominant load was the weight of the structure itself. As the construction often took years, warning of impending structural failure would be given by the cracking and spalling of the work in progress allowing repairs to be made as part of the building process. However, structural failures did occur and some evidence still exists.

For example Snefru (reign 2613-2589 BC) was the first king of Egypt of the 4th dynasty. He began building a pyramid at Dahshaur with a slope of 56°. As building progressed structural faults became apparent so the slope was changed abruptly to 43°, to allow the pyramid to be completed. He subsequently constructed a second pyramid, the Red pyramid, which had a slope of 43°. Both these pyramids still stand. The later and better-known pyramids at Giza have similar slopes to the Red pyramid.

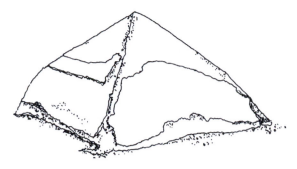

Fig. 0.6 'Bent' pyramid at Dahshaur

Nearly four thousand years later a great church building programme took place in Northern Europe, the result of which included the Gothic cathedrals. Again it is hard to know exactly what structural design process was used, but the masons had to be experts in geometry to ensure that the whole masonry structure fitted together, especially the complex vaulting systems – *"it would perhaps be somewhat exaggerated to speak of the rationalism of medieval architects for this supposes an organisation of knowledge that was certainly lacking"*.[4] As the masons tried to glorify God with higher structures with bigger windows, problems with the slenderness of the masonry began to appear. The limit was passed with the cathedral of Saint-Pierre at Beauvais in Northern France. It was conceived as the largest and tallest cathedral to be built, but various parts collapsed during construction. The cathedral was never completed; only the choir and transept remain standing. Close inspection of the surviving structure reveals numerous cracks and repairs.

Fig. 0.7 Saint-Pierre at Beauvais

Many other famous large-scale buildings have suffered structural problems such as the St. Sophia in Istanbul, St. Peter's Basilica in Rome and St. Paul's cathedral in London. The fact that there were structural problems with many of these large buildings should not automatically lead to criticism of the designers who produced amazing structures that have basically stood the test of time.

0.4 The search for structural understanding

The generally accepted view nowadays is that the behaviour of physical phenomena can be explained by a rational scientific approach. This view is relatively recent, in the past magical explanations were used. However, magical explanations do not provide predictive information and this is what structural designers need.

The idea of logic and rational explanations began with the Greek philosophers Plato (428-348 BC) and Aristotle (384-322 BC) but it was another Greek, Archimedes (290/80-212/11 BC), who is considered the founder of theoretical mechanics. One of his nine treatises is called 'On the equilibrium of planes' which deals with centres of gravity (see section **3.2**) and the 'law of the lever' (see section **1.5**), though it is not totally clear this was his own work or copied from earlier unknown authors.

Fig. 0.8 Archimedes

No further attempts to understand theoretical mechanics are known to have been made until the work of the mysterious Jordanus Nemorarius. This was the name given in the Renaissance to the author of a 12th or 13th century mathematical manuscript. The equilibrium of a lever and the action of a weight on an inclined plane are discussed in this work. It is not surprising that Leonardo da Vinci (1452-1519) also tried to contribute to the understanding of structures.

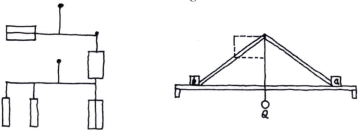

Fig. 0.9 Diagrams by Jordanus (left) and Leonardo (right)

The popular view of Leonardo da Vinci is that he was an artistic genius, which he was, and the inventor of everything, but his ambition was to be a recognised engineer and architect,[5] and it was by engineering that he earned his living. As an engineer and inventor he was no better than other contemporary engineers – Francesco di Giorgio for example [6] – and almost all of the technical drawings in his notebooks were copied from other sources.[7] However, Leonardo da Vinci was different in one aspect; in the late 1480s[8] he began to realise that there could be a physical understanding of the materials he used and this would inform and improve his engineering work. He made a number of tests on structures[9] and tried to draw conclusions from them. However, it is unclear whether these tests provided him with any useful quantative information. His work was unpublished; his observations being recorded in his numerous notebooks, so other engineers were unable to profit from or to extend his work.

More than 100 years passed before further advances are recorded. Then two remarkable men Simon Stevin (1548-1620) and his better known contemporary Galileo Galilei (1564-1642) both investigated, amongst many other things, aspects of structural behaviour.

Fig. 0.10 Stevin (left) and Galileo (right)

Stevin correctly stated the triangle of forces (see **Chapter 14**) and Galileo tried to discover what happened inside a beam.

Fig. 0.11 Galileo's bending test

Although the findings of both Stevin and Galileo were published, they remained in the realm of research and were unused by the structural designers of the time.

The idea of elasticity, or springiness, of engineering materials, essential to the understanding of structural behaviour (see **Chapter 5**), was stated independently by Robert Hooke (1635-1703) and Edme Mariotte (1620-1684). Hooke came to the idea in 1660 but only published it in 1678 as *Ut tensio sic vis* (as the pull so the stretch), having previously published it, in 1676, in the form of an indecipherable anagram as *ceiiinosssttuv!* This is now known to all engineers as Hooke's Law. Mariotte, who published the result in 1680, also attempted to discover what happened inside a loaded beam though he did not arrive at the correct understanding. This had to wait for another sixty to a hundred years.

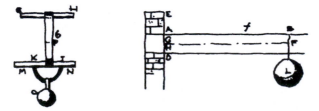

Fig. 0.12 Tests made by Edme Mariotte

The correct mathematical description of a beam needed the **differential calculus,** the most important tool in the mathematical theory of engineering. This was developed simultaneously and independently by Isaac Newton (1643-1727) and the German mathematician Gottfried Wilhelm Leibniz (1646-1716), however neither of them applied it to the theory of structures.

Fig. 0.13 Leibniz (left) and Newton (right)

The clarification of the mathematical theory of the beam was made by the brilliant Swiss mathematician Leonhard Euler (1707-1783) whose principal interest was the behaviour of 'elastic curves'.[10]

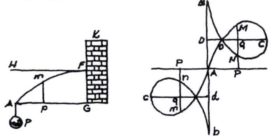

Fig. 0.14 Euler's elastic curves

The curves investigated by Euler were of little immediate use to the engineer as they took the forms shown in the diagram, though his work proved invaluable in the long run. A clearer explanation of beam behaviour was made by the French mathematician, physicist and military engineer Charles Augustin de Coulomb (1736-1806). In 1764 he was sent to Martinique, in the West Indies, where he spent nine years fortifying the island. During this time he also made numerous experiments and theoretical discoveries all of which were included in his famous paper written in 1776.[11] The conceptual explanations, given in section **3.4**, for the behaviour of a beam are due to his description.

So finally, towards the end of the 18th century, there existed a mathematical theory that described, and could be used to predict, the engineering behaviour of a simple beam. The understanding of shear stresses, see section **3.5**, came later, in 1858, with the clarification by WJM Rankine (1820-1872),[12] (the explanation of shear stresses in built-up sections (see section **4.3, I** beams for example) had to wait for the 1950s[13]). This had exercised some of the most brilliant minds over several centuries. Of course this lack of a predictive theory did not prevent thousands, probably millions, of beams being used in buildings all over the world. These were sized by experience, some local rule of thumb or perhaps just what came to hand, and probably most served their purpose. In 1826 the lecture notes of the mathematician and engineer CLM Navier (1785-1836) were published.[14] These were a summary of known structural theory together with original material. In these notes Navier formulated a general mathematical theory of elasticity which was the foundation of the modern approach.

0.5 The modern approach to structural design

The modern approach to the design of structures is to check any proposed design by making numerical calculations. These calculations are based on a mathematical theory that describes the physical behaviour of the system. Using known values such as the dimensions, the loads and the properties of the material to be used, a specific calculation can be made. The numerical result of this calculation indicates whether the proposed design will perform satisfactorily or not.

The **idea that numerical calculations** for a structure **could be made** is considered by several authors[15, 16] to have originated from the request, by pope Benedict XIV in 1742, from three mathematicians for a report on the reasons for the cracking of the dome of St. Peter's Basilica in Rome. According to H Straub[17] it *"must be considered as epoch-making in the history of civil engineering"*.

The **idea of training engineers** began in France with the founding, in 1671, of the Académie Royale d'Architecture that taught as much engineering as architecture. In 1672 the Corps du Génie (the French army engineering corps) was formed and in 1716 the Corps des Ponts et Chaussées. There were no textbooks so the professor of mathematics, B de Belidor (1693-1761), wrote several including the first one on engineering.[18] In 1747 the École des Ponts et Chaussées, the first ever engineering school, was founded to train military engineers. The first technical school in Britain was the Royal Military Academy, founded in 1741 at Woolwich. John Muller (1699-1784), the first director, wrote a textbook based on the work of Belidor.

As well as these events, the rapid acceleration of industrialisation, with the discovery of cheap ways to produce iron (see section **5.2**) and the introduction of steam power, first to factories and then to railways, required new types of structures to carry previously unimagined loads. Now, unlike massive stone structures, the new iron structures were light in comparison to the loads they had to carry and there was no time, or money, to see whether a new railway bridge would collapse when the train arrived.

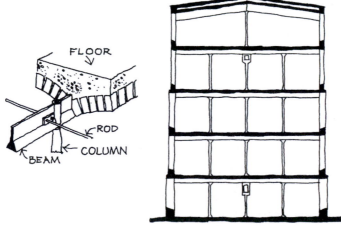

Fig. 0.15 Bage's mill 1796 detail and section

The 19th century was the century in which the modern approach emerged because a correct theory of structural behaviour had finally been discovered and there was a practical need to have predictive methods of calculating structures. Numerous mathematicians, physicists and engineers developed structural theory throughout the century;[19] however, actually applying the theory to specific projects was more difficult. Many tests were made to obtain correlations between theoretical predictions and actual behaviour[20] but during the century, especially the latter half, confidence in theoretically based numerical calculations increased until it became the way to check the adequacy of a particular structure.

Famous engineers of the 19th century, such as Robert Stephenson (1803-1859) and Isambard Brunel (1806-1859)[21] in Britain and Gustave Eiffel (1832-1923) in France calculated their structures. Without modern calculating aids these calculations had to be carried out by hand. To this end many handbooks were produced providing standard formulae for common structures, plus tables of allowable loads on elements such as beams, columns and slabs.

Fig. 0.16 Royal Albert Bridge, Saltash 1859 by IK Brunel

Today detailed hand calculations have largely been superseded by calculations made by computer programs; however, conceptual hand calculations should still form the basis of conceptual choices. How this can be done is explained in **Chapter 14**. But first the behaviour of structures **must be understood conceptually**.

0.6 The conceptual understanding of structural behaviour

The conceptual understanding of how structures behave when loaded can be achieved **without the need for any mathematics**. The conceptual understanding is gained by finding the answers to a series of questions about the structural behaviour.

- **What is the function of a structure?**

The most common answer to this question would be to **carry loads**. Whilst there is truth in this it needs to be extended to the concept of carrying loads from one place to another, which is **transferring loads**. A simple example illustrates this. If people want to cross a stream then a plank could be used as a bridge. Whilst people are on the bridge their weight (**the loads**) are transferred from a point over the water, which cannot directly support them, to points on the banks that can.

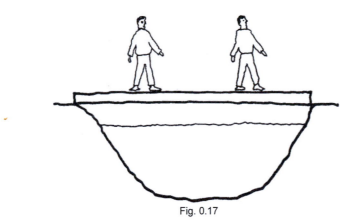

Fig. 0.17

The purpose of the plank is to **transfer** the point of load application to the point of load support. The plank does this by acting as a **structure**. This load transferring function is the main purpose of all structures, whether it is a chair or the Forth railway bridge.

- **What are the loads and the load paths?** – see **Chapter 1**

The source of loads on buildings is a combination of **natural loads,** that is those caused by nature – snow, wind, gravity, etc. – and those caused by the specific use of the building, which are **useful loads**. In the case of the simple plank bridge, the natural load is the bridge's own weight and the useful load is the weight of the people on the bridge.

Each load on a building structure is eventually supported by the foundations of the building, which is where the building joins the 'rest of the world'. In the case of the plank bridge the **rest of the world** is the banks of the river. The sequence of structural elements that join a specific load to the foundations is called the **load path**. The load path may be different for different loads. For example the load from the weight of people standing on the first floor of a five storey building will not be exactly the same as for those standing on the fourth floor.

- **How does the structure transfer loads?** – see **Chapters 1, 2 & 7**

The structure transfers loads by **forces that exist within each element** in the load path and by **forces between the elements** where they meet.

- **What are these forces in the structural elements?** – see **Chapters 2, 3, 4, 5 & 7**

There is more than one way of regarding the forces in structural elements; however, in the majority of cases, the force in an element can be considered to be a combination of a force **along** the element, a force **across** the element, a force **bending** the element and, sometimes, a force **twisting** the element.

The idea of conceptual analysis is to identify which of these forces are acting on any particular element of any structure for any load. The modern approach finds numerical values for these forces and from known data checks if each element can support these forces and so verify that a proposed structure is satisfactory.

- **Does the structure have overall stability?** – see **Chapter 6**

When people amuse themselves by building towers of children's bricks or playing cards they build the tower higher and higher until it collapses – 'like a pack of cards'.

This loss of overall stability can occur in a number of ways in building structures and clearly they must be avoided.

- **Is any element too slender?** – see **Chapter 6**

If a column is short and fat, increasing the load on it will eventually cause it to 'squash', but if the column is long and thin it will 'buckle' at a load lower than the 'squash' load. For a structure to be satisfactory, slender elements must be identified in any load path to ensure that they will not buckle in some way.

References - Introduction

1	B Rudofsky – **Architecture without architects** – Academy Editions 1964, p4 of the Preface
2	L Mumford - **The city in history** – Penguin 1966
3	RW Mainstone – **Structural theory and design before 1742** – Architectural Review April 1968, – p 303-310
4	**Vol.1 – A history of technology & invention** – Crown Publishers 1969 – ISBN 0-517-507277, p 536
5	M White – **Leonardo the first scientist** – Little Brown & Company 2000 – ISBN 0-349-11274-6, p 111
6	P Galluzzi - **The career of a technologist IN Leonardo Vinci: Engineer & Architect** – Montreal Museum of Fine Arts 1987 - ISBN 2-89192-084-8, p 41-43
7	B Gille – **The renaissance engineers** – Lund Humphries 1966 – ISBN 0-262-05024-5
8	Ref.6- p 72-76
9	SP Timoshenko – **History of strength of materials** – Dover 1983 – ISBN 0-486-61187-6, p 31-36
10	ibid. – p 31-36
11	A de Coulomb – **Essai sur une application des règles de maximis & minimis etc** – Mémoires de Mathématique et de Physique, l'Académie Royale des Sciences par divers Savants – 7, 343-382 – 1776
12	WJM Rankine – **Applied mechanics** – Griffin 1858
13	J Heyman – **Structural analysis; a historical approach** – Cambridge University Press 1998 – ISBN 0-521-62249-2, p 48-49
14	CLM Navier - **Lectures of the application of mechanics** – Paris 1826
15	RJ Mainstone - **Development of structural form** - Penguin 1975 – ISBN 0 14 00 65032 E, p 283
16	H Straub – **History of Civil Engineering** – Leonard Hill Ltd 1952, p 111-116
17	ibid. - p 116
18	BF de Belidor – **The science of engineering** – Paris 1729
19	TM Charlton – **A history of theory of structures in the nineteenth century** – CUP1982 – ISBN 0-521-23419-0
20	D Smith – **Structural model testing and the design of British railway bridges in the 19th century** – Transactions of the Newcomen Society 48 – p 73-90
21	D Beckett - **Brunel's Britain** – David & Charles 1980 – ISBN 0-7153-7973-9, p 99

CHAPTER 1 *Loads and load paths*

A structure's main function is to **transfer loads**, but before considering the form of a structure, a clear idea of what loads it has to transfer is required: in other words an answer to the question **what are the loads?**

The sources of loads can be divided into **natural, useful** and **accidental** loads. Natural loads occur due to the existence of the structure in the world; useful loads are ones that occur from the purpose of the structure; and accidental loads occur from the misuse of the structure.

1.1 Natural loads

All structures on the surface of the Earth have to resist the force of **gravity**. This force acts through a body in a line joining the body with the centre of the Earth. However, at the local level these forces can be considered vertical.

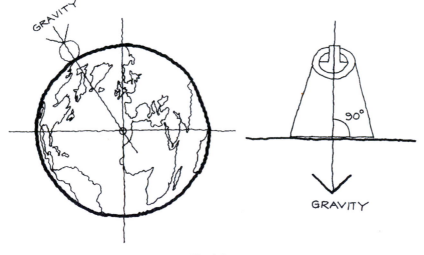

Fig. 1.1

So the first source of **natural** loads is the **gravity load**. For the example of the plank across the stream - see **Fig. 0.17** – this means that the plank has to transfer its own weight, usually called **self-weight**, to the support points.

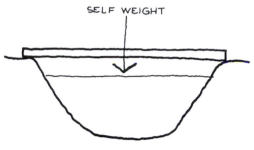

SELF WEIGHT

Fig. 1.2

Due to regular and continuous changes in atmospheric pressure from place to place on the Earth's surface air flows across the surface of the Earth, that is, wind. All structures built on the Earth's surface have to resist forces from wind. Near to ground level the wind can be considered to blow along the surface: this is not true for the whole of the atmosphere, as any pilot knows.

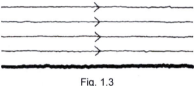

Fig. 1.3

If an obstruction is placed in the path of the wind it alters the pattern of the wind flow. This is why kites and planes fly and boats sail. If the object is fixed to the Earth's surface, like a building, the wind must flow around and over it.

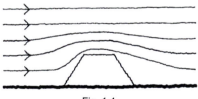

Fig. 1.4

How the wind flows around and over an object depends both on the wind speed and the shape of the object. These are the basic questions considered by the complex subject known as **aerodynamics**. But the alteration in wind flow pattern will always cause a **force** on the interrupting object.

It is an intellectual feat to see the alteration of the wind flow pattern around and over a building as a force or **wind load**. But this view allows the action of the wind on a building to be clear.

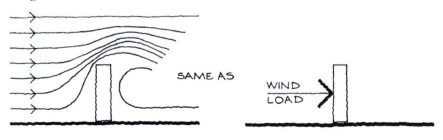

SAME AS

WIND
LOAD

Fig. 1.5

This effect can readily be felt by holding a flat object in the flow of a stream. This is why canoes and people can propel themselves through water.

Although the pattern of wind flow around buildings is complex (very!) the resulting loads from the alteration of wind flow are predominately at right angles to the surfaces of the building.

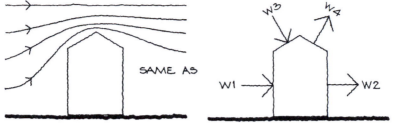

Fig. 1.6

So, for the pitched roofed building shown in **Fig. 1.6**, the alteration in wind flow will cause four loads. The loads **W1** and **W2** are on, and at right angles to the walls, and the loads **W3** and **W4** are on, and at right angles to the roof slopes. These are **wind loads**.

As far as buildings and their supporting structures are concerned, **gravity** and **wind** loads are two types of **natural** loads they always have to resist.

There are other natural loads that the structure may have to resist. These are **earth** or **water pressure, earthquakes, temperature**, and **ground movement.**

If the local shape of the Earth's surface is altered to site the building, as it often is, then parts of the building and its structure may be subject to loads from **earth pressure**. This is because the natural surface has found a shape that is at rest (not over geological time of course). So, rather like the wind flow, an alteration will cause forces. If dry sand is piled into a heap, there is a maximum slope for the sides.

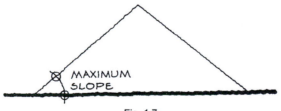

Fig. 1.7

What is happening inside the heap is complex, and is further complicated by the addition of water (which is why sand castles can be made). If, however, a heap with a vertical side is required, forces are needed to keep the heap in the **unnatural** shape.

Fig. 1.8

This is usually done by building a (retaining) wall. Because the heap wants to return to a natural shape, shown by the dotted line in **Fig. 1.8**, the wall must hold back all the sand above the dotted line in **Fig. 1.9.**

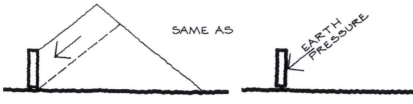

Fig. 1.9

This causes loads on the wall. In buildings, this occurs when the building has a basement, or is built into a sloping site.

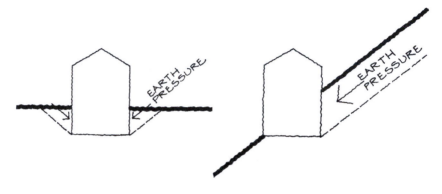

Fig. 1.10

In these cases the structure has to resist **natural** loads from **earth pressure**.

Under the surface of the Earth, depending on the local geology and climate, there will be, at some level, water. The top level of this water is called the **water table**. This level may be at the surface in swamps, bogs and beaches, or many metres down in deserts. If the siting of the building interrupts the natural water table, an **unnatural water table** is created around and under the building.

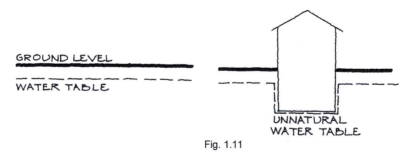

Fig. 1.11

Not only are the walls loaded by the water pressure but it also causes **upward** loads on the floor. The building is trying to **float**.

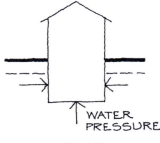

Fig. 1.12

The structure has to resist natural loads due to **water pressure**.

The general shape of the surface of the Earth is the same over the life-span of most buildings, but may alter slightly due to climatic or geological changes. As the building is attached to the surface of the Earth, local changes will force a change in the shape of the structure, as the building is hardly likely to prevent the Earth changing shape. In particular, load may be caused if the local shape changes differentially. It is **not obvious** how this causes a load on the structure, if indeed it does. For example, suppose the plank bridge has a support in the stream.

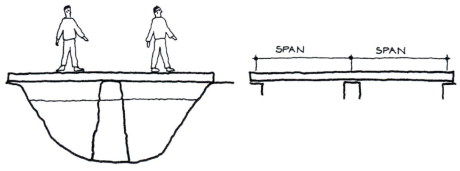

Fig. 1.13

If this central support were to sink into the stream bed, depending on the fixing, it may pull the plank down (load it) or cease to be a support at all.

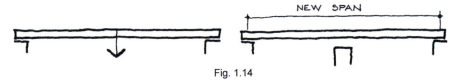

Fig. 1.14

So **ground movements** can alter the load-carrying behaviour of a structure, and so can be considered, in a rather roundabout way, to load the structure.

Another form of ground movement that can load a structure is an earthquake. Earthquakes are caused by sudden internal movements within the Earth's crust. This causes a shock to the system and results in shaking the crust of the Earth over a certain area. The Earth's surface will both bounce up and down and move backwards and forwards.

HORIZONTAL   VERTICAL

Fig. 1.15

In general the vertical movement is small compared with the horizontal movement. A building, during an earthquake, undergoes an experience similar to a person standing unaided on a cakewalk.

Fig. 1.16

Again, it is not obvious where or what the load is but the effect, as far as the building or the person is concerned, is the same as being pushed horizontally to and fro with the foundations (feet) kept still.

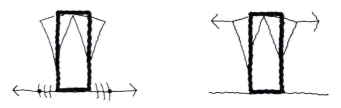

Fig. 1.17

So earthquakes cause horizontal loads similar, to some extent, to wind loads.

The last type of natural load is caused by differential dimensional changes in the structure. All structural materials expand when heated and contract when cooled. As structures are often exposed to the ambient climate, their **temperature** may vary considerably, from a hot summer day to a cold winter night, and in some cases this may cause loads. An example illustrates how this may happen. Suppose a structure consists of two parts firmly joined by a spanning structure.

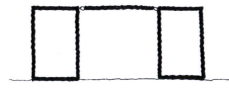

Fig. 1.18

As the temperature varies, the spanning structure will expand and contract. As it is firmly joined to the supporting structures, it will push them and pull them causing loads.

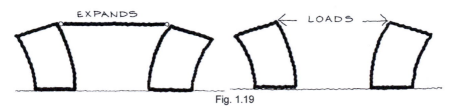

Fig. 1.19

So, as with ground movements, temperature, in a rather unobvious way, may be a load. To avoid these loads, bridges are often provided with systems of sliding bearings at the tops of the supporting columns. On large bridges these can often be seen.

A successful structure must be able to resist the effects of some or all of these natural loads for the whole of its useful life. On the whole, these loads cannot be avoided and are an integral part of the structure's existence.

1.2 Useful loads

Unlike natural loads, which cannot be avoided and so must be tolerated, **useful loads** are ones that are welcomed. These loads happen because the building and hence the structure have been constructed for a useful purpose.

With the plank bridge, it has been constructed for people to cross the stream. If it couldn't do this it would be of no use, so the previous figures can be re-drawn showing **natural** and **useful loads**.

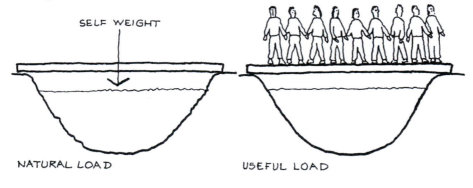

Fig. 1.20

The amount of useful load can be altered by how many people are 'allowed' on the bridge at any one time; and whether people are allowed to take their pet elephants on the bridge. It is often practical for the useful load to be the maximum load that is likely to occur. Practically the useful load would be a bridge full of people, but no elephants allowed.

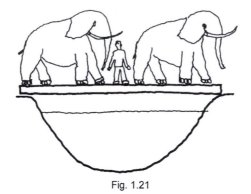

Fig. 1.21

So, unlike natural loads, there is a choice for useful loads. Of course if everyone using the bridge had an elephant (or a car), it would be sensible for the useful load to be a bridge full of people or full of elephants. As gravity acts on the people and the elephants, the effect of this useful load will be towards the centre of the Earth, or locally vertical.

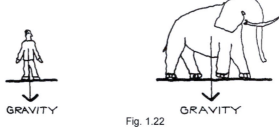

GRAVITY   GRAVITY

Fig. 1.22

Unlike natural loads, useful loads can vary enormously, depending on the use of the building which may have to carry anything from railway trains to sleeping people.

Whilst the majority of useful loads act vertically, sometimes they act horizontally. It may be useful to store sand, grain or water and these will cause useful earth or water pressure loads.

Fig. 1.23

Also, rather like earthquakes, machinery housed in a building may tend to shake a building sideways, causing another type of useful horizontal load.

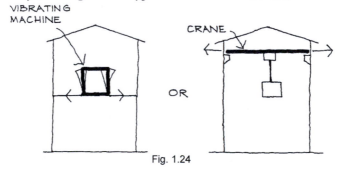

Fig. 1.24

Again, industrial processes may increase or reduce the ambient temperature, giving 'useful' temperature loads.

1.3 Accidental loads

The occurrence of **accidental loads** is inextricably bound up with concepts of **safety** see **Chapter 6** for a detailed explanation. How safe anything is, driving a car or drinking water, is a matter for society to decide, or at least keep under review. If accidents are thought to be likely and unavoidable then the structure should be able to resist loads that these accidents cause. For instance, in a multi-storey car-park, it is likely and unavoidable that someone will hit the edge barrier whilst parking.

SAME AS

Fig. 1.25

The edge barrier should be able to cater for 'run of the mill' collisions but not suicide attempts. Similar situations occur at railway stations and ship berthing jetties.

Another unavoidable accident is a minor (!) explosion. Minor explosions in kitchens and bomb factories are of different orders of magnitude, but both should be expected and allowed for. Other unavoidable accidents are crowd panics which require the installation of panic barriers, or tanks bursting which require lower structures to carry the extra liquid load.

It is impossible for an individual to decide which accidents, and hence accidental loads, are unavoidable and which aren't, and any society is never clear about this. Compare the numbers of people killed on the roads in 'unavoidable' accidents and the relatively few killed in train 'disasters'.

1.4 Loading summary

The major function of a structure is to transfer loads and the main sources of these loads have now been identified. Whilst each load or set of loads can be considered to act independently, buildings are usually loaded by combinations of the various loads. As the building must carry any combination it is usual to consider a range of combinations called **load cases**.

The only load case that will always be present is the **natural gravity load**. That is the effect of gravity on the building construction and to this load must be added **all other loads**. All the other loads that have been identified may or may not be acting at any particular time. Therefore an almost endless variety of load combinations may act. For example:

- **Loadcase 1** – Natural gravity load + Useful gravity load on all floors
- **Loadcase 2** – Natural gravity load + Wind load in a particular direction
- **Loadcase 3** – Natural gravity load + Useful gravity load on some floors + Natural temperature load

However, the purpose of considering these different load cases is not to find as many load cases as possible but to ensure that the building structure will safely carry all possible load cases. This apparently contradictory statement means that only the load cases that cause the biggest effect on the structure need to be considered. In other words only the **worst load case** is of interest. This presents two difficulties that are:

1   One load case may cause the biggest effect on one part of the structure whereas another load case may have the biggest effect on another part, so there may be more than one worst load case.
2   How can the worst load case or cases be found without considering **every** possible load case?

Unfortunately there is no automatic process to overcome these difficulties for every situation but guidance is given in technical documents. For buildings it is usual to consider:

1   Natural gravity load + Maximum useful gravity load
2   Natural gravity load + Wind load in direction 1
3   Natural gravity load + Wind load at right angles to direction 1

It is unusual to have to consider loads due to earth or water pressure, ground movement, temperature or accident. But for particular types of building or sites these may have to be considered, and incorporated into the load cases. For example, for a two-storey factory building, the following loads would be considered for the structural design.

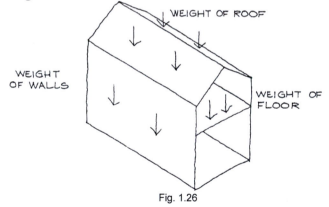

Fig. 1.26

The ground floor often bears directly on to the ground and does not load the structure.

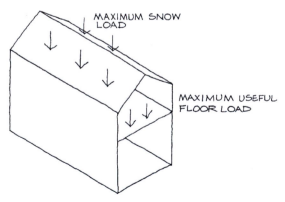

Fig. 1.27 Maximum useful gravity load

The natural gravity plus maximum useful gravity loads usually, but not always, give the **worst vertical load**.

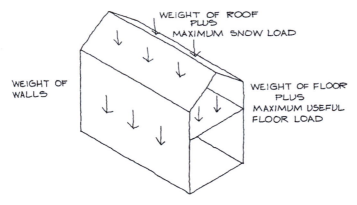

Fig. 1.28 Worst vertical load

The combination of natural gravity load and the maximum wind loads usually gives the **worst horizontal load**.

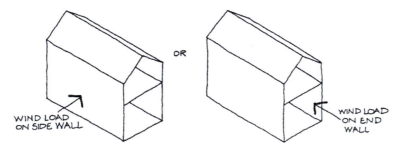

Fig. 1.29 - Worst horizontal load

It may seem surprising that only two directions are chosen for the wind, because, after all wind blows in any direction. So the maximum wind load, which has been decided, can act in **any** direction.

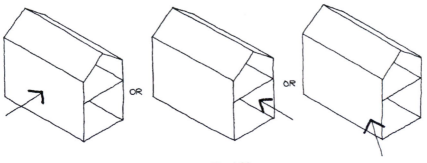

Fig. 1.30

But if the building structure is strong enough to carry the maximum wind load separately in two perpendicular directions, then **all** other wind loads can be considered to be smaller proportions of the maximum loads.

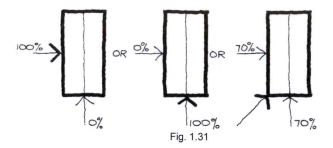

Fig. 1.31

The same principle of **load combinations** applies to all buildings.

1.5   Reaction loads

In the same way that people stand on a floor and usually don't fall through, buildings also have to stand on something strong – the foundations.

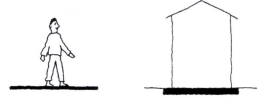

Fig. 1.32

But what is the floor doing to stop people from falling through? What it is doing is to provide a **reaction force**, or a **reaction load**. The idea of reactions is due to Issac Newton who, in 1687, stated three fundamental laws, which together with his discovery of gravity, provided the basis of what has come to be known as **Newtonian mechanics**. These were used extensively by scientists in their pursuit of knowledge about the natural world. They formed the backbone of physics and still provide the backbone of structural engineering thought.

(It was only at the beginning of the 20th century that Albert Einstein postulated a system of mechanics that were non-Newtonian. This system came to be known as **relativity**, which is used for calculations about the Universe. Fortunately structural engineers can still use Newtonian mechanics for building structures on the Earth.)

One of Newton's three laws (the third), states:

- **To every action there is always an equal and opposite reaction.**

So when a person stands on a floor, the weight of the person pushes down on the floor with a force equal to their bodyweight. For equilibrium, the floor must push back with an **equal and opposite force**.

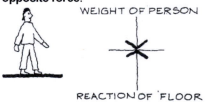

WEIGHT OF PERSON

REACTION OF FLOOR

Fig. 1.33

An understanding of this statement is fundamental for an understanding of how building structures carry loads.

Whilst it is true that the load and the reaction have to act at the point of the application of the load, a structure transfers the load to another point. Returning to the example of the plank bridge:

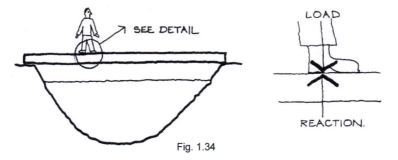

Fig. 1.34

The reaction to the person's weight is **in the structure**, and the structure transfers this reaction to the banks.

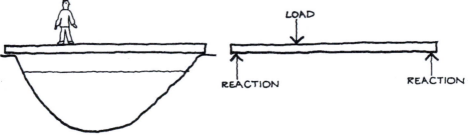

Fig. 1.35

Because of Newton's law, the numerical sum of the loads and the reactions must be equal.

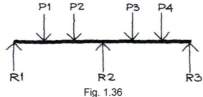

Fig. 1.36

For vertical equilibrium of the 2-span beam in **Fig. 1.36**:

- **P1 + P2 + P3 + P4 = R1 + R2 + R3**

When loads are acting horizontally, a reaction is required for equilibrium. It is to upset this equilibrium that tug-of-war contests are held.

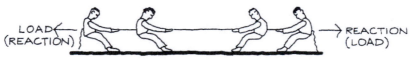

Fig. 1.37

Here it is unclear which is the load and which is the reaction. This is why the (applied) load and the reaction (load) should be thought of as a balanced system of loads.

REACTION ←────┤├──────────────→ LOAD

Fig. 1.38

Here the pull of the team is the (applied) load and the tree provides the reaction (load).

Not only are there vertical and horizontal reactions there are also **moment** reactions. What is a moment? A moment is a **force times a distance**. Moments abound in structural engineering but the concept of a moment is often found hard to understand. However, it is because of moments that things can be weighed or people can enjoy see-saws.

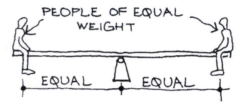

Fig. 1.39

The fun in see-sawing can only be enjoyed if the people are of equal weight and sit at an equal distance from the support. This is because they are in moment equilibrium.

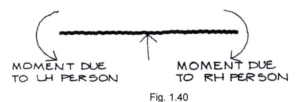

Fig. 1.40

In other words, the left-hand person causes an **anti-clockwise** moment and the right-hand person causes a **clockwise** moment about the central support. Because both people are of equal weight and are sitting at equal distances from the support, the anti-clockwise and clockwise moments are equal in magnitude but opposite in direction and so are in **moment equilibrium**. By pushing from the ground this equilibrium is upset and the people 'see-saw'.

The same principle can be used for weighing scales, this time to find the unknown weight of some goods.

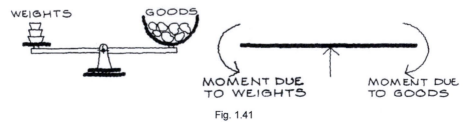

Fig. 1.41

To balance the scales the moments must be equal. As the distances are equal the weights must equal the weight of the goods.

The idea of **moment reaction** occurs at the support of a **cantilever**.

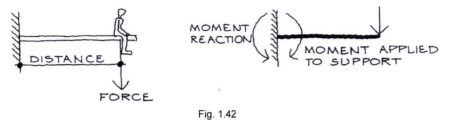

Fig. 1.42

The person sitting on the end of the cantilevered plank causes a moment at the support (**force × distance**). The fixing of the plank must balance this moment with a moment reaction, otherwise the plank will rotate away from the wall.

Moment reactions are also required to prevent flag poles, fences and signs from being blown over by the wind.

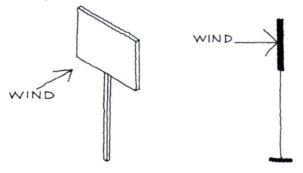

Fig. 1.43

In this case the post is acting as a **vertical cantilever** from the ground. The wind force acting on the sign at some height (distance) above the ground causes a moment at ground level, so the post must be dug into the ground to provide a moment reaction.

Fig. 1.44

Notice that the moment reaction is in the opposite direction to the moment caused by the wind force × height.

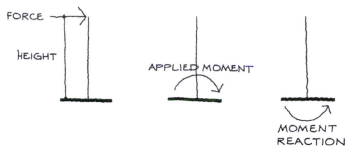

Fig. 1.45

Many structures require more than one type of reaction. Using the example of wind blowing on a sign, the support must provide **vertical, horizontal** and **moment reactions**. These resist the **weight** of the **sign**, the **wind load** and the **wind moment**.

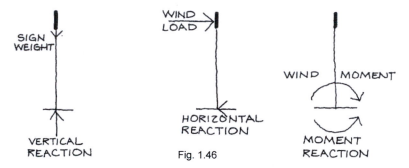

Fig. 1.46

The idea of moment equilibrium also plays a part in apportioning vertical reactions for spanning structures. Suppose a weightless plank spans between two weighing scales and a person stands at different points along the plank.

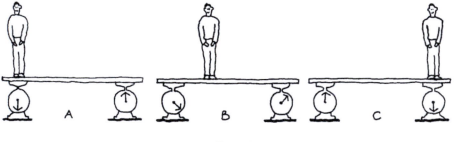

Fig. 1.47

The person is the load and the reaction forces occur at the supports on the weighing scales. As the person moves from position **A** to **B** and then to **C**, the readings on the scales will vary, giving the values of the reactions for each position. But the fact that the sum of the readings on the scales for each position will equal the weight of the person **does not indicate how they are shared**. If the person stands in position **A**, directly over the left-hand weighing scale, it is reasonable to expect this scale to give a reading of **100%** of the person's weight and the right-hand weighing scale to give a reading of **0%** of the person's weight. But **vertical equilibrium** would equally be satisfied by the right-hand scale reading **100%** of the person's weight and the left-hand scale reading **0%**.

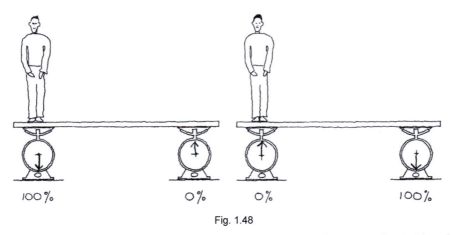

Fig. 1.48

This seems unlikely to be true, but why not? The answer is because only 100% at the left-hand scale gives moment equilibrium. But where are the moments? These are far from obvious, but suppose the left-hand weighing scale was removed.

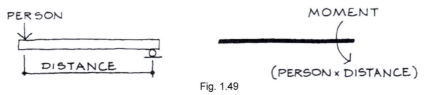

Fig. 1.49

Now the person causes an anti-clockwise moment about the right-hand weighing scale and the plank would hinge about the right-hand end. To prevent this, the left-hand weighing scale provides a reaction that causes a clockwise moment about the right-hand weighing scale.

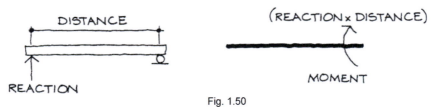

Fig. 1.50

As these two moments must balance, the left-hand reaction must balance the person's weight, as the distance from the right-hand end is the same for the load and the reaction so:

Person's weight $\times$ **length of plank = left-hand reaction $\times$ length of plank**

So the left-hand diagram of **Fig. 1.48** gives vertical **and** moment equilibrium whereas the right-hand one gives vertical equilibrium **but not** moment equilibrium. So **every time there are loads on structures there must be reactions (vertical, horizontal and moment) and these reactions must balance the loads.**

In other words:

- **Sum of vertical loads = Sum of vertical reactions**
- **Sum of horizontal loads = Sum of horizontal reactions**
- **Moments due to loads = Moments due to reactions**

These three statements must be true for all structures and the understanding of these statements unlocks the door to an understanding of structures.

1.6   Load paths

To understand how loads are transferred through complex structures the **concept of load path** is used. This is basically a sequence of loads and reactions between structural elements. The important point here is one element's reaction to the next element's load.

For the simple example of a beam on two walls, the reactions of the beam 'cause' loads on the walls.

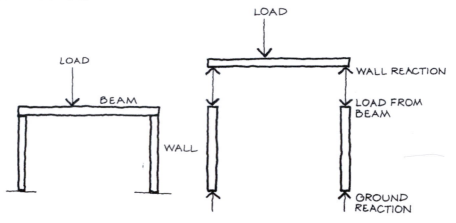

Fig. 1.51

The double-headed arrow between the beam and the walls represents the reaction and the load. The **upper arrow** represents the wall providing a **reaction** to the beam and the **lower arrow** represents the beam causing a **load** on the wall.

Fig. 1.52

Fig. 1.53 shows a more complicated situation of two beams supported by walls, all sitting on a longer beam.

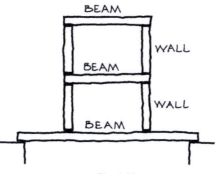

Fig. 1.53

First, what are the loads? These are natural, the self-weight of the beams and walls, and useful, the loads applied to the beams.

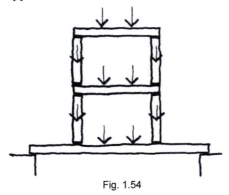

Fig. 1.54

Loads **P1**, **P2** and **P5** are the self-weight of the beams and **P3** and **P4** the self-weight of the walls. Loads **P6**, **P7** and **P8** are the loads applied to the beams. For vertical equilibrium, all the loads **P1** to **P8** must be balanced by the reactions of the lowest beam.

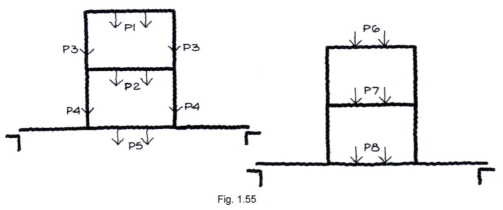

Fig. 1.55

For the lowest beam:

The sum of the reactions = P1 + P2 + P3 + P4 + P5 + P6 + P7 + P8

But how do the loads get to the reactions? First the upper beam.

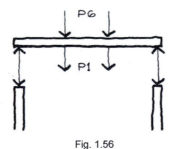

Fig. 1.56

Loads to the upper walls = P1 + P6

The upper walls are loaded by the loads on the upper beam plus their self-weight.

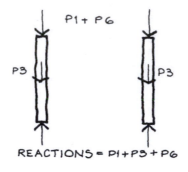

Fig. 1.57

The tops of the lower walls are loaded by and provide a reaction to the upper walls and the middle beam.

Fig. 1.58

So for the lower walls,

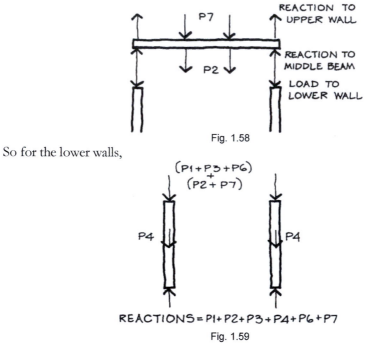

REACTIONS = P1+ P2+ P3 + P4+ P6 +P7

Fig. 1.59

And the reactions to the lower walls are:

Load from the upper wall + Load from the middle beam + Self-weight of the lower wall

Reaction = (P1 + P6 + P3) + (P2 + P7) + P4

The lower beam is not only loaded by its self-weight, **P5**, and the applied load, **P8**, but also by providing reactions to the lower walls.

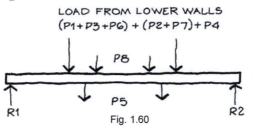

Fig. 1.60

So for vertical equilibrium of the lower beam:

The **REACTIONS** = Self-weight of the upper beam
+ Self-weight of the middle beam
+ Self-weight of the lower beam
+ Self-weight of the upper walls
+ Self-weight of the lower walls
+ Useful load on the upper beam
+ Useful load on the middle beam
+ Useful load on the lower beam

that is:

R1 + R2 = P1 + P2 + P3 + P4 + P5 + P6 + P7 + P8

The load path of load **P6** can now be identified. First the upper beam transfers the load to the upper wall, which transfers it to the lower wall, which transfers it to the lower beam, which transfers it to the supports.

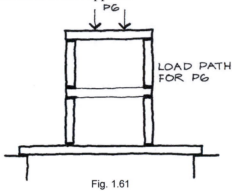

Fig. 1.61

And for **P2**, the self-weight of the middle beam:

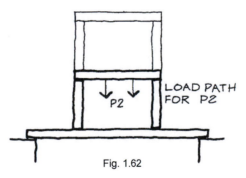

Fig. 1.62

The load path joins the load from its **point of application** to the **final support point**. There are two facts to be considered about load paths.

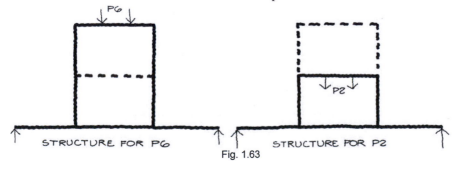

Fig. 1.63

Firstly **all loads** must and will have a load path from their point of application to the final support. The structural designer must identify these paths for **all loads** and **all load cases**.

Secondly, as the function of the structure is to transfer loads, then the **load path is the structure** for each load. So the answer to the question **'what is the structure?'** may vary with each load. For the loads **P2** and **P6** the structures are different.

The identification of vertical load paths for most buildings is relatively straightforward. Oddly it can be quite complex for 'simple buildings' like houses.

Not only do vertical loads need load paths but so do horizontal loads. These loads are usually caused by wind. How does the signboard shown in **Fig. 1.64** resist wind forces? The main wind load is caused by the wind blowing on the actual sign, and only the load path for this load is considered. This means the effect of the wind on the rails and posts is ignored.

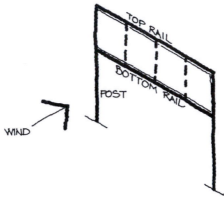

Fig. 1.64

The actual signboard spans horizontally between the vertical stiffeners and the stiffeners act as vertically spanning beams supported by the top and bottom rails.

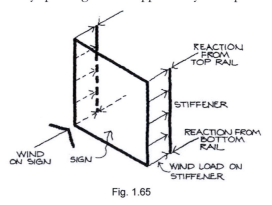

Fig. 1.65

The reactions from the stiffeners become horizontal loads on the top and bottom rails. These rails act as horizontally spanning beams supported by the vertical end posts.

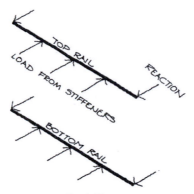

Fig. 1.66

The reactions from the top and bottom rails now cause loads on the vertical posts that act as vertical cantilevers from the ground. For the signboard, the wind load path is the whole structure.

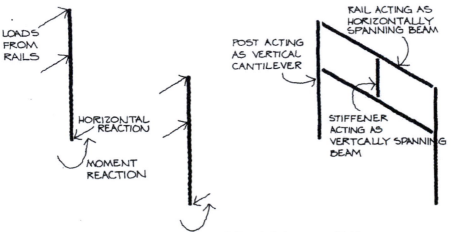

Fig. 1.67 Loads on post (left) and whole structure (right)

But even in simple buildings the load paths for vertical and horizontal loads are rarely the same. As the **load path is the structure**, this means there are usually **different structures** resisting vertical and horizontal loads.

CHAPTER 2   *Internal forces*

So far, loads, reactions and load paths have been identified for structures. But how does the structure transfer the load to the reaction? And what happens to the structure when it transfers loads? The structure transfers loads by **forces** that are **in the structure** and these forces cause **stresses** in the structural material. The structure also deforms under the effect of the loads, and the size of the deformation depends on the **stiffness** of the structure.

2.1   Axial forces

To illustrate the idea of **internal force** consider a simple column supporting an end load.

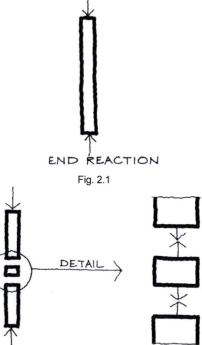

END LOAD

END REACTION

Fig. 2.1

What happens to a typical **slice** of the column?

DETAIL

Fig. 2.2

The **slice** is being squashed, or compressed, and furthermore **all slices** are being squashed.

.

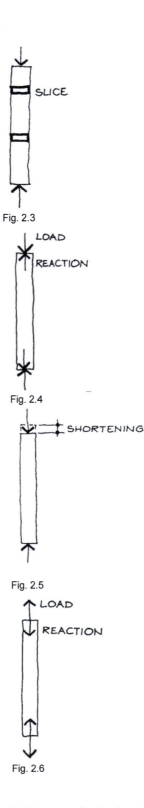

SLICE

Fig. 2.3

LOAD

REACTION

The column transfers the end load to the reaction by a system of 'squashed slices', or to use the engineering description, the column is
in compression.

Fig. 2.4

SHORTENING

Not only is the column in compression but also deforms by **shortening**. This happens because each slice becomes thinner on being squashed.

Fig. 2.5

LOAD

REACTION

If the direction of the load is reversed then each slice is being stretched, and the end load is transferred to the reaction by a system of 'stretched slices'. Or, to use the engineering term, the column is **in tension**.

Fig. 2.6

Forces that stretch or compress elements in the direction of their longitudinal axis are called **axial forces** and these always act **along** the element.

2.2　Bending moments and shear forces

Looking again at the load path for load **P6** (see **Fig. 1.61**), the walls supporting the upper beam are in compression.

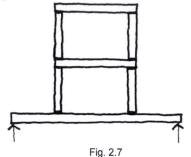

Fig. 2.7

But what is happening to the upper and lower beams? These beams are transferring the loads to the supports by a combination of **bending moments** and **shear forces**. Although bending moments and shear forces act together, conceptually they can be considered separately. To understand what is happening to the beam it helps to see what happens to a slice.

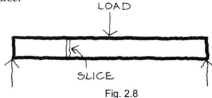

Fig. 2.8

Each side of the slice is being bent by a moment.

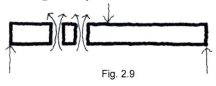

Fig. 2.9

The moments at the slice are the forces multiplied by their distances from the slice.

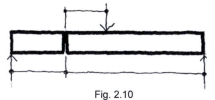

Fig. 2.10

So the moments on the slice are:

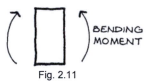

Fig. 2.11

This causes the slice to be squashed at the top and stretched at the bottom. In other words the **top of the beam is in compression** and the **bottom in tension**, and a pair of bending moments is bending the slice.

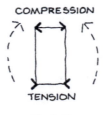

Fig. 2.12

Because the top is in compression it **shortens**, and because the bottom is in tension it **lengthens**. These effects cause the sides to **rotate**.

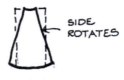

Fig. 2.13

In general, the size of the bending moment varies from slice to slice. This varying size can be represented by drawing lines at right angles to the beam, with the length of the line indicating the **size of the bending moment.**

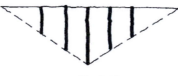

Fig. 2.14

Because there is a bending moment at every slice and the beam is 'made' of slices, there is a bending moment at every point of the beam. A clearer picture of the bending moments on the beam can be obtained by joining the ends of all the bending moment size lines shown in **Fig. 2.14**. This diagram is called a **bending moment diagram.**

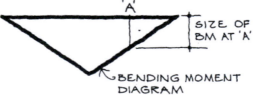

Fig. 2.15

And because **each slice changes shape**, as shown in **Fig. 2.13**, the beam takes up a bent shape.

Fig. 2.16

Bending moments in a beam resist the effects of the moments caused by external loads, and reactions acting at different distances from each other. Bending moments **do not** resist the vertical effect of loads on beams; **shear forces** resist these. When a **rectangle** is distorted by an angular change into a **parallelogram**, it is **sheared**.

Fig. 2.17

Returning to a slice of a beam, not only does the slice have to transfer the bending moments from one face to the other, it also has to transfer the vertical load from one face to the other.

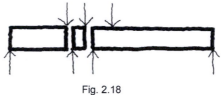

Fig. 2.18

The beam either side of the slice has to be in **vertical equilibrium**.

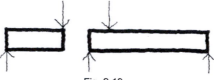

Fig. 2.19

And the balancing forces themselves have to be balanced by forces on the face of the slice.

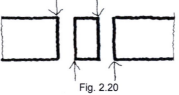

Fig. 2.20

It is these pairs of **up and down forces** that are called shear forces, because their effect is to shear the slice.

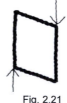

Fig. 2.21

Like bending moments, shear forces will, in general, vary along a beam. So, in a similar way to bending moment diagrams, **shear force diagrams** can be drawn.

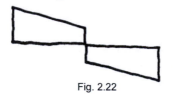

Fig. 2.22

2.3 Structural diagrams

So far structures have been drawn realistically, that is beams and columns with depth and width. But it much easier just represent structural elements like beams, columns, trusses and frameworks by just using a single line to represent the element these are called **structural diagrams**. This is an essential step in moving away from pictures of structures into the world of engineering, a step not always easy to make. **Fig 2.23** shows how structures are shown using just lines to represent structural elements.

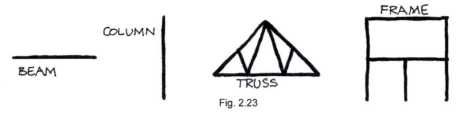

Fig. 2.23

But the diagrams in **Fig. 2.23** do not show how the elements are joined together, or how they are joined to their supports.

To aid the process of using structural concepts, structural designers have evolved standard names and symbols for the different types of structural joints. Joints that can transfer all forces are called **fixed** or **encastre** joints, joints that transfer forces but no bending moments are called **pin** joints, and joints that only transfer a force in a specific direction are called **sliding** joints. These joints are drawn on structural diagrams in a standard way.

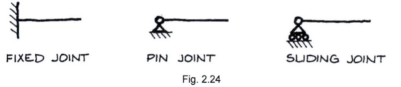

FIXED JOINT   PIN JOINT   SLIDING JOINT

Fig. 2.24

This allows structural designers to draw diagrams of structures that make their structural behaviour clear. The familiar simple structures of a cantilever beam and a simply supported beam can now be drawn as **structural diagrams**.

CANTILEVER   SIMPLY SUPPORTED BEAM

Fig. 2.25 Structural diagrams

These joint symbols can be used to show how more complicated structures are joined together or how they are joined to the foundations. It should be noted that under the right-hand support of the simply supported beam, there are two circles that represent rollers that allow the beam to expand; this is a convention, but also means if the beam was heated it could expand without restraint.

As a general rule triangulated structures like trusses are normally assumed to have members pin-jointed together – a **pin-jointed truss**. Framed structures, like a portal frame – a goal post – see section **2.5**, have their members joined together rigidly – in fact frames depend on this joint rigidity for their lateral stiffness – **rigid-jointed frames**.

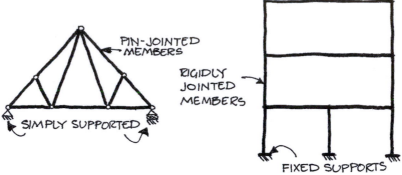

Fig. 2.26 Pin-jointed truss and a Rigid-jointed frame

These joint symbols indicate **idealised joints**, so pinned joints allow rotation movement without any restraint whereas fixed joints hold the end of the member absolutely rigid – in real structures these conditions are only attained by very special joints; in general real joints are between the two – see section **11.6**. How to model foundations - see **Chapter 8** – present a special problem, because ascertaining the rigidity of the soil which supports the foundation is a complex matter and beyond the scope of this book.

Using these symbols, the structural diagrams of the curved structure make it obvious which is the arch and which is the curved beam.

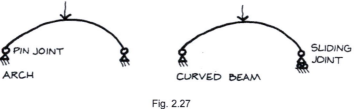

Fig. 2.27

2.4   Signs of structural forces

The **Fig. 2.28** shows two cantilevers that are exactly the same except the loads are being applied in **opposite** directions. Some agreement has to be made to distinguish the fact that cantilever **A** is being bent down, and cantilever **B** is being bent up.

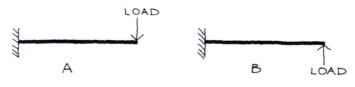

Fig. 2.28

It could be agreed by deciding that cantilever **A** deforms in a **negative** way, causing negative bending moments and vice versa for cantilever **B**.

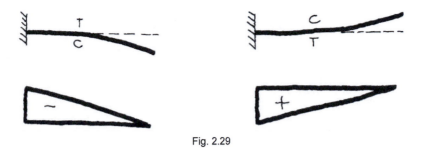

Fig. 2.29

In **Fig. 2.29** the bending moments have been drawn on the **tension side** of the beam. Although these decisions are supposed to aid clarification, this is not always the case. Especially as the decisions about positive and negative are made by personal whim. However, they have to be made and adhered to or the bending moment diagrams become chaotic.

Similar decisions have to be made about shear forces, but here the situation is more incomprehensible. As shear forces are pairs of forces, the sign decisions have to be made about these pairs. A possible sign convention is shown in the following figure.

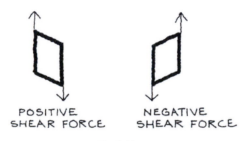

POSITIVE
SHEAR FORCE

NEGATIVE
SHEAR FORCE

Fig. 2.30

Again this decision is made by personal whim. Using the stated sign conventions the bending moment and shear force diagrams can be drawn for a simple beam with point load, and these diagrams show the signs of the bending moments and shear forces.

LOAD

BENDING MOMENT
DIAGRAM

SHEAR FORCE
DIAGRAM

Fig. 2.31

Sets of diagrams like this that give engineers pictures of what is happening inside a structure. **The conceptual meaning of sets of bending moment and shear force diagrams is central to the understanding of structural behaviour.** Being able to sketch the correct shapes for these is a skill to be learnt, as is being able to calculate numerical values – guidance on how to obtain these skills is given in **Chapter 14**. A deep understanding of structural behaviour is only obtained when the correct diagrams can be drawn for real or proposed structures.

2.5 A simple plane frame

For the more complicated structure of a goal-post, known as a **portal frame,**
diagrams can be drawn showing what is happening inside the structure when it is
loaded.

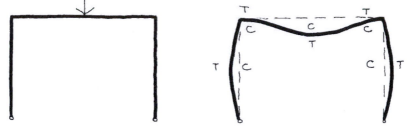

Fig. 2.32

Here, although there is only vertical load there are **horizontal reactions**. These exist
because otherwise the legs would move apart at their bases.

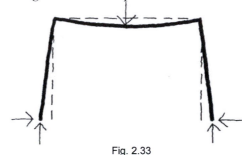

Fig. 2.33

The deformed shape (**Fig. 2.32**) shows which sides of the legs and cross-bar are in
tension and compression. Using this as a guide the bending moment diagram can be
drawn.

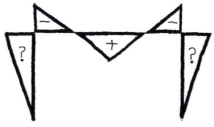

Fig. 2.34

The bending moment diagram is drawn on the tension side of the legs and cross-bar.
Although the sign convention used for the beam shown in **Fig. 2.29** can be used for
the cross-bar, it is unclear what sign should be given to the bending moments in the
legs. Not only will there be bending moments in the frame but there will also be axial
forces and shear forces. There are axial forces in the legs due to the vertical load and
an axial force in the cross-bar due to the horizontal reaction.

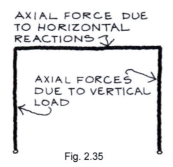
Fig. 2.35

As well as the bending moment diagrams, an **axial force diagram** can be drawn on the portal frame. For axial forces there is no agreed convention for the sign of axial forces or even the way the diagram should be drawn! In some ways the sign convention for axial forces is simpler than for bending moments and shear forces because compression forces are either positive or negative, and similarly for tension forces. Traditionally, axial force diagrams are drawn with a system of arrows on the structure, with numbers written alongside the member indicating the size of the force. To be consistent axial force diagrams should be drawn in the same way as bending moment and shear force diagrams. Both types of diagrams are shown in **Fig.2.36**. The arrow convention is for **arrows pointing away** from the end of a member to indicate compression and, for the diagram, compression is assumed to be positive.

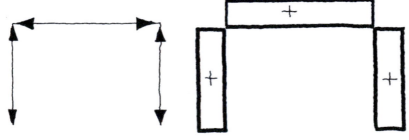
Fig. 2.36

Also a **shear force diagram** can be drawn, here the beam sign convention shown in **Fig. 2.31** can be used for the cross-bar but again, as for the case of the bending moment, the sign of the shear force in the legs is unclear.

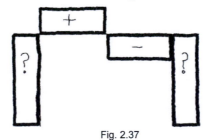
Fig. 2.37

It is impossible to have fully consistent sign conventions and diagrams without having agreed local and global axes systems for the whole structure. The importance of this point becomes clear when computer programs are used to find the forces in a structure, and this is commonplace these days.

Further understanding of how the internal forces are acting on a structure can be obtained by considering the parts of a structure as **free bodies**. In the case of the portal frame, the **free bodies** are the beam and the two legs.

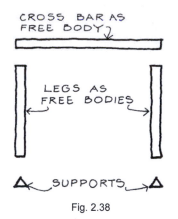

Fig. 2.38

The forces acting on these free bodies to keep them in equilibrium are shown in **Fig.2.39**.

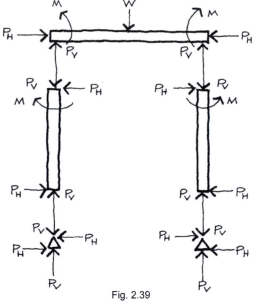

Fig. 2.39

The meaning of this bewildering set of forces is easier to understand by considering the forces due to the load and the forces due to the horizontal restraint separately. For the vertical load **W**, its effect on the beam is balanced by the end forces P_v. These in turn cause forces equal to P_v on the tops of the legs that are balanced by forces, also equal to P_v, at the bottom of the legs. The forces at the bottom of the legs are balanced by forces on the supports that, in turn, are balanced by the reactions.

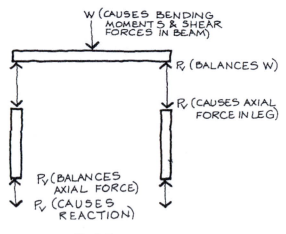

Fig. 2.40

The reasons for the existence of **M** and **P$_H$** are less clear. They exist because the joints between the legs and cross-bar are **stiff**, that is, the joints are **at right-angles before and after loading**. Due to the vertical load **W**, the cross-bar bends and the ends rotate. To maintain the right-angles at the joints, the legs want to move outwards, as is shown in **Fig. 2.33** (if this did happen **M** and **P$_H$** would not exist). But the connection at the bottom of the legs prevents horizontal movement and this causes the legs to bend.

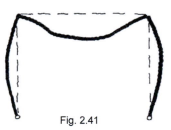

Fig. 2.41

And just looking at one leg:

Fig. 2.42

This effect can be simulated by holding one end of a flexible stick between two fingers of one hand and rotating the other end with the other hand.

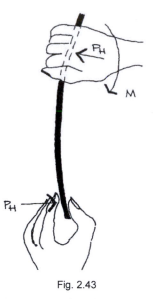

Fig. 2.43

So the effect of connection is to cause bending moments in the leg due to **M** and shear forces due to **P$_H$**. A free body diagram can be drawn showing the effect of **M** and **P$_H$** on all the parts of the structure.

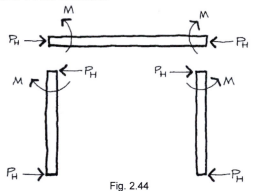

Fig. 2.44

The diagrams showing the bending moments, shear and axial forces can be separated into those caused by the vertical load **W**, and those caused by the horizontal restraint of the legs. Firstly the effect of the vertical load with no horizontal restraint at the base of the legs.

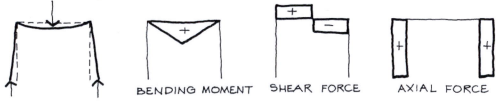

BENDING MOMENT   SHEAR FORCE   AXIAL FORCE

Fig. 2.45

And secondly the effect of pushing the bottom of the legs together.

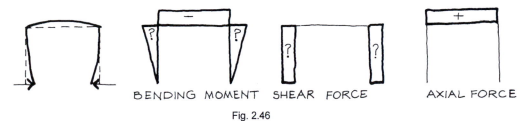

BENDING MOMENT   SHEAR FORCE   AXIAL FORCE

Fig. 2.46

As both effects happen together, the diagrams can be combined to give the complete picture.

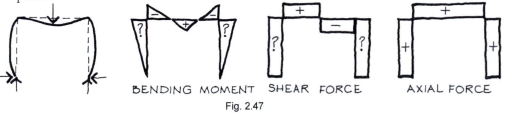

BENDING MOMENT   SHEAR FORCE   AXIAL FORCE

Fig. 2.47

It is sets of diagrams like these, together with the magnitude of all the forces, that provide the engineering information on how any structure behaves under any form of loading.

2.6   Slabs

The concepts of bending moments, shear and axial forces are not confined to one-dimensional elements, such as beams and columns; they can be applied to all structural forms. For instance a two-dimensional element such as a floor slab resists lateral loads by a system of internal bending moments and shear forces.

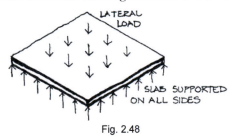

Fig. 2.48

Because the slab is two dimensional, bending moments and shear forces can be considered as acting in two separate directions. For example a rectangular slab, supported on all sides and loaded by a central point load, will span in two directions.

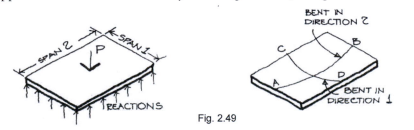

Fig. 2.49

A 'strip', **AB**, of the slab acts rather like a beam spanning from **A** to **B**. This strip will have bending moment and shear force distributions that can be represented by bending moment and shear force diagrams.

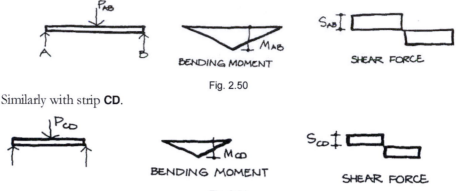

Fig. 2.50

Similarly with strip **CD**.

Fig. 2.51

Because the whole slab is carrying the load **P**, the amount of load the strips **AB** and **CD** carry is less than **P**. The diagrams drawn for the strips can be compared with those shown in **Fig. 2.31**. These diagrams can be drawn for the two strips.

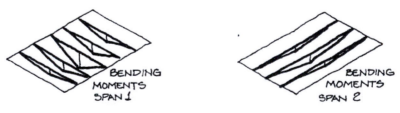

Fig. 2.52

Remember that this is for one strip in each direction and the width of the strip is arbitrary. For the real slab, these bending moments and shear forces will vary continuously throughout the slab. Unfortunately this is difficult to show as a clear diagram, but an idea can be given by drawing the diagrams for a series of strips. In the next diagram, bending moments are drawn for the two directions for a series of strips.

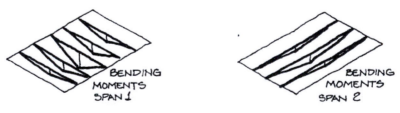

Fig. 2.53

Similarly a series of shear force diagrams could be drawn.

2.7 The structural action of load paths

Often beams support the edges of floor slabs and columns support the beams. The slab spans two ways on to the beams and the beams, together with the columns, form a series of portal frames.

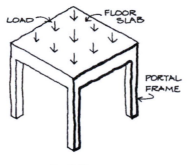

Fig. 2.54

The slab carries the load to the beams by a system of bending moments and shear forces acting in two directions. At the edges of the slab there are vertical reactions that balance the load on the slab. In turn, these reactions cause loads on the portal frames.

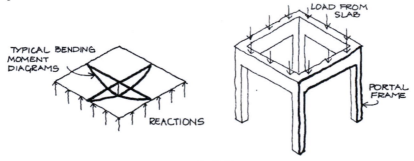

Fig. 2.55

The portal frames resist these loads by internal bending moments, and shear and axial forces. These internal forces are distributed throughout the portal frames and are summarised by diagrams like those shown in **Figs. 2.45-47**. The columns are now part of two portal frames.

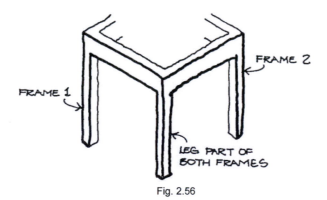

Fig. 2.56

The bending moments and shear forces from the action of portal **FRAME 1** are in the plane of **FRAME 1** and those from **FRAME 2** are in the plane of **FRAME 2**.

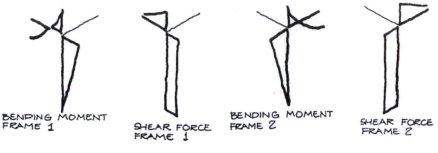

BENDING MOMENT FRAME 1   SHEAR FORCE FRAME 1   BENDING MOMENT FRAME 2   SHEAR FORCE FRAME 2

Fig. 2.57

As the column can't bend in two different directions at the same time it actually bends in a third direction that is not in the plane of **FRAME 1** or **FRAME 2**.

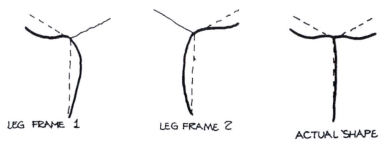

LEG FRAME 1   LEG FRAME 2   ACTUAL SHAPE

Fig. 2.58

This illustrates the fact that whilst it may be conceptually convenient to view the slab supports as a series of portal frames, the structure acts in a way that is most structurally 'convenient'.

The example of the slab supported by beams and columns, shown in **Fig. 2.54**, has a simple load path. With the new concepts of structural actions it can be seen that this load path carries the loads by a sequence of these structural actions.

Now two essential skills required for the understanding of structures have been presented and these are:

- **Identifying the load path for each load — this is what carries the load**

- **Identifying the sequence of structural actions in the load path — this is how the load is carried.**

To see how the concept of structural actions shows how the load path carries the load, the earlier example of the wind-loaded signboard, see **Fig. 1.64**, is re-examined using these concepts.

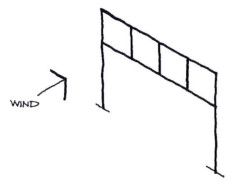

Fig. 2.59

The sign itself is a two-dimensional structural element which is supported by three stiffeners and the posts. As these lines of support are parallel, the element acts like a one-dimensional element.

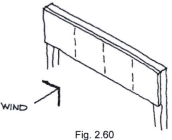

WIND

Fig. 2.60

The bending moments and shear forces caused by the wind vary along the sign but are constant across it.

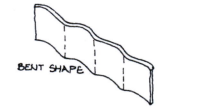

BENT SHAPE

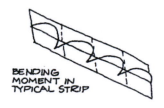

BENDING MOMENT IN TYPICAL STRIP

Fig. 2.61

It may be clearer to draw as a view from above.

BENT SHAPE

BENDING MOMENT DIAGRAM

SHEAR FORCE DIAGRAM

Fig. 2.62

The reactions from the sign load the stiffeners, and these act as beams spanning between the rails. Bending moment and shear force diagrams can be drawn for a typical stiffener.

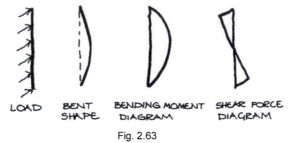

LOAD   BENT SHAPE   BENDING MOMENT DIAGRAM   SHEAR FORCE DIAGRAM

Fig. 2.63

The reactions from the ends of the stiffeners act as three point loads on the top and bottom rails. These act as beams spanning between the posts so bending moment and shear force diagrams can be drawn for the rails.

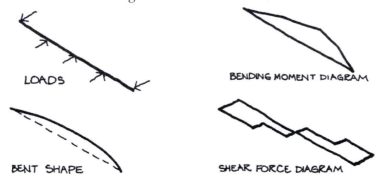

LOADS   BENDING MOMENT DIAGRAM

BENT SHAPE   SHEAR FORCE DIAGRAM

Fig. 2.64

The posts act as cantilevers carrying the loads from the ends of the rails plus the load from the sign. The bending moment and shear force diagrams are drawn for the posts.

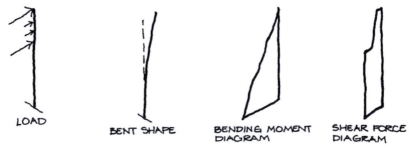

LOAD   BENT SHAPE   BENDING MOMENT DIAGRAM   SHEAR FORCE DIAGRAM

Fig. 2.65

So each part of the load path transfers the load by some form of structural action – these may be bending moments and shear forces or axial forces or some combination of these. Not only is the load path the structure, but also as a sequence of internal structural actions, the **load path acts as a structure**.

2.8   Twisting forces

The internal forces that are axial forces, bending moments and shear forces are the 'usual' forces. However, there is another internal force that **twists** a structural element about its longitudinal axis. This internal force is a moment and is called a **torque** or, more commonly, a **torsional moment**.

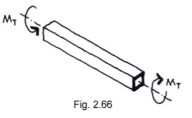

Fig. 2.66

That this internal force is a moment, that is a force acting at a distance, can be seen by considering an element loaded by equal and opposite forces applied to the element by rigid arms.

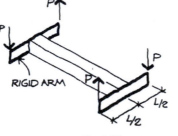

Fig. 2.67

Here the torsional moment applied to each end of the element is:

$$2(P \times (L/2)) = P \times L = M_T$$

There are no other forces in the element as all the loads are equal and opposite.

Torsional moments are often applied in daily life, think of the action of a screwdriver or a spanner (torque wrench), they are rarely used as part of the primary load carrying systems in building structures however, they can occur. Consider a slab cantilevering from a beam that is spanning between two columns.

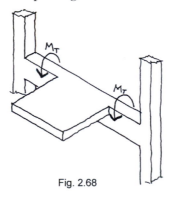

Fig. 2.68

But torsional moments frequently occur as a result of the geometry of the structure. In the case of the structure shown in **Fig. 2.54** the supporting beams will be subjected to these 'secondary' torsional moments. The beam will rotate due to the connection with the slab and with the column. At each point the rotation will vary so that the beam is being twisted which will cause these secondary torsional moments.

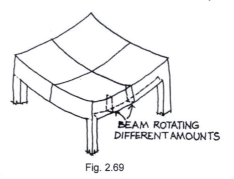

BEAM ROTATING
DIFFERENT AMOUNTS

Fig. 2.69

These types of torsional moments, those that are not part of the primary load carrying system, are usually regarded as **secondary effects** and are ignored at the 'discretion' of the structural designer provided there is confidence that they will not cause unwanted results.

In the case of beams curved in plan, torsional moments are part of the primary load carrying system in all cases and cannot be ignored – see section **3.7**.

2.9   Summary

It is the prediction of the structural behaviour of the load path that is the major skill required for successful structural engineering design. When structures are proposed, the structural action of each load path must be predicted as part of the proposal. The more complex the proposed structure, the more difficult it is to predict the structural behaviour of the load paths. In very complex structures it may even be difficult to identify the load paths. Severe problems can arise in the design process when complex structures with unpredictable structural behaviour are proposed. A prime example of this was the structural design of the Sydney Opera House (see section **12.7**) for which thirteen different structural schemes were proposed before an acceptable structural design was found; this took six years and an estimated 375,000 hours of engineering design time. Often it is wise to propose simple, and therefore easily predictable structures, unless there is ample time and money during the design process for the inevitable modifications to be made.

CHAPTER 3   *Structural element behaviour*

In this chapter the behaviour of the structure that is part of a load path is examined in detail. The understanding that is obtained from this examination makes it clear how parts of structures resist the internal forces. It also gives guidance on the best shape or **structural form** for any particular part of the load path. The choice of overall structural form for any particular structure is one of the basic tasks of the structural designer but before the behaviour of whole structural forms can be understood, the behaviour of very simple structures must be clear. To do this it is helpful to think of structures being **assemblies of elements.**

3.1   Structural elements

For structural engineering convenience, elements are considered to be one dimensional, two dimensional or three dimensional. The basic element can be thought of as a rectangular block, with sides of dimensions **A, B** and **C.**

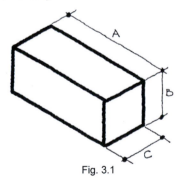

Fig. 3.1

If the three dimensions are very approximately equal then such an element is a **three-dimensional element**. Examples of three-dimensional elements are rare in modern building structures but often occur in older buildings, such as wall buttresses or thick stone domes.

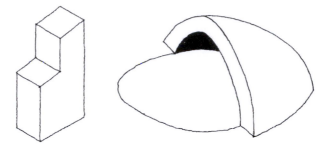

Fig. 3.2

If one of the dimensions, say dimension **B**, is small compared with dimensions **A** and **C**, then the element is a **two-dimensional element**.

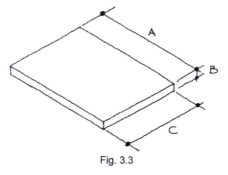

Fig. 3.3

Many parts of modern building structures are two-dimensional elements such as floor slabs, walls or shell roofs.

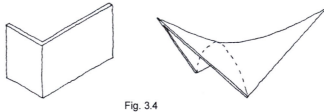

Fig. 3.4

If two of the dimensions of the basic element, say **B** and **C**, are small compared with dimension **A**, then the element is a **one-dimensional element**.

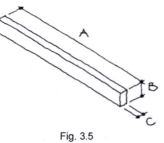

Fig. 3.5

One-dimensional elements are used abundantly in nearly all buildings; examples are beams, bars, cables and columns. Using the concept of elements, structures can be conceived as assemblies of elements. Examples can be found both in traditional and modern structures.

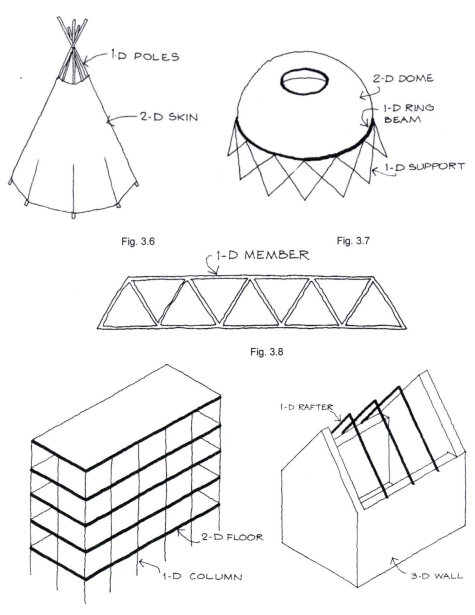

1·D POLES

2-D SKIN

2-D DOME

1-D RING BEAM

1-D SUPPORT

Fig. 3.6

Fig. 3.7

1-D MEMBER

Fig. 3.8

1-D RAFTER

2-D FLOOR

1-D COLUMN

3·D WALL

Fig. 3.9

Fig. 3.10

Nowadays structures are usually conceived and designed as assemblies of structural elements. This means the structural behaviour can be quantified by considering the behaviour of each **structural element** in each load path.

3.2   Concepts of stress and stress distribution

For any structure, all the elements that make up each load path must be strong enough to resist the internal structural actions caused by the loads. This means detailed information is required about the structural behaviour of different materials and of the structural elements.

To obtain this knowledge a new concept has to be introduced, this is the concept of **stress** and the related idea of **stress distribution**. Stress is a word in common usage but for engineering it has a particular meaning and that is **force per unit area**. Stress distribution describes how the sizes of stresses vary from unit area to unit area.

To begin to understand these ideas it is helpful to look at the **slice of a column** shown in **Fig. 2.2**.

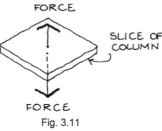

Fig. 3.11

Suppose the cross-section of the slice is gridded into squares of the same size (unit squares), then a force can be attached to each square. If the slice is divided into **25** unit squares, so the force shown in **Fig. 3.11** is divided into **25** forces per unit area, f_1 to f_{25}.

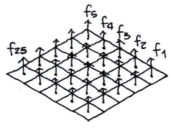

Fig. 3.12

For equilibrium, the numerical sum of the sizes of the twenty-five forces per unit area must equal the total force on the cross-section. So far there is no requirement that any of the forces per unit area, f_1 to f_{25}, are numerically equal. **Fig. 3.12** is redrawn as **Fig. 3.13** showing a possible **pattern of variation** for f_1 to f_{25}.

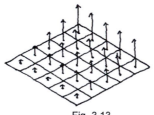

Fig. 3.13

The length of each force arrow indicates the size of the force in each unit square and it can be seen that these forces (stresses) vary in a pattern. Suppose, for clarity, just one strip of squares is drawn and the tops of the arrows are joined with a line.

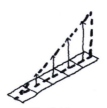

Fig. 3.14

As can be seen the resulting shape is a triangle, so along this strip there is a **triangular stress distribution**. **Fig. 3.13** shows the stresses varying in both directions across the cross-section so the tops of all the arrows can be joined with lines as shown below.

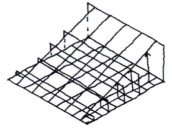

Fig. 3.15

These lines show triangular shapes in one direction and rectangular ones in the other direction.

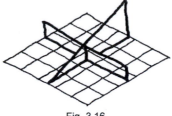

Fig. 3.16

It usual to simplify these diagrams of stress distribution by just drawing the outline along the edges.

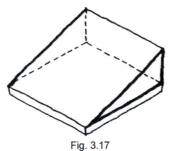

Fig. 3.17

Notice that the stress distribution is drawn right across the section. The stress distribution shown in **Fig. 3.17** is **triangular** in one direction and **uniform** in the other. Uniform, or constant, stress distribution means that the sizes of the stresses do not vary in that direction.

In general there is no restriction on how stresses vary across any cross-section of any structure, except that the sum of the stresses must be equal to the internal force acting at the section and the internal force acts at the **centre of gravity** of the stresses. This new concept of centre of gravity has been used, in a different way, for the see-saw (see **Fig.1 .39**). Suppose a see-saw has people of different weights all along its length, their weights are indicated by their sizes.

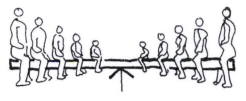

Fig. 3.18

In this figure the see-saw is divided into ten equal spaces and, to balance, pairs of people of equal weight sit at equal distances from the balance point.

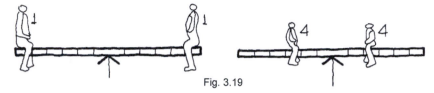

Fig. 3.19

Two such pairs are shown. Provided the equal pairs sit at equal distances from the balance point, the order of the pairs does not matter. **Fig. 3.20** shows two different seating arrangements both of which balance. That is because the centre of gravity of the ten people is at the balance point of the see-saw.

Fig. 3.20

As the seated height of the people relates directly to their weight, these diagrams are conceptually similar to the diagrams of stress distributions. For instance the left-hand seating arrangement shown in **Fig. 3.20** relates to a **triangular stress distribution.**

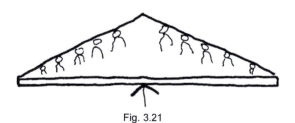

Fig. 3.21

If the seating arrangement were altered to have all the heaviest people at one end, **Fig. 3.22**, then the balance point would have to be moved.

NEW BALANCE POINT

Fig. 3.22

The new balance point will be nearer the end of the heavier people than the lighter. This is because the centre of gravity of this new seating arrangement is no longer at the centre of the see-saw. In the same way the internal force at any point of any structural element must act at the centre of gravity of the stress distribution. Where stresses vary in two directions across the section, the centre of gravity will also vary in two directions.

This new concept of stress allows checks to be made along each load path to ensure that it is strong enough to resist the internal forces caused by the loads. This is checked by making sure that the stresses in the structural elements that are in the load path are less than the **maximum allowable** (or **usable**)**stress** allowed for the structural material being used. In other words the structure must not be **over-stressed**. How a maximum allowable stress is decided is far from straightforward and is discussed later.

Using the concepts of load path, structural action and maximum stress, the main parts of the **process of structural design** can be outlined. Once the reason for the existence for the structure has been identified – building, water tank, bridge – then the process is used as follows:

Step 1   Choose a structural form and material or materials.

Step 2   Identify the loads that the structure has to carry.

Step 3   Find the structural actions in the load path for each loadcase.

Step 4   Check that each load path is not over-stressed.

The details of the process of structural design are examined later but now the concept of stress has been explained, the main steps of the process can be stated. This gives the basic framework that allows the overall behaviour of structures to be understood or designed.

The main point about the size of stresses is that they can be varied without altering the force. Carrying out **step 4** of the design process may indicate that some part of a load path is over-stressed. If this is the case then it may be convenient to alter the structure locally, by altering the geometry, so that the stress is reduced below the maximum stress that is allowed.

This idea is used widely in everyday life; stresses are increased or reduced purposely. For example, the weight of a person may be constant, but the stress under the person's feet will vary with the area of the shoe in contact with the ground. This variation may have good or bad effects. **Fig. 3.23** shows three types of shoes, normal shoes, high heeled shoes and snow shoes.

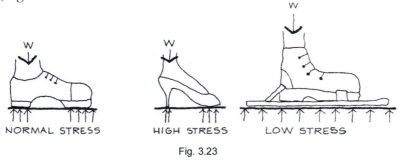

Fig. 3.23

Normal shoes cause normal stresses and can be used on surfaces that can resist these stresses. High heeled shoes, as they provide a much smaller area to carry the same weight, cause higher stresses under the shoe, particularly under the heel. With very slender (stiletto) heels the stresses can be high enough to permanently damage some types of normal floor surfaces. Where stresses must be kept low, for walking on snow for instance, the area under the foot must be increased. This is why snow shoes prevent people from sinking into snow.

The meaning of 'comfortable' shoes, beds and chairs etc. is partly based on limiting the stresses on the human body to 'comfortable' ones. Padded chairs with large seat areas are more comfortable than hard chairs with small seat areas.

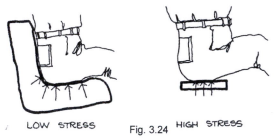

LOW STRESS   Fig. 3.24   HIGH STRESS

The idea of deliberately **altering** stress sizes by geometric methods is also widely used in many other objects used by humans. For example drawing pins are provided with large heads, to allow comfortable stresses on the thumb, and pointed shafts to cause high stresses under the point. The point stress is so high that the base surface fails and allows the drawing pin to be driven in.

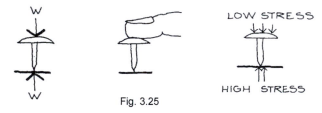

Fig. 3.25

The important idea is that for equilibrium, the force on the head must equal the force on the point, but the stresses vary. The stresses are varied by changing the geometry (of the drawing pin). The provision of handles, points, sharp edges and wide shoulder straps are all familiar devices for deliberately raising or lowering stresses.

Returning to engineering structures, the task is to provide a structure that will carry the prescribed loads down the load path with 'comfortable' stresses everywhere. Depending on the material used, the size of the comfortable stress will vary. For instance as steel is stronger than timber, the allowable (comfortable) stress for steel is higher than for timber. So, in a general sort of way, timber structures will have larger structural elements than steel structures if they are to carry the. same load

As it is usually impractical to arrive at satisfactory structures by guesswork or by testing whole structures, the modern approach is to calculate the size of the stresses on each loadpath and to check that all the stresses are within set limits. For this to be a practical proposition rather than a research project, many simplifying assumptions have to be made. These assumptions allow what is usually known as **Engineer's theory** to be used for stress calculations. Some of these assumptions are concerned with the nature of the material from which the structure is made. These are:

- **The material is isotropic.** This means that the mechanical behaviour of the material is the same in all directions.

- **The material is linear elastic.** An elastic material is one which after deforming under load returns to exactly the same state when the load is removed. If an elastic material deforms as an exact proportion of the load then it is linear elastic. This is discussed further in **Chapter 6**.

There are also assumptions about the geometry of the structure. These are:

- **The structure is homogeneous.** This means that is there are no cracks, splits or holes or other discontinuities in the structure.

- **The deflections of the loaded structure are small.** This means that using the shape of the unloaded structure for calculations to determine structural behaviour will not lead to any significant errors. This does not apply to very flexible structures; think for example of a washing line.

- **Plane sections remain plane.** This rather cryptic statement means that certain parts of a structure that are flat before loading are still flat after loading. This is explained more fully in this chapter.

The Engineer's theory is used for most structural design because it leads to simple stress distributions in structural elements when they are subjected to internal forces of bending moments, shear and axial forces.

3.3 Axial stresses

An axially loaded structural element has axial internal forces and these cause axial stresses across the element (see **Figs. 3.11** and **12**). Using the Engineer's theory this leads to a very simple stress distribution.

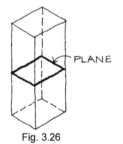

Fig. 3.26

This plane cross-section remains plane after the column is axially loaded. This is visually implied in **Fig. 2.2** where a slice of a loaded column is shown. What the **plane sections remain plane** assumption means in this case is that the flat faces of the unloaded slice are flat after the slice is loaded.

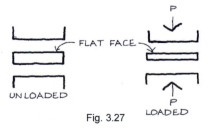

Fig. 3.27

This assumption gives a very simple stress distribution for an axially loaded column. Because the loaded faces remain flat, all parts of the column cross-section deflect by the same amount.

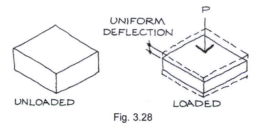

Fig. 3.28

Because the deflections are equal over the cross-section, the stress (load/unit area) is the same everywhere, in other words there is a **uniform stress distribution**.

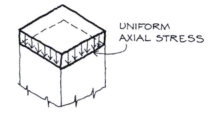

Fig. 3.29

The uniform stress over the cross-section of an axially loaded column gives a very simple relationship between force and stress and this is:

- **Axial stress = Axial force divided by the cross-sectional area**

This means that for a given force, the size of the stress can be varied by increasing or decreasing the cross-sectional area of the column.

The assumption that plane sections remain plane also gives guidance as to when a structural element should be regarded as one, two or three dimensional (see **Figs. 3.1, 3.3** and **3.5**).

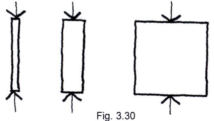

Fig. 3.30

The assumption implies that the whole cross-section is equally stressed. **Fig. 3.30** shows three columns each subjected to a local load. For the widest column it does not seem reasonable to assume that the whole cross-section is equally stressed or even that the whole cross-section is stressed.

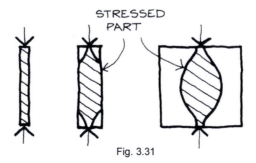

Fig. 3.31

This figure shows the stressed part of the three columns. Very approximately the stress 'spreads out' at about 60°. This means that for the widest column, plane sections do not remain plane. The faces of the loaded slice of the widest column **do not remain plane.**

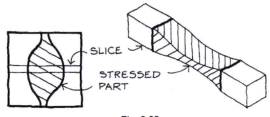

Fig. 3.32

From an engineering point of view this gives guidance as to whether structural elements are one, two or three dimensional. Where simple stress distributions are reasonable then elements can be regarded as one dimensional, but where the stress distributions are no longer simple, the elements are two or three dimensional. In **Fig. 3.32** the widest column has to be regarded as a two dimensional element. This effect can be seen by pulling on progressively wider and wider sheets of paper. The stressed part of the paper will become taut; the unstressed areas will remain floppy.

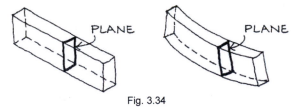

Fig. 3.33

3.4 Bending stresses

Where parts of the load path are spanning elements, beams and slabs, the elements will have internal bending forces (moments). The top and bottom surfaces of these elements become curved; however, plane cross-sections still remain plane.

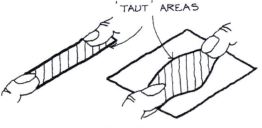

Fig. 3.34

Again looking at unloaded and loaded slices (see page **39**), the plane sections can be identified.

PLANE CROSS-SECTIONS

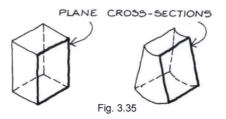

Fig. 3.35

By viewing the slice from the side it can be seen that the plane sections rotate.

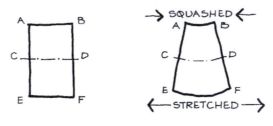

Fig. 3.36

When the slice is bent by an internal bending moment, **AB** is squashed, **EF** is stretched and **CD** remains the same length. Because the cross-sections remain plane, the amount each part of the slice is squashed or stretched varies directly with the distance it is from **CD**.

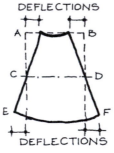

Fig. 3.37

As the structural material is linear elastic, the force is directly proportional to the deflection, so the maximum compression is at **AB** and the amount of compression decreases constantly from **AB** to **CD**. Similarly the maximum tension is at **EF** and the tension decreases constantly from **EF** to **CD**. The maximum compression is at the top of the slice and the maximum tension is at the bottom of the slice and at **CD**, the change point, there is neither compression nor tension. Using this information a stress distribution diagram can be drawn for the side view of the slice.

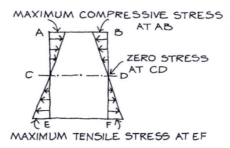

Fig. 3.38

If it is also assumed that these stresses that are caused by an internal bending moment do not vary **across** the beam, a three-dimensional diagram of the stress distribution of the compressive and tensile stresses can be drawn.

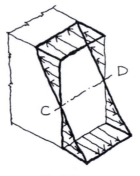

Fig. 3.39

This stress distribution, which is based on the assumptions of **linear elasticity** and **plane sections remaining plane**, is widely (but not exclusively) used in structural engineering. It can be viewed as being in two parts, a triangular distribution of compressive stress and a triangular distribution of tensile stress. **Figs. 3.21** and **3.22** explain how a stress distribution balances a force at the centre of gravity of the stress distribution. The two parts of the stress distribution give a new concept which is the **moment as a pair of forces**. In **Figs. 2.9** to **2.12** a bending moment is shown as a rotating force. Now the bending moment acting on a slice of a beam can be thought of in three alternative ways – as a rotating force, as a double triangular distribution of compressive and tensile stresses, or as a pair of forces.

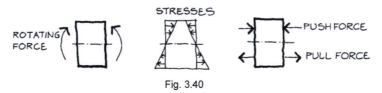

Fig. 3.40

This figure illustrates a **key concept** in the understanding of structural behaviour and applies, often disguised, to almost all structures. These three alternative views are logically connected by the various concepts that have been introduced; really **three steps** have been made.

Step 1   Connects the idea of a bending moment in a beam with plane sections remaining plane and the sides of the slice of a beam rotating.

Fig. 3.41

Step 2   Connects the deflection of the slice caused by the rotation of the sides to ideas of linear elasticity and stress distribution.

Fig. 3.42

Step 3 This uses the idea that if a force causes a stress distribution, then where there is a stress distribution there must be a force. And this force must act at the centre of gravity of the stress distribution.

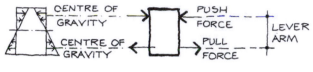

Fig. 3.43

In this figure the **distance** between the **push forces**, which are the effect of the compressive stresses, and the **pull forces**, which are the effect of the tensile stresses, is called the **lever arm**. Remembering that any moment is **a force times a distance**, the push and pull forces 'give back' the bending moment. Here, rather confusingly, the force can be the push or the pull force and the distance is the lever arm.

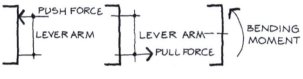

Fig. 3.44

The push and pull forces and the lever arm show how by altering the local geometry of the beam, the **size** of the stresses can be altered for any bending moment. From **Fig. 3.44** two statements can be made about the sizes of the forces from the requirements of equilibrium. Firstly the forces on each face must be in horizontal equilibrium.

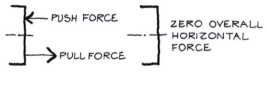

Fig. 3.45

So the first statement is:

- **the size of the push force must equal the size of the pull force.**

Secondly, from moment equilibrium, the bending moment must equal a force times the lever arm. So the second statement is:

- **the size of the push force times the lever arm must equal the size of the pull force times the lever arm must equal the size of the bending moment**

The size of the bending moment is 'fixed' by the position of the element in the load path and the size of the loads the load path has to carry. So, from the second statement, if the lever arm is made bigger, the push (or pull) force is smaller and vice versa.

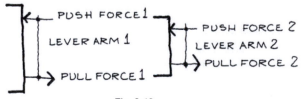

Fig. 3.46

Because of statement two, the size of **PUSH FORCE 1** times **LEVER ARM 1** must equal **PUSH FORCE 2** times **LEVER ARM 2**. As **LEVER ARM 1** is bigger than **LEVER ARM 2** then **PUSH FORCE 1** will be smaller than **PUSH FORCE 2**. The relationship between the size of stresses and forces is dependent, for any force, on the area and the shape of the distribution. For bending stresses the distribution shown in **Fig. 3.39** has been used.

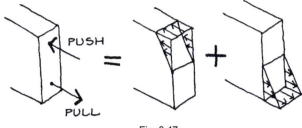

Fig. 3.47

All the compressive stresses (force per unit area) on the upper part of the beam must add up to the push force, and all the tensile stresses on the lower part of the beam must add up to the pull force. By varying the **depth** and therefore the lever arm, the size of the push and pull forces can be altered, which means the sizes of the stresses can be altered. This is only true if the width of the beam is not altered. The size of the stresses can also be altered by varying the **width** because this alters the area. Or the size of the stresses can be altered by varying both the depth and the width.

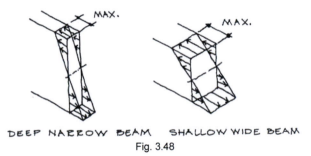

DEEP NARROW BEAM   SHALLOW WIDE BEAM
Fig. 3.48

Unlike axially loaded elements that are equally stressed over the whole cross-section (**Fig. 3.29**), beams bent by moments have varying stresses that are at a maximum at the top and bottom. As all structural materials have a maximum usable stress, rectangular solid beams like those shown in **Fig. 3.48** are **under-stressed** except for the top and bottom faces.

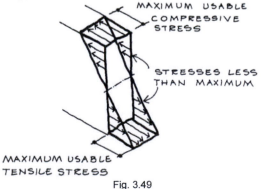

Fig. 3.49

It is one ambition of structural design to try and stress all parts of a structure to the **maximum usable stress** of the structural material being used. In this way no structural material is wasted. This is a sensible ambition provided it does not lead to geometrically complex structures that are expensive to build.

Not only can material be wasted within the depth of a beam but it can also be wasted along its length. Suppose a beam of constant depth and rectangular cross-section is used to carry a load over a simple span. The size of the bending moment will vary along the length of the beam.

Fig. 3.50

For this simple structure, the maximum stress only occurs at one place where the bending moment is at its maximum. Almost the whole of the beam has bending stresses less than the maximum. This contrasts sharply with a column with end loads. Here the whole of the cross-section and the whole of the length of the column can be at maximum stress and so none of the structural material is wasted.

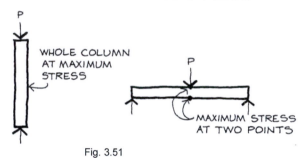

Fig. 3.51

To try and make beams more **stress effective**, non-rectangular shapes have been developed. Although there is some visual evidence that ancient builders were aware of the effect of cross-sectional shapes on the bending performance of beams, the pioneers of modern engineering in the early 19th century took some time to evolve efficient shapes. As the maximum stresses for bending are at the top and bottom of a beam, more efficient beam sections have more structural material here. These efficient sections are I, channel or box sections.

'I' BEAM   CHANNEL   BOX

Fig. 3.52

The exact details of these shapes depend on the structural material used, as the methods of construction are different. Furthermore where bending efficiency is not of paramount importance or for a variety of other reasons, such as cost and speed of construction, other shapes such as tubes, rods and angles may be used.

To understand why the shapes shown in **Fig. 3.52** are **bending efficient** it is helpful to compare an **I** shaped section with a **+** shaped section. Both have the same depth and the same cross-sectional area.

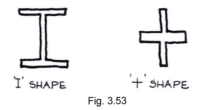

'I' SHAPE   '+' SHAPE

Fig. 3.53

As plane sections are assumed to remain plane, and both sections are assumed to have the same maximum usable stress, the side view of the stress distribution is the same as **Fig. 3.38** for both the sections.

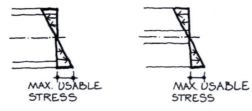

MAX. USABLE   MAX. USABLE
STRESS   STRESS

Fig. 3.54

However, if the three-dimensional stress diagrams are drawn, similar to **Fig. 3.39**, dramatic differences appear.

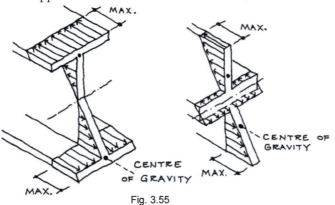

Fig. 3.55

The **I** section has large areas of the cross-section with stresses near to the maximum, but the **+** section has large areas with stresses near to zero. This means that the push and pull forces of **Fig. 3.43** are much bigger for the **I** section than for the **+** section. Also the positions of the centres of gravity of these stresses are different and this gives the **I** section a larger lever arm than the **+** section.

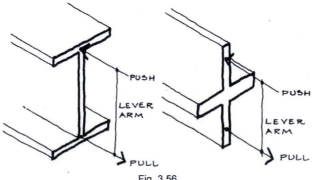

Fig. 3.56

The maximum bending moment a beam with any particular cross-section can carry is given by the second statement stated on page **70,** and this moment is:

• **the push force, with the maximum usable stress, times the lever arm**

which is the same as:

• **the pull force, with the maximum usable stress, times the lever arm**

Both the lever arm and the push force (or pull force) are greater for the **I** section than for the **+** section. Because of this, if beams have the same depth, the same cross-sectional area and the same maximum usable stress, then those with **I** sections will be able to resist larger bending moments than those with **+** sections. Although **I** beams, as they are called, can be made from timber or reinforced concrete they are readily made from steel. Due to the bending efficiency of **I** beams they are very widely used in steel construction as any visit to a steel construction site will show.

By adopting more efficient cross sections, more structural material is used at, or near to, the maximum usable stress. But as the size of the bending moment usually varies along a beam, higher stresses can be achieved away from the position of maximum bending moment by reducing the width or the depth of the beam.

BENDING MOMENT DIAGRAM   BEAM   DEPTH REDUCED

Fig. 3.57

By reducing the depth the lever arm is reduced, so that the push and pull forces are higher for the smaller bending moment. Reducing the width has the effect of reducing the stress area for the push and pull forces and so increasing the stresses.

Building a beam with an **I** section and varying the depth or width to keep the bending stresses high where the size of the bending moment reduces, is an efficient use of structural material compared with using a solid rectangular section of constant depth and width. Whether it is worthwhile using the more complex bending efficient beam depends on cost, both of the material and cost of construction. It is common to see beams of varying depth used for road bridges but unusual in building structures. It is also common to see steel **I** beams, but timber structures, particularly in houses, nearly always use timber beams of rectangular cross-section of constant width and depth.

As with columns (see section **3.3**), the assumption that plane sections remain plane is not always valid. There are two situations where it may not apply. The first is when the span of the beam is not more than about five times the depth of the beam. As the plane sections are no longer plane, the bending stress distribution is not the one shown in **Figs. 3.38** and **3.39**.

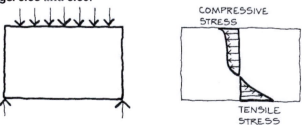

COMPRESSIVE STRESS

TENSILE STRESS

Fig. 3.58 – bending stress in a deep beam

These beams, called **deep beams**, cannot be regarded as one-dimensional elements but are two-dimensional elements (see figure **3.3**).

If a beam is not deep but is made from an **I** or similar section, again plane sections may not remain plane. If the widths of the top and bottom parts of the section are increased eventually they will become **too wide** and not all of the section will be stressed by the bending moment.

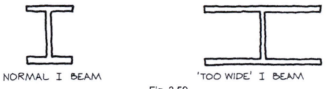

NORMAL I BEAM   'TOO WIDE' I BEAM

Fig. 3.59

For a normal **I** beam the bending stresses are assumed to be constant across the top and bottom parts, but for wide beams only part of the beam may be stressed and the stress is not constant across the beam.

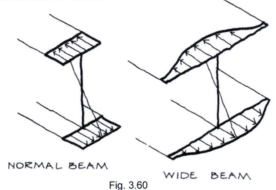

NORMAL BEAM   WIDE BEAM

Fig. 3.60

The effect that causes this varying stress across wide beams is called **shear lag** and the part of the beam that is stressed is often called the **effective width**.

3.5   Shear stresses

Axial forces cause axial stresses (see **Fig. 3.29**) and bending moments cause bending stresses (see **Fig. 3.39**), so it is not unreasonable to expect shear forces to cause **shear stresses**. Shear stresses resist vertical loads so it is to be expected that shear stresses act vertically. For the vertical shear force acting on the face of the slice of the beam, ideas similar to those shown in **Fig. 3.12** can be used. Here, unlike the column, the shear stresses (force per unit area) act in line with the face of the slice.

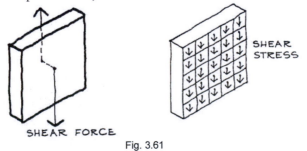

SHEAR STRESS

SHEAR FORCE

Fig. 3.61

Unfortunately the distribution of shear stress cannot be deduced from the straightforward assumptions that were used for axial and bending stress. At the top and the bottom the shear stress must be zero otherwise there would be vertical shear stresses on the surface of the beam, which is impossible. So what shape is the distribution of shear stress? Mathematical analysis shows that for a rectangular beam the shear stress distribution has a curved shape, accurately described as **parabolic shear stress distribution**. The maximum is at the middle of the beam and it is zero at the top and bottom and is constant across the width of the beam.

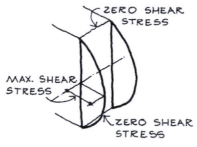

Fig. 3.62

It is common to assume for practical structural engineering design that the shear stress distribution is rectangular rather than curved. This means that this shear stress is 50% less than the maximum shear stress and that there are vertical shear stresses at the top and bottom faces. In spite of these inaccuracies this assumption is thought to be worthwhile as it simplifies the numerical calculation of shear stresses.

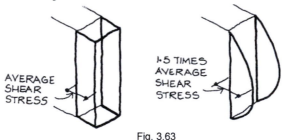

Fig. 3.63

With this assumption there is a similar relationship between shear force and shear stress as that used for the axial forces and stresses (see pages **65-66**) and this is:

- **Shear stress = Shear force divided by the shear area**

The term **shear area** is introduced because for non-rectangular cross-sectional shapes the **vertical area** is used rather than the total area.

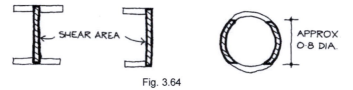

Fig. 3.64

This figure shows typical shear areas for a few common structural cross-sections and illustrates the general idea of vertical shear area.

3.6   Torsional stresses

When a one-dimensional element is twisted by torsional moments (see section **2.8**) the internal forces in the element cause torsional stresses. To see what is happening, cut a slice from a circular bar that is being twisted by torsional moments.

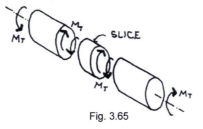

Fig. 3.65

If the circular cross-section is divided into small areas by radial and circumferential lines then each area has a force in the tangential direction to the circumference. Compare this with the diagram for shear stresses – **Fig. 3.61.**

Fig. 3.66

At the centre these tangential forces are zero and it is assumed that they increase linearly towards the outside of the bar. Compare this with the variation of bending stresses shown in **Fig. 3.38.**

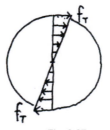

Fig. 3.67

If a circular tube, with a wall thickness that is 'small' compared with its diameter, is twisted by torsional moments, then it could be considered reasonable that the tangential stresses are constant across the wall of thickness **t**.

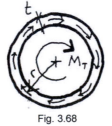

Fig. 3.68

In this case the relationship between the torsional moment, **M$_T$**, and the tangential torsional stress, **f $_T$**, is particularly simple;

Torsional moment = Circumference at wall centre x wall thickness x torsional stress

or $$M_T = 2\pi r \times t \times f_T$$

The tangential torsional stresses in circular elements can be thought of as a number of **loops** or **circles of constant stress**, with the stress in each circle being proportional to the distance from the centre. The circular tube is then a special case of just one circle of constant stress.

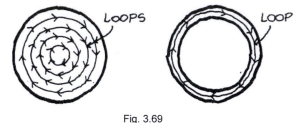

Fig. 3.69

As far as torsional stresses are concerned, circular rods and tubes are special cases because their cross-section is symmetrical about **all** radial axes. The faces of slices cut from these elements are flat (plane) before being twisted and remain flat after the element has been twisted – this is a special case and is not true for sections of other shapes. This should be compared with the idea of plane cross-sections shown in **Fig. 3.35** for the case of a bent beam. If a rod with an elliptical cross-section is twisted, the face of a slice that is flat before the rod is twisted by a torsional moment will not remain flat. In this case the face will deform into a curved surface technically called a **hyperbolic paraboloid**. In other words the **cross-section warps** and the element deforms unequally in the longitudinal direction.

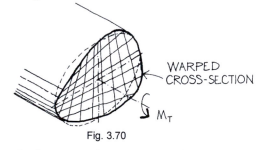

Fig. 3.70

In the case of elliptical rods, the torsional stresses can still be thought of as a series of loops but in this case these loops are elliptical.

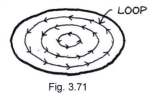

Fig. 3.71

In the case of a rectangular bar, the loops are not all of the same shape and the cross-section warps in a more complex manner.

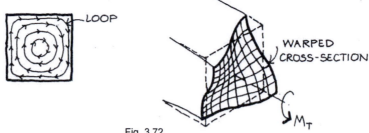

Fig. 3.72

Where cross-sections of an element are made up of a number of rectangular elements which do not form any type of tube – **I** beams and channels for example – they are called open sections (see **Fig. 3.52**). For these sections the torsional stresses are loops round the whole section and the cross-section warps.

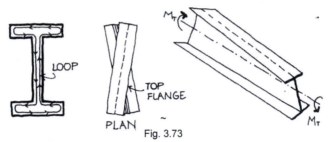

Fig. 3.73

The torsional behaviour just described has two important features that are:

• **the torsional stresses form 'loops' within the section**

• **in general a plane cross-section warps when the element is twisted**

This type of torsional behaviour is often called **Uniform Torsion** or **St. Venant's Torsion** (after the French mathematician Adhémar JCB de Saint-Venant (1797-1886) who presented the mathematical theory of torsion in 1853). Torsion is looked at again, from a different point of view, in the next chapter.

3.7 Curved elements

When structural elements are curved vertically or horizontally the internal forces, axial forces, bending moments and torsional moments cannot always be considered as separate internal forces as they can be interconnected. To see how this happens, two cantilevers, one curved vertically, one curved horizontally and each loaded at the end with a point load **P**, are considered.

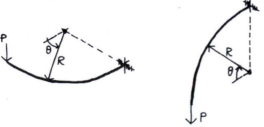

Fig. 3.74

Looking at the horizontal cantilever, first consider an 'L' shaped cantilever with straight elements **AB** and **BC**. Using definition that a bending moment is a distance times a force – see page **27** – the bending moment will increase linearly along **AB** and be constant along **BC**. There will be no twisting effect in element **AB** but a constant one in element **BC**. The bending moment and torsional moment diagrams are drawn in the next figure. A constant shear force of **P** also exists, but the diagram is not drawn for this structure.

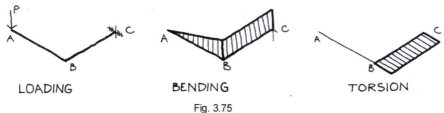

LOADING   BENDING   TORSION

Fig. 3.75

But with the curved cantilever, the bending and torsional moments are present throughout the element and vary continuously as trigonometrical functions of the angle θ.

LOADING   BENDING   TORSION

Fig. 3.76

A similar approach is used for the vertical cantilever, firstly an 'L' shaped cantilever is considered. In this case only an axial force exists in element **AB** whereas bending moments and shear forces exist in element **BC**.

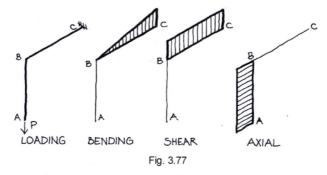

LOADING   BENDING   SHEAR   AXIAL

Fig. 3.77

Like the horizontal curved cantilever, all the forces in the vertical cantilever are present throughout the element again varying as trigonometrical functions of the angle θ.

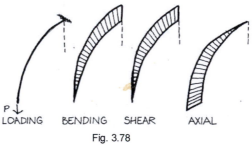

LOADING   BENDING   SHEAR   AXIAL

Fig. 3.78

If a curved member is bent to a tight radius, the distribution of stresses across the section, even using the assumption of the **Engineer's theory** (see page **64-65**), will not be linear, however the linear distribution is accurate enough for most situations. Curved elements are not considered further in this book – the interested reader should consult the specialised literature. This brief section has been included to show how a structure with curved elements has a more complex and interactive behaviour than those structures that only have straight elements.

3.8   Combined stresses

When a one-dimensional element is part of a load path it will have internal forces and these may be axial forces, bending moments or shear forces. These internal forces can be thought of as distributions of axial stress, bending stress and shear stress. With the simplifying assumptions that have been made these stresses have very simple **stress distributions.**

For axial forces and axial stresses:

Fig. 3.79

for bending moments and bending stresses:

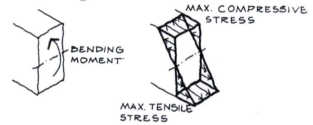

Fig. 3.80

and for shear forces and shear stresses:

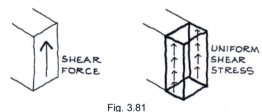

Fig. 3.81

Figs. 2.45-2.47 shows how axial forces, bending moments and shear forces vary around a portal frame when it is loaded with a point load. Each part has an axial force, a bending moment and a shear force, causing distributions of axial stresses **and** bending stresses and shear stresses. Can these stresses be combined to give the total stress distribution? One way is to combine the stresses on the face of a slice; this type of combination is frequently used in engineering.

This way of combining stresses is relatively straightforward as it **just adds** stresses that are in the same direction on the face of the slice. Both axial stresses and bending stresses act at right angles to the face of the beam, which is along the beam, so they are combined by adding the stress distributions together.

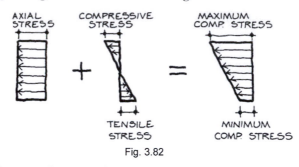

Fig. 3.82

In this figure because the size of the axial compressive stress is bigger than the maximum tensile bending stress, the whole of the cross-section is in compression. The effect of combining the stresses gives a combined **maximum stress** and a combined **minimum stress**. The sizes of these stresses are:

- **Maximum stress = Axial compressive stress** plus **Maximum compressive bending stress**
- **Minimum stress = Axial compressive stress** minus **Maximum tensile bending stress**

Because the shear stress is at right angles to the face of the slice, it is not added to the axial and bending stresses but is kept separate. Depending on the relative sizes of the axial and bending stresses and whether the axial stress is tensile or compressive, the combined stress distribution is all tensile, tensile and compressive, or all compressive.

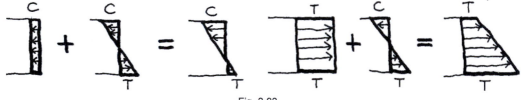

Fig. 3.83

The axial stress distribution can be thought of as an axial force acting at the centre of gravity of the axial stress distribution and the bending stress distribution can be thought of as a pair of **push-pull forces** acting at the centres of gravity of the tensile and compressive parts of the bending stress distribution.

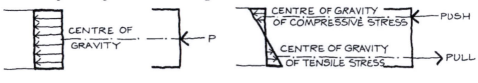

Fig. 3.84

As the stress distributions have been combined to give one stress distribution, can the forces be combined to give one force? If so what is this force and where does it act? As **Fig. 3.45** shows the push equals the pull so the combined force can only be the axial force. But this force must act at the centre of gravity of the combined stress distribution.

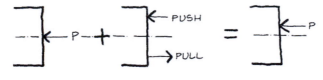

Fig. 3.85

And this centre of gravity is not at the centre of gravity of the axial stress.

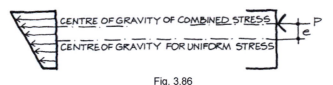

Fig. 3.86

The effect of the moment is to 'move' the axial force by a distance, **e**, from the centre of gravity for uniform axial stress. This distance **e** is called the **eccentricity** and with this new concept many common engineering situations can be better understood.

Before combining the forces there was an axial force **P** and a bending moment **M**. Now there is an axial force **P** that has 'moved' by a distance, the eccentricity **e**. What has happened to **M**, the bending moment? The bending moment still exists but now as **P** times **e**. This is the by now familiar force **P**, times distance **e**.

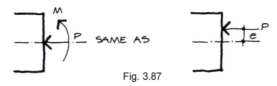

Fig. 3.87

This idea of the axial force acting at an eccentricity can be used for both internal forces and external forces. If a structural element has an internal axial force and a bending moment then this can be viewed as being the same as the axial force being applied at a point eccentric from the centre of gravity for uniform stress. Alternatively if an external axial load is applied to a structural element at a point eccentric from the centre of gravity for uniform axial stress then this can be viewed as being the same as applying an **axial load plus a moment**. This gives a very simple relationship between axial force, bending moment and eccentricity, which is

- **bending moment = axial force times the eccentricity**

or

- **eccentricity = bending moment divided by the axial force**

Suppose a beam is supported on a wall as in **Fig. 1.52**. Then, for the wall only to have uniform axial stress from the reaction of the beam, the beam must be supported exactly at the position of the centre of gravity for this uniform stress distribution.

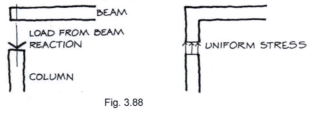

Fig. 3.88

This is usually impossible in any real structure unless very precise precautions are taken. This means the reaction from the beam that the wall is supporting, will be applied to the wall at an eccentricity. So the wall is loaded by an axial load plus a bending moment.

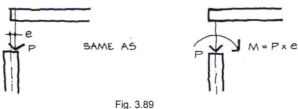

Fig. 3.89

In this figure the eccentricity is within the width of the wall but this will not always be the case. What happens at the base of a garden wall or any other free-standing wall, when the wind blows? The axial force is caused by the weight of the wall itself and the bending moment is caused by the wind blowing horizontally on the wall.

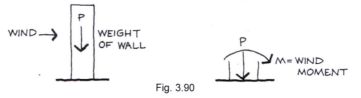

Fig. 3.90

Here the eccentricity could be of any size depending on the relative sizes of the axial force caused by the weight of the wall and the moment caused by the wind. The left diagram in **Fig. 3.91** show a cross-section with only compression stresses, whilst the right diagram shows compressive and tensile stresses. This means that the eccentricity is greater in the right diagram.

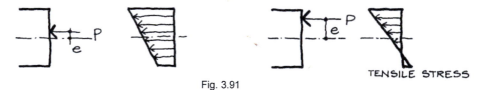

Fig. 3.91

For rectangular sections the eccentricity must be kept within the **middle third** of the cross-section if there is to be **no tensile stress**.

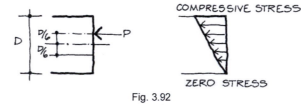

Fig. 3.92

This has very important consequences for structures made from structural materials such as masonry or mass concrete that cannot carry significant tensile stresses. For structures made from these materials, axial forces must be **kept** within the central part of the cross-section or the structure will crack or collapse. This is why brick chimneys and walls sometimes blow over in high winds.

This way of combining stresses makes it easy to check that the stresses in a structure are within the limits of the usable stress for the material. Of course all parts of every load path have to be checked in this way for all load combinations to ensure that the stresses in the structure are always within the limits of the material.

CHAPTER 4 *Advanced concepts of stress*

In the last chapter the concept of stress was introduced and it was shown how axial forces, bending moments and shear forces could be related to stress distributions in a structural member. By making simplifying assumptions, the **Engineer's theory** in particular, simple stress distributions were obtained. At the end of the chapter the idea of combining stresses was used to show how axial loads and moments are related. Most engineering design is carried out just using these concepts, however, the idea of stress can be used to understand more complicated structural behaviour.

This chapter could be omitted on first reading, but the concepts used in this chapter give a deeper understanding of structural behaviour. These concepts can be used to understand more complicated structures than those made of simple beam and column elements, but they also give deeper insights into how simple structures behave.

4.1   Principal stresses in one-dimensional elements

Section **3.8** of the last chapter gave one way of combining stresses, but there is another way of combining stresses at points in a structure by using the idea of **principal stress**. The idea of principal stress is both conceptually and mathematically more difficult than just adding the axial and bending stresses and keeping the shear stresses separate, but it does give much more information on how a structure acts.

To try and understand how a structure acts, slices of the structure have been examined and the idea of stresses has been presented as the effect of forces acting on the face of a slice. The structure does not 'know' that the human brain has decided that it is stressed by axial, bending and shear stresses, nor does it 'think' that it is made up from a series of slices. When a structural element is loaded by being part of a load path it deforms. Some parts squash and others stretch and internal forces do exist. However, the idea that three types of stress exist on the face of a slice cut at right angles to the length of the element is simplistic.

To get a better idea of what is happening inside a structure a 'small part' of the structure is examined. This is similar to the approach used for slices cut at right angles to a one-dimensional structural element only this time there is no restriction on the position of the part examined. This approach can apply to one, two or three-dimensional elements.

What is meant by a small part is usually taken as a small cube. How small is small is never stated explicitly but it is larger than molecular size but small enough for stresses not to vary across the faces of the cube. Because the stresses do not vary, a stress on a face can be represented by a single **force arrow**.

As before, if a beam is subjected to lateral loads it resists these by internal forces called bending moments and shear forces. Using simplifying assumptions these cause constant shear stress and linearly varying bending stresses on a face cut at right angles to the length of the beam.

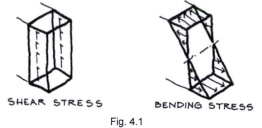

SHEAR STRESS   BENDING STRESS

Fig. 4.1

If two small cubes are cut from the beam, one near the top and one near the bottom, then these cubes would be subjected to axial stresses from the bending moment and shear stresses from the shear force.

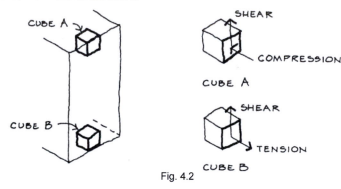

Fig. 4.2

Because the cubes have been cut from a beam rather than a more general structure and because they have been cut at right angles to the length of the beam, it seems that only two of the six faces of the cube have been stressed. Each of the two faces is stressed with a shear stress and an axial stress.

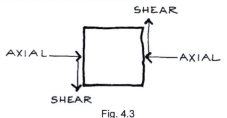

Fig. 4.3

The cube is in horizontal equilibrium and vertical equilibrium as the stresses balance but the cube is not in moment equilibrium, as the shear stresses are tending to rotate the cube.

SAME AS

Fig. 4.4

As this cannot happen there must be other stresses to balance the rotation. These 'new' stresses are shear stresses on the top and bottom faces of the cube.

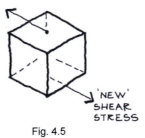

Fig. 4.5

So the small cubes when cut from the beam in the positions shown are stressed by axial stresses, vertical shear stresses and the new **horizontal shear stresses**. For moment equilibrium the horizontal shear stresses must be numerically equal to the vertical shear stresses. Because there are no forces across the beam there are no further stresses.

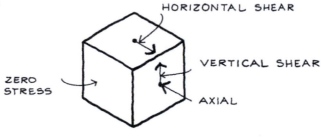

CUBE A

Fig. 4.6

Before exploring these ideas further the effects of **rotating cubes** must be clear. If a square flexible sheet is pulled on two opposite sides it will stretch and if pushed it will squash.

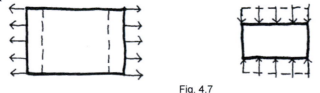

Fig. 4.7

If the sides of the sheet are subjected to shear forces, the sheet will take up a lozenge (or parallelogram) shape.

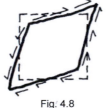

Fig. 4.8

Draw a square on the sheet at **45°** to the sides. If the sheet is pulled on one pair of opposite sides and pushed on the other pair, then the square sheet becomes a rectangle, but the square drawn on the sheet becomes lozenge shaped.

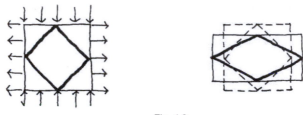

Fig. 4.9

And if the sheet is subjected to shear forces, the square sheet becomes lozenge shaped and the square drawn on the sheet becomes a rectangle.

Fig. 4.10

This shows that for push and pull forces the sheet 'thinks' it is in tension and compression but the drawn sheet 'thinks' it is in shear. When the sheet has shear forces on the sides the situation is reversed and the drawn sheet 'thinks' it is in tension and compression. So, depending on how the element is cut from the structure, the type and the sizes of the stresses depend on the angle at which it is cut. The sheet example illustrates the two-dimensional case (as in the beam). In general, the element is a cube and the stresses are in three directions, the concept of rotating is the same but the diagrams would be distorted cubes.

When shear stresses are absent, that is, there are **only axial stresses**, these stresses are called **principal stresses**. At some point in a structure a small cube positioned in some particular direction will, in general, have axial and shear stresses acting on the faces of the cube. To find the principal stresses at this point the cube must be rotated so that the shear stresses are zero. For the previous examples, push and pull forces cause principal stresses so no rotation is needed, but for shear the element must be rotated by 45°.

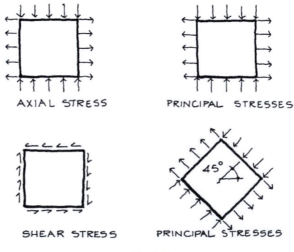

Fig. 4.11

Generally, at any point in a structure, axial and shear stresses will exist. Depending on the numerical size of these stresses, the cube will have to be rotated a specific amount for the shear stresses to be zero. The stresses on the rotated cube will be principal stresses.

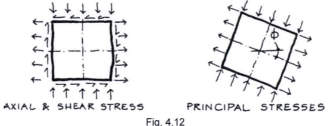

AXIAL & SHEAR STRESS   PRINCIPAL STRESSES

Fig. 4.12

As the stresses vary in type and size from point to point of a structure under load, the principal stresses will vary in size and direction from point to point. To see what information principal stresses give, it is helpful to look at a simple beam loaded with a constant lateral load.

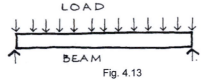

LOAD

BEAM

Fig. 4.13

The beam transfers the lateral load to the supports by a system of internal forces that, in this case, are bending moments and shear forces. As before, the variation in the size of these forces is shown by bending moment and shear force diagrams.

MAX. MOMENT
AT MID-SPAN

MAX. SHEAR
AT SUPPORT

BENDING MOMENT
DIAGRAM

SHEAR FORCE
DIAGRAM

Fig. 4.14

If the beam has a rectangular cross-section, the stresses on a face at right angles to the length of the beam are those shown in **Figs. 3.49** and **3.62**. That is, linearly varying for bending and curved (parabolic) for shear.

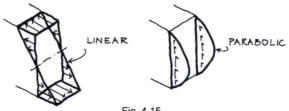

LINEAR   PARABOLIC

Fig. 4.15

The size of the bending moment and shear force vary along the length of the beam so the size of the stresses varies both across the depth and along the length of the beam. For bending stresses, the maximum is at the top and bottom faces in the centre of the beam and the shear stress is at a maximum at mid-depth at the ends of the beam.

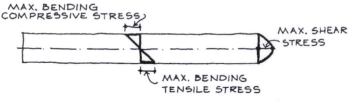

Fig. 4.16

For the top and bottom faces, the shear stress is always zero, and at the centre of the beam the bending stress is always zero. For these points on the beam, the principal stresses are horizontal, or at 45°, see **Fig. 4.11**.

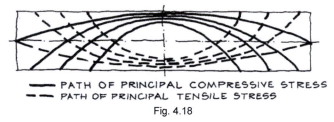

Fig. 4.17

For other points on the beam, the size and direction of the principal stresses can be calculated and these can be plotted. To indicate how the directions of these stresses change, lines can be drawn connecting the stresses at each point.

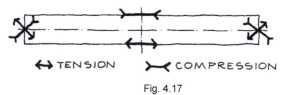

Fig. 4.18

The paths of stress (sometimes called **stress trajectories**) show that for this load case near the middle of the beam the principal stresses are nearly horizontal whilst near the supports the influence of the shear forces causes the stress paths to curve. The size of the stress varies along each path. **Fig. 4.18** shows that for the beam shown in **Fig. 4.13,** the two sets of principal stresses act in a series of **arch- like** curves – each curve crossing at right angles with every other curve.

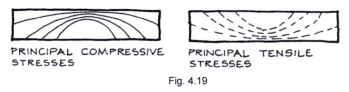

Fig. 4.19

These diagrams give a far clearer picture of what is happening to the beam than do a series of bending moment and shear force diagrams.

If a rod is subjected to a torsional moment, as shown in **Fig. 3.65**, then the rod will have principal stresses. The explanation follows directly from **Figs. 4.2** to **4.6**, which deal with vertical shear.

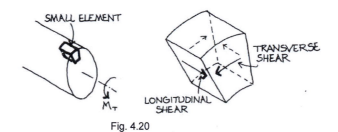

Fig. 4.20

A 'small element' of the torsionally loaded rod will become lozenge shaped which can be interpreted as 'diagonal' principal stresses – see **Fig. 4.11**.

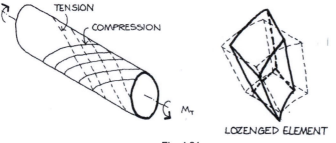

Fig. 4.21

The 'lozenging' of the element can be thought of as being 'caused' by principal tensile and compressive stresses whose direction is at 45° to the longitudinal axes. Therefore a torsional moment is resisted by principal stresses that 'spiral' around the rod.

4.2   Principal stresses in two-dimensional elements

Pictures of the paths of principal stress can be drawn for any structure including those for which bending moment and shear force diagrams do not apply. Suppose a **plate** (a two-dimensional element) has a hole in it, and the plate is stretched in one direction. The principal stress paths give a clear picture of how the plate behaves under this loading.

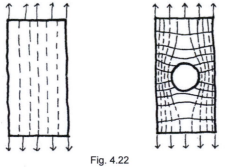

Fig. 4.22

For the plate without a hole the lines of tensile stress are parallel, but for the plate with the hole these lines have to curve around the hole. Because the lines of principal tensile stress curve there are curved lines of principal compressive stress near the hole.

Using the idea of principal tensile and compressive stresses diagrams can be drawn showing how a column 'changes' into a beam. Both a column and beam are considered to be one-dimensional elements, but the intermediate stages are two-dimensional elements.

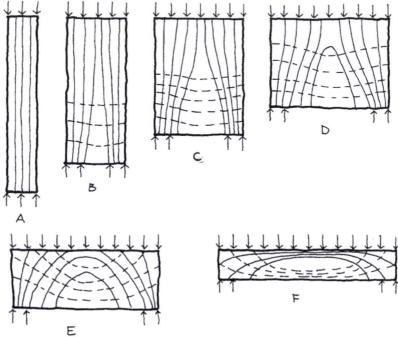

Fig. 4.23.

Fig. 4.23A shows the stresses for a column, a one-dimensional element, and **Fig. 4.23F** shows the stresses for a beam, also a one-dimensional element. **Figs. 4.23B to E** show the stresses for various intermediate stages, and all these are two-dimensional elements. Whilst bending moment, axial and shear force diagrams make sense for the column and beam they cannot usefully be drawn for the intermediate structures.

Without the use of a computer program it is very laborious to calculate numerical values for the magnitude and direction of principal stresses. However, it is possible to make relatively simple calculations by introducing fictitious compressive and tensile members – struts and ties. **Fig. 4.23D** shows a structure that resembles a deep beam – see **Fig. 3.58**. By introducing a tie, shown dashed, and struts,[1] shown as full lines, it is possible to approximate the two-dimensional element with a simpler structure.

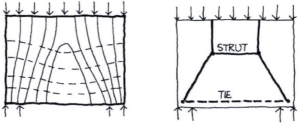

Fig. 4.24 Principal stresses and strut and tie model

What the actual cross-section is for each strut and tie obviously cannot be determined precisely so **engineering judgement** has to be used. However, even without needing to make numerical calculations, drawing possible strut and tie models can lead to an increased conceptual understanding of these two-dimensional structures.

Principal stresses can also be drawn for curved elements like a shell. If a curved shell is spanning between end supports and loaded laterally the pattern of principal stresses will be similar to those for the beam shown in **Fig. 4.18** but the stresses will be curved across the shell.

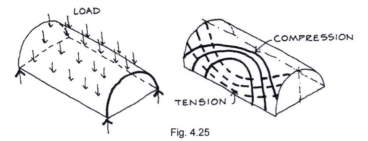

Fig. 4.25

As with the beam, the two sets of tensile and compressive stresses act as **arch-like** curves. The compressive stresses move together at the top of the centre of the shell whereas the tensile stresses move together at the bottom.

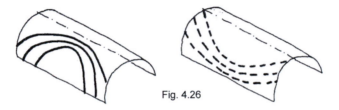

Fig. 4.26

It is often quite difficult to calculate the size and direction of the principal stresses for structures in general, however, if the pattern of the paths of the principal stresses can be visualised this gives a clear picture of how the structure is acting. With materials such as concrete or masonry, which cannot resist significant tensile forces, principal stress paths show where problems may occur or tensile reinforcement is needed.

4.3   The role of shear stresses in beams

When beams do not have simple rectangular cross-sections, as is often the case, the actual behaviour can be quite complex. **Fig. 3.52** shows a number of common non-rectangular shapes used for beams and **Fig. 3.55** shows the distribution of the bending stresses for an **I** beam. **Fig. 3.64** illustrates the idea of shear area used in the simple design of non-rectangular cross-sectional shapes.

The idea of the new shear stress shown in **Fig. 4.5** is crucial to the understanding of the complex behaviour of beams with non-rectangular cross-sections. Although this shear stress is required for the equilibrium of a small cube cut from a beam, what does it contribute to the behaviour of a beam with a rectangular cross section? Suppose there are two beams of equal depth, one on top of the other and separated by a perfectly slippery surface.

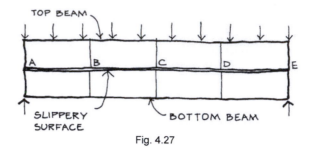

Fig. 4.27

The bent shape of the two beams will be the same, with the top of each beam shortening and the bottom lengthening (see **Fig. 2.13**). This means **ABCDE** of the top beam gets longer and **ABCDE** of the bottom beam gets shorter. Note that point **C** is at midspan.

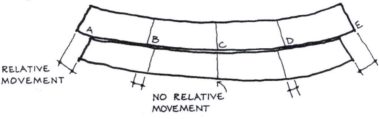

Fig. 4.28

Along the slippery surface **ABCDE** there will be a relative movement between the top and bottom beams. At midspan the movement is zero and the relative movement increases to become a maximum at the ends **A** and **E**. If the two beams are to act as one beam there would no relative movement along **ABCDE**. If this movement is to be zero there must be a force to stop the movement and the force will be proportional to the relative movement. So the force will be zero at midspan and a maximum at the ends.

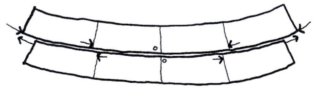

Fig. 4.29

It is the existence of these forces that causes the new shear stress. Because it is acting along the beam it is often called **horizontal shear** (or in timber design rolling shear). It is this horizontal shear stress that alters the bending stress distribution from a 'two beam' to a 'single beam' one.

Fig. 4.30

Not only does the size of the horizontal shear stress vary along the beam but it also varies within the depth of the beam. The size of the stress at any point within the depth of the beam is related to the size of the horizontal force being transferred. This force is due to the change in size of the bending stress across a slice. The difference in the size of the bending stresses has an out of balance horizontal force on any horizontal cut and this force is balanced by the horizontal shear stresses at the cut.

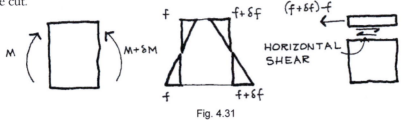

Fig. 4.31

By taking a series of horizontal cuts across the slice, the size of the horizontal shear stresses can be found. At the top and bottom faces of the beam this stress is zero whilst at mid-depth it is at a maximum. The actual shape of the distribution is parabolic, the same shape as the distribution of the vertical shear stress (see **Fig. 3.62**).

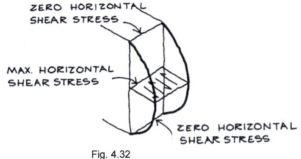

Fig. 4.32

If an **I** section is used for a beam the horizontal shear stress still exists but the distribution is rather different. Because of the changed distribution of bending stresses, the largest part of the bending stress is in the top and bottom flanges (see **Fig. 3.55**). The maximum horizontal shear stress is still at mid-depth, but because the section is 'made up' of flanges and a web, the horizontal shear force has to be transmitted from one part of the beam to another. If the section is 'exploded' it can be seen how the horizontal shear forces 'join' it together.

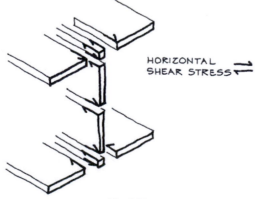

Fig. 4.33

What is happening is that the change in push force in each half of the top flange is being transmitted to the top of the web by a horizontal shear force.

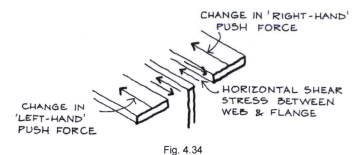

Fig. 4.34

The total change in flange force is then transmitted by a horizontal shear force to the web underneath the flange.

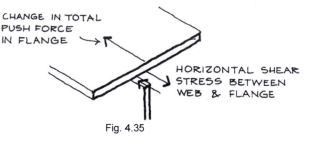

Fig. 4.35

At the mid-depth of the beam, the total change in web and flange force is being transmitted by a horizontal shear force.

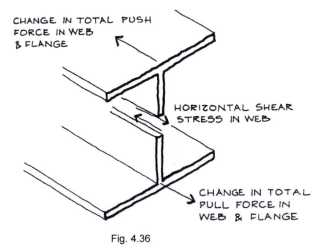

Fig. 4.36

Similarly for the change in bending tensile forces. Note that the word force has been used rather than stress because the stress will depend on the relative thickness of the flanges and the web. The horizontal shear stress in the web is balanced by the vertical shear stresses, but the horizontal shear stresses in the flange are acting in the plane of the flange and have to be balanced by shear stresses acting **across** the flange.

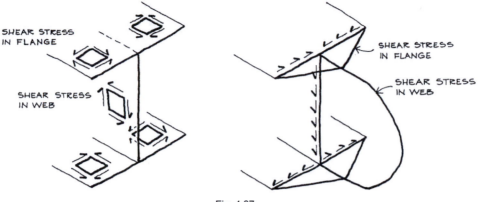

Fig. 4.37

The cross flange shear stress is zero at the outer edges and increases linearly towards the web. Because the web shear under the flange is the sum of the change of both the left and right-hand push forces, there is an increase at this point. The stress in the web then varies parabolically with a maximum at mid-depth. These shear stresses can be plotted on the cross-section. These shear stresses in built-up sections are often called the **shear flow**. Strictly the shear flow is a force, as it is the shear stress times the thickness.

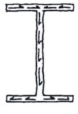

Fig. 4.38

The horizontal forces in each flange are in horizontal equilibrium and the vertical shear stresses are in vertical equilibrium with the shear force. However, if a channel section is used for a beam, the shear flow can be obtained from the diagram for the **I** beam.

Fig. 4.39

Here, although the horizontal forces in each web are in overall equilibrium, these forces are some distance apart which means there is a moment.

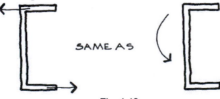

SAME AS

Fig. 4.40

This moment is trying to twist the channel rather than bend it. This example of the channel has been introduced to show how structural actions can become complicated, even for a **simple beam** and a **simple section** like a **channel**.

4.4   Effect of beam cross-section

The reason the channel wants to twist and the **I** beam does not, is because the **I** beam is symmetrical about a vertical line and the channel is not.

LINE OF SYMMETRY

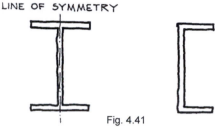

Fig. 4.41

More generally the effect of the cross-sectional shape of a structural element interacts with the type of loading to produce different types of structural behaviour. This structural behaviour can become extremely complicated for general shaped elements. The important point is to appreciate what causes simple or complex behaviour.

For axially loaded elements, if all parts are to be equally stressed, i.e. uniform stress distribution (see **Fig.3.29**), then the load has to be applied to the element at a particular point. This point is confusingly called the centre of gravity of the cross-section, a better term is **centre of area**. This point is the same point that balances a uniform stress distribution. To illustrate this concept imagine a tee shaped platform carrying people of equal weight equally spaced on the platform.

Fig. 4.42

These people are supposed to represent a uniform stress distribution. But where is the balance point? Unlike the see-saw the balance point has to be found in two dimensions. Two pictures can be drawn, one along the tee and one across it.

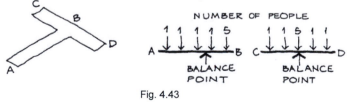

Fig. 4.43

In the **AB** direction the balance point will be nearer **B** than **A**, but for the **CD** direction the loading is symmetrical so the balance point is midway between **C** and **D**. The balance points are really lines and these lines intersect   at the centre of area.

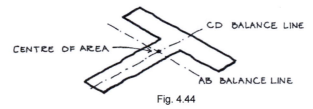

Fig. 4.44

So, if the axial loads are applied through the centre of area, a uniform stress distribution will be caused. If another shaped cross-section (or platform) is used then the centre of area will move. The balance lines will always be along any axes of symmetry, so for shapes with two axes of symmetry the centre of area will be at the intersection of the axes.

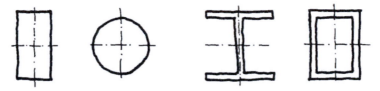

Fig. 4.45 Doubly symmetric sections

Notice that for the box section the centre of area is not actually within the cross-section. Where there is only one axis of symmetry, the unsymmetrical balance line will vary with the geometrical dimensions of the cross-section.

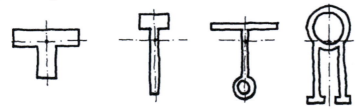

Fig. 4.46 Singly symmetric sections

And where there is no axis of symmetry, the centre of area can only be found by calculation.

Fig. 4.47 Unsymmetric sections

For each cross-sectional shape there is only one position for the centre of area, and the position depends on the shape and, if the section is not doubly symmetric, the dimensions of the cross-section. In other words the centre of area is a **section property**. In actual structures it is not easy to ensure that axial loads are always applied through the centre of area.

As well as affecting the behaviour of elements when axially loaded the cross-sectional shape also affects the way they behave when they bend as beams. When a beam bends, part of the cross-section is in compression and part is in tension (see **Fig. 3.38**). Where the stress changes from compression to tension the stress is zero.

The question is where is this point? And the answer is where it needs to be to satisfy horizontal equilibrium (see **Fig. 3.46**). This is not a helpful answer, but if no simplifying assumptions are made the position of zero stress is not easy to find. If the **Engineer's theory** (see pages **64-65**) is used the position can be found. With this theory plane sections are expected to remain plane, and the structural material to be linear elastic. This results in the points of zero stress due to bending being in a straight line. Because this is a line of zero stress it is often called the **neutral axis**. For a rectangular beam loaded laterally there has been a tacit assumption (see section **3.4**) that the neutral axis is across the beam at mid-depth.

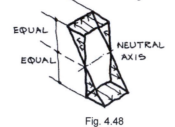

Fig. 4.48

Because the horizontal (push/pull – see **Fig. 3.45**) forces must balance, then, for cross-sections that are symmetric about a horizontal axis that are being loaded vertically, the neutral axis will be at mid-depth.

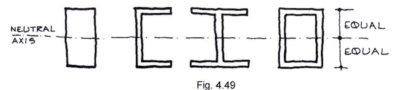

Fig. 4.49

Because of this symmetry, the stress due to bending at the top of the section will be equal to the stress at the bottom of the section.

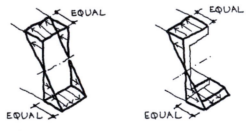

Fig. 4.50

For sections that are not symmetrical about a horizontal axis, the neutral axis will not be at mid-depth, but where will it be? Surprisingly and very fortunately it passes through the centre of area.

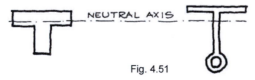

Fig. 4.51

As the **Engineer's theory** is being used, the bending stresses vary linearly with the depth of the beam. Where the neutral axis is not at mid-depth this linear variation means that the stresses at the top and the bottom will no longer be equal.

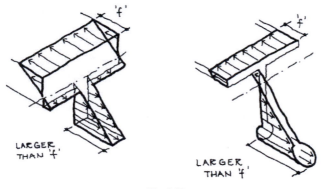

Fig. 4.52

It may seem fortuitous that the neutral axis passes through the centre of area, but this is not so. To see why consider a cross-section in two parts, one double the area of the other. The centre of area is the balance point for constant stress over the whole area of the cross-section. In this case it means the stress **f** is constant over the two parts of the section.

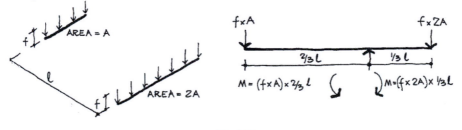

Fig. 4.53

The force in each part of the cross-section is the area multiplied by the constant stress **f**. The moments about the balance point (see **Fig. 1.41**) will be equal if the position is as shown in **Fig. 4.53**. For bending, plane sections remain plane and due to linear elasticity the stress is directly proportional to the movement. For this section, if it is rotated about the balance point (centre of area — see **Fig. 3.37**) the movement of one part will be twice that of the other. This means where the movement is double, the stress will be double.

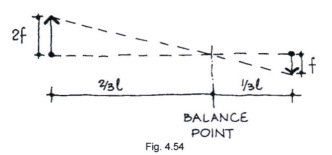

Fig. 4.54

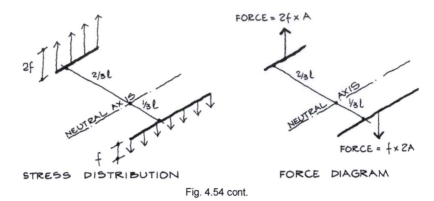

Fig. 4.54 cont.

This diagram shows that for the part of the section with area **A**, the stress is **2f** giving a force of **2fA** in one direction. For the part of the section with an area of **2A** the stress is **f** giving a force of **2Af** in the opposite direction. Therefore the push/pull forces are equal and opposite as required for horizontal equilibrium (see **Fig. 3.45**). This in principle is why the neutral axis goes through the centre of area, and this principle applies to a cross-section of any shape or any number of parts.

4.5   Biaxial bending

Whilst the neutral axis goes through the centre of area, its position rotates depending on the loading. For a rectangular beam loaded **vertically** the neutral axis is **horizontal**, that is at right-angles to the load direction. The same is true for the beam if it is loaded **horizontally**. The associated stress diagrams due to bending are drawn as before.

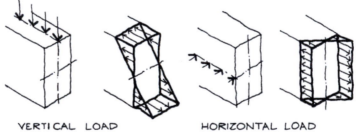

VERTICAL LOAD   HORIZONTAL LOAD

Fig. 4.55

If both the vertical and horizontal loads (not necessarily of the same size) are applied to the beam simultaneously, the beam will have a **new neutral axis**. The position of this neutral axis can be found by adding together the two bending stress diagrams. This addition is similar to the addition of stresses shown in **Fig. 3.82**.

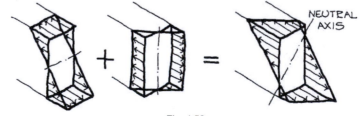

Fig. 4.56

Whilst this is relatively straightforward, what is not obvious is that now, except for a few special cases, the new neutral axis is not at right-angles to the axis of loading. Why is this? The answer is the beam has 'provided' push-pull forces at the centres of gravity of the now rather odd-shaped stress distributions. These forces are also on the line of the load axis. This neutral axis is no longer at right-angles to the load axis which means that the beam does not deflect in the direction of the load.

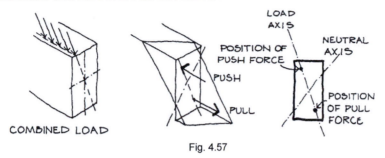

Fig. 4.57

The reason for this is that any cross-section will have axes of bending called **principal axes**, and these are another section property. When the load is applied through a principle axis, the neutral axis will be at right-angles to the load axis but for loads in other directions this will not be true. To predict the bending behaviour of beams of different cross-sections, the positions of the principal axes need to be known. They intersect at the centre of area but in what direction do they go? They will go through an axis of symmetry, so for sections with an axis of symmetry, the directions of the principal axes are clear.

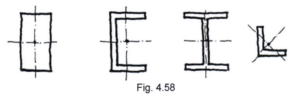

Fig. 4.58

For sections with no axis of symmetry, the direction can only be calculated.

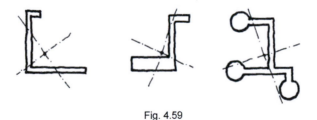

Fig. 4.59

When a beam bends there will be bending stresses and, except for very special cases, there will also be shear stresses. The effect of shear stresses on beams has been described in section **4.3**. **Fig. 4.40** shows that shear stresses may also cause twisting even when only vertical loads are present. This is because of another section property called the **shear centre**. The shear centre is the point through which the load axis must pass to avoid any twisting caused by the shear stress distribution. (Conversely the shear centre is the point about which the section will twist if loaded with twisting loads – see sections **2.8** and **3.6**.) For doubly symmetric or skew symmetric cross-sections, the shear centre will coincide with the centre of area. For cross-sections with only one axis of symmetry, the shear centre will be on this axis of symmetry but will not in general coincide with the centre of area.

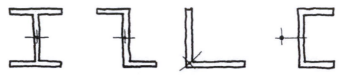

Fig. 4.60 Shear centres

Three important **section properties** of cross-sectional shapes have been identified, and these are:

- **Position of the centre of area**

- **Directions of the principal axes**

- **Position of the shear centre**

For doubly symmetric cross-sections these properties are readily found, but for general cross-sectional shapes these properties can only be found by calculation.

Knowing these section properties, the distributions of axial, bending and shear stress can be drawn provided the assumptions of the **Engineer's theory** are used. Even when the Engineer's theory is used, for structural elements of general cross-sectional shape, the structural behaviour is quite complex. If the element itself is curved or varies in cross-sectional shape along its length, engineering analysis, both conceptual and mathematical, rapidly becomes extremely difficult. This analysis is the subject matter of advanced texts or even research papers.

4.6   Torsion and warping of open sections

Some of the effects of twisting one-dimensional elements have already been described in sections **2.8, 3.6** and **4.1**. In section **3.7** it was seen that torsion can also occur in curved elements. For **Uniform Torsion**, see section **3.6**, the two important features were noted as the formation of 'loops' of torsional stress and the warping of non-circular sections.

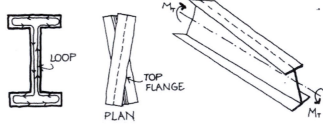

Fig. 4.61 Torsion loops and warping of a built-up section

It can be seen why tube-like sections are torsionally stiff for uniform torsion, and built-up sections are not. For a tube, the resistance to the torsional moment M_T is due to the circumferential torsional stresses times the radius – see page **78**. The same thing is happening in the **I** beam, but the lever arm is now very small as it is within the thickness of the flange or web.

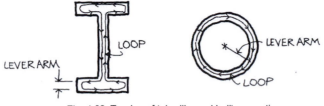

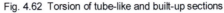

Fig. 4.62 Torsion of tube-like and built-up sections

If however a built-up section is supported in such a way that it cannot warp, the torsional rigidity increases enormously. This can be seen by considering a cantilever **I** beam, which is supported in a way that prevents the flanges displacing longitudinally, and is loaded by a torsional moment. In this case the torsional moment is resisted by the top and bottom flanges acting as horizontal cantilevers.

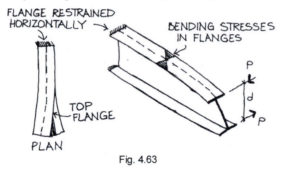

Fig. 4.63

The torsional moment $\mathbf{M_T}$ can be thought of as a pair of point loads **P** acting on the flanges, giving the moment $\mathbf{P} \times \mathbf{d}$. Now the torsional moment is being resisted by longitudinal stresses rather than spiral principal stresses. Although this case of horizontal restraint, or **warping restraint**, may seem an unusual one in fact it is very common in building structures. This is because a torsional moment applied between the supports of a beam gets this restraint because the flanges act as horizontal beams, even if there is **no longitudinal restraint** at the support.

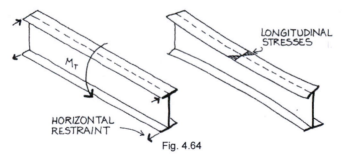

Fig. 4.64

Few computer programs in current use take this common situation into account.

4.7 Composite elements and pre-stressing

Often structural elements are made from more than one type of structural material to form composite structural elements. These combinations are made to exploit the different qualities of the materials to produce an element that performs better than one made from only one material. The usual combination is of a relatively cheap material such as concrete or masonry with a relatively expensive material such as steel. In these elements, the concrete or masonry carries the compressive stresses and the steel carries the tensile stress.

By far the most common form of composite construction for building structures is **reinforced concrete**. Reinforced concrete, together with structural steelwork, is widely used throughout the world for a great variety of structures, both large and small. Because concrete has no useful engineering tensile strength, the steel, usually called **reinforcement** or **re-bar**, is placed in areas of the structural element where calculations predict tensile stresses. This is where diagrams like **Fig. 4.18** are useful. This shows that there are tensile stresses along the bottom of the beam near the centre and these slope near the ends of the beam. So, to make a reinforced concrete beam, there would be longitudinal reinforcement in the bottom of the beam and sloping reinforcement towards the ends.

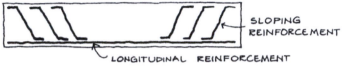

Fig. 4.65

Historically the sloping bars shown in **Fig. 4.65** were used, but it is now more usual to resist the sloping tensile stresses by vertical reinforcement. This vertical reinforcement is bent into rectangles called **links**. The reinforcement is made into a cage by tying the bars together with wire.

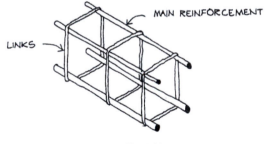

Fig. 4.66

The cage is placed into a mould, or form, and the wet concrete is poured around the reinforcement, thus forming a composite element. As the concrete dries it shrinks and **grips** the reinforcement. To aid this grip the reinforcing bars are often made with a rough pattern.

Fig. 4.67

When the composite beam is bent by a moment, the principle of push-pull forces (see **Fig. 3.43**) still applies, but because concrete cannot resist tensile stresses, the pull force is resisted by tensile stresses in the reinforcement.

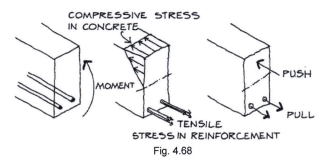

Fig. 4.68

For the steel and concrete to act compositely, the steel must not slip in relation to the concrete. This is the same effect as that shown in **Fig. 4.30** for horizontal shear stresses. The relative slip is resisted by horizontal shear stresses on the face of the reinforcement; these stresses are often called **bond stresses**.

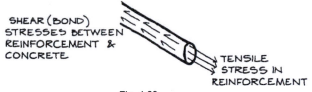

Fig. 4.69

The behaviour of reinforced concrete when subjected to shear forces is very complex but, as can be seen from the principal stress diagram (**Fig. 4.18**), in areas of high shear there are diagonal tensile stresses. In unreinforced concrete these would cause cracks at right angles to the lines of tensile stresses.

Fig. 4.70

The role of the diagonal reinforcing bars or links is to provide tensile strength across these lines of tensile force.

Fig. 4.71

Although in theory concrete only needs reinforcement in areas of tensile stress, except for very minor elements, it is usual to provide a complete cage of reinforcement. The reinforcement that resists the tensile stresses is called the **main reinforcement** and the other reinforcement is called **nominal reinforcement**. For the portal frame shown in **Fig. 2.32,** loaded on the cross-beam, the bending moments cause tensile bending stresses in both the cross-beam and the columns.

| LOADING | BENDING MOMENT DIAGRAM | POSITIONS OF TENSILE STRESS |

Fig. 4.72

Here the main reinforcement is placed in areas of tensile stress, but for practical reasons whole cages of reinforcement would be used for the cross-beam and the columns.

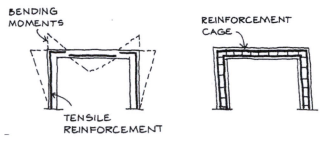

Fig. 4.73

It is not always possible to provide continuous reinforcement in areas of tensile stress, so reinforcing bars are 'joined' by **lapping**. The bars are laid next to each other in the mould, and the concrete is poured around both bars. The force is transmitted from one bar to another by bond (shear) stresses in the surrounding concrete.

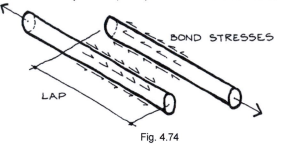

Fig. 4.74

By lapping bars, parts of the reinforced concrete structure can be cast in a preferred sequence. In the case of the portal frame, the sequence would be foundations, columns and then the cross-beam. Bars would be left projecting from each part to be lapped with the reinforcement of the next part.

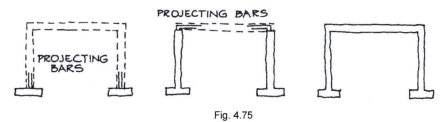

Fig. 4.75

Whilst reinforced concrete is the most common form of composite construction, structural steelwork and reinforced concrete can also be combined to form structural elements. This form is frequently used in spanning structures where the floor slab, a two-dimensional reinforced concrete element, is also used as part of the main beams by acting compositely with the one-dimensional structural steel elements.

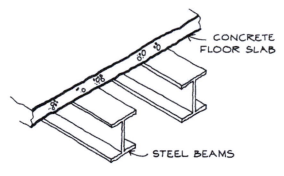

Fig. 4.76

To achieve composite action, the slab is joined to the top of the floor beams by what are known as **shear connectors**. These are pieces of steel, usually in the form of studs, welded to the top of the beam.

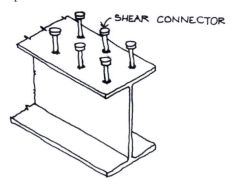

Fig. 4.77

The concrete slab is cast around the shear connectors and these prevent the slab and the top of the steel beam moving in relation to each other. This allows horizontal shear stresses to develop between the slab and the steel beam as is explained on page **95.**

Fig. 4.78

Now the floor beam is the steel beam and the concrete slab. By the addition of the shear connectors, the concrete slab becomes part of the compression flange.

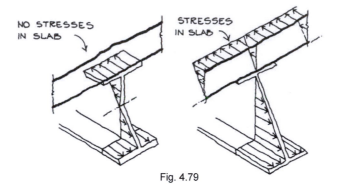

Fig. 4.79

Another form of composite construction is to **pre-stress** materials such as concrete (or less often masonry). This is a technique that causes stress in structural elements **before** they are loaded. Like the addition of reinforcement, the purpose of pre-stressing is to add tensile strength to elements made of materials that can only resist compressive stresses. The principle can be illustrated by stressing together some match boxes with an elastic band. This pre-stressed element can now act as a beam.

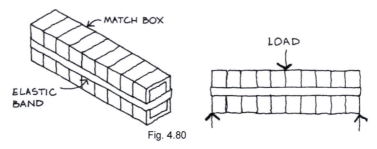

Fig. 4.80

Here the stretched elastic band causes compressive stresses between the match boxes **before** there are stresses due to beam action. When the lateral load is applied it is resisted by internal push-pull forces that cause tensile and compressive bending stresses (see **Fig. 3.40**). Provided the numerical size of the pre-stressed compressive stress is equal or greater than the bending tensile stress the match boxes, with the pre-stress, will act as a beam. The stresses due to pre-stress and bending can be combined as shown in **Fig. 3.83**.

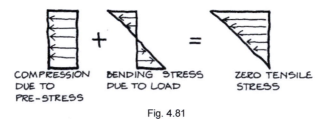

Fig. 4.81

Exactly the same principle is used to make pre-stressed concrete elements. The pre-stress is caused by tensioning the steel reinforcement, and this can be done in two ways called **pre-tensioning** and **post-tensioning**. For pre-tensioning the steel reinforcement is tensioned by jacking against strong points fixed to the ground, then the concrete is poured around the tensioned reinforcement. When the concrete has hardened the jacks are released.

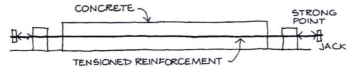

Fig. 4.82

When the jacks are released the stretched reinforcement tries to shorten. But, because the hardened concrete has shrunk around tensioned reinforcement (see **Fig. 4.69**), it prevents the reinforcement shortening and by doing this goes into compression. So in the case of pre-tensioned pre-stressed concrete there are bond (shear) stresses between the (tensioned) reinforcement and the concrete before any load is applied.

Fig. 4.83

Concrete can also be pre-stressed after it has hardened, this is called post-tensioning. The concrete element is made with a hole through it, this hole is usually called a duct. The reinforcement to be stressed is then threaded through the duct, in many cases the reinforcement is put in the duct before the concrete is cast. When the concrete is hard enough the reinforcement is tensioned by jacking it against the end of the concrete element. This causes tension in the reinforcement and compression in the concrete. When the required tension force has been obtained, the reinforcement is **locked off** and the jacks removed. There are several methods of locking off, and these depend on the proprietary method being used.

In the pre-tensioned method, the force in the tensioned reinforcement is transferred to the concrete along the whole length of the element but in the post-tensioned method, the force is transferred at the jacking points. This can sometimes require special end details to make sure the concrete is not over-stressed locally.

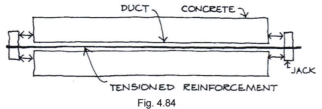

Fig. 4.84

In the same way as eccentric applied loads cause axial stresses and bending stresses (see **Fig. 3.87**), if the tensioned reinforcement does not go through the centre of area of the section, then the pre-stress will not be a constant axial stress. This can be an advantage as it can increase the size of the compressive stress in the part of the element that will have tensile stresses due to the applied load.

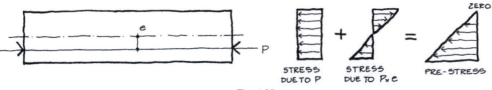

Fig. 4.85

The idea is that the stress distribution due to pre-stress is completely reversed under maximum applied lateral load. This means that, for a simple beam element, the stress at the top is zero due to pre-stress, and the stress at the bottom due to pre-stress and applied load is zero.

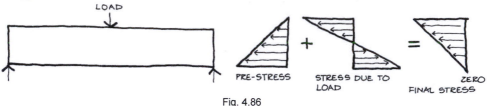

Fig. 4.86

The effect of the eccentrically applied pre-stress is to apply a moment to the element and this moment can be used to counteract the effect of the bending moment caused by the self-weight of the element. For concrete elements, the self-weight is a significant part of the total load. By careful adjustment of the pre-stress force and its position, the stress distribution due to pre-stress and self-weight can be made triangular, with zero stress at the top face.

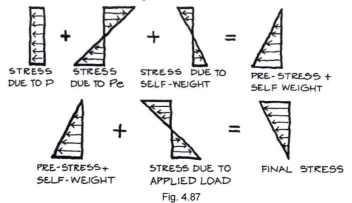

Fig. 4.87

When the maximum live load is applied, the stress diagram is reversed as before. It is usual for the maximum compressive stresses to be the maximum allowable stress for the concrete. By using pre-stress in this way, the concrete member can be used more effectively than a reinforced element, because the maximum stress in a reinforced element has to include both self-weight and live load. Because of this, the pre-stressed element can carry higher loads, or alternatively be shallower for the same load than a reinforced element.

The pre-tensioning method means that the pre-stressing reinforcement has to be straight, but there is no restriction on the shape of a duct that can be cast into a concrete element. This means that the post-tensioning method allows the position of the pre-stressing force to be varied along the element. As lines of principal tensile stress are rarely straight, the ducts can be cast into the concrete along these lines.

LINES OF PRINCIPAL
TENSILE STRESS

DUCT

Fig. 4.88

This has the advantage of putting compressive stresses into the element which directly counteract the tensile stresses caused by the applied load.

The method of pre-tensioning is ideally suited to the production of **standard** pre-stressed elements made in pre-casting yards. These types of elements are used extensively as floor spanning members or beams, usually called lintols, over openings in masonry walls. The method of post-tensioning is slower so its use in building structures is relatively rare and is limited to unusually large elements in major buildings. It is used extensively for large bridges. Often these are made from a number of pre-cast units that are stressed together exactly like the matchboxes (see **Fig. 4.80**).

Composite action can also be used to increase the 'size' of a beam in a masonry wall. This is done by making the masonry that is built on top of the concrete beam act with the beam.

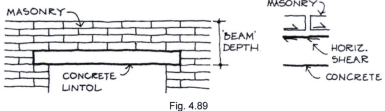

Fig. 4.89

This is similar in principle to the action between the concrete slab and the steel beam shown in **Fig. 4.78**. Here the horizontal shear stresses that are essential for the composite action are resisted by the mortar joints, the beam and the masonry units (bricks or blocks).

Many other examples of composite action could be given but the essential point is to understand the role played in the total structural action of the element by the different materials. This is done by understanding how each part of the element is stressed when it acts as part of a load path.

As buildings are constructed by joining together a variety of elements, walls, floors, windows, stairs, etc. it is important to be sure that loads do go down the chosen load paths and not into non-loadbearing elements that are not capable of carrying the loads. This is really composite action in reverse. For example, the portal frame when loaded will deflect. If the portal frame is glazed as part of the building design, the glazing would try and prevent the portal frame from deflecting. This means that the glazing is acting compositely with the portal frame to 'make' a two-dimensional wall element.

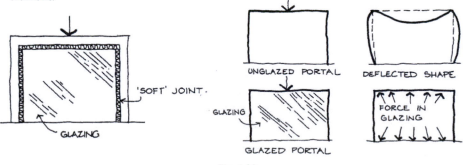

Fig. 4.90

Unless the glazing is designed to be part of the load path, it may fail as it tries to carry a share of the load due to composite action. In these cases special 'soft' joints or other devices must be introduced to prevent the composite action. These are exactly opposite to the idea of the shear connectors shown in **Fig. 4.77**. In this case the joint between the glazing and the portal frame must be designed so that the portal frame can deflect without loading the glazing.

4.8   Summary

This section shows how structural elements act when they are loaded as part of a load path. This behaviour has been characterised by the stress distribution at each point of the element. These stresses are caused by the structural actions, axial bending and shear forces described in **Chapter 3**. The stress distributions in this section have been obtained by using the **Engineer's theory**. These assumptions have been used by several generations of structural designers. Whilst the Engineer's theory is still widely used, non-elastic theories are now also used. These theories are outlined in **Chapter 6**.

Part of the skill of designing structures is the prediction of the stress distribution in each element as it acts as part of a load path (or paths). The accuracy of prediction will vary depending on the stage of the design process. For instance the exact size of elements may not need to be calculated at preliminary stages. However, it should be clear to the structural designers that the proposed types of elements, shells, slabs, **I** beams etc., will act effectively as their part of the **load path**. This is clarified if the stress distribution is known in principle. For instance if load-bearing walls are used at different levels and they cross at angles, then the whole wall will not be effective (see **Fig. 3.31**).

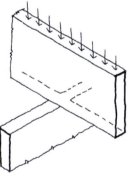

Fig. 4.91

Or again if an element is acting as a beam, then an **I** section is better than a **+** section (see page **73**), and it might be worthwhile to vary the depth (see **Fig. 3.57**).

The central point is that structural design is not the result of a logical process but the result of an imaginative concept. For this concept to be successful it must be informed by a conceptual understanding of how the imagined structure will behave.

References – Chapter 4

1   J Schlaich, K.Schäfer, M. Jennewein – **Towards a consistent design of structural concrete** – PCI Journal 32, N° 3, May/June 1987 – p 74-150

CHAPTER 5   *Structural materials*

To build any structure, whether it is a chair or the Forth Bridge, it has to be constructed of a suitable material. That is a material that at least has the necessary structural properties. The two basic properties that are required are: **strength and stiffness.** Because the structure has to transfer forces it has to be **strong enough**, and because, on the whole the structure is expected to maintain its shape, it has to be **stiff enough**.

Strangely, strength and stiffness of a material are unrelated. The reason for this is that the molecular structure varies from material to material. However structural designers usually consider the macroscopic rather than molecular level of behaviour. The behaviour of materials at the molecular level is the concern of material scientists and is beyond the scope of this book.

5.1   Types of material behaviour

Engineering materials are classified by comparing the relationship between **strength** and **stiffness** or stretchiness. Everyone is familiar with stretching rubber bands or pulling pieces of Plasticine®. After being stretched the rubber band and the piece of Plasticine behave quite differently. The rubber band returns to its original size whereas the piece of Plasticine stays stretched.

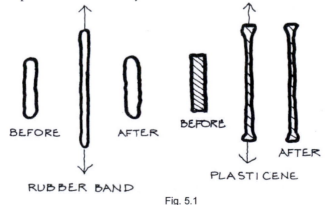

Fig. 5.1

This is because the rubber is **elastic**, hence elastic band, and Plasticine is **plastic**. Elastic and plastic are technical engineering terms. The elastic and plastic behaviour are best described by drawing graphs of the **load/deflection** behaviour.

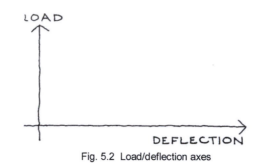

Fig. 5.2 Load/deflection axes

It is usual to plot the load on the vertical axis and to plot the deflection on the horizontal axis. If the load/deflection graph is plotted for an elastic band, the deflection will increase with load.

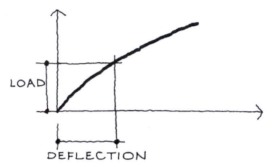

Fig. 5.3 Load/deflection graph of an elastic band

However, once a piece of Plasticine starts to stretch, it can be continuously stretched with a constant load. So the load/deflection graph is more or less a horizontal line.

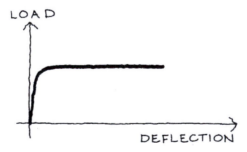

Fig. 5.4 Load/deflection graph of a piece of Plasticine

Naturally it is preferable for structures to act elastically rather than plastically when loaded, otherwise the structure would be permanently deformed.

Some materials can be both elastic and plastic, steel for example. This can readily be demonstrated with an ordinary paper clip. When being used to hold papers together the clip acts **elastically**, returning to its former shape when the papers are removed. But the clip can easily be permanently deformed by being bent out of shape – to achieve this steel acts **plastically**. The load/deflection graph has two parts, an **elastic part** and a **plastic part**.

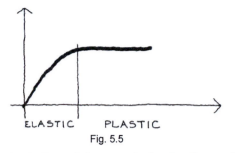

ELASTIC   PLASTIC

Fig. 5.5

Some materials will act elastically and then, on further loading, suddenly break. Glass and plaster are examples of these materials. These materials are called **brittle** materials. This type of material is unsuitable for important structural elements as accidental overloading may cause sudden, and therefore catastrophic, failure.

To aid the process of numerical structural design, structural materials are idealised, where possible, as **linear elastic/perfectly plastic** materials.

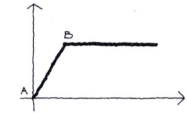

Fig. 5.6 Load/deflection graph of a linear elastic/perfectly plastic material

For this **idealised** structural material the load/deflection graph consists of two **straight** lines. A sloping line **AB**, which is the linear elastic part, and a horizontal line, starting at **B**, which is the perfectly plastic part. The fact that **AB** is straight means the **load is directly proportional to the deflection**. So if the load doubles then the deflection doubles. In the **AB** part of the graph, how load is proportionally related to deflection is given by a number. This number varies from material to material, and indicates how stretchy it is. It is named after Thomas Young (1773-1829), and is known as **Young's modulus of elasticity**; often denoted by **E**. A low number or low **E** indicates a material is **stretchy**, and a high number or high **E** indicates a material is stiff. For example the number for timber is low and the number for **steel** is high.

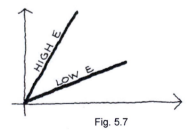

Fig. 5.7

At point **B**, on **Fig. 5.6**, the material's behaviour changes from linear elastic to perfectly plastic; this point is called the **yield point**. From point **B** the material deflects (forever) under constant load. The vast majority of building structures are expecting to spend their entire useful lives within the elastic part of their behaviour. Otherwise the structure would change shape permanently after every loading, and this would be rather inconvenient.

5.2   Actual structural materials

Every stiff physical object is a structure; the choice of suitable materials is immense. A slice of toast, a pair of shoes, flowers, aeroplanes and bicycles are all structures. However, for a building structure the choice of suitable materials is very limited. This is because the materials must be strong, stiff, durable and cheap. These are relative terms, but building structures must be strong and stiff enough to carry the required loads without deflecting excessively; they must be sufficiently durable to last for the structure's useful life and cheap enough to make the structure affordable. Because building structures consume considerable amounts of material they, unlike materials for musical instruments and racing cars, must be cheap which means plentiful.

Few materials comply with these requirements in any culture at any historical time. The original traditional buildings were constructed from **natural** materials. These were vegetation (trees, grass, leaves, etc.), animals (skins and less commonly bones), rocks and stones (including caves) and, in the case of the Inuit people, ice and snow. Slowly **man-made** materials were evolved, so mud-dried bricks and woven cloth were used and stones were shaped rather than used as found. Later, kiln-dried bricks and lime-based mortar and concrete were used. Even though bronze, first smelted about 4500 BC and iron first smelted about 2500 BC, are strong, stiff and durable, they were far too expensive for use in building structures. Even as late as 1750 AD the use of iron nails was rare. Thus, for thousands of years building structures were constructed of timber, brick and stone.

This was changed by what is wrongly called the **Industrial Revolution**; a better word would be evolution (because it took about 150 years). In 1709, Abraham Darby (1678-1717) discovered a method of smelting iron ore using coal (actually using coke, a product of coal). Previously iron ore, which is plentiful, was smelted using charcoal which was neither cheap, and as the supply of trees ran out, nor plentiful. This crucial discovery meant that iron became a plentiful and cheap material. Therefore iron, or more correctly **cast iron**, could be used for building structures. This was dramatically demonstrated by the erection, in 1779, of the Iron Bridge at Coalbrookdale in Shropshire. What is revolutionary about this bridge, which still stands, was not its size or method of construction, but the fact that it is wholly constructed of iron. See also section **12.2**.

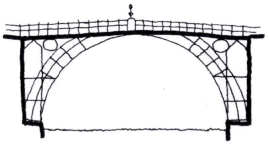

Fig. 5.8 Iron Bridge at Coalbrookdale

The evolving manufacturing and transport industries required a variety of new types of buildings and structures. These included mills, bridges, workshops, chimneys and railway buildings.

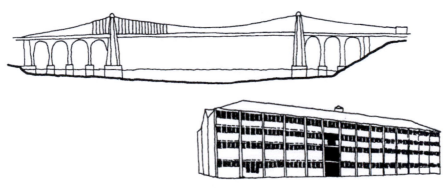

Fig. 5.9 Menai Straits Bridge and The Boat Store at Sheerness

Because the size of these structures and the magnitude of the loads were much greater than traditional buildings, there was pressure to produce both new types of structure and new structural materials. After the availability of cast iron, **wrought iron**, due to Henry Cort (?1741-1800) in 1784 and later **steel**, due to the Bessemer process (1850) became cheap enough for building structures. About 1811, Joseph Aspdin (1778-1824) invented artificial **cement** made from Portland stone, which allowed strong mortars and mass concrete to be made. In 1892, François Hennebique (1842-1921) patented the use of concrete reinforced with iron and steel, now known as **reinforced concrete**. Thus by about 1900 all the 'modern' building structural materials were available.

Nowadays, building structures are constructed using concrete, both mass and reinforced, timber, brick or block masonry and steel. So a combination of new materials, steel and concrete, and traditional materials, brick and timber are used. Cast iron, wrought iron and stone are now rarely used for building structures. Although there are constant efforts being made to find **new materials** for building structures, none have been found, mainly due to lack of cheapness. Many developments have taken place since 1900 but these have mainly been either new uses or methods of design and construction.

On the whole the behaviour of structures in the real world is too complicated to be modelled by structural theory, so theories are derived that are based on various simplifying assumptions. This provides theories that are simple enough (but not necessarily simple) to be used for structural design.

Although structural theory exists that can predict behaviour of structures built of non-linear elastic materials, computations are enormously simplified if **linear elasticity** is assumed. But is this a valid assumption for the limited range of materials used in building structures?

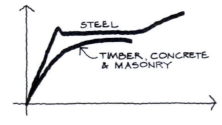

Fig. 5.10

The figure shows that only steel, and mild steel at that, closely approximates the idealised linear elastic/perfectly plastic behaviour. However, all exhibit some type of elastic behaviour at the beginning of the load/deflection graph. Therefore, for design rather than research purposes, **steel, concrete, timber and masonry are assumed to be linear elastic**. This means that 'ordinary' structural theory can be used for the structural design of all the commonly used materials. (It should be noted that **Fig. 5.10** only shows the relative shape of the load/deflection graphs rather than the relative numerical values.)

The most important concept to grasp for an engineering understanding of structural materials is the **load/deflection behaviour**. For designing structures it is also necessary to know the **strength** of the materials. Of the four common structural materials steel is the strongest with concrete, masonry and timber very roughly the same strength as each other. All the materials can vary considerably in strength depending on the process of manufacture, or in the case of timber, the species. Again steel is the stiffest material with concrete about one tenth, masonry about one twentieth and timber about one thirtieth as stiff as steel. Again these values, apart from steel, vary considerably.

Not all the materials are equally strong in tension and compression; that is pulled or squashed. Steel and timber are equally strong in tension, but masonry and concrete, although strong in compression, are very weak in tension; so weak in fact that their tensile strength is usually ignored in structural design. This difference in material behaviour has a great influence on the choice of structural form, because if the loaded structure has to carry tensile forces then steel or timber must be used.

Another influential characteristic is the **strength to weight ratio**. The self-weight of structures constructed from steel or timber is usually not more than 15% of the total load carried, whereas the self-weight of masonry and concrete structures can be 40% of the total load carried. This is because steel and timber have high strength to weight ratios and masonry and concrete have low strength to weight ratios, so **timber** and **steel** are **lightweight materials** and **masonry** and **concrete** are **heavyweight materials**.

5.3   Non-structural effects

Structural materials also have **non-structural** characteristics which influence their use in structures. These include behaviour due to temperature change, exposure to fire, exposure to climatic changes, and dimensional changes due to moisture variation. The common structural materials behave quite differently under these influences. Because these material characteristics are non-structural they do not directly affect the structural performance of the materials, but they strongly influence their use for structures.

Temperature change and moisture variation both cause a change of size of a structure. This would not matter if the structure could just grow or shrink but usually there is a **differential change** in size between different members of the structure, which causes stresses. See also **Figs. 1.18** and **1.19**.

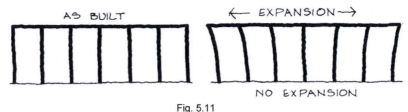

Fig. 5.11

To avoid these effects, structures are jointed, which means a change in structural form.

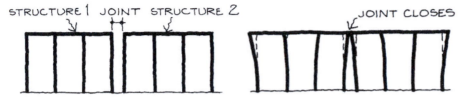

Fig. 5.12

Structural materials also behave differently when exposed to fire. Steel, masonry and concrete are all **incombustible** when exposed to ordinary fires, but timber **burns**. But oddly, timber structures can be more fireproof than steel structures.

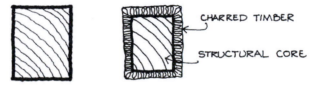

Fig. 5.13 Timber before and after burning

When large timber sections burn, the fire chars the outer surface and the charring rate is known. The timber underneath the charred surface maintains its structural strength so, during a fire, timber members lose strength for geometric reasons.

Whilst steel does not burn, its structural behaviour changes at temperatures of about 550°C, quite a usual temperature in ordinary fires. At these temperatures, steel loses most of its strength and stiffness and ceases to act structurally, hence the 'mass of tangled steelwork' after a fire.

If structures are required to be fireproof, as they often are, then steel and timber structures need special attention. Timber structures have to be checked for strength using the structural member sizes after they have been charred, and steel structures need some form of protection to keep the steel below the critical temperature.

Nothing lasts forever, but structures have to be **durable**. How durable varies with the use of the structure, and it is not easy to make accurate predictions for durability. Again when exposed to climatic changes, the common structural materials behave differently.

In the presence of moisture and oxygen steel will **corrode** (or rust). Unlike other metals, such as copper or aluminium, the corrosion does not form a protective layer but is progressive until the steel literally rusts away. The products of corrosion, iron oxides, are less dense than steel so the corroded steel expands, this can crack or spall any material, such as masonry or concrete, in which it is embedded. To prevent this corrosion, steel can be coated with materials that inhibit the corrosion process.

These materials can be other metals, such as zinc or aluminium, or special corrosion inhibiting paints. Ordinary paints do not have any corrosion inhibiting properties.

Whilst masonry and concrete may last for hundreds of years, they may also deteriorate in a short time if attacked by frost and chemicals. If moisture is present in small cracks, it may freeze and expand. This can cause further cracking and possibly spalling of the face of the concrete or masonry. Also many chemicals can attack masonry and concrete causing various forms of deterioration. These chemicals may be present in the atmosphere, ground, be part of an industrial process or even be present in the constituents (for instance polluted mixing water or contaminated aggregates).

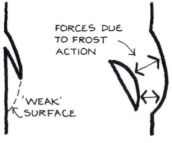

Fig. 5.14

Although concrete may be attacked by chemicals and frost it is more frequently attacked by the corrosion of the steel with which it is commonly reinforced. It is perhaps illogical to strengthen concrete with steel reinforcement only to find the rusting reinforcement destroying the concrete. This only happens if moisture and oxygen can penetrate the concrete sufficiently to allow this corrosion to occur. The growing interest in the repair of concrete structures indicates that this is neither a small nor rare problem. This problem could be solved by using stainless steel reinforcement but unfortunately, except for special circumstances, this material is not cheap enough.

Rather like masonry and concrete, timber can last for hundreds of years. But timber can also deteriorate, usually due to attacks from animals or plants. Various animals, such as insect larvae or termites, eat the timber. Various plants, mainly fungi, can grow in the timber. The action of these plants and animals alters the structure of the timber. This alteration usually means that the timber can no longer serve its constructional purpose. Some species of timber are more readily attacked than others; susceptible timbers can be preserved with various forms of chemical treatment. But the best way of ensuring timber is durable in building is to avoid using it in positions where attack is possible.

Not only do the material properties affect the choice for a particular structure, the choice is also affected by the process of building with the material. The four main structural materials are available in quite different forms.

The shape and size of steel structures is almost unlimited (think of super-tankers). Steel is generally available in various standard forms, these are plates of standard thicknesses and rolled members of particular cross-sectional shapes and sizes. Whilst these can be assembled into structures of any size they are usually fabricated in workshops rather than the final site. The size of the largest part is usually limited by the maximum size that can be transported.

Like steel, concrete structures are unlimited by size or shape. Concrete can either be formed on site, in-situ concrete, of made off site in special pre-casting yards –

pre-cast concrete. Again like steel, the maximum size of pre-cast parts is limited by transport restrictions.

Timber sizes are determined by the natural size of trees. Larger timber structures can be made by laminating timber. This technique involves gluing natural sized timber together to form large structures. Laminated timber can also be made into curved or bent structures.

Fig. 5.15

Theoretically, the size of masonry bricks and blocks is not limited, but masonry is constructed manually. This means the size of individual units is limited by human dimensions of the bricklayers, both their size and strength. Strangely this has resulted in bricks sized to be held in one hand whilst blocks come in a range of sizes, including some dense concrete blocks that are so heavy that it takes two people to lift them.

This section shows that the choice of a particular structure, made from a particular structural material, cannot be made without consideration of the non-structural behaviour. For example, the non-structural behaviour may restrict choice in highly corrosive or highly flammable environments. Again restrictions of size may require joints or complete separation of structural elements, thus altering the structural behaviour. When proposing a structural system for a particular application, the structural designer must be sure that the chosen system satisfies the requirements of the non-structural behaviour.

CHAPTER 6   *Safe structures and failure*

A major aim of structural design is to provide structures that are strong enough, that is, they can carry the loads imposed on them by their use without failure. This may seem obvious, but there are many difficulties associated with this simple requirement, and unless they are resolved, the possibility of failure remains.

6.1   Basic concepts of safety

In industrial societies, building structures are expected to be very safe and the occurrence of failures, especially causing loss of life, must be almost unknown. To achieve this, the possibility, or more correctly the probability, of failure must be quantified. This is attempted by using a **statistical approach**.

The first question to be answered is how big is the load on a particular structure? If this question cannot be answered, then all attempts at structural design will be meaningless. But accurate answers can only be obtained if the use of the building is somehow controlled. For example, the density of water does not vary so, for a water tank, the load from the liquid can be known accurately, unless someone decides to store mercury in the tank. This illustrates the difficulty of knowing how a structure will be loaded during its life, which may be 100 years or more.

Other important loads such as those from snow or wind are beyond the control of humans, so can never be 'known'. To overcome this serious problem, attempts are made to estimate possible loads from natural phenomena by making a statistical analysis of past records. In many areas of the world no useful records exist so the prediction of these loads becomes hazardous.

To understand how real structural design is done the basic principles of the statistical approach must be understood. These principles attempt to use past data to predict **probable future data**. Because the prediction is one of **probability** it is, by definition, uncertain. To illustrate the principles a non-structural engineering example is used. Anyone who has visited ancient buildings may have noticed that the heights of doorways are often lower than those of modern buildings. This is often explained by the 'fact' that people were smaller when these buildings were constructed. So how high should a doorway be? Should every doorway be high enough for the tallest person who ever lived – Robert Wadlow (1918-1940) who was 272cm (8ft 11in) tall – to walk through upright?

Fig. 6.1

As this person was so tall, 'most' people would agree that all doorways do not need to be this high. But what percentage of doorway users should be able to walk through the doorway upright? For convenience, most users should be able to walk through the doorway upright. To arrive at an actual height some data are needed. Suppose 100 randomly chosen adults have their heights measured. There will be an average height, but how much shorter or taller than the average height will any person be? The first step is to draw a **histogram** of the data. This is a diagram that shows how many of the 100 people there are of each height. If the heights are taken for 4cm intervals and the number of people in each height interval is recorded, the histogram can be drawn.

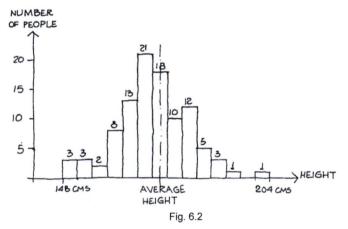

Fig. 6.2

All the histogram does is to record the **distribution** of the heights of the **population**, as the sample is called. In this population there is one person over 2m tall, so if all doorways used by the group were made 204cm high everyone could walk through all doors upright, but if they were made 192cm high, 98 people could walk through upright and 2 could not.

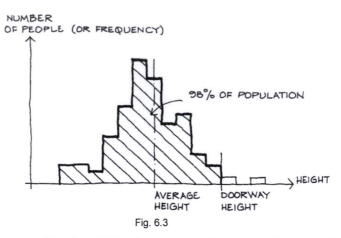

Fig. 6.3

It may seem reasonable that 98% of the population can walk through all the doorways upright and the chosen door height is 14cm higher than the average height. This choice has not used probability because the heights of **all** the users are known. But can the data be used to predict anything? Is a random sample of 100 people enough? In **Fig. 6.3** the histogram is 'heaped' around the average height but would this always be true and would the average height be 174cm? Suppose the top of the histogram is made into a smooth curve by joining the middle of each step to the next.

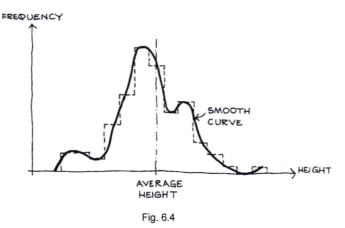

Fig. 6.4

If a mathematical expression could be found for this rather odd-shaped curve it would be called a **probability density function**. From the mathematical expression for the curve, the **mean** can be calculated and so can something called the **standard deviation**. In this case the standard deviation would be a length in centimetres. By adding or subtracting a number of standard deviations to the mean, a relationship can be established between the mean, a number of standard deviations and a percentage of the population.

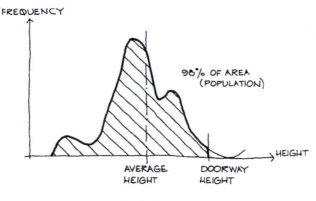

Fig. 6.5

As the population increases in size the size of the interval can be reduced and the smooth curve may become simpler. Anticipating this simplification a bell-shaped probability density function is often used. This is called the **normal** curve and it is the probability density function of the **normal** (or **Gaussian**) **distribution**. This is used as it is straightforward to calculate the standard deviation, and two standard deviations from the mean give 98% of the population.

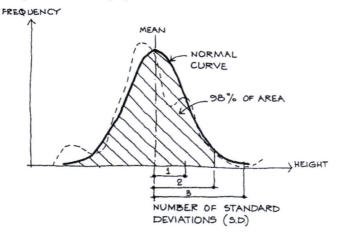

Fig. 6.6 Normal distribution

Using the standard calculations for the normal distribution (often available on pocket calculators) any data can be processed to produce the **mean** and the **standard deviation**. So the data used to draw the histogram could be processed as a normal distribution to give the mean and the standard deviation.

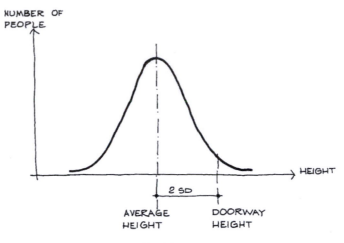

Fig. 6.7

This approach is used to decide what loads a structure should carry and how strong the structure should be. Instead of measuring the heights of people, a population of 'identical' structures could be tested. Suppose the structure is a solid rectangular cube of a particular size. If 100 of these cubes were made and then tested by loading them in some way, opposite faces for instance, the results could be analysed statistically.

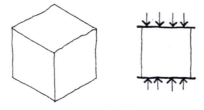

Fig. 6.8

If the failure strength of each cube is recorded, it may seem reasonable to expect the histogram of the failure loads to approximate to a normal distribution.

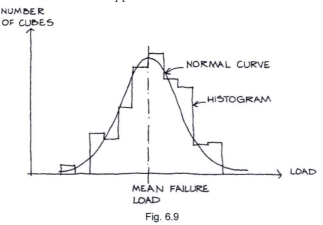

Fig. 6.9

Now, unlike the door, it is the **lowest** strength that is required. Using the same 98% criterion used for the doors, this would be two standard deviations from the mean.

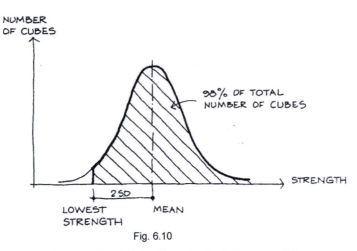

Fig. 6.10

The **lowest strength** is the one that 98% will attain. So it is reasonable to assume for these concrete cubes, that if they are always made in the same way, there will be a 98% probability that they will be at least as strong as the lowest strength. As this can be calculated, it provides some information on the likely strength of these cubical structures.

As structural materials are regarded as **linear elastic/perfectly plastic** (see **Fig. 5.6**) the test on the concrete cube finds point **B** of **Fig. 5.6**.

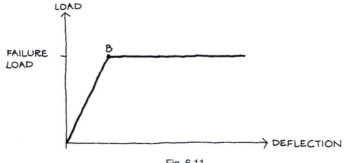

Fig. 6.11

This statistical approach could be used to find the 'lowest strength' of any structure, provided a large enough number of identical structures could be tested. Practically this means that only very simple structures, like the cube, can be tested. These simple tests are used to give information about structural materials rather than whole structures.

As well as knowing the lowest strength that a structure may have, the **highest load** that a structure has to carry must also be decided. The loads that a structure has to carry are the weight of the construction, the loads from the use of the building and the loads from natural phenomena. How much the weight of the construction varies can be found in the same way as the strength of the cubes.

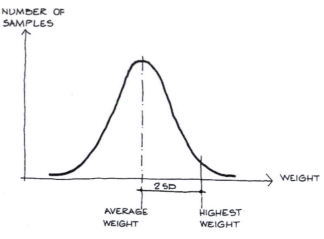

Fig. 6.12

To establish the loads applied to buildings from their use, surveys have to be carried out over a period of time. This period is called the **return period**.

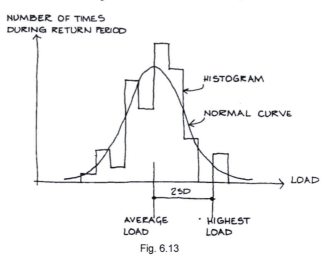

Fig. 6.13

Naturally to carry out these surveys thoroughly is a vast undertaking. The results of these are now codified in many countries and these loads are available as standard data.

A similar approach is used for natural phenomena such as wind or snow loading if sufficient data are available over a long return period. Twenty years is the minimum return period. For wind, the maximum daily wind speed is recorded and the histogram of the data is approximated by a normal distribution.

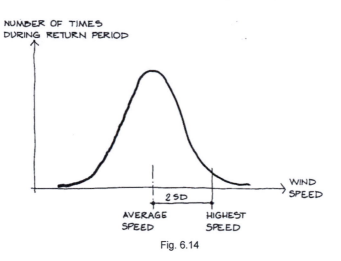

NUMBER OF TIMES
DURING RETURN PERIOD

WIND
SPEED

2 SD

AVERAGE
SPEED

HIGHEST
SPEED

Fig. 6.14

The same approach can be taken with other natural phenomena, like the depth of snow or height of sea waves. This again assumes that the data are collected over a sufficiently long return period, and the data exhibits the characteristic of the normal distribution. There are other natural phenomena, such as earthquakes, that are hard to predict statistically. Although areas of seismic activity can be mapped – see **Fig.15.35** – earthquakes are a geological phenomenon so the statistical analysis has to be carried out over geological time. This problem also occurs with freak weather conditions such as hurricanes which occur regularly but too infrequently to provide enough data for accurate prediction. So, whilst it is valid to attempt to predict loading by statistical methods, it is not surprising that for some occurrences these may be inaccurate.

By using the normal distribution to describe what is meant by a highest load (**Fig. 6.13**) and a lowest strength (**Fig. 6.10**), the concept of a **safe structure** is available. This concept combines two bell-shaped curves, one for the **structure strength** and one for the **structure load**.

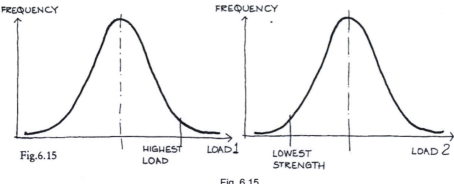

FREQUENCY

FREQUENCY

Fig.6.15

HIGHEST
LOAD

LOAD 1

LOWEST
STRENGTH

LOAD 2

Fig. 6.15

LOAD1 is the load the structure **has to carry** and **LOAD2** is the load the structure **can carry**. Provided **LOAD1** (the highest load) is less than **LOAD2** (the lowest strength) the structure will not fail, so the two diagrams can be drawn overlapping.

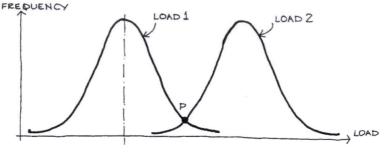

Fig. 6.16

At point **P** the highest load coincides with the lowest strength so the structure will fail. This is a statistical possibility and depends on the accuracy of the data used for the curves, and on how many standard deviations are used to relate the highest/lowest values to the mean. As the failure condition, point **P**, has been found, the concept of **factor of safety (F.o.S)** can be used. The factor of safety is actually a number. As the load at **P** is a real possibility, and the strength at **P** is also a real possibility, there is a **real possibility of failure**. For building structures this is unacceptable as society has decided they should be very safe, hence sayings such as 'safe as houses'. The factor of safety moves the curves of **Fig. 6.16** apart by the numerical factor. This means **LOAD1** (the highest load) and **LOAD2** (the lowest strength) are now **numerically different**.

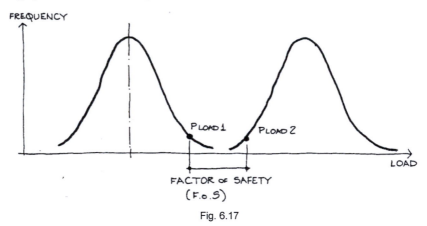

Fig. 6.17

The idea of **designing**[*] the structure can now be used, in other words somehow matching the loads that are expected to be applied to the structure with the strength of the structure and the factor of safety. This can be done in three ways, which are:

- **Elastic (or Permissible Stress) Design**
- **Collapse (or Plastic) Design**
- **Limit State Design**

Basically this means moving the two curves of **Fig. 6.15** together in three different ways to find a position for **P** that is a **design criterion**.

---

[*] Here the word **designing** means only matching loads, strength and the factor of safety

For the **elastic** method, the actual load (**LOAD1**) is used but the failure strength, (**LOAD2**) is divided by the factor of safety to give an **elastic strength**.

This is the same as moving the point **B** of **Fig. 6.11** down the elastic part of the graph of the load/deflection behaviour to a point that is the failure strength divided by the factor of safety.

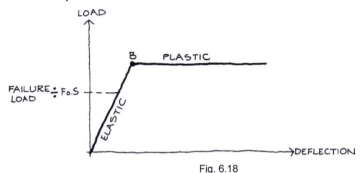

Fig. 6.18

This also has the effect of moving the P_{LOAD2} curve of **Fig. 6.17** to the left, so P_{LOAD1} and $P_{LOAD2} \div$ **F.o.S** coincide.

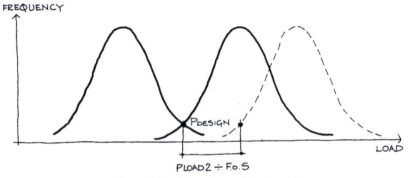

Fig. 6.19 Elastic (or Permissible stress) design

Now the structure is designed to make sure that $P_{LOAD2} \div$ **F.o.S** is greater then P_{LOAD1}. This gives the **design criterion** represented by P_{DESIGN} on **Fig. 6.19**. Because for design, the structure is on the elastic part of the load/deflection graph (see **Fig. 6.18**) this design procedure is called **elastic design**.

The **collapse** method is the opposite procedure, which is P_{LOAD1} multiplied by the **F.o.S** to give the **collapse load**. That is, the real load is multiplied by the factor of safety to give the load at which the structure is expected to collapse. This has the effect of moving the **LOAD1** curve of **Fig. 6.17** to the right, so that P_{LOAD2} and $P_{LOAD1} \times$ **F.o.S** coincide.

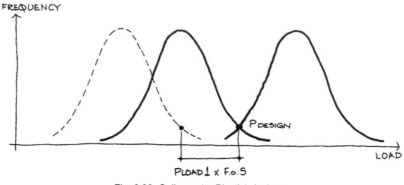

Fig. 6.20 Collapse (or Plastic) design

Now the structure is designed to make sure that P_{LOAD2} is greater than P_{LOAD1} × F.o.S which gives the **design criterion** represented by P_{DESIGN} on **Fig. 6.20**. As, for design, the structure is now at the collapse point (point **B** of **Fig. 6.18**) of the load/deflection graph, this design procedure is called **collapse design**.

The third method, called **limit state design**, moves both the **LOAD1** and the **LOAD2** curves of **Fig. 6.17**, one to the right and one to the left. Now the overall factor of safety is composed of two **partial safety factors** and these are:

- **Partial load factor called gamma f (γ_f)**

- **Partial material (strength) factor called gamma m (γ_m)**

With this combined method the position of P_{DESIGN} is found by multiplying P_{LOAD1} by γ_f and dividing P_{LOAD2} by γ_m. This effectively moves both curves of **Fig. 6.17**, one to the right and one to the left.

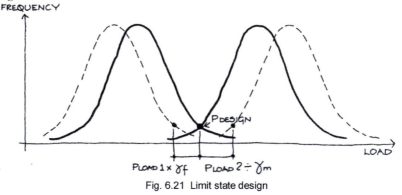

Fig. 6.21 Limit state design

In **Limit state design** the partial safety factors can be varied to take account of a number of factors that affect the variability of both the loading and the strength. The point called P_{DESIGN} is a **limit state** and the limit state method allows a number of different limit states to be considered. This is done by varying γ_f and γ_m.

The existence of three methods of designing structures suggests there is a choice of method giving three different designs, and there is some truth in this. The choice of method depends on the designer's preference although the choice may be dictated by legislation in some places. All three methods ensure a safe structure is designed, but there may be some slight variation in the actual designs.

The complexity of the numerical design of structures can often lead to a desire to achieve a high degree of numerical accuracy. This can obscure the fact that all the ideas of designing safe structures are based on the statistical interpretation of what may be quite inadequate basic data. Furthermore the histograms of the data may not be accurately modelled by the shape of a normal distribution probability density function. This point is made by JE Gordon(1913-1998)[1] who, on statistically analysing the strength of airframes tested during World War II, found the probability density function was not the normal curve but approximately square.

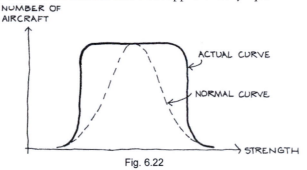

Fig. 6.22

6.2 Types of structural collapse

For structures to collapse under load they have to become a mechanism. That is, the structure will undergo a gross movement before coming to rest in its collapsed state. For example, if a portal frame (see **Fig. 2.32**) has four hinges and is loaded by a horizontal load, it will collapse sideways as they rotate. When the frame has collapsed it is no longer a mechanism, as it can no longer move.

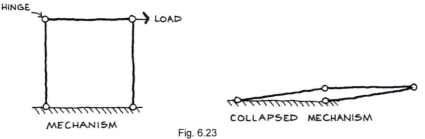

Fig. 6.23

In this example, the four-hinged portal is not a structure but a mechanism. For structures to collapse they have to **become mechanisms**. This can happen suddenly or gradually. These two types of collapse can be compared with the two types of material behaviour described in **Chapter 5**. The sudden collapse can be compared with the sudden failure of **brittle** materials, and gradual collapse with the **plastic** phase of elastic/plastic materials.

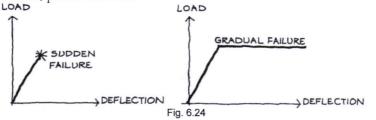

Fig. 6.24

Sudden collapse can occur for two reasons:

- **The structural material is brittle**
- **The structure loses overall stability**

Structural designers try to avoid using brittle materials, but this is not always possible. Although masonry and concrete exhibit some plastic behaviour, the plastic phase is quite short (compared with ductile materials such as steel), so collapses can be sudden. Because of this, the factor of safety for these materials is high. Ductile metals such as steel can also become brittle, this can happen due to a very high number of repeated loadings, or high loading rates at low temperatures. With steel these problems are avoided by limiting the types of steel used in building structures.

The loss of overall stability can occur when the **disturbing force**, the loading, exceeds the **restoring force** due to gravity. Suppose a cantilever structure is anchored by a counterweight.

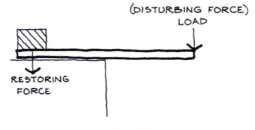

Fig. 6.25

Gravity acting on the counterweight causes a force that can balance loads on the cantilever.

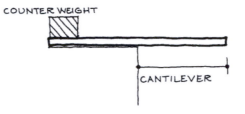

Fig. 6.26

If the load is increased until the disturbing force exceeds the restoring force, the cantilever structure will tip, becoming a mechanism, and collapse.

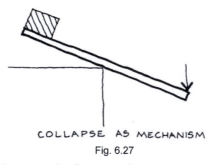

COLLAPSE AS MECHANISM
Fig. 6.27

This can also happen horizontally, for example, a retaining wall can slide.

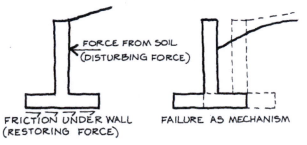

FORCE FROM SOIL
(DISTURBING FORCE)

FRICTION UNDER WALL
(RESTORING FORCE)

FAILURE AS MECHANISM

Fig. 6.28

The wall moves until the load on the back of the wall is reduced to the restoring force. Strangely, structures can also collapse due to a loss of overall stability due to their own weight. This is what happens when a 'tall' stack of bricks suddenly collapses.

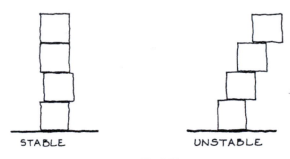

STABLE

UNSTABLE

Fig. 6.29

This happens due to the **Pe effect** shown in **Fig. 3.89**. As the stack grows higher, the centre of gravity of each brick starts to deviate from the centre of gravity of the brick below.

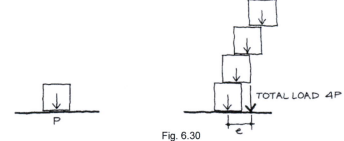

P

TOTAL LOAD 4P

Fig. 6.30

e

The lowest brick of the toppling stack provides the restoring force and the bricks above the disturbing force.

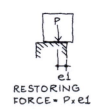

P

e1

RESTORING
FORCE = P x e1

P

e2

DISTURBING
FORCE = P x e2

Fig. 6.31

And, as before, when the disturbing force exceeds the restoring force, the structure collapses.

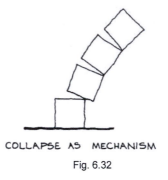

COLLAPSE AS MECHANISM

Fig. 6.32

Really **Fig. 6.32** is just another version of **Fig. 6.27**. What is important to notice in these overall stability collapses is that the structural elements do not fail, but the load path loses stability. So the cantilever, the wall and the individual bricks have not failed by losing strength as structural elements, but they have become part of an unstable load path. For overall stability, the **factor of safety** can be expressed as:

- **F.o.S = Restoring force ÷ disturbing force**

6.3   Plastic behaviour

For structures to collapse **gradually** they have to be behaving plastically at some part of the load path, and this plastic behaviour must cause the structure to become a mechanism. To see how this happens look again at the beam shown in **Fig. 2.31**.

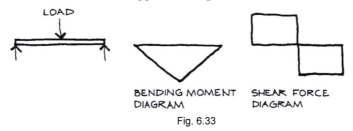

BENDING MOMENT DIAGRAM   SHEAR FORCE DIAGRAM

Fig. 6.33

In **Chapter 3**, the linear elastic stress distribution (**Fig. 3.39**) was given. It was noted that there was a point of maximum stress at the top and bottom faces at the point of maximum bending moment (**Fig. 3.50**). As the load on the beam is increased, the stress at these points will eventually reach point **B** of **Fig. 5.6**. That is the maximum elastic stress; this is often called the **elastic limit.**

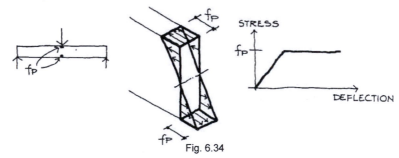

Fig. 6.34

The stress f_p (force per unit area) is the stress at which the structural material starts to act plastically. As the load is further increased, the point becomes a **zone of plastic stress**. This zone occurs as parts of the beam adjacent to the original point of maximum stress reach the elastic limit and become plastic.

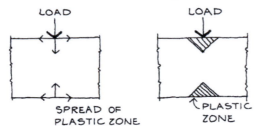

Fig. 6.35

Because the stress cannot exceed the elastic limit, the stress distribution in the plastic zone changes from that shown in **Fig. 3.49**.

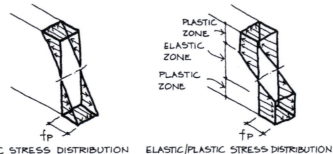

ELASTIC STRESS DISTRIBUTION   ELASTIC/PLASTIC STRESS DISTRIBUTION

Fig. 6.36

As the load is increased further, the depth of the plastic zone increases until the beam achieves **full plasticisation**.

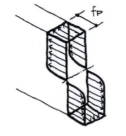

PLASTIC ZONE

Fig. 6.37

When full plasticisation is reached the beam cannot be stressed further and a **plastic hinge** has formed. The beam now collapses gradually as it becomes a mechanism rotating about the plastic hinge.

COLLAPSE MECHANISM

Fig. 6.38

The bending moment at the formation of the plastic hinge is called the **plastic moment**. The ratio between the elastic moment, **M$_e$**, the moment at the elastic limit, and the plastic moment, **M$_p$**, varies with the cross-sectional shape. For a rectangular cross-section the ratio is 1.5. The behaviour of the beam through the loading range can be illustrated by drawing a graph of the bending moment plotted against the central deflection.

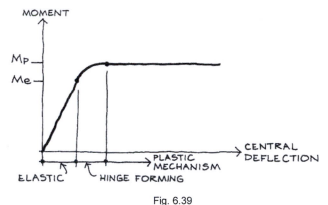

Fig. 6.39

What happens to the structure is that a local failure of an element in the load path causes the structure to become a plastic mechanism. The prediction of the plastic mechanism forms the basis of the **collapse design method**. For the simple beam the elastic behaviour directly predicts the plastic mechanism.

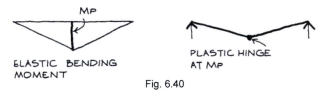

Fig. 6.40

But for slightly more complicated structures, such as a two-span beam, the formation of one plastic hinge will not cause the structure to become a plastic mechanism.

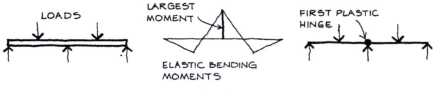

Fig. 6.41

Here the first plastic hinge forms at the central support but the structure is not yet a mechanism.

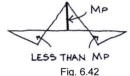

Fig. 6.42

The load on the structure can be increased until one of the span moments reaches the plastic moment. A second plastic hinge now forms and the structure becomes a mechanism and collapses.

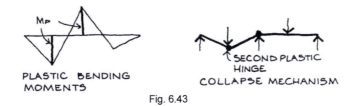

PLASTIC BENDING
MOMENTS

SECOND PLASTIC
HINGE
COLLAPSE MECHANISM

Fig. 6.43

For a pitched portal frame loaded both horizontally and vertically there are three different possible collapse mechanisms. Which one will form depends on the rates of loading for each load.

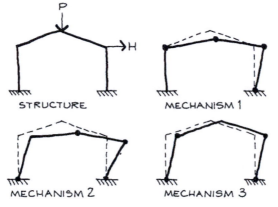

STRUCTURE   MECHANISM 1

MECHANISM 2   MECHANISM 3

Fig. 6.44

This idea of plastic hinges can be used for laterally loaded two-dimensional structures to predict collapse mechanisms. The plastic moment, instead of being at a point forming a plastic hinge, is along a line. This **line of plastic moment** is usually called a **yield line**. For a rectangular slab spanning between opposite supports the yield line position is similar to that of the hinge in the beam shown in **Fig. 6.38**.

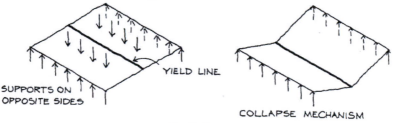

YIELD LINE

SUPPORTS ON
OPPOSITE SIDES

COLLAPSE MECHANISM

Fig. 6.45

For this simple case, the position of maximum bending moment is in a straight line across the slab which gives the position of the yield line. A plan of the slab showing the yield line (or lines) is called the **yield line pattern**. For the slab shown in **Fig. 6.45** the yield line pattern has just one line.

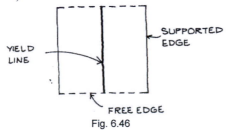

YIELD
LINE

SUPPORTED
EDGE

FREE EDGE

Fig. 6.46

A **free edge** of a laterally loaded slab is one that is unsupported. If the rectangular slab is supported on all sides then it will span two ways (**Fig. 2.49**). This will cause bending moments in two directions (**Fig. 2.53**).

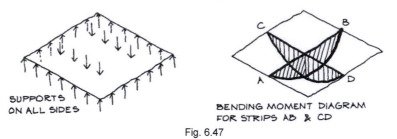

Fig. 6.47

But, what is the yield line pattern? While the slab is acting elastically the maximum bending moment will be at the centre, but as the load is increased the slab will become plastic at this point, the moment cannot be increased (see **Fig. 6.39**) and a yield line begins to form.

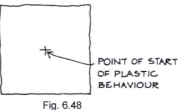

Fig. 6.48

But how will the yield lines grow into a yield line pattern that allows the slab to collapse? For the one-dimensional structure shown in **Figs. 6.43** and **6.44**, the hinges allowed the structure to fold into a collapse mechanism. Similarly the slab must be able to fold to be able to collapse. As the supported sides must remain level, the fold lines (yield lines) must go to the corners.

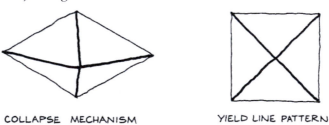

Fig. 6.49

The fact that the yield lines go diagonally across the slab is because, it is necessary for the fold pattern, but these are also lines of **principal moments**. The idea of principal moments is not described here, but it is similar to the idea of principal stresses (section **4.1**). Moments are applied to the **sides of a small element** and this is rotated in plan to find the maximum and minimum moments on each side.

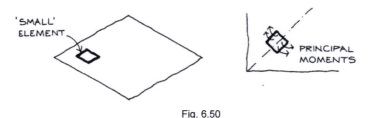

Fig. 6.50

142 Chapter 6

For a square slab with a uniform load the yield line pattern may be obvious, but a rectangular slab can be folded in several different ways.

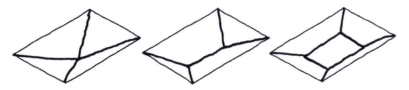

Fig. 6.51 Collapse mechanisms

These three different foldings of the slab give three different yield line patterns and three different collapse loads.

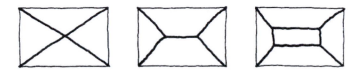

Fig. 6.52 Yield line patterns

Because the mathematical prediction of the elastic behaviour of slabs (usually called **plates** in the technical literature) is difficult, or often impossible, the mathematical elastic analysis of slab structures is not usually carried out as part of structural design. In contrast, **yield line analysis**, developed for reinforced concrete by the Danish engineer FW Johanssen, is relatively simple to carry out. Of course the correct yield line pattern must be chosen to make sure that the lowest collapse load is calculated.

The collapse mechanisms for these one- and two-dimensional structures rely on the formation of plastic hinges (yield lines) at positions of maximum bending moments. The formation of these hinges allows geometrically simple foldings of the structure into a collapse configuration. This means that these simple types of structural collapse are only possible if internal axial forces are absent or negligible and the geometry of the structure allows a simple folding.

For instance the ideas of plastic hinges and folding do not give any guidance on how a simple column collapses. Again the ideas of yield lines give no guidance on how the curved shell shown in **Fig. 4.25** collapses. To see how these structures collapse, the effect of **axial forces** must be examined.

6.4   Axial instability

When a straight one-dimensional structural element is loaded by axial end loads, it either stretches or squashes (see page **37**). If the structural material is linear elastic/perfectly plastic (**Fig. 5.6**) the element deforms elastically as the load is increased until the elastic limit is reached. The element then becomes plastic and deforms without limit under the collapse load. Because the axial stress distribution is assumed to be uniform (**Fig. 3.29**) the whole of the cross-section becomes plastic at the collapse load.

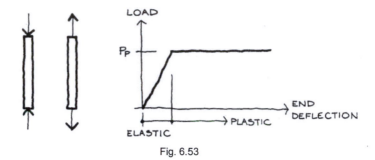

Fig. 6.53

At collapse load **P$_p$** the element fails by 'endless' stretching or squashing. This is always true for elements in tension but for elements in compression it is only true for certain types of element. This is because compressed elements can be affected by the **Pe effect** which caused the stack of bricks, shown in **Fig. 6.29**, to topple. If there are two columns of the same cross-section, made of the same material, and one is **short** (stocky) and the other is **long** (slender), the difference in length will not alter the collapse load, **P$_p$** of **Fig. 6.53**. Both will resist axial forces by uniformly distributed axial stresses. As the cross-sections and the material are the same, both columns will become **plastic** at the same load.

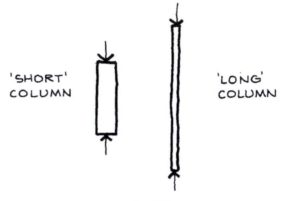

'SHORT' COLUMN

'LONG' COLUMN

Fig. 6.54

But a simple experiment with a slender rod will show, as the end load is increased that a slender rod begins to bow, that is, it starts to bend.

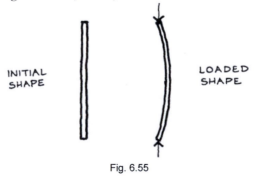

INITIAL SHAPE

LOADED SHAPE

Fig. 6.55

The rod (column) is still carrying load but because the rod is bent, the **internal forces** are **axial** and **bending moments**. The size of the bending moment depends how much the axial load bends the column. So far the behaviour of structures has been described using the **unloaded shape** of the structure, and the deflection has not altered the behaviour. This assumption is part of the **Engineer's Theory** mentioned on pages **64-65**, and this theory makes no distinction between stocky and slender columns. For this distinction to be made, a more sophisticated theory is required. The general name for this bending behaviour under axial load is **buckling** (buckle means to bend out of shape). Because of the technical difficulties of buckling it has fascinated and frustrated mathematicians and engineers for over 200 years. The first mathematical analysis was carried out by the great Swiss mathematician Leonhard Euler (1707-1783), who used it as an illustration of the calculus of variations which he was developing – see **Fig. 0.14**. His work remained unknown to engineers for over 100 years but such was its importance, Euler's name (pronounced 'oiler') is still associated with the buckling behaviour of structures.

But why has the initially straight rod (column) buckled? According to Euler's analysis, the **perfectly straight** rod will remain straight under increasing load until the **Euler buckling load** is reached.

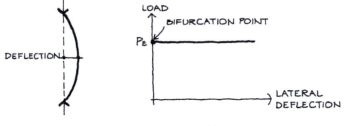

Fig. 6.56

The rod can then either buckle or stay straight. The Euler buckling load is often called the **elastic critical load**, and the point on the load/deflection graph where the rod can buckle is called the **bifurcation point**. The deflection is now the lateral deflection and not the axial deflection of **Fig. 6.53**.

Euler's analysis was based entirely on mathematical theory, and the fact that the rod has a choice at the bifurcation point is a 'quirk' of the mathematics, no real rod behaves like this. Euler's analysis also required that the rod is perfectly straight, but real rods are not, they are **imperfect**. The reason that a stack of bricks topples (**Figs. 6.30** to **6.32**) is that it cannot be perfectly made, stacked or loaded. These imperfections cause the 'e' of **Fig. 6.30** and the toppling of the stack. Similarly columns cannot be made perfectly or loaded perfectly. This means columns are never perfectly straight, as Euler's theory requires, but are always bent (imperfect).

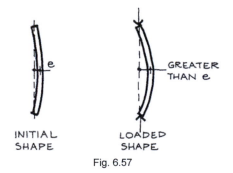

Fig. 6.57

This imperfection **e** has the same effect on the column as that shown in **Fig. 3.89**.

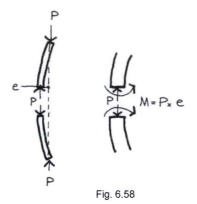

Fig. 6.58

In the case of the eccentric loading shown in **Fig. 3.89,** the eccentricity **e** remains constant no matter how big the axial load **P** becomes, and the **Engineer's theory** applies. For the imperfect column, as the axial load increases the dimension **e** increases, so the bending moment, **M = P × e**, also increases. If the Engineer's theory is used for an imperfect column, the bending moment in the column is **Pe** where **e** is the initial imperfection. As the axial load increases, the increase in **e** is ignored, and the moment increases in direct proportion with the load.

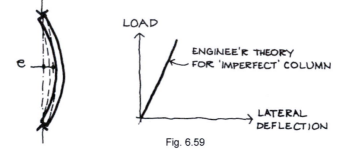

Fig. 6.59

If the effect of the increase in **e** due to increasing load is taken into account, the load/deflection behaviour is not represented by the straight line of **Fig. 6.59** but by a curve. As the axial load reaches the Euler buckling load (**P$_E$**, the **elastic critical load**) the curve meets the horizontal line of **Fig. 6.56**.

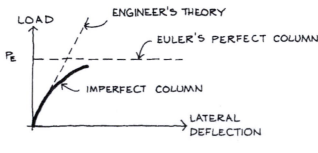

Fig. 6.60

The **slenderness** of a column depends on the length, the structural material and the cross-sectional shape. As the buckling effect causes a bending moment in the column, the better the column is at resisting bending, the less slender it will be. Unlike a beam that is loaded in a particular direction, a column can buckle in any direction, so columns that are good at resisting bending in any direction will be the least slender. For the same reasons for preferring **I** sections to **+** sections for beams (see page **73**), columns with circular tubular sections are the least slender and those with **+** sections the most slender. This was not realised by 19ᵗʰ century engineers who frequently used **+** section columns. And as the column becomes more slender, the elastic critical load $\mathbf{P_E}$ reduces.

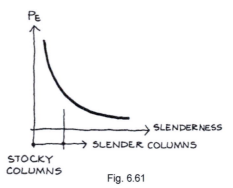

Fig. 6.61

This figure indicates a point on the slenderness axis where a column alters from a stocky column to a slender column. For a stocky column the buckling effect can be ignored, and the Engineer's theory can be used to predict the column behaviour. As is explained later, the reason that this distinction can be made is because stocky columns fail at loads well below their elastic critical loads.

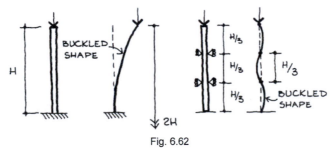

Fig. 6.62

Columns that are cantilevers or horizontally restrained within their height will have buckled shapes that are different to each other, and to the column shown in **Fig. 6.57**.

For the cantilever, the slenderness would be based on a length of **2H**, whereas for the column restrained at third points, the length would be **H/3**, a sixfold difference. So, depending on how a column is joined to the rest of the world, a column could be stocky or slender. To make sure that the appropriate theory is used, the following questions must be answered for **all parts of structures in compression**.

- **What is the buckled shape?**
- **Is the structure slender?**

And as with many structural engineering questions they are easier to ask than to answer.

For columns, the whole structure buckles into a shape that depends on how the column is joined to other parts of the total structure. But how does a beam buckle? As already explained, when a beam is loaded, part of the beam is in compression and part is in tension (**Fig. 3.36**).

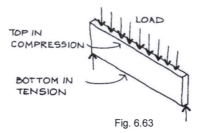

Fig. 6.63

For this simple beam, the whole of the top of the beam is in compression, so it will be the top part of this beam that will buckle. As the bottom is in tension it can only be displaced by an external force, so the top can only buckle sideways.

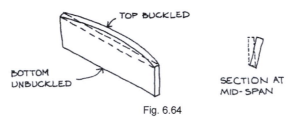

Fig. 6.64

If, like the column in **Fig. 6.62**, the top of the beam is restrained at third points, the top of the beam will buckle into a different shape.

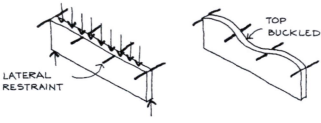

Fig. 6.65

Having found the buckled shape, it has to be decided whether the compressed part of the structure is slender or stocky. As with the column, this depends on the (buckled) length, the structural material and the cross-sectional shape. The compressed part of the beam buckles by a combination of sideways bending and twisting (**Fig. 6.64**), so this type of bucking if often called **lateral-torsional buckling**. The resistance to this buckling depends on the torsional stiffness of the beam. Beams that have cross-sections that are good at resisting this combined action are the least slender. For solid rectangular beams, deep narrow sections are more slender than square ones, for non-rectangular sections, tubes or sections with wide flanges are less slender, and **+** sections are more slender.

Where stress effective sections (see page **72**) are used, flanges or webs that are in compression may have buckled shapes in part of the element; this is often called **local buckling**. If an **I** beam is used for a simple beam, compressive stresses will be high in the top flange at the centre of the beam and in the web at the supports.

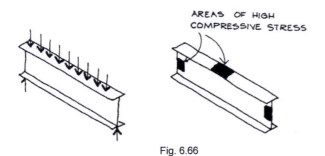

Fig. 6.66

So the top flange or the web could buckle locally in these areas of high compressive stress.

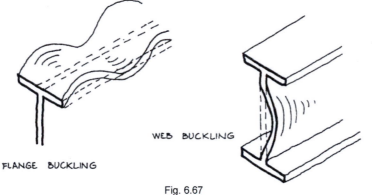

FLANGE BUCKLING

WEB BUCKLING

Fig. 6.67

This local behaviour can happen anywhere in a structure if there are high compressive stresses and the structure is **locally slender**. This could happen in the wall of a box column or the crown of a cylindrical shell.

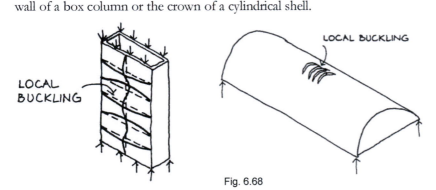

LOCAL BUCKLING

LOCAL BUCKLING

Fig. 6.68

These various forms of buckling can be combined by considering slenderness in the compressed part of the structure. Whether it is local is then a matter of definition rather than concept. For the box column, the whole of the wall has buckled locally.

As with other structural engineering concepts, slenderness has to be quantified before it can be a factor for making structural decisions. The importance of identifying slenderness is shown by redrawing **Fig. 6.60**.

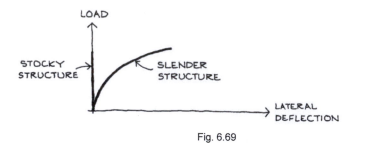

Fig. 6.69

Although a stocky structure will not be perfect, the imperfections can be ignored for structural design, and axial forces only cause axial shortening and uniform axial stress. For a slender structure, imperfections cannot be ignored for structural design, and axial forces cause axial shortening and lateral displacement, hence non-uniform axial stresses. Most importantly the bending of slender structures under axial forces means the type of collapse will be different from a similar stocky structure and **at a lower load**.

Whether elastic, collapse or limit state design methods are used (see page **132**), to be successful they all depend, in one way or another, on the collapse strength of the structure. Structures collapse by becoming mechanisms (see section **6.2**) and if they are slender, the bending due to axial forces must be considered in the formation of these mechanisms. This bending may cause a slender structure to collapse in quite a different way to a similar but stocky structure. For example the two columns shown in **Fig. 6.54** will collapse differently. The stocky structure, the short column, will collapse by squashing as the axial stress reaches the elastic limit and becomes plastic. The slender structure, the long column, will collapse when a plastic hinge (see **Fig. 6.38**) forms in the column bent by the effect of the axial load.

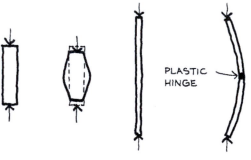

Fig. 6.70

A structure will always collapse due to plastic behaviour before the **elastic critical load** is reached. The more slender the structure, the nearer the collapse load will be to the elastic critical load. Recent research into the behaviour of steel columns has been collated to produce a graph showing the relationship between the collapse load and the elastic critical load (also see **Fig. 14.46**).

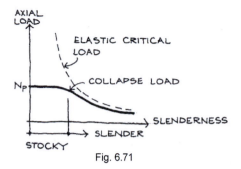

Fig. 6.71

In **Fig.6.71**, **N_p** is the squash load of a stocky column, which is the maximum collapse load of the column. As the column becomes more slender, the collapse load reduces and is nearer the elastic critical load which is also reducing with increased slenderness. For beams the situation is similar, that is, a stocky beam will collapse with a plastic hinge when the bending moment reaches **M_p** (see **Fig. 6.40**). As the beam becomes more slender, the effect of buckling on the part of the beam in compression (see **Fig. 6.65**) reduces the collapse moment. A diagram similar to **Fig. 6.71** can be drawn for beams.

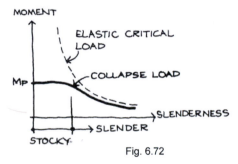

Fig. 6.72

These diagrams show that if the failure strength of a column or a beam (**P_{LOAD2}** of **Fig. 6.17**) is calculated without considering slenderness, then the factors of safety used in the design process may be dangerously wrong. In fact safe structures have collapsed for this reason. One of the best known collapses of this type was the failure, in 1907, of the St. Lawrence Bridge in Canada.[2] This bridge collapsed twice during construction with the loss of 88 lives. As the bridge structure was being cantilevered out, one of the compression elements failed as a mechanism caused by the buckling effect.

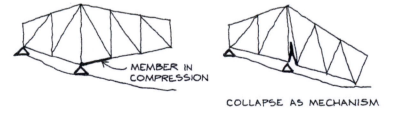

COLLAPSE AS MECHANISM

Fig. 6.73

Slender structures may have a light appearance but are rarely light in terms of structural material. This is because the permissible stress of the structural material has to be reduced to avoid the possibility of buckling-induced collapses. Slenderness in structures presents the designer with a number of practical difficulties:

- The theoretical analysis is mathematically difficult and at present incomplete.

- The matching of theoretical predictions to laboratory experiments is also incomplete and has only been attempted for elementary structures such as beams and columns.

- The design process does not automatically identify parts of the structure that are slender.

The first two difficulties mean that the structural designer may not have reliable technical data for use in quantitative analysis. The third difficulty means that the structural designer must be able to **identify** structures, or parts of structures, that are slender.

The various aspects of the effect of buckling on structures has generated a vast amount of technical literature. Unfortunately in most introductory texts, the buckling effect on structures is either ignored or treated as an isolated topic. Although the basic behaviour of structures can be understood without considering the buckling effect, it leads to a naive understanding of structural design. This is because both overall conceptual design and detail design are concerned with the control of slenderness, by either the choice of element or the specific introduction of slenderness-controlling elements, or systems.

A simple example explains how this happens. At the end of a simple beam, the shear force is at its maximum – **Fig. 2.31**. If the chosen beam has an **I** section, then this shear force is mainly carried by the web, **Fig. 4.37** and the web may buckle locally, **Fig. 6.67.**

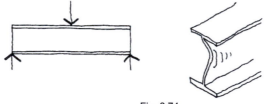

Fig. 6.74

This buckling behaviour may have to be controlled by making the web thicker, choice of element, or by adding slenderness-controlling elements. As the web wants to bend sideways, these extra elements need to stiffen the web against this bending.

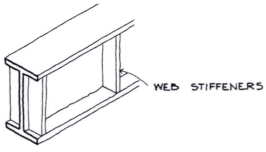

WEB STIFFENERS

Fig. 6.75

In effect, the stiffener now acts as a beam spanning between the top and bottom flanges, and because it is stiff in the direction that the web wants to buckle, it prevents the web buckling. These web stiffeners can often be seen on steel railway bridges or other large steel beams.

Although the most widely used structural materials are still steel, concrete, timber and masonry (see section **5.2**) there is an increasing availability of these materials with higher strengths. This may result in more slender structures, but to use the higher strengths, more slenderness-controlling strategies are needed.

6.5   Relationship of structural theories

No matter what theories of structural behaviour are proposed, a real loaded structure will behave in a way that suits the structure and not the theory. To design structures by using a theory there are two conditions. The predictions of the theory must have a **reasonable correlation** with the behaviour of real structures, and the theory must be **simple enough** to be usable as a part of the design process. But how close is a reasonable correlation, and how simple is simple enough? There is no definitive answer to these questions, but by comparing how the various theories apply to a simple structure, an opinion can be formed. The simple structure used for this comparison is the portal frame shown in **Fig. 2.32**. The loads are applied both vertically and horizontally.

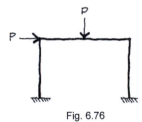

Fig. 6.76

The structural material is idealised as linear elastic/perfectly plastic (see **Fig. 5.6**). The behaviour shown in **Fig. 5.10** indicates the reasonable correlation obtained by this idealisation. Under the loading, the portal frame will deflect sideways at the beam level.

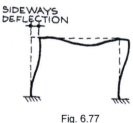

Fig. 6.77

As the size of the loads, **P**, is varied, the size of the horizontal deflection will also vary. The response of this deflection to the variation of the load will indicate how the frame is behaving. The most widely used theory for the prediction of structural behaviour is the **linear elastic theory**; this uses the assumptions of the **Engineer's theory**. This analysis predicts that the size of the deflection will vary in **direct proportion** to a variation in the size of the load. There is no limitation to the size of load, which means that there is no prediction of collapse. This theory predicts a **linear** response.

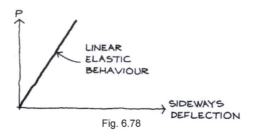

Fig. 6.78

For simple framed structures, the **rigid/perfectly plastic theory** can be used. This assumes a collapse mechanism from which a collapse load is predicted. For the portal frame with the loading shown in **Fig. 6.76**, the collapse mechanism would have four hinges.

Fig. 6.79

This theory predicts a collapse load, and at this load the frame would deflect without limit. This theory would not predict the frame's behaviour before collapse.

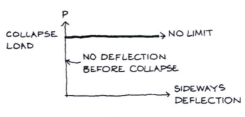

Fig. 6.80

The predictions of these two theories can be combined to give a **linear elastic/ perfectly plastic** response.

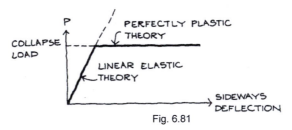

Fig. 6.81

These theories can also be combined to predict **linear elasto-plastic** behaviour. Really this is just alternating applications of the two theories. The linear elastic theory is used until the largest elastic moment equals the plastic moment (see **Figs. 6.41** and **6.42**). The structure used for analysis is now modified by the formation of the first plastic hinge but acts elastically until the second plastic hinge forms. Again the structure for elastic analysis is modified and another hinge forms, this process is repeated until the frame becomes a mechanism. Each phase of elastic analysis will only predict the position of the next plastic hinge and will not automatically identify the collapse mechanism. The response alters with the formation of each hinge.

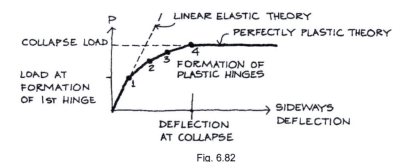

Fig. 6.82

This elasto-plastic analysis gives additional information such as the loads at which each hinge forms. The formation of the first hinge, which is a form of local failure, may occur at a load that is much lower than the collapse load. Because now there is a deflection history, the rotations at each hinge are predicted.

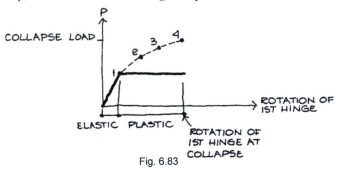

Fig. 6.83

In a real structure, there may be a limitation on the rotation of a plastic hinge due to a lack of ductility. This may cause the first hinge to fail due to excessive rotation before the final hinge forms to cause the collapse mechanism. In this case the failure would not be the frame collapse, but a local collapse and the collapse load would be lower.

An analysis which takes into account the bending moments and deflections caused by the **Pe** effect (see **Figs. 6.57** and **6.58**), the response will be **non-linear** and will follow a similar curve to that shown for the imperfect column in **Fig. 6.60**. An elastic critical load can also be predicted for the frame under the specific loading, and this limits the size of the load the frame can carry.

So an alternative elastic analysis can be carried out for simple frames that take the buckling effect into account; this is a **non-linear elastic** analysis.

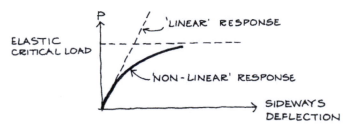

Fig. 6.84

The elastic critical load will always be greater than the collapse load as **Figs. 6.71** and **6.72** show for columns and beams. However, the elasto-plastic analytical process can use the non-linear elastic analysis between the formation of plastic hinges. The response will be similar to that shown in **Fig. 6.82** except the behaviour between hinge formation will now be non-linear.

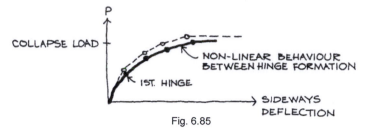

Fig. 6.85

This theory may predict a collapse load that is lower than the one predicted by the linear theory as the buckling effect may increase the bending moments at critical sections. This will cause the hinges to form at lower loads. The responses predicted by the five types of analysis can be compared by combining **Figs. 6.81, 6.82** and **6.85** into one diagram.

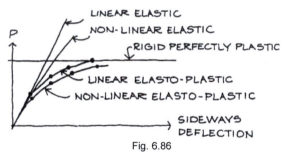

Fig. 6.86

The analytical dilemma facing the structural designer is now clear. A reasonable correlation between theory and real behaviour is best obtained by the use of the non-linear elasto-plastic analytical process which predicts the response shown in **Fig. 6.85**. The only general theory that is simple enough for general use is the linear elastic theory which predicts the response shown in **Fig. 6.78**.

The reasonable correlation of the non-linear elasto-plastic theory is approximate as it idealises the true material behaviour, ignores local buckling effects, ignores the effect of residual stresses and ignores the effect of axial and shear stresses on the formation of plastic hinges. Theories that take account of these effects are in the realm of research rather than structural design. The linear elastic theory is only simple enough for quite simple structures unless computing facilities are available. In spite of these shortcomings, the linear elastic theory can be used, because the difference in the predicted behaviour and the actual behaviour is small in the phase before the formation of the first plastic hinge.

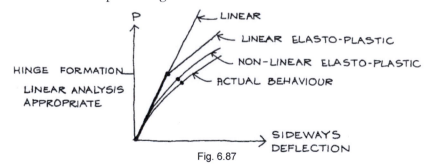

Fig. 6.87

As the majority of building structures are expected to behave elastically during ordinary use, their behaviour is adequately predicted by the linear elastic theory. However, safe structures can only be designed by using factors of safety against collapse (see pages **132-134**). The factors of safety are applied to linear elastic analysis by the use of a range of numerical coefficients. These coefficients are based on current analytical and experimental research and take account of the non-linear effects of material and structural behaviour. These coefficients are published in technical documents specifically prepared for structural design and are called **Codes of Practice**. In countries that have sufficient technical resources, these are prepared as national codes and their recommendations are often legal requirements as they are part of national building laws. In Europe, the national codes are being superseded by trans-national European codes.

It should be noted that the approach to safe structures outlined in this chapter assumes that the original structure remains intact for all loading cases. Under extreme loading, due to earthquakes, accidents or malicious actions for example, part of the structure may be so damaged that it longer serves any load-carrying function. In such cases the approach to the safety of the structure is quite different, and is examined in **Chapters 15** and **16** .

References – Chapter 6

1   JE Gordon – **Structures or why things don't fall down** – Penguin 1978 p 328

2   RM Francis – **Quebec Bridge** – Conf. Canada. Soc. Civil Eng. Vol III, 1981 – p 655-677

CHAPTER 7   *Geometry and structural behaviour*

A structure may be considered to be an assembly of elements and these elements can be one, two or three dimensional. Depending on whether the loading is lateral or axial, each element has a particular type of structural behaviour (see **Chapter 3**). This behaviour may also be affected by the slenderness of parts of the structures that are axially loaded, as this can lead to instability (see section **6.4**).

The structural behaviour of any structure is dependent on a number of factors and these are:

- **The shape of the structure**
- **The type of loading on the structure**
- **The slenderness of the structure**

To conceive structures, the structural designer must be able to understand the consequences of structural geometry and structural assembly. This can be achieved by knowing how structures can be varied geometrically, and understanding the overall behaviour of different assemblies of elements.

7.1   Geometry of structures

For structures to exist in the real world they must have a shape or **form**. Not only must the overall structure have a **geometry**, but also each part of the structure must have a shape or form.

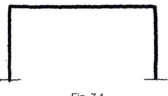

Fig. 7.1

For a simple goal post structure, there is a choice for the cross-sectional shape for the posts and the cross-bar. They could be rectangular, circular or any other shape. Furthermore, the posts and cross-bar could have the same (constant) cross-section throughout their length, or a variable (that is, tapered, etc.) cross-section.

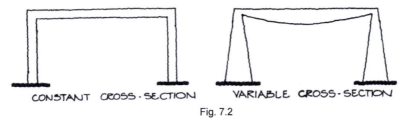

CONSTANT CROSS-SECTION   VARIABLE CROSS-SECTION

Fig. 7.2

Or again the basic goal post geometry could be altered by sloping the posts or curving the cross-bar.

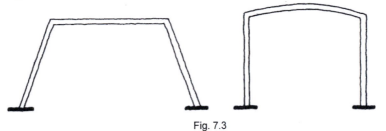

Fig. 7.3

It is worth making a distinction between **defined** and **organic geometry**. What is meant by a defined geometry is one whose shape can be expressed mathematically. Examples are rectangles, circles, ellipses and so on. Thus with a defined geometry the exact shape can be determined by mathematical calculation. This contrasts with organic geometry which has no mathematical basis. All natural objects such as trees, fish, humans, rocks and beetles have this geometry. This geometry can be created by drawing or modelling the structure without mathematical constraints. The exact numerical geometry can, if necessary, be obtained by measuring the drawing or model. This is often done for such natural objects as car body shape

Traditional building tends to use organic geometry, for example tepees, igloos and thatched cottages, and this is part of their charm and 'naturalness'. This is not to say that traditional building has random geometry, often traditional geometry complies with a strict geometry, but it is not mathematically based. This contrasts with civilised building which has a strict defined geometry. Often the geometry is something of a fetish. Research has highlighted the amazing accuracy of the geometry of the ancient Egyptian Pyramids and Classical Greek temples. Indeed the main secrets of the masons who built the great Gothic cathedrals were geometric.

Many attempts have been made to build modern civilised organic buildings, such as the original scheme for the Sydney Opera House – see section **12.7**. However, these attempts appear contrived rather than natural.

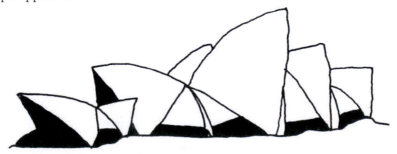

Fig. 7.4 Sydney Opera House

There are obvious advantages for a civilised society to use defined geometry. This is because civilisation uses extended lines of communications and a defined geometry is easier to communicate than an organic one. The majority of civilised building structures are based on rectilinear forms, and there are practical and economic reasons for this. Due to the lack of skill of the designers, the vast array of non-rectilinear, but still mathematically based geometries are rarely used. Again, because the engineering analysis of non-rectilinear structures is difficult, therefore time-consuming and costly, engineering designers prefer rectilinear geometries.

7.2　The behaviour of structural systems

To understand the overall behaviour of any structural system it must be clear how the basic concepts apply. These concepts are:

1 **The function of a structure is to transfer loads** (see page **11**)
2 **The load path is the structure for each load** (**section 1.6**)
3 **The structure transfers loads by forces in the structure** (see **Chapter 2**)
4 **Forces in the structure can be considered as a combination of axial forces, shear forces and bending moments** (see **Chapter 2**)
5 **The structure must have overall stability** (see **section 6.2**)
6 **Collapse initiated by slender structures must be avoided** (see **section 6.4**)

The choice of structural materials, concepts of structural safety and the stress distribution all affect the actual design, but not the overall behaviour of the structural concept.

The first step towards understanding the overall behaviour is to extend the concepts of direct forces, shear forces and bending moments to more complex structures than the beam element. The behaviour of a simple spanning beam can be characterised by drawing the bending moment and shear forces diagrams (see **Fig. 2.31**). The shape of these diagrams will depend on the pattern of loading and the magnitude on the size of the span and the loads. Looking yet again at the simple beam with a central point load, the bending moment and shear force diagrams are those shown in **Fig. 7.5**.

BENDING MOMENT DIAGRAM　　SHEAR FORCE DIAGRAM

Fig. 7.5

These diagrams plot the size of the internal forces which balance slices of the beam (**Figs. 2.9** and **2.18**).

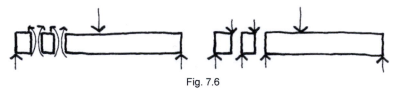

Fig. 7.6

It is important to understand the equivalence of bending moments with push-pull forces acting a lever arm apart (**Figs. 3.40** and **3.43**).

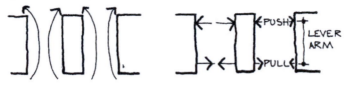

Fig. 7.7

These concepts have been explained by their effect on a simple, beam but a more general statement is:

- **When any structure carries loads over a span, bending moments and shear forces, or THEIR EQUIVALENT, will be present.**

The key is to find **THEIR EQUIVALENT**. Suppose that instead of using a beam to transfer the load **P** to the support points, a loose cable is used. As anyone who has hung out washing knows, the line changes shape as each item is hung up. For a central point load, the shape is particularly simple.

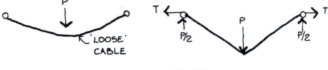

Fig. 7.8

The cable will be in tension (a direct force), and the supports must be capable of resisting vertical and horizontal loads. This seems to be a completely different structure from a beam, so where is the equivalent of the bending moment and shear force? Where is the push force and where is the pull force? Using the slicing technique of a section, what happens to a slice of cable?

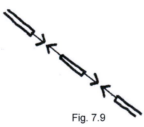

Fig. 7.9

Everything is nicely balanced, but suppose that the sloping forces are thought of as a combination of horizontal and vertical forces.

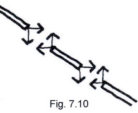

Fig. 7.10

Now the vertical forces on the slice look rather like shear forces.

Fig. 7.11

But where is the bending moment? All there is are some pull forces and these are not in the same line.

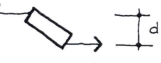

Fig. 7.12

The push force is in mid-air in line with the supports.

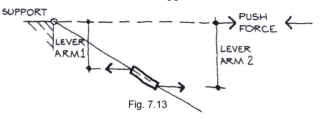

Fig. 7.13

This seems completely unreasonable, after all how can there be a push force in mid-air? Clearly it isn't there as such, only conceptually, and this allows the comparison with a bending moment and bending moment diagram.

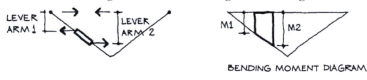

Fig. 7.14

Because the force in the cable cannot vary, the variation in the size of the bending moment is achieved by the variation in lever arm. This rather fantastic concept makes more sense if a strut is introduced to **hold the supports apart**.

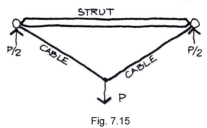

Fig. 7.15

Now the supports only resist vertical forces, and the tension force **T** of **Fig. 7.8** becomes a compression force in the strut.

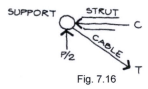

Fig. 7.16

Now the strut/cable assembly can be sliced.

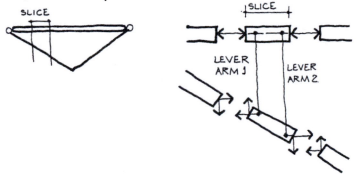

Fig. 7.17

The whole structure could be turned upside down, with sloping struts and a horizontal tie.

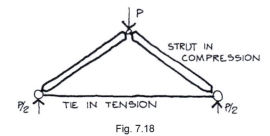

Fig. 7.18

Here a slice would show that the shear is now carried by the vertical force in the sloping strut and the tensile force in the tie. This is the pull force of the bending moment. If the supports can resist horizontal forces, then the tie could be removed.

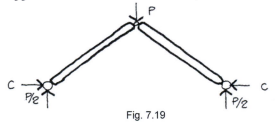

Fig. 7.19

A slice of this structure would now require a pull force in mid-air to allow comparison with a bending moment. These five different structures, all carrying the same load over the same span provide a basic palette of structural types. These five structures are:

1   A beam
2   A hanging cable
3   A hanging cable with a compression strut
4   Sloping struts with a straight cable
5   Sloping struts

Structures **3** and **4** are **trusses**, and are simple forms of the structure shown in **Fig. 3.8.** Structure **5** is an **arch**, these are usually curved shapes. These five structures can now be compared for the structural actions of bending moments and shear forces.

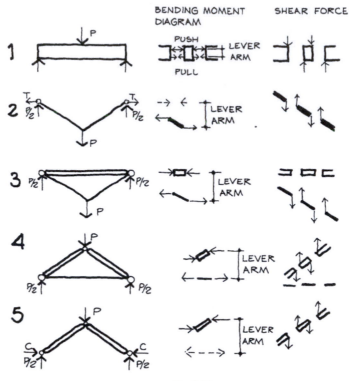

Fig. 7.20

It is worth noting that in structures **3** and **4,** the shear forces are carried by the sloping members, the horizontal member making no contribution.

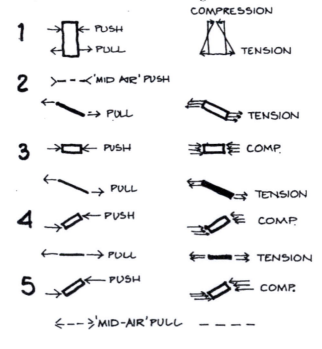

Fig. 7.21

Similarly the stress distribution for shear for structures **2, 3, 4** and **5** is the 'vertical' stress in the sloping member.

Fig. 7.22

For a beam, the paths of principal stress give arch-like curves for tension and compression (see **Fig. 4.19**).

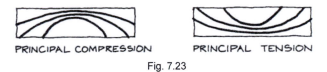

PRINCIPAL COMPRESSION   PRINCIPAL TENSION

Fig. 7.23

Because of the simplicity of the stress paths of the structures **2** to **5**, they only crudely approximate the beam patterns. For comparison they are drawn on beam shapes.

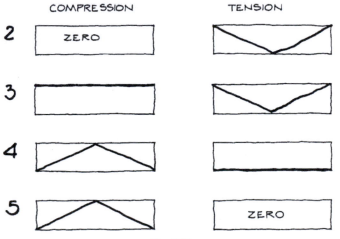

Fig. 7.24

All these structures are in two dimensions but they can be extended to form similar three-dimensional structures.

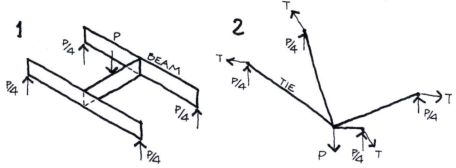

Fig. 7.25 continued on next page

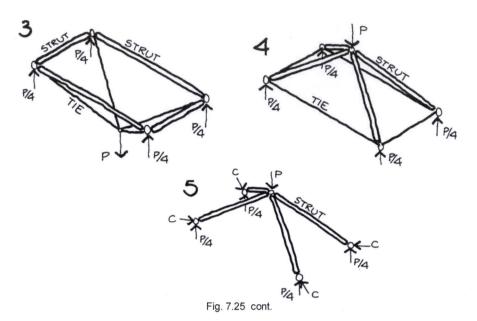

Fig. 7.25 cont.

Structure **1** now has bending moments and shear forces in two directions.

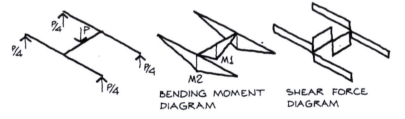

BENDING MOMENT DIAGRAM   SHEAR FORCE DIAGRAM

Fig. 7.26

For the tetrahedron-shaped structures, it is difficult to draw the slices and the push and pull forces but **M1** and **M2** must exist – see **Fig. 7.14**. These structures can be thought of as having four simple triangles.

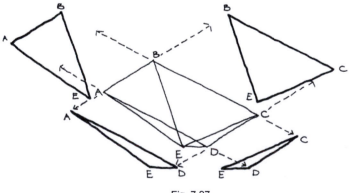

Fig. 7.27

The inclined triangles share the inclined members **AE**, **BE**, **CE** and **DE**. The inclined trusses **ABE** and **DCE** resist the bending moment **M1**, and **ADE** and **BCE** resist the bending moment **M2**. This is achieved by the horizontal part of the tension force in the inclined ties **AE**, **BE**, **CE** and **DE**. The push forces are supplied by the compression forces in the struts **AB**, **BC**, **CD** and **DA**.

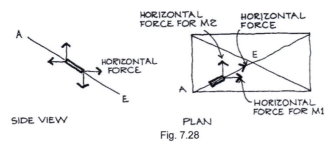

SIDE VIEW   PLAN

Fig. 7.28

Because the structure is now **three-dimensional,** the five basic **two-dimensional** structures can be combined to form many different structural systems. Here are three (the bold numbers indicate the type of structure used – see **Fig. 7.20**):

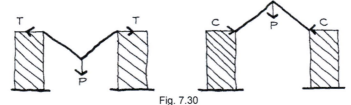

Fig. 7.29

These simple structures can also be used to illustrate concepts **5** and **6** (see page **160**). Structures **2** and **5** depend for their action on the existence of the support reactions **T** and **C** shown in **Fig. 7.20**. These reactions could be resisted by massive blocks.

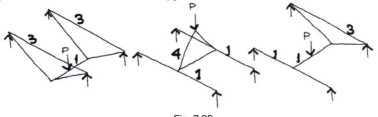

Fig. 7.30

The massive blocks must be stable under the disturbing forces that tend to turn the blocks over.

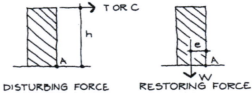

DISTURBING FORCE   RESTORING FORCE

Fig. 7.31

From page **138** the **factor of safety** would be:

-     **F.o.S = Restoring force ÷ disturbing force**

The structure could fail by the blocks overturning or sliding.

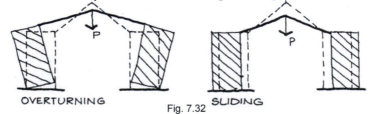

OVERTURNING   SLIDING

Fig. 7.32

Again structures **4** and **5** could fail by falling over sideways if there was eccentricity in the construction.

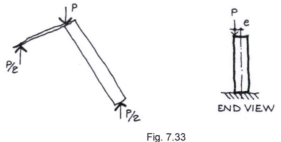

Fig. 7.33

If the dimension **e** was significant then the truss would lose overall stability.

In structure **1**, if the beam was slender then a collapse could be initiated by lateral buckling of the top of the beam (see **Fig. 6.64**). In structures **3**, **4** and **5** if the compression struts are slender then a collapse could be initiated by overall buckling of the strut (see **Fig. 6.55**). This is what happened in the collapse of the Quebec Bridge (see **Fig. 6.73**).

7.3   Trusses and frames

It is now possible to see how the concepts of bending moments and shear forces enable the structural action of a variety of physically dissimilar structures to be understood. In **Fig. 7.20** the structures **3** and **4** are trusses and trusses can be made in a range of **triangulated** arrangements of straight members.

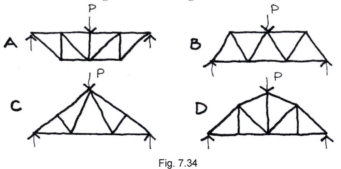

Fig. 7.34

These trussed structures are used widely, and can be seen in all types of buildings; particularly as roof structures. As with the simple trusses, the sloping members carry the shear forces and also part of the push-pull forces of the bending moment, whilst the horizontal members only carry the push-pull forces. This can be shown by examining the forces in **truss type A**.

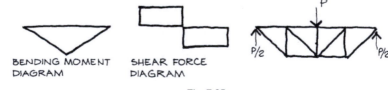

BENDING MOMENT   SHEAR FORCE
DIAGRAM   DIAGRAM

Fig. 7.35

If the truss is sliced then the slice of the truss must be in equilibrium with the bending moment and the shear force.

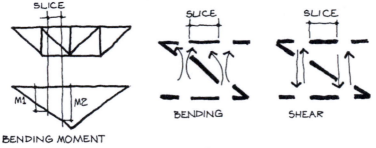

BENDING MOMENT

Fig. 7.36

Of the three truss members cut by the slice, only the sloping member has a vertical force and can carry shear.

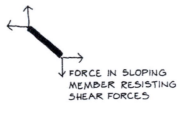

Fig. 7.37

The forces in the top and bottom members only contribute to the push-pull forces, but there is also a contribution from the sloping member. So there are three push-pull forces.

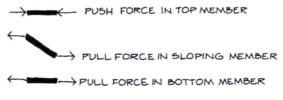

Fig. 7.38

As the forces do not vary along each member, the variation from **M1** to **M2** comes from the variation in the lever arm caused by the different positions of the pull force in the sloping member.

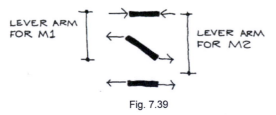

Fig. 7.39

This shows the top member in compression and the bottom and sloping members in tension. The complete distribution of compression and tension forces for such a simple truss is relatively easy to discover.

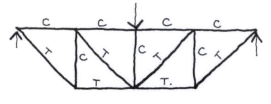

Fig. 7.40

Again the forces in the members can be considered to be paths of principal stress (see **Figs. 7.23** and **7.24**). Because the truss is now more beam-like, the paths are more beam-like.

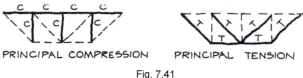

PRINCIPAL COMPRESSION   PRINCIPAL TENSION

Fig. 7.41

For this truss there is overall stability but there are several possibilities that slender parts could initiate collapse. The whole of the top part of the truss could buckle laterally, similarly to the top of a beam.

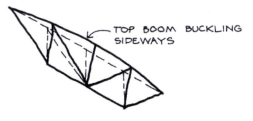

Fig. 7.42

Or any of the seven members that are in compression could buckle individually.

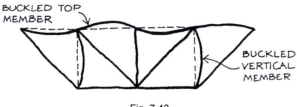

Fig. 7.43

Sometimes it is more convenient, for practical reasons, to support this type of truss at the level of the bottom member.

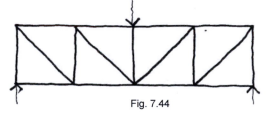

Fig. 7.44

The pattern is not altered, but the extra vertical members are in compression, basically just transferring the reaction force. The extra horizontal members are unloaded.

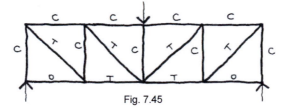

Fig. 7.45

This would be altered if the diagonals were reversed.

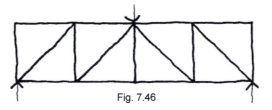

Fig. 7.46

The force pattern is similar for the top and bottom members but the forces in the diagonals now change from tension to compression and vice versa for the verticals.

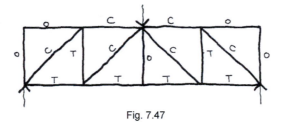

Fig. 7.47

This shows how a structural designer can alter, to some extent, the force pattern by choice of structural arrangement. But the truss still has to provide vertical forces for shear and push-pull forces for bending moments. This means the top and bottom members will always have tension and compression forces.

The trusses have axial forces in the individual members of the truss, but a beam has bending moments and shear forces. As has been explained, there are similarities between the structural action of spanning trusses and beams, but physically they are quite different. It is possible however to physically change them into one another. Suppose a beam has small holes drilled through it and a truss has thicker members with large joints.

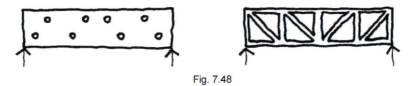

Fig. 7.48

These two structures do not appear to be similar and it would quite reasonable to expect the beam to act like a beam and the truss like a truss. In the region of the small holes, the beam stresses would be slightly altered and in the region of the joints the direction of the direct forces may be altered. But the overall behaviour would be **beam-like** and **truss-like**. However, if the holes in the beam were made larger and the members of the truss made thicker, the behaviour would change.

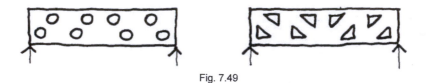

Fig. 7.49

Both these structures have to carry bending moments and shear forces but the stress distributions are no longer like beams or trusses. The large holes in the beam will invalidate the assumptions made for a beam (section **3.4**). The thick members and the large joints mean that the truss members will no longer only carry axial forces because the joints are no longer pinned. By making the holes in the beam square, or removing the truss diagonals, the structures become the same – a **frame**.

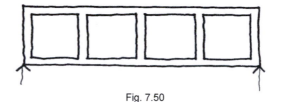

Fig. 7.50

But how does this unbeam-like/untruss-like structure carry the overall bending moments and shear forces? Again, slice the structure.

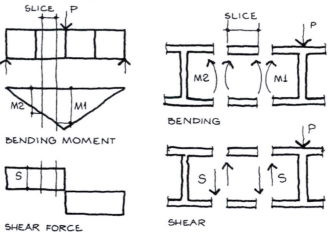

Fig. 7.51

Now the top and bottom parts of this structure have to carry the effects of **M1** and **M2** by axial push-pull forces and also the shear forces.

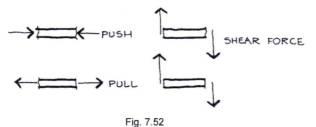

Fig. 7.52

It may appear that these are the only forces that act on the structure, but by carrying the shear forces, the top and bottom members are also subjected to bending moments – this is far from obvious. In the truss with diagonals, the individual members may be joined to each other in such a way that they are hinged to one another. This is called **pin-jointed**. However, if the frame was pin-jointed, it would be a mechanism and collapse.

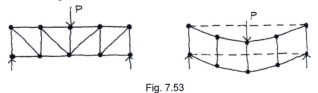

Fig. 7.53

But if the frame members have stiff joints, the structure will not collapse. What is preventing the collapse? It is the stiffness of the joints stopping each panel lozenging, but to do this the stiff-jointed members must bend.

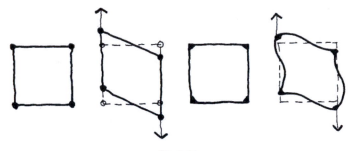

Fig. 7.54

Each member bends into an **S shape**, with the maximum bending moments at each end and a zero bending moment in the middle. Drawing the bending moment on the tension side of each member gives a rather confused bending moment diagram for the whole panel.

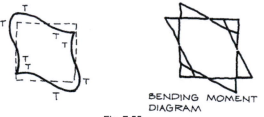

BENDING MOMENT
DIAGRAM

Fig. 7.55

Not only are there bending moments in all members of the structure but there are also (horizontal) shear forces in the vertical members.

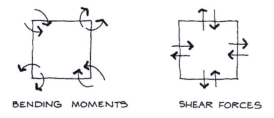

BENDING MOMENTS   SHEAR FORCES

Fig. 7.56

This should not be too surprising as this is similar to the horizontal shear forces that were required for the beam (see **Fig. 4.29**).

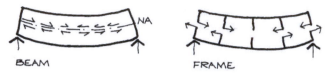

BEAM   FRAME

Fig. 7.57

For the whole frame, the bending moments are a sequence of those shown in **Fig. 7.55** for one panel. For clarity, the bending moment diagram is split into two, one for the top and bottom members and one for the vertical members.

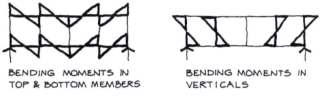

BENDING MOMENTS IN   BENDING MOMENTS IN
TOP & BOTTOM MEMBERS   VERTICALS

Fig. 7.58

In the truss, the variation in the overall bending moment either side of the slice was catered for by the variation in the lever arm (see **Fig. 7.39**). The lever arm varied because of the varying position of the force in the sloping member. In the frame this is achieved by the bending moments in the top and bottom members. The axial forces are constant in each panel and cater for the overall moment at the point of zero moment in the top and bottom members.

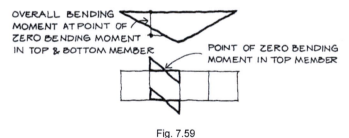

OVERALL BENDING
MOMENT AT POINT OF
ZERO BENDING MOMENT
IN TOP & BOTTOM MEMBER

POINT OF ZERO BENDING
MOMENT IN TOP MEMBER

Fig. 7.59

For each panel, the overall bending moment is the sum of the moment due to the axial forces **plus** or **minus** the bending moments in the top and bottom members.

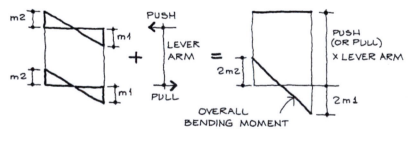

$m2$ PUSH
        $m1$ LEVER   +   ARM   = $2m2$
$m2$ $m1$ PULL

OVERALL
BENDING MOMENT

PUSH
(OR PULL)
X LEVER ARM

$2m1$

Fig. 7.60

This frame action with bending moments at the stiff joints which connect the individual members of the frame is used widely in structural engineering. The portal frame (see **Fig. 2.32**) is a common example of a framed structure. It is the loss of joint stiffness by the formation of plastic hinges (see **Fig. 6.44**) that causes frame structures to collapse.

Three types of structure have been identified – beams, trusses and frames.* Each type carries the overall bending moment and shear forces of **Fig. 7.5**: beams by internal forces of bending moments and shear forces; trusses by internal forces of axial tension and compression, and frames by internal forces of bending moments, shear forces and axial forces. This means that if any part of a load path has to carry an overall bending moment and shear forces, then any of these types of structure can be used. For example, the vertical legs of the sign board shown in **Fig. 1.64** could be **beam-like, truss-like** or **frame-like**.

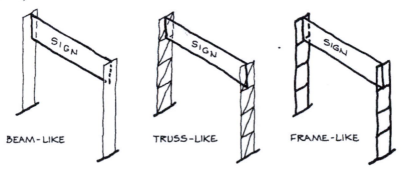

Fig. 7.61

Or again the portal frame (see **Fig. 2.32**), whilst itself a frame could also be beam-like, truss-like or frame-like.

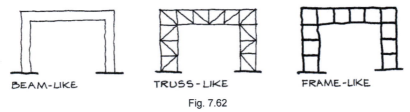

Fig. 7.62

The types can be mixed to make a portal frame with beam-like legs and a truss-like beam, or any other mixture.

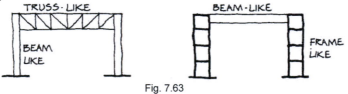

Fig. 7.63

All these portal frames are the same. That is they all have to carry the applied load, and do so by overall bending moments and shear forces. Where part of the structure is beam-like, they are carried by internal bending moments and shear forces, where it is truss-like, they are carried by internal axial forces and where it is frame-like, they are carried by frame action. Even one structural element could be a mixture of structure types.

---

* this type of spanning frame is often called a Viereendel girder

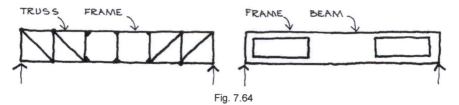

Fig. 7.64

By using these mixtures, a great variety of structural systems are available to the structural designer.

7.4 Cables and arches

There is another type of structural behaviour which is not beam-like, truss-like or frame-like but **funicular**. Funicular comes from the Latin for rope – *funis*. The behaviour has already been described for the washing line/cable structure (see **Fig. 7.8**). For a cable (or rope), the shape of the structure changes with a change in the load pattern.

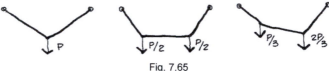

Fig. 7.65

This is because the cable is flexible and can only have internal forces of axial tension. It would be rather surprising if the cable took up different shapes from those shown in **Fig. 7.65**.

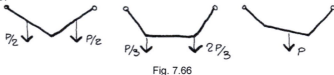

Fig. 7.66

The shapes shown in **Fig. 7.66** would require that the structure was stiff rather than flexible, then the structure would be a frame – but a cable is not a frame it is a funicular structure. Like any spanning structure it has to carry the overall bending moment and shear forces. For a cable this has already been described on pages **161-162**. If a cable is loaded by a uniformly distributed load, the cable will take up a parabolic shape. This is the **funicular shape** for this load pattern.

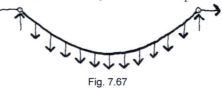

Fig. 7.67

If the load is non-uniform then other curved shapes would be the funicular shapes.

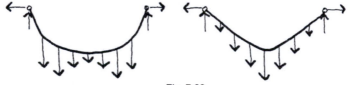

Fig. 7.68

Because all these cables are in direct tension, if they were turned upside down they would be in direct compression.

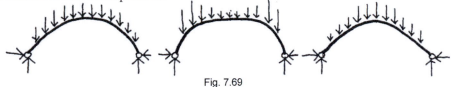

Fig. 7.69

Of course this would not be possible for a cable, but if the structure could carry compression then the funicular shape obtained from the hanging cable gives the correct shape for an arch that is in direct compression everywhere. Although the arch was the main spanning structure for construction from the Roman period to the 19th century, the idea of inverting cables to find arch shapes was only stated in 1675 by the English genius and eccentric Robert Hooke (1635-1703). There is a sketch in the British Museum by Christopher Wren (1632-1723) – see **Fig. 12.10**, of a funicular line drawn on the dome of St. Paul's, but there is no direct evidence that he used this for the design. The first application of this principle seems to have been by G. Poleni (1683-1761) in 1748, as part of his investigation into the structural behaviour of the dome of St. Peter's in Rome. He used a loaded chain to determine the funicular shape of the dome.

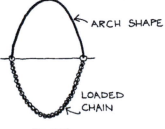

Fig. 7.70

If an arch is built to the shape of the funicular line for a particular loading, the whole of the arch will be in direct compression. If, however, the loading changes, or the arch is built to the wrong shape and the funicular line moves outside the arch, then the arch will have to maintain its shape by frame action or collapse.

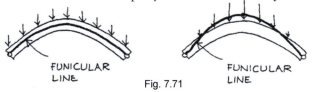

Fig. 7.71

Because funicular arches are in direct compression, they are suited to materials that are good in compression but have little tensile strength, that is, brick, stone or mass concrete. To ensure that tensile stresses or cracks do not occur with arches made of these materials, it is important to keep the funicular line within the middle third of the cross-section (see **Fig. 3.92**).

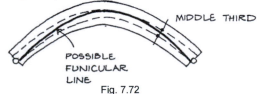

Fig. 7.72

As the funicular line changes shape with a change in loading, for compression only arches the load variation can only be small. For heavyweight structures the permanent load is usually large compared to the applied load. If this is not the case, the arch structure must be capable of resisting the bending moments and shear forces that result from the frame action required to maintain the arch shape. It must be remembered that funicular structures need supports that can provide a horizontal reaction. In fact funicular structures must be seen as a combination of the funicular part and the horizontal restraint. Casual viewing of a curved structure does not always reveal whether the structure is an arch or just a curved beam.

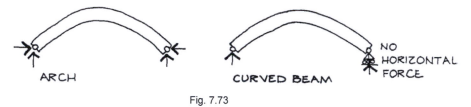

Fig. 7.73

7.5   Three-dimensional structures

Beam-like, truss-like, frame and funicular structures can be two-dimensional or three- dimensional. For three-dimensional structures the basic principles of the different types of behaviour still apply. The structure now has overall bending moments and shear forces in two directions. Schematically this can be illustrated for a structure, rectangular in plan and supported at the corners.

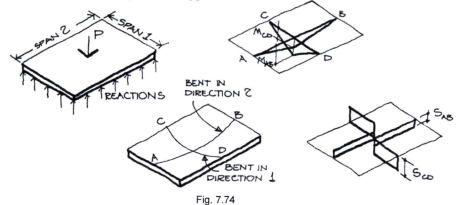

Fig. 7.74

This has already been described for slabs (see section **2.6**). The basic pattern of behaviour will be the same. The different types of structure can be used to span a rectangle, and be supported at the corners.

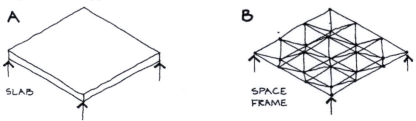

Fig. 7.75. continued on next page

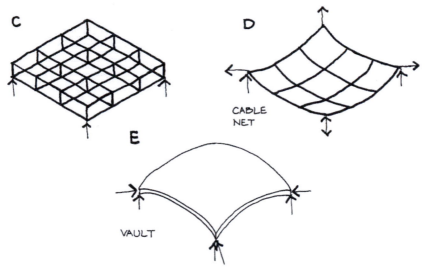

C

D

CABLE
NET

E

VAULT

Fig. 7.75 contd.

The three-dimensional truss is often called a **space frame**, the cable system a **cable net** and the curved surface a **shell** or **vault**. Structures **D** and **E** are funicular surfaces which will be a different shape for each different loading pattern if bending moments and shear forces are to be avoided.

The action of each type of structure follows from the two-dimensional types. The slab resists the loads by internal forces of bending moments and shear forces like a beam. The space frame resists load by axial forces in the individual members, the top and bottom members resisting the bending push and pull forces and the diagonal members resisting the shear and the bending. The three-dimensional frame has axial forces with bending moments and shear forces at the stiff joints. The cable net only has axial tension forces, and the shape varies with loading pattern. The shell is the cable **net turned upside down**. Provided the shell is a funicular shape, the loads will be resisted by compression forces only. Like the two-dimensional funicular structures the supports of the cable net and the shell must be able to resist horizontal as well as vertical forces.

The variety of structures that can be derived from these basic types is almost limitless. Not only is there a choice for the overall structural system, but every part of the structure can be one of the different types. This is just an extension of the ideas shown in **Figs. 7.61** to **7.64**. However, these structures must not be conceived visually; the conception must be based an understanding of the structural behaviour. This is illustrated by **Fig. 7.73**, as it is no good expecting a curved structure to be a funicular structure unless the supports can resist horizontal forces; again a truss without diagonals has to behave as a frame, therefore must have stiff joints (**Fig. 7.54**).

7.6   Prevention of axial instability

Even if the conception of a structural system is based on an understanding of structural behaviour, the structure may be slender and prone to buckling-initiated collapse. Part of conceptual design is to provide stiffness against these slenderness-induced failures. The designer must ensure that parts of the structural system that are in compression have **stiffening structures** to keep the slenderness within sensible limits. The example of a beam with a **U-shaped** cross-section illustrates this point.

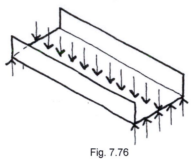

Fig. 7.76

The structure has to resist the overall bending moment due to the load. As it is a beam-like structure, this bending moment will cause longitudinal tension and compression stresses and the compression stress will be in the top part of the structure.

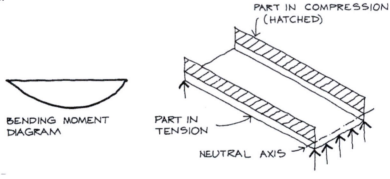

BENDING MOMENT DIAGRAM

PART IN COMPRESSION (HATCHED)

PART IN TENSION

NEUTRAL AXIS

Fig. 7.77

If the top part is slender it could buckle sideways initiating collapse. To prevent this, the top of the structure must have some lateral stiffness. This stiffness could be continuous or discrete. Continuous stiffness can be provided by giving the top lateral stiffness or by making the joints between the vertical and horizontal parts of the 'U' stiff.

LATERALLY STIFF TOP

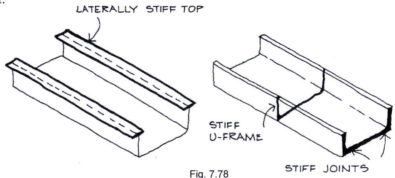

STIFF U-FRAME

STIFF JOINTS

Fig. 7.78

For the stiff top structure to buckle sideways the top must deflect sideways and this is resisted by the top acting as a horizontal beam. For the stiff jointed 'U' to buckle, the 'U' must open or close, and this is resisted by bending moments at the stiff joints.

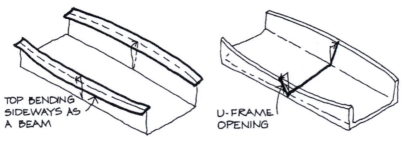

TOP BENDING
SIDEWAYS AS
A BEAM

U-FRAME
OPENING

Fig. 7.79

Alternatively the structure can have discrete stiffening structures which have the effect of providing lateral restraint at each point.

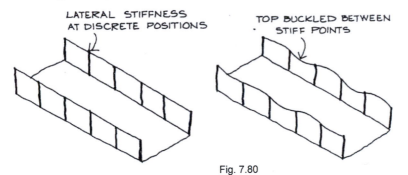

LATERAL STIFFNESS
AT DISCRETE POSITIONS

TOP BUCKLED BETWEEN
STIFF POINTS

Fig. 7.80

Again these stiffening structures can be beam-like or truss-like.

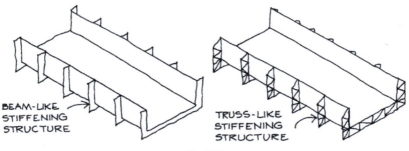

BEAM-LIKE
STIFFENING
STRUCTURE

TRUSS-LIKE
STIFFENING
STRUCTURE

Fig. 7.81

The stiffening **U-frames** provide stiffness in the same way that the continuously stiff-jointed structure does, but at discrete points. This shows that if the structural concept was the **U-shaped** structure, it would be incomplete **as a concept** without the provision of stiffness against buckling. How any structure is stiffened against buckling-initiated collapse is a matter of choice for the designer, but it must be part of the concept rather than something that is added at a later stage to **make the structure work**. If the structural designer is unable to conceive where this stiffening is required then the original concept is likely to be flawed. Radical re-design may be required at the detail design stage, often with unfortunate results for the initial concept; for instance at the WD & HO Wills factory in Bristol.[*]

---

[*] Architectural Review, October 1975, p 196-213

Using all the concepts that have been described it is possible to understand how building structures behave when they are loaded. This understanding does not give any quantitative information about the structures. It does not answer questions about the sizes of the individual structural elements; this information can only be obtained by numerical calculations.

Because structures are built into buildings, it is not usually possible to see how the structure acts without additional information such as drawings or written descriptions. If this information is available, usually from technical journals, then the concepts can be used to understand how any particular building structure works. Investigating the behaviour of existing structures gives the inexperienced designer important insights into how building structures are designed and built. Because there is such an enormous variety of possible structures, this knowledge does not mean that all designs need be to slavish copies – **but perhaps a good copy is better than an ill-conceived innovative one.**

CHAPTER 8 *Below-ground structures*

There are basically two types of below ground structures; foundations and basements. Whilst all the basic engineering principles apply, there are also specific aspects that have to be addressed. The basic cause is that unlike the structures described so far, where there was a choice of structural geometry and material, the ground under any building has to be used, and this will have its own unique properties.

All building structures rest on the surface of the Earth, and the foundations are the final part of the structure. Loads imposed on the planet Earth by buildings are trivial, but locally the behaviour of the surface of the Earth matters. The purpose of the foundations is to ensure that the stress on the local surface is within the **safe bearing stress** of the soil. The concept of foundations is the same as using snowshoes – **Fig. 3.23.**

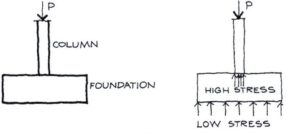

Fig. 8.1

This shows the basic concept that the foundations are structures that **transfer** the building loads to the **rest of the world**, that is part of the planet that is unaffected by the building.

In **Fig. 1.9** and **1.10** it showed how earth can act as a horizontal load on a structure, and this is discussed later in the chapter. **Fig. 1.10** is shown again as **Fig. 8.2.**

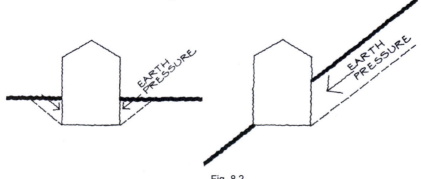

Fig. 8.2

But before concepts that relate to below ground structures can be discussed, the nature of what is under and around the structure has to be explained.

8.1   Structure of the planet Earth

The planet Earth is roughly spherical and rather like an onion with five layers. The only layer of interest is the outermost layer called the **crust, or lithosphere**. This crust is not contiguous, but is divided into eight major sections called **tectonic plates**. It is along the junctions of the plates that most volcanoes are located, and the slow movement of the plates is the source of earthquakes.

The thickness of the crust varies from 5 to 70 kilometres, and is made from two types of rock. Under the oceans the **oceanic crust** is made of rocks like **basalt**, whilst on land the **continental crust** is made of rocks like **granite**. Both granite and basalt are **igneous rocks**, which are formed by cooled magma or lava. This means that if a hole is dug in the surface of the Earth rock will eventually be found, this is called the **bedrock**. This rock may be many metres below the ground level, so the foundations are usually placed on the layer that lies between the bedrock and the surface. This layer above the crust is complex and very variable in depth.

8.2   Above the crust – the pedosphere

The layer above the crust – technically called by the little-known term the **pedosphere** – is basically composed of fragments from the bedrock that have been detached over millions of years by various form of weathering and erosion. These fragments are often transported by air, water or glaciers, and during this process can become mixed with other material. Deeply buried material can become rock-like, these are **sedimentary rocks**. Typical sedimentary rocks are **limestone** and **sandstone**.

The molten rock below the crust can also appear in this layer, as lava flows out through weaknesses in the crust such as volcanoes, and then cools and solidifies in this layer. This 'new' **igneous rock** can flow over existing sedimentary rocks, and can itself be subjected to weathering processes. A typical igneous rock from volcanic action is **basalt**, though there are many others.

If high temperatures, more that 150°C, and high pressures occur in this layer, both sedimentary and igneous rocks can be altered and become **metamorphic rocks**. For instance **limestone** can become **marble**.

Of course not all the material is changed into forms of rock; some remains **unconsolidated,** as loose material. The particle size of this material varies enormously, from less than **0.002mm, clay particles**, to **0.06mm, silts**, to **2mm, sand**, to **60mm, gravel**, to **200mm, cobbles** and then **large boulders**. These different sizes are often mixed up in various proportions so there can be silty sand, sandy gravel, clayey sand and so on. This unconsolidated or loose material is called **soil**.

Water is also present in parts of the pedosphere, because when rain falls some of it may soak into the ground. The top surface of this water is called the **water table**, which may be level or sloping. How water is retained or flows underground is dependent on the porosity of the underlying material. If there is an underlying basin of impervious material, then the water may be trapped.

Water may also be trapped within some types of material, particularly where there are clay particles. If water is poured over a heap of large stones, apart from a small part that wets the surfaces of the stones, all the water will drain away. However, with a heap of very small particles, this will not happen as the wetted area of the particle is enormous compared with its volume.

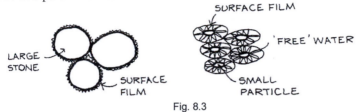

Fig. 8.3

The water does not drain away, but is adsorbed onto the surfaces of the particles. Complex electro-chemical actions between the wetted particles now cause them to cohere together to form a **clayey soil**. This allows soils to be divided into **freely-draining soils – non-cohesive** or **granular soils** and **non-draining soils – clayey soils** (**clayey soils** are soils with particles in general not bigger than **0.002mm** and include **clay, marls** and **some silts**). The difference can be physically experienced by squeezing handfuls of wet sand and clay. The water is readily squeezed from the sand but cannot be squeezed from the clay. This is because the proportion of **free water** in clayey soil is small, and the diameters of the drainage paths are also small which causes very low permeability.

The layered structure of the planet is often replicated in the pedosphere, where there are layers, or **strata**, of different types of rocks or soils. And in areas where plants grow, there is a top level of soil called **topsoil**. Here the rock fragment-based soil is mixed with organic matter, which provides nutrients for the plants that grow on it. This stratum is usually very shallow, rarely being more than 200mm thick.

The ground below any proposed building site will most likely be composed of organic topsoil, followed by several different strata of non-organic soils and below that rock, and eventually the bedrock.

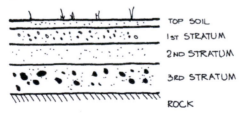

Fig. 8.4 Idealised profile

The pedosphere is often very complex, and rarely consists of neat uniform strata of easily classified soils and rocks. This has given rise to a number of specialised subjects such as **geology, rock mechanics, engineering geology** and **soil mechanics**. These are mostly outside the scope of this book. What is explained here are the conceptual ideas and procedures that allow the basic ideas of below-ground structures to be understood.

8.3   Geotechnical site investigations

Unlike materials for structures, the ground under any proposed building cannot be specified; what is there has to be established. Most importantly the engineering properties of the subsoil have to quantified, so that eventually numerical calculations can be made to determine the size of the structural elements. In other words the site has to be investigated geotechnically.

There are essentially four stages in any geotechnical site investigation.

- **Desk-based research**
- **Excavating trial pits, sinking boreholes, carrying out insitu tests and obtaining samples**
- **Laboratory testing of site samples**
- **Preparing a geotechnical report, with or without engineering guidelines**

These investigations can range from the very simple, that may only require a few pits to be dug, and no laboratory work, to ones of huge complexity requiring deep boreholes, and a whole range of sampling and testing, resulting in reports in several volumes. The size of any investigation is usually commensurate with the size of the proposed project. The investigation for a single house is unlikely to be on the same scale as one for a number of high-rise buildings with deep basements. The extent and complexity of any investigation is likely to be decided between the structural designer, the geotechnical investigation specialist and the client.

The first task is to try and obtain paper information to give an idea as what is likely to be encountered. In many areas there are geological maps, however these need specialist interpretation, and rarely give useful detailed information, just a general idea. If there has been relatively recent construction in the vicinity, probably there was a geotechnical report, so a copy may be obtainable; alternatively geotechnical investigation specialists can be contacted to find if they have worked in the area. Other sources are local building authorities and contractors.

Though not directly related to the ground conditions, the preliminary desk study should establish the presence of any underground services. This is done by contacting the suppliers of services such as water, electrical, gas, drainage services and possibly others.

The next step, with or without any prior information, is the physical investigation of the site. This is usually done by digging a number of trial pits up to about 4m deep, and/or sinking a number of narrow boreholes. These are typically 100 to 150mm diameter, and are bored driving a tubular casing or drilling; these can reach a depth of 100m. Insitu tests can be carried out and samples taken both from pits and boreholes. In boreholes the levels of any groundwater can be recorded.

The samples are tested in the laboratory where a range of tests can be carried out. To a non-specialist these tests can appear arcane, and their description is outside the scope of this book.

The geotechnical report is usually prepared by a specialist, and will describe the general geotechnical conditions of the site. Records of boreholes and trial pits will be included together with the results of tests. If requested, the report will also offer advice on suitable types of below-ground structures, together with numerical design parameters.

Needless to say, starting any project without a geotechnical investigation and report is a recipe for disaster, which can cause endless delays and spiralling costs. Obviously the more thorough the investigation the less chance of problems, but these are expensive so often a careful balance has to be struck between getting enough information without spending money unnecessarily.

8.4 Soil as a structural material

For the design of structures considered so far what is known as the **Engineer's Theory** has be used – see page **64-65**. This assumes that the structural material is **isotropic** and **linear elastic**, it also assumes that the structure is **geometrically defined** and **homogeneous**. For the soil acting structurally to support loads from a building, none of these helpful assumptions are likely to be true. This means that the way soil acts as a structure has to be viewed differently

There are two basic differences between the behaviour of structural elements and the structural behaviour of soil. The first is that the part of soil loaded by the foundations of a structure cannot act in isolation in same way a column can. The loaded part of the ground is affected by adjacent unloaded parts of the ground.

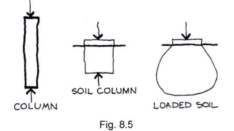

Fig. 8.5

How much of the adjacent soil is affected by the load is hard to determine, but it can be significant. To see why this happens, look at two simplified models of soil. One is of unlinked elastic coil springs and the other of elastic spheres. Both are in pits with completely rigid sides.

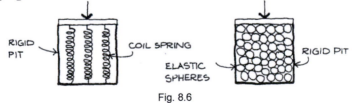

Fig. 8.6

For the first model the behaviour is quite simple. As the load is applied through the rigid foundation each coil spring deflects vertically under its share of the load. As the load increases so does the deflection. The bottom and sides of the pit do not move.

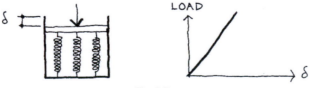

Fig. 8.7

This model assumes that the soil under the foundation **does** act as an isolated structure; the springs. This is the same as assuming there are finite columns of elastic soil under the foundation, which act as springs, and that soil outside the rigid box is unaffected.

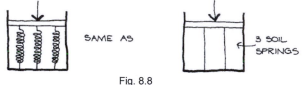

Fig. 8.8

The second model using elastic spheres is more complex as there are three phases of behaviour. The pit of elastic spheres will not be tightly packed, so the load causes compaction of the spheres. This compaction can be seen by shaking a jar of rice or sugar and noting the depth before and after shaking.

UNCOMPACTED   COMPACTED

Fig. 8.9

The second effect is the restriction on the shape into which the spheres can deform. Because the spheres are touching each other and the sides of the pit, each sphere cannot deform freely.

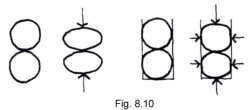

Fig. 8.10

As the confined spheres are compressed, the restriction on their lateral deformation causes horizontal loads on the rigid pit walls. As the spheres deform, the foundation moves down into the pit, this reduces the overall volume of the pit and the size of the voids between the spheres.

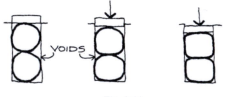

Fig. 8.11

When all the voids are filled the pit will be completely filled with the elastic material. This is quite a different structure from the pit filled with barely touching spheres. This means that the pit filled with elastic spheres will have three phases of behaviour.

Phase 1   Reduction of voids by compaction.
Phase 2   Deformation of spheres until the voids are filled.
Phase 3   Deformation of the elastic material that fills the pit.

This gives a three-part load/deflection diagram.

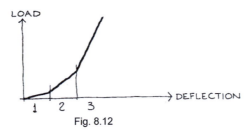

Fig. 8.12

It is possible to find single-sized spherical stones occurring naturally, these can be seen on some shingle beaches. For this soil, the model of elastic spheres is reasonable but the rigid pit restriction is not. A new model of this soil would be an infinitely wide layer of elastic spheres with finite thickness. This layer rests on a rigid base.

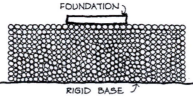

Fig. 8.13

As the foundation is loaded, the spheres compact locally. Then the touching spheres begin to deform. With no rigid pit walls the adjacent, unloaded spheres have to provide lateral forces.

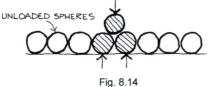

Fig. 8.14

The lower spheres will provide the lateral force if they are heavy enough. Each layer of spheres transfers its load to a lower layer and each lower layer will have more spheres.

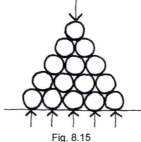

Fig. 8.15

In this way the area of loaded spheres increases with depth, and the level of load in the spheres reduces.

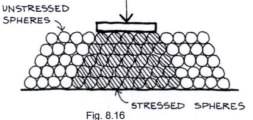

Fig. 8.16

As soil is not usually made from elastic spheres and there is not a rigid base, the stressed volume under a single foundation becomes bulb-shaped.

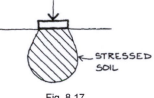

Fig. 8.17

For an elastic sphere to deform into an elastic cube, thus filling all the voids, the material has to be very elastic. A stone sphere could not deform into a cube as it would split first. If the foundation load is increased, the highly stressed spheres will fail, or the lateral forces required will become too high for the unloaded spheres, and these will heave upwards.

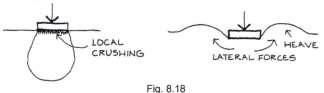

Fig. 8.18

The load/deformation curve can be drawn for this model, and again this has three phases.

Phase 1   Reduction of voids by compaction.
Phase 2   Deformation of spheres.
Phase 3   Failure by crushing or heaving.

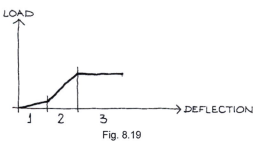

Fig. 8.19

So far the models have been used to understand the behaviour of the **soil skeleton**. If, as is often the case, there is water in the soil, the behaviour of the soil skeleton **plus water** has to be modelled. The behaviour of this composite structure can be quite different from the behaviour of the soil skeleton. Fill the pits of the first two models with water and assume that the foundations fit into the pits in a watertight manner. This is called a **fully saturated soil**.

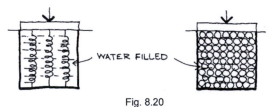

Fig. 8.20

Water is almost incompressible, so the load from the foundations is carried by water pressure in both models, with almost no deformation. This is called the

development of excess pore water pressure. The behaviour will be altered if holes are made in the foundation which relieve the water pressure, and allow some water to escape.

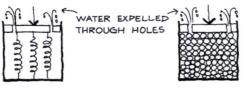

Fig. 8.21

Now the water that is filling the voids in the soil skeleton has a **drainage path**. This is called the **drainage of excess pore water pressure**. As the water is expelled from the voids, the soil skeleton carries the load as before. This is the **full dissipation** of **excess pore water pressure**. This is the end of **consolidation**, so the soil is **consolidated**. If the holes are large the water will be expelled immediately, and the soil will act like the coil spring model with no water – see **Fig. 8.7**.

But if the holes are very small, the water will take time to seep through. Initially the water will carry the entire load, but as the water pressure is gradually reduced by seepage, the load is transferred to the coil springs. Now the deformation is **time-dependent**, and under a constant load will deform in a non-linear way until the springs are carrying the entire load.

In the water-filled soil skeleton, the pressure of the water in the voids is called the **pore water pressure**. Before loading, the pore water pressure is just the hydrostatic head, but the loads cause an increase in the pore water pressure. This increase is relieved by the drainage until the pressure returns to the hydrostatic pressure. The speed of the drainage is called the **seepage rate**. The smaller the drainage holes, the longer it takes. In a real soil there is no rigid pit so the water drains away laterally as well as vertically.

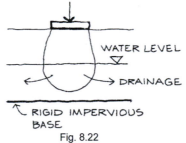

Fig. 8.22

Even with the first model, the presence of water and a low seepage rate dramatically alters the soil structure behaviour. With all the variations of underlying strata, particle size and shape and rate of loading, if water is present the soil structure behaviour of a real soil can be complex.

For non-cohesive soils, water may or may not be present, but in clayey soils water is **always** present, unless it has completely dried out and turned to dust. If a clayey soil is loaded by a foundation, the load is initially carried by an **increase** in pore water pressure. As with granular soils, the pore water pressure in cohesive soils reduces by draining laterally to unstressed areas. But due to the extremely low seepage rate in cohesive soils this may take years.

8.5   Rock as a structural material

In some areas rock can be found near the surface of the earth. This can be the original granite bedrock or strata of sedimentary, metamorphic or igneous rocks. Rocks are different from soils in that the particles are solidly joined – **cemented** – together, however this does not necessarily mean a rock is a strong or a solid material. So if foundations are to be built on rock these two qualities have to be determined.

Strength	Field indication	Examples
Extremely strong	Chipped with hammer	Granite, basalt
Very strong	Many hammer blows to break	Sandstone, limestone, gneiss
Strong	More than one hammer blow to break	Marble, schist, slate
Medium strong	One hammer blow to break	Siltstone, shale, **concrete**
Weak	Can be dented by pointed hammer	Chalk, rocksalt
Very weak	Crumbles under hammer blow	Mudstone

Table 8.1 – Rock classification

The specific type of rock can only be determined by a specialist and its strength by carrying out compression tests on samples. There is no international standard for classifying rock strength, but **Table 8.1** gives some guidance.

To give some idea of relative compressive strengths, extremely strong rock has about **ten times** the compressive strength of concrete whereas weak rock may have only a **tenth** of the strength of concrete. These strengths are given for **solid** or **intact rock,** so the table shows that most intact rocks will be adequate for most foundation loads.

However rocks near the surface may not be intact for a number of reasons. These include porous rocks that may be saturated with water, rocks that have been weathered over geological time which can weaken the cementing of the particles, or rocks that are fissured. All these can seriously reduce their strength in comparison to their intact strength.

As with soils, the accurate assessment for rocks as a foundation material is complex, and requires specialist advice.

8.6   Foundations for vertical loads

The most common form of below-ground structure is the one shown in **Fig. 8.1**, an isolated foundation under a column. There are, however many variations on this simple theme of trying to transfer vertical loads in a highly-stressed superstructure to the rest of the world via a much lower-stressed part of the pedosphere.

The most common forms of support for vertical loads are **strip** or **pad footings;** these have been used, in various forms, since time immemorial. Single **padstones,** brick walls widened to form **stepped footings, mass concrete bases** poured in brick walls widened to form **stepped footings, mass concrete bases** poured in excavated pits, and **reinforced concrete slab bases** have all been used. Nowadays the reinforced slab base is probably the most widely used, but mass concrete bases can still provide a cheap and effective alternative.

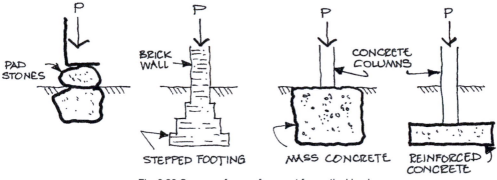

Fig. 8.23 Common forms of support for vertical loads

For the engineering design of these bases a simple **uniform stress distribution** is assumed on the underside of the base. This is exactly the same as the axial stress described in section **3.3 Axial stresses**. One of the main aims of a site investigation is to provide a numerical value for the **safe bearing pressure**, expressed in force per unit area. The required area for this type of base can then be calculated from:

Base area required = Load from the column ÷ the safe bearing pressure

If the base is to be made of reinforced concrete then the bending moment, for design purposes, can be calculated by assuming the base slab cantilevers from the face of the column, being loaded by the pressure under the base – see **Figs. 1.42** and **2.28**.

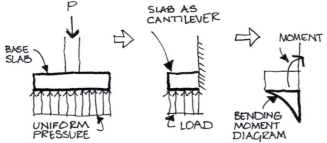

Fig. 8.24 Design of simple base

Sometimes, where columns are closely spaced, or the safe bearing pressure is low, bases designed by this simple method may 'overlap,' in which case a combined base has to be used. The simple pressure distribution under the base is still used but now:

Base area required = Load from both columns ÷ the safe bearing pressure

Now the centre of the base has to coincide with the **centre of gravity** of the **columns loads** – see **Figs. 3.18** to **3.22**.

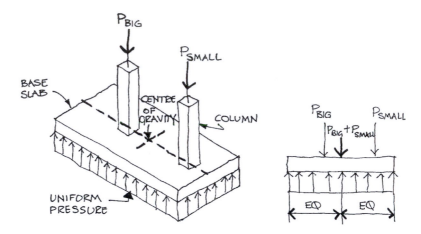

Fig. 8.25 Combined base

If the safe bearing pressure, due to poor ground conditions, is so low that the individual bases are so big they constantly overlap, it can be advantageous to make the whole area of the building one single foundation, this is called a **raft foundation**. For small buildings this is often just a simple reinforced concrete slab, but for larger buildings it may be necessary to make the raft foundation a cellular structure stiffened by a grillage of beams.

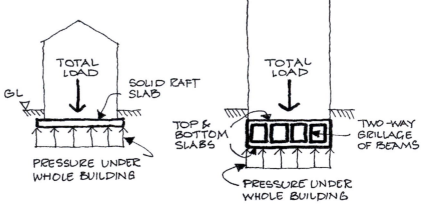

Fig. 8.26 Raft foundations

Whilst the idea of raft foundations is a simple concept, and building them is not especially difficult, there is a problem with their engineering design. This is due to the prediction of the pressure distribution under the foundation. It is no longer realistic to assume a simple distribution, as was assumed for the isolated bases, because now the relative stiffnesses of the raft and the underlying soil determine the distribution. If the raft is flexible and the underlying soil is stiff, then the pressure will be concentrated under the loads, whereas if the raft is stiff and the soil soft, the distribution will be more uniform.

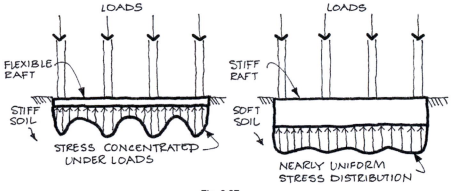

Fig. 8.27

The different pressure distributions shown in **Fig. 8.27** are just another example of the shoes shown in **Fig. 3.23.** While simple in concept, the detailed calculations required to arrive at the correct distribution are fraught with difficulty, because it is not easy to accurately calculate the stiffness of a concrete structure, and it is even more difficult to calculate the stiffness of any given subsoil. It is for this reason that raft foundations are not widely used, though hybrid versions such as combining piles with a raft to make a piled raft, are sometimes used.

There is an alternative for carrying vertical loads that require overlapping individual bases, and that is to increase the base size in the vertical direction rather than in the horizontal direction. This is done by using **piled foundations**. A **pile** is a relatively **slender column-like element** that goes down deep into the ground under a building. Piles have been used at least since Roman times, and can be made of timber, steel or concrete.

There are three ways of putting – **installing** – piles into the ground: by hammering them in – **driven piles**, by filling pre-bored holes with concrete – **bored piles**, and by screwing them in – **screwed piles**. The piles carry vertical load in two ways; by the friction between the soil and the surface of the pile – **friction piles**, and by the end of the piles bearing on a strata that is deep below the building – **end-bearing piles**. As a general rule the strength of soils increases with depth.

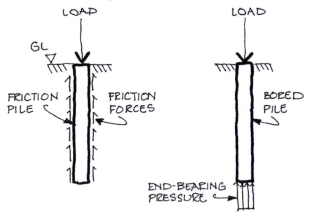

Fig. 8.28 Pile types

The capacity of a pile can be increased by increasing the size of the end of the pile: this can be done in two ways. By using special equipment, a conical base can be formed at the end of a bored pile – **under-reamed pile**. The second method, developed by the Belgian engineer Edgard Frankignoul (1882-1954) in 1909, drives an empty steel tube into the ground using a concrete plug – **Franki pile**. When a pre-determined depth is reached, more concrete is added and driven out of the end of the tube to form a bulbous base. Concrete is then poured into the tube as it is withdrawn, to form the pile shaft.

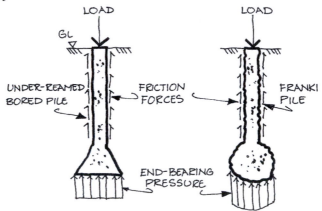

Fig. 8.29 Under-reamed and Franki piles

For the simple design of piles, the **load capacity of a pile** is calculated by adding the **friction forces** to the **end-bearing forces**, so:

Load capacity = Area of pile shaft × friction + Area of pile base × end bearing pressure

Design values for friction and end-bearing pressure are usually given in the site investigation report. Unusually for the design of structural elements, it is commonplace to carry out a **full-scale load test**. A **test pile is installed** and loaded with the design load. Deflections are monitored over time to check that they will be small under working loads. Then it is usual to load the pile to failure; the criterion for failure is when deflections increase rapidly under load.

Often the load capacity of one pile is less that the applied load, so several piles are installed in **pile groups** under each column or other vertical load-carry elements – walls or lift shafts for example. The transfer of the vertical load to the pile group is made using a **pile-cap** - a thick concrete element. A simple method of finding the forces in a pile cap is to use the strut and tie model – **Fig 4.24**.

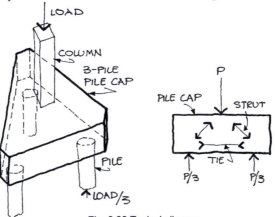

Fig. 8.30 Typical pile cap

This section has outlined the basic options for carrying vertical loads to the ground under a building. Simple methods for calculating vertical load-carrying capacities have also been described. It should be borne in mind that foundation engineering is a vast and often complex subject, with many variations on the solutions presented here.

It should be noted that foundations may also have to carry **horizontal loads** from **wind loads, horizontal reactions** from structures, or for other reasons. It is not easy to give simple rules for carrying these loads. Often, considering friction on the underside of bases, or the foundations, pile caps or piles pushing against the surrounding soil may be sufficient. In other cases specific horizontal structural elements may be needed to resist these forces – to tie together the feet of portal frames, P_H in **Fig. 2.39** for instance. Numerical calculations are needed to give guidance here.

8.7 Earth Retaining Structures

Every building meets the ground, so they all need some form of foundation, but there are other forms of below-ground structures where spaces are required below ground level - **basements**. For these to be built, earth retaining structures are needed. As well as loading the ground vertically, these structures are **loaded horizontally by the ground**, as has already been shown in **Fig. 8.2.**

To give limits on what the horizontal stresses that any ground exerts, it is helpful to see what stresses are required to support a block of a completely solid material like rock, and a completely liquid one. Assuming the depth of the block is **D** and the density of the material is gamma, **γ**, then the **vertical stress** under each block will be **D times γ**. The vertical face of the solid material will be kept in place with **zero horizontal stress**. But due to **hydrostatic stress** the liquid material requires a horizontal stress **linearly varying** from **zero** at the top to **D times γ** at the base.

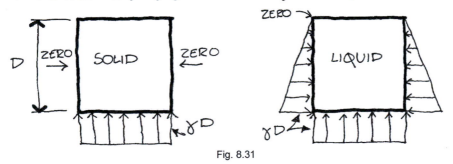

Fig. 8.31

As **Fig. 8.31** shows, the **percentage** of the density **γ** of the material that is **required as a horizontal stress** to maintain the shape of the block varies from **zero**, for the solid material, to **one** for the liquid one. Whilst the ground conditions for a basement could be solid rock, or an almost liquid swamp, most are built in some form of non-cohesive or cohesive soil, so the fraction of the density that acts horizontally must be between **0** and **1**.

If a perfectly dry granular soil like sand is poured onto a flat surface it will form a conical heap, the sides of which make an angle – usually called **phi** or **φ** – with the flat surface – the maximum slope in **Fig. 1.7.** This angle **φ**, in the case of granular soils, approximates the **angle of internal friction**. Assuming such a soil, and making further simplifying assumptions, in 1857 WJM Rankine proposed a mathematical formula that related **φ** to what is now known as **Rankine's active coefficient**, usually denoted K_A. Typical values are around a third. So using $K_A = 0.33$, and assuming that the weight of the soil is constant, and the lateral earth pressure increases linearly with depth, the **earth pressure** and can be calculated as:

Earth pressure = soil density × depth × K_A ≈ 0.33γD

Using this approximation, the horizontal load – the lateral earth pressure – on the walls of a basement can be calculated. The walls now act as **one** or **two way spanning slabs** – see section **2.6** – and all the principles of structural behaviour apply. **Fig. 8.32** shows a **2 level basement**, with the **lateral earth pressure** and the consequent **loading** and **bending moment diagrams** on the basement walls.

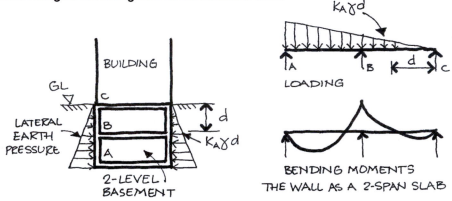

Fig. 8.32

There are two further important points to note about the structural design of such basements. The first is the importance of the role played by the internal horizontal structures, which have to act as **structural supports** to the walls by providing **propping forces**. These structures have to provide a balanced and continuous system, in other words a **complete load path**. This means the forces have to be carried – **diverted** – around any substantial openings. As basements are often used for car parking, their access ramps require long openings in the floor. So care has to be taken that the floor structure can carry the diverted propping forces – this is often done by **horizontal beam action** in the floor structure.

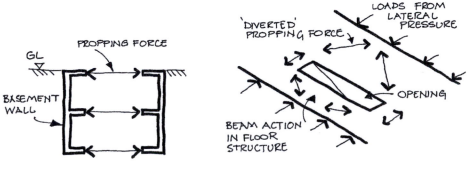

Fig. 8.33

The second point concerns basements that are built below the water table, as can often happen near rivers, lakes and the sea. Here not only are the basement walls subjected to an extra lateral load from the hydrostatic water pressure but the **floor of** the basement is also **subjected to an upward pressure**. If the downward pressure due to the **self-weight of the base slab is less** than the **upward water pressure**, then the base slab has to span between the vertical walls, which act at supports – **Fig. 8.34.**

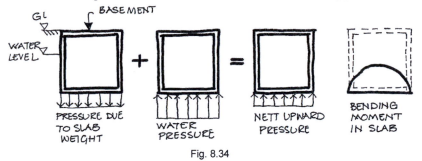

Fig. 8.34

If the water table is high, and the building above ground is light, **the downward minimum total vertical load minus the upward load due to the water pressure on the base has to be downward**, otherwise the building can rise out of the ground until the water pressure is reduced – in other words the **building can float** – see **Figs. 1.11** and **1.12**. To avoid this **extra weight** may have to be added to the building, usually by thickening the base slab or walls, or using an anchoring system.

The basements considered so far have to be built in an excavation that is wider than the structure; usually the excavation has sloping sides to prevent the soil from collapsing. When basements become **deep**, this method starts to become difficult to use for practical and economic reasons. For this situation, another method can be used, which is to construct the **vertical walls from ground level** and then dig out the soil between the walls. There are two basic types of these walls are called **diaphragm walls** and **contiguous pile walls**.

To construct a diaphragm wall, special excavating machines make deep slots in the ground. To prevent the slots collapsing they are filled with thixotropic slurry. Reinforcement cages are lowered into the slurry filled slots, then the slots are filled with concrete by concreting from the bottom of the slot using a tremie. The fresh concrete rises in the slot, displacing the thixotropic slurry. When all the slots have been concreted, a continuous wall has been constructed – see **Fig. 8.35** left.

Contiguous pile walls are basically a row of slightly interlocking bored piles. First primary piles are installed, leaving gaps between them. After the concrete in primary piles has hardened, secondary piles are bored between them. See **Fig. 8.35** right.

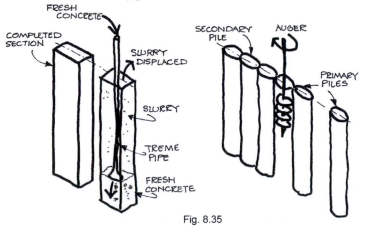

Fig. 8.35

After the installation of the walls is complete, excavation begins **top down**. As the excavation proceeds, the walls, loaded with lateral earth pressure, **act as cantilevers** above the level of excavation. When the cantilever bending moment reaches a calculated value, **temporary horizontal supports** are installed. After the excavation is completed, the permanent horizontal structures are constructed **bottom up**.

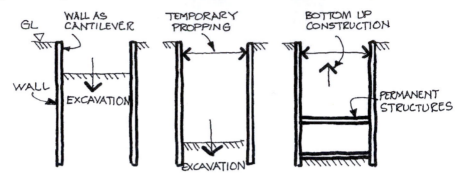

Fig. 8.36 Deep basement construction

It has been possible to approach the structural behaviour and design of the structures to carry vertical loads – individual bases, raft and piles foundations – using fairly simple concepts, as it has with normal basements. With deep basements this is no longer possible. The lateral pressure distribution behind the walls is complex, and changes during the various stages of construction. Furthermore as these are often installed in cohesive soils – clayey soils – the idea of Rankine's active coefficient K_A no longer applies, so these structures are definitely in the realm of the expert.

8.8   Ground movement effects

Like all structural materials, when soil is loaded is will deflect; this deflection is usually called **settlement** (see section **8.4** and especially **figs 8.12** and **8.19**). In most cases the settlement of foundations is assumed to be minimal, and the effect ignored. However, there are various situations where the ground movements cannot be ignored, for instance where the soil is **loosely compacted** or **water is present**; each presenting different behaviour.

For loosely compacted soils, when load is applied the air between the soil particles is driven out and the soil particles are more closely packed together – **compacted** – see **fig. 8.9**. It is unusual to place foundations on loosely compacted soil; however, where filling material is placed to make up levels under ground-bearing slabs, it is usual to mechanically compact it to prevent future settlement.

Where there is water present with a drainage path, any applied load is initially carried by an increase in the **pore-water pressure**, in the water that occupies the pores between the soil particles. Over time, this increased pressure is dissipated as the water migrates outwards from the loaded area. This causes the particles to become more densely packed and the soil to settle – this is called **consolidation**. In free-draining granular soils this effect is immediate, but in clayey soils, due to the small size of the pores, it can take years before it is completed.

If the predicted settlement is not minimal, then this movement can affect the superstructure. If all the foundations of a structure settled equally, this would have no effect on the structure. But this is unlikely, as what happens is **differential settlement**. This has the effect of **imposing deflections** on the superstructure. Consider the effect on a **simple portal frame** – see section **2.5** – where one foundation settles more than the other. This will cause **bending moments**, and consequential **shear forces** in the frame – see **Fig. 8.37**.

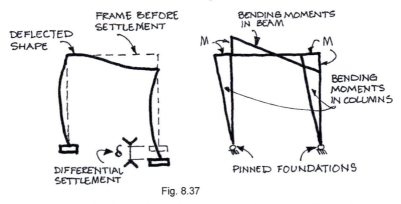

Fig. 8.37

Note that in **Fig. 8.37**, the bases have been assumed not to offer resistance to rotation, in other words they only supply a **pin joint** – see **Fig. 2.24** – to the **base of the columns**, which means the **bending moment** there is **zero**. How much resistance to rotation simple bases offer is a complex matter, and is not discussed here.

Load causes consolidation and subsequent settlement. But this can also occur where there are layers of clayey soil under the foundation level, that become drier over time. This removal of water will reduce the size of the pores in the soil, so the soil will reduce in volume, and hence cause downward movement – settlement. This drying can be caused by seasonal variations or the removal of moisture by other means such as tree roots.

Most effects of ground movements occur due to the ground settling, that is going down, but the ground can also come up, which for some structures will induce moments and shear forces. When a **clayey soil** is loaded, the **pore water pressure** is eventually reduced and the soil is **consolidated** with a smaller volume. If the load is then reduced by excavating the soil above the layer of **clayey soil**, over time the **pore water pressure** increases, causing the volume to increase and the soil to **heave**.

For an underground building the **heave** has a similar effect as that of **water pressure**, as shown in **Fig. 8.34**, only this time it is not an immediate effect, but can take years.

8.9   Summary

In summary four broad statements can be made about soil as a structural material and the design of below-ground structures: these are:

- **Many below ground structures can be designed using simplified processes.**
- **The engineering behaviour of many real soils is difficult to formulate analytically. Many aspects are not fully understood and these are subjects for research by specialists.**

- It is much more common to have problems with below ground structures than with the superstructure.

- There many techniques and types of below-ground structure that have been omitted in this introductory chapter: these include rock anchors, tension piles, temporary sheet piles, piled rafts and many others, details of which can be found in specialised texts

Further reading

John Atkinson – **An Introduction to the mechanics of soils and foundations** – McGraw-Hill College 1993

FGH. Blyth and, Michael de Freitas - **A Geology for Engineers**, CRC Press; 7th edition 1984

Percival Leonard Capper and W. Fisher Cassie - **The Mechanics of Engineering Soils -** E. & F.N. Spon 5th edition 1969

TW Lambe and RV Whitman – **Soil Mechanics** - Wiley 1969

Karl Terzaghi, Ralph B. Peck, Gholamreza Mesri, - **Soil Mechanics in Engineering Practice (Civil Engineering)**,1996, 3rd Edition, Wiley-Interscience - The classic text by the 'father of soil mechanics' Karl Terzaghi

MJ Tomlinson – **Foundation Design and Construction -** Longman Group United Kingdom; 7th edition 2001

Estimating Soil Texture -
http://culter.colorado.edu/~kittel/SoilChar%28%26RibbonTest%29_handout.pdf – useful practical guide to soil type identification

CHAPTER 9　*Behaviour of a simple building*

Buildings are constructed to alter the environment locally by enclosing space, and building structures give strength and stiffness to the enclosing elements. The simplest building is a single enclosed space, or a single space building. If the function and behaviour of the structure of a single space building is understood, then understanding building structures of more complex buildings is relatively straightforward. Although many buildings have many spaces, factories, sports halls, theatres and churches are all examples of buildings which are often essentially a single space.

The shapes of single spaces could be cubic, spherical or any defined or organic geometry (see section **7.1**). However, the majority of new buildings are rectilinear for a number of practical reasons, so the **basic structure** is the structure for a cubic single space. The explanation for the behaviour of the structure for this single space uses the **six basic concepts** which are:

1　　The function of a structure is to transfer loads
2　　The load path is the structure for each load
3　　The structure transfers loads by forces in the structure
4　　Forces in the structure can be considered to be a combination of axial and shear forces and bending moments
5　　The structure must have overall stability
6　　Collapse initiated by slender structures must be avoided

An understanding of how these six essential concepts apply to the structure of a single space can be used to understand the structures of more complex buildings such as houses, hotels, offices or arts centres. Not only does the application of these basic concepts give an understanding of structural behaviour, but it also provides a basis for the more difficult process of structural design. The design process is more difficult than understanding the behaviour of existing structures, as the concepts have to be used simultaneously to produce the design.

9.1　Basic structure and loading

As these concepts apply to the whole of the structure they must be applied to every part of the structure; from each weld or bolt to the whole structure. So that the concepts can be applied to a specific example, the basic shape of the building is assumed to be rectangular with a simple pitched roof.

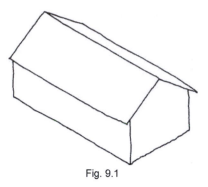

Fig. 9.1

The building has a roof covered with corrugated metal sheeting, with walls of brickwork. The main structure is steelwork, the floor is of pre-cast concrete, and the foundations are of in situ concrete. This type of building is used widely throughout the world for factories and warehouses.

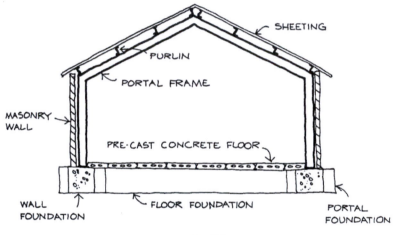

Fig. 9.2

To avoid the endless use of the word **concept** in the rest of this section, concepts are put into square brackets. **So [2] in the text will mean that concept 2** – the load path is the structure – applies.

To start at the beginning **[1]**, what are the loads? The sources of loads will be gravity, the wind and the use of the space. Gravity and use will apply vertical loads (see **Figs. 1.28** to **1.31**).

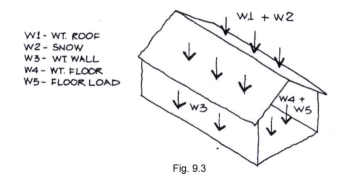

W1 - WT. ROOF
W2 - SNOW
W3 - WT WALL
W4 - WT. FLOOR
W5 - FLOOR LOAD

Fig. 9.3

Wind will apply loads at right-angles to the roof and walls.

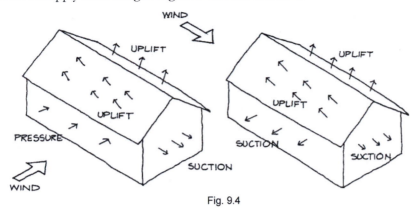

Fig. 9.4

Whether the wind causes an uplift force on the roof depends on the slope angle of the roof.

Although all these loads are applied to the building at various times, not all the loads will be applied simultaneously, so the structure must be safe under all **load combinations** (see pages **21-24**). Even for such a simple building there can be numerous different combinations. Here three combinations will be considered.

Loadcase 1   Maximum vertical load on the roof and floor.

Loadcase 2   Minimum vertical load on the roof and floor plus wind load on the side elevation.

Loadcase 3   Minimum vertical load on the roof and floor plus wind load on the end elevation.

Because of **[2]** the structure for each loadcase may be different, so **[2]** has to be applied to each loadcase. As the space is three dimensional, the structure has to be three dimensional, however each element is either one or two dimensional (see pages **58-59**) and will act as one-dimensional or two-dimensional structures. For this structure the elements can be identified as one or two dimensional, and so can their actions.

Element	Type	Action
Roof sheet	2D	1D
Wall	2D	2D
Steel frame	1D	1D
Pre-cast floor	2D	1D
Foundations	1D	1D (?)

It may seem odd that two-dimensional elements like the roof sheeting or the floor units act as one-dimensional structures, but this is because of the way they are connected to the rest of the structure.

Before each load path **[2]** is identified, the structural behaviour, **[3]** and **[4]**, of each element can be clarified. Firstly the roof sheeting, this is two dimensional, but spans unidirectionally.

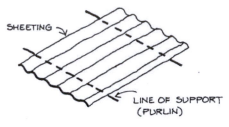

Fig. 9.5

The wall is connected vertically for vertical loads and is connected laterally for horizontal loads.

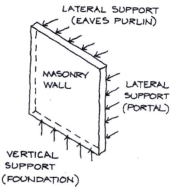

Fig. 9.6

The steel frame consists of several different parts. The purlins, the portal frames, the roof wind bracing, the wall wind bracing and the gable posts.

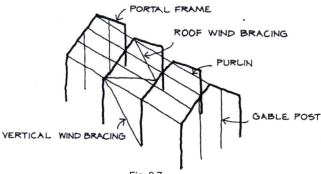

Fig. 9.7

The pre-cast concrete floor units are two-dimensional elements, but span unidirectionally.

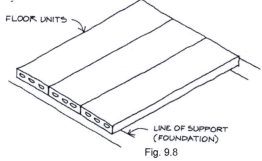

Fig. 9.8

The foundations are one-dimensional elements, but their structural action, rather surprisingly, is one or two dimensional!

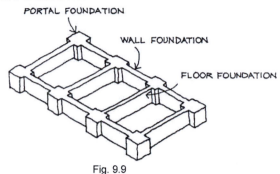

Fig. 9.9

The identification of the structural elements often provides important clues to the behaviour of the structure, but for built structures this identification usually requires more information than can be provided by visual inspection. Having identified all the structural elements, it is possible to see how they become parts of load paths [2], how the structure transfers loads [3], and what type of internal forces there are in each element [4].

For **Loadcase 1**, maximum vertical load, every element will be involved because all the elements have self-weight due to gravity. Is usual to chase loads down a building, so the roof load path has to be identified.

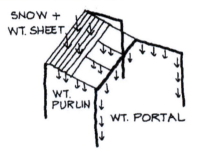

Fig. 9.10

The vertical load on the roof, snow load and the self-weight of the sheeting, is supported by the roof sheeting which spans from purlin to purlin.

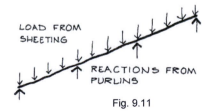

Fig. 9.11

The reactions to the sheeting become loads on the purlins, the self-weight of the purlins must be added to the sheeting reactions. The purlins span between the portal frames.

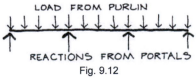

Fig. 9.12

Now the reactions to the purlins become loads on the portal frames, again the self-weight of the frames must be added to these loads. These loads are carried by the frame action of the portal frames to the foundations.

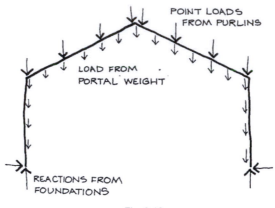

Fig. 9.13

The foundations are loaded by the reactions to the portal frames plus the reactions to the self-weight of the walls and the reactions to the floor units.

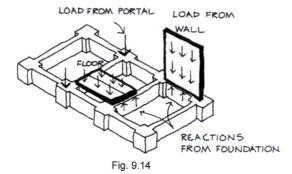

Fig. 9.14

The loadcases for the wind load include the minimum vertical load, which is the self-weight of the building construction. As the load paths for these loads are the load paths for **Loadcase 1**, only the load paths due to the wind loads are described. When the wind blows on the side elevation, the walls are loaded horizontally and the roof sheeting is loaded at right-angles to the roof slope — these loads are shown in **Fig. 9.4**. Again the roof sheeting spans between the purlins but the walls span both vertically, from the ground to the eaves, and horizontally between the portal frames or gable posts.

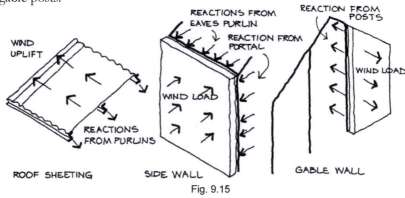

Fig. 9.15

The loads on the intermediate portals are due to the reactions to the purlins and the side walls. The self-weight of the sheeting, purlins and the portal frames must be added to the wind loads.

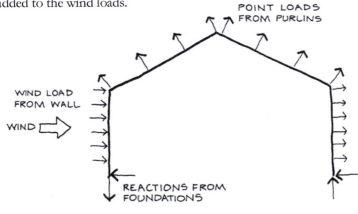

Fig. 9.16

For the end portals, the reactions from the wind load on the gable walls must be added to the loads from the wind on the side walls shown in **Fig. 9.16**.

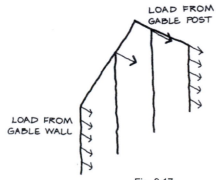

Fig. 9.17

Because the outward loads on the end walls are approximately equal, there is no overall effect along the building. The loads across the building do have the overall effect of a horizontal load.

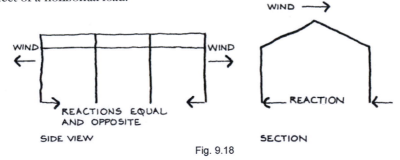

Fig. 9.18

When the wind blows on the end wall there is uplift on the roof and equal and opposite outward wind loads on the side walls. The loads on the intermediate portals are similar, but not the same as those shown in **Fig. 9.16**.

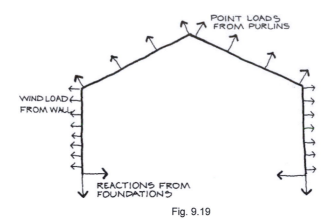

Fig. 9.19

The loads on the end portals are similar to those on the intermediate portals plus loads from the gable wall. The gable wall loads are similar to those shown in **Fig. 9.17**. However, the overall load situation is the opposite of that shown in **Fig. 9.18**, there is now an overall force along the building, but no overall force across the building.

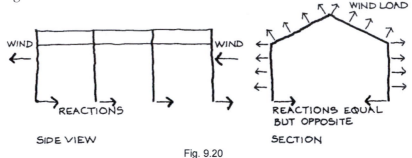

SIDE VIEW   SECTION

Fig. 9.20

For the wind loads, the foundation loads are the reactions required by the portal frames, the gable posts and the wall panels. Again it must be remembered that the self-weight loads must be added to these wind loads.

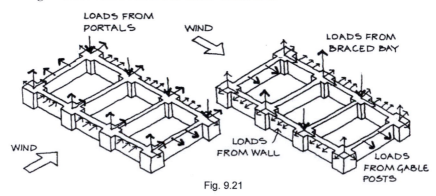

Fig. 9.21

It is now possible to see how each part of the structure carries the loads **[4]** and how stability effects are dealt with – **[5]** and **[6]**. There are two approaches to this, either the whole of the load path for each loadcase can be investigated, or each part of the structure can be investigated for all the loadcases. Because it is usual to design structures element by element, the second approach will be used here. As structures are usually designed **roof down**, the order of elements would be:

1	Roof sheeting
2	Walls
3	Purlins
4	Portal frames
5	Windbracing
6	Pre-cast concrete floor
7	Foundations

9.2   The roof and walls

For the roof sheeting only two of the three loadcases will apply because there will be a maximum downward loadcase and a maximum upward loadcase.

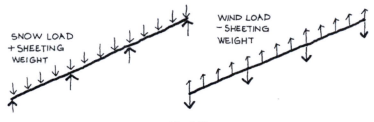

Fig. 9.22

The sheeting spans as a three-span beam between the four rows of purlins, and this spanning action will cause shear forces and bending moments in the sheeting. Shear force and bending moment diagrams can be drawn for these internal forces [3]. For brevity only the downward loadcase is shown.

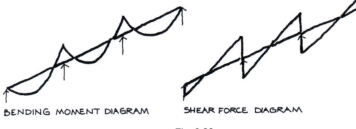

BENDING MOMENT DIAGRAM   SHEAR FORCE DIAGRAM

Fig. 9.23

As the sheeting is beam-like, there will be bending stresses and shear stresses in the sheeting. The sheeting is corrugated so that it can carry these stresses in an efficient way, the bending stresses will be at a maximum at the top and bottom of the corrugations and the shear stresses will be a maximum at the mid-depth of the section [4].

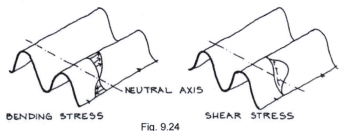

BENDING STRESS   SHEAR STRESS

Fig. 9.24

Behaviour of a simple building   211

The overall stability [5] of the sheeting is provided by the fixings to the purlins. These must be strong enough to prevent whole sheets being sucked off by the upward wind loads. Due to the shape of the sheets, lateral buckling (see page 181) will not occur, but local buckling [6] could initiate collapse. This could occur at the point of maximum compressive stress, or at the point of maximum shear stress.

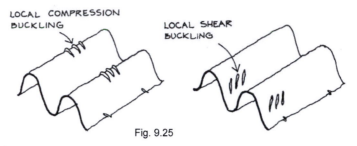

Fig. 9.25

Possible problems due to local buckling are prevented by providing a suitable thickness for the roof sheeting.

The walls are not loadbearing in the sense that they are part of the main structure however, they do have to transfer [1] wind loads to the portal frames. They also have to carry their own weight.

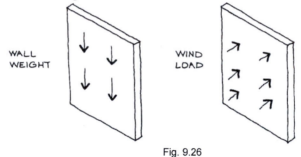

Fig. 9.26

The self-weight load is applied vertically and causes axial forces [3] and compressive stresses [4] in the wall. The wind load is applied horizontally and causes shear forces and bending moments [3] in the wall. As the wall is connected horizontally on all sides (Fig. 9.6), the wall spans in two directions, this means that these internal forces [3] will also be in two directions (see section 2.6).

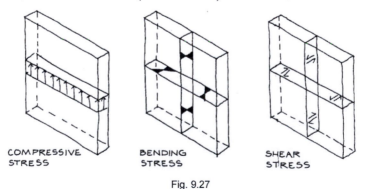

Fig. 9.27

Because brickwork has very limited tensile strength, the size of the bending moments in the wall is limited by the tensile bending stress. The bending stress depends on the span of the wall and the thickness of the wall. As walls can only be built in specific thicknesses, it is usual to choose a thickness and then limit the span. If the spacing between the main portal frames means the span of the wall is too big, then additional supports can be used to reduce the wall span.

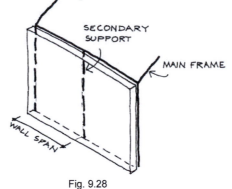

Fig. 9.28

The windload can cause bending in the wall panels in either direction so the walls must be fixed positively to the support framework, otherwise a panel could be blown (actually sucked) over [5]. The wall could also collapse by buckling [6] under its own weight if it is too thin. This form of buckling would be similar to the buckling of the wall of a box-column (**Fig. 6.68**).

The function of the purlins is to transfer the sheeting loads to the portal frames [1]. How much load depends on the spacing of the purlins along the sheet.

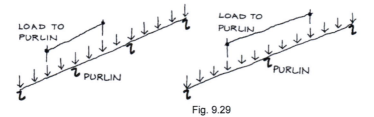

Fig. 9.29

The purlins are beams spanning between the portal frames so they have shear forces and bending moments like any other beam [3] and [4].

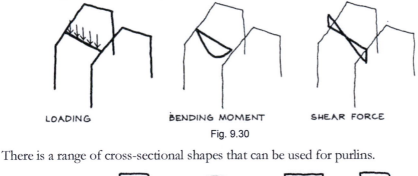

LOADING   BENDING MOMENT   SHEAR FORCE

Fig. 9.30

There is a range of cross-sectional shapes that can be used for purlins.

ANGLE   ZED   TUBE   I   CHANNEL

Fig. 9.31

If the chosen purlin is slender then the possibility of the compression flange buckling sideways [6] must be examined. Under downwards load, the roof sheeting acts as a stiffening structure to prevent lateral buckling of the compression flange. Under upward wind loading, the bottom flange is in compression and could buckle between the supports.

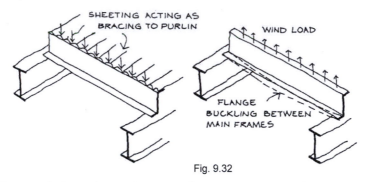

Fig. 9.32

If the span is long, then a discrete stiffening structure can be used to provide lateral restraint to the bottom flange. This is often done by bracing the bottom flange of each purlin to the top flanges of the adjacent purlins with a rod.

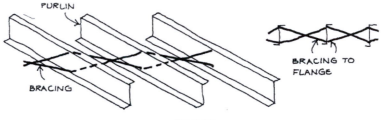

Fig. 9.33

This bracing reduces the slenderness of the bottom flange of the purlin which now has to buckle between support points.

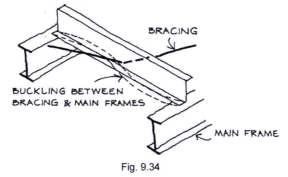

Fig. 9.34

9.3 The portal frames

The portal frames carry the loads from the purlins (**Fig. 9.30**) and the lateral loads from the walls [1]. This is done by frame action of the portal; this frame action only acts across the building. This means that the portal can only carry loads that are applied across the building, not loads that are applied along it.

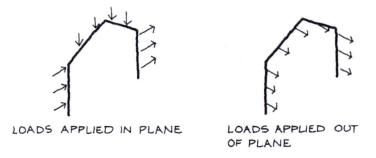

LOADS APPLIED IN PLANE

LOADS APPLIED OUT OF PLANE

Fig. 9.35

The three loadcases cause different load patterns on the portal frame **[1].**

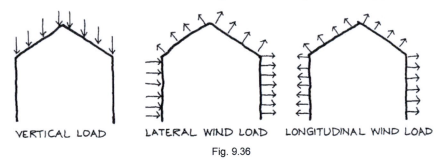

VERTICAL LOAD   LATERAL WIND LOAD   LONGITUDINAL WIND LOAD

Fig. 9.36

These load patterns will cause axial forces, shear forces and bending moments in the beam-like members that make up the portal **[4].** The size of these internal forces will vary along the members of the frame and can be represented by axial force, shear force and bending moment diagrams similar to those shown in **Fig. 2.47**. There will also be vertical and horizontal reactions at the base of the portal frame.

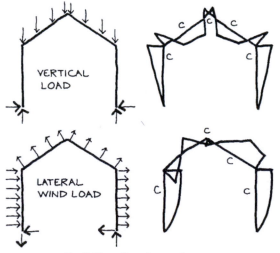

VERTICAL LOAD

LATERAL WIND LOAD

Fig. 9.37 continued on next page

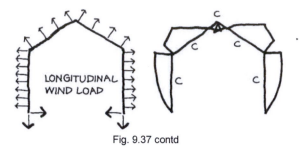

LONGITUDINAL
WIND LOAD

Fig. 9.37 contd

This figure only shows the bending moment diagrams, but there will be a direct force and shear force diagram associated with each of these bending moment diagrams. The positions of the tensile and compressive stresses are also shown on the diagrams. It should be noted that these vary quite dramatically from loading to loading, as do the directions of the reactions at the support of the frame. Under wind loading, one vertical reaction is up and the other is down. This indicates that the whole frame could overturn under wind loading [5].

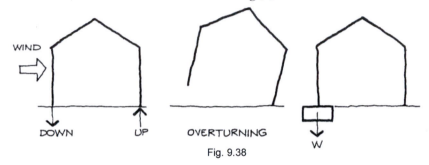

WIND

DOWN   UP   OVERTURNING
                                        W

Fig. 9.38

If the frame and the cladding is light', the frame may need to be held down by the weight of the foundations. Where there are compressive stresses in the frame, the possibility of buckling-initiated collapse [6] must be investigated. Because different loadcases cause compressive stresses in different parts of the structure, each case must be considered separately. For compressive stresses in the top of the roof part of the frame, the purlins act as discrete stiffening structures and, depending on the connection, the walls may prevent the outside of the legs buckling.

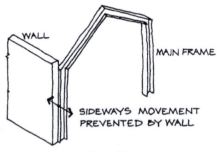

WALL

MAIN FRAME

SIDEWAYS MOVEMENT
PREVENTED BY WALL

Fig. 9.39

Under vertical load, the inside of the legs, the eaves and the ridge have compressive stresses, and are not restrained in an obvious way. Under sideways wind load, different parts of the frame have compressive stresses and again some of these are unrestrained.

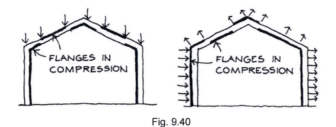

Fig. 9.40

Any of these areas of compression could buckle laterally if they were too slender.

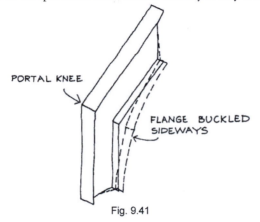

Fig. 9.41

9.4 The wind bracing system

The steel portals resist the force due to the wind acting on the side of the building, but they cannot resist horizontal loads caused by wind loads on the gable walls (**Fig. 9.35**). The forces along the building are resisted by truss-like structures called **wind bracing**. These truss-like structures are a combination of the members of the portal frame, and bracing members specifically introduced to resist the longitudinal wind forces - hence wind bracing.

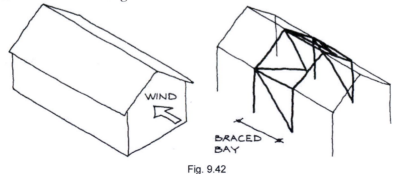

Fig. 9.42

The wind force on the end walls has to be strutted or tied to the braced bay.

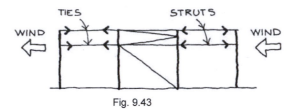

Fig. 9.43

These struts and ties may be the purlins **[2]**, in which case they have to be designed to act as part of this load path, or they may be extra members added to the roof structure solely for this purpose. The bracing in the roof is a truss-like structure often called a **wind girder**. The vertical bracing is also a truss-like structure which acts as a cantilever from the ground. For calculations of the wind bracing see **Example 14.21** in **Chapter 14**.

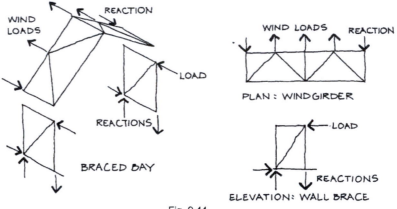

Fig. 9.44

The portal frames become part of the truss-like structures **[2]**. The roof parts of the frames become the top and bottom members of the wind girder, and the legs of the portal frames become the vertical members of the cantilever trusses.

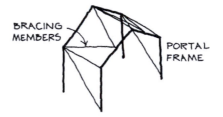

Fig. 9.45

The cantilever side bracing requires upward and downward reactions. These are the push-pull forces of the cantilever bending moment.

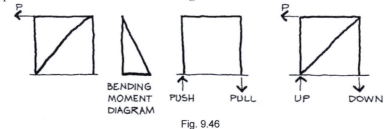

Fig. 9.46

As with the portal frame, the whole frame could overturn [5]. If the self-weight is low, then the downwards reaction is provided by the weight of the foundations.

Fig. 9.47

These truss-like bracing structures resist the shear forces and bending moments [4] caused by their spanning action by tensile and compressive forces in the individual elements of the trusses. As the wind direction is usually reversible, all the members of the bracing system will be in compression or tension for one of the wind directions. This means all parts of the bracing system have to be checked for the possibility of buckling-initiated collapse [6] (section **6.4**).

9.5   The floor structure

Like the purlins, the floor units span as simple beams between the lines of foundations [1] and [2]. The units are beam-like, so the shear forces and bending moments are carried by shear stresses and bending stresses in the units – [3] and [4].

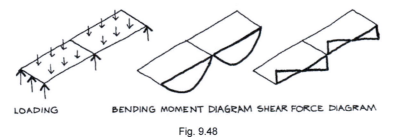

Fig. 9.48

As concrete is a heavyweight material and floors usually only have downwards loads there is no problem of overall stability [5]. As no part of the structure is slender there will be no slenderness-initiated collapse [6].

9.6   The foundations

The most common form of foundation for this type of simple building would be individual bases under each portal leg – these are described in section **8.6**. Nowadays reinforced concrete slabs bases are usually used, but mass concrete bases could be an alternative. In the case of this building the foundations also have to provide weight against uplift and resistance to horizontal forces.

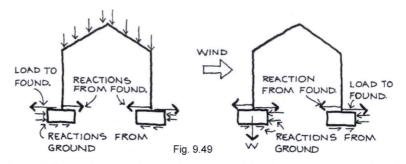

Fig. 9.49

The horizontal forces due to side wind are resisted by friction on the underside of the foundations and earth pressure on the sides of the foundations.

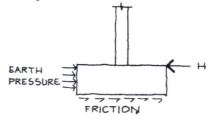

Fig. 9.50

Where the horizontal forces are acting in opposite directions, the friction and earth pressure can resist them, but if the force is high then a specific tie member may be required to resist spreading of the portal supports.

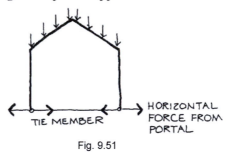

Fig. 9.51

If the supports of a portal frame move, the distribution of bending moments will alter radically. This is similar to the difference between an arch and a curved beam (**Fig. 7.73**).

9.7 Summary

This example of a structure for a single space building illustrates how different load paths are needed for different loadings and how concepts of axial forces, shear forces and bending moments are used to understand the behaviour of each load path. The type of stress in each part of the structure depends on whether it is part of a beam-like or truss-like structure.

How any building structure behaves can be found by using the conceptual analysis used for this simple example. **It also shows how a structural designer has to choose the structure for every part of the structural system**. For instance, the chosen purlins were steel and beam-like, but truss-like steel or beam-like timber purlins could have been chosen. It is these choices, and their consequential effect on the structural behaviour of the whole structural system, that is the essence of structural design.

CHAPTER 10 *Real structures*

The way any structure behaves under loading can be understood by using the six basic concepts (page **203**). The behaviour of the **basic structure** for a single space building was analysed in detail, by repeatedly applying these concepts to each part of the building. This process can be used to analyse any structure, provided sufficient technical information is available.

Because the process of structural design currently used for building structures is relatively recent, the structures of older buildings are often different in concept from more recent ones. Any building structure will act in the way that suits the structure. So the designer's concept must reflect realistic structural behaviour. Recent designs answer questions raised by considering the six basic concepts, but for structures built before about 1850 the process was different. In older structures the design was based on traditional practice (rule of thumb, experience) and by the use of geometric concepts rather than structural ones. The geometry was used to size structural elements by using relationships based on proportions rather than structural behaviour. This means that the behaviour of structures conceived in this way is often difficult to clarify, their exact behaviour can even be a matter of debate amongst interested academics.

The six structures chosen for conceptual analysis are mainly from the period of engineering design, because structural behaviour tends to be easier to clarify. The chosen structures are:

- **Durham Cathedral**,[1,2] England, completed 1133
- **The Palm House**,[3,4,5] Kew Gardens, England, completed 1848
- **Zarzuela Hippodrome**,[6] Madrid, Spain, completed 1935
- **CNIT Exposition Palace**,[7] Paris, France, completed 1960
- **Federal Reserve Bank**,[8] Minneapolis, USA, completed 1973
- **Bank of China**,[9] Hong Kong, completed 1990

These projects have been chosen because they all have very clear, but different structural forms. Each structure is conceptually analysed in outline using the six basic concept process. These analyses demonstrate how these universal concepts apply to structures that are quite different geometrically and materially.

10.1 Durham Cathedral

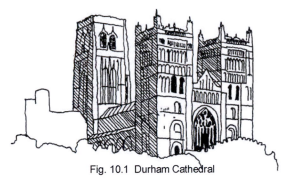

Fig. 10.1 Durham Cathedral

The period of the early Middle Ages, which is from the 11th to 15th centuries, saw an enormous programme of church building in Western Europe. The buildings ranged from small parish churches to the famous, and not so famous, cathedrals. Their style is now known as Gothic, and Gothic architecture has been, and still is, a subject of considerable academic and popular interest. This interest covers the historical, symbolic and aesthetic aspects of these churches and cathedrals.

There is also an interest is how the cathedrals were built and what technical knowledge the builders had. But the study of these aspects is hampered by the lack of documentary evidence of the building process. Although written material survives from this period, none of it relates to technology, so either it was considered unimportant, or never existed. As there was no concept of scale technical drawings the masons and carpenters must have worked from models and full-size templates.

The modern concepts of structural engineering had not been formulated, so the builders could not have known about stress, or bending moments, but they must have known about gravity and force. Technical knowledge that did exist came from the Greeks, but this had been lost in Western Europe during the so-called Dark Ages so the builders of the cathedrals were really pioneers.

The plan of Durham Cathedral follows the usual Latin cross plan of the Gothic style.

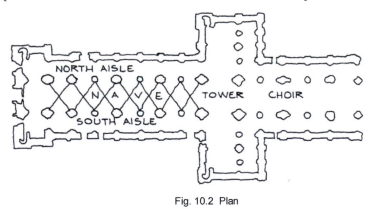

Fig. 10.2 Plan

The cross-section also follows the usual pattern for Gothic cathedrals.

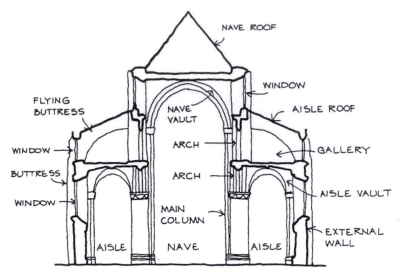

Fig. 10.3 Cross-section

The main parts of the cross-section are the roof, the main vault (ceiling), the internal and external 'walls', the side aisle roofs and vault.

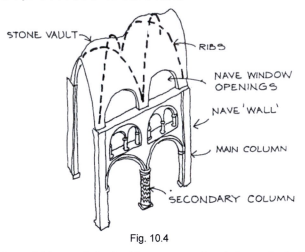

Fig. 10.4

One of the main ambitions of the builders was to flood the cathedrals with natural light, so the internal and external walls have numerous perforations, which means that the walls are more like colonnades.

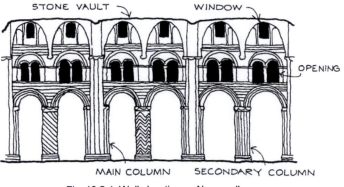

Fig. 10.5-1 Wall elevations – Nave wall

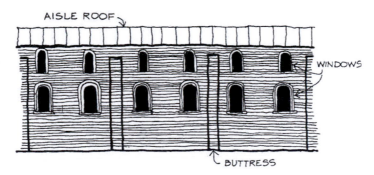

Fig. 10.5-2 Wall elevations – External wall

The structures of the roofs of the nave and the side aisles are of timber. These structures span between the internal and external walls.

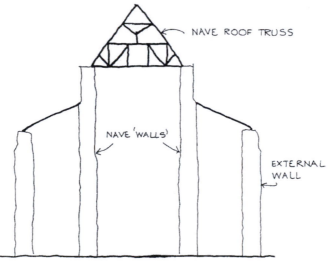

Fig. 10.6 Roof structures

Below these roofs are stone vaulted ceilings, and it is this vaulting that is one of the main interests in cathedral architecture. To allow light into the cathedral and to permit circulation at ground level, each bay of the nave vaulting is only supported at the corners.

Fig. 10.7 Vaulting system

Most of the cathedral structure is built of masonry, and because masonry can only carry compressive forces most of the structure must be in compression. The exception is the timber roof structures. The cathedral is essentially a single space with the main loading being from self-weight, snow and wind. As masonry is a heavyweight material, and the structure is massive, self-weight is the major load.

Compared with this load, snow and wind loads are negligible.

The main roof structure and the stone ceiling vaulting are independent structures spanning across the nave. The timber roof structure is a rather complicated structure which spans unidirectionally across the nave whereas the stone ceiling vault spans in two directions (**Fig. 7.75 E**). As both are spanning there will be associated bending moment and shear force diagrams.

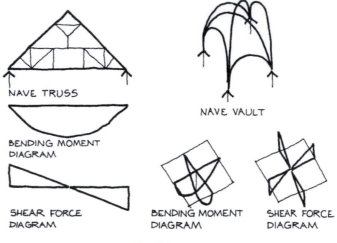

Fig. 10.8

The roof structure is truss-like, so the push-pull forces are taken by the sloping and bottom members and the shear resisted by the sloping member (**Fig. 7.18**).

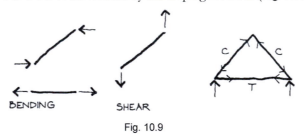

Fig. 10.9

The vault, however, is funicular (see section **7.4**) and the push-pull forces are carried by compression in the vault and by tension in mid-air (**5** of **Fig. 7.21**). The shear is carried by the vertical component of the sloping compression force.

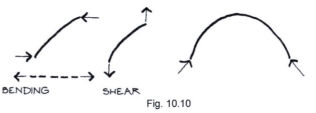

Fig. 10.10

Because the vault acts in two dimensions, these forces will also be in two dimensions. The spans of these vaults are not great, only **9.75m** across the nave at Durham, smaller than many ancient Islamic mosques. However, the height of the nave is quite considerable, **21.4m** at Durham. It is this height that causes the major structural difficulty as the 'tension in mid-air' is supplied by a sloping thrust at the level of the vault supports.

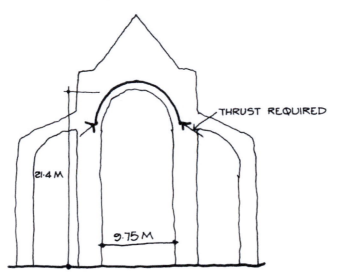

Fig. 10.11

And this thrust becomes a load on the nave/external wall structure.

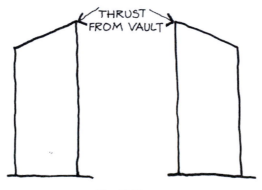

Fig. 10.12

These walls are cantilevers from the ground, and the sloping thrust can be regarded as a combination of a vertical and a horizontal force applied to the top of the wall. This causes axial forces plus a bending moment and a shear force.

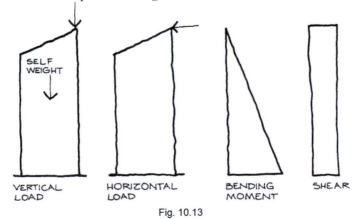

Fig. 10.13

This action is just another example of an axial load acting at an eccentricity to cause a moment (**Figs. 3.89** to **3.91**). Because the wall is of masonry the thrusts must be kept within the wall section.

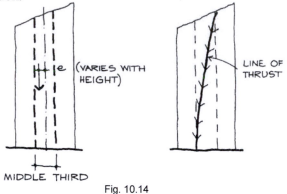

MIDDLE THIRD

Fig. 10.14

The line of thrust cannot be as shown in **Fig. 10.14** as the nave/external wall is not solid across the building, so the thrust is carried by a **flying buttress** which joins the tops of the nave and external walls.

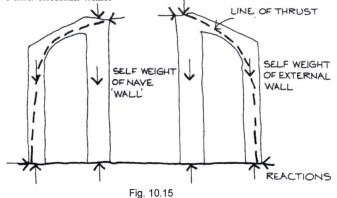

Fig. 10.15

In this way the wall can be perforated. This system of flying buttresses became more and more complex as the Gothic period progressed, and culminated with the cathedral at Beauvais. Here the height of the nave was **48m** and the vault thrust was taken by three tiers of buttresses.

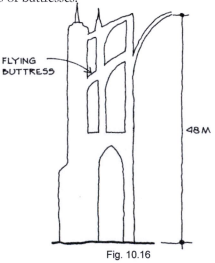

Fig. 10.16

Beauvais, see **Fig. 0.7,** is often considered the final achievement of the Gothic builders, though this view must be tempered by the fact that various parts of the cathedral collapsed, and it was never completed.

Whilst the forces across the structure are taken by the nave and external walls and the flying buttresses, because the vault is two dimensional there are also forces along the nave.

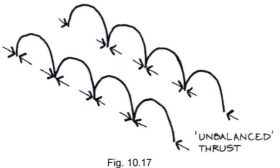

Fig. 10.17

As the main force is due to self-weight, the forces along the nave balance one another, that is until the end. At the ends are more solid constructions, the main tower and the West tower, and the weight of these resist the end thrusts.

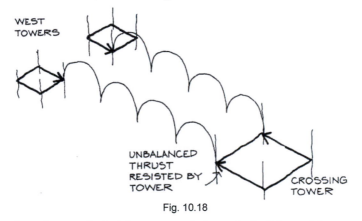

Fig. 10.18

The marvel of these cathedrals' structures is how the builders, without concepts of stress and moments, were able to balance the various thrusts and keep them within the funicular lines. They occasionally failed to manage this, with consequent collapses.

10.2 The Palm House

Glasshouses were a building type that came into existence in the 19th century being an extension of the 18th century orangeries and conservatories. As with all new building types, their emergence depended on a number of factors, technical, economic and social. The first substantial structure built of iron was the Ironbridge at Coalbrookdale in 1779 (see page **118**): by the 1840s, iron, both cast and wrought, were routinely used for structures. During this period there were also advances in the production of glass. It was the availability of iron and glass at reasonable prices that were the technical and economic factors that made glasshouses possible. During the 19th century there was also a rise in interest in science, and this gave the impetus to the expansion of numerous scientific establishments. It was under these circumstances that plans for a Palm House at the Botanic Gardens at Kew were drawn up. These initial plans were abandoned and Decimus Burton (1800-1881), the designer of the Winter Gardens in Regent's Park, was asked to draw up plans for a new design.

Decimus Burton had already worked with the Irish iron founder Richard Turner (1798-1881), an astute and ambitious businessman, who ensured that the Commissioner of Works for the new Palm House asked him for a proposal for the new building. His proposal was quite different to Burton's design and was similar to the final design. For many years the design was attributed to Decimus Burton, but it is now recognised that the main influence on the design was Richard Turner.

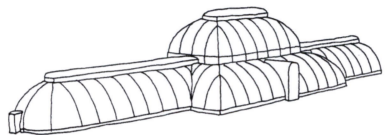

Fig. 10.19 The Palm House at Kew

The design was influenced by the work of George MacKenzie (1780-1848) and John Loudon (1783-1843), who had both promoted, for horticultural reasons, the advantages of curved glasshouses and the Palm House is curved in all directions. Turner's design also used the recently patented wrought iron **deck beam**.

Fig. 10.20 – Deck beam

The production of these beams was, in turn, made possible by the invention of the steam hammer by James Nasmyth (1808-1890) in 1839. The deck beam was the forerunner of the ubiquitous I beam (see page **72**). The deck beam was so-called as it was used to support decks in the new iron ships. The Palm House was the first building to use this new structural element.

Like the builders of Durham Cathedral, the builders of the Palm House were principally concerned with natural light. But Turner and Burton had a new structural material, wrought iron, which was much stronger than stone and could also resist substantial tensile stresses. In the 1840s, structural design was in its infancy and no evidence of the existence of technical calculations for the Palm House has ever been found, but Turner wrote *"…complete principle of mechanics for Stability"*, and beams were subjected to tests, but for what load is not known.

To understand the structural behaviour the first step is to simplify the complex three-dimensional shapes into three parts; the end caps, the barrel vaults and the central transept.

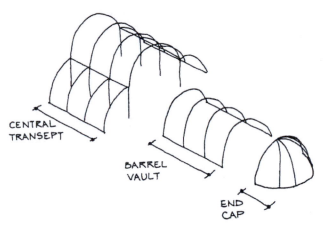

CENTRAL
TRANSEPT

BARREL
VAULT

END
CAP

Fig. 10.21 – Simplification of the structure

Although these parts are connected together, they do act fairly independently. The major loads on the Palm House are self-weight, snow and wind loads. Due to the curved shapes, the intensity of these loads vary continuously. The loading is conceptually similar to that on the **basic structure** (**Figs. 9.3** and **9.4**), but with no differentiation between wall and roof.

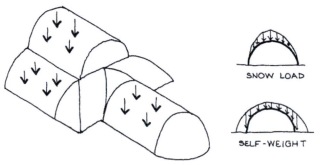

SNOW LOAD

SELF-WEIGHT

Fig. 10.22

The overall distribution of wind pressure is complex and can only be obtained from wind tunnel tests, a technique not available to the original designer. Across the barrel vault sections the pressure distribution is similar to **Fig. 9.4.**

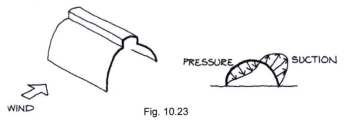

WIND

PRESSURE   SUCTION

Fig. 10.23

Around the end caps and the central transept, the wind pressure distribution is more complicated, but there will be areas of positive pressure and areas of suction. Again, the structural behaviour of the end caps and the transept is more complicated than the barrel vaults. By regarding the barrel vaults as separate structures, a conceptual analysis can be carried out on this area. This closely follows the analysis of the roof and portal frame of the **basic structure** (see section **9.2** and **9.3**).

Initially the loads are carried by the glazing (glass cladding). These loads are self-weight, snow and wind loads and the glass carries these loads by spanning between the curved glazing bars.

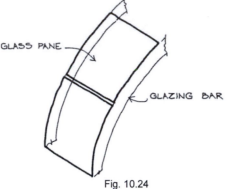

GLASS PANE

GLAZING BAR

Fig. 10.24

The load and the structural behaviour of the glass vary from area to area. The self-weight and the snow load are always vertical, whereas the wind load is normal (at right angles) to the surface.

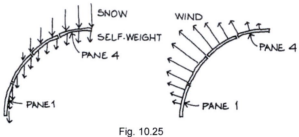

SNOW

WIND

SELF-WEIGHT

PANE 4

PANE 4

PANE 1

PANE 1

Fig. 10.25

For example **pane 2** may have the highest wind load whereas **pane 4** may have the highest snow load. All the panes have the same self-weight but near the crown this loads the pane across its width (a beam) but at the ground it loads the pane along its length (a wall).

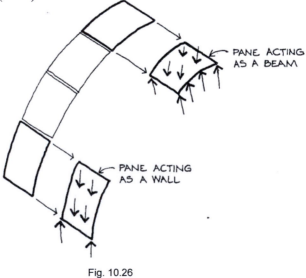

PANE ACTING AS A BEAM

PANE ACTING AS A WALL

Fig. 10.26

To cater for the changing loading patterns and structural behaviour the glass panes, as structures, could be altered throughout the glass house. For a building this is too complicated, so the **worst** case will determine the glass design. Depending on the numerical values, this could be at the crown under self-weight and snow load, or at an intermediate point under self-weight and wind load. In each of these cases the pane will act as a beam-like structure spanning between the glazing bars. This means the glass pane will have a bending moment and a shear force with the associated stresses.

LOADING   BENDING MOMENT DIAGRAM   BENDING STRESSES IN GLASS

Fig. 10.27

Like the spacing of the purlins of the **basic structure** (**Fig. 9.5**), the spacing of the glazing bars is chosen by the designer. Greater spacing means less glazing bars but thicker glass to keep the stresses in the glass within set limits; closer spacing means thinner glass but more glazing bars. There is no correct spacing.

The glazing bars are curved and run from the ground to clerestory windows. The glazing bars are supported by the intermediate tubular purlins for inward loads but not for 'outward' loads. An outward load is a wind suction force. The reason for this one-way support is because the glazing bars just rest on rods which in turn just rest on the tubular purlins.

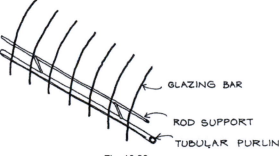

GLAZING BAR

ROD SUPPORT

TUBULAR PURLIN

Fig. 10.28

This odd arrangement of glazing bar support shows that the designers were unaware of the suction effects of wind load. It also means that under inward load the glazing bar spans, as a beam, from purlin to purlin but for net outward load they have to span from ground to clerestory level. This is done by the glazing bar acting as a funicular structure in tension – a hanging cable (**Fig. 7.8**).

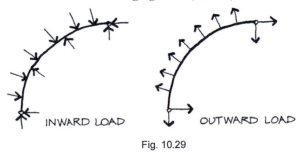

INWARD LOAD   OUTWARD LOAD

Fig. 10.29

When the purlins are loaded they span between the arch frames, but they also have a rather strange feature as they are pre-stressed (see section **4.7**). Pre-stressing is common for concrete but rare for steelwork. At the Palm House, the purlins are stressed by the stretching of an internal iron rod.

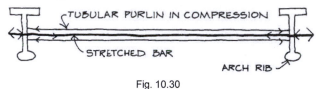

Fig. 10.30

Under inward, load the purlin system is the rod and the pre-stressed tubular purlin.

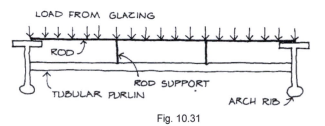

Fig. 10.31

The rod spans as a three-span beam loaded by the reactions from the glazing bars. The rod support reactions become point loads on the pre-stressed tubular purlins.

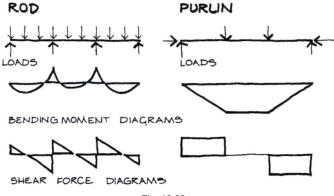

Fig. 10.32

The stresses in the rod are as for a beam but those in the purlin are altered by the pre-stress compression (**Fig. 3.83**).

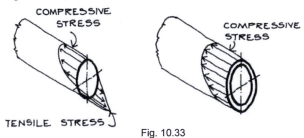

Fig. 10.33

The different inward/outward load behaviour of the purlin system means the loads on the arch frame are very different for the snow load and wind load cases.

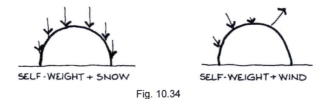

SELF-WEIGHT + SNOW

SELF-WEIGHT + WIND

Fig. 10.34

These frames act like curved portal frames and not like funicular arches so their behaviour is similar to the portals of the **basic structure** (**Fig. 9.37**). This behaviour can be represented by axial force, shear force and bending moment diagrams. Only the bending moment diagrams are shown.

SELF-WEIGHT + SNOW
BENDING MOMENT DIAGRAMS

SELF-WEIGHT + WIND

Fig. 10.35

The behaviour of the central transept is quite different and has to be viewed three dimensionally.

Fig. 10.36

The cross-section has an arch frame, two half-arch frames and two columns.

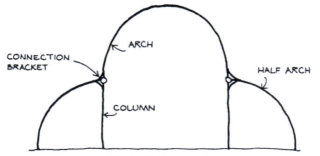

CONNECTION BRACKET

ARCH

HALF ARCH

COLUMN

Fig. 10.37 Cross-section

There are six of these frames and each is loaded by loads that are similar to those applied to the barrel vaults.

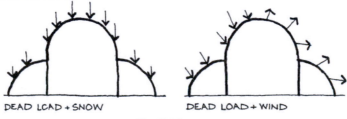

DEAD LOAD + SNOW

DEAD LOAD + WIND

Fig. 10.38

Real structures 235

These frames could act independently, rather like more complicated versions of the barrel vault arch frames.

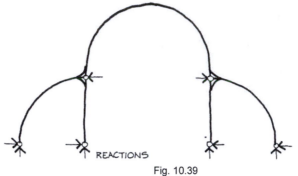

Fig. 10.39

However, the structure of the central transept acts as a three-dimensional structure and this means that not only are the cross frames supported at the ground in the vertical and horizontal directions but they are also supported horizontally at the gallery level. This additional horizontal support allows the top arch frame to act in the same way as the barrel vault arch (**Fig. 10.35**) and the side arch frames to act in a similar way. Again this behaviour can be represented by axial force, shear force and bending moment diagrams, and again only the bending moment diagrams are drawn.

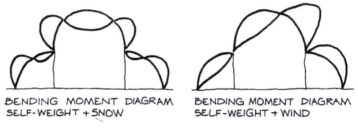

BENDING MOMENT DIAGRAM
SELF-WEIGHT + SNOW

BENDING MOMENT DIAGRAM
SELF-WEIGHT + WIND

Fig. 10.40

The horizontal reactions from the frames at gallery level become loads on the gallery which acts as a horizontal beam spanning between the main arch frames at each end of the transept.

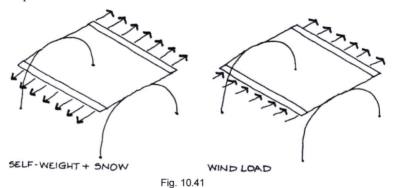

SELF-WEIGHT + SNOW   WIND LOAD

Fig. 10.41

Like any other beam, the gallery has bending moments and shear forces.

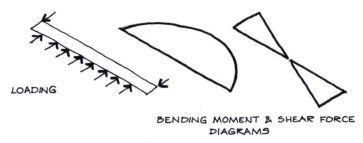

LOADING

BENDING MOMENT & SHEAR FORCE
DIAGRAMS

Fig. 10.42

The reactions from the beam become loads on the main arch frames. In the case of the vertical load, the reactions from the gallery beams do not produce any load on the arch frame, but the reactions from the wind load do cause a horizontal load applied to the arch crown.

VERTICAL LOAD   WIND LOAD

Fig. 10.43

The main arch frames resist these loads by acting as curved frames. The structure for the wind load on the central transept acts like the bracing system used for the wind load on the end wall of the **basic structure (Fig. 9.45)**.

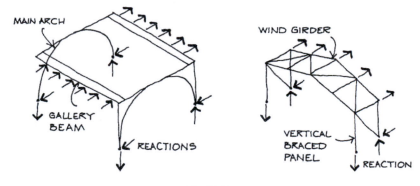

MAIN ARCH

GALLERY
BEAM

REACTIONS

WIND GIRDER

VERTICAL
BRACED
PANEL

REACTION

Fig. 10.44

The gallery beam spans horizontally, as does the wind girder of the **basic structure**, and each cause horizontal loads on the vertical structural elements – the main arch frames and the vertical braced panels. This is another example of similar structural behaviour, but quite different structural geometries. It is the ability to recognise these systems of structural action rather than geometry, that is a key to understanding how whole structures act.

The wind load acting on the Palm House, when the wind blows along it, is resisted by the end caps and the transition structures at the central transept. These wind forces cause internal forces in the various half-arch frames, which again could be represented by axial force, shear force and bending moment diagrams.

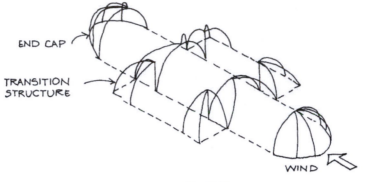

END CAP

TRANSITION
STRUCTURE

WIND

Fig. 10.45

As the structure is of iron it is quite slender, so all parts that are in compression under any loading must be examined for the possibility of buckling-initiated local or overall collapse (see section **6.4**). The structure must be examined element by element as was the **basic structure**.

The Palm House looks like a modern structure, and is renowned for its beauty and elegance, however its designer did not use the current rational approach. As none of the arches are near to the correct funicular shape for the loadings, a portal frame would have been more structurally appropriate. This approach can be seen at Kew with the more recent Australian and Princess Diana glass houses.

At the time of the design, the 1840s, there was considerable technical knowledge about the theoretical behaviour of structures. This knowledge was not widespread, and consequently not routinely used for structural design. It is probably for this reason that no calculations were done by the original designers but in the 1980s the Palm House was completely dissembled, refurbished and re-assembled. As part of this process the structure was checked using modern analytical and wind tunnel techniques. This work showed that the original design is adequate, and that no structural strengthening was required. The term re-assembled is used rather than rebuilt, because the Palm House is a kit of over 7000 iron parts. The refurbishment allowed the technical and organisational genius of Richard Turner to be seen in its totality for the first time.

10.3   Zarzuela Hippodrome

The engineered structures of the 19th century were predominately of cast and wrought iron, and towards the end of the century, of steel. The first use of reinforcing concrete with metal is usually attributed to Joseph-Louis Lambot (1814-1887), with his boat in 1849, and Joseph Monier (1823-1906) with his garden boxes in 1865 but the idea was proposed by François Coignet (1814-1888) in 1828. But it was only at the end of the 19th century that concrete, reinforced with steel, began to be used widely. This was due to the pioneering work of the French engineer François Hennebique and architect Auguste Perret (1874-1954). By the 1930s, the use of reinforced concrete structures was commonplace in Europe.

Because concrete structures can be formed **in situ** by pouring wet concrete into moulds, virtually any shape can be made. Again, the reinforcing bars can be placed anywhere in the concrete and the density of the bars can be continuously varied. This means that these in situ reinforced concrete structures are quite different in concept from iron or steel ones. They are no longer an assembly of elements as the one-, two- or three-dimensional parts can be joined by smooth geometric transitions. If the structure is formed from complex shapes the conceptual analysis can be very difficult, so where possible the structure may be approximated by an assembly of elements.

The structure of the Zarzuela Hippodrome was designed by the celebrated Spanish engineer Eduardo Torroja (1899-1961), and was built in 1935, just in time to be damaged, but not destroyed, in the Spanish civil war.

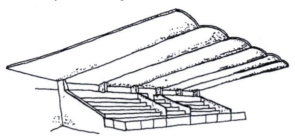

Fig. 10.46 Zarzuela Hippodrome

The building is essentially a grandstand with a betting hall underneath the seating. A cross-section through the building shows the functions of the various parts clearly.

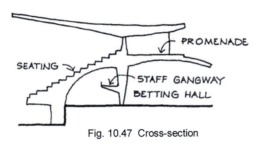

Fig. 10.47 Cross-section

This section can also be used to show where the loads are applied to the structure. As the structure is of reinforced concrete, a heavyweight material, the self-weight of the structure is a major load. Even though the roof structure is thin, its self-weight is still greater than any upward wind load.

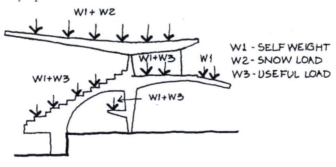

Fig. 10.48 Vertical loads

The main supporting structures are frames which are spaced regularly along the building.

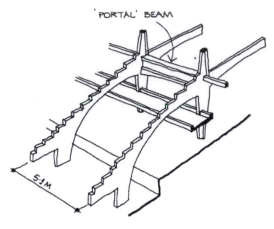

Fig. 10.49

Although much more complex in shape, these frames can be compared with the portal frames of the **basic structure (Fig. 9.7)**.

The roof of the grandstand is a shell **(Fig. 3.4)**. Concrete shells were pioneered by the German engineers Franz Dischinger (1887-1953) and Ulrich Finsterwalder (1897-1988) in the 1920s, are examples of vaulted structures **(Fig. 7.75E)**. Because the shell is thin it cannot resist significant bending moments, so shells are only successful if they are good funicular shapes. If the shape of a shell deviates from a funicular shape, it may have to be thickened to resist the internal stresses caused by the bending moments. This makes a shell an inappropriate structural form. Sydney Opera House (see section **12.7**) and the TWA terminal at Idlewild airport in New York are well-known examples of inappropriate shapes for shell roofs. As the roof is spanning, overall bending moments and shear forces exist.

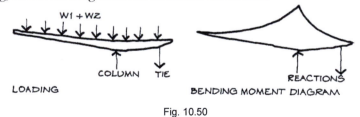

Fig. 10.50

A shell is a two-dimensional structure so this shell roof spans along the building as well as across it.

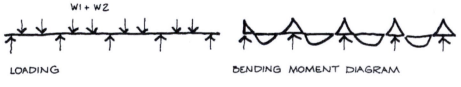

Fig. 10.51

For the roof to act as a funicular structure, rather than a beam-like structure, these bending moments and shear forces must be carried by internal axial forces. The pattern of these axial forces is complex ,and was too difficult to be found by the mathematical techniques available at the time of the design. This meant that the designers had to resort to carrying out a load test on a large scale model. Testing was extensively used by engineers in the 19th century, but it is slow and expensive compared with mathematical analysis. These tests enabled the direction and magnitude of the principal stresses (see sections **4.1** and **4.2**) to be identified. The reinforcement was placed in a simplified pattern of the principal **tensile** stresses.

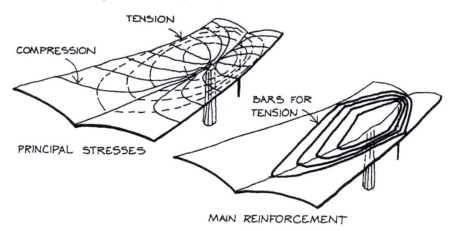

Fig. 10.52

The internal forces that result in the principal tensile and compressive stresses provide the push-pull forces that resist the overall bending moments and shear forces. At the column support where the overall moments and shear are at a maximum.

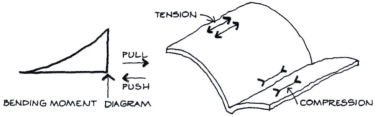

Fig. 10.53

Unlike a beam (**Fig. 3.43**) these forces are not vertically above one another, the tensile force is at the crown and the compressive force in the valley. The curved geometry of the shell roof provides the depth between these forces, which is the lever arm.

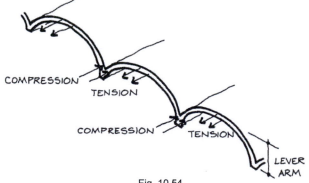

Fig. 10.54

Although the shells act as cantilevers from the support columns, the patterns of the principal stresses show that the structural action is two dimensional in the curved surface. The action of the roof causes up and down forces on the columns (**Fig. 10.50**) and these become loads on the transverse frames (**Fig. 10.49**). The other loads on the frames are from the reactions to the grandstand seating, the promenade floor and the staff gangway.

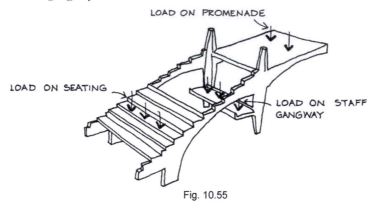

Fig. 10.55

The structural action of the transverse frames is similar to the portal frames of the **basic structure** and the arch frames of the Palm House. The frames resist the loads by internal forces which are bending moments, axial forces and shear forces. These can be represented by the appropriate diagrams. Only the bending moment diagram is shown.

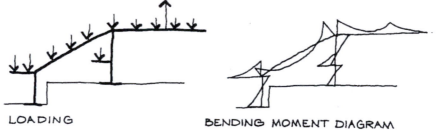

LOADING   BENDING MOMENT DIAGRAM

Fig. 10.56

Frame action is dependent on **stiff** joints and these joints are able to resist bending moments. This stiffness is readily achieved with in situ reinforced concrete by placing reinforcing bars **through** the joint for the push-pull forces.

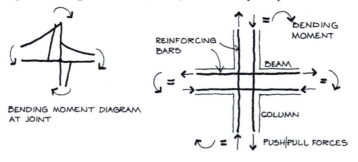

Fig. 10.57

Notice that the bending moment can change direction either side of a joint. This happens, for example, where the cantilever beam supporting the staff gangway connects to the column. If this was not a stiff joint, the beam could not be a cantilever.

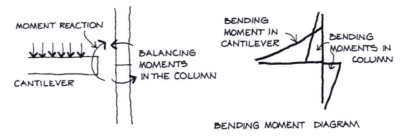

Fig. 10.58

The arrangement between the roof and the promenade beam shows how the designer's understanding of structural behaviour means an effective structure is provided. The secret is the roof tie which provides the pull for the roof structure, and thus reduces the cantilever moment in the promenade beam. If the tie was removed, large bending moments would be required to resist the roof load and the load on the promenade. For calculations for the tie see **Example 14.22** in **Chapter 14**.

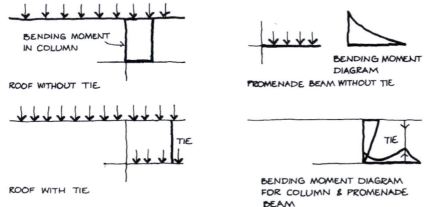

Fig. 10.59

As the building is basically open, the loads from the wind along the building are small, but all structures need some lateral strength or they could just fall over sideways. Here this lateral strength is again provided by frame action. This is achieved by using special longitudinal members, portal beams, which have stiff joints with the columns.

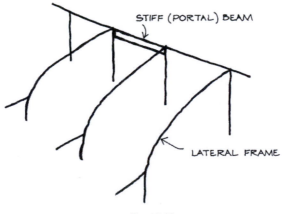

Fig. 10.60

Rather like the **basic structure (Fig. 9.43)**, one bay is made stiff. This is done with the stiff joints forming a portal frame instead of using a diagonal bracing member.

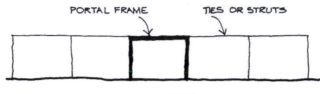

Fig. 10.61

Because concrete is a heavyweight material, concrete structures rarely have problems of overall stability. Also stresses in concrete structures are usually quite low, which means the elements have to be stocky to carry the loads, so they are rarely slender enough to initiate collapse by buckling.

This structure, unlike the Palm House, was designed by an engineer who was very conscious of the structural behaviour and who took considerable trouble to investigate and quantify it. Where this was not possible by using analytical techniques, scientific tests were carried out. An alternative would have been to redesign the roof so that analytical techniques available at the time could have been used.

10.4   CNIT Exposition Palace

In 1950, the Federation of Industries decided that a permanent exhibition centre should be built. This centre would provide space for temporary and permanent exhibitions for all types of French industrial equipment. It would be the *Centres National des Industries et des Techniques*; hence CNIT. A site was chosen 7km from the centre of Paris at La Defense. The design for the centre was carried out by the architects Camelot, de Mailly and Zehrfuss. Their design was triangular in plan and had a roof that spanned between the apexes of the triangular plan, without intermediate supports.

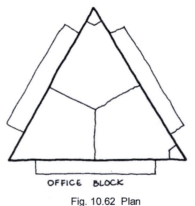

Fig. 10.62 Plan

The span of the roof is **218m** on each face of the triangular plan. This was the longest roof span ever built using the final choice of construction; this was a concrete double shell.

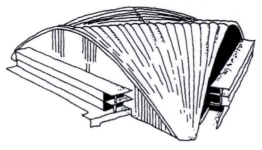

Fig. 10.63 CNIT Exposition Palace

A four-storey office block is built within each façade, with the space between office block and the roof closed with a glazed facade. The structure of the office blocks is separate from the roof structure. In the late 1980s the office blocks were removed and an hotel and a shopping complex were built under the original roof.

A number of leading engineering designers were asked to submit proposals for the roof structure. Seven proposals were submitted, three using steel as the structural material, three using reinforced concrete and one proposed a composite design using steel and concrete (**Fig. 4.76**). The scheme chosen was of concrete, and was submitted by Entreprises Boussion whose technical director was Nicolas Esquillan (1902-1989).

Their proposal was for a vaulted structure of reinforced concrete. To save weight, the structure of the roof was of honeycomb construction, with thin top and bottom surfaces spaced apart by a two-way arrangement of vertical webs. The whole roof is divided into three kite-shaped sections by a three-way joint.

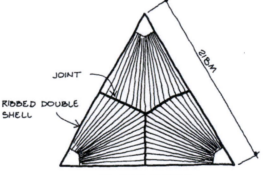

Fig. 10.64 Roof plan

Because the roof is of concrete, as with the roof of the Hippodrome, self-weight is the dominant loading. Although the wind causes loads, the building is so large that high wind pressures do not occur over the whole roof at any one time. For the effect of gravity load, the bending moments are similar to those in a triangular slab supported at the corners.

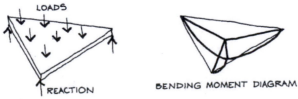

Fig. 10.65

One kite-shaped section of the slab roof could be regarded as acting as one half of a simple beam.

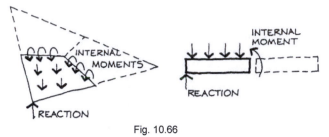

Fig. 10.66

If the roof was a flat slab then these bending moments would be resisted by push-pull forces within the depth of the slab (**Fig. 3.40**), but the roof is not flat, it is curved. The curve of the roof is the funicular shape for the self-weight; this shape is called a **catenary**. Because of this, the bending moment and the shear forces are resisted by axial forces in the structure, which follow the funicular line.

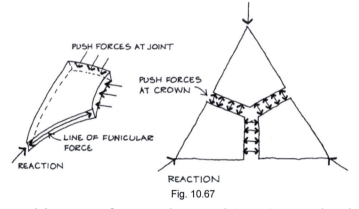

Fig. 10.67

The top and bottom surfaces are also curved in section, so that the surface is corrugated.

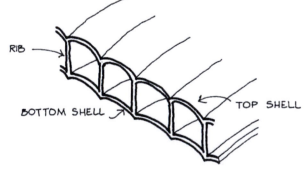

Fig. 10.68

The plan dimensions of the structure reduce towards the supports but the axial force does not; this would mean that the stresses could increase as there is less structure to carry the forces. This is avoided by concentrating the longitudinal webs and by increasing the thickness of the top and bottom skins.

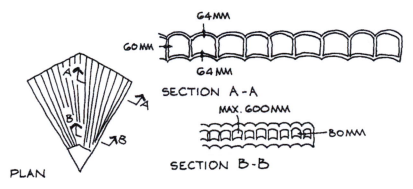

64 MM

60 MM

64 MM

SECTION A-A

MAX. 600 MM

80 MM

SECTION B-B

PLAN

Fig. 10.69

To prevent the centre of the roof being excessively high, the curve of the roof is kept quite flat, which reduces the overall lever arm.

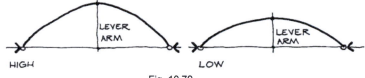

LEVER ARM

HIGH

LEVER ARM

LOW

Fig. 10.70

As the shape of the vault is a catenary, the radius of the roof varies from point to point. At the crown the radius is **91m** but at the supports it is **424m**.

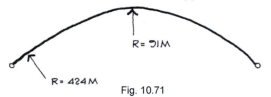

R = 91M

R = 424 M

Fig. 10.71

The radius at the supports is twice as large as the one used for the bridge at Sando in Sweden. When this bridge was built in 1943, it was the largest concrete arch in the world, and also had the largest radius of curvature. As the curve is flat, constructional inaccuracies could lead to the roof seriously deviating from the funicular line, so great care was taken with the geometry during construction.

Concrete structures are rarely slender but this structure is slender locally and globally, so the possibility of buckling-initiated collapse was carefully checked. The whole roof can buckle in symmetric and asymmetric modes.

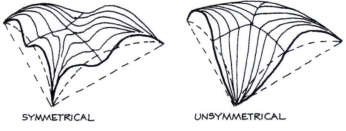

SYMMETRICAL

UNSYMMETRICAL

Fig. 10.72

As the whole of the cross-section is in compression, a collapse could be initiated by either the top or bottom surfaces buckling locally between the diaphragms.

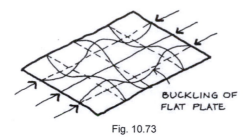

BUCKLING OF
FLAT PLATE

Fig. 10.73

This buckling pattern requires alternate panels to buckle in opposite directions. This could happen if the panels were flat but this local buckling pattern is prevented by the local curvature of the panels. This curvature means that local buckling takes place at the local crowns (**Fig. 6.68**), and this requires a much higher load than the alternate panel buckling. This was the reason that this local curvature between the diaphragms was introduced.

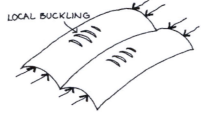

LOCAL BUCKLING

Fig. 10.74

Not only are the main parts of the roof in compression due to the arch action, but the triangular geometry and the rib arrangement cause compression across the shell at the crown joint. This is far from obvious.

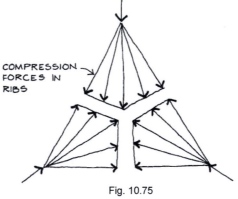

COMPRESSION
FORCES IN
RIBS

Fig. 10.75

Because of the fan-shaped pattern of the shells, the axial forces at the joint meet at varying angles. At the facade they are in line but the angle varies towards the centre.

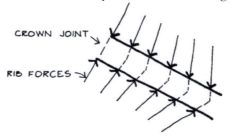

CROWN JOINT

RIB FORCES

Fig. 10.76

At the centre, the third section balances the forces, but elsewhere there is no balancing force as there are special rollers between the shells.

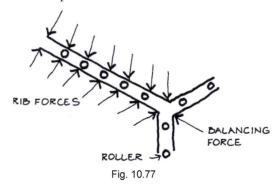

Fig. 10.77

These angled forces cause a varying compression force in the top edge members of each shell section. These edge members, the crown walls, are strengthened to carry these forces.

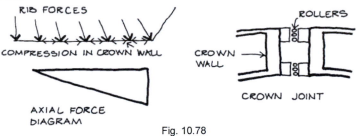

Fig. 10.78

To maintain the overall compression in the shell, the support points must provide horizontal as well as vertical reactions (**Fig. 7.19**). These horizontal reactions from the pull forces that resist the overall bending moment.

Fig. 10.79

If the shell was built between rigid abutments, natural rock for example, then the horizontal reactions could be provided by the foundations. Although the site of the building has natural rock near the surface, site limitations and the construction of underground railways in the future prevented direct use of the foundation rock for horizontal reactions.

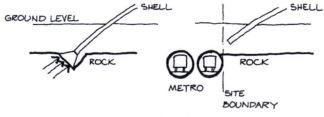

Fig. 10.80

The horizontal reactions are provided by special tie members (compare with **Fig. 9.51**). These run along the lines of the facades.

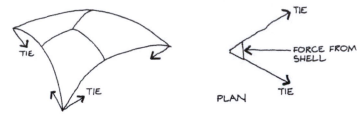

Fig. 10.81

The level of the tie at the foundation was too high along the facades, so it had to be diverted to a lower level.

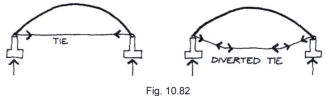

Fig. 10.82

This diversion of the tie members requires an additional tie member at the point of change in direction. This is another example of a cable shape for a particular loading.

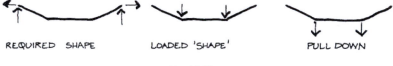

Fig. 10.83

The pull-down members are anchored in the underlying rock by excavating undercut holes so the concrete of the tie is wedged in the rock.

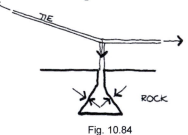

Fig. 10.84

The sides of the shell are enclosed by the four-storey office blocks and glazing.

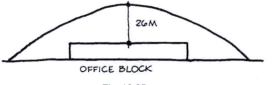

Fig. 10.85

The facade supports are substantial steel structures as they have to span up to 26m from the roof of the office block to the shell roof.

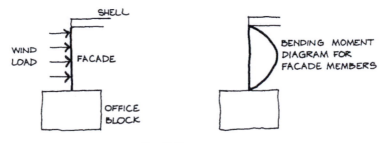

Fig. 10.86

Because the top of the shell moves vertically under different loads, there is a special joint between the shell and the facade structure to prevent the facade steelwork becoming part of the roof load path (compare with **Fig. 4.90**).

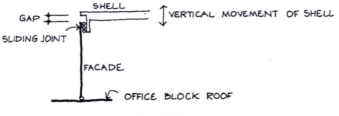

Fig. 10.87

The CNIT Exposition Palace is an enormous building, and the design and construction was a considerable undertaking. Using the six basic concepts listed on page **203**, together with the necessary technical information, the structural behaviour can be understood conceptually.

10.5 Federal Reserve Bank

Most office buildings are enclosures of cellular spaces (offices) and the building is usually planned on a rectangular grid with vertical columns at the grid intersections. The structure of the floors is an arrangement of beams and slabs carrying the loads to the columns by bending moments and shear forces.

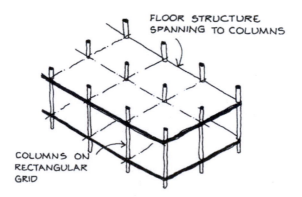

Fig. 10.88 – A standard office structure

The vertical loads are carried directly to the ground by the columns. Horizontal wind loads, which are substantial for the taller office buildings, can be resisted by a variety of structural systems. For wind loads, any building is essentially a cantilever from the ground with lateral loads (wind) and axial loads (self-weight, etc).

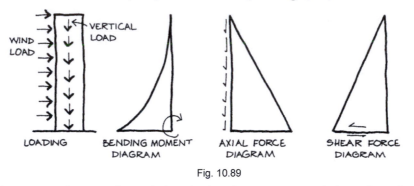

Fig. 10.89

The structural system for resisting the bending moment and shear force from the lateral wind load can be beam-like, truss-like, frame-like or, in the case of guyed structures, almost funicular.

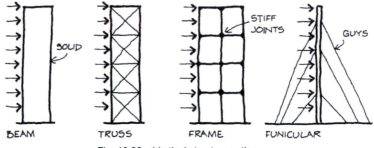

Fig. 10.90 – Vertical structure options

Where beam or truss structures are used, they restrict circulation so they are placed near lift shafts or at the ends of the building.

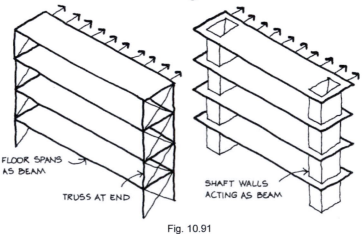

Fig. 10.91

The Federal Reserve Bank in Minneapolis, designed by architects Gunnar Birkets and Associates with engineers Skilling Helle Christiansen and Robertson, was completed in 1973. It is a ten-storey office building with underground car parking and bank vaults, quite a standard arrangement. But this building is far from standard, as the whole of the office block spans across a three-storey height space under the building. Creating this space under a ten-storey building means that the column loads, which would normally be supported by the ground have to be transferred laterally. The building now has to span across the space.

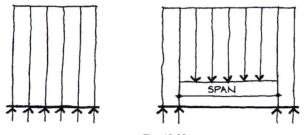

Fig. 10.92

And the loads are transferred by internal forces of bending moments and shear forces.

LOADING   BENDING MOMENT   SHEAR FORCE
               DIAGRAM   DIAGRAM

Fig. 10.93

As the design requires the building to span across the space, the structural designers had to choose a suitable structural system. There is no 'correct' system, just the chosen one. The choices for spanning structures are the four types: beam-like, truss-like, frame-like or funicular. As the building that spans is ten storeys high even with one type, say truss-like, there are further choices. A roof-level truss with hung floors, or trusses at two levels supporting columns are examples of possible choices.

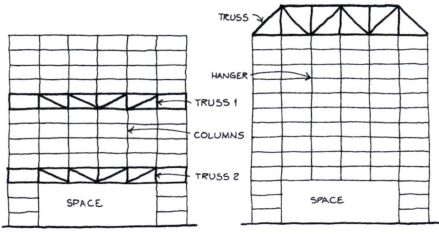

Fig. 10.94

The actual choice for the structure was quite unusual; they chose a funicular structure – a hanging cable. The cable is the whole depth of the ten-storey office building.

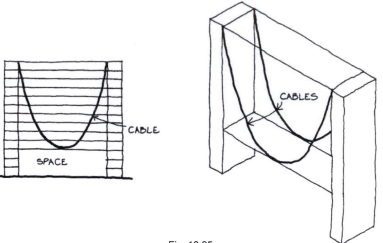

Fig. 10.95

This choice means that a horizontal force must be provided at roof level so that the cable can resist the bending moment.

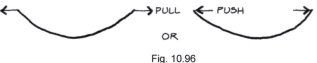

Fig. 10.96

In a suspension bridge, the mid-air push force (**Fig. 7.13**) is resisted by tensile forces in the back stays, but this would be inconvenient for this building, so a strut is used to provide the push force (**Fig. 7.15**).

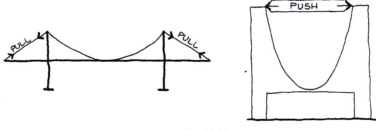

Fig. 10.97

A truss-like structure has been chosen for the strut. The floor trusses span across the building on to vertical members. These vertical members transfer the floor truss reactions to the cable. The vertical members above the cable are in compression whilst the members below are in tension.

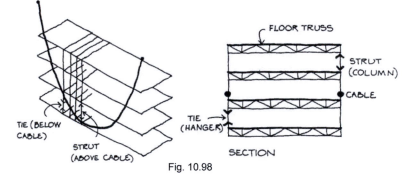

Fig. 10.98

At each end of the cable/strut structure there are vertical reactions (**Fig. 7.15**), which are resisted by thirteen-storey high concrete towers. The complete spanning structure is the cable, the strut and these end towers. The construction of the facade visually emphasises the presence of the cable part of the spanning structure.

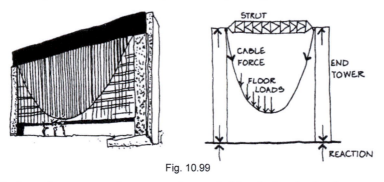

Fig. 10.99

Not only does the structure have to resist vertical loads, but it also has to act as a cantilever to resist wind loads. The cantilevering action is done by the concrete end towers. Because of the vertical load from the cable structure, the forces at the base of the towers are always compressive. This is another example of combining axial and bending stresses (**Fig. 3.82**). For the calculation of the stresses in the towers see **Example 14.23** of **Chapter 14**.

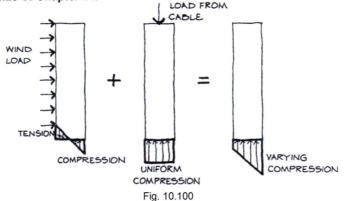

Fig. 10.100

The wind load path starts at the cladding system, and ends at the base of the cantilevering end towers. The cladding system spans vertically from floor to floor. The floors are loaded by the reactions of the cladding system, and span as horizontal beams between the end towers. The end towers are loaded at each floor level by the reactions from the floors acting as horizontal beams. The end towers carry these loads by acting as cantilevers from the ground.

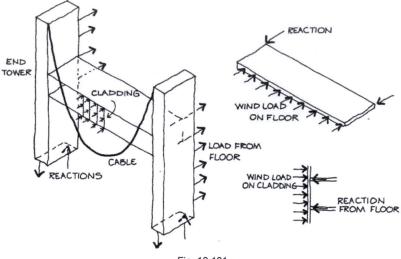

Fig. 10.101

The end towers are considered to be concrete I-beams and this affects the planning of the accommodation in the towers.

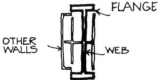

Fig. 10.102 Plan on end tower

One of the main problems for the structural designer in using these core areas as vertical cantilevers is to ensure that the accommodation requirements allow horizontal shear forces to develop between the flanges and the web (**Fig. 4.33**).

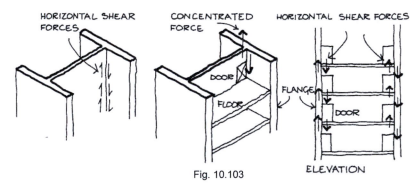

Fig. 10.103   ELEVATION

For a cable to act as a funicular structure it must change shape with a change of load pattern (**Figs. 7.67** and **7.68**). In this building the main load is the uniform vertical load from the building construction, but the pattern can vary when different layouts of furniture and equipment are adopted on each floor and, of course, the occupants tend to move about. For an ideally flexible cable, each change would require a change in funicular shape and this would be difficult to achieve for a cable that is part of a building. The cables in this building can act as bending elements for the relatively small bending moments that are required to keep the cable in its basic shape. This is achieved by constructing a **composite cable** of a cable acting with a curved steel I-beam.

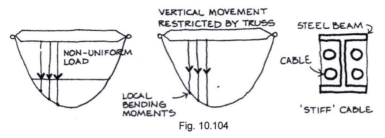

Fig. 10.104

Whilst there are only small variations in the load of the completed building, this is not the case during construction. Great care was taken by the builders to control the cable shape during construction as the cables were gradually loaded by the building elements. This was done by stressing the cable part of the cable in stages as the load was applied.

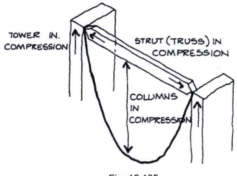

Fig. 10.105

There are a number of parts of the structure that must be checked to ensure that buckling-initiated collapse does not occur (see section **6.4**). The parts that are in compression are the roof level strut, the end towers and the columns. The roof level truss-like strut could buckle in a number of ways.

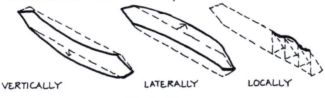

Fig. 10.106

The towers could also buckle locally, or as a complete structure.

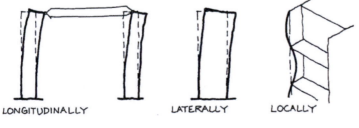

Fig. 10.107

It is unusual to be able to see all the parts of the structural system clearly when a building is complete, however, as can be seen, this photograph taken during construction clearly shows the structural system.

Fig. 10.108 photo: Balthazar Korab

The Federal Reserve Bank is unusual as the major structural action is visually expressed by the completed building. The structure is extraordinary for an office block, and it is not easy to understand why the designers went to such trouble and expense to span over a rather bleak plaza.

10.6 Bank of China

The headquarters building for the Bank of China in Hong Kong was designed by the architect IM Pei and the structural designers were the engineers LE Robertson Associates of New York. When it was completed in 1990, it was the fifth tallest building in the world, and the tallest building outside New York and Chicago.

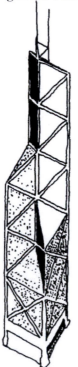

It is a massive building, 52m square on plan rising to a height, including the antennae, of 368m above road level. The gross area of the building is 133,000sq.m and there are 70 storeys.

As buildings become taller, the plan dimensions do not increase at the same rate. The reason for this is that although office workers rarely work by natural light, there is a psychological need for windows, for 'outside awareness'. This means that everyone needs to be no further than about 18m from a window. This limitation on plan dimension causes taller buildings to be more slender than shorter ones.

The combination of increased height and slenderness has two effects on the structural design of tall buildings. The first is the fact that wind speeds increase with height, with a consequent increase in the wind loads on the faces of the building. The second is that all buildings act as cantilevers from the ground to carry the wind loads (**Fig. 10.89**) and, as the structure becomes more slender, this cantilevering behaviour under wind load tends to dominate the choice of structural system.

Fig. 10.109 Bank of China

Four structural systems are shown in **Fig. 10.90** for resisting lateral loading from wind, and two of these systems are shown in **Fig. 10.91** for the slender direction of a rectangular building. For a square building, like the Bank of China, there is no slender direction.

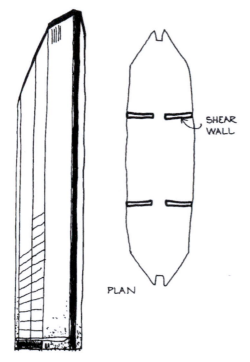

PLAN

SHEAR WALL

Early, very tall buildings, like the Chrysler and Empire State buildings in New York were designed as framed structures (**Fig. 10.90**). The lateral flexibility of these buildings was reduced by non-loadbearing external and internal wall elements. The idea of using a vertical, beam-like structure — a **shear wall** — to carry the wind loads was first used by Pier Luigi Nervi (1891-1979) in the structural design of the Pirelli tower in Turin in Italy.

Fig. 10.110 Pirelli Tower

As the external cladding became lighter and commercial pressures demanded column-free internal spaces, the wind-resisting structure was sometimes moved to the façade of the building. The pioneer of this structural system was Fazlur Khan (1929-1982), who first used it for the De Witt Chestnut building in 1965. He also used this concept for the better-known John Hancock Center built in Chicago in 1970.

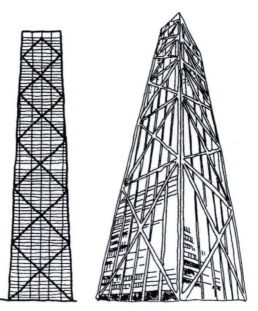

Fig. 10.111 John Hancock Center

Moving the wind-resisting structure to the external facade meant that the floors could be structure-free apart from the necessary stair/lift cores. The perimeter columns take the vertical loads directly to the ground.

Fig. 10.113 John Hancock Center

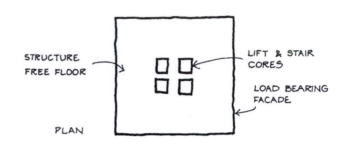

STRUCTURE
FREE FLOOR

LIFT & STAIR
CORES

LOAD BEARING
FACADE

PLAN

Fig. 10.112 Plan of John Hancock Center

The Bank of China building uses the concept of the braced façade, but with several important innovations. Before explaining the structural action, it is helpful if the external shape of the building is understood. Essentially it is a cubical building with a pyramid roof, but with each quadrant **slid down** by different amounts.

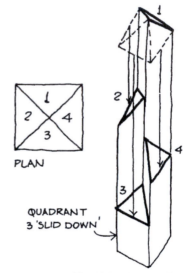

PLAN

QUADRANT
3 'SLID DOWN'

Fig. 10.114 Bank of China

This sliding means that the floor plan varies with the height.

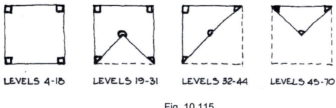

LEVELS 4-18   LEVELS 19-31   LEVELS 32-44   LEVELS 45-70

Fig. 10.115

The John Hancock Center uses the whole façade for the windbracing structure, but the Bank of China building uses a **megastructure** as the primary load path for both the wind loads **and** the vertical loads.

This is really the same idea as the use of purlins and portal frames for the **basic structure** described in **Chapter 9**. The purlins are part of the secondary structure with the portals acting as a megastructure by carrying both the wind loads **and** the vertical loads.

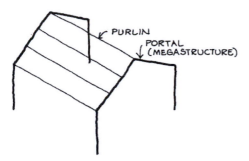

Fig. 10.116 Basic structure

The Bank of China is a **stack of five twelve-storey buildings**, each of which is supported by the megastructure.

There are four megacolumns, one at each corner, but due to the changing floor shape, a fifth central megacolumn is required above **level 25**.

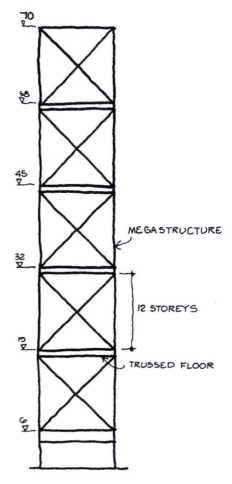

Fig. 10.117 Bank of China - megastructure

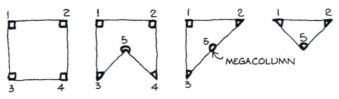

Fig. 10.118 Bank of China – floor plans

Amazingly, the central megacolumn does not continue below **level 25**, its load being transferred to the corner megacolumns by a pyramid structure.

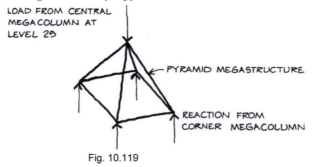

Fig. 10.119

At the bottom of each twelve-storey building is a storey-height trussed floor. This acts as the 'foundation' for the twelve-storey building, transferring the load to the megacolumns.

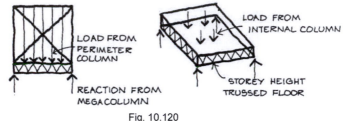

Fig. 10.120

The vertical loads in the perimeter columns are transferred directly into the facade megastructure at the points of structural intersection.

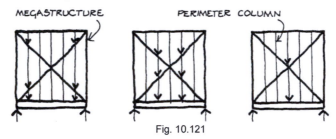

Fig. 10.121

Hong Kong is in an area of very high winds – typhoons – and these cause wind loads that are approximately twice the wind loads carried by the Chicago and New York skyscrapers. These loads are resisted by the truss action of the facade megastructures. These external facades are cross-braced trusses.

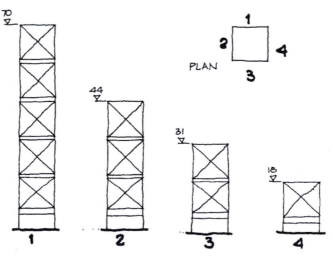

Fig. 10.122 Elevations of 'square' facades

At the higher levels there are also external facades on the plan diagonals. These facades have diagonally braced trusses.

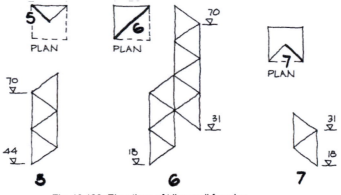

Fig. 10.123 Elevations of 'diagonal' facades

The vertical loads from the floors are transferred to the four corner megacolumns. These loads counteract the tension forces caused by the wind loads on the facade megatrusses. This maintains upward reactions at the base of the building under wind loading.

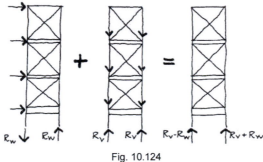

Fig. 10.124

This is another example of the role of combined stresses (section **3.8**). Although the external columns can carry tension forces it is difficult to provide substantial downward reactions at foundation level.

At the bottom of the tower, the horizontal wind load as well as the vertical load has to be transferred to the ground. In the Bank of China this is done by providing horizontal and vertical structures to transfer these forces to concrete walls that are below ground. These are the perimeter walls of the basement. There are five elements in the load path for the horizontal wind forces. These are:

1   The façade megatrusses
2   A horizontal steel diaphragm structure at level 4
3   A vertical steel/concrete core between level 4 and the foundation
4   A horizontal concrete diaphragm structure at level 0
5   Vertical concrete perimeter basement walls

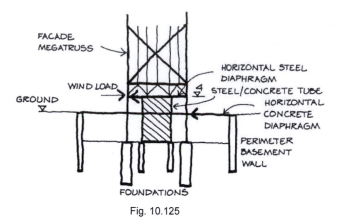

FACADE
MEGATRUSS

WIND LOAD

GROUND

HORIZONTAL STEEL
DIAPHRAGM

STEEL/CONCRETE TUBE

HORIZONTAL
CONCRETE
DIAPHRAGM

PERIMETER
BASEMENT
WALL

FOUNDATIONS

Fig. 10.125

At **level 4** the horizontal wind loads from the facade megatrusses are transferred to the vertical steel/concrete core by forces in the plane of the steel diaphragm structure.

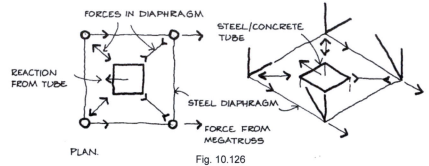

FORCES IN DIAPHRAGM

REACTION
FROM TUBE

PLAN.

STEEL/CONCRETE
TUBE

STEEL DIAPHRAGM

FORCE FROM
MEGATRUSS

Fig. 10.126

The core transfers these horizontal loads by shear forces in the core walls to the concrete diaphragm at **level 0**.

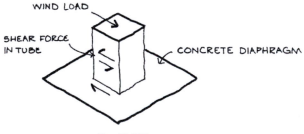

WIND LOAD

SHEAR FORCE
IN TUBE

CONCRETE DIAPHRAGM

Fig. 10.127

There are also vertical forces in the core caused by the push-pull forces from the bending moment. These are carried down to separate core foundations.

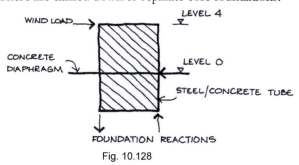

WIND LOAD

LEVEL 4

CONCRETE
DIAPHRAGM

LEVEL 0

STEEL/CONCRETE TUBE

FOUNDATION REACTIONS

Fig. 10.128

The horizontal forces in the **level 0** concrete diaphragm are transferred to the top of the vertical basement by forces in the plane of the diaphragm structure. The forces in the walls are transferred to the ground by friction forces on the faces and the base of the walls.

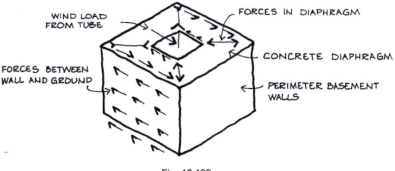

Fig. 10.129

The weight of the structural steel required for the structure of the Bank of China building was far lower than that used for other tall buildings built in the Far East. This was partly achieved by the efficiency of the overall structural form, but a significant contribution was made by the way the megastructure joints were constructed. At any joint in a structure, the forces in the elements have to be transferred through the joint, and the cost of these joints is often a substantial proportion of the total structural cost. This is particularly true for three-dimensional structures due to the geometrical and structural complexities at the joints. This was overcome in the Bank of China building by using composite steel and concrete construction for the joints and members of the megastructure.

The façade megatrusses shown in **Figs. 10.122** and **10.123** were built as individual **plane** trusses with simple joints. Where they met at the corners to form the three-dimensional megastructure, they were connected by casting concrete around them to form the megacolumns, and the joints of the megastructure.

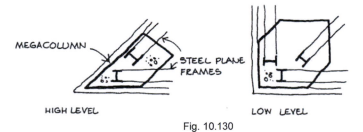

Fig. 10.130

Both the structural concepts and the finished appearance of the Bank of China are clear and simple. However, it should be appreciated that this was achieved by bold design decisions, and a vast amount of complex detailed structural design.

References – Chapter 10

1   G Cook – **Portrait of Durham cathedral** – Phoenix House 1948 (out of print)
2   J Fitchen – **The construction of Gothic cathedrals** – University of Chicago Press 1961 – ISBN 0 226 252203 06102-3
3   S Minter – **The greatest glass house** – HMSO 1990 – ISBN 0 11 250035 8
4   JL Guthrie et al – **Restoration of the Palm House** – Proceedings of ICE December 1988 – p1145 -1191
5   E Diestelkamp – **Richard Turner and the Palm House at Kew Gardens** – Transactions of the Newcomen Society 54, 1982 – p 1-26
6   E Torroja – **The structures of Eduardo Torroja** – Dodge Corp 1958 (out of print)
7   N Esquillan – **Shell vault of the exposition palace Paris** – Journal of Structural Division of ASCE January 1960
8   **Structure of the Federal Reserve Bank** – Architectural Record October 1971 – p106- 109
9   LE Robertson et al – **Structural Systems for the Bank of China** – Proceedings of the Fourth Conference on Tall Buildings – Vol 1 – 1988

CHAPTER 11 *Structural conception*

Having an understanding of how structural systems work, what structural materials are available and what loads structures must carry does not lead to an automatic method of how to design, or more accurately how to **conceive** a structure. But as the structure is an essential part of any building, and its **conceptual choice** may be part of the architectural design, the conception of the structure or the structural system is often not only made on the basis of structural economics. The interplay between structures and architecture is often complex and indeed the relationship between the engineer and the architect can lead to misunderstandings. How and why this is so, is discussed in **Chapters 12** and **19**. The present chapter shows how a **conceptual understanding** of structures can inform the process of **conception of structures** in buildings.

The term **structural designer** is used to describe the person who is responsible for the **structural concept**. This person may or may not be responsible for all the detail design and calculations for the final structure.

11.1   Structures in buildings

The only role of the structures of a crane or bridge is to carry the load, whereas the structure of a building fulfils other roles. Under the current method of building design, the designer is usually more than one person, so the structural designer is part of a team. Often each member of the design team is primarily concerned with a different aspect of the overall design. A building is essentially a space that is protected from the natural environment and is constructed for a specific use. The structure of the building is part of the building construction, and plays the role of giving the construction sufficient strength to withstand the loads to which the whole building is subjected. These loads are caused by natural phenomena such as wind and gravity, and by the use of the building.

The structure is part of a building and should not be conceived in isolation, but as part of the whole design. However, it plays a specific role, that of providing strength. Whilst the structure of a building is part of the construction, the **concept** of the structure is not. Frequently design decisions are made before the structural concept is clear, often the physical size of structural members is considered without reference to an overall structure. Often the role of structural design is seen as arriving at the physical size of structural elements rather than considering an overall design strategy.

So the structural designer of building structures is frequently faced with a difficult task. Not only is the structural design part of a whole, over which he or she may have no direct control, but the actual size and appearance of individual parts is often proscribed by others, who have no concern for their structural action.

The structural designer must keep two principles firmly in mind, and these are:

- **There is no correct structure**
- **All loads must have a load path**

The first principle is often the cause of much difficulty to inexperienced designers because everyone likes to get the right answer, choose the correct structure, and it is conceptually important to realise that this is not possible. The obverse is that the chosen structure, provided that it satisfies all the requirements of the building design, is the **correct structure**. Before the structure is chosen, alternatives may be considered, but these rarely eliminate themselves so the designer must choose the correct structure.

The second principle is obvious as a principle, but frequently non-structural requirements alter the chosen structural concept. This means that load paths may need to be altered locally or globally. It is essential that the consequences of any alterations are accepted. A simple example illustrates this point. Suppose part of a building has floors that span on to edge beams, and these beams span between columns that are spaced at regular centres.

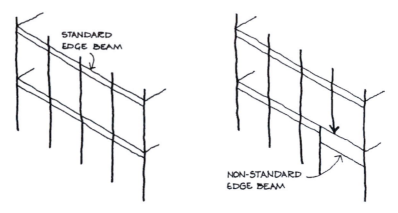

Fig. 11.1

If for some non-structural reason a column at ground level has to be moved then the upper columns will have to be carried by a beam at first floor. The beam at first floor carrying the load from the columns above will have to be far stronger and therefore bigger than the other edge beams.

The two basic principles do not give any guidance on how to conceive a structure for a building, however, the building design does. The use of a building may determine the span of the floors or roof, as the internal space requirements often determine the positions of vertical supports. An office space can have internal vertical supports but planning flexibility suggests these should be columns rather than walls. An auditorium, however large, can have no internal supports but does require, for sound isolation, heavy perimeter walls. A tall building needs vertical access, these can be grouped into stair and lift towers that can be used by the structural designer to resist horizontal wind loads. These are simple examples that show how non-structural requirements for a building can guide a structural designer towards decisions about possible structural concepts.

11.2   Conceptual load paths

Before decisions are made about a particular structure, the load paths for the different load cases must be identified. Because the load path for any loading **is the structure** it must be clear how each load path structure acts. Building structures provide the strength and stiffness for the building enclosure and this means that there must be load paths to transfer **vertical** and **horizontal loads** (see section **1.6**). The structure transfers the loads by parts of the load path spanning to support points. As buildings are three-dimensional objects the structure also has to be three dimensional, even though parts of the structure may be considered as two-dimensional.

For gravity loads the load paths are conceived **top down**. This is because each part of the building has to be supported by the structure below and also support the building above – just like a stack of bricks. To act as a load path the structure must be **complete** – that is, no structural gaps.

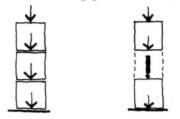

Fig. 11.2 Complete (left) and incomplete (right) load paths

A solid brick column could support a statue but is not much use as a building structure; however, the idea of a complete load path can be applied to a stack of tables.

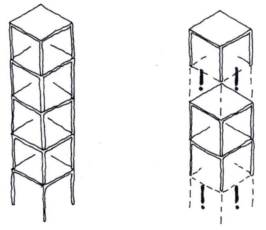

Fig. 11.3 Complete (left) and incomplete (right) load paths

The idea of a complete gravity load path may seem obvious for stacks of bricks or tables, but for complex buildings it may be far from clear. For example, a hotel requires different types of space at different levels.

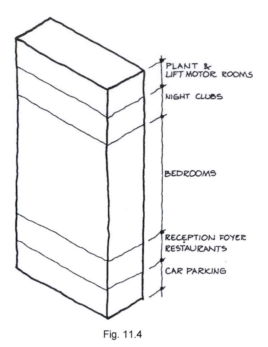

Fig. 11.4

Each part has to support all the loads from above, but each type of space suggests different types and spacing of vertical structure. Bedrooms have walls at close spacings whereas a car park needs widely spaced columns that allow an efficient car parking layout. It is rare that the position of vertical structure for differing uses coincides, this means that vertical loads will have to be diverted laterally by transfer structures, or the position of the vertical structure will have to be a compromise.

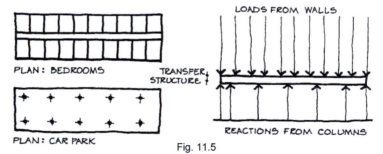

Fig. 11.5

A similar principle applies for horizontal loads, usually caused by wind loading. For horizontal loading, the building cantilevers from the ground and the cantilever structure must be complete from roof to foundation.

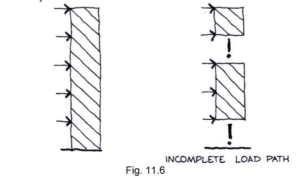

Fig. 11.6

As the wind can blow from any direction, the wind load paths must be complete in three dimensions.

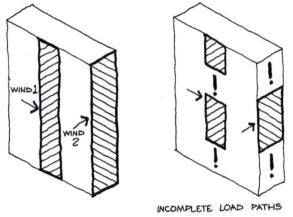

INCOMPLETE LOAD PATHS

Fig. 11.7

For wind loads there are also horizontal structural elements which transfer wind loads to the vertical cantilever structure. These may be glazing, walls, floors or roofs acting as structural elements, and again these must act as complete load paths.

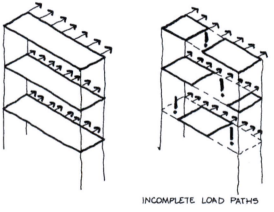

INCOMPLETE LOAD PATHS

Fig. 11.8

During the design development of a building, or as part of alterations to an existing building, part of a load path may need to be removed.

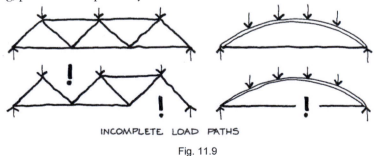

INCOMPLETE LOAD PATHS

Fig. 11.9

It is clear for the structures shown in **Fig. 11.9** which part has been removed, but when a structure is part of a building it may be far from clear. For example the St.

Pancras station in London has a large curved roof. The structure of this roof is an arch and the horizontal thrust at the spring points is provided by a tie across the building at the level of the platforms. Access may be required through the platforms to the lower level by stairs or ramps and these will cut the tie. It is not obvious, without investigation, that the platform structure acts as a tie, or whether the roof is an arch or a curved beam (**Fig. 7.73**). If access is required, then the tie forces must be provided with a new load path in the region of the opening.

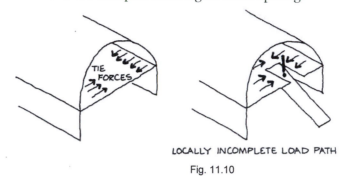

LOCALLY INCOMPLETE LOAD PATH

Fig. 11.10

It must be clear to the structural designer that the completeness of **all** load paths is achieved, and that non-structural requirements do not interrupt them.

11.3 Load path geometry

The idea of conceptual load paths is to establish a path of structure through a building for every load case, but conceptual load paths give no information about the actual geometry of the load paths. The geometry of the load path will determine the type of structural behaviour of the load path, which is beam, frame, truss or funicular behaviour. The conceptual load path has to act structurally, and its geometry gives guidance to its behaviour.

The choice of load path geometry is dependent on many aspects of building design – use, economics, aesthetics, local skills or planning laws are examples. The structural designer must be aware of what type of structural behaviour will result from a choice of load path geometry and what effect this will have on the structural details. As there is no correct load path, there is no correct load path geometry, just the chosen one. However if the load path geometry is chosen on the basis of a particular type of structural action then alteration to the load path geometry, either locally or globally, will have structural consequences. Problems on particular projects can often be traced to misconceptions of the structural action of a chosen geometry. This can be illustrated by a simple example. Suppose a building is to have, for non-structural reasons, a pitched roof with overhanging eaves.

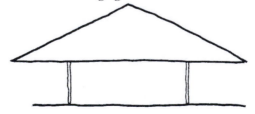

Fig. 11.11

For vertical loads, the conceptual load path for the roof is a central span with two side cantilevers. The conceptual structural behaviour is characterised by the bending moment diagram.

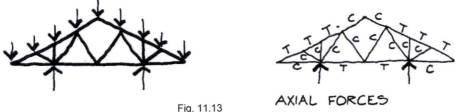

LOADING   BENDING MOMENT DIAGRAM

Fig. 11.12

Because of the overall form it would seem sensible to choose a load path geometry that gave truss-like structural behaviour – that is, to use a roof truss.

Fig. 11.13   AXIAL FORCES

A truss-like structure carries the bending moments and shear forces from the conceptual load path by axial forces, tensile and compressive, in the members of the truss. This leads to choices of structural elements that are suitable for axial forces. If during the design process it is decided, for non-structural reasons, to have a sloping rather than horizontal ceiling line, then this will affect the structural geometry.

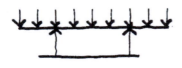

Fig. 11.14

The conceptual load path (**Fig. 11.12**) is unaltered, but the chosen load path geometry is no longer suitable. A new load path geometry has to be chosen which can act as a beam-like structure.

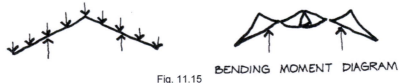

BENDING MOMENT DIAGRAM

Fig. 11.15

Beam-like behaviour needs elements that can resist internal forces that are bending moments and shear forces rather than axial forces. These beam-like elements will have a different geometrical shape to those chosen for the truss. Provided it is realised that this is a change in load path geometry as well as a change in building geometry then, it is just part of the design process.

This simple example illustrates how important it is to understand that an alteration in load path geometry, whilst not affecting the efficacy of the conceptual load path, may have a profound effect on the type of structural behaviour.

11.4 Overall structural behaviour

Building structures are always subjected to a number of different loads and these can act in different combinations and in different directions. These loads act vertically and horizontally. The structure must provide load paths for all these loads from the point of application to the reaction from the ground. How these loads are 'chased' has been a recurrent theme of this book, first introduced in section **1.6**. For a simple building the various load paths are examined in detail in **Chapter 9**. The load paths for a number of real structures are given in **Chapter 10**. The load path for each load case **is** the structure and, depending on the load path geometry, it will have a particular type of structural action.

Essentially there are four types of structural action for spanning members. These are **beam-like**, **truss-like**, **frame-like** and **funicular**; **Chapter 7** explains how these different types act.

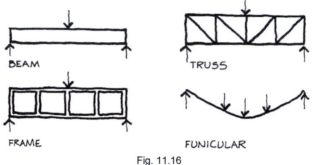

Fig. 11.16

The structures shown in **Fig. 11.16** can only be a part of an overall structure as this has to enclose space. To do this a vertical element, a column, must be added.

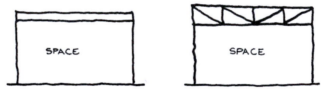

Fig. 11.17

The columns carry the vertical loads for the gravity load case, but they must also provide the overall lateral stability and in doing so act as spanning structures themselves. This can be done by making the structure a portal frame, or by cantilevering the columns from the ground, or both.

Fig. 11.18 Pinned portal (left) cantilever columns (centre) fixed portal (right)

These structures enclose space, are stable and can carry vertical and horizontal loads.

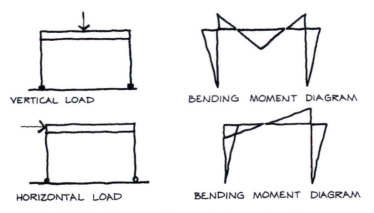

VERTICAL LOAD   BENDING MOMENT DIAGRAM

HORIZONTAL LOAD   BENDING MOMENT DIAGRAM

Fig. 11.19 Bending moment diagrams for the pinned portal

The beam-like spanning structure has become a portal frame. For both vertical and horizontal loads there is a bending moment in the **column** which means it acts as a spanning structure.

The structural designer, when conceiving a structure has to be aware how the whole structure acts under each load case, and how the choice of structural geometry causes the structure to act in different ways. This can be illustrated by examining the structure for a single-storey space.

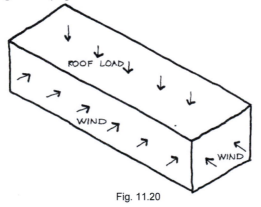

Fig. 11.20

The structure will have to carry vertical loads applied to the roof and wind loads which can act in any horizontal direction. As this building is just a flat-roofed version of the building considered in detail in **Chapter 9**, the structure already chosen (**Fig. 9.7**), would be one choice.

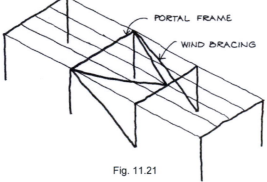

Fig. 11.21

But other choices can be made. The roof structure could be a three-dimensional space frame (**Fig. 7.75B**), supported on perimeter columns.

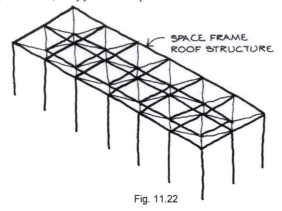

Fig. 11.22

The columns, as with the portal frame, have to provide stability against overall collapse, and also be part of the load path for horizontal loads.

Fig. 11.23

Because the space frame is triangulated in the horizontal plane, it can act as a **wind girder** in any direction.

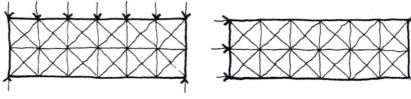

Fig. 11.24 Plans

Some columns could be chosen just to carry vertical loads whilst others, say the corner columns, could also provide stability and carry the horizontal loads.

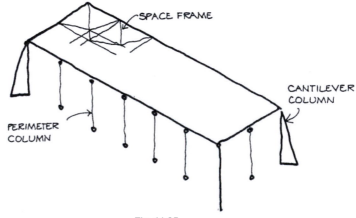

Fig. 11.25

The corner columns act as cantilevers from the ground so they are spanning structures.

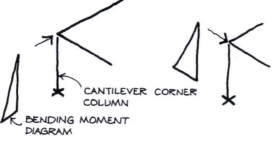

CANTILEVER CORNER COLUMN

BENDING MOMENT DIAGRAM

Fig. 11.26

To carry the bending moments in these corner columns, which act in more than one direction, a three-dimensional, truss-like structure could be chosen. The columns that only carry vertical loads could be simple tubular struts.

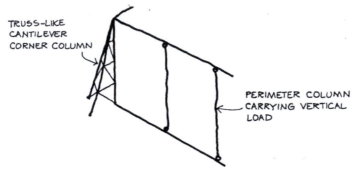

TRUSS-LIKE CANTILEVER CORNER COLUMN

PERIMETER COLUMN CARRYING VERTICAL LOAD

Fig. 11.27

Two quite different structures have been chosen for this simple building, and **both are correct** as they have been conceived by using an understanding of the overall structural behaviour. Many other structures could be chosen to support the enclosure of this simple space. All these structures would be correct provided the choice of geometry was based on an understanding of the overall structural behaviour.

11.5   Choice of materials and elements

In **Chapter 5** four basic materials were identified as being suitable for building structures, these were steel, timber, concrete and masonry. The reason that the choice is limited is that the materials have to be cheap. They also have to be durable, easily altered or repaired, and to be constantly available. This is because buildings are expected to last a long time, be relatively maintenance free, and to be altered without recourse to specialist suppliers or technology. The situation is quite different for non-building structures. For instance, aircraft structures are very expensive, have a specific life and are regularly maintained by specialists who have ready access to the latest technology.

Fortunately this lack of choice of suitable materials has not resulted in a lack of variety either in building structures, or in the buildings they hold up; after all building structures have rarely been built of anything else. The structural designer has to be aware which material is suitable for any chosen structure. Ideally the structural form and the structural material are conceived simultaneously. As each of the four materials are more suitable for different structural types, the material choice is often implicit. Timber and steel are strong compared with their weight, so are suitable where tensile forces are large. Where loads are compressive, masonry or mass concrete are suitable. These materials can be used for spanning structures if they are used compositely with tensile material, steel, or are pre-stressed (see section **4.7**). Non-structural characteristics such as combustibility, or susceptibility to chemical attack may influence choice (see section **5.3**). It is also necessary to know how the material can be joined (see section **11.6**).

With so many caveats, the inexperienced designer can feel there are more problems than solutions, so some broad guidance is needed. The main guidance is from structures that exist, but each time and place favours different solutions. These will depend on material availability and the presence of suitable expertise in the chosen material. Concrete is made by mixing cement, aggregate and clean water, so difficulty in obtaining any of these at an affordable price will preclude the use of concrete. The use of reinforced concrete also needs suitable steel reinforcement, expertise and technology to cut and bend the bars, and material to make the formwork. These are usually readily available in industrialised areas, but may not be available in remote rural areas. The choice will then be between local materials or the cost of transporting non-local materials, technology and expertise.

In the description of the action of structural systems (see sections **7.2** to **7.5**) no mention was made of materials. The chapter on real structures (**Chapter 10**) describes both structural systems, and the use of various structural materials such as stone, wrought iron, reinforced concrete and steel.

As most parts of a structural system are required to span under some load case (see section **11.4**), the structural designer must be aware of how the chosen structural material caters for the resulting internal forces. The beam-like, truss-like and frame-like spanning structures all require tensile strength in some part of the structure so for example, masonry or mass concrete cannot be used. Beams and trusses of steel or timber are commonplace.

Fig. 11.28

Frames also require tensile strength, and simple frames such as portal frames (see section **2.5**) are made from both steel and timber. Multi-storey frames (see **Fig. 10.90**) and spanning frames (see **Fig. 7.50**) are often made of steel or reinforced concrete.

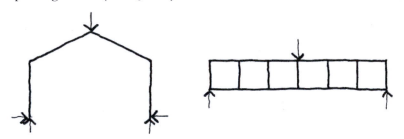

Fig. 11.29

There are two types of funicular structures (see section **7.4**), hanging and arching. The hanging funicular structures are in tension so timber or steel are suitable, but due to jointing problems timber is rarely used. For arches, mass concrete or masonry is very suitable, and this form of tension-free spanning structure was the major form until the end of the 18th century.

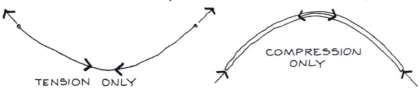

Fig. 11.30

Although structural materials are commonly used on their own, they are also frequently combined to form composite materials or structures (see section **4.7**). Since the 1920s, concrete reinforced with steel rods, usually called **rebar**, has become, together with steel, a widely used structural **material** for building structures. Although heavy compared with its strength, reinforced concrete is used for beams, slabs, frames, shells and even trusses. Great care has to be taken to ensure there is rebar in all areas of tension. This means that the structural designer has to decide the size and position of every bar.

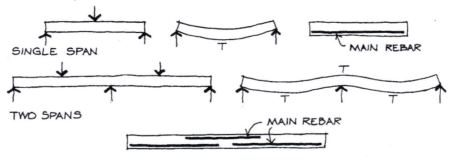

Fig. 11.31

An alternative to rebar is **pre-stress** (see pages **111-112**). Here the tensile stress caused by the structural actions is reduced to zero by using internal steel tendons to apply compressive stresses.

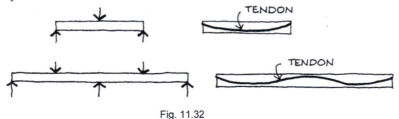

Fig. 11.32

Reinforced and pre-stressed concrete are often regarded as composite structures, but there are other ways of making composite structures. Two examples have already been given, that of steel beams with concrete slabs (see pages **109-110**) and the use of reinforced concrete with masonry (see page **113**). A further example is the composite behaviour of structural steelwork and concrete used in the Bank of China (see section **10.6**) to form mega reinforced concrete.

Two different materials, or two forms of the same material, can be combined to make composite elements. A steel plate can be used with timber to form a flitch beam. Timber **I** or box beams can be made using ordinary timber sections with plywood sheeting.

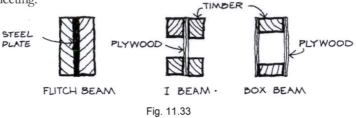

Fig. 11.33

There is also a choice for the shape of the structural element. An element's section shape should be stress effective (see page **72**), the effect of cross-section shape is explained in section **4.4**. Section shape also has an effect on axial stability (see section **6.4**). Elements can also be shaped over their length (see **Fig. 3.57**).

Each of the four, or five if reinforced concrete is classed as a structural material, can be shaped in different ways. Mass and reinforced concrete can be made into almost any shape, limited by the skill of the makers of the formwork and the patience of the designers and the fixers of the rebar.

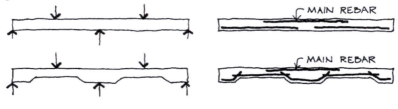

Fig. 11.34

In shaping reinforced concrete for structural efficiency, the benefit must be available to the client in the form of lower cost – this is often difficult to judge as building costs vary continuously.

Structural steelwork is available in simple bars, rods and plates of different sizes. In industrial areas **standard sections** are available. They are made by rolling hot steel into a variety of cross-sectional shapes – hence **hot rolled sections**. The size and shape may vary by producer, or may comply with a national standard. In areas where a national standard applies the choice is easy for the structural designer, but where the sections are obtained from various sources, the exact size and shape may only be known as construction begins. The usual range of hot rolled sections are angles, channels, I sections, tees, round and square tubes. Sizes vary from 50 to 1000mm.

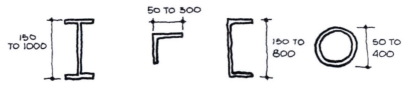

Fig. 11.35

With the use of cutting and welding equipment, these sections can be altered to form structurally efficient structures. This is commonly done at the knee joint of portal frames.

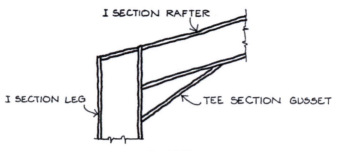

Fig. 11.36

Steelwork fabricators cut and weld steel as part of normal operations but, as with complex reinforced concrete structures, the cost of complexity must be outweighed by an overall saving.

Timber is normally cut, or converted to use the correct term, into lengths with a rectangular cross section. In some areas the sizes are standard, which is an advantage to the structural designer. The structural performance of timber varies greatly between different species. There are two basic types – hardwood and softwood. In the Northern hemisphere, structural timber is predominately softwood, but in the tropics and the Southern hemisphere structural timber is usually hardwood. Timber sheet materials are also available in many parts of the world as plywood, chipboard and hardboard, and these can be used structurally. Structural timber is most often used as simple beams with a rectangular cross-section or made into simple trusses. These can be on a large scale, for instance timber structures have been used for the construction of airship hangars.

Masonry, in the form of mud dried bricks, is one of the oldest building materials. The strength and size of blocks and bricks varies widely. The strength of masonry, rather than the units themselves, is usually limited by the strength of the mortar in which the bricks or blocks are laid. Sizes of the basic units vary but tend to be standard in an area, and this will determine the overall sizes of masonry structures, as it is far better to use whole units rather than cut them.

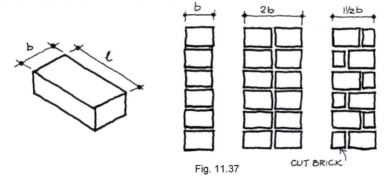

Fig. 11.37   CUT BRICK

The key to a sensible choice for a structural material is local availability and expertise. This often dictates the range of structural forms which can be used economically in any area at a particular time, requiring the structural designer to be aware of the cost and availability of materials before structural decisions are made.

Structural designers sometimes tire of the usual materials and yearn for 'new materials'. The new materials are usually sought from more high-tech industries such as aerospace. Although this pursuit of new materials is clothed in acceptable notions such as progress or innovation, often the purpose is to gain attention for the user of the 'new' material. Sometimes these new materials make their appearance in new forms of construction such as tent structures or structural glass facades.

Tent buildings date from pre-history, see **Fig. 0.2**, but from the 1970s stressed tents have been promoted by a number of designers. These require durable, strong fabrics which are now available as Teflon coated glass fibre. This material is not cheap, and has no application in ordinary buildings.

Another new material is toughened laminated glass which can be used as a structural element in a glass facade. This type of glass, originally developed for the windows of cars and aeroplanes, is now used as **fins** for strengthening glass-only facades.

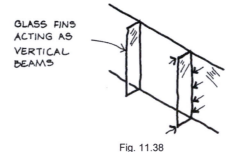

GLASS FINS
ACTING AS
VERTICAL
BEAMS

Fig. 11.38

The use of new materials produces expensive structures for clients who want attention-seeking designs. Of course there are proper innovations, new materials and processes. In the past, the introduction of iron, steel, welding and pre-stressing were all innovations that made significant differences to the way building structures were conceived and constructed. At present, the choice of structural material for most building structures is still between steel, timber, masonry or concrete, mass, reinforced or pre-stressed.

11.6 Element connection

The load path for each load case has to be complete – there can be no gaps (see section **11.2**). It is rare that this can be achieved without having to join parts of the structure together. They may be joints between similar or different structural materials, or they may be joints between major structural elements.

A structure transfers load by internal forces and at points of support the internal forces are balanced by reaction forces.

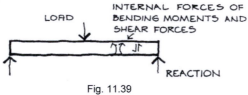

LOAD

INTERNAL FORCES OF
BENDING MOMENTS AND
SHEAR FORCES

REACTION

Fig. 11.39

The reactions may balance axial or shear forces or bending moments. For a cantilever beam with vertical and horizontal loads, the reactions provide vertical and horizontal forces and a moment reaction.

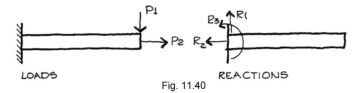

LOADS   REACTIONS

Fig. 11.40

Like points of support, joints have to transfer the internal forces to the adjacent part of the structure. Suppose, for the cantilever shown in **Fig. 11.40**, there is a joint in the beam.

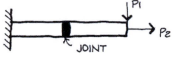

Fig. 11.41

At the joint, the forces are the same as the forces at the **cuts** in a beam (see **Figs. 2.9** and **2.18**), except now the joint is a cut.

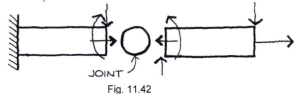

Fig. 11.42

The joint in the cantilever beam has to transfer axial and shear forces and a bending moment. For a simple spanning beam, a joint at the end only has to transfer shear forces.

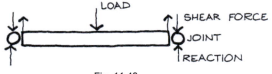

Fig. 11.43

Whilst a joint is the connection between two, or more, parts of a structure it is still part of the load path, so calling it a joint is arbitrary from the conceptual point of view. But how the elements are joined together may affect the structural behaviour. For example, a two-span beam may be continuous over the central support. At this support there is a bending moment as well as shear forces.

LOAD   BENDING MOMENT DIAGRAM   SHEAR FORCE DIAGRAM

Fig. 11.44

If a joint is made between the two spans that can only carry shear forces then the structural behaviour will be altered. The structure now acts as two, adjacent, simply supported beams.

LOAD   BENDING MOMENT DIAGRAM   SHEAR FORCE DIAGRAM

Fig. 11.45

The difference between an arch and a curved beam (**Fig. 7.73**) is dependent on the structural designer's choice of joint at the support points. If the designer chooses joints that can transfer vertical and horizontal forces then the curved structure will act as an arch. If the joints can only transfer vertical forces then it will act as a curved beam.

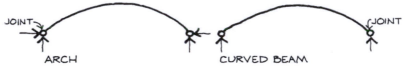

Fig. 11.46

Choosing the position and types of joints is part of the process of conceiving structures. The structural designer has to introduce joints to allow the transport and erection of the different structural elements. What structural behaviour these joints need is determined by how the structure is expected to behave at the joint positions and the practical considerations of the joint details.

How are the symbolic joints in the structural diagrams – see section **2.3** – to become real joints in real structures? This largely depends on the structural material being used at the joint. Structural masonry is constructed by jointing the individual bricks or blocks to each other by introducing a bed of mortar between them.

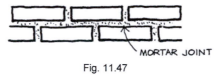

Fig. 11.47

Steel can be joined by welding, by heating the metal at the joint and introducing molten steel. It is joined so that the material becomes continuous at the joint.

Fig. 11.48

Welding is best carried out under workshop conditions, so welded joints in steel structures are used to make steelwork elements that are transported to the site.

When reinforced concrete is constructed in its final position, that is, built in situ, joints are made simply by casting new concrete around reinforcing bars that have been left projecting from the part to be joined.

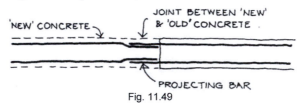

Fig. 11.49

The ease with which joints can be made in this way is one of the main reasons for the widespread use of reinforced concrete.

As trees grow they form joints, branch to trunk, as part of the growing process. There is currently no way of growing cut pieces of timber into timber structures so it has to be joined by other means.

When different materials are to be joined, mechanical fixings have to be used. These are of two basic types – **specific strong object** or **glue**. Examples of specific strong objects are bolts, screws and nails, whilst the range of glue types is enormous. Nowadays there is strong glue that will bond together almost any combination of materials.

To be able to design joints, the structural action must be clear to the designer. Like structures in general, **there is no correct joint**, but a number of choices. There is a load path through a joint and these can often be complex. The choices and load paths are illustrated by considering a joint between two steel I sections that are part of a beam.

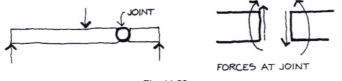

Fig. 11.50

The forces that are to be transferred through the joint are a shear force and a bending moment. The bending moment, push-pull forces, is mainly transferred by horizontal tensile and compressive stresses in the flanges (see **Fig. 3.55**) and the shear forces by vertical shear stresses in the web (see **Fig. 4.37**).

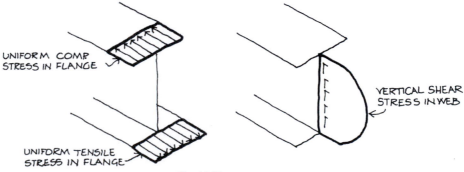

Fig. 11.51

Conceptually the joint is made by joining the flanges to take the tension and compression and the webs to take the vertical shear.

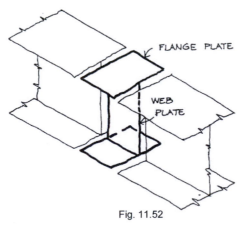

Fig. 11.52

One choice would be to weld the whole section together.

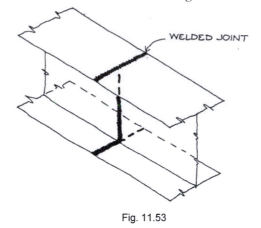

Fig. 11.53

For making joints on site, bolted connections are usually preferred. For this a number of options are available. Loose flange and web plates can be used to **splice** the beams together.

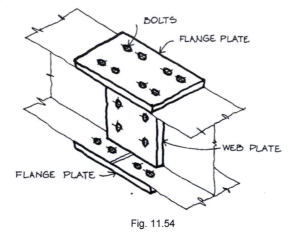

Fig. 11.54

As an example of a joint load path consider the bottom flange plate. The tensile loads in the flanges are transferred to the flange plates by shear forces in the shafts of the bolts.

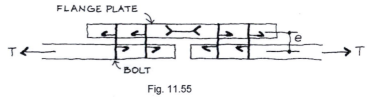

Fig. 11.55

There is an eccentricity in the load path that may cause some local bending in the plate.

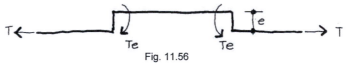

Fig. 11.56

The uniform tensile stress in the flange is transferred into the flange plate at the specific positions of the bolts.

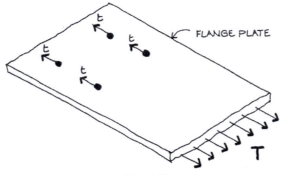

Fig. 11.57

For horizontal equilibrium **4** × **t** = **T**, but at the bolt positions, the tensile stress is altered from a uniform distribution to a non-uniform stress distribution.

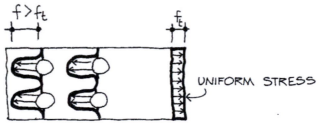

Fig. 11.58

As the area near the bolts is smaller than the whole flange, the stresses are higher than the uniform stress. There is a maximum allowable (or usable) stress for the steel (see **Fig. 3.54**) and the high stresses concentrated at the bolts must not exceed this. This indicates that it is better to make the joint in a part of the beam where the stresses are less than the maximum.

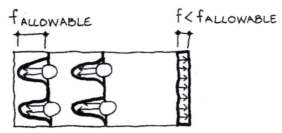

Fig. 11.59

A similar joint could be made by welding the plates to one of the beams in the fabrication shop and bolting them to the other beam on site. Another type of bolted joint can be made by welding plates across the ends of both beams then bolting the plates face to face on site.

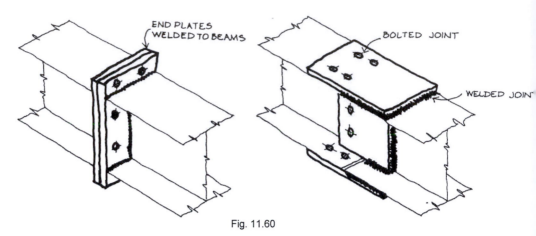

END PLATES
WELDED TO BEAMS

BOLTED JOINT

WELDED JOINT

Fig. 11.60

For this joint, the load path is quite different to the load path in the plated joint. In this joint, the load transfer causes bending moments in the end plates and the bolts carry shear and tension.

There are many **standard** ways of joining elements and these are given in technical guides. The positioning and behaviour of joints in structures can affect the overall behaviour of the structure, so the structural designer should consider them as part of the structural concept rather than an additional requirement.

11.7   Structures and building construction

The structure of a building, whilst fulfilling the specific role of giving strength and stiffness to the building enclosure, is not physically a separate part of the building construction.   The structural elements form part of building elements, and the structural designer needs to know how **the structure** will relate physically to the other elements, often designed by other members of the design team. During the design process, the structural designer often has to modify the structural design to accommodate design developments carried out by other members of the design team.

For any rigid object, gravity forces cause internal forces. In this sense all parts of the building are structures, but the structural designer is usually concerned with the **primary structure**. This is a rather nebulous concept, as all the load paths have to be complete from the point of load application. For instance, when the wind blows on a building causing wind loads, these are often applied to the window panes. Except for unusually large panes, the structural designer is not concerned with the pane as a structure. What constitutes the primary structure usually becomes clear during the design process.

Sometimes parts of the structure fulfil a dual purpose, as part of the enclosure and part of the primary structure. This is particularly true for masonry walls, which are part of the enclosure as well as acting as part of the primary vertical load path. This can cause difficulties as more than one member of the design team may be concerned with their design, and each member may not be aware of the dual role. For example, the inner leaf of a cavity wall may carry floor loads, and thus require a specific strength. Other members of the design team are concerned with the thermal insulation that the inner leaf provides. To obtain the required thermal insulation the strength may be reduced. Or in domestic buildings some internal walls may be loadbearing whilst others are only space-enclosing elements. As the construction may be similar for both walls this can lead to confusion.

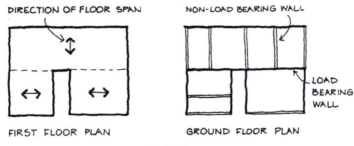

Fig. 11.61

Even with specific structural elements such as reinforced concrete columns in an office building, the building construction can influence their shape and position. This is especially true for the columns that support the floor perimeter.

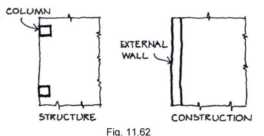

Fig. 11.62

There are various options, not always chosen by the structural designer. The columns can relate to the external enclosure in a number of ways.

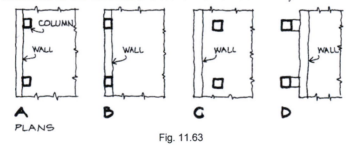

Fig. 11.63

In **A** the columns are positioned just inside the external wall which means the inner face is not flush. This will affect the layout of furniture, loose or built-in. In **B** the columns are within the wall and the wall may need extra width to accommodate the column.

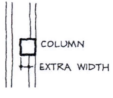

Fig. 11.64

To reduce this width, the column size needs to be the minimum possible, which may make the column slender (see page **144**).

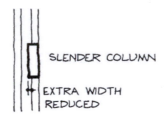

Fig. 11.65

In **C** the columns are placed within the building, which means that the floor has to cantilever past the columns thus locally altering the structural behaviour.

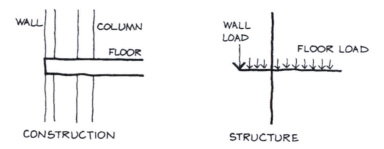

Fig. 11.66

In **D** the column is placed outside the building so it has to be connected to the floor it is supporting by a beam that penetrates the external wall.

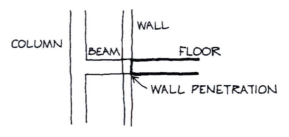

Fig. 11.67

This beam needs a hole in the wall which is a potential source of rain penetration. To combat this, complicated waterproofing details have to be devised and built correctly. The beam can also create a **cold bridge** conducting heat from the building or cold into the building. This can cause local condensation with consequent deterioration of materials. As with structural design in general ,there is no correct position for the column and many buildings have been constructed with columns in all the positions shown in **Fig. 11.63**.

Another aspect of building construction that frequently affects the structure is the installation of environmental services. These range from small wires for telecommunications, to large ducts for air handling, and all these may need openings somewhere in the primary structure. Many services are run at ceiling level.

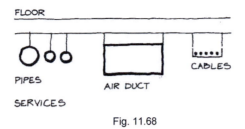

FLOOR

PIPES
AIR DUCT
CABLES

SERVICES

Fig. 11.68

These services are often concealed from the general building user by installing a suspended ceiling below the services.

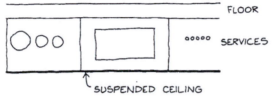

FLOOR
SERVICES
SUSPENDED CEILING

Fig. 11.69

These diagrams appear simple but services run in all directions. If there are downstand beams or trusses for large spans, the services may have to run through them to keep the construction depth to a minimum.

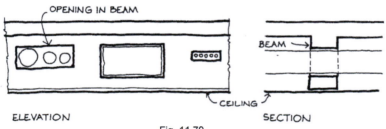

OPENING IN BEAM
BEAM
CEILING
ELEVATION
SECTION

Fig. 11.70

Depending on the size and position of these openings the beam may turn into a frame (see **Fig. 7.64**). Where trusses are used, the diagonals may need to be removed locally which affects the structural behaviour (see **Fig. 7.64** again).

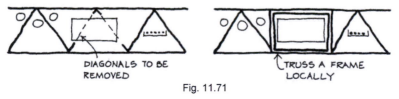

DIAGONALS TO BE REMOVED
TRUSS A FRAME LOCALLY

Fig. 11.71

Often ducts for small pipes have to run in reinforced concrete floors to supply perimeter radiators.

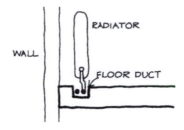

Fig. 11.72

These ducts cause considerable complexity for the reinforcement as well as weakening the structure locally.

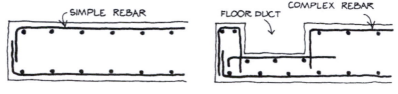

Fig. 11.73

With these local alterations to the primary structure, the structural designer must ensure that the conceptual load paths are complete, and the structure at the positions of the local alterations is still strong enough to transfer the internal forces.

These examples show how the designer of building structures needs knowledge of building construction to anticipate the relationship of the primary structure to the whole construction, and to be able to discuss this relationship with other members of the design team. This knowledge is not easy to acquire, especially as the structural designer rarely designs the building construction. The successful designer sees the primary structure as part of the whole design, and expects that the design process will require alteration to the initial structural design. These alterations will often be made by members of the design team who do not understand the structural concepts, so may be unaware of their effect. Local alterations can usually be made with some added local complexity, but if an alteration in structural concept is required then it has to be made and its consequences accepted. Because of the inevitable alterations needed during the design process, it is unwise to size the structural elements so tightly that small alterations cause major structural problems. This is not being uneconomic, just sensible.

CHAPTER 12 *Structures and built form*

In **Chapter 10** a number of well-known buildings were examined to see how their structures behaved conceptually. In **Chapter 11** some parameters that affected the conception of structures were looked at together with how **the structural concept** related to the total building construction. When indigenous, vernacular or traditional buildings were, or are built, it is likely that those involved see the project as a conceptual whole; there is no perception of a separate **structural concept**. Nowadays the structural concept is usually thought of as applying to the **primary structure**, if it can be clearly identified as a separate entity, and this primary structure is considered to be within the domain of the structural engineer. The engineer makes calculations to arrive at satisfactory sizes. Secondary structures, partition walls and window frames for example, are usually within the domain of the architect and are rarely subjected to calculation procedures.

The idea that the primary structure can be viewed conceptually as a separate entity is relatively recent, really only since sometime towards the end of the 19th century. It is the direct result of the formation, in the 19th century, of separate professions for architects and engineers, which led to an increasingly divergent conceptual view of the role of structures within the built form. These divergent views have led to some strange and often inappropriate structures, because the primary structure is often conceived from two quite different points of view; that of the architect and that of the engineer. The architectural conception is frequently based on a visual or sculptural understanding, often poorly informed by any real understanding of actual structural behaviour. On the other hand the engineering concept is aimed at providing direct load paths at the lowest cost, with little or no interest in the aesthetic aspects.

In this chapter these divergent strands are critically examined from various conceptual and non-chronologically historical perspectives. The underlying questions that always have to be asked are:

- How is the built form related to the conceptual behaviour of the structure?
- What could the designer know about the structural behaviour and how did this influence the design?

These questions are not specifically answered, but the reader, already armed with a conceptual understanding of the structural behaviour of buildings, should be constantly asking these questions about the projects and the approaches presented. Of course these questions should always be asked and answered in a mature and sensible way about any building project.

12.1 The masonry dome and Christopher Wren

Before the arrival of industrialisation, the only available structural materials were timber and various types of stone or brick. As timber is perishable and combustible, its architectural contribution was mainly in vernacular buildings. These were not built for posterity, so historical timber structures that have accidentally survived are usually for buildings such as housing, small churches and barns. Where buildings were so important that they were to last forever, stone or brick was chosen. This is not to say that structural timber was not used in some of these buildings, the roof structures of Gothic cathedrals for example – see **Fig. 10.6**, but these did not have a major effect on the built form.

The main restriction on built form imposed by the available materials before industrialisation was the dimensional limitation of spanning structures. Those of timber, in the absence of efficient jointing methods, were limited to the available lengths of natural timber. Stone spanning structures, in the form of arches or vaults, were also limited due to the requirement of resisting abutment forces. The spans of Gothic cathedrals were quite modest, 9.75m in the case of Durham Cathedral, however their heights were impressive, 48m at Beauvais – see **Fig. 10.16**. It is the soaring internal heights that are the wonder of Gothic architecture and to achieve this, complex forms of external buttressing were required, and these in turn dominate the external built form – see **Fig. 0.7**. Little is known about either the construction methods[1] used for the great Gothic buildings, or what technical knowledge was available.[2,3] This is not to say that the builders of the Gothic cathedrals were not only masters in name but masters in fact. One of the few Gothic documents to have survived is the notebook of Villard de Honnecourt (1175?-1240?). There is dispute as to whether this notebook is of a master mason, or a traveller who sketched.[4]

Fig. 12.1 Page from Villard de Honnecourt's sketchbook

Before the Gothic period, spans were similarly modest. In Greek architecture they were limited by the span of timber beams or stone lintels. The Romans, with arches and barrel vaults, achieved few large spans, an exception being the dome of the Pantheon. This dome, which still stands, was built in 120 AD and has an internal diameter of 43m, supported on a circular wall.

Domes did not become part of Gothic architecture, but were used mainly on a small scale in Byzantine architecture, and subsequently in Islamic architecture. But a large dome was used for the roof of the cathedral of St. Sophia, built in Istanbul between 532 and 537. The diameter of the dome was 31m, smaller than the

Pantheon, but it was higher. The dimension to the top of the dome was 50m, and it was supported on four piers instead of a continuous wall. Much later, in the 17th century, the amazing Gol Gumbaz,[5] with a diameter of 42m, was built in southern India.

In Western Europe, large domes first reappeared during the Renaissance. Two themes relevant to engineering and architecture emerged in the Renaissance and continued to be important up to, and to some extent, beyond the coming of industrialisation in the 18th century. Firstly, there was an interest in trying to find rational explanations for how things work – the solar system or the human body, for example. Secondly, there was a great interest in Greek and Roman civilisation and culture, which came to be known as Classical.

An important part of the quest for rational explanations and knowledge of Classical culture was to study the original texts, many of which had been suppressed or lost during the early Christian period. From the point of view of engineering and architecture, the most important find was the *"Ten Books on Architecture"* written by Vitruvius (1st century BC), discovered in the 14th century, and still in print[6] after 2000 years. But Vitruvius said nothing about domes.

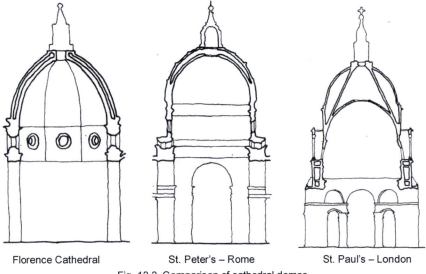

| Florence Cathedral | St. Peter's – Rome | St. Paul's – London |

Fig. 12.2 Comparison of cathedral domes

Buildings with large domed structures continued to be a rarity, the three most notable being those of Florence Cathedral, St. Peter's Basilica in Rome and St. Paul's Cathedral in London. These domes are different from one another, but each is considered to be the work of a single designer. The earliest was for Florence Cathedral, which was built between 1420 and 1436. The cathedral itself had been begun over hundred years earlier by Arnolfo di Cambio (c1240-c1310) and in 1418 a competition was held to find someone to finish it. The winner was Filippo Brunelleschi (1377-1446), who had trained as a goldsmith and sculptor. The outstanding task was the construction of the massive cupola on the eight piers that had already been built.

The construction of the new cathedral in Rome, called St. Peter's Basilica, took even longer, the foundation stone was laid in 1506, and the cathedral was only finally completed in 1667. The dome was originally designed by Donato Bramante (1444-1514), the first architect who had trained as a painter; however the dome that was built is essentially to the design of Michelangelo (1475-1564), who had also trained as a painter. His dome was far higher than the one projected by Bramante, but was only completed after Michelangelo's death. In contrast, St. Paul's Cathedral was designed by one man, Christopher Wren (1632-1723), who was originally a professor of astronomy. It was completed in 1710, although by that time the 78 year old Wren was no longer the architect.

All these major domes, from that of the Pantheon to St. Paul's stand today, but all have suffered some form of structural problem. In the case of St. Paul's, the problems have been with the supporting structure rather than with the dome. So what are the problems that confront the designer of a large stone or brick dome? There are basically two:

- **Control of tension forces in the dome or its supports**
- **Resolution of the geometry of the dome with the supporting structure**

Leonardo da Vinci (1452-1519) had already noted the tensile behaviour of a dome "*...after the manner of a pomegranate or orange which splits into many parts lengthwise...*",[7] as no doubt had many others.

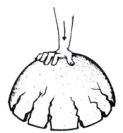

Fig. 12.3 The tensile behaviour of a dome

In a very limited sense, domes are three-dimensional arches, see section **7.4**, but not only do stresses travel down the dome – **arch-like stresses** – but also around – **hoop stresses**. These hoop stresses have a horizontal component in the radial direction and these components act as supports to arching action.

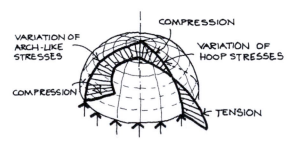

Fig. 12.4 The variation of hoop and arch-like stresses in a dome

As can be seen from the figure, under self-weight – the major load for masonry domes – tensile hoop stresses exist in the lower part of the dome. Because masonry has very limited resistance to tensile stresses, this means specific tensile resisting elements have to be introduced in the lower part if cracking is to be avoided. If a dome cracks radially at the lower level, it can still remain stable provided the supports can resist horizontal forces. The formation of the radial cracks in the lower part means that the individual pieces of structure between the cracks now act as **arching segments** supporting the uncracked cap.

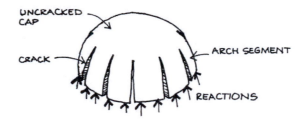

Fig. 12.5 A cracked dome with supporting **arch segments**

Nearly all early domes cracked; these include the domes of the Pantheon in Rome, the dome over Florence Cathedral and the dome over St. Peter's. It was the cracking of the dome of St. Peter's that is considered to have originated structural calculations – see section **0.5**. The domed roof of the St. Sophia partially collapsed in 558.

The second problem to be solved for domed roofs was the geometric arrangement of the vertical supports, basically three geometric solutions were used.

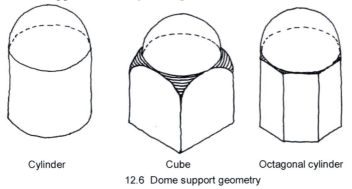

Cylinder   Cube   Octagonal cylinder

12.6 Dome support geometry

The circular wall defines the usable space and was used for the Pantheon, but for the other domes, that were part of larger spaces, the four or eight column solutions were used, based on the geometry of a cube or an octagonal cylinder. At St. Sophia and St. Peter's, four columns with pendentives were used, whereas Florence and St. Paul's used eight columns. The eight-column solution avoids the use of pendentives, but has to transfer the circular dome support geometry to the octagonal geometry of the columns; this was done by providing a sufficiently wide octagon so that the dome fitted onto it.

The great domes of the Pantheon, St. Sophia, Florence Cathedral and St. Peter's were all complete before Christopher Wren undertook the task of designing the dome of the new cathedral of St. Paul's. It is not easy to understand how Wren came to be the designer of the new cathedral. A man of formidable intellect, at 28 he was already the prestigious Savilian Professor of Astronomy at Oxford University; a brilliant career as an astronomer must have been assured. His involvement with buildings began with two strange events that occurred in 1661. He was consulted about repairs to the decrepit original St. Paul's Cathedral and, more oddly, the newly restored king, Charles II, suggested that he go to Tangier to supervise the rebuilding of the fortifications. As one of his biographers notes *"How and why should a newly appointed young professor of astronomy, with no track record as a surveyor, have been asked out of the blue to leave Oxford and work as a military engineer?... For that matter, why should his advice have been sought on the repair of St. Paul's?"*[8]

After the destruction of the original St. Paul's Cathedral in the Great Fire of London in 1666, Wren, after some political manoeuvring, was asked to design a new cathedral. He made four designs, the first, known as the Greek Cross, was approved by the king in 1672. He modified his design to produce what is known as the Great Model, and it was this that was presented to the actual client, the Commission, in 1674. The Commission rejected it and Wren cried when he received the news. The Commission, like most clients, wanted something that would suit their purpose and be in use as soon as possible, and they really didn't care what it looked like. Wren's proposed design did not suit the Anglican liturgy and that was that; however, the final design would also have a large dome.

By looking in some detail at the dome structure and its supports, which are more complex than either Florence Cathedral or St. Peter's Basilica, some assessment can be made of Wren's ability to integrate essential structural elements into his overall design. The dome and its supporting structure, whilst conceptually simple, is complex in some of its details.

The dome is shown schematically in **Fig. 12.7**. Working down from the top, the following elements can be identified:

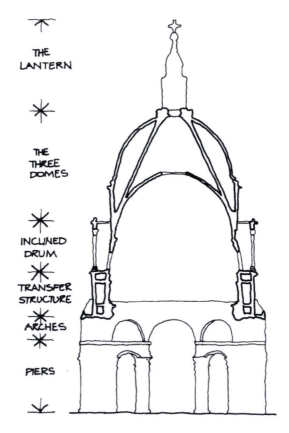

THE
LANTERN

THE
THREE
DOMES

INCLINED
DRUM

TRANSFER
STRUCTURE

ARCHES

PIERS

Fig. 12.7 The main elements of the dome structure of St. Paul's

The lantern – this weighs in the region of 850 tons (8500 kN).

The domes – there are three of these, an outer timber dome with the lower vertical part in stone, a conical brick dome and an inner nearly hemispherical brick dome.

The Wren chain(s) – where the domes meet there are iron chains around the whole structure (it is not clear whether Wren put one or two chains around the domes).

The inclined drum – this carries the three dome structure.

The transfer structure – this is a complex structure with inner and outer drums connected by 32 radial walls.

The 1920s chains – During extensive repairs two new chains were added around the transfer structure.

The support arches – As the spacing between the piers are not equal, there are four main arches over the larger spacing, and arches at two levels over the smaller spacing.

The piers – there are eight of these, unequally spaced, supporting the whole structure.

As far as the structure is concerned, not all the elements shown are of equal importance. The main structural elements are the conical dome and inclined drum, the chain(s), the double drum transfer structure, the support arches and the piers.

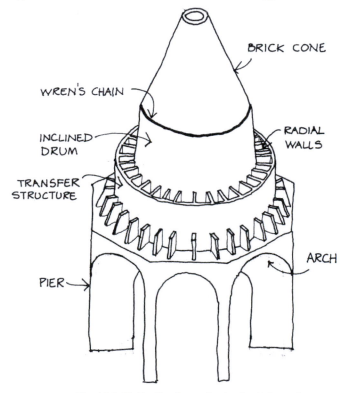

Fig. 12.8 St. Paul's - the main structural elements

Like Brunelleschi and others before him, Wren acted as both architect and engineer, because in his time engineering and architecture were not distinct professions. Because of this, the interplay between built form and structure are not easy to separate. As **Fig. 12.7** shows, there are strong elements of built form, such as the lantern, that perform no structural function, whereas there are structural elements, such as the brick cone, which are structural but not part of the discernible built form. The questions are; did Wren provide a sensible structural system to support his chosen built form, and why did he think it was sensible? The answers are not clear.

To assess how sensible the structure is, some understanding of its behaviour is needed. Of the three domes, the outer timber framed dome is supported by the cone, whereas the inner brick dome is an independent structure. They all come together at a common point, where outward thrusts are resisted by circumferential tension in Wren's chain(s). Below this level the load is predominantly vertical on a circular plan. These loads are carried by the inner drum in mainly vertical compression. At the bottom of this drum is the transfer structure.

Assuming that the inner and outer drums and the cross-walls act as an integral unit, the action depends on the stiffness of the supports – the arches. To see how this structure might act, two extreme cases can be considered, one where only the inner drum is supported and another where only the outer drum is supported.

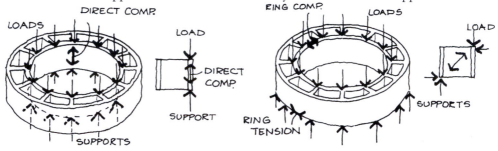

Fig. 12.9 Transfer structure models

If the structure is only supported by the inner drum, then only this drum will be loaded. If the structure is only supported by the outer drum, then the entire load has to be transferred by the radial walls, and this causes diagonal forces in these walls, and horizontal forces top and bottom. These in turn cause a ring compression in the top and a ring tension in the bottom. The actual support of the two drums is neither of these; however, it seems likely that most of the load would be carried by the inner drum, so the majority of the load in the piers would be near their inner faces. This structure seems overcomplicated, which makes it difficult to identify clear load paths, the key to sensible structural conception.

On what basis Wren decided, either qualitatively or quantitatively, that his structural concepts were correct is hard to assess. There are no surviving calculations or experimental models, things that given Wren's abilities one might expect to have been made. The only evidence of structural analysis that exists is a sketch of a thrust line drawn on a section of an earlier scheme for the domes. In **Fig. 12.10** Wren's line is contrasted with the profile of hanging a chain with the correct loads. Actually these funicular thrust lines make far more sense for arches than domes.

Robert Hooke (1635-1703), who was a lifelong friend of Wren, had proposed that a hanging chain gave the shape for an arch – see **Fig.7.70**. An arch is not a dome as has been shown, and some think there is no definite connection between Hooke's catenary and the dome,[9] but Wren and Hooke were close friends and collaborators, and there is an entry in Hooke's diary noting that Wren was altering his dome design according Hooke's arch principle.[10]

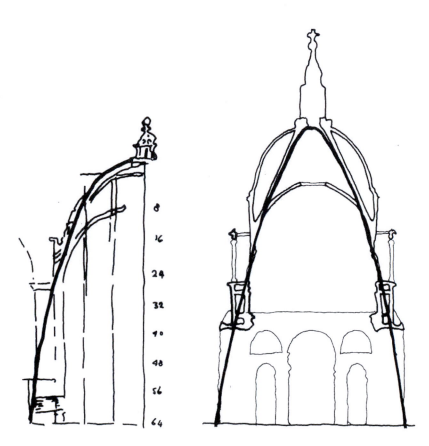

Fig. 12.10 Wren's thrust line (left) and that of a weighted chain (right)

Wren's achievements were remarkable, and he is regarded by many as Britain's greatest architect, but his reputation as a great structural engineer seems less secure. Some have given him a place of honour in the history of structural engineering,[11] prompting Dr Thurston[12] to state that Wren *"…was simply a great natural mathematician, and it was possible that Wren was, in the same way, such a great genius that he was able to determine what was required without the need for elaborate mathematics".* This is clearly overstating the case.

There have been many structural problems with St. Paul's Cathedral, mainly with the dome support structures. Wren himself was made aware of one of these when cracks appeared in the eight large piers that support the main dome. They were **bursting** due to the load. The piers, following usual practice, were built from a stone outer **box** filled with rubble but, as Wren realised, the smaller upper piers were loading the rubble and not the stone of the lower piers. This produced the effect shown in **Fig. 8.9**, but here the **rigid pit** was the stonework of the lower piers which was unable to resist the lateral forces from the rubble, and so cracked, or **burst**.

There were problems due to differential settlement of the piers, as not all the foundations had been taken down to an adequate bearing stratum. But the main structural problems were with the load transfer structure between the domes and the supporting piers. There is no evidence that Wren had a clear conceptual understanding of the structural behaviour of this structure, however he decided to place extensive iron work in it. Much of this failed, causing severe cracking and, after years of running repairs, the whole structure was renovated and strengthened between 1925 and 1930.[13]

Wren intended to publish a treatise on architecture, which was to have included his thoughts on the behaviour of structures, but he never got round to it. He stated in a report on Westminster Abbey that *"It is by due Consideration of the Statick Principles, and the right Poising of the Weights of the Butments to Arches, that good Architecture depends"*.[14] His only known attempt at structural analysis was for the abutments of an arch, and this was totally flawed.[15] He was brilliantly clever, a very able mathematician, an imaginative and dedicated experimenter and his friend Hooke was also all of these, so it is difficult to understand why Wren did not make more progress with useful aspects of structural design.

12.2 The arrival of the skeletal structure

In 1709 Abraham Darby first produced iron by using coke, a coal derivative, rather than charcoal. Charcoal was becoming prohibitively expensive with the almost complete deforestation of Great Britain. This new process was the foundation of the Industrial Revolution. Iron, now being an affordable material, allowed the development of machinery which in turn gave rise to the steam engine that provided the energy for industrialisation. In 1779 Darby's grandson Abraham Darby III built the Iron Bridge at Coalbrookdale, see **Fig. 5.8**, and in 1802 the first railway locomotive.

For structures and the built form, the arrival of affordable iron and the new demands of industry changed everything. Firstly with cast iron and then, with the more tension-resistant wrought iron, high strength to weight ratio structural elements, in the form of bars, rods, angles and other standard sections, became available. Secondly industrial demands brought new built forms into being; factories, railway stations, cranes and railway bridges, with structures that often had to support previously unimagined large loads, the weight of railway trains or stationary steam engines and so on. So instead of the structural self-weight being dominant, as with large masonry structures, it was now low compared with the load carried; a totally new situation. These structures, made as assemblies of relatively slender high-strength iron elements joined by metal fastenings, were **skeletal structures**.

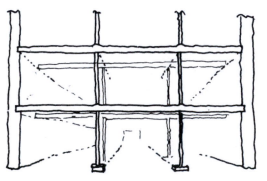

Fig. 12.11 Mill with simple internal iron framing 1801

The ability of iron skeletal structures to permit the construction of huge buildings in an incredibly short time was amply demonstrated by the erection of the Crystal Palace[16] in London in 1851 – *"... the mid-nineteenth century touchstone"*.[17] In 1849 Henry Cole (1808-1882) proposed to Prince Albert that a great international exhibition should be held in London. A site was chosen, Hyde Park, and the date set, 1851, giving less than eighteen months to stage the biggest show the world had ever seen.

In January 1850 a Building Committee was formed that included the architects, Thomas Donaldson (1795-1885), Robert Cockerell (1788-1863) and Charles Barry (1795-1860), and the engineers Isambard Brunel (1806-1859) and Robert Stephenson (1803-1859). An open international competition was held for the design of the building, and 245 entries were received. After the Committee had examined the entries, they announced that none was acceptable and they would design the building themselves. The design produced by this high-powered committee was a monstrous hybrid surmounted by a 62m (200 feet) diameter, 46m (150 feet) high dome designed by Brunel. When the scheme was presented to the public there was an outcry that put the whole idea of the Great Exhibition in jeopardy.

Fig. 12.12 The exhibition building designed by the Committee

The project was rescued by the remarkable Joseph Paxton (1801-1855). Lacking even elementary education, he had started as a gardener's boy on the estates of the Duke of Devonshire. By the time of the exhibition he was a wealthy man, the manager of all the Duke's estates and a railway company director. Visiting his friend John Ellis, in June 1850, he mentioned his doubts about the proposed exhibition building and noted he had some ideas of his own and was wondering if it was too late to submit a design. Ellis took Paxton to meet Cole. Paxton learned from Cole that the Committee would consider a proposal provided it could be submitted, with detailed drawings, within two weeks. Paxton replied that the drawings would be ready in nine days. Three days later, at a Midland Railway board meeting, he sketched his scheme for the building that was to be 569m (1848 feet) long by 138m (450 feet) wide. When his scheme was presented to the Committee they accepted it.

Fig. 12.13 Joseph Paxton's sketch scheme

The chosen contractors, Fox and Henderson, took possession of the site on 30th July 1850 and this enormous building was ready nine months later. Everything was designed on a grid with high repetition of parts.

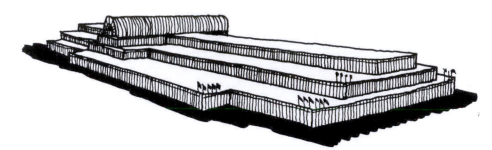

Fig. 12.14 The Crystal Palace in Hyde Park

The exhibition was thought to be a great success, and the building a great achievement, but it could have turned out rather differently. The frame, in spite of its enormous number of iron structural elements, was not sufficiently stiff against horizontal wind loads. Although some braced bays were introduced, see **Fig. 9.42**, they were inadequate, and stiffness was supplied by the portal action of the joint between the columns and the trusses. This was criticised in 1850 by many people, including the Astronomer Royal George Airy (1801-1892).

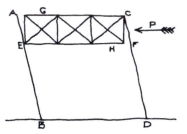

Fig 12.15 The portal action of the Crystal Palace

The critics were right, and when the building was dismantled and re-erected at Sydenham in South London it was stiffened, but not sufficiently, because a large part of it blew down in 1861. Surprisingly this did not come to the attention of the public.[18] The rest of the building stood until 30th November 1936, when it was totally destroyed by fire.

Fig. 12.16 The Sheerness Boat Store

A building constructed only nine years later, in the obscurity of Sheerness naval dockyard, in North Kent, took the idea of the skeletal iron frame forward. The Sheerness Boat Store,[19,20] built in 1859, and still in use, has all the features of what would now be considered a modern building.. The external envelope was non-loadbearing, with strip glazing and cladding panels. This revolutionary building was designed by Colonel GT Green (1807-1896), who was neither a civil engineer nor an architect, but a military engineer.

It is clear that the horizontal stability was provided by the bolted beam/column connections, these beams are called **transverse bracing girders** on the original drawings. This modern skeletal structure showed how iron could provide a minimal primary structure that gave floors uninterrupted by loadbearing walls, and external glazing patterns that were unrestricted.

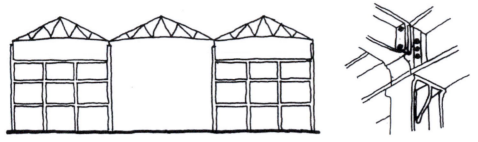

Fig. 12.17 Section and connection detail

Meanwhile in the rapidly industrialising United States of America, a new building form was evolving – the skyscraper. The first skyscraper is usually considered to be the Home Insurance Company Building built in 1884-85, 11 storeys high; it was designed by William Le Baron Jenney (1832-1907). Jenney had studied in Paris, at the *École Centrale des Arts et Manufactures*, which trained *'ingénieurs civils'* or *'constructeurs'*. During the American Civil War he served as a military engineer. He practised as an **engineer-architect** in Chicago (1868-1905), and is regarded as the father of the Chicago School. These Chicago buildings had iron or steel frames with external elevations clad with a variety of materials, really much larger versions of the pioneering Sheerness Boat Store.

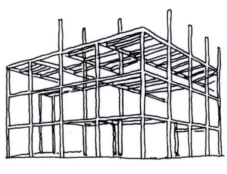

Fig. 12.18 Home Insurance Company Building and skyscraper construction

Towards the end of the 19th century, a new structural material – reinforced concrete – appeared.[21] The idea of reinforcing concrete with metal was not new, but it was only in 1892 that the French engineer François Hennebique (1842-1921) patented a complete building system. This system had virtually all the features of reinforced concrete structures that are used today.

The early reinforced concrete structures were similar to the iron ones in that they were mainly skeletal; beams and columns supporting concrete slabs. The slabs were regarded as separate elements spanning from beam to beam. Reinforced concrete structures had an advantage over steel ones as they were fire-proof, whereas structural steel needed some form of fire protection; also it was *"cheaper than anything available before"*.[22]

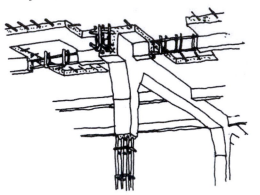

Fig. 12.19 The Hennebique reinforced concrete system

So in something like a hundred years, the idea of a separate steel or reinforced concrete primary structure became a reality. It had also brought into existence specialists in the design of these structures – the engineers – and this caused at least one architect to lament, in 1907[23] that *"...where elaborate steelwork enters the architect's design he has to employ an engineer...there remains only one conclusion, that a joint production of this sort cannot be a complete success...".*

12.3 Engineers, architects, decoration and theory

The traditional professions were medicine, law and theology, but the process of industrialisation saw new groups emerging who also wanted their activities to be regarded as professions, amongst them were architects and engineers. Up to the end of the 18th century, architects, or surveyors as they were often called, were solely responsible for all aspects of building design.[24] They were strongly supported by master craftsmen who would often include the engineering design of masonry and timberwork as part of their contract. The term **engineer** was reserved for members of army engineering corps. Even then the line was not firmly drawn, with many prominent architects undertaking engineering work and military engineers often being responsible for the design of buildings.

John Smeaton (1724-1792) was the first person in Britain to call himself a **civil engineer**, a term he used to distinguish himself from the military engineers. In 1771 he founded the *Society of Civil Engineers*, and amongst the eleven founder members one, Robert Mylne (1733-1811), was an architect. The *Society of Civil Engineers* remained a learned society, and over the years recruited military engineers and more architects. Gradually it became an elite dining club for senior canal builders so, on 2nd January 1818, eight younger men met and founded the ***Institution of Civil Engineers***. After the election, in 1820, of the eminent engineer Thomas Telford (1757-1834) as president, the new institution expanded rapidly due to his energy and organisational ability. In 1828, the institution was granted a charter which gave it a legal existence.

As other countries industrialised, institutions for engineers were founded. In the early stage of institutionalisation, architects and engineers often formed joint bodies: for instance in Switzerland the *Société Suisse des Ingénieurs et des Architectes* in 1837; in Austria the *Osterreichischer Ingenieur und Architektenverein* in 1848; and the *American Society of Civil Engineers and Architects* in 1852. But in general the institutionalisation process formed **separate institutions for engineers and architects.** In Britain, the *Institute of British Architects* was formed in 1834 from the *Society of British Architects* and received a royal charter in 1837.[25] In 1868 in the USA, the '*and Architects*' was dropped to give the *American Society of Civil Engineers*, as the *American Institute of Architects* had been formed in 1857.

As time passed the roles and duties of the two professions became mutually exclusive. For instance, in Britain, in 1938, a government act reserved the use of the term **architect** for those with the requisite qualifications. In some countries both architects and engineers have managed to get both these terms protected by law, and frequently use Architect or Engineer as titles. Often technical submissions will not be accepted by the authorities unless they are signed by qualified architects and engineers – thus the division between architects and engineers is a legal requirement.

A basic reason for the division was the appearance of a mathematically based theory for the behaviour of loaded structures. At the beginning of the 19th century, the correct mathematical description of the behaviour of structures had been presented, principally by a number of brilliant French mathematicians and engineers – see section **0.4**. However this presentation, in the form of what are known as differential equations, did not actually provide engineers with 'answers' because the solution of the equations was another matter, nor could they be understood without special training. By the end of the 19th century, calculation procedures had been established for many common forms of skeletal structure. These were applied routinely by engineers to obtain numerical predictions that provided the required dimensional structural information. Learning these theoretically based calculation procedures became an increasing part of an engineer's training.

Not everyone was happy with this steadily increasing theoretical content. One of the founders of the École Centrale des Arts et Manufactures, Théodore Olivier (1793-1853), himself a *Polytechnicien*, heavily criticised the École Polytechnique[26] considering "*...that the sacred tradition of engineering education had been undermined by excessive devotion to pure theory...*". Over the years other engineers made similar criticisms, for example from 1952 "*...a new resource – structural theory has been added to the equipment of the structural engineer...But in acquiring that theory the engineer had temporarily or partially lost his sense of architecture and proportion*",[27] or in 1979 "*The danger in this arises when the designer's energy goes into the equations rather than the actual construction. The designer risks becoming a mere analyst...*",[28] and in 2003 "*At college students get a diet of theory, theory, theory*".[29]

This increasing interest in theory resulted in engineers gradually losing their aesthetic role. In 1844 Richard Turner, the engineer for the Palm House – see section **10.2** – added so much decoration to the structure that the architect Decimus Burton objected to "*...his use of a Gothic style and numerous ornamental details* *in fretwork, crockets etc*".[30] Twenty years later a military engineer, Captain Francis Fowke (1823-65)[31] was able to win an open architectural competition for a museum complex at South Kensington, which included a natural history museum, and a museum to house the collection of the Commissioner of Patents.

Fig. 12.20 Captain Fowke's entry for the Museum Competition

But by 1884, when the French engineer Gustave Eiffel (1832-1923)[32] made his proposal for a 300m tower, an architect had to decorate it. The tower was initially the idea of engineers Émile Nouguier (1840-1897) and M Koechlin (1856-1946), both of whom worked for the Eiffel Company, but "*Not long afterwards the two engineers asked the architect Sauvestre to give architectural form to their quick sketch, in short, to make the pylon a tower*".[33] Amongst other things he added the arches to the base. These were decorative and did not form part of the basic structure.

Fig. 12.21 The initial concepts of the engineer (left) and the architect (right)

During the design process the architect's decorated tower, which initially had been accepted, was altered "*...in particular the shape of the four huge arches of the base was changed...**more clearly asserting the dominance of the engineer's art over that of the architect**"*.[34] (Author's emphasis)

Fig. 12.22 The final design (left) and the built design (right)

By the end of the 20th century the loss of interest in the aesthetic aspects of design by engineers meant that architects were thought to be designing bridges, *"When completed, the Millau viaduct, designed by British architect Norman Foster, will be the highest in the world…".*[35]

With the technical aspects of structures, architects went in the opposite direction to engineers. As RJM Sutherland (1922-2013) wrote about beam design in the 19th century *"…it is hard to visualise the architects having either the time or the inclination to master it, let alone the necessary grasp to do the sums".*[36] By 1986 architects often sought engineer's advice for a house *"Even here, most architects, myself included, will take the advice of a structural consultant for domestic problems".*[37] And in 2003 a professor of architecture, Sarah Wigglesworth (b1957), stated that *"I am absolutely hopeless with structures. I know nothing about them at all".* [38]

Thus it is often unclear who should have responsibility for the essential task of structural conception as neither architects nor engineers have made understanding it a priority. This cannot be an ideal arrangement, and it has had, and continues to have, unfortunate consequences.

12.4   Architects embrace engineering

When the new structural materials appeared, steel and reinforced concrete, which provided specific load carrying systems rather than the ambiguous loadbearing systems of the Renaissance period, even renowned architect Norman Shaw (1831-1912) *"…could not find a way of harnessing the revolutionary achievements of Victorian structural engineering to create a new architecture for his time".*[39] But after the First World War, young architects appeared who thought they could – they came to be known as the Modern Movement. The principal groups were the Bauhaus[40] in Germany, De Stijl[41] in Holland, the Constructivists in Russia[42] and the Purists[43] in France. From these groups, trying to build a new society based on modern or revolutionary art and architecture, the Germans Ludwig Mies van der Rohe (1886-1969) and

Walter Gropius (1883-1969), and the Swiss-French Charles-Édouard Jeanneret (1887-1965), who became better known as Le Corbusier, emerged as the founders. In 1928 a unifying organisation called the *Congrès Internationaux de l'Architecture Moderne*, usually denoted C.I.A.M, was formed.

Fig. 12.23 Typical Modern Movement architecture

Perhaps the most influential was Le Corbusier. With the destruction of the First World War already in evidence, he felt a rationalised approach to housing, based on mass production principles, would be needed. To this end, in 1915, he produced a system he called Domino or Dom-ino. The drawing of this system, based on a simple reinforced structure, became a Modern Movement icon and Le Corbusier kept *"...a picture of it on his wall next to a photograph of the Parthenon: both central to his lifelong production"*.[44]

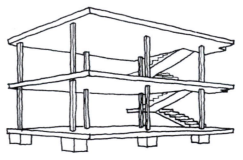

Fig. 12.24 The Dom-ino system

In 1917 he left Switzerland for Paris where he met Amédée Ozenfant (1886-1966). Son of a building contractor and reinforced concrete pioneer, Ozenfant was a painter and intellectual who ran a fashion shop – and he became the other Purist. They started an avant-garde magazine, *L'Esprit Nouveau*, and to increase the number of 'contributors' they frequently penned articles under pseudonyms, thus Jeanneret became Le Corbusier. In 1923 the book *"Vers une architecture"* [45] was published, which was based on a number of articles written by Ozenfant and Jeanneret under the joint pseudonym Le Corbusier-Saugnier.

The book, with the incorrect English title *"Towards a new architecture"*, is considered one of if not the most important document of the Modern Movement, and is essential reading. It attacks recent architecture and holds up the work of engineers as things of beauty from which architects should take inspiration. The opening paragraph reads: *"The Engineer's Æsthetic, and Architecture, are two things that march together and follow one from the other: the one being now at its full height, the other in an unhappy state of regression"*. But for Kenneth Frampton (b1930) *"While 'Vers une architecture' fails to sustain a tight, consequential argument, its importance as an overall primer in*

Purist aesthetic theory resides in the fact that here for the first time the fundamental split between engineering and architecture is set forth in dialectical terms".[46]

Fig. 12.25 Typical illustration from Vers une architecture

In 1926 Le Corbusier published his *"Five Points of a New Architecture"*,[47] which were:

1   **pilotis** – columns that lift the building clear of the ground
2   **plan libre** – interior planning free from loadbearing walls
3   **façade libre** – exterior cladding freed from loadbearing functions
4   **fenêtre en longeur** – the horizontal strip window
5   **toît jardin** – the roof garden gaining land lost under the building

These could only be made possible by the use of a structural frame rather than any form of traditional loadbearing walls with the usual timber floor and roof structures. In this way the 'New Architecture' demanded an engineer's structure rather than that of the craftsman. Le Corbusier also wanted every part of his architecture to be based on an engineering aesthetic so, where possible, mass-produced windows, radiators and other items would be used, but frequently these had to be handmade to look mass-produced.

In spite of Le Corbusier's dedication to technology, many his projects failed technically, including the Cité de Refuge and the Pavillon Suisse, both in Paris. For these Le Corbusier and his cousin and partner Pierre Jeanneret roughly followed the five points. The **façade libre** became fully glazed on some elevations. When the proposals for the Pavillon Suisse were presented to the client M. Jungo he considered that the structure was inadequate and sought a second opinion from Dr. Ritter of Zurich Polytechnic. He was shocked by the **pilotis** and considered the scheme to be *"quite useless in its present form".*[48] After construction, environmental problems appeared in both buildings, the glazed facades turning some of the interiors into unusable ovens – the greenhouse effect - which had been known for years. Remedial work had to be carried out on both buildings. But Le Corbusier considered them successful, with any problems due to the buildings not being run properly.

Fig. 12.26 Pavillon Suisse 1931

The buildings of Mies van der Rohe and Walter Gropius also used the structure aesthetically in perhaps a more obvious way than Le Corbusier, especially with steel structures. But *"Architects like Mies van der Rohe believed they were akin to engineers, designing rational structures…but it was no more the product of objective scientific method than any other architecture"*.[49]

Fig. 12.27 Crown Hall at IIT by Mies van der Rohe

Often, as at the Crown Hall, the primary structure was placed outside the building to **express the structure**. Apart from being the worst position for the structure from the point of view of the waterproofing, it could introduce stability problems. The main horizontal beams of the Crown Hall have unrestrained upper flanges, see **Figs. 6.64** and **65** and section **7.6**, which means extra material is used to provide stiffness for this secondary effect. When it was impractical to express the primary structure, a **decorative expressed structure** would be placed on the outside of the building.

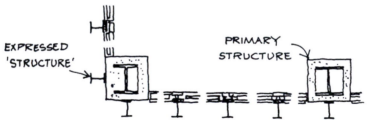

Fig. 12.28 Plan detail of Lake Shore Drive

The work of the Modern Movement, from the point of view of technology and the use of structure, reveals a puzzling situation. For instance Le Corbusier, who had taken private lessons in maths and engineering, states clearly and frequently that engineering solutions hold the key to modern architecture, but he seemed incapable of applying them successfully. Frequently he tried to introduce technical innovations that were ineffective or worse, and he was unable to learn from these mistakes.

He wanted to be a reinforced concrete expert, but seemed to have no conceptual grasp of structural behaviour or, in fact, environmental control, or even building technology. Hence he left a trail of buildings with technical problems that others had to try to resolve. In spite of his desire to incorporate modern technology into architecture, he still saw architecture and engineering as quite separate thought processes, and in 1942 he produced a diagram showing this.

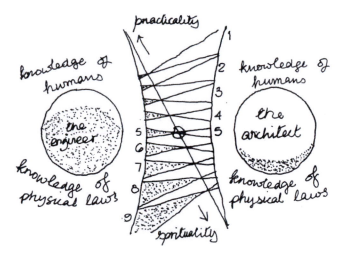

Fig. 12.29 An interpretation of Le Corbusier's view of the Engineer-Architect relationship

A basic idea of the Modern Movement was to introduce modern technology and materials into buildings to provide better environments and more durable buildings built faster and at a lower cost. Admirable aims but rarely achieved in the hands of Modern Movement architects because *"They were for allowing technology to run its course, and believed they knew where it was going, even without having bothered to acquaint themselves with it very closely"*.[50] In other words the Modern Movement's real concern with technology was the visual aspects of a machine aesthetic rather than its technical functionality.

12.5 Engineering as fantasy

As has been stated several times, a built form cannot exist without a structure. The structure will influence the built form either in a demonstrative or a non-demonstrative way. Le Corbusier's houses were explicitly dependent for their built form on a structure of reinforced concrete, but perhaps with the exception of the 'pilotis' the structures were non-demonstrative, whereas for the built form of the Eiffel Tower the structure is defining. In each case the structure has to fulfil its load-carrying function. But if a design is drawn with no intention of building it, then any structure the design implies, does not have to fulfil this function, and so can be a structural fantasy.

In 1784 the influential French architect Étienne-Louis Boullée (1728-1799)[51] made a design for a Cenotaph for Isaac Newton that was to be an empty sphere of 150m diameter, more than three times bigger than the largest existing dome, St. Peter's with a diameter of 43m. The section, see **Fig. 12.30**, is similar to St. Peter's double dome, see **Fig. 12.2**, and shows a thickness of 7.5m as opposed to St. Peter's 3m. Boullée has been criticised as a megalomaniac because of his grandiose proposals, but apparently *"…these should be seen as visionary schemes rather than practical projects"*.[52] Some 150 years later, Albert Speer (1905-1981) Hitler's chief architect, projected a 300m diameter dome as part of his plan to re-build Berlin.[53] In fact, it was to be built as the eighth wonder of the world, and an engineering scheme existed.

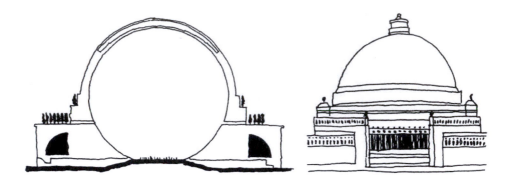

Fig. 12.30 Fantastic domes by Boullée and Speer

The designs of Futurist Antonio Sant'Elia (1888-1916)[54] and Constructivist Vladimir Tatlin (1885-1953)[55] are also scarce in structural detail. Both produced powerful images of built forms that are endlessly reproduced in architectural books; Sant'Elia in 1914 with his New City, and Tatlin, in 1920, with his tower for the Third International.

Fig. 12.31 Futurist and Constructivist fantasies

The New City is based on engineering imagery, but not even plans exist and *"...even for him it was a dream and not a practical reality".*[56] Tatlin whose tower was to be 400m high, that is 100m higher than the then tallest structure in the world, the Eiffel Tower, is an optimistic jumble of structural elements. Apparently Tatlin thought it was a practical project, but *"...the tower was the conception of a sculptor rather than an engineer".*[57] Sant'Elia was killed in the First World War, but Tatlin went on to try to build a human-powered flying machine based on his studies of geese; needless to say it never flew.

The American Buckminster Fuller (1895-1983) had little time for architects in general *"Architecture is voodoo. The architects don't initiate anything"* [58] and Modern Movement architects in particular.

Fig. 12.32 Fuller's design for a 100 storey office block suspended from spokes of a wheel

He variously described himself as machinist, sailor, engineer, astronaut or 'trim tab', but was in effect an inventor who had several patents to his name. During 1927 due to business and family traumas he remained silent, his 'year of silence', during which he used 'four-dimensional thinking'. He summarised these thoughts in a privately published and distributed essay called 4D,[59] which few of the recipients understood. The impenetrable prose was interspersed with drawings of fantastic buildings.

Later in his life Fuller returned to mega-structures which included 3km diameter domes over cities and 1.7km diameter 'cloud structures' that would float around the world like hot air balloons, each housing thousands of people. In between, he came up with numerous smaller scale technical ideas, some of which worked and some that did not. Lacking technical training he seemed unable to subject his ideas to cold rational analysis.

In the 1960s, partly influenced by Fuller, a group of young mainly British architects, who became known as Archigram, produced a number of images of futuristic cities. Their work was based on Pop Art imagery and comic book science fiction and included the 'Walking City' and the 'Plug-in-City'. The *"Plug-in-City did not solve any immediate problems, nor was it intended to be built. Rather it explored and expressed ideas, beliefs..."*.[60]

But for architect and detractor Denise Scott-Brown (b1931), their work was just another iconographic use of real engineering *"...or the oil-derricks, pumps and cranes of San Pedro harbour..."*.[61] Most members of Archigram subsequently pursued careers as teachers of architecture rather, than the designers of built projects.

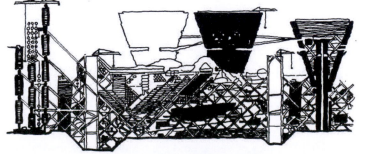

Fig. 12.33 The Plug-in-City from 1964

Not all fantasies have to be on a mega scale; a British firm called Future Systems spent years producing images based stylistically on aerospace technology. In an article written in 1983 called 'Skin', architects David Nixon and Jan Kaplicky (1937-2009), in the midst of photos of aeroplanes and their own drawings complained that *"One of the problems of designing innovative structures is the reluctance of many structural engineers to get involved: …it just means we have to get a different type of engineer"*.[62]

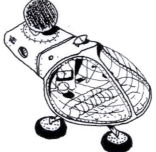

Fig. 12.34 Future Systems' 45° House

It was only in 1999 that Future Systems managed to use an 'aero-type' stressed skin structure for a building; this was for Lords Media Centre.[63] The whole structure is made of aluminium, and had to be fabricated by boat builders. The main reason for the stressed skin being used was intellectual rather than structural.

It is interesting to note that all these projects were drawn to explore or express ideas, but what ideas one might ask? If these ideas were about actually building anything, then why the avoidance of any credible engineering content? But in spite of their inapplicability to real buildings, these projects had an enduring impact on architects, whilst being totally ignored by engineers.

12.6 Engineered curved structures

The engineering skeletal frame of steel or reinforced concrete functions best if the individual elements are straight. Straight elements are also easier to construct, and consequently are the most economical. Overall rectangular arrangements are also preferred for similar reasons, roof slopes being obtained by using triangular shaped trusses. Whilst curved shapes, both for single elements and overall geometry, could be used, there are few strictly functional advantages. But as was seen with the dome, the structural behaviour of curved structures is not straightforward. If the behaviour of curved structures is properly understood then, for some specific structures, they can have some engineering advantages. During the 20th century, a few engineering designers did understand this behaviour and were able to use it advantageously.

Concrete, in its initial wet state, can take almost any geometric form, all that is needed is the necessary shaped formwork. In the 1920s German engineer Franz Dischinger (1887-1953), who worked for the German contractors Dyckerhoff & Widmann A.G, realised that a thin curved concrete structure, in other words a shell, could be both strong and cheap. Working with Zeiss engineer Walter Bauersfeld (1879-1959) they designed, and built, a thin hemispherical shell in

Munich. They took out a patent for their system called Zeiss-Dywidag, and also formulated a mathematical theory for domical shells. Joined by the mathematically gifted Ulrich Finsterwalder (1897-1987)[64] in 1922, he extended the theory to shells of other shapes. This enabled their company to build, between 1925 and 1962, an amazing 3,101,537sq.m of shell roofs.[65] It is important to note that these roofs were built to enable contracts to be won on a cost basis.

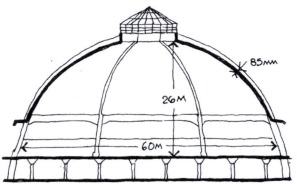

Fig. 12.35 The roof of the market at Basel built in 1932 by Dischinger & Finsterwalder

Although their shells were thin, the 'thinness' could not be seen. But with the Cement Hall, designed by Robert Maillart (1872-1940) and built in 1939 for an exhibition in Zurich, the 'thinness' of shells could be seen. The work of the engineers Dischinger and Finsterwader did not have any significant impact on architecture, but Maillart's shell did, probably because the visual thinness of shells gave another opportunity to express the structure. Maillart built no more shells, and the Cement Hall was demolished after the exhibition.

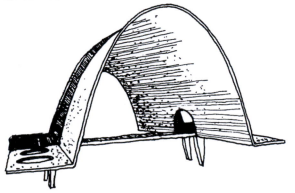

Fig.12.36 The Cement Hall by Robert Maillart

Architectural interest in shell structures was rekindled in the 1950s when the work of Félix Candela (1910-1997)[66] began to be published widely in the architectural press. Candela caused excitement in both architectural and engineering circles, not only for the range of shell roofs he had built, but also for the imaginative forms he created. In 1936 he had been awarded a travelling scholarship and hoped to go to Germany to work with the shell specialists Finsterwalder and Dischinger. Almost on the day of his planned departure, the Spanish Civil War started. An enthusiastic republican he fought on the losing side and, choosing exile rather than oppression, landed in Mexico in 1939 with little more than the clothes he stood up in. After ten years of various work, mostly related with construction, in 1950 he formed a company with his friend Fernando Fernandez called Cubiertas Ala, SA. The company was to specialise in industrial buildings, but first they built an experimental shell roof in the patio of a factory owned by Fernandez's father.

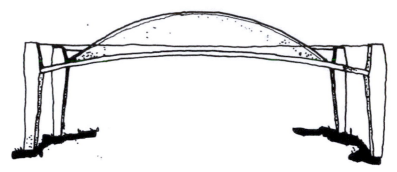

Fig. 12.37 Candela's first shell structure

Thus began the career of one of the greatest shell builders of the 20th century. Over the next twenty years Candela built a huge number of shell roofs. Working with other architects and engineers Candela would be responsible for the form and calculations of the shell roofs. The vast majority of his shells were based on the shape of the **hyperbolic paraboloid**, or hypar for short.

This is the name given to a geometric surface that can be generated by straight lines. If a square grid is drawn on a plane, with each grid intersection point being given coordinates, then the surface is defined by its distance from the plane at each point. In the case of the hypar, the vertical distance from the plane equals the product of the coordinates.

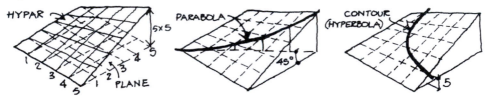

Fig. 12.38 Hyperbolic paraboloid geometry

Lines drawn on the surface of the hyperbolic paraboloid that are not directly above the basic gridlines will not be straight but curved. Two special curves may be drawn, **parabolas** and **hyperbolas**, which give the surface its name. If lines are drawn at 45° to the grid on the plane, the lines on the surface that are vertically above are parabolas. Lines on the surface that join points of equal height – contours – are horizontal hyperbolas.

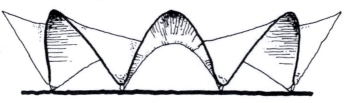

Fig. 12.39 The shell roof of Xochimilco restaurant.

As this form can be generated from straight lines, concrete formwork can be erected economically, or at least could be in Mexico at that time. Candela, often working on quite moderate projects, was able to produce an almost endless variety of beautiful and elegant shell roofs. These were often based on hypars; tilted, cut on the parabolas or hyperbolas, or many joined together. The roof over the Xochimilco restaurant, built in 1957, is perhaps one of the most beautiful shell roofs ever built – it is now severely compromised by banal extensions.

Candela was an architect, but in designing and building his shells he acted as an engineer-contractor. His company would build these shell roofs, often on the basis that it was the lowest cost solution. Whilst his shells were admired by architects, engineers were sometimes less happy. In 1954, Candela wrote an article entitled *"stereo-structures"*,[67] in which he outlined his conceptual understanding of structures, and in the same year presented two papers at the Massachusetts Institute of Technology. Both the article and his papers were strongly attacked by eminent engineers,[68] who accused him of making conceptual and mathematical errors, to which Candela replied,[69] pointing to his dozens of shells, *"there they are and they seem to work"*.[70] It was not that Candela had no knowledge of the mathematical analysis of shell structures, but he thought that this analysis could be simplified by using his conceptual understanding. His shells stood, but this does not show that he or his critics were right, because many factors can make the behaviour of a real structure significantly different to that of an idealised one. By the end of the 1960s, Candela stopped building shells and, in 1971, emigrated to the United States where he taught in various universities.

Curved structures in the form of framed domes were promoted by Buckminster Fuller; the geodesic dome. After various failures both technical and financial, and success with the Dymaxion Deployment Unit during the Second World War, in 1948 he was invited to tutor at a Summer School at Black Mountain College. Here he got students to build a 15m diameter geodesic dome from Venetian blinds slats – it collapsed. In spite of this failure the following year he was invited to direct the Summer School.

But what is a geodesic dome? A geodesic is the shortest line joining two points on a surface. If the curved surface is spherical, then all these curves are the same – that is, circles of the same diameter as the sphere.

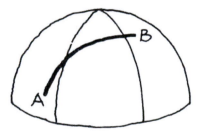

Fig. 12.40 Geodesic line joining points A and B

The idea of the geodesic dome was to create a geometry on the surface of the sphere whose nodes would be joined by geodesic lines. Fuller did this by using an icosahedron. It was known before Plato that there were only five regular solids; the tetrahedron, the cube, the octahedron, the dodecahedron and the icosahedron which has twenty faces of equilateral triangles. These solids can be put 'inside' a sphere so that their vertices touch the surface. If the faces are then 'pushed' out to the surface, the sphere is divided into regular curved regions.

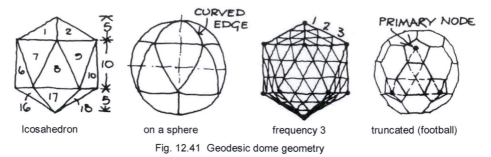

| Icosahedron | on a sphere | frequency 3 | truncated (football) |

Fig. 12.41 Geodesic dome geometry

Each face of an icosahedron can be subdivided with more equilateral triangles which generate more geodesic lines; the number of subdivisions is called the frequency. With this subdivision there are pentagons around the primary nodes and hexagons between them, this derived form is called a truncated icosahedron and is often used for footballs.* Fuller managed to patent these domes, and his application showed a dome based on an icosahedron divided with a frequency of 16.

Thousands of geodesic domes have been built, mainly by the US military, who use them for easily transported temporary accommodation and radar domes. They have also been used for many other purposes, from houses and garden greenhouses to the US pavilion for the 1967 EXPO at Montreal.

Fig. 12.42 Gardener with a geodesic greenhouse

However, it must be stressed that the geodesic dome is, in all its various configurations, just a structure transferring loads. It has no special structural qualities, its advantages being purely geometrical. The groups of members and connectors have the same geometry, but the forces in the members vary with their position in the structure so the cross-sections cannot, for economy's sake, all be equal. As the members cannot be continuous, every joint has to be designed to transmit the full force.

The geodesic dome was the beginning of Buckminster Fuller attaining *"…almost legendary status amongst architects and architectural students all over the world"*.[71] Whilst Fuller's approach was in some ways similar to that of an engineer, he never attained any special status amongst engineers, probably due to his penchant for incomprehensible statements like *"There are many ways of rendering geodesic structures, but all represent closed systems in which compression is comprehensively encompassed by tension. In principle, this emulates the structuring of the universe."*[72]

---

* This geometry becomes clearer if a simple model is made of a 3-frequency icosahedron

Occasionally, engineers would use curved forms based on the successful example of the suspension bridge that is a hanging roof.

Fig. 12.43 Hanging roof by Schnirch, 1824

The pioneer for these roofs was Bedřich Schnirch (1791-1868)[73] working in Moravia in the early part of the 19th century. In 1824 he proposed a hanging roof for a theatre in Strážnice. In 1896 the Russian engineer Vladmir Shukov (1853-1939)[74] designed and built three pavilions with hanging roofs at Nižnii Novgorod.

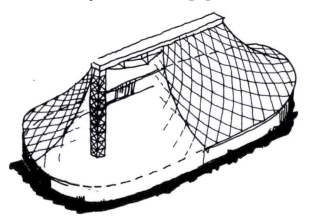

Fig. 12.44 Shuckov's pavilion at Nižnii Novgorod 1896

In 1961 the contractors Shimitzu won a design and build contract for a stadium to be built as part of the Tokyo Olympic Games. The structure, designed by the engineers Yoshikatsu Tsuboi (1907-1990) and Mamoru Kawaguchi (b.1932), was, with a span of 126m, the longest spanning hanging roof built at the time.[75]

Considered by many to be one of the outstanding buildings of the 20th century, the stadium combines a brilliantly clear structural form with an architectural statement of great beauty. This combination, on this scale, is almost unknown and so it seems a pity that the architect involved, Kenzo Tange (1913-2005) had to claim the credit for the engineering *"What made me personally decide on this structural method was the possibility I saw in it of creating an open form".*[76]

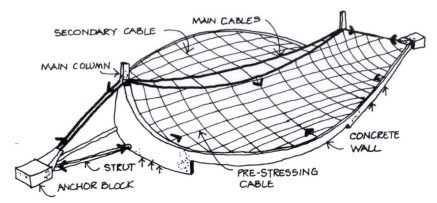

Fig. 12.45 Tokyo Olympic stadium structural system

But hanging roofs were rarely used, mainly due to their cost. Whilst a hanging cable is a very economic structural element in terms of material, it needs a horizontal reaction to function structurally, see **Fig. 7.67**, and the structure that provides this, often high above ground level, is not usually cheap.

In looking at these structures that created curved built forms, it should be noted that:

- **They were used to give value for money**
- **They provide sensible and direct load paths**
- **Methods of calculation were available before conception**

These are the fundamentals of the engineering approach to built form.

12.7 Engineering fantasy becomes reality

After the Second World War, Le Corbusier started to depart from his five principles and his projects took many different forms. From a structural point of view one of the oddest was the Phillips Pavilion for the 1958 Brussels World Fair.[77] Phillips, the Dutch electrical and electronics firm, contacted Le Corbusier in 1956, and asked him to design their pavilion. He replied *"I will not make a pavilion for you but an Electronic Poem…"*.[78] It can be argued that the project was not really designed by Le Corbusier, but by Iannis Xenakis (1922-2001),[79] a Greek engineer who had been working for Le Corbusier for ten years, now better known as an composer of avant-garde electronic music.

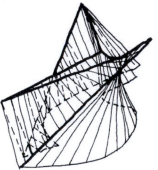

Fig. 12.46 Perspective of an early model of the Phillips Pavilion

After various ideas for the form of the pavilion had been examined, the shape evolved into a number of interlinked hyperbolic paraboloids, see **Fig. 12.38**. With the geometry defined, a method of construction was needed. The initial idea was that the intersection lines between the curved surfaces would be made as a structural steel frame, with some extra vertical supports. The curved surfaces would be made from a flexible sheet material supported on a network of cables. There were only two problems with this approach, first the engineers decided that they could not calculate the forces in the frame, and second it was discovered that the level of sound insulation required a thickness of at least 5cm of concrete. So the curved surfaces had to become some type of shell.

Formwork for a hypar can be made by using narrow flexible pieces of wood laid along the straight lines, each piece being slightly twisted. But casting concrete at an angle steeper than about 40° needs formwork for **both** surfaces, which for a hypar is difficult.

The design and the designers were saved by Hoyte Duyster, a Dutch engineer with the contractor Strabed, who had a rare combination of imagination, practicality and theoretical ability. Working with engineers at Delft University, led by Professor Vreedenburgh, he undertook the final design. His solution was to form the shells from pre-cast concrete elements fitted between pre-stressing cables, which followed the straight generators of the hypars.

When everything was in place, the elements and cables would be made into a shell by concreting the joints. As the structure could not be calculated, structural load tests had to be carried out at Delft University. The structural tests showed that the structure did not need the vertical columns, so these were omitted.

To make the elements, each diamond having a slightly different curvature, the hypar shapes were made in sand and the elements cast on top.

Fig. 12.47 Load test and element production

The structure needed a forest of scaffolding to support all the individual elements until they could be concreted together.

Fig. 12.48 The scaffolding and the completed Phillips Pavilion

Opinions about the structure are divided. A Professor of Architectural Theory writes *"The solution was not only very efficient; from the point of view of structure, it was also conducive to simplifying the process of physical construction"* [80] whereas a Professor of Engineering writes *"The Le Corbusier building, small as it is, could not be understood as a structure. The reason is simple; the building is more a work of sculpture. Le Corbusier's form did not spring from structural imagination, and even some of the finest thin shell engineers in the world could not clearly explain its behaviour"*.[81]

In 1956, an international architectural competition was held for the design of a centre for the performing arts to be built in Sydney in Australia. This new centre, which became known as Sydney Opera House, was to give the popular Sydney Symphony Orchestra a new home. Sydney Opera House is now so famous that it is difficult to think of Sydney without it, rather like Paris without the Eiffel Tower. The winning project, chosen by a panel made up of four architects, was the one submitted by Jørn Utzon (1918-2008).

Fig. 12.49 Sydney Opera House – Utzon's competition entry

The design and building of the Sydney Opera House was far from a simple matter, and the story has been told many times from various points of view. [82-86] The immediate problem was to give the client some assurance on the technical aspects of the design, and in particular the dramatic roof structure. Utzon had conceived these roofs, *"apparently unaided by structural engineering advice"*.[87] But on arriving in Sydney shortly after winning the competition he was able to announce that *"The roof of the opera house will be made of concrete a few inches* thick…..This is a very economical method of construction"*.[88] He had a clear idea of how they should look saying *"I wanted to see a smooth concave surface, like the inside of an egg shell"*.[89]

---

* I inch = 2.54 cm

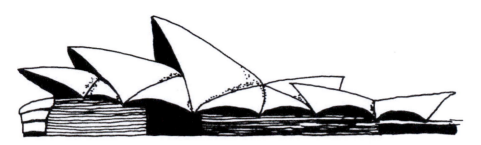

Fig. 12.50   Model of Utzon's competition scheme showing thin shells

To provide the client with his scheme worked up in more detail Utzon, who had already been contacted by Ove Arup (1895-1988), recommended that Ove Arup & Partners be appointed to act as structural engineering consultants. Ove Arup was already known in architectural circles for having a design rather than a calculation approach to structures in buildings, and his senior partner, the brilliant engineer Ronald Jenkins (1907-1975), had been responsible for a number of concrete shell roofs. But when the more detailed scheme, that came to be known as the Red Book, was presented to the client in March 1958, all the structural engineers could do was to comment that *"The superstructure of the Opera House consists partly of a series of large shells. The structural design of the latter is obviously quite a problem and has only just been touched on...".*[90]

The major problem was not the roof, though with almost any other project it would have been, but Utzon's attempts to reconcile the irreconcilable – to design a concert hall that was also an opera house. This ultimately led to his resignation in 1966 under circumstances that will always have different interpretations. The scale of the difficulties that the project designers and constructors had to overcome is measured by the facts. The project took 16 years to design and build (1957 to 1973), the final cost was $A102,000,000 whilst the original budget, set artificially low for political reasons, was just under $A10,000,000, and the structural engineers worked for an estimated 375,000 man hours on the engineering design – equivalent to one man working for nearly 200 years. But the interest here is not the whole project, but the roof.

The shells proposed by Utzon did not comply with any of the basic requirements of a shell roof. Think of a child's balloon or a bird's egg, they are smooth, but burst or break when loaded with point loads. These shells were not smooth, nor did they have mathematically defined shapes, making calculations impossible. They were supported at points, and were subjected to concentrated loads from the acoustic ceiling units and ultimately, the heavy tiling units. All this was quickly recognised by the engineers who noted that *"...Utzon's intuitive technical assessment turned out to be erroneous. He had visualized the roof as thin shells...".*[91]

The first scheme prepared by the engineers used geometry based on the parabola, and with the shells replaced by ribbed structures stabilised longitudinally by 'louvre' walls. These were required as some of the 'shells' in Utzon's scheme were unstable as rigid bodies in the longitudinal direction.

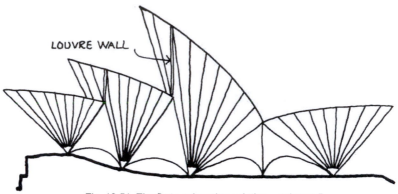

LOUVRE WALL

Fig. 12.51 The first engineering solution – scheme B

To provide Utzon with his *smooth concave surface, like the inside of an egg shell,* Jenkins, certainly one of the best shell engineers in the world at the time, tried to find a 'shell-like' solution. This was not a shell as such, but a double shell with an internal steel structure. See **Fig. 10.68** for a comparison.

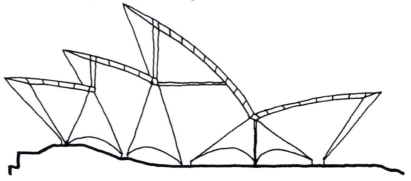

Fig. 12.52 'Shell like' engineering solution – scheme C

The analysis of this structure required Jenkins and his talented team to work at the limit of what was possible; the 'usual' problem of getting answers from complex theory.

When Utzon had time to examine the result of this work he decided he did not like it as he *"…considered the steel skeleton to be structurally dishonest"*.[92] The idea of **structural honesty**, a Modern Movement edict, makes no sense to anyone who has a conceptual understanding of structural behaviour. With the rejection of the 'architect required shell-like' scheme Jenkins understandably lost interest, and his chief and very able assistant, H Møllmann, ironically also Danish, was so incensed that he resigned and went back to Denmark.

Amazingly Ove Arup supported the architect's decision, so a new team was formed under J Zunz (b1923). This team, which saw the project to completion, initially continued to refine Jenkins' scheme, whilst also developing a ribbed scheme.

The final scheme was based on the geometry of a sphere, and used a ribbed structure that was made of pre-cast elements stressed together after erection, which made it suitably honest. This structure was so heavy that the supporting structure, which had already been built, had to be strengthened.

Fig. 12.53 The final engineering solution – scheme M

In terms of dimensions, there was nothing spectacular about the span, or the height of the roof of Sydney Opera House. In **Fig. 12.54**, the maximum cross-section dimensions are compared with the roofs of St. Pancras railway terminus in London built in 1868, and the CNIT exhibition hall, built in 1958 and described in section **10.4**.

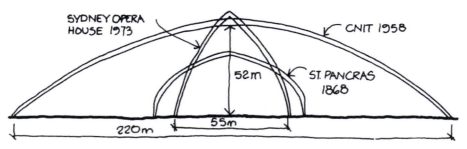

Fig. 12.54 Span comparisons

Clearly such competent engineers as Ove Arup & Partners would not require six years of work, or twelve different schemes for a roof of these dimensions. But the leaders of the engineering design were convinced that this effort was justified on architectural grounds, which seems questionable; it could never be justified on any others. Ove Arup put the whole process succinctly and rather poetically *"You may say…you should have brought Utzon down to earth. I could answer: not while there was a chance of his pulling us up to heaven".* [93]

Needless to say subsequent opinions about the roof of Sydney Opera House are divided. For architects it is technological poetry *"…Utzon demonstrated how technology can transcend itself and blossom into works of art. What is "clearer" and at the same time more poetical than the Sydney shells."* [94] But for engineers, it is a technical disaster *"…many of the most prominent thin shell concrete structures designed during the 1950's by architects generally were not thin, far overran their cost estimates and often performed badly…",* [95] and even Candela remarked that *"…the Sydney Opera House is a tragic example of the catastrophic consequence of this attitude of disdain for the most obvious laws of physics".* [96]

In 1971 an open competition was held for a new centre for the visual arts to be built on the Plateau Beaubourg in Paris. It was named the Pompidou Centre. The winners were the unknown architects Renzo Piano (b1937), Richard Rogers (b1933) and Gian Franco Franchini (1938-2009).[*] The winning submission showed a strong Archigram influence, see **Fig.12.33**, and incorporated structural features such as a steel structure partly fireproofed by the internal circulation of cooling water, floors that would move up and down and a floor structure of only 1.6m depth spanning nearly 50m.

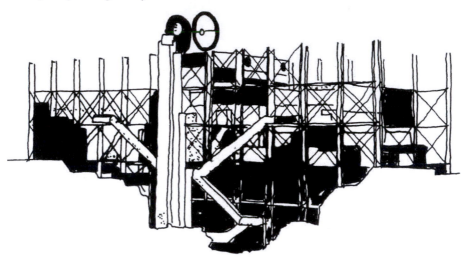

Fig. 12.55 The competition entry

The structure of the winning scheme also had another rather surprising feature in that it was a mechanism under horizontal loads, see **Fig. 6.23**, in other words the building would have fallen down.

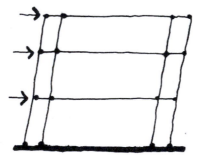

Fig. 12.56 Sway mechanism of the competition entry

All this might just have been understandable if it were not for the fact that the entry was prepared under the guidance of two engineers, Ted Happold (1930-1996) and Peter Rice (1935-1992). As the winning design was to be built, all these questions had to be addressed. In a paper written about the structure, the engineers, noted that their concept would not work *"Either solution had serious disadvantages, either by increasing an already excessive span or by seriously complicating problems of connections…"*.[97]

The solutions referred to were either joining the trusses with moment connections, which would have reduced the mid-span moment but generated high forces in the connecting pieces. Alternatively, the trusses could be simply supported between points mid-way between the two columns, thus increasing the span. Neither

---

[*] the inclusion of Franchini was apparently an administrative error.

solution was practical. In the same paper it was also noted that *"the design of the structure was of the greatest importance from the architectural standpoint"*[98] which makes it all the more incredible that the scheme design engineers, calling the initial design *"merely a rough draft"*,[99] could have got it so wrong.

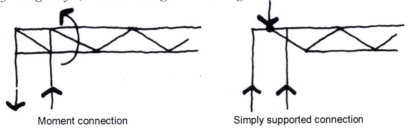

Moment connection   Simply supported connection

Fig. 12.57 Unsatisfactory truss connections

Both the ideas of the floors moving and the trusses being unprotected against fire had to be abandoned. This caused difficulties with the truss design, as it now had to be wrapped in fireproofing and still appear slim and elegant. The external skin had to incorporate fire-proof panels which reduced the planned transparency. The steel work outside the skin needed a sprinkler system for fire protection; this was activated by sensors on the steelwork set to operate when the steelwork reached a preset temperature. The structure also had to be made stable under horizontal loads applied in either the longitudinal or the lateral direction.

The floor system and column arrangement were modified, the spacing between the 'columns' became 6m, and the outer 'column' became a tie. The trusses were aligned with the columns, deepened to 2.3m, and supported on cantilever brackets that were called 'gerberettes,'* which became emblematic of the structural brilliance of the project.

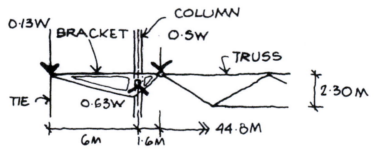

Fig. 12.58 Floor support details and forces

The matter of horizontal stability also had to be resolved. **Fig. 12.59** shows how stability was attained for horizontal forces applied in the longitudinal direction. The internal steel and concrete floor plate acted as a stiff diaphragm, but horizontal bracing had to be introduced in the external area to transmit the forces to the façades.

---

* named after the German engineer Heinrich Gerber (1832-1912)

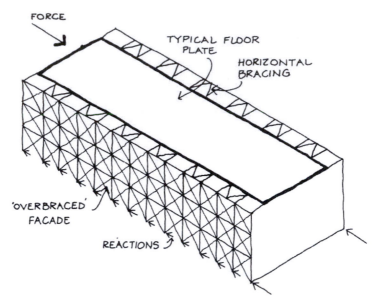

Fig. 12.59 Longitudinal stability

The competition design showed façades completely braced in every bay by rod cross-bracing; this was retained. As section **9.4** explains only one vertical braced bay is actually required for stability. At the time of building rod cross-bracing, the rods, only being able to resist tensile forces, had largely been superseded by a single diagonal that could resist both tensile and compressive forces, as this was easier to build and cheaper.

Even after the post-competition alterations had been made, the building was still a lateral mechanism. There was no possibility of making the lateral structures into moment-resisting frames whilst maintaining the architectural appearance, so the building also had to be braced laterally.

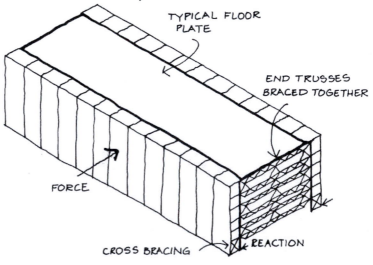

Fig. 12.60 Lateral stability

Again the steel and concrete floor plates acted as stiff diaphragms, this time spanning the whole length of the building. To make the end bays stiff the standard truss arrangement was modified by linking them vertically with diagonal members. At the ground level, stability was achieved by introducing substantial cross-bracing in the two outer bays. As the 'standard' trusses in the end bays are subjected to quite different forces, these trusses are not standard at all. The overall appearance of these end bays is not one of structural clarity.

Having made all these modifications to the competition design, the main columns were not braced sufficiently by the lateral structural system for the buckling length to be the distance between floors, which is the usual situation. The buckled shapes for the main columns, the **buckling length**, was calculated to be nearly three times the floor to floor height. When the buckling length or 'effective length' increases there is always a consequent reduction in allowable stress, see **Fig. 15.46**. This means that the structural member will be less efficient in terms of material.

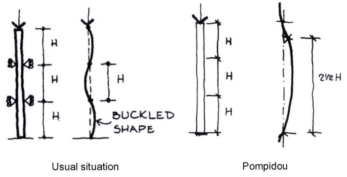

Usual situation   Pompidou

Fig. 12.61 Buckling shapes of the main columns

The Pompidou Centre is visited by more people than the Eiffel Tower. It is an example of what became known as High Tech[100] architecture: but when asked about High Tech, the eminent, and eminently sensible, engineer Frank Newby (1926-2001) put it bluntly *"I don't think high-tech has made any contribution to the development of structures at all...architects just started using structure as decoration...".*[101] This comment could equally be applied to the other two projects described here. However, the designers, if not already famous as in the case of Le Corbusier, all went on to have illustrious careers.

It is hard to know what to make of this situation. In the 19th century, designers – whether architect or engineer, the distinction was only just being made – confronted new building forms and structural materials with commonsense and economy. Hence, previously unimaginable projects such as the Crystal Palace and the Eiffel Tower were designed and built in astonishingly short periods.

With the projects described here, all built in the second half of the 20th century; the opposite seems to have happened. None were a new type of building; an exhibition space, two concert halls or some art galleries and a library, but all involved enormous difficulty and effort both for the design and the construction - hardly progress. In the case of the Phillips Pavilion, the concept seemed to have been based purely on a geometric shape derived without any thought for the actual construction. The concept of Sydney Opera House was partially based on a complete misunderstanding of the structural behaviour of shells. The structure for the Pompidou Centre was central to the architectural concept, and was prepared with constant engineering input, yet the structure of the competition winning scheme wasn't even stable.

12.8 Guggenheim, computers and beyond

In 1997, the Guggenheim Museum designed by architect Frank Gehry (b.1929)[102] opened in Bilbao. It has proved to be a great attraction for visitors from all over the world. It was conceived as a shape without mathematically defined geometry, and no attempt was made to provide structural stability – the structural engineer's task was to make it stand up.

Fig. 12.62 Guggenheim Museum – Bilbao

The engineers noted that *"...the architectural themes of fractured and irregular building masses were explicitly at odds with the normal structural engineering precepts of stability, organisation and regularity...".*[103] So they had to bring structural order to chaos. Having chosen structural steel as the material, order was imposed by making horizontal and vertical lines of structure on a 3m by 3m 'grid'.

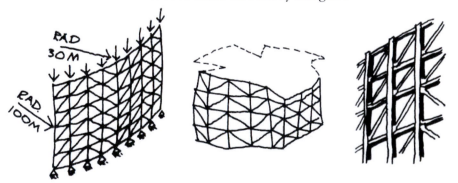

Fig. 12.63 Guggenheim Museum – Structural concept and detail

As can be seen, the structural concept is simple and sensible within the context of the randomly changing geometry. Sub-structures were shop fabricated and site bolted. The diagonals were tubes and not rod cross-bracing, as has been the economical practice for years and the steelwork connections were 'engineering' rather than 'aesthetic'. All this was possible because the structure was not visible.

The design and building of the Guggenheim could not have been easy, but unlike those involved in the projects described in section **12.7,** the designers had a certain advantage which was computers. Computers, invented in the 1940s, were a commonplace tool by the end of the 20th century. In the case of the Guggenheim Museum it allowed the architect and engineer to function almost independently. The architect conceived the form of the building using three-dimensional models without any thought for the structural behaviour. To turn the architect's free form model into computer information, the model was scanned using a digitizing wand. This information was imported into a program called CATIA, first used it in 1977 to design the Mirage fighter jet. Unlike the pre-computer age, when engineers needed mathematically defined shapes for structural analysis, modern structural analysis programs work on a coordinate basis. The engineers, having the geometric coordinates of the form, could, having decided on the sensible strategy shown in **Fig. 12.63**, construct their computer model.

And even with the help of computers, unusually shaped buildings are not necessarily easy to build. The Downland Gridshell is a modest single-storey building with an incredibly complex structure made from green oak laths. A brief report [104] on the project includes *"...the slivers of timber that are the basic components of the roof...were laboriously cut into short sections..."* and *"It was repetitive and time consuming work requiring a tremendous amount of patience..."* and *"All the time the carpenters worked to printouts from the engineers...".*

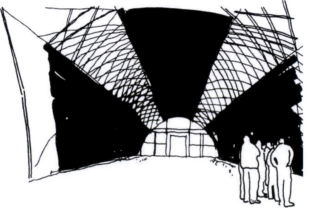

Fig. 12.64 The Downland Gridshell

Projects like this are often called innovative (which actually means something different, rather than better), but there is no useful innovation here; in the future modest single-storey work spaces will not have gridshell structures of green oak laths. However, it provides the engineers with a 'challenge' and shows that they are capable of producing 'exciting' and 'interesting' structures, meanwhile giving the client a building that will be neither easy to alter nor to extend.

Nor did computers help directly with the design of a small building designed by Norman Foster, the Business Promotion Centre in Duisburg. Because the *"The complex geometry of the perimeter beam caused huge problems on site......After several ill-fated attempts and costly delays, Hoch Tief, one of Germany's leading contractors gave up...".* [105] And again with Nicholas Grimshaw's new building at Zurich airport, which has a roof that is a *'croissant on stilts'* which for the engineers *"...developing the croissant into a form to which numerical and engineerable properties could be applied was a huge challenge...".* [106] It is interesting to see the use of the word **challenge** where **problem** would be more apt.

The program that Gehry used, CATIA, describes digital models using parametric Bézier curves and 3D surface algorithms. The parameters of these functions can be freely adjusted, making a surface accurate at any scale. Such programs allowed architects to create curved shapes without any need to make physical models. The shapes can be altered easily by changing the parameters of the Bézier curves, and this gave rise to a whole new ism of architecture that was called **parametricism**, or **parametric design**. This new way of creating shapes had no relationship with the conception of building structures. An architect who largely built her reputation on parametricism was Zaha Hadid (1950-2016). An early excursion into this new ism was the Phæno Science Center in Wolfsburg, completed in 2005 – see **Fig. 12.65**.

Fig. 12.65 – The Phæno Science Center

In this case, unlike with the Guggenheim Museum where the structure was hidden, this building's structure was, substantially, the architecture. To achieve this, 27,000 cubic metres of self-compacting concrete were poured in one of the world's largest pieces of hand-crafted formwork. And the engineer, Hanif Kara (b1982) needed two years of intense computer analysis before he was sure it would stand up – see page **528**.

 All this is part of a relatively new approach of engineers to architecture where they see themselves if not as servants, but as enablers, *"Helping architects achieve their dreams"*[107] as engineers Mark Whitby (b1950) and Bryn Bird (b1946) put it in 1988, or another engineer, Mario Salvadori (1907-1997)[108] *"I have had the good fortune to serve architects in the structural development of their dreams"*. Whereas one would have thought that engineers should ensure that the client gets sensible and cost effective engineering.

When Gothic cathedrals were built, they were built by master builders. Later people like Brunelleschi and Wren and many others could also be regarded in the same way. They worked with no distinction between engineering and architecture; as **engineer-architects**. With the rise of professions, the engineer-architect became almost extinct, Francis Fowke and William Le Barron Jenney being rare examples in the 19th century. In the 20th century it was often considered impossible for one person to be able carry out both duties, or rather see architecture and engineering as a single entity, but some did manage it – Owen Williams (1890-1969)[109] for example.

Fig. 12.66 Boots 'Wets' Factory 1930-32

In 1929, he was appointed the **engineer** and the **architect** for the new Dorchester Hotel to be built in the centre of London. His appointment was heralded by newspaper headlines such as *"Engineer instead of Architect"*.[110] Throughout the 1930s he worked on numerous projects as an **engineer-architect**. These projects included houses, flats, office and industrial buildings. The best known are probably his factory designs for the pharmaceutical firm Boots.

In 1931 Williams wrote that *"I do not believe that an architect as an architect can collaborate with an engineer as an engineer"*[111] and Gavin Stamp (b1948) wrote *"...Williams stands out and apart from Modern Movement architects in Britain for his lack of cant and for his sound, practical knowledge of building"*.[112] In fact he twice declined invitations from the MARS group, the British section of C.I.A.M, having scant respect for architects, and they repaid him by regarding him with a certain disdain. Commenting, in 1938, on the Boots factory the American critic Henry Russell Hitchcock (1903-1987) wrote *"his buildings remain ambivalent; brilliant seen from the point of view of the engineer, but tasteless and confusing in their architectural expression"*.[113] Williams' factory for Boots appears in many architectural histories but his later work does not; however, he continued working to the end of his life on both buildings and civil engineering projects, always as an engineer-architect. And more recently Santiago Calatrava (b.1951)[114] has become well known working as an engineer-architect.

Could the engineer-architect come back in some form to provide designs where the design concept automatically incorporates technical requirements without the intervention of specialists? Strangely computers could help this, especially with structures, but also with other engineering aspects. Before the introduction of user friendly programs for structural analysis in the early 1980s, engineers had to make hand calculations based on theory. This was onerous and difficult to apply to complex structures. When confronted with structures such as the Phillips Pavilion or Sydney Opera House even the best engineers had to carry out model tests in laboratories, an expensive and time-consuming process. Computer programs have changed this to a large extent and now someone who has a conceptual understanding can enter data into a computer and understand the output. This output can be checked against simple hand calculations that are explained in **Chapter 14**. See also **Chapter 19** for more on the architect/engineer relationship.

It also means that architects could get involved more knowledgeably in the structural aspects of their work and would not expect that *"Our architecture comes out of our engineering and our engineering comes out of our engineers"* [115] as architect Michael Hopkins (b1935) stated in 1985. Architects would no longer have to claim that they have an 'intuitive' understanding of structures – this is the *"perception of truth without reasoning or analysis"* [116] – the two things that allow the correct understanding of structural behaviour. After admitting she knew nothing about structures, see page **309**, Professor Sarah Wigglesworth stated her approach was *"totally, totally intuitive"*,[117] Dutch architect Dirk Jan Postel (b1957) also thinks that *"it is much better if you have intuition about form and structure"*.[118] Jørn Utzon had an intuitive feeling for structure that cost the client dearly. This 'intuition' should be replaced by a conceptual understanding which is quite a different matter and which, even in the now traditional architect/engineer relationship, would save hundreds of hours currently wasted by talking at cross purposes. And it would also make statements by architects such as *"Architecture is only made possible through structure"* [119] or *"Structure should create the architecture"*[120] more credible.

By means of various examples, this chapter shows how chosen structural systems affect any built form, and how important it is that the choice is made on the basis of conceptual understanding. Without conceptual understanding it is not possible to make the numerically predictive calculations that save time and give confidence. Clear conceptual understanding has not always been available, so for example Wren could not approach his designs completely on this basis, with some consequent problems – see pages **297-301**. When limited understanding became available in the 19th century, with skeletal structures, numerical calculation procedures emerged but this coincided, and was partly the cause of, the unfortunate split between engineers and architects.

This split has meant that the architectural profession has largely abandoned the idea of understanding structural behaviour in a mature way, and has fallen back on an aesthetic approach based on intuitive understanding. Hence conceptually flawed projects like the Phillips Pavilion, Sydney Opera House and Pompidou Centre are built, but with great difficulty due to their inherent conceptual misconceptions. In spite of this, they were lauded in the architectural press. Meanwhile engineers, who are constantly honing their calculating skills, now enormously empowered by computers, feel they should rise to the challenge of making these misconceptions work. This situation, which causes technical and financial problems with many projects, can only get better when everyone involved in the design process has a sufficient understanding of both technical and aesthetic aspects.

Perhaps instead of, as Berthold Lubetkin (1901-1990) put it, *"...experiment for the sake of difference...endless, aimless pursuit of one stunning novelty leapfrogging over another..."*,[121] more attention should be paid to the edict of HD Thoreau (1817-1862) that *"The most interesting buildings are the most unpretending"* [122] whilst always bearing in mind FM Cornford's famous Principle of the Dangerous Precedent that states that *"Nothing should ever be done for the first time"*.[123]

References – Chapter 12

1   J Fitchen – **Building construction before mechanization** – MIT Press 1988 – ISBN 0-262-06102-3
2   J Heyman – **How to design a cathedral** – Proc. ICE 1992, 92, Feb – p 24-29
3   RJ Mainstone – **Engineering a cathedral** – The Structural Engineer/Vol 72/N°1/4 January 1994 p 13-14
4   CF Barnes Jr. – **Villard de Honnecourt** – Macmillan Dictionary of Art 1996 – Vol 32 – p 569-571
5   J Fergusson – **History of Indian & Eastern Architecture** – John Murray 1910 – Vol II p 273-277
6   Vitruvius – **The ten books on architecture** – Dover Books 1960 – ISBN 486-20645-9
7   E MacCurdry – **The notebooks of Leonardo da Vinci** – Jonathan Cape 1938 – p 430
8   A Tinniswood – **His invention so fertile: A life of Christopher Wren** – Pimlico 2002 – ISBN 0-7126-7364-4 –   p 95
9   H Dorn & R Mark – **The architecture of Christopher Wren** – Scientific American July 1981 – p 138
10 J Heyman – **The science of structural engineering** – Imperial College Press 1999 – ISBN 1-86094-189-3 – p 41
11 SB Hamilton – **The place of Sir Christopher Wren in the history of structural engineering** –Transactions of the Newcomen Society XIV -1933-34 – p 27-42
12 ibid. p 39
13 CS Peach & WG Allen – **The preservation of St. Paul's Cathedral** – RIBA Journal XXXVII N° 18 – 9th August 1930 – p 668-9
14 see ref.9 p 137
15 RJ Mainstone – **Developments in structural form** – Architectural Press 2001 – ISBN 0-750-6545-11 – p 284
16 P Beaver – **The Crystal Palace** – Hugh Evelyn Ltd. 1970
17 N Pevsner – **The sources of modern architecture and design** – Thames & Hudson 1968 – p 11
18 R Mallet – **The record of the international exhibition 1862** – The Practical Mechanic's Journal Special Edition 1862 – p 60
19 K Ackermann – **Building for Industry** – Watermark Publications 1991 – ISBN 1-873200-12-9 – p 24-26
20 AW Skempton – **The Boat Store, Sheerness and its place in structural history** – Transactions of the Newcomen Society Vol. XXXII – 1959-60 – p 57-78
21 JW de Courcy – **The emergence of reinforced concrete, 1750-1910** – The Structural Engineer Vol. 65A/N° 9/September 1987
22 see ref.19 – p 45
23 Martin S Briggs – **Iron, Steel & Modern Design** – Architectural Review Vol 21 1907 – p 226
24 J Heyman – **Wren, Hooke & Partners** – Proc. First Int. Congress on Construction History – Madrid 2003
25 A Mace – **The RIBA Guide to its archive and history** – Mansell Publishing Ltd. 1986 – ISBN 0-7201-1773-9
26 JH Weiss – **The making of technological man** – MIT Press 1982 – ISBN 0-262-23112-3 – p 173
27 AW Skempton – Proc. ICE. Vol 1. Pt III, 1952 – p 405
28 DP Billington – **Robert Maillart's Bridges** – Princeton Univ. Press 1979 – p 47
29 C Wise in New Civil Engineer, 29 May 2003 – p 38
30 EJ Diestelkamp – **Richard Turner and the Palm House at Kew Gardens** – Transactions of the Newcomen Society 54, 1982 – p 4
31 see Chapter Five of – **Survey of London Vol XXXVIII – The Museums Area of South Kensington & Westminster** – Athlone Press 1975
32 H Loyette – **Gustave Eiffel** – Rizzoli International Publications Ltd. 1985 – ISBN 0-8478-0631-6
33 ibid. p 111
34 ibid. p 122
35 **THE WEEK** – 31 May 2003 – p 7
36 RMJ Sutherland – **The age of cast iron 1780-1850: Who sized the beams?** – Essay in **The Iron Revolution** – ed. Robert Thorne – p 28
37 HW Rosenthal – **The teaching of structure** – Building Design. 17th October 1986 – p14
38 O Popovic Larsen & A Tyas – **Conceptual structural design** – Thomas Telford 2003 – ISBN 0-7277-3235-8 – p 82
39 A Service – **Edwardian Architecture** –Thames & Hudson 1977 – p 14
40 M Droste – **Bauhaus** – Taschen 1993 ISBN 3-8228-0295-6

41   various – **De Stijl: 1917-1931 Visions of Utopia** – Phaidon Press Ltd. 1982 – ISBN 0-7148-2438-0
42   C Lodder – **Russian Constructivism** – Yale University Press 1983 – ISBN 0-300-02727-3
43   CS Eliel et al – **L'esprit nouveau - Purism in Paris 1918-25** – Harry N Abrams Inc. 2001
44   WJR Curtis – **Le Corbusier: Ideas and forms** – Phaidon Press Ltd. 1986 – ISBN 0-7148-2790-8 – p 43
45   Le Corbusier – **Towards a new architecture** –The Architectural Press 1927
46   K Frampton – **Le Corbusier** – Thames & Hudson 2001 – ISBN 0-500-20341-5 – p 29
47   see ref.44 – p 105
48   see ref.44 – p 69
49   L Hellman – **Architecture for beginners** – Unwin paperbacks 1986 – ISBN 0-04-7200033-2 – p 109
50   R Banham – **Theory & design in the first machine age** – Architectural Press 1962 – p 329
51   J-M Pérouse de Montclos – **Étienne-Louis Boullée** – Flammarion 1994 – ISBN 2-08-010075-0
52   **Enc. Brit. Micropædia Vol. 2** -15th Edition – p 423
53   L Krier – **Albert Speer: Architecture 1932-1942** – Aux Archives D'Architecture Moderne1985
54   C Tisdall & A Bozzolla – **Futurism** – Thames & Hudson 1977 – Ch 6
55   see ref.42 – p 7-18
56   see ref.54 – p 132
57   B Risebero – **Modern architecture and design** – MIT Press 1983 – ISBN 0-262-68046-7 – p 167
58   New York Times – 23 April 1967
59   R Buckminster Fuller – **4D Time lock** – Biotechnic Press 1970
60   B Lawson – **How Designers Think** – Architectural Press 1980 – I SBN 0-85139-852-9 – p 65
61   D Scott-Brown – Journal of American Institute of Architects July 1968 – p 230
62   D Nixon & J Kaplicky – **Skin** – Architectural Review vol CLXIX Nº 1037 July 1983 – p 54-59
63   S Lyall – **Masters of Structure** – Laurence King Publishing 2002 – p 96-103
64   **Schalen und Behälter** in **Festschrift** – **Ulrich Finsterwalder** – Verlag G Braun Karlsruhe 1973 – p 75-94
65   ibid. p 81
66   C Faber – **Candela/ Shell builder** – Architectural Press 1962
67   F Candela – **Stereo-structures** – Progressive Architecture – June 1954 – p 84-93
68   **p/a views – critical discussion of stereo-structures** – Progressive Architecture – June 1954 – p 84-93
69   **critical discussion of stereo-structures parried by Candela** – Progressive Architecture – August 1954 – p 15-16
70   see ref.66 – p 14
71   M Pawley – **Buckminster Fuller** – Trefoil Publications Ltd. 1990 – ISBN 0-86294-160-1 – p12
72   J Meller ed. – **The Buckminster Fuller Reader** – Jonathan Cape 1979 – p 292
73   J Kadlcak – **Statics of suspension cable roofs** – Balkema 1995 – p 2-4
74   ibid. p 5-7
75   Y. Tsuboi & M. Kawaguchi – **Suspension structure for the Tokyo Olympics** – Proc. of Symposium on High-rise & Long-span structures – Japanese Soc. for the Promotion of Science – Sept. 1964
76   P Rianni – **Kenzo Tange** – Hamlyn 1970 – p 35
77   M Trieb – **Phillips Pavilion: Space calculated in seconds** – Princeton Press 1996
78   N Matossian – **Xenakis** – Kahn & Averill 1986 – ISBN 0-900707-82-8 – p 110
79   ibid.
80   A Tzonis – **Le Corbusier: The poetics of machine and metaphor** – Thames & Hudson 2001 – ISBN 0-500-283-192 – p 227
81   D Billington – **The tower and the bridge** – Princeton 1983 - ISBN 0 691 02393 – p 169
82   J Yeomans – **The other Taj Mahal** – Longmans & Green 1968
83   **The Arup Journal** – October 1973
84   F Fromont – **Jørn Utzon et l'Opéra de Sydney** – Gallimand 1998
85   Y Mikami – **Utzon's sphere** – Shokokusha Tokyo 2001 – ISBN 4-395-00712-0
86   B Murray – **The saga of the Sydney Opera House** – Spon 2003 – ISBN 0-415-32522-6
87   see ref.83 – p 5
88   see ref.82 – p 42
89   see ref.85 – p 58
90   see ref.82 – p 51
91   ON Arup & GJ Zunz – **Sydney Opera House** – The Structural Engineer March 1969 – p 101
92   A Holgate – **The art in structural design** – Clarendon Press 1986 – p 20
93   Discussion on paper by ON Arup & GJ Zunz – **Sydney Opera House** – The Structural Engineer ,October 1969, Nº10, vol.47 – p 421
94   C Norberg-Schulz & Y Futagawa – **Jørn Utzon - Sydney Opera House 1957-73** – Global Architecture Nº 54 – ADA Edita 1980
95   see ref.81 – p 170
96   see ref.86 – p 13
97   P Rice & L Grut – **Main structural framework of the Beaubourg centre** – acier/stahl/steel 9/1975 – p 298

98 ibid. p 297
99 ibid. p 297
100 C Davies – **High Tech Architecture** – Thames & Hudson 1988
101 M Pawley – **The secret life of the engineers** – Blueprint March 1989 – p 36
102 H Iyengar et al – **The structural design of the Guggenheim Museum, Bilbao, Spain** – The Structural Engineer vol 78/Nº 12 20 June 2000 – p 20-27
103 ibid. p 20
104 **Small project - winner** – British Construction Industry Awards – October 2002
105 G Bramante – **The Columbus Egg** – World Architecture Nº 33 – p 89
106 A Mylius – **Clockwork croissant** – New Civil Engineer 27.02.2003 – p 22
107 **Helping architects achieve their dreams** – NCE CONSULTANTS FILE April 1988
108 D Gans ed. – **Bridging the gap** – Van Norstrand Reinhold 1991 – ISBN 0-442-00135-5 – p xiii
109 D Cottam – **Owen Williams** – Architectural Association 1986 – ISBN 0-904503-71-2
110 ibid. p 53
111 ibid. p 163
112 ibid. p 11
113 see ref.19 – p 71
114 L Molinari – **Santiago Calatrava** – Skira 1999 – ISBN 88-8118-525-3
115 see ref.101 – p 36
116 **The Chambers Dictionary** 1993 – p 879
117 see ref.38
118 see ref.38 – p 91
119 see ref.19, p 177
120 R Thorne – **Structural stylists** – Building Design June 24 1988 – p 16
121 A3 Times No.10 Vol 4 1988 – p18
122 HD Thoreau – **Walden** – Princeton 1971
123 FM Cornford – **Microcosmographia Academica** – Metcalfe & Co. 1908

CHAPTER 13 *Structures in existing buildings*

So far the process of structural conception and design has assumed that choices can be made both for the basic structural concept, for the material and for the form of individual structural elements. This changes fundamentally when existing buildings are involved. The process of structural design is applied to existing buildings for several reasons, the most common being:

- **The building is exhibiting signs of structural failure**
- **There is a change of use that means higher loadings will be imposed**
- **A new use requires structural alterations**
- **A new use requires an extension to the existing building**

Whichever of these are the reason, they all have the same starting point; **the existing building**. What is required is a **structural appraisal**. This comes in two parts. The first part is called the **structural investigation**, and is carried out to answer the question **what is the structure?** The second part is called the **structural assessment**, which is carried out to answer the question **how strong and stiff are the existing load paths?** Confusion can be caused by using terms such as structural survey, structural investigation, structural assessment and structural appraisal without stating clearly what they entail. Here the word survey is NOT used, and the other terms are used strictly as defined.

13.1   Structural investigation

The main purpose of structural investigations is to answer the question **what is the structure?**

There are many similarities between structural investigations and geotechnical site investigations – see section **8.3** – and indeed a geotechnical site investigation may also be required. So there are four similar stages for a structural investigation:

- **Desk-based research**
- **Physically examining the structure and obtaining samples**
- **Laboratory testing site samples**
- **Preparing a report**

For existing structures, desk-based research is a complex issue as there are many possible avenues that may be explored. The starting point for this is the history of the building. However visual inspection, and a little local knowledge, should readily establish whether the building is **traditional** or **engineered**.

As explained in section **0.5 – The modern approach to structural design**, this approach is likely to have been used for buildings that have iron or steel structures, beginning in the nineteenth century, and similarly for reinforced concrete structures, which were introduced towards the end of the same century. Often these engineered structures are not visible in a finished building, but the presence of slender individual columns and large spans indicates such a structure is present.

When the building has been constructed using what are generally termed traditional methods, the situation is radically different. The use of such methods is usually obvious from the presence of short spans, walls with small openings and tiled pitched roofs. The engineering approach was usually applied to timber and masonry structures later than those of iron, steel or concrete, though when and to what is not easy to establish. As a guide, the first British code of practice for masonry – CP111 – only appeared in 1948, whilst one for timber – CP 112 – only in 1952. This is not to say that engineering principles were never applied to timber and brick structures before these dates, however as it is far harder to identify brick or timber in a building as part of an engineered structure, than a steel or concrete one.

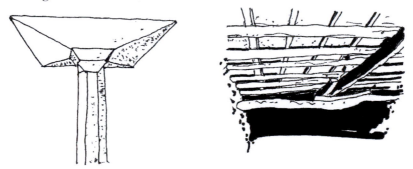

Fig. 13.1 Engineered and traditional structures

The reason that this distinction is so important is that traditional buildings were not based on an understanding of structural mechanics, but on **rules of thumb**, which often left some elements **over-designed** according to current engineering practice, whereas other elements were **under-designed**. This is often a source of difficulty when calculations are being made to justify a historic structure.

So the first step in the investigation is to make a preliminary visual inspection, taking the opportunity to make a thorough photographic record. The next step is to obtain documentary information. Depending on the age of the building, and whether the structure is engineered or not, there are a number of routes.

For engineered buildings there will have been working drawings produced for fabrication and construction. However the chances of these existing are surprisingly rare, as they are often destroyed, sometimes almost casually. Possible sources are building control authorities, the original architects, engineers or contractors.

For non-engineered structures, depending on the age, the possibility of any drawings existing is effectively zero. However, there are sources of information such as histories of building construction, and publications of various learned bodies.

For instance there are very few drawings extant for Georgian terrace houses, however their construction is well-documented, which greatly aids any structural investigation. In contrast a full set of working drawings for Penn Station in New

York still exist; this is despite the fact it was completed in 1910, and infamously demolished in 1963.

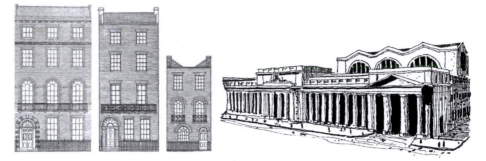

Fig. 13.2 Georgian terrace and Penn Station

Armed with whatever documentary information there is available, and knowledge of the nature of the proposed intervention, the scope of the structural investigation can be determined. As structures are normally hidden from view, these often need to be physically exposed, which if the building is still in use can cause difficulties. In some countries historic buildings may have a special legal status, which means physical investigations require official permission. Often the foundations need to be investigated, which requires excavation and quite possibly carrying out a geotechnical investigation – see section **8.3.**

There are several reasons for exposing the structural elements of the existing structure, which are:

- **Understanding the structural arrangement**
- **Establishing the structural materials used**
- **Determining the size of structural elements**
- **Taking samples for laboratory analyses**
- **Carrying out non-destructive testing**

Understanding the structural arrangement requires an initial assessment from any documentary data and the visual appearance of the building. This should indicate what type of structure the building has: traditional timber floors, metal roof trusses, reinforced concrete frame for instance. Then the basic determination of structural materials and element sizes will give a clearer idea of the whole structural scheme.

However visual inspection and the measurement of the overall size of structural elements cannot give all the information about the structure. For this, non-destructive testing and/or the laboratory testing of samples is invaluable.

With masonry, small samples of the bricks themselves and the mortar will indicate their strength, but other, less obvious factors can influence the strength of a brick wall. The bonding of the wall and the method of laying the bricks is important. To speed construction various features are used, most of which reduce the strength. These include laying the bricks 'frog down,' or shell bedding them. Where walls are made of two leaves, how the leaves are connected or bonded together can affect overall strength. The two leaves maybe insufficiently bonded together, or original metal wall ties may have corroded away.

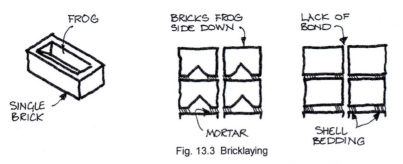

Fig. 13.3 Bricklaying

With brick walls it is also important to find out how walls are connected to horizontal structures, as this will affect their effective length – see **Fig. 6.62** – and consequently their load capacity. Radar can been used to determine the presence of voids or metallic inserts in masonry; however, especially if the masonry is damp, radar cannot give precise information, but will indicate where intrusive examination should be done. Other means of obtaining information about hidden details are metal detectors and borescopes.

When confronted with a metal structure, depending on its age the metal will be cast iron, wrought iron or steel, or more unusually aluminium. The investigation not only has to determine the shape and sizes of the individual members, but samples have to be taken to determine the engineering properties of the metal. Also important are the connection details, which may be difficult to view, and again the engineering properties of bolts and/or rivets need to be established. Expert visual examination can often determine the date of a metallic structure, which may indicate likely mechanical properties.

Existing concrete structures present an obvious difficulty; it is not easy to see through concrete. A concrete structure may be constructed in several ways. It could be a steel structure cased in concrete, a common way of providing fire-protection up until the 1970s. It can be a normal reinforced structure, possibly it could be pre-stressed – see section **4.7**. Pre-cast concrete elements may be present, especially in concrete floor structures.

For concrete structures it is important to know what is inside the concrete, which in the absence of original drawings, clearly presents problems. With good access it is possible to see metal inside concrete using an electrical phenomenon known as eddy currents. Handheld devices have been developed with eddy current sensors that react when a metal object is encountered. These can be used to identify the position of reinforcing bars, and may indicate their diameter, but not the steel grade. The type of steel can only be determined by taking a sample.

For timber structures the first step is to identify the species, and estimate the stress grade. In timber engineering, timber is graded for the presence of naturally occurring defects, knot, splits, shakes or grain density. This can be done visually, provided the surveyor is experienced. More difficult is to determine the joint details, as these are made in numerous different ways. In older structures, the traditional joints of mortise and tenon and lap joints are common, often strengthened with wooden pegs, nails, screws and assorted pieces of metal. With adequate access, visual inspection can furnish the joint details.

Since World War Two, starting in the United States, modern structural timber joints were developed that use nail-plates, toothed connectors, split-ring connectors, joist hangers and many other specially shaped pieces of metal. Some of these can be seen whereas others – toothed and split-ring connectors – see **Fig. 13.4** – are hidden inside the structure.

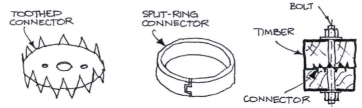

Fig. 13.4 Timber connectors

Timber members may not be simple solid elements but can be built up from layers like plywood or laminated beams – see **Figs. 5.15** and **11.33**. Timber can also be used to make I-beams and box-beams, often using plywood or other timber sheet material as the webs. Plywood, or even plasterboard can be part of a load path that carries wind load by acting as wind-bracing – see section **9.4**.

During a structural investigation, a proprietary structural system may be encountered. These have been used, in various forms, since the nineteenth century, indeed what are now considered standard reinforced concrete structures were originally called the 'Hennebique system' – see **Fig. 12.19**. As these systems come and go due to commercial and other pressures, their presence and details can be confusing. If the date of the building is known, contemporary technical literature can provide useful information. An example is the Metropolitan Floor used in the United States between 1899 and the 1930s, shown in **Fig. 13.5**.

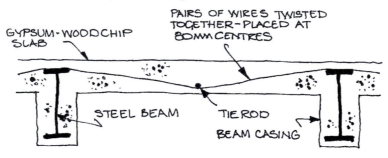

Fig. 13.5 Metropolitan Floor

If the reason for the structural investigation is because the **building is exhibiting signs of structural failure**, then recording these signs is an important part of the investigation, but this should be part of any investigation. Typical signs are cracks in brickwork or concrete, or deflection of beams or floors, or the leaning of columns or walls that are visible to the naked eye. It may be necessary to monitor these over time, to check whether the structure is still moving. There are numerous electronic devices that can measure and monitor these movements.

Another sign of structural failure is the degradation of the structural material. The corrosion of steel used in steel sections, as reinforcement in concrete or as wall ties to connect separate leaves of masonry, can lead to structural failure. Concrete can be attacked by chemicals and timber by fungi and insect larvae. See also section **5.4 Non-structural effects**.

Like geotechnical investigations, structural investigations come in all shapes and sizes. For example if a new opening is to be made in an existing internal wall, a single visit may determine that the wall is non-loadbearing, so no further investigation is needed. At the other end of the scale, structural investigations carried out on Gothic cathedrals or nuclear power stations, for whatever reason, are likely to be lengthy, detailed, time-consuming and expensive.

13.2   Structural assessments

The objective of a structural investigation is to obtain physical information about the existing structure of a building. As already noted the structural assessment then takes this information and applies engineering principles so that the important question, **how strong and stiff are the existing load paths** can be answered.

The arrangement of the structure, the sizes of structural elements and the characteristics of the structural material are known from the investigation. Deciding the acceptable allowable stresses for the structural materials might require consultation of historic documents. It might seem straightforward to calculate using accepted calculation procedures – see **Chapters 14** and **17** – the strength and stiffness of the load paths. Here the presence of engineered and non-engineered structures makes a big difference.

Engineered structures, this generally means steel, iron or concrete structures will probably have been designed using simple concepts of simply supported beams, or two-dimensional trusses or frameworks. To appraise the strength and stiffness of the load paths, the initial design has to be replicated, but using modern codes of practice as a first step. This can be problematic as modern codes often demand higher loads, especially wind loads, than earlier ones, and are not framed with earlier structural engineering practice in mind.

Often proprietary structural elements are used in engineered structures whose strength was justified by load tests, but finding documentary evidence, even if the proprietary product is identified, can be difficult. For example, the Metropolitan Floor was just one many systems used in steel buildings in the early part of the nineteenth century. Shown in **Fig. 13.5**, the Metropolitan system was a catenary floor – see **Fig. 7.8** – and was approved by testing in 1899, both for loads and fire resistance. Current codes of practice do not include catenary floors nor gypsum/ woodchip 'concrete' as fire resistance, so showing how such a floor is still adequate is not straightforward, though it can be done. Because of such difficulties, many clients and engineers prefer the removal of unfamiliar structural elements rather than their re-use, but this is not necessarily cost-effective, and is a poor excuse for demolishing historic structures that have functioned satisfactorily for decades.

Where the building has a non-engineered structure, it is far more difficult to identify simple structural models that follow currently accepted design procedures. This is because the original builders did not think of the structure as something separate from the complete building. Nor did they have an understanding of structural behaviour that was based on the principles outlined in this book. This often resulted in structures whose structural behaviour is hard to understand using the basic concepts. This is true even where the structure is easy to see, for instance in the barn, built in 1426, shown in **Fig. 13.6.**

Fig. 13.6 Medieval barn structure

Clearly these 'non-engineering' designers were aware that loads had to be carried, but how was based on cumulative experience, and related **rules of thumb**. It is easy to romanticise the understanding that these earlier builders had of structural behaviour, but it is well to remember that what remains are the structures that did not collapse, but many did – see section **0.3**. However complicated it is to find structural load paths that can be checked against engineering theory, because a structure has been there a long time it be concluded that it not tiptoeing to collapse.

Fig. 13.7 A structure that has tiptoed to collapse

In **Fig. 13.6** the fact that the designers knew that the structure needed to be braced laterally and longitudinally is evident. But engineering designers tend to avoid curved elements and connections where the members do not meet at a single point – a node. This is to avoid complicated load transfer models that are difficult to understand. A good example showing evidence of structural understanding coupled with a non-engineering approach is the load-bearing trussed partition used in some houses in the 18th and 19th centuries. In a diagram from a 1797 book on carpentry – see **Fig. 13.8** – the understanding is evidenced by the presence of diagonal trussing members. But the non-engineering approach is shown by the lack of complete triangulation, and members not meeting at nodes.

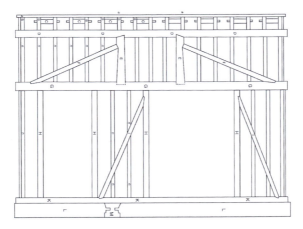

Fig. 13.8 Diagram from 1797 book

The structural assessment part of the structural appraisal report will identify load paths in the existing building; identify the type and strength of the structural materials used, and pinpoint parts of the existing structure that need strengthening or repair. This could mean making structural elements stronger or stiffer, reducing the span and/or increasing the capacity of joints.

13.3   Structural strengthening

Where parts of an existing structure are found to be inadequate, then they need to be strengthened or replaced. Structural elements, beams, columns, walls and foundations, can be strengthened by altering the cross-section, changing the material or adding material of a different kind. This can be done in numerous different ways: extra steel can be welded or bolted to steel members, concrete members can be enlarged, timber members can be strengthened with plywood decking or steel plates, etc. External steel rods can be added to concrete, steel or timber beams. Strips of stiff, strong modern materials such as fibre reinforced polymer (FRP) or carbon fibre can be bonded to concrete, timber or steel. **Fig. 13.9** shows just a few of the many ways that beams can be strengthened. Some of these methods can also be applied to columns.

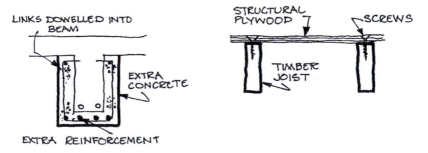

Fig. 13.9 -1 Examples of structural element strengthening

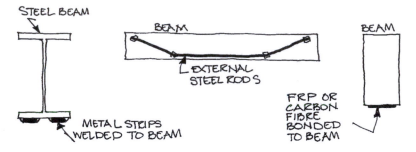

Fig. 13.9-2 Examples of structural element strengthening

Frequently joints in steel and timber structures have to be strengthened either because rust or types of rot have degraded the strength or, as is often the case with traditional timber joints, they are under-strength. Again there are many ways of doing this. For instance the rotten ends of joists supported by a brick wall are cut at the face of the wall, and supported on new metal joist hangers. Or a steel column, rusted-through at its base, is burnt off and welded to a new fabricated piece – see **Fig. 13.10**.

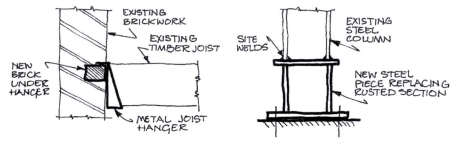

Fig. 13.10 Types of joint strengthening

Existing foundations may need to be enhanced for various reasons. This includes inadequate strength, or that they are not deep enough to avoid seasonal movement. To resolve these problems new foundations are often inserted under the existing ones; this is called **underpinning**. The use of underpinning is more than 100 years old; a famous historical example is the underpinning of the walls of Winchester Cathedral, carried out between 1906 and 1911 almost single-handedly by deep-sea diver William Walker (1869-1918).

Traditional underpinning excavates under the existing foundation, and then pours a larger and deeper mass concrete foundation. To avoid large scale temporary works to hold up the existing wall and foundation, construction proceeds in short lengths, with construction proceeding by alternate sections.

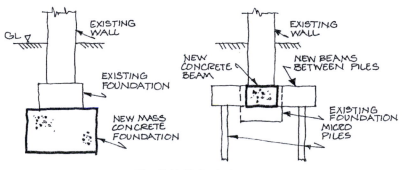

Fig. 13.11 Underpinning

There are modern alternatives, using mini-piles for instance. These are placed either side of the existing foundation and are linked by beams that pass through the wall. A new concrete beam links these beams, and continuously supports the wall – see **Fig. 13.11**.

Often strengthening has to be introduced **within the original load path**, in which case an important part of the process is **load transfer**. Clearly **a load path must be available at all times**, so during strengthening a **temporary load path** is required. After the new load path has been constructed, in a space previously occupied by part of the original load path, the load has to be **transferred**. The load transfer process is shown in **Fig.13.12**.

Here **A** shows the original structure and load path. By introducing temporary supports, **B**, a temporary load path is introduced and the new structure can be built. When it is ready, a cement-based material, often called dry-pack, **C**, is put between the new structure and the existing to form a solid joint, which allows the temporary supports to be removed. The dry-pack remains part of the final strengthened load path **D**.

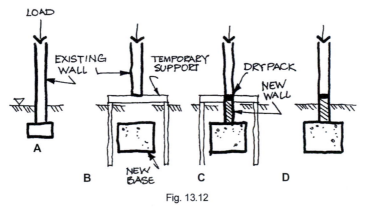

Fig. 13.12

Although there are numerous different reasons and different ways of strengthening structures, whenever the new strengthening elements are part of what was the original load path, the process shown in **Fig. 13.12** always has to be followed conceptually. This is to ensure that there is **a load path** at every stage of the strengthening process.

An extraordinary case of strengthening an existing structure was when the already-constructed supporting structures for the Sydney Opera House roof, which had been designed to support thin shells, were found to be unable to support the weight from the final roof design. Strengthening was done by removing the existing concrete from the supporting structures by using explosives, so more reinforcement and concrete could be bonded to the original reinforcement.

13.4   Structural interventions

Where an existing building is being altered in a way that changes the original load paths, new load paths have to be introduced. These alterations are almost invariably to take away existing structure to create wider spans or new openings. This means that loads have to be diverted to a new structure, which needs new load paths to the foundations. Above the new openings **new spanning members** have to be introduced. At their supports, locally applied loads usually require a form of **padstone** to ensure the existing structure is not locally overstressed. This load may then be dispersed through lower existing structure, or may require a new load path all the way to the foundations.

A simple example

Consider the four-storey masonry wall shown in **Fig. 13.13**. Uniformly distributed loads are applied to the wall at each level from floors spanning onto the wall. There is a small existing opening at each level, but two new large opening are to be made at **level 2** and **level G**. At points **A**, **B**, **C** and **D**, the new spanning members will cause concentrated loads – shown by bold arrows. Under **A** and **B**, the loads can disperse through the existing wall between **levels 1** and **2**. At **level G** the loads from **D** can disperse through the panel of masonry between the new opening and the existing opening. But the concentrated load at **C** needs a new load path all the way to the foundations.

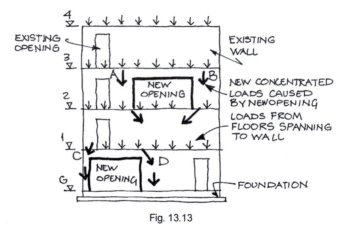

Fig. 13.13

New beams are required over the new openings, and under the beams new load-spreading padstones are needed. New stronger masonry may be needed on **level 2**, between the existing and new openings. Under the padstone at **D**, new vertical structure could be required and the foundation may need to be strengthened locally. The rest of the existing structure between **levels G** and **1** could remain unaltered. All this would depend on detailed numerical calculations. The structural interventions are shown in **Fig. 13.14**.

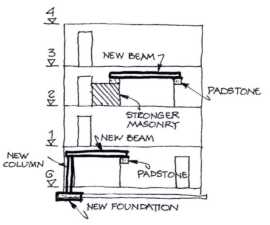

Fig. 13.14 Structural interventions

Figs. 13.13 and **14** show the essential conceptual ideas for structural interventions. A structural appraisal is carried out to give technical information about the existing structure. New structures are introduced locally where alterations are being made – in this case new beams over the new openings. The existing structure is checked locally for overstressing, and new elements are introduced if this is the case. New padstones are shown under the new beams, and new stronger masonry replaces the existing masonry at **level 2** under the left-hand end of the new beam. Altered load paths are checked down to the foundations – here the existing masonry between **levels 1** and **2** is deemed adequate, as are the existing masonry and foundations between **levels G** and **1** to the right-hand side of the new opening. However the higher loads to left of the new opening at **level G**, now require a new structure, a column. This has to be supported on a new foundation.

13.5   Structures for additions

Structural additions can be above, below, alongside or within the existing building; each type of addition has its own requirements but all have the basic requirement, that existing load paths within the building must be maintained, or new structure has to be introduced that provides alternative paths.

Where an addition is built **under** an existing building – a new basement – a number of factors influence the construction. They depend on whether the new basement is **A**, within the existing buildings perimeter, **B**, on it or **C**, outside it – simplistically shown in **Fig.13.15**. In each case the major requirement is provide a foundation design that provides support for the existing building.

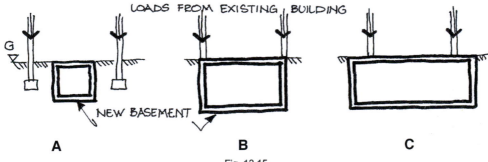

Fig. 13.15

In case **A**, provided the new basement is far enough from the existing foundations, it can be an independent structure. Case **B** will require that the existing vertical structure be underpinned – see section **13.3**. In case **C**, it would be possible to construct the new basement walls independently, then provide new beams, a form of underpinning, to carry the existing loads to new basement walls. The basement can then be excavated top-down. The details of the construction of all these cases are dependent on the scale of the existing building, however, conceptually, the same principles apply. The design of the basement itself must follow the concepts outlined in section **8.7**.

Where the addition is **above** the existing building – new floors – then existing load paths have to carry extra loads. One way of reducing the impact of extra floors is to make new loads as small as possible. In this way it may be possible to restrict the increase to a small percentage of the existing total load – not more that 10% is a common rule of thumb – which can mean no additional work is needed on the existing structure.

Where this is not possible, the load paths identified in the structural appraisal need to be checked in detail. This is normally limited to vertical structural elements, as existing spanning elements are not normally affected. The concepts of strengthening have already been outlined in section **13.3**.

New structures **alongside** an existing one are not likely to have much impact, unless the new structure spans onto the existing one. Here again the principles of checking load paths and strengthening apply. Where the new structure is totally independent of the existing one, care must be taken to avoid new foundation loads overloading existing ones. Quite possibly at points of support, new foundations may be required similar to that shown at ground level in **Fig. 13.14**.

An extreme situation of a new structure alongside an existing one is in a practice called **façadism**. This is when the whole of the existing building is demolished except for the external façades; often only the street one is kept. The reason for this curious process is basically an unresolved dispute between supporters and opponents of modern architecture. When a non-modern building is no longer useful and demolition is proposed, it is often considered by a large number of people that at least the façade should remain. So a compromise is reached whereby a completely new building is constructed behind the façade; this can result in an unhappy compromise – a type of Frankenstein building – disliked by both parties – see **Fig. 13.16**.

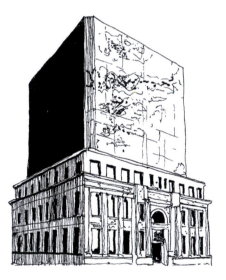

Fig. 13.16 A 'Frankenstein' building

That aside, for the engineering, a modified form of the principles shown in **Fig. 13.12** has to be followed. Now the whole of the façade has to be supported, horizontally to resist wind loads on the now temporarily free-standing façade, and quite possibly its self-weight also has to be supported vertically to allow the construction of new foundations or basements. Then the new building is constructed behind the façade. When it is complete, the existing façade has to be linked to the new structure which will then carry the horizontal wind loads and the self-weight of the existing façade – see **Fig. 13.17**.

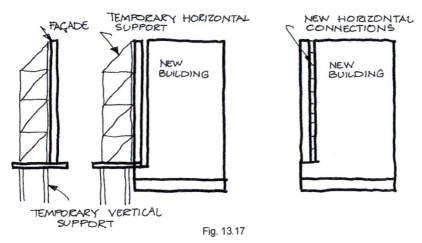

Fig. 13.17

There are various ways of treating façades; they can be totally incorporated into the new building or they can be kept outside the new building as a semi-free-standing element. In either case the structural connections between new and old have to be durable and cope with forces caused by temperature effects. Where the façade is of ageing masonry, the most common case, how discrete structural connections can be made that will resist tension forces, due to wind suction – see **Fig. 9.4** – need careful consideration.

Where new structures are required **inside** an existing building, once again all the principles apply, with special attention being made to any connections between the new structures and the existing ones.

13.6   Two examples

Seeing how structural engineering concepts apply to actual buildings is not always easy. With existing buildings, seeing how concepts apply to strengthening, repairs and alterations can be even more difficult due to the wide variety of structures encountered, and the different ways interventions are done. To help make this connection, two real projects are briefly described.

York Minster strengthening

York Minster – see **Fig.13 18** – in the North of England is the second largest Gothic cathedral in Northern Europe, and was built between 1230 and 1472; it replaced a Norman church built in 1080.

Fig. 13.18 York Minster

In 1407 the central tower collapsed and had to be rebuilt, and during the ensuing centuries the building suffered from religious vandalism, fires and neglect. By 1967 parts of the building were leaning dangerously, and large cracks had appeared indicating that the building, especially the central tower, was close to collapse, so something had to be done.

What was done, by an engineering team led by Poul Beckmann (b1924) and David Dowrick, was to make a painstaking investigation of the building to discover the reasons for the structural problems, and then propose and supervise appropriate remedial works. The whole project took seven years, and entailed engineering analysis and design of the highest quality, for which Beckmann and Dowrick were awarded the prestigious Telford Gold Medal by the Institution of Civil Engineers.

The basic problem was that the size of some of the foundations meant that the stresses on the soil – see **Fig. 8.1** – were too high under the tower, and there were big differences between foundation pressures under different parts of the building. This meant that the deflection of the ground – the **settlement** – was uneven, causing what is called **differential settlement**. Using sophisticated back analysis the **settlement history** of the whole building, from the date of the construction of the Norman church in 1080AD to the time of the analysis, was calculated – see **Fig. 13.19**.

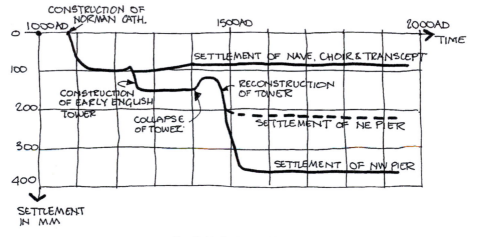

Fig. 13.19 Settlement history

What this showed, and site observations confirmed, was that some parts of the building had settled **100mm**, whereas the central tower had settled unevenly between **220mm** and **370mm**. Further analytical work was done that produced a theoretical structural model that predicted the observable movements of the superstructure. In other words the engineers had **understood the structural arrangement** by producing a sophisticated **predictive model**. With the building understood structurally, it was possible to make proposals for remedial work; obviously this was to be extensive and is described in detail elsewhere – see *Further Reading*. Here only one aspect of the work is explained.

As the size of the foundations under the central tower resulted in high foundation stresses leading to large settlements, what was required were bigger foundations to reduce the foundation stresses and minimise future settlement, so the existing foundations needed to be enlarged. This was done by building concrete 'extensions' to the existing foundations and joining the new to the old with **prestressing bars** –

see **Fig. 4.84** – which would ensure the old and new foundations acted as one structural element – see **Fig. 13.20**.

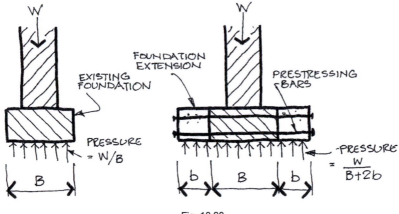

Fig. 13.20

Fig. 13.20 shows what is required; however building the foundation extensions does not alter the pressure distribution under the old foundations. The foundation extensions have to be loaded and the existing foundations have to be unloaded; there has to be a **load transfer**. This is shown conceptually in **Fig. 13.12**, but in this case there are no temporary supports to carry the whole load. This was done was by putting **prestressing flat jacks** under the new foundation extensions. Flat jacks are basically circular metal balloons. Initially thin, with the top and bottom faces almost touching, they are put between two structural elements. The jack is then pumped up hydraulically to force the faces apart, thus loading the structural elements.

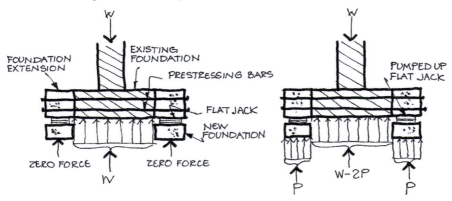

Fig.13. 21 Foundation details

Fig. 13.21 shows how the load is transferred. Initially the reaction to the total load **W** is provided by the stresses under the existing foundation whose sum equals **W** and there is **Zero Force** under the foundation extensions. The flat jacks are then inflated causing a load **P** between the foundation extension and the concrete pressure pad. Now the sum of the stresses under each pressure pad is equal to the jack load **P**. As the existing and foundation extensions now form one structural element, the stresses under the previously existing foundation are reduced, so that their sum is equal to **W – 2P**.

What this very brief description of the structural remedial work carried out on the York Minster shows is how the basic concepts of a thorough investigation followed by understanding and analysing the existing structure were the key to making appropriate remedial proposals, and how the proposals themselves required imaginative engineering. It is perhaps hard to convey just how much surveying work was required, and the level of intellectual effort needed to understand the structural behaviour.

Royal Exchange Theatre, Manchester

One of the most unusual structural interventions was the construction of a new theatre in-the-round inside the Royal Exchange in Manchester, a Northern English city. The current building is the much modified third exchange building, all the exchange buildings being built as trade centres for the Lancashire textile trade. The third was constructed between 1867 and 1874 in a Neo-classical style, and was extensively modified between 1914 and 1931 to create what was claimed to be the largest trading space in the world. It took a direct hit from a bomb during WWII and was subsequently partially rebuilt in yet another modified form. It closed for business in 1968 but fortunately was spared demolition, a fate which was suffered by many fine old buildings in that era.

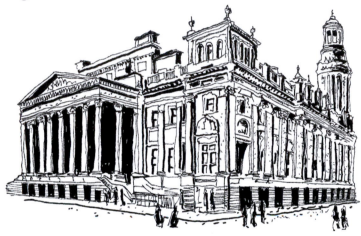

Fig. 13.22 The Royal Exchange in the nineteenth century

In 1972 it was decided to build a new theatre within the old trading hall. It was to be sited under the existing central glazed dome within a rectangle of 30m by 21m. The corners of this rectangle were defined by the existing 3m square masonry pillars that supported the domed roof.

The first task was to understand the existing structure. Here the design team was extraordinarily lucky as the architects for the 1914 to 1931 alterations, Bradshaw, Gass and Hope, were still in business and had all the original drawings. Examination of these showed that the existing floors could not support the extra load from the two new seating galleries and a new roof. However this examination showed that the brick pillars could support additional load, and this became the controlling factor for the structural intervention. The only option was to design a building for which the seating galleries and the roof would be supported on the existing pillars, with the total load restricted to the pillars' extra capacity.

An all-steel trussed structure was designed, made from tubes ranging in diameter from 90mm to 270mm. The total load of 150 tons was carried to the pillars by 4.7m deep primary trusses. Spanning onto these were 4.7m deep secondary trusses. These trusses made up the supporting structure for the subsidiary steel structure of the theatre. This was built inside the 30m by 21m square created by supporting structure. To ensure that the extra load was applied to the centre of the pillar, 500mm wide slots, 2.75m high and 1.83m deep, were cut into the pillars to allow the ends of the trusses to be positioned correctly. The new supporting structure is shown in **Fig. 13.23**.

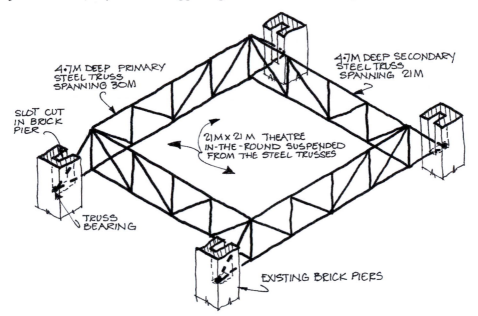

4·7M DEEP PRIMARY STEEL TRUSS SPANNING 30M

4·7M DEEP SECONDARY STEEL TRUSS SPANNING 21M

SLOT CUT IN BRICK PIER

21M x 21M THEATRE IN-THE-ROUND SUSPENDED FROM THE STEEL TRUSSES

TRUSS BEARING

EXISTING BRICK PIERS

Fig. 13.23 The supporting structure of the Theatre in the Manchester Royal Exchange

Due to the lightness of the theatre construction, the main loading was due to its use, and this caused larger than normal static deflections. Whilst the static deflections were considered acceptable, they indicated that there could be problems with the dynamic behaviour of the theatre structure – see **Chapter 15**. The calculated **natural frequencies** of this structure were in the range that could be troublesome, so, in the absence of significant damping – see section **15.3** – it was decided to add specific damping elements. These were similar to car shock absorbers, and were located at the joints between the theatre structure and the supporting structure. This is an example of the philosophy outlined in **Chapter 15**; that is to identify the possibility of potential dynamic problems, and, if necessary, take preventative measures as part of the initial design.

13.7 Conclusions

Few books on general engineering design devote much space to the role of structural design with reference to existing buildings. With the increased interest in the conservation of historic buildings, coupled with the financial and environmental advantages of reusing existing buildings rather than replacing them, the importance of structural design related to existing buildings has become more important.

Although all aspects of structures in existing building must follow the same behaviour as those in new structures, there is no longer the freedom of choice there is for designing a new structure. Here the roles of the structural investigation and assessment are of critical importance. As with geotechnical investigations, this work has to be thorough, but as this can be slow and expensive there is often pressure to save on it. This is a false economy, as the cost of rectifying the construction problems this can cause will be far higher than the savings made by less-than-thorough investigations and assessments.

Because new structures in existing buildings are rarely on show, it may appear that the options that design offers are pedestrian and mundane, whereas the opposite is true, as the two examples show. Designing structures for alterations to existing buildings often requires more ingenuity and imagination than is needed for new structures, which, whilst not designing themselves, usually have hundreds of precedents. There are many special products, structural and otherwise, to aid the renovation of existing buildings, but every renovation requires a combination of intelligence, imagination, and engineering common sense. The fact that most of this remains hidden from view does not detract from the possible elegance of the solutions.

Further reading

Poul Beckmann and Robert Bowles – **Structural Aspects of Building Conservation** – Elsevier Butterworth-Heinemann – 2nd Edition 2004. **NOTE**: This book gives detailed information about all aspects of the repairs made to **York Minster**.

BRE Digest 366 – **Structural Appraisal of existing buildings including for a material change of use** – 2012

Building and Construction Authority – **Periodic Structural Inspection of Existing Buildings** – 2012

M Bussell – **Appraisal of existing iron and steel structures** – Steel Construction Institute – 1997

M Bussell, D Lazarus and P Ross – **Retention of masonry façades: best practice guide** – Concrete Industry Research and Information Association – 2003

David Dowrick – **The use of prestressing in the foundation strengthening at York Minster** – Ground Engineering Nov.1970, p14-17

Michael Forsyth (ed.) – **Historic Building Conservation** in 3 volumes.

    Volume 1 – Understanding Historic Building Conservation – Wiley-Blackwell – 2013

    Volume 2 – Structures & Construction in Historic Building Conservation – Wiley-Blackwell – 2014

    Volume 3 – Materials & Skills for Historic Building Conservation – Wiley-Blackwell – 2012

Barry Haseltine – **The evolution of the design and construction of masonry buildings in the UK** – Proceedings of the 15th International Brick and Block Masonry Conference – 2012

Jacques Heyman – **The Stone Skeleton: Structural Engineering of Masonry Architecture** – Cambridge University Press – 1995

Institution of Structural Engineers – **Appraisal of existing structures** – ISE 3rd Edition 2010

Susan Macdonald (ed.) – **Concrete: building pathology** – Blackwell Science – 2003

Peter Ross – **Appraisal and repair of timber structures** – Thomas Telford 2002

James Sutherland, Dawn Humm and Mike Chrimes (eds.) – **Historic Concrete** – Thomas Telford 2001

CHAPTER 14 *A simple approach to calculations*

In this chapter the concepts of structural behaviour are used to give a simple approach to calculations that check the fundamental points of any proposed structural system. No more than the usual arithmetic operations and simple algebra are used. The ability to make basic calculations gives 'the designer' the self-sufficiency, not only to conceive structural schemes, but also to arrive rapidly at sizes for the principal elements. Clearly these simple calculations will be re-done in detail for the final scheme, but what is intended here is to show how, what are sometimes called 'back of an envelope' calculations, are made. Of course envelopes should not really be used, as all calculations are extremely important project information and should be numbered and filed in a proper manner see section **19.4**. To gain full benefit from this chapter all the exercises should be done.

Calculations, even for a small project can be lengthy, so it is essential to be clear at all times just exactly what the point is of the current step. In section **0.6** the following questions were asked:

- **What is the function of the structure?**
- **What are the loads and the load paths?**
- **How does the structure transfer the loads?**
- **What are the forces in the structural elements?**
- **Does the structure have overall stability?**
- **Is any element too slender?**

The core of the book, **Chapters 1** to **7**, show conceptually how these questions are answered and **Chapters 9** and **10** show how the concepts apply to the structures of real projects. Now, with the conceptual understanding, the questions asked in the **Introduction**, and returned to in **Chapter 9**, can be put more succinctly as:

- **What is the structure?**
- **What are the loads?**
- **Is the structure strong enough?**

To which has to be added:

- **Is the structure stiff enough?**

14.1 The basic questions

Before actual numbers are introduced, a strategy is required to answer the basic questions given above.

- **What is the structure?**

To enable calculations to be made the proposed structure has to be idealised by a **structural diagram** – see section **2.3**. Below **Fig. 14.1** shows them for a **cantilever** and a **simply supported beam**.

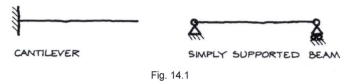

Fig. 14.1

These two structures form the basis for the simple approach to calculations.

• **What are the loads?**

Chapter 1 dealt at some length with the nature and source of structural loads. To do calculations, specific values are needed, and these are available for most situations.

• **Is the structure strong enough?**

Actually this question should really be:

• **Are the stresses in the structure acceptable?**

This is really the central question. The answer involves all the concepts described in **Chapters 2** to **6**, and is what is usually called **structural analysis.** This, together with **section design**, are the core subjects of official structural engineering. They are used in this chapter in a simplified form to find the magnitude of the internal forces - axial, shear and bending moments – and to check that the stresses in each element are within those permitted.

• **Is the structure stiff enough?**

Nothing has been said so far about stiffness except from the point of view of slenderness – see section **6.4**. Here the phenomenon of buckling was examined in some detail. This is an important aspect of stiffness, but when in use the structure must not deflect 'too much'. This is not really a conceptual question as it is obvious, and 'just needs to be calculated to see if it is within acceptable limits'.

14.2   Units

When calculations are carried out, the numbers represent the **size** of a 'physical' quantity – length, axial force and area are examples. To calculate the loading on a structure not only must the physical size of the structure be known, but also the size of loads – that is, the size of **forces**, and units for measuring them are needed.

In the past many systems of measurement have been used. These systems were often local, or national, but engineering now uses an international system of measurement called the Système International, or **SI** for short. This system is based on the metric system, which uses units like metres and kilograms, but it also uses a unit of measure for force called the **Newton**. This unit is only used for calculations in physics and engineering, so is not widely known. The reason for its existence is to clarify the old problem of trying to distinguish between **mass** and **force**. They are related by the famous equation stated by Isaac Newton:

Force = Mass × Acceleration

In the **SI** system, the standard measure of mass is the **kilogram** and the standard measure of length is the **metre**. As acceleration is the rate of change of velocity, it is measured is metres per second per second or **m/s^2**. The definition of a **Newton** is, from Newton's equation, the force required to accelerate **1 kilogram** by **1 m/s^2**.

$$1 \text{ Newton} = 1 \text{ Kilogram} \times 1 \text{m/s}^2$$

As the acceleration, **g**, due to gravity is known to be **9.81 m/s^2**, the force exerted by a mass of one kilogram on the surface of the earth is:

$$1 \text{kg} \times g = 1 \text{kg} \times 9.81 \text{m/s}^2 = 9.81 \text{N}$$

As 9.81 is almost 10, **1 kilogram can be thought of as causing a force of 10N**. Here calculations are only made for structures with static loads rather than dynamic loads – see **Chapter 15** – so there is no need to be concerned about mass and force, so loads and forces can all be measured in Newtons. In the SI system there are certain names and prefixes for useful multiples:

1000 times – kilo (k)   **1,000,000 times – mega (M)**

In structural design, it is often convenient to use units of force that are larger than the Newton:

1 kiloNewton = 1kN = 1000N   **1 megaNewton = 1MN = 1,000,000N**

These are used to keep the number of zeros that appear in the calculations under control. The **kiloNewton** is commonly used, and for large structures, **megaNewtons** are used. Forces can now be expressed as single forces in **N**, **kN** or **MN**, as forces per length in **N/m**, **kN/m** or **MN/m**, and as forces per area as **N/m^2**, **kN/m^2** or **MN/m^2**.

Description	Units	Description	Units
Loads on an area	kN/m^2	Loads along a beam or truss	kN/m
Concentrated loads	kN	Reaction forces	kN
Axial or shear forces	kN	Bending and torsional moments	kN.m
Stresses in an element	N/mm^2	Foundation stresses	kN/m^2

Table 14.1   Typical units

14.3   Real loads

No calculation for structures makes sense if the wrong load is used. Calculating the load on a structure is not usually a fascinating process, but it has to be right. In **Chapter 1**, three types of loads were identified: **Natural loads** – section **1.1**; **Useful loads** – section **1.2**; and **Accidental loads** – section **1.3**. In this chapter only **Natural** and **Useful** loads will be considered. It might seem difficult to decide what load wind, snow or the use of a room for an office will cause, but fortunately all this has been 'decided' by various authorities and form part of official **Building Codes** in many countries; therefore no hard decisions are required. This official quantifying of loads is relatively recent, mainly during the 20th century; before that, those responsible for the calculations had to decide for themselves what appropriate loads would be. Only three types of **natural loads** are used here; **gravity, snow** and **wind**.

Gravity loads that act vertically are due to the self-weight of the building construction, which includes the weight of the structure itself – see **Fig. 1.20**. The basis for the calculation of these loads is the **density** of the materials in **kN/m^3**. It is possible to find the density of any type of material in engineering handbooks – some are given in **Table 14.2**.

Material	kN/m³	Material	kN/m³
Water	10	Stone	27
Soil	18	Glass	28
Concrete	25	Steel	77
Brickwork	20	Aluminium	27
Plaster	18	Timber	7

Table 14.2 Typical densities of building materials

With this information, it is a simple matter to calculate the weight of any construction. Extra information can be obtained from technical literature.

Example 14.1   Calculate the gravity load of the weight of the floor construction shown in the figure. Note the dimensions are shown in millimetres but are converted to metres for the calculation.

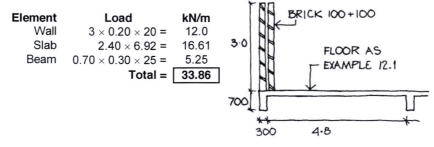

Material	Load	kN/m²
Timber	$0.022 \times 7 =$	0.15
Screed	$0.060 \times 22 =$	1.32
Concrete	$0.200 \times 25 =$	5.00
Plaster	$0.025 \times 18 =$	0.45
	Total =	6.92

Example 14.2   Calculate the gravity load on the beam under the wall shown in the figure. The floor construction is as Example.14.1

Element	Load	kN/m
Wall	$3 \times 0.20 \times 20 =$	12.0
Slab	$2.40 \times 6.92 =$	16.61
Beam	$0.70 \times 0.30 \times 25 =$	5.25
	Total =	33.86

How wind acts on a building is a complex matter but has been simplified so that a static **wind load** can be calculated for any 'normal' building. There are a number of factors that influence the calculated wind load and these are:

1   **Geographical location**
2   **Local topography, height and size of building**
3   **Shape of building**

The basic data is the **basic wind speed, V**; this depends on the geographical location and is obtained from a wind map. This wind speed is then modified, by published factors, **S**, for the type of local topography – city, outskirts, open countryside, the height – wind speed increases with height – and the overall size of the building. The basic wind speed is multiplied by the factor to give the **design wind speed, Vs**. The wind pressure, **q**, is then obtained from: $q = 0.613 \times V_s^2 \times 10^{-3}$ **kN/m²**, where the wind speed is in metres per second, and 0.613 is half the density of air in kg/m³. This load is then applied to the surfaces of the building after being multiplied by a pressure coefficient **Cp**, that takes into account the shape of the building.

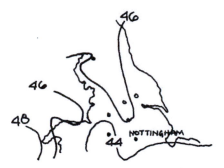

Fig. 14.2 A wind map showing contours of Basic Wind Speed **V**

Height – m	City	Outskirts	Country
10	0.62	0.74	0.88
20	0.75	0.90	0.98
30	0.85	0.97	1.03
50	0.98	1.04	1.08
100	1.10	1.12	1.16

Table. 14.3 – Typical **S** factors

Element	C_p - windward	C_p - leeward
Wall	+0.7	-0.3
Roof slope 0°	-0.8	-0.6
Roof slope 10°	-1.1	-0.6
Roof slope 20°	-0.7	-0.5
Roof slope 30°	-0.2	-0.5
Roof slope 50°	+0.2	-0.5

Table 14.4 Typical coefficients C_p

The plus signs in **Table 14.4** indicate that the wind is causing a pressure on the element and minus signs suction.

Example 14.3   Calculate the wind loads on a building 10m high with a pitched roof of 20°. The basic wind speed, from the wind map is 44m/s and the building is on the outskirts of a city.

∴ Basic wind pressure **q = 0.613 × (0.74 × 44)^2 × 10^{-3} = 0.65kN/m^2**

Element	$q \times C_p$	kN/m^2
Wall - windward	0.65 × (+0.7)	+0.46
Wall - leeward	0.65 × (-0.3)	-0.20
Roof windward slope	0.65 × (-0.7)	-0.46
Roof leeward slope	0.65 × (-0.5)	-0.33

Useful loads obviously depend on the use and are tabulated in the various national codes. Typical loadings for different uses are given below.

Use	kN/m²
Residential use	2.0
Offices	2.5
Shops, showrooms, laboratories	3.0
Theatres, cinemas	4.0
Dance halls, churches, gymnasiums	5.0
Plant rooms, storage areas	6.0

Table 14.5 Typical useful floor loads

People = 2.5kN/m²

Depending on the use of the space, the floor load for its use must be added to the gravity load from the construction. Sometimes additional loads are added to take account of loads from services or non-loadbearing partitions. Typical values are **0.3kN/m²** for service loads and **1.4kN/m²** for partitions. It is more common in calculations to call the gravity loads the **dead load (DL)** and the useful load the **live load (LL)** and in calculations these are often kept separate.

Example 14.4   Calculate the **live load**, the **dead load** and the **total load** for the floor shown which is to be used for a laboratory.

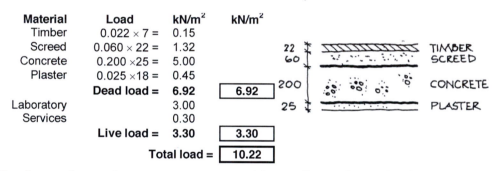

Material	Load	kN/m²	kN/m²
Timber	$0.022 \times 7 =$	0.15	
Screed	$0.060 \times 22 =$	1.32	
Concrete	$0.200 \times 25 =$	5.00	
Plaster	$0.025 \times 18 =$	0.45	
	Dead load =	**6.92**	6.92
Laboratory		3.00	
Services		0.30	
	Live load =	**3.30**	3.30
	Total load =		10.22

Roofs may also need to support **snow loads**. These will vary due to the slope and the geographical location. The density of fresh snow is **1.0kN/m³**. Many countries produce **snow maps** similar to wind maps.

In terms of calculations, loads are somewhat problematic because at the initial stages of a project there may be many unknowns that will affect the loading. In many countries there are loading codes some of which, especially for wind and snow, can be quite complex. Therefore it is always sensible to **err on the safe side** when computing the loads. The values shown in this section are 'typical' and are given to allow basic calculations to be made, where possible reference should be made to the applicable code.

14.4   The beam and the cantilever

In this section the bending moments and shear forces are calculated for a simply supported beam and a cantilever. These structures are shown in **Fig. 14.1**. This is the beginning of structural analysis; trying to find more and more general methods for doing this occupied engineers for a large part of the 19th century, and all of the 20th.

A simple supported beam has a span of **L**, and carries a uniformly distributed load of **w** per unit length. The bending moment and the shear force are required at each point of the beam. First the reaction forces are required and then the moments and shears are found at a point **x** from the support by considering moment and vertical equilibrium.

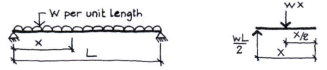

Fig. 14.3 Simply supported beam

At the position **x** along the beam, the bending moment, M_x, will be equal to the sum of all the moments from the left, or from the right. That is, from the left, the reaction **wL/2**, times the lever arm **x**, minus the load **w** × **x**, times the lever arm **x/2**, which is the equation:

$$M_x = w \times L/2 \times x - w \times x \times x/2$$

And the shear force, S_x, is the sum of the vertical forces. That is, from the left, the reaction, **wL/2**, minus the load, **w** × **x**, this is the equation:

$$S_x = w \times L/2 - w \times x$$

To find the bending moment and the shear force at the support, M_{SUP} and S_{SUP}, **x** = **0** is entered into the equations and at the centre for M_{CEN} and S_{CEN}, **x = L/2**, these give:

$$M_{SUP} = 0 \text{ and } S_{SUP} = wL/2 \quad \text{and} \quad M_{CEN} = wL^2/8 \text{ and } S_{CEN} = 0$$

Example 14.5   The beam in Example 14.2 is simply supported and spans 4.8m. The slab live load is as Example 14.4. Calculate the bending moment at the centre and the shear force at the supports, also calculate the values for the bending moment and shear force 1.3m from the support. Draw the bending moment and shear forces diagrams showing the values.

Total uniformly distributed load (**UDL**) on the beam = Dead Load (**DL**) + Live Load (**LL**)
= 33.86 + 2.4 × 3.30 = **41.78kN/m**

Force	Calculation	Result
S_{SUP}	(41.78 × 4.8) ÷2	100.27kN
$S_{1.30}$	100.27 − (41.78 × 1.3)	45.96kN
M_{CEN}	(41.78 × 4.8^2)÷ 8	120.33kN.m
$M_{1.30}$	(100.27 × 1.3) − (41.78 × 1.3^2)÷2	95.05kN.m

100.27 kN
45.96 kN

SFD

95.05 kN.m   120.33 kN.m

BMD

Note that the abbreviations **SFD** and **BMD** have been used for **Shear Force Diagram** and **Bending Moment Diagram**, and these will be used from now on.

The approach used for the simply supported beam can be used for the cantilever. A cantilever has a span of **L**, and carries a uniformly distributed load of **w** per unit length. The bending moment and the shear force are required at each point. First the reaction forces are required and then the moments and shears are found at a point **x** from the support by considering moment and vertical equilibrium.

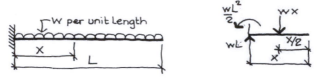

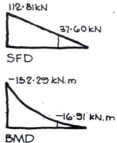

Fig. 14.4 A cantilever

So, following the process used for the simply supported beam, the bending moment and shear force at a distance **x** from the support are:

$$M_x = wL \times x - wL^2/2 - wx \times x/2 \quad \text{and} \quad S_x = wL - wx$$

To find the bending moment and the shear force at the support, M_{SUP} and S_{SUP}, **x=0** is entered in the equations and at the free end for M_{END} and S_{END}, **x = L**, these give:

$$M_{SUP} = -wL^2/2 \text{ and } S_{SUP} = wL \quad \text{and} \quad M_{END} = 0 \text{ and } S_{END} = 0$$

Example 14.6   A cantilever of 2.7m is loaded as Ex.14.5. Calculate the bending moment and the shear force at the support, and 1.8m from the support. Draw the bending moment and shear forces diagrams showing the values.

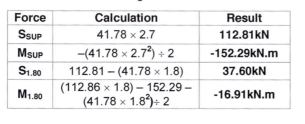

Force	Calculation	Result
S_{SUP}	41.78×2.7	112.81kN
M_{SUP}	$-(41.78 \times 2.7^2) \div 2$	-152.29kN.m
$S_{1.80}$	$112.81 - (41.78 \times 1.8)$	37.60kN
$M_{1.80}$	$(112.86 \times 1.8) - 152.29 - (41.78 \times 1.8^2) \div 2$	-16.91kN.m

Exercise 14.1   Check the values of the bending moments and shear forces calculated for the simply supported beam and the cantilever, in the examples above, by considering the forces to the **right**.

Exercise 14.2   Calculate values at regular intervals along the simply supported beam and the cantilever and draw shear force and bending moments to scale.

Exercise 14.3   Recalculate the values of the shear forces and bending moments assuming the concrete slab is 300mm thick and the live load is for an office with allowances for services and partitions.

In the calculations carried out so far the values of the reaction forces, **wL/2**, for the beam and $-wL^2/2$ and **wL**, just 'appeared'. These are true for a **UDL** of **w** along the whole of the element but suppose the loading is different. A simply supported beam with a **partial UDL** and **point load** is shown in the figure.

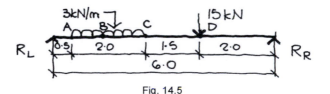

Fig. 14.5

The loads shown ignore the weight of the beam and the numbers are simple to aid the explanation. Now, before the values of shear forces and bending moments can be calculated, the values of the reactions, **R_L** and **R_R**, have to be known. These are calculated using the concepts explained in section **1.5** for the man on the plank.

They are found by considering moment equilibrium about the right-hand and left-hand supports respectively and equating clockwise and anti-clockwise moments.

Example 14.7 For the beam shown in Fig. 14.5 calculate reactions, R_L, R_R, bending moments M_B, M_D, and the shear forces, S_B, S_D at the positions shown. Draw the bending moment and shear forces diagrams showing the values.

First about the right-hand support for R_L:

$$R_L \times 6.0 = (3 \times 2.0) \times (3.50 + (2.0 \div 2)) + (15 \times 2.0)$$

$$\therefore R_L = (27 + 30) \div 6.0 = 9.50 \text{kN}$$

and about the left-hand support for R_R:

$$R_R \times 6.0 = (3 \times 2.0) \times (0.50 + (2.0 \div 2)) + 15 \times 4.0$$

$$\therefore R_R = (9 + 60) \div 6.0 = 11.50 \text{kN}$$

$$R_L + R_R = 9.50 + 11.50 = 21 \text{ kN}$$

$$\therefore \text{ Sum of reactions = Total load (checks)}$$

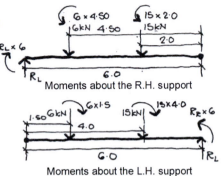

Moments about the R.H. support

Moments about the L.H. support

As the reactions are known, the shear force and the bending moment can be calculated at any point on the beam. This is done in exactly the same way as before by considering the vertical and moment equilibrium at the position on the beam where the values are required. The calculations are made using the equilibrium to the **left**.

Force	Calculation	Result
S_B	$9.5 - (3 \times 1.0)$	6.50kN
M_B	$(9.50 \times 1.5) - (3.0 \times 1.0^2)/2$	12.75kN.m
S_D	$9.50 - (3 \times 2.0)$	3.50kN
M_D	$(9.5 \times 4.0) - (3 \times 2.0 \times 2.5)$	23kN.m

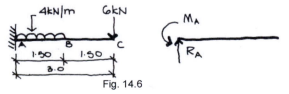

Exercise 14.4 Calculate all the values for the shear forces and bending moments shown on the diagrams. Check by calculating from the **right**. Calculate intermediate values and draw the diagrams to scale.

For cantilevers, the calculation of the reactions is simpler. As there is only one vertical reaction it must equal the total load. The moment reaction is equal to the moment due to all the loads.

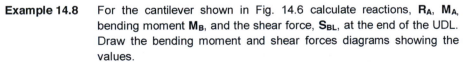

Fig. 14.6

Example 14.8 For the cantilever shown in Fig. 14.6 calculate reactions, R_A, M_A, bending moment M_B, and the shear force, S_{BL}, at the end of the UDL. Draw the bending moment and shear forces diagrams showing the values.

Force	Calculation	Result
R_A	$6 + (4 \times 1.5)$	12kN
M_A	$-(6 \times 3.0) -$ $((4 \times 1.5^2) \div 2)$	−2.5kN.m
S_B	$12 - (4 \times 1.50)$	6kN
M_B	$-22.5 - ((4 \times 1.5^2) \div 2)$ $+ 12 \times 1.50$	−9kN.m

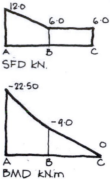

The pinned and fixed supports of the beam and cantilever are idealisations that are rarely found in real structures – see **Chapter 10**. In the case of the cantilever, instead of having a fixed support, the usual case is for a cantilever to be an extension of a supported beam. So a simply supported beam can cantilever beyond its support. To see how this affects the reactions, shear forces and bending moments, the beam shown in **Fig. 14.5** and the cantilever shown in **Fig. 14.6** can be combined to give the structure shown in **Fig. 14.7.1**.

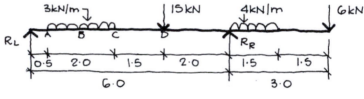

Fig. 14.7.1

Example 14.9   For the beam and cantilever shown in Fig. 14.7.1 calculate the reactions, bending moments and the shear forces at the same positions shown in Examples 14.7 and 14.8. Draw the bending moment and shear force diagrams showing the values.

The reactions, shear forces and bending moments for the beam and cantilever have already been calculated independently, but the effect of the cantilever support moment now has to be taken into account. The loads on the cantilever apply a moment to the support and this is balanced at the support by the equal and opposite support moment. The beam now provides the resistance for the cantilever moment. The effect on the beam is to apply a clockwise moment to the right-hand end. This is the same as the concept explained in **Figs. 2.42-43**. This applied moment causes equal and opposite reactions at the left- and right-hand supports of the beam and a constant shear force in the beam itself. These moments and reactions are shown in **Fig. 14.7.2**.

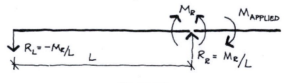

Fig. 14.7.2

In this case; **M_A = 22.50kN.m** and **R_L = −M_A/L = −22.50 ÷ 6.0 = −3.75kN**, the minus sign indicating that the reaction is downwards.

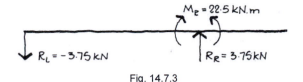

Fig. 14.7.3

For vertical equilibrium $R_R = -R_L$ and, as well as a constant shear force, there is also a linearly varying bending moment in the beam due to the effect of the cantilever. The values of the bending moments, due to the cantilever, are given at the positions for which the bending moments have been calculated for the load on the beam; these are calculated directly by proportional triangles.

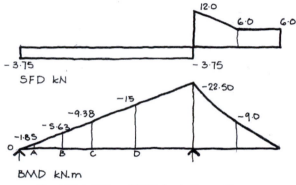

Fig. 14.7.4 SFD and BMD due to the cantilever

The final reactions and the complete shear force and bending moment diagrams can now be drawn by simply adding, with respect to sign, the values given in **Fig. 14.7.3** to those given in **Example 14.7**.

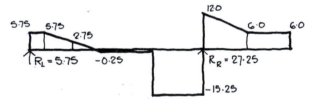

Fig. 14.7.5 Final Reactions and SFD

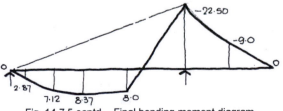

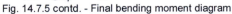

Fig. 14.7.5 contd. - Final bending moment diagram

In **Fig. 14.7.5**, positive and negative values appear on both the shear force and bending moment diagrams. **Figs. 2.30** to **2.37** show how a sign convention for shear forces and bending moments can be introduced. **Fig. 14.7.6** shows how this sign convention applies to the beam and cantilever.

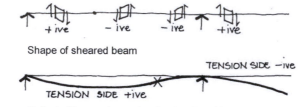

Shape of sheared beam

TENSION SIDE −ive

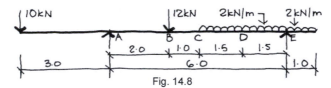

TENSION SIDE +ive

Deflected beam shape showing tension side

Fig. 14.7.6 Shear force and bending moment sign convention

Exercise 14.5   For the beam and cantilevers shown in **Fig. 14.8** do all the calculations and draw all the diagrams that were done for **Example 14.9.**

Fig. 14.8

(Partial answers: R_A = 24.33kN , R_E = 5.67kN , M_A = –30.0kN.m, M_C = 1.0kN.m)

It is essential that these examples are thoroughly understood, and that all the exercises in this section are done before proceeding. This understanding may be reinforced by inventing further exercises, particularly using real loads. The understanding of this section can be used as a basis for carrying out simple calculations for an amazing array of structures, as will be shown in the following sections.

14.5   More complex beams

For the beam and the cantilevers, all the forces, shear forces and bending moments were calculated using Newton's third law which is

- **To every action there is an equal and opposite reaction.**

Which leads to the following statements for **equilibrium** – see page **29**

- **Sum of vertical loads = Sum of vertical reactions**
- **Sum of horizontal loads = Sum of horizontal reactions**
- **Moments due to loads = Moments due to reactions**

These statements must always be true everywhere in every structure. As there were no horizontal loads on the beam or cantilever only two of these statements were used.

Suppose a beam of span **L**, loaded with a **UDL** of **w**, has a pinned joint at the right-hand support, but instead of a pin joint at the left-hand support it has a fixed support. There are now three reaction forces; vertical forces R_L and R_R at the supports plus a moment reaction M_L at the fixed support.

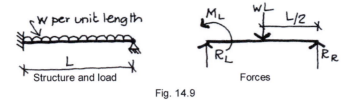

Structure and load   Forces

Fig. 14.9

Note that in **Fig. 14.9** the moment caused by the **UDL** has been shown as the total load **wL** acting at its centre **L/2**. Now the equilibrium conditions for vertical forces and moments can be used:

$$R_L + R_R = w \times L \qquad \text{and} \qquad M_L + R_R \times L = (w \times L) \times L/2$$

There are three unknowns to be calculated, R_L, R_R and M_L, but there are only two equations from the equilibrium conditions. This is a basic difficulty in structural analysis, but it is avoided here because simplification is required, not mathematical analysis. What can be done? A possibility is to make one of the unknowns zero. If $R_R = 0$ is chosen then the structure becomes a cantilever, or if $M_L = 0$ is chosen the structure becomes a simply supported beam, both of which have already been calculated.

$R_R = 0$; Cantilever $M_L = 0$; Simply supported beam

Fig. 14.10

The forces calculated from either of these structures will be in equilibrium and so will be satisfactory from the statical point of view; that is they are **statically admissible solutions**. But the deflections caused at the supports seriously violate the geometric conditions because δ_R or θ_L are not zero, so they are **kinematically inadmissible solutions**.

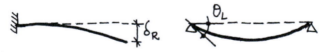

Fig. 14.11 Inadmissible deflections

However, it is possible to alter the structure in another way that allows the forces to be calculated from the equilibrium conditions. This can be done by introducing a pin joint within the length of the beam. This turns the structure into a simply supported beam with one end supported by a cantilever.

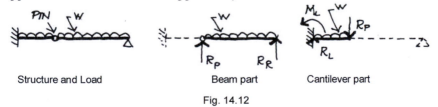

Structure and Load   Beam part   Cantilever part

Fig. 14.12

Finding the forces in this structure follows directly from the previous examples. First the reaction forces are found; then these are used to calculate the shear forces and bending moments at any point. This is illustrated by making the calculations for the structure shown in **Fig. 14.13**.

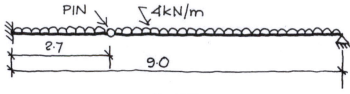

Fig. 14.13

Example 14.10 For the structure shown in **Fig. 14.13** calculate reactions, bending moments and the shear forces. Draw the bending moment and shear force diagrams showing the values

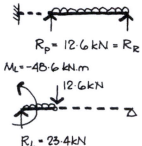

Force	Calculation	Result
R_P	$(4 \times 6.3) \div 2$	**12.6kN**
R_R	$(4 \times 6.3) \div 2$	**12.6kN**
R_L	$12.6 + (4 \times 2.7)$	**23.4kN**
M_L	$-(12.6 \times 2.7) -$ $((4 \times 2.7^2) \div 2)$	**−48.6kN.m**

The shear force and bending moment diagrams and the deflected shape can now be drawn.

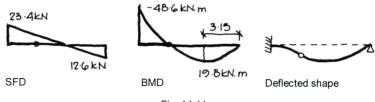

Fig. 14.14

The shear forces and bending moments calculated again provide a **statically admissible solution** and the deflected shape does not violate the support geometry. But, of course, the calculations have not been done for the original structure, but one modified by the insertion of a pin. Now three statically admissible solutions have been identified, the cantilever, the simply supported beam and the inserted pin structure. In **Fig. 14.15** the bending moment diagrams, together with the values of the reactions, are shown for these solutions. The last diagram is the result of a calculation based on the mathematical theory – see **Chapter 17**.

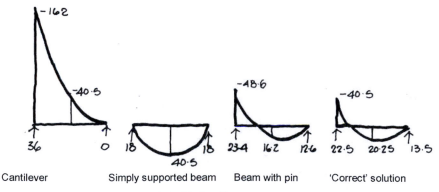

Fig. 14.15 Statically admissible bending moment diagrams and reactions

Clearly the cantilever and simply supported beam solutions are nothing like the correct solution, shown on the far right of the figure, whereas the inserted pin structure gives values within 20%. Why is this? The reason is that the pin was inserted close to the true position of the **point of contraflexure**. In **Fig. 14.7.5** the **BMD** is shown for the structure of a beam with a cantilever, and in the beam span the sign of the bending moment changes from positive, in the left-hand part, to negative, in the right-hand part. So at one point the bending moment is zero, and at this point the deflected shape changes, as is shown in **Fig. 14.7.6**. This is the point of contraflexure and it 'functions' as a pin. As **Fig. 14.15** shows, if a pin is inserted to make it possible to use the equations of equilibrium to calculate the forces, and the pin is close to the actual point of contraflexure, the calculated forces will be approximately correct, which is good enough for the simple approach.

Another important point is the role of the bending moment calculated as if the load were applied to a simply supported beam of the same span. This is often called the **free bending moment**. For this example it can be seen how the simply supported **BMD** can be added to the support **BMD** to give the final **BMD**.

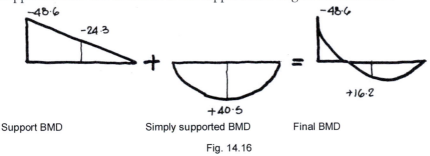

| Support BMD | Simply supported BMD | Final BMD |

Fig. 14.16

When the forces can be calculated from statics, the structure is said to be **statically determinate**; otherwise it is **statically indeterminate**. The insertion of the pin into the statically indeterminate structure, shown in **Fig. 14.12**, made it statically determinate. To show how this can be used for a more complex beam, calculate the forces in the four-span beam shown in **Fig. 14.17**.

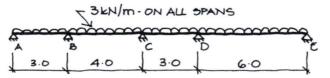

Fig. 14.17 Statically indeterminate 4-span beam

If pins were inserted at supports **B**, **C** and **D** there would be four simply supported beams – a statically determinate system which violates the continuity of the beams. Using the previous example as a guide, insert pins to the right of **B**, **C** and **D** at a distance from the support of 20% of the span.

Fig. 14.18 Statically determinate 'inserted pin' 4-span beam

Example 14.11 For the structure shown in Fig.14.18 calculate bending moments and the shear forces. Draw the bending moment and shear force diagrams showing the values.

The support moment at **D** can now be calculated as before so:

$$M_D = (3 \times 2.4) \times 1.20 + 3 \times 1.20^2 \div 2 = \textbf{10.80kN.m}$$

But the calculation for the support moment at **C** also has to take into account the moment at **D** already calculated, as this causes a reaction at the pin between **C** and **D** so:

$$M_c = ((3 \times 1.2) \times 0.60 + 3 \times 0.6^2 \div 2) - ((10.8 \div 2.4) \times 0.6) = \textbf{0kN.m}$$

Having calculated all the support moments, the bending moment diagram can be drawn. The values at mid-span have been added.

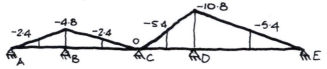

Fig. 14.19 Support BMD

The free bending moment diagrams for each span can be added to this diagram to give the final **BMD**.

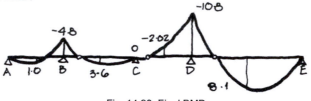

Fig. 14.20 Final BMD

The **SFD** can also be drawn. The shear in each span is the **SFD** for the span as a simply supported beam with an 'adjustment' for the effect of the support moment – this is as shown in **Fig. 14.7.3**.

$$S_{DE} = (3 \times 6.0) \div 2 + 10.8 \div 6.0 = \textbf{10.8kN} \text{ and } S_{ED} = (3 \times 6.0) \div 2 - 10.8 \div 6.0 = \textbf{7.2kN}$$

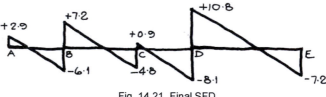

Fig. 14.21 Final SFD

For comparison the 'mathematically correct' final **BMD** is shown in **Fig. 14.22**.

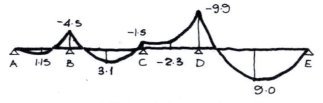

Fig. 14.22 'Mathematically correct' final BMD

The values obtained from the inserted pin structure agree reasonably with the 'correct' figures except the bending moment **M$_C$**, which is **0** instead of **−1.5**. This may seem a gross error, but this simplified approach is only trying to get a first idea of the sizes of forces and it should be borne in mind that the 'correct' figures are not correct for the actual structure for various reasons. Few building structures have perfect pin supports, the loads cannot be known with complete accuracy, the material properties of the structure may vary and so on; all these will alter the 'correct' answer.

Exercise 14.6   1 Calculate all the forces for the example in detail.
2 Calculate the forces for different positions of the pins and draw BMD and SFD.
3 Find positions of pins to give the 'correct' answer.
4 Draw the SFD for the 'correct' answer.

14.6   Simple frames

The calculation of forces in beams is used widely for parts of buildings, but often it is important to consider structural frames acting in two dimensions. Again the insertion of 'contraflexural' pins can yield useful results. Let a simple frame, as already described in section **2.5**, be loaded by a concentrated load of **40kN**. To find the bending moment, two pins are inserted at the positions of the 'guessed' points of contraflexure.

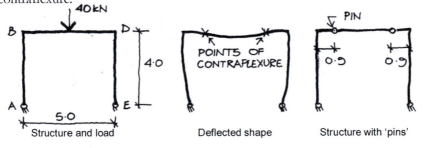

Fig. 14.23 Simple frame with vertical load

It should be noted that if a real structure had these four pins it would become a mechanism, see **Fig. 6.23**. But these are not real pins, they are points of contraflexure, that is, of zero moment.

The bending moments at the corners are calculated first, these are the shear forces at the pins multiplied by the cantilever length **0.9m**. Therefore the bending moment $M_B = -(40 \div 2) \times 0.9 = -18kN.m = M_D$, which, using the previous calculation procedures, allows the **BMD, SFD** and **AFD** (axial force diagram) to be drawn.

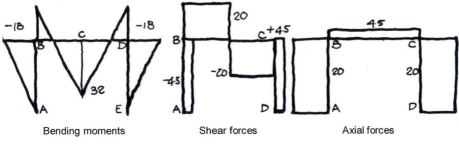

Bending moments   Shear forces   Axial forces

Fig. 14.24 Simple frame force diagrams

To clarify how these forces are in equilibrium they can be shown on a free-body diagram, similar to **Fig. 2.39**.

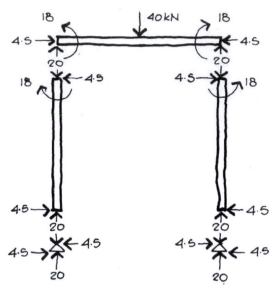

Fig. 14.25 Free body forces (kN and metres)

If the same frame is loaded with a horizontal load applied to joint **B**, then the beam will take up a double curved shape with a point of contraflexure at the centre. So a pin is inserted here, again making the structure statically determinate.

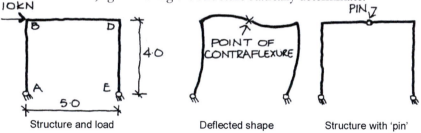

| Structure and load | Deflected shape | Structure with 'pin' |

Fig. 14.26 Simple frame with a horizontal force

The bending moments in the legs are due to the horizontal force acting at the support; this is considered to be shared equally between the legs so horizontal equilibrium is given by:

$$H_A + H_E = 10kN \quad \text{so} \quad H_A = H_E = 5kN$$

giving the moments at the top of legs as

$$M_B = M_D = 5 \times 4.0 = 20kN.m$$

These values allow all the other forces to be calculated and the force diagrams to be drawn.

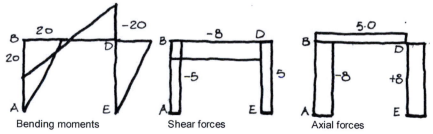

| Bending moments | Shear forces | Axial forces |

Fig. 14.27 Simple frame force diagrams for a horizontal load

If both the loads are acting together then the previous calculations would be done and the results 'added' together. So the bending moment diagrams for each load are 'added' by adding the various values, with respect to sign and the combined **BMD** is drawn.

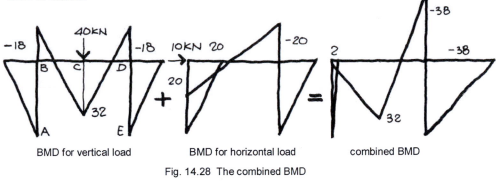

BMD for vertical load   BMD for horizontal load   combined BMD

Fig. 14.28 The combined BMD

Exercise 14.7 1 Calculate all the forces for the example in detail.
2 Draw the SFD and AFD for the combined load case
3 Draw the forces on free body diagrams for the horizontal load and the combined load case.

Sections **14.4**, **14.5** and **14.6** show how it is possible to calculate the internal forces in relatively simple beam and frame structures made from one-dimensional elements. It is essential that these three sections are thoroughly understood, as in more complex structures this interplay of bending moments, shear and axial forces constantly appears.

14.7 Calculation of stresses in beams and columns

In the previous sections, the values of three types of internal forces have been calculated for the beam and frame structures. For these structures to be strong enough to carry the calculated internal forces, the stresses caused by them must always be less than the allowable (usable) stress for the material. So two values are required, first the actual stress in the structure, f_{act}, and second the allowable stress, f_{all}. The calculations must show that $f_{act} < f_{all}$ is true for all parts of the structure for all load cases and combinations.

In this chapter only three internal forces are considered to be part of the simple approach, bending moments, shear and axial forces. Biaxial bending, see section **4.5**, and torsion, see sections **3.6** and **4.6**, are not treated here. Knowing the value of the internal forces, two questions have to be answered:

•   **What are the values of the actual stresses?**
•   **What are the values of the allowable stresses?**

The actual stresses, f_{act}, are calculated from the forces for each type of force as follows:

Axial forces, **N**, cause axial stresses, f_{ax}, and these are calculated by assuming this stress is constant over the cross-section, **A**, see **Fig. 3.29**. Therefore the actual axial stress, f_{ax-act}, is calculated by dividing the axial force, **N**, by the cross-sectional area **A**.

$$f_{ax-act} = N \div A$$

Shear forces, **S**, cause shear stresses, f_{sh}, and these are calculated by assuming this stress is constant over the shear cross-section, A_{sh}, see section **3.6**. Therefore the actual shear stress, $f_{sh\text{-}act}$, is calculated by dividing the shear force, **S**, by the shear cross-sectional area A_{sh}.

$$f_{sh\text{-}act} = S \div A_{sh}$$

Bending moments, **M**, cause bending stresses, f_{bm}, which are calculated by assuming this stress varies linearly across cross-section, with maximum values at the outer faces, see section **3.4**. The maximum actual bending stresses, $f_{bm\text{-}act}$, are calculated by dividing the bending moment, **M**, by a quantity called the **section modulus, Z**.

$$f_{bm\text{-}act} = M \div Z$$

The **section (or elastic) modulus**, is a property of the cross-section. In general this quantity has to be derived mathematically and the formulae and specific values are widely available. For a rectangular section of width **b** and depth **d** the section modulus $Z = bd^2/6$.

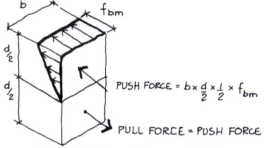

Fig. 14.29 Rectangular beam push/pull forces

The expression for the section modulus for a rectangular beam can be derived by considering the push-pull forces caused by the linear stress distribution, see **Figs 3.42-43** and **14.29**. To calculate the push force, the area property of a triangle is used, that is the **area = ½ × height × base**. So the push force is the **stress volume**. To calculate the size of the lever arm between the push and pull force the fact that, for a triangle, the centroid is **1/3** of the height above the base, is used.

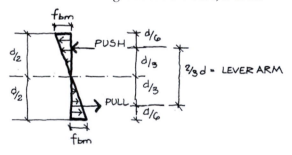

Fig. 14.30 Rectangular beam lever arm

That $Z = bd^2/6$ is found from these two diagrams and the following simple algebra:

$$M = \text{push force} \times \text{lever arm} = (b \times d/2 \times 1/2 \times f_{bm}) \times (2/3 \times d) = (bd^2/6) \times f_{bm}$$

$$f_{bm} = M \div (bd^2/6) = M \div Z \quad \text{and} \quad Z = bd^2/6$$

Example 14.12   Calculate the actual stresses in the beam at **B** for the structure shown in **Fig. 14.24**. The beam has a rectangular cross-section with **b** = 150mm and **d** = 300mm. The internal forces are shown in **Fig. 14.24**.

Sect. Prop.	Calculation	Result		Stress	Calculation	Result
A	150×300	$45{,}000\,mm^2$		$f_{ax\text{-}act}$	$4.5 \times 1000 \div 45{,}000$	$0.1\,N/mm^2$
A_{SH}	150×300	$45{,}000\,mm^2$		$f_{sh\text{-}act}$	$20 \times 1000 \div 45{,}000$	$0.44\,N/mm^2$
Z	$150 \times 300^2 \div 6$	$2{,}250{,}000\,mm^3$		$f_{bm\text{-}act}$	$18 \times 1{,}000{,}000 \div 2{,}250{,}000$	$8.0\,N/mm^2$

To convert the forces to Newtons and millimetres, the axial and shear forces have to be multiplied by 1000, and the bending moment by 1,000,000. To avoid all these zeros large numbers can be written in exponential form. There are two ways of writing this:

$$1000 = 10^3 = \text{E3} \qquad \text{and} \qquad 1{,}000{,}0000 = 10^6 = \text{E6}$$

where the numbers **3** and **6** represent the number of zeros, so:

$$f_{bm\text{-}act} = 18 \times 1{,}000{,}000 \div 2{,}250{,}000 = 18\,\text{E6} \div 2.25\,\text{E6} = 8.0\,N/mm^2$$

The results show that the stress due to the bending moment is much higher than the axial and shear stresses, this is quite common.

Example 14.13 Repeat the calculation of Example 14.12 for a steel **I** section. Check the stresses in a European section **IPE 180**. The section properties for these sections are obtained from standard tables.

Sect. Prop.	from table		Stress	Calculation	Result
A	$23.95\,\text{E2}\,mm^2$		$f_{ax\text{-}act}$	$4.5\,\text{E3} \div 23.95\,\text{E2}$	$1.9\,N/mm^2$
A_{sh}	$11.25\,\text{E2}\,mm^2$		$f_{sh\text{-}act}$	$20\,\text{E3} \div 11.25\,\text{E2}$	$18\,N/mm^2$
Z	$146.3\,\text{E3}\,mm^3$		$f_{bm\text{-}act}$	$18\,\text{E6} \div 146.3\,\text{E3}$	$123\,N/mm^2$

It is instructive to look at the bending and shear of the **I** beam with only the flanges resisting the bending, and the full depth of the web resisting the shear, see **Figs. 3.56** and **3.64**.

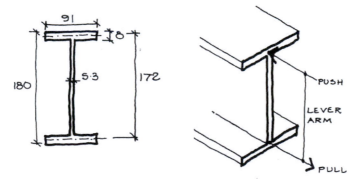

Fig. 14.31 Details of IPE 180

Push force = Pull force = Moment ÷ Lever arm = $18\,\text{E6} \div 172 = 104.7\,\text{E3}\,N$ so:

$$f_{bm\text{-}act} = 104.7\,\text{E3} \div (91 \times 8) = 144\,N/mm^2 \qquad \text{and}$$

$$f_{sh\text{-}act} = 20\,\text{E3} \div (180 \times 5.3) = 21\,N/mm^2$$

which gives approximately the same values as those obtained by using the section properties obtained from the tables.

Exercise 14.8   **1** Calculate the stresses in the various examples using a variety of different sections.

2 Draw stress diagrams like those shown in **Fig. 3.82**.

The stress distribution shown in **Fig. 14.30** assumes that the structural material is homogeneous, this is one of the assumptions of the Engineer's Theory, and is true for metals and true enough for timber but is not true for concrete used for a beam. If concrete is used to make structural elements that are subjected to tensile stresses then it has to be reinforced with steel bars, see section **4.7**. **Fig. 14.29** can be re-drawn to show the push force and the pull forces in a reinforced concrete beam.

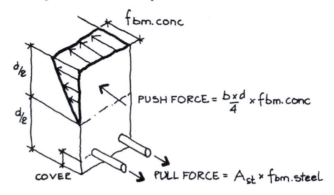

Fig. 14.32 Push and pull forces in concrete beam

The neutral axis is shown at a depth of **d/2**. In the technical literature there is a lot of detail about the depth of the neutral axis and the shape of the stress distribution in the concrete, but for the simple approach, the details given in **Fig. 14.32** are sufficient. If the distance from the bottom of the beam to the centre of the reinforcement is known (chosen), it is usually from about **40mm** to **70mm**, then the lever arm dimension can be calculated.

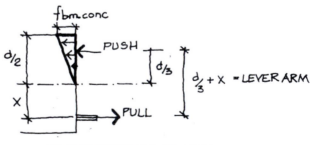

Fig. 14.33 Concrete beam lever arm

Using the information from these two diagrams it is possible to calculate the force in the rebar.

Example 14.14   Calculate the force in the reinforcement due to the bending moment in the beam of **Example 14.12**. Assume the cover = 40mm

$$M = 18kN.m ; \quad \text{lever arm} = d/3 + x = 300/3 + (150 - 40) = \textbf{210mm} \quad \text{so}$$

$$\text{Force in reinforcement} = 18 \text{ E6} \div 210 = \textbf{86 E3 N}$$

$$\text{Stress in reinforcement} = f_{bm.st\text{-}act} \div A_{st} \text{ where } A_{st} = \text{Area of the reinforcement}$$

Having calculated the actual stresses in the structure they have to be checked against the allowable stresses for the material to ensure the chosen section is adequate. Before these are given it should be clear which method of design is being used. In section **6.1** three approaches are explained and are illustrated in **Figs. 6.19, 20** and **21**. Until the late 1970s virtually all calculations were carried out using **permissible stress design**, since then it has been generally superseded by **limit state design**. Limit state design multiplies the loads by factors, typically **1.5**, and divides the ultimate stress by factors, typically **1.3**[1]. The factors are given in technical codes. For the simple approach outlined in this chapter it is better to ignore the limit state partial factors, and work with the unfactored loads and the permissible stresses. **The most important point to remember is to state clearly in the calculations which approach is being used.** In limit ltate terminology calculations using the unfactored loads is called the **serviceability limit state** or **SLS** for short.

Material	Grade	Tensile stress	Comp. stress	Shear stress
Structural steel	Mild steel	165	155	120
	High tensile	230	215	160
Concrete		-	7	0.4 – max 4
Reinforcement	Mild steel	140	140	140
	High tensile	260	260	260
Timber	Average	6	6	0.7

Table 14.6 Permissible stresses in N/mm^2

Using these stresses it is possible to check whether a structural member is adequate. In reinforced concrete beams it is usual to check that the concrete is adequate, and then size the reinforcement from the force, thus obtaining the cross-sectional area required. If the compressive or shear stresses are exceeded in a concrete element it is possible to give additional strength by adding compression or shear reinforcement.

The stresses given in **Table 14.6** are based on 'usual' grades of the material; it is possible to encounter material with both higher and lower usable stresses. Generally 'mild steel' is used for structural steelwork and 'high tensile' steel for reinforcement. Compressive stresses have to be reduced, often considerably, when elements are slender, see section **14.10**.

14.8 Triangulated structures

Structures made from beams and columns are probably the structural form used most commonly in buildings but, especially for roof structures, trusses are often used. Some typical trusses are shown in **Fig. 7.34**. Trusses are usually supported like simply supported beams or cantilevers, and the truss geometry itself is usually a sequence of triangles. The structural elements of the truss, for calculation purposes, are considered to be pinned to each other so that the elements only have axial forces. All this means that trusses are almost always **statically determinate**, so the forces can be found from the equilibrium statements given on page **370**.

In the past, graphical methods were popular for finding forces in trusses but nowadays hand calculations either find the forces from considering joint equilibrium or the equilibrium at a cut, see **Fig. 7.36**. Both require the concept of **resolution of forces** (or its equivalent the **force triangle**). This concept is shown in **Fig. 7.10**. The basis for all these calculations are the well known trigonometrical relationships for a right-angled triangle between the hypotenuse and the sine and cosine of the angle θ.

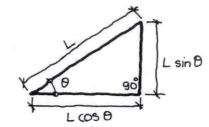

Fig. 14.34 Trigonometrical relationships for a right-angled triangle

Using these relationships it is possible to resolve a diagonal force into **vertical** and **horizontal components** which is equivalent to drawing a **triangle of forces**.

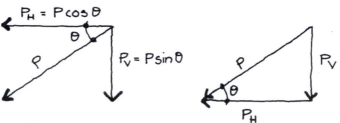

Fig. 14.35 Force components and triangle of forces

This idea can be reversed to find two forces that resist a third force.

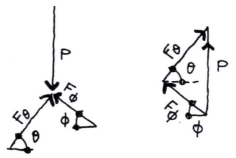

Fig. 14.36 Three forces at a point

A separate triangle of forces can be drawn for each 'resisting' force F_θ and F_φ.

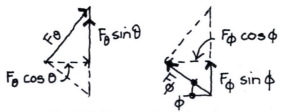

Fig. 14.37 Force triangles for F_θ and F_φ

From **Fig. 14.37** the horizontal and vertical equilibrium conditions can be written as:

$$F_\theta \cos \theta = F_\varphi \cos \varphi \qquad \text{and} \qquad F_\theta \sin \theta + F_\varphi \sin \varphi = P$$

Example 14.15 Calculate the forces F_1 and F_2 for the arrangement shown in the figure.

For horizontal equilibrium: $F_1 \cos 30° = F_2 \cos 45°$ so

$0.866\ F_1 = 0.707\ F_2$ giving $F_2 = 1.225\ F_1$

For vertical equilibrium: $F_1 \sin 30° + F_2 \sin 45° = 10$ kN

so $0.5\ F_1 + 0.707\ F_2 = 10$kN: substituting $F_2 = 1.225\ F_1$ gives

$F_1 = 7.32$kN   and $F_2 = 8.97$kN

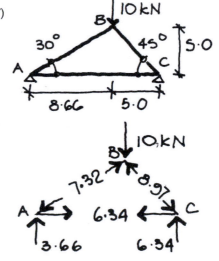

This example shows how forces in two members meeting at a joint can be found from joint equilibrium.

Example 14.16 Calculate the forces in the truss shown in the figure from joint equilibrium.

Find reactions R_A and R_C (as for beam – page 367)

$13.66 \times R_A = 10 \times 5.0$ so $R_A = 3.66$kN

$13.66 \times R_C = 10 \times 8.66$ so $R_A = 6.34$kN

Equilibrium at joint A

Vertical: $F_{AB} \sin 30° = 3.66$ so $F_{AB} = 7.32$kN

Horizontal: $F_{AB} \cos 30° = F_{AC}$ so $F_{AC} = 6.34$kN

Equilibrium at joint C

Vertical: $F_{CB} \sin 45° = 6.34$ so $F_{CB} = 8.97$kN

Horizontal: $F_{CB} \cos 45° = F_{CA}$ so $F_{CA} = 6.34$kN

Equilibrium at joint B – as Example 14.15

As the forces have been calculated at the joints, it is now possible to draw a diagram showing the forces in the truss members. Compression is shown as positive and tension is shown as negative.

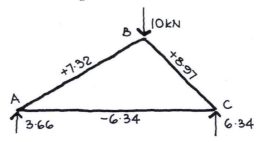

Fig. 14.38 Axial forces (kN) for Example 14.16

To find the forces from the equilibrium of a slice the **BMD** and **SFD**, calculated as though the truss is a beam, are used.

Example 14.17 Calculate the forces in elements **AB** and **AC** of the truss used in **Example 14.16** by considering the equilibrium of the truss cut, for example at 4.33m from joint **A**.

Draw the BMD and SFD as though the truss was a beam. Note: the reactions R_A and R_B calculated previously are used.

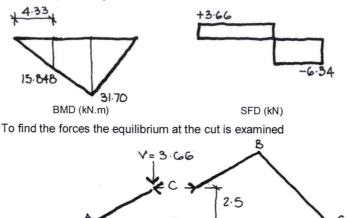

BMD (kN.m)   SFD (kN)

To find the forces the equilibrium at the cut is examined

The vertical force **V = 3.66 kN**, and the horizontal forces **C** and **T** are found from:

C = T = Moment ÷ Lever arm = 15.848 ÷ 2.5 = **6.34 kN**

The force in **AC** is given directly from **T**: F_{AC} = T = **6.34kN** (tension)

The force in **AB** is given by the force triangle so:

F_{AB} = C ÷ cos 30° = V ÷ sin 30° = **7.32kN** (compression)

For the simple approach the equilibrium at a cut is often quicker. The maximum bending moment and shear force are calculated from which the maximum top, bottom and diagonal member forces are rapidly calculated.

Exercise 14.9   Verify the forces shown for the truss in **Fig. 14.39**. Hint: calculate the reactions then find the forces in the members at the supports. Then proceed to joints where there are only two unknown forces.

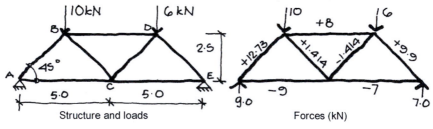

Structure and loads   Forces (kN)

Fig. 14.39 Truss and forces for Exercise 14.9

The results should also be checked by slicing the truss at several positions and following the procedure of **Example 14.17**.

14.9   Deflection and stiffness

It is an everyday experience to find materials that are hard such as stone or concrete, or soft such as rubber, plastic, and that 'thin' things are easier to bend or stretch than 'thick' ones. But for calculations these experiences have to be quantified, for the material and for the element.

As the **Engineer's theory**, see page **64-65**, is being used the material is assumed to be linear elastic, which means that the stiffness of the material can be characterised by a number. This number is called the **modulus of elasticity**, or **E**, and has the dimensions of force per area; usually **N/mm²** is used. Stiffer materials have higher values for **E**; see **Fig.5.7**.

Material	Modulus of elasticity – N/mm²
Steel	210 E3
Concrete	Approx. 14 E3
Timber – softwood	Average 9 E3
Timber – hardwood	Average 14 E3

Table 14.7   Values of modulus of elasticity

As can be seen the only definite value is for steel. The value for concrete is approximate because it is dependent on the mix, type of aggregate, amount of water, age, and other factors. The values for timber vary with the species and because timber is a natural material, each piece is slightly different. This shows that any calculations for structural movement due to load can only be approximate.

To relate the values of **E** to loads, another definition has to be introduced, that of **strain**. If two short columns of the same length and cross-section are made of different material but carry equal loads, the column with a material of lower **E** will compress more.

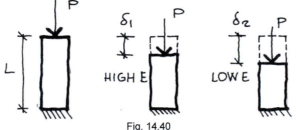

Fig. 14.40

The column with the lower **E** will compress more but how can they be compared numerically? The answer is to compare the strains. **Strain**, usually written **ε**, is defined as **the ratio of the deflection to the original length**. In this case, the ratio of δ_1 : **L** will be smaller than δ_2 : **L** because the **E** is higher. Now **Hooke's Law**, see page **7**, can be stated in terms of **stress, f, strain, ε,** and the **modulus of elasticity, E,** as:

Stress = Modulus of elasticity times **strain**   or   **f = E × ε**

Stiffness of a structural element has a particular meaning in calculation and is defined by the relationship:

Force = Stiffness times **deflection**   or   **P = K × δ**

With these definitions it is now possible, by simple algebra, to find expressions for the axial stiffness and the deflection of a column. This is done as follows:

Stress = Force divided by **Area**   and   **Strain = Deflection** divided by **Length**

or $f = \dfrac{P}{A}$ and $\varepsilon = \dfrac{\delta}{L}$

which, substituting for stress and strain in Hooke's Law, gives

$$\frac{P}{A} = E \times \frac{\delta}{L} \qquad \text{rearranging gives} \qquad P = \left(\frac{EA}{L}\right) \times \delta = K \times \delta$$

where **K** is the **stiffness** of the column with units of force per length – **kN/m.** This expression can also be arranged to give the deflection:

$$\delta = \frac{PL}{EA} \qquad \text{and stiffness} \quad K = \frac{EA}{L}$$

Example 14.18 Calculate the axial deflection and the stiffness of the column shown for values of **E** of **60 E3** and **5 E3 N/mm²**.

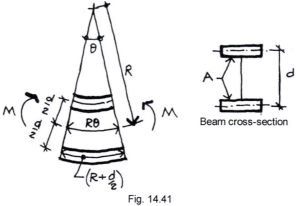

E		Calculation	Result
60E3	δ	(200E3×4E3) ÷ (60E3×300²)	0. 15mm
	K	(60E6×0.3²) ÷ 4	1.35 E6 kN/m
5E3	δ	(200E3×4E3) ÷ (5E3×300²)	1.78mm
	K	(5E6×0.3²) ÷ 4	112 E3 kN/m

Note: The calculations for δ are in **N** and **mm** but for **K** they are in **kN** and **m**.

To understand numerically how the bending of a beam is related to a vertical deflection, a rather artificial situation, from a practical point of view, is examined. A beam composed of two equal flanges, each with area **A** and a distance **d** apart, is bent by a moment **M**.

Fig. 14.41

Looking at a small slice of the beam it is assumed that it is bent into a circular shape by **M**, and the radius of the neutral axis is **R**. The length of the neutral axis, which does not change length due to bending is **Rθ** – see **Fig. 3.36**, but the length of the bottom flange has increased to **(R + d/2)θ**. As the unbent length was **Rθ**, the **strain** in the flange can be found as follows:

$$\varepsilon = \frac{(R+d/2)\theta - R\theta}{R\theta} = \frac{d}{2} \times \frac{1}{R} = \frac{d}{2} \times K$$

The strain is as before, the extension divided by the original length, this time of the flange. The reciprocal of the radius **R** is **K** (the Greek letter kappa) and is the **curvature** of the beam at the slice. Now the stress in the flange can be found from Hooke's Law as:

$$f = E \times K \times \frac{d}{2}$$

As the moment **M** is the force in the flange times the lever arm **d**, the moment can be written in terms of **E, A, d** and **K**, as

$$M = f \times A \times d = E \times K \times \left(A \times \frac{d^2}{2} \right) = E \times I \times K$$

Now the moment on the slice is given in terms of the **modulus of elasticity**, the **curvature** and the **moment of inertia, I**. This new term **moment of inertia** is borrowed from dynamics and is the part inside the brackets. It should really be called, and sometimes is, the **second moment of area**, as it is the area multiplied twice by the distance to the neutral axis, so, in this case:

$$I = 2 \times A \times \left(\frac{d}{2} \right)^2 = A \times \frac{d^2}{2}$$

Algebraic expressions and actual values for different shapes and standard cross-sections are widely available in technical literature. The above examination not only used an **I** beam without a web but only looked at a 'slice'. What about a whole beam? If a whole beam had the same moment at every point then the vertical deflection can be found.

Consider a beam of span **L** with equal and opposite moments **M** applied at each end. At every point the bending moment is the same, **M**, so the slice is the whole length of the beam and the beam is bent into a circular arc.

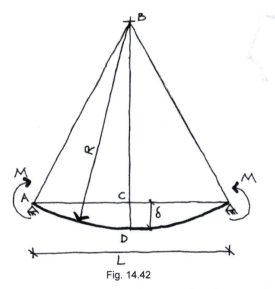

Fig. 14.42

The deflection, δ, can be found from an application of Pythagoras' theorem as:

$$\delta = CD = BD - BC = R - \sqrt{(AB^2 - AC^2)} = R - \sqrt{(R^2 - (L/2)^2)}$$

The radius, **R**, can be found from the moment, span and the moment of inertia of the beam. So for a given beam the deflection can be found.

Example 14.19   Calculate the central deflection for the beam shown. The section is made of steel and the flanges have the same dimensions as an **IPE 180**, see **Fig. 14.31**.

$$I = 91 \times 8 \times \frac{172^2}{2} = 1077\text{E4mm}^4$$

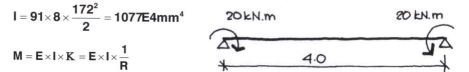

$$M = E \times I \times K = E \times I \times \frac{1}{R}$$

rearranging $R = \dfrac{E \times I}{M}$ so, working in Newtons and millimetres, **R** is calculated as:

$$R = \frac{210\text{E3} \times 1076\text{E4}}{20\text{E6}} = 112980\text{mm} \qquad \therefore \quad \delta = 112980 - \sqrt{(112980^2 - 2000^2)} = 17.7\text{mm}$$

So the central deflection, for this rather artificial case, can be calculated from an examination that just uses simple geometry. As in most beams the size of the bending moment varies along the beam; the radius **R**, shown in **Fig. 14.41**, will be different for each point. In other words the curvature **K** is not constant, which means Pythagoras' theorem, used for **Fig. 14.42**, will not apply. To find deflections in these cases a more complex analysis is required. Alternatively the algebraic expressions given in technical handbooks can be used.

As a beam with a constant bending moment is unusual in real structures it might seem that this approach is of little use. It does not give the 'correct' deflection for beams loaded differently but it can act as a guide. Supposing, for **Example 14.19** the correct value of **I**, obtained from tables is **1317 E4 mm⁴**, then the deflection will be reduced in proportion to the increased value for **I**, that is:

$$\delta = \frac{1077\text{E4}}{1317\text{E4}} \times 17.7 = 14.5\text{mm}$$

Alternatively the calculations could be re-done with the new value. But how does this value compare with deflections calculated using more complex analysis for loads of different types? Below a comparison is made between the calculated value and values for three other loadings.

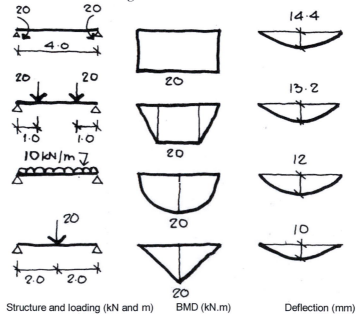

Structure and loading (kN and m)   BMD (kN.m)   Deflection (mm)

Fig. 14.43 Comparison of deflections

Unsurprisingly the nearer the shape of the **BMD** is to a rectangle, the closer the values are. For the central point load the 'constant moment approach' overestimates the deflection by 44%. Given the fact that at the preliminary stages many other values are approximate, loading, actual material or even the dimensions, this is acceptable for the first stage and provides a guide. Having calculated a deflection does it show that the structure is stiff enough? Guides to acceptable deflections are given in many codes, but they are not always clear. As a general guide the following limitations are typical for deflections due to the **live loads**.

Structure	Maximum deflection
Cantilever	Length/180
Beams (with brittle finishes)	Span/360
Beams in general	Span/250
Horizontal per storey	Storey height/300

Table 14.8 Maximum permissible deflections for live loads

As can be seen from the calculations a beam's stiffness is directly related to the value of **EI**, that is, the product of the **modulus of elasticity** with the **moment of inertia**. As it is rarely practical to alter **E**, stiffness is altered by **I**, that is, changing the dimensions of the structural cross-section. In general it is not easy to calculate deflections, and this simple approach can only indicate some key values. However these should show whether a chosen structure is sufficiently stiff.

14.10   Slenderness and axial stability

A structure must be sufficiently stiff for the deflections under load to be acceptable, but there is an additional stiffness requirement; parts of the structure that are axially loaded must have sufficient stiffness to prevent buckling-initiated collapse. The ideas of axial stability and slenderness are explained in section **6.4** so here it is only necessary to indicate how to calculate the slenderness and how this affects the permissible stress.

As buckling is due to an element bending under an axial load, 'slenderness' is partially dependent on its bending stiffness, that is **E** × **I**. It is also dependent on its **effective length L$_E$**. The effective length is dependent on how the ends of the member are supported; the four classic cases are shown.

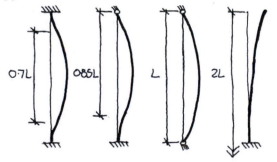

Fig. 14.44 Effective length for different support conditions

These effective lengths are for elements supported 'ideally', that is fully fixed or with perfect pins, which do not occur in real structures. The designer has to decide on what is a reasonable effective length. Whilst resistance to buckling is dependent on the **EI**, slenderness is calculated by dividing the effective length by the **minimum radius of gyration, r_{min}**. The radius of gyration is another term borrowed from dynamics. When a mass **m** is rotated at a radius **r** then the moment of inertia is given by **mr^2**. The moment of inertia **I** was defined on page **387**, so if the mass is considered to be the cross-sectional area **A** then the radius of gyration can be calculated.

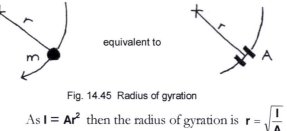

equivalent to

Fig. 14.45 Radius of gyration

As **$I = Ar^2$** then the radius of gyration is $r = \sqrt{\dfrac{I}{A}}$

In the mathematical analysis of buckling, the minimum radius of gyration plays a central role in defining slenderness. To avoid the possibility of buckling, the allowable stress in an axially loaded member has to be reduced by a factor that is related to the slenderness of the element. These have been calculated and are available in technical codes. Due to the material, the values of **E**, and the maximum allowable stress, there is some variation in the value of the reduction factor. The typical range for the relationship between this factor and the slenderness is shown in **Fig. 14.46**. These curves are the envelope of values obtained from a number of technical publications. The range is due to modifications introduced to take into account initial defects such as lack of perfect straightness. This is another example of how the basis for numerical calculations is not exact.

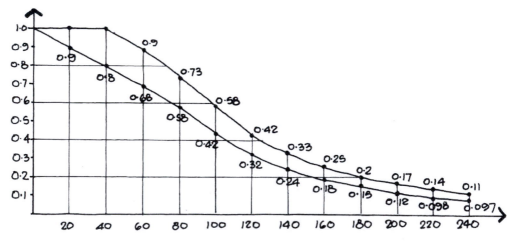

Fig. 14.46 Reduction factors plotted against slenderness ratio L_E/r_{min}

When **r** is found it has to be the **minimum value**, so the minimum value of **I** has to be used.

Example 14.20   Calculate the allowable axial load that a mild steel column, supported as shown, can carry if it is:

1   An IPE 180
2   A circular tube (CHS) of dia. 168.3mm and wall thickness 5mm

Assuming the connection to the concrete foundation is a pin joint and the connection to the concrete super-structure is nearly fixed then:

L$_E$ = 0.9 × 4.0 = 3.60m

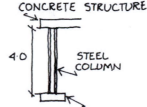

CONCRETE STRUCTURE

4·0   STEEL COLUMN

CONCRETE FOUNDATION

Section properties from tables are:

Section	A mm^2	I$_{min}$ mm^4	Calculation	r$_{min}$ mm
IPE 180	23.95 E2	100.9 E4	√(100.9 E4 ÷23.95E2)	20.5
168.3 CHS	25.7 E2	856 E4	√ (856 E4 ÷25.7E2)	58

Calculate the slenderness; find the reduction factor using an average value.

Section	Calculation	L$_E$/r$_{min}$	factor	Calculation	f$_{all}$ N/mm^2
IPE 180	3.6 E3 ÷ 20.5	176	0.2	0.2 × 155	31
168.3 CHS	3.6 E3 ÷ 58	62	0.8	0.8 × 155	124

Calculate the allowable axial load, **N$_{all}$**, from **A** and **f$_{all}$**.

Section	Calculation	N$_{all}$ kN
IPE 180	31 × 23.95 E2 ÷ E3	74.3
168.3 CHS	124 × 25.7 E2 ÷ E3	319

Exercise 14.10   Repeat the calculations of Example 14.20 for the following sections:
1   HEA 120A
2   150 x 100 rectangular tube (RHS) with wall thickness of 5mm

The material is mild steel and the section properties are:

Section	A mm^2	I$_{min}$ mm^4
HEA 120A	25.34 E2	230.9 E4
150 x 100 RHS	23.9 E2	396 E4

Exercise 14.11   Compare capacities of the four sections in terms of the weight of material used. The weights are given in **kg/m**.

IPE 180	168.3 CHS	150 x 100 RHS	HEA 120 A
18.8	20.1	18.7	19.9

Where other parts of structures are in compression, such as the flanges and webs of beams, diagonals of trusses for example, the allowable stress will be reduced if they are slender. And the reduction will be as dramatic as shown in **Fig. 14.46**. Technical literature provides guidance for many situations, but stresses can often be checked approximately by considering the part in compression as an 'axial member'.

14.11   Four examples of simple calculations

To see how the simple approach can give useful information with the minimum of calculation, some examples, all of which have already appeared in the book, are now given. Parts of these real structures are calculated. These are:

- **Simple building,** the wind bracing system section sizes
- **Zarzuela Hippodrome,** the roof structure tie
- **Federal Reserve Bank**, stresses at the base of the end tower
- **Centre Pompidou,** floor truss section sizes and deflection

As exact dimensional information is not available for all these examples, reasonable assumptions are made as necessary.

Example 14.21

A Simple Building – (see Chapter 9)

Calculate the sizes of the elements of the wind-bracing system that resist the longitudinal wind forces.

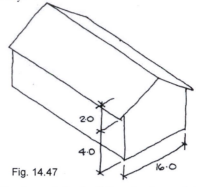

Fig. 14.47

The basic wind speed is assumed to be **50m/s** and the building is situated in the country. The relevant dimensions are shown in **Fig. 14.47**. The bracing structure is shown in **Fig. 14.48**. Only the section sizes of the diagonal members are required as the other members are part of the portal frames.

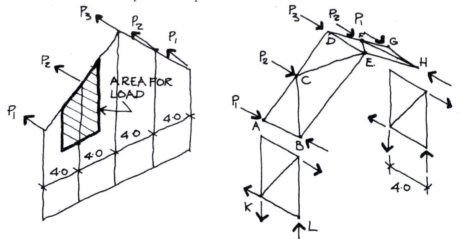

Fig. 14.48 Wind load and bracing structure

The first step is to calculate the wind load.

	Symbol	Calculation	Result
Basic wind speed	V	given	50m/s
Coefficient	S	Table 14.3	0.88
Design wind speed	V_s	0.88 × 50	44m/s
Wind load	q	0.613 × 44^2 E-3	**1.2kN/m^2**

Then forces, **P$_1$**, **P$_2$** and **P$_3$** on the bracing structure.

	Symbol	Calculation	Result
Wind load on end walls	$q \times C_p$	1.2 (0.7 - (-0.3))	kN/m^2
P$_1$	Area × q	4/2 × 4/2 × 1.2	**4.8kN**
P$_2$	=	4 × 5/2 × 1.2	**12.0kN**
P$_3$	=	4 × 6/2 × 1.2	**14.4kN**

For the purposes of the calculation of forces, the truss is assumed to be flat. The forces are found by considering the equilibrium of the joints. 'Vertical' and 'Horizontal' are used to distinguish the directions, not the position in the building.

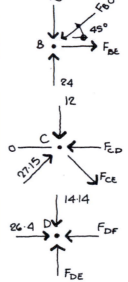

Joint B

Direction	Equilibrium	Force
'Vertical'	$24 - 4.8 = F_{BC} \sin 45°$	$F_{BC} = 27.15$kN
'Horizontal'	$F_{BE} = F_{BC} \cos 45°$	$F_{BE} = 19.20$kN

Joint C

Direction	Equilibrium	Force
'Vertical'	$27.15 \sin 45° =$ $12 + F_{CE} \sin 45°$	$F_{CE} = 10.18$kN
'Horizontal'	$F_{CD} =$ $(27.15 + 10.18) \sin 45°$	$F_{CD} = 26.40$kN

Joint D

Direction	Equilibrium	Force
'Vertical'	Equal to the load	$F_{DE} = 14.40$kN
'Horizontal'	Equal to F_{CD}	$F_{DF} = 26.40$kN

The forces in the horizontal truss that forms part of the wind-bracing are summarised in the diagram.

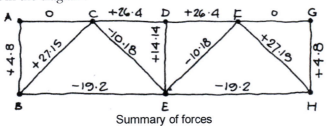

Summary of forces

Now structural sections can be chosen for the diagonal members, circular hollow sections (**CHS**) are usual, and the actual stress, f_{act}, calculated.

Element	N_{act} kN	CHS	A mm^2	Calculation	f_{act} N/mm^2
AB	4.80	60.3 × 3.2	5.74 E2	4.80 E3 ÷ 5.74 E2	8.4
BC	27.15	114.3 × 3.6	12.50 E2	27.15 E3 ÷ 12.5 E2	21.7
CE	10.18	76.2× 3.2	7.33 E2	10.18 E3 ÷ 7.33 E2	13.9
DE	14.40	60.3 × 4.0	7.07 E2	14.40 E3 ÷ 7.07 E2	20.4

The allowable stresses, f_{all}, is calculated and checked against the actual stresses to make sure that $f_{all} \geq f_{act}$ is true for all elements. As wind is reversible all elements are designed for compression.

Element	L_E mm	r_{min} mm	Slenderness	Coeff.	f_{all} N/mm^2
AB	4.0 E3	20.2	198	0.15	155 × 0.15 = 23.3
BC	5.7 E3	39.2	145	0.3	46.5
CE	5.7 E3	25.8	220	0.12	18.6
DE	4.0 E3	20	200	0.15	23.3

This shows that $f_{all} \geq f_{act}$ is true for all elements. The sizing of the vertical structure is left as an **Exercise**.

Example 14.22   The Zarzuela Hippodrome (see section 10.3)

Design the tie down for the roof.

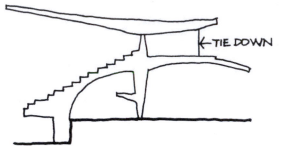

Fig. 14.49 Typical cross-section

The roof structure is considered to be a simply supported beam with two cantilevers. This means that the forces can be calculated from equilibrium as the structure is **statically determinate**. The spacing of the columns and ties is **5.1m**, and the thickness of the shell roof varies from **55mm** to **125mm**, there are no finishes; assume average thickness of **100mm**. Therefore the load will be the self-weight of the concrete roof plus an allowance for snow, assume **0.6kN/m²**.

Element	Load	kN/m
Roof	$0.1 \times 5.1 \times 25 =$	12.8
Snow	$0.6 \times 5.1 \times 1.0 =$	3.1
	Total =	15.9

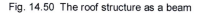

Fig. 14.50 The roof structure as a beam

Calculate the bending moments, shear forces and reactions for loads on each span separately.

Span AB

Force	Calculation	Result
S_{BA}	-15.9×13	−206.7kN
M_{BA}	$15.9 \times 13^2 \div 2$	−1343.6kN.m
S_{BC}	$1343.6 \div 5.25$	255.9kN
R_B	$206.7 + 255.9$	462.6kN
R_C	$= -S_{BC}$	−255.9kN

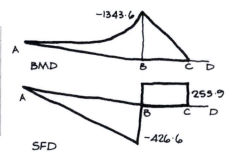

Span BC

Force	Calculation	Result
S_{BC}	$15.9 \times 5.25 \div 2$	41.7kN
S_{CB}	$-15.9 \times 5.25 \div 2$	−41.7kN
M_{max}	$15.9 \times 5.25^2 \div 8$	54.8kN.m
R_B	$= S_{BC}$	41.7kN
R_C	$= -S_{CB}$	41.7kN

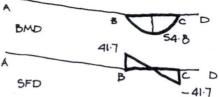

Span CD

Force	Calculation	Result
S_{CD}	15.9×1.75	27.8kN
M_{CD}	$15.9 \times 1.75^2 \div 2$	−24.3kN.m
S_{BC}	$24.3 \div 5.25$	−4.6kN
R_B	$= S_{BC}$	−4.6kN
R_C	$27.8 + 4.6$	32.4kN

Now the tie down force can be calculated from the sum of the reactions R_c.

Tie down force = N_{act} = Sum of R_c = −2 55.9 + 41.7 + 32.4 = −181.8kN

Note that this force includes the effect of snow on spans **BC** and **CD** which reduces the total force. To take account of the possibility on less snow take a design force of **200kN**. From this, the diameter of a mild steel tie can be calculated.

$$A_{req} = N_{act} \div f_{all} = 200\ E3 \div 155 = 1290mm^2$$

$$\therefore \text{ use 42 dia. tie } (A_{act} = 1385mm^2)$$

Example 14.23   The Federal Reserve Bank (see section 10.5)

Calculate the stresses at the base of the end towers, for vertical and wind loads.

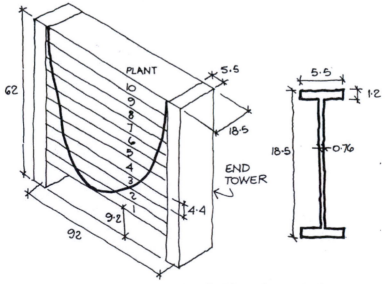

Fig. 14.51 Main dimension of building and tower structure

Calculate a typical floor load using assumed values.

Component	kN/m^2
Self-weight	4.0
Finishes	1.2
Live load	3.0
Partitions	1.5
Total	**9.7**

Calculate the load to the façade per floor, from the floor and the cladding.

Element	Load	kN/m
Floor	9.7 × 18.5 ÷ 2	89.7
Cladding	1.2 × 4.4	5.3
	Total	**95**

Calculate the load to one tower, assume **14** floors (to take into account plant loads and roof) and roof truss weight of **1200kg/m**.

Element	Load	kN
Floors	14 × 95 × 86.5 ÷ 2	57,522
Truss	12 × 92 ÷ 2	552
	Total	**58,074**

Calculate the typical floor load in the tower.

Component	kN/m^2
Self-weight	5.0
Finishes	3.0
Live load	4.0
Total	**12.0**

Calculate the load due to the weight of the tower; this is the self-weight, the weight of non-loadbearing walls and the weight of floors.

Element	Load	kN
Self-weight	(2 × 1.2 × 5.5 + 0.76 × (18.5-2×1.2)) × 25 × 62	39,426
Other walls	(18 × 4 × 0.2) × 25 × 62	22,320
Floors 12N°	12 × (5 × 18) × 12.0	12,960
	Total	**74,706**

Using the total vertical load on the tower and dividing it by the gross cross-section of the structure, the axial stress is calculated.

Total load = N_{act} = 2 × 58,074 + 74,706 = **190,854kN**

Total area = A_{act} = 2 × 1.2 × 5.5 + 0.76 × (18.5 − 2×1.2) = **25.44 m^2**

Axial stress = $f_{ax\text{-}act}$ = 190,854 E3 ÷ 25.44 E6 = **7.5N/mm^2**

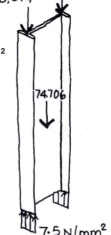

58,074

58,074

74706

7·5 N/mm^2

To assess the wind load assume the basic wind speed is **50m/s**.

	Symbol	Calculation	Result
Basic wind speed	V	assumed	50m/s
Coefficient	S	Table 14.3	1.04
Design wind speed	V_s	1.04×50	52m/s
Wind load	q	0.613×52^2 E-3	**1.66kN/m^2**

Calculate the total wind load on the building, ignore the space under the central part and use a total coefficient of **1.0**.

$$\text{Total load} = W_{win} = (92 + 5.5) \times 62 \times 1.66 = \textbf{10,035kN}$$

The two towers act as cantilevers from the ground, so the cantilever moment for each tower is:

$$\text{Moment per tower} = M_{win} = (10,035 \div 2) \times 62 \div 2 = \textbf{155,542kN.m}$$

The stress due to the wind moment can now be calculated from the push pull force in the flanges and the area of the flange.

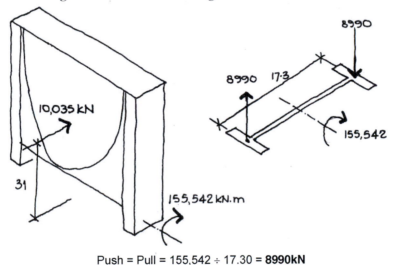

$$\text{Push} = \text{Pull} = 155,542 \div 17.30 = \textbf{8990kN}$$

and

$$\text{Flange stress} = f_{bm\text{-}act} = 8990 \text{ E3} \div (5.5 \times 1.2) \text{ E6} = \textbf{1.36N/mm}^2$$

It is now possible to combine the flange stresses at the base of the tower to give the maximum and minimum stress.

$$\text{Maximum stress} = f_{max} = f_{ax\text{-}act} + f_{bm\text{-}act} = 7.5 + 1.36 = \textbf{8.86N/mm}^2$$

and

$$\text{Minimum stress} = f_{min} = f_{ax\text{-}act} - f_{bm\text{-}act} = 7.5 - 1.36 = \textbf{6.14N/mm}^2$$

This shows that the stresses are acceptable for concrete in compression, see **Table 14.6**, and that there are no tensile stresses at the bottom of the tower.

Exercise   Recalculate the axial forces and stresses ignoring Live Loads and allowances for finishes and partitions. Check the combined stresses.

Example 14.24 The Pompidou Centre – (also see pages 327-331)

Calculate the forces in the floor structure and size the top and bottom members of the truss shown in **Fig. 14.52**. Estimate the central deflection under live and partition loads.

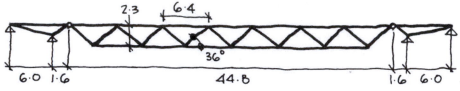

Fig. 14.52 Floor structure of Centre Pompidou

Calculate a typical floor load using published information and assumed values.

Component	kN/m^2
110 mm slab	2.8
Finishes	1.2
Live load	5.0
Partitions	1.2
Total	**10.2**

Calculate the load on the truss and add an assumed truss self-weight of **1000kg/m**, the trusses are spaced at **12.9 m**.

Element	Calculation	kN/m
Floor	10.2 × 12.9	131.6
Truss self-weight	assumed	10.0
	Total	**141.6**

Calculate the maximum bending moment and shear force. Calculate the truss forces in the top and bottom members; these are the push/pull forces. The forces in the end diagonal members resist the shear and are calculated using the triangle of forces.

$$\text{Maximum moment} = M = w \times L^2 \div 8 = 141.6 \times 44.8^2 \div 8 = \textbf{35,525kN.m}$$

$$\text{Push force} = \text{pull force} = M \div d = 35,525 \div 2.3 = \textbf{15,445kN}$$

$$\text{Maximum shear force} = S = w \times L \div 2 = 141.6 \times 44.8 \div 2 = \textbf{3171kN}$$

$$\text{Maximum diagonal forces} = S \div \sin 36° = 3171 \div 0.587 = \textbf{5395kN}$$

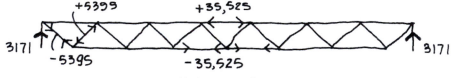

Maximum truss forces

Now it is possible to choose structural elements for the top, bottom and diagonal members and check the actual stresses, **f$_{act}$**. Twin circular tubes are used for the top member, and twin circular bars for the bottom member. The diagonal members are single bars and tubes. This is the arrangement used in the actual project.

Element	N$_{act}$ kN	Section	A mm^2	Calculation	f$_{act}$ N/mm^2
Top	15,445	2 × 437 × 32 CHS	85.4 E3	15.45 E6 ÷ 85.4 E3	181
Bottom	−15,445	2 × 220 dia. bar	76 E3	15.45 E6 ÷ 76 E3	203
Diag. tens	−5395	180 dia. bar	25.5 E3	5.4 E6 ÷ 25.5 E3	212
Diag. comp	5395	406 × 25 CHS	30 E3	5.4 E6 ÷ 30 E 3	180

The allowable stresses, f_{all}, are calculated using high tensile steel.

Element	L_E mm	r_{min} mm	Slenderness	Coeff.	f_{all} N/mm^2
Top	6.4 E3	151	42	0.9	194
Bottom	-	-	-	-	215
Diag. T	-	-	-	-	215
Diag. C	3.9 E3	135	29	0.95	204

This shows that $f_{all} \geq f_{act}$ is true for all elements.

The deflection is calculated using the constant moment approach used for the beam on page **387**. The deflection is only for the live load and the partition load so the bending moment, M_{defl}, has to be reduced in proportion to this load to the total load.

$$M_{defl} = (((5.0 + 1.2) \times 12.9) \div 141.6) \times 35,525 = \textbf{20,066kN.m}$$

Calculate the moment of inertia, **I**, of the truss from the area of the main members, see page **387**. As the areas are not equal this calculation is not quite true, but it is sufficiently accurate for this simple approach. The larger area is used.

$$I = A \times \frac{d^2}{2} = 85.4E3 \times \frac{2300^2}{2} = \textbf{2.25E11mm}^4$$

Calculate the radius from the moment, moment of inertia and the modulus of elasticity, see page **388**.

$$R = \frac{EI}{M_{defl.}} = \frac{210E3 \times 2.25E11}{20,066E6} = \textbf{2,354,729mm}$$

Now, using Pythagoras' theorem, see page **387**, the deflection can be calculated.

$$\delta = 2,354,729 - \sqrt{(2,354,729^2 - 22,400^2)} = \textbf{106mm}$$

Which is equivalent to the **span ÷ 422**.

14.12 Summary

It has been shown how it is possible to make significant calculations, on two pages or so, using no more than the basic arithmetic operations. Apart from the conceptual understanding and some basic technical data, all that was needed was some simple algebraic manipulations and elementary trigonometry. However, the essential point is the conceptual understanding, which makes sense of the numbers and how they relate. No calculations should be done if the underlying concepts are not understood.

Some new quantities were introduced strain, moment of inertia, section modulus and radius of gyration. Most of these arose almost naturally, without the need for new concepts. With these it is possible to make links to the relationships that form the basis of the mathematical treatment of structural behaviour.

- **external loads to internal forces or equilibrium**
- **stresses to internal movements (strains)**
- **internal movements to deflections of the structure**

For axially loaded elements, these three relationships have been given as:

- **external loads to internal forces** or **P = A × f**
- **stresses to strains** or **ε = E × f**
- **internal movements to deflections** or **δ = ε × L**

In the case of the beam, the same relationships exist but here the internal force is the moment, **M**, and the internal movement the curvature, **K = 1/R**.

- **external loads to internal forces** or, for example **M$_x$ = wL/2 × x − wx × x/2** (see page **366**)
- **stresses to strains** or **M = E × I × K**
- **deflections to internal movements** or $\delta = R - \sqrt{(R^2 - (L/2)^2}$

In all mathematical theories, these relationships appear and are related to define various forms of governing equations. Unfortunately these relationships are often hidden in the mathematics, so whilst following any mathematical development it is always worthwhile asking where and how these relationships are appearing.

As can be seen, assumptions were being made continually in the calculations so exact numerical accuracy, with many significant figures, is not required but the numbers must be of the correct magnitude. In some ways numerical calculations are an expression of ignorance, in the sense that sizes of structural members are unknown until they are calculated.

Some form of simple calculations should always be done at the outset of a project, not only to test initial ideas. but to provide a check on subsequent more detailed calculations. Structural computer programs, especially with graphical output, can be a great help in understanding structural behaviour, and simple models can be checked against initial hand calculations.

With the availability of programs that can accept enormous structural models, there is an unfortunate tendency to put whole buildings into the computer before the basic behaviour is understood – this should always be avoided – see **Chapter 18**. Quite often whole building models are unnecessary, as adequate analysis can be done with a number of simple smaller models. When complex analysis is required, the results must always be reviewed against the structural behaviour predicted by simplified calculations, and significant differences properly understood.

Reference – Chapter 14

1   A Beal – **Factors of ignorance?** – The Structural Engineer, Vol. 79/No. 20 16 Oct. 2001 – p 15-16

CHAPTER 15 *Dynamic behaviour*

One textbook on structural dynamics notes that there is a widely held belief that this subject is too difficult to be part of structural engineers' knowledge; this opinion is offered, as most books on it are mathematically dense, but this book does not follow the approach of using mathematical descriptions from the outset. However, for the design of any real structure, numerical calculations, based on mathematical theory, are essential – the later self-contained **Chapter 17** entitled ***The mathematical basis*** allows the interested reader to grasp the essentials of the mathematical fundamentals.

The conceptual ideas that explain structural behaviour for **static loads**, and how these inform design decisions, takes up the bulk of this book. This is done by diagrams and verbal explanations, with numerical values, which are essential for verifying any actual design, being introduced only in **Chapter 14** *A simple approach to calculations*. However, due to the complexities of the dynamic behaviour of structures, diagrams and verbal explanations are insufficient, so a slightly more technical approach has to be taken.

Under loads, structures deflect – they move; but structures are generally designed so that these movements are small, in the order of one three-hundred-and-sixtieth of the span of a beam – **span/360** – so that they are normally imperceptible to the users. Effectively, structures stay still – they do not vibrate. The main reason for investigating the dynamic behaviour of a structure is **to make sure that any vibration effects are tolerable**. Naturally, a clear quantitative definition is difficult. When a structure vibrates it may cause three problems:

- **The occupants might suffer from mild to severe discomfort**
- **Vibration sensitive technical equipment or procedures may be adversely affected**
- **The structure, or other parts of the building, may suffer permanent damage, or even collapse**

Unlike static behaviour, the mathematical description of the dynamic behaviour of even the simplest structure cannot be made without recourse to advanced mathematics, in particular the **differential calculus** – see sections **17.1** and **17.2**.

This chapter has to introduce numerous special terms which only apply to dynamic behaviour, and, unlike the rest of the book, mainly explains dynamic behaviour by using **graphs**.

The essential quantity for dynamic behaviour is **time**. Any pictorial representation of this behaviour usually includes this variable, so many of the graphs plot some important quantity against time. As well as the usual quantities of interest for structural behaviour, deflection, force, etc., there are new quantities. Two of these are the **velocity** of the moving structure, and the **acceleration**. Acceleration is important because this quantity is often used to characterise human discomfort.

These plots against time frequently take the form of a **sine curve** (or sine wave), as the mathematical description. The differential calculus, predicts dynamic behaviour will follow such a curve (**Sine is a trigonometrical function of angle** and is described in numerous elementary mathematical texts.[*]) Here it is the shape of the curve that is of interest, as it characterises the dynamic response of a simple structure against time. When plotted against an angle θ, the **value of sine θ** varies smoothly between **+1** and **–1**, taking these values at odd multiples of **90°**, and taking the value **0** at even multiples of **90°**. A sine curve is shown in **Fig. 15.1**.

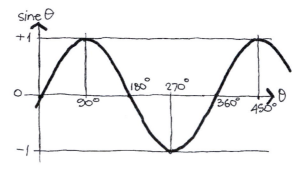

Fig. 15.1 Sine curve

For instance, this curve characterises the dynamic behaviour of many quantities for the simplest system – **Simple Harmonic Motion** – see next section. Depending on various factors, dynamic quantities are also characterised by a similar curve called a **cosine curve**; this is basically a **sine curve** displaced by **90°**, see **Fig. 15.2**.

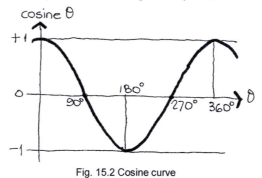

Fig. 15.2 Cosine curve

These curves have three important qualities which relate to the dynamic behaviour of structures; these are:

- **They oscillate between a fixed maximum, +1, and a fixed minimum, –1**
- **They continue in the angle θ direction, without coming to an end**
- **The curves are smooth, there are no breaks, steps or sudden changes of direction**

While these curves show the behaviour for the simplest systems, the behaviour of more complex situations are characterised by more complex curves. But in many cases they are complex versions of **sine** and **cosine** curves; the reasons for this lie within the mathematical analysis, which is beyond the scope of this book.

---

[*] see https://en.wikipedia.org/wiki/Sine_wave, for instance

15.1 Simple harmonic motion

The basic principles of dynamic behaviour are best explained by examining how a simple idealised vibrating system acts. The system chosen is a **mass** suspended vertically from a **spring**. Here the spring is assumed to be **weightless** and the whole system is in a **vacuum**. When the mass is motionless, the **force** in the **spring** is **equal** to the **weight** of the **mass** – this is the **equilibrium position**. If the mass is displaced vertically **above** the equilibrium position by a distance **d** and then released, the mass will move **downward** to the equilibrium position. It will then continue downwards to a distance **d below** the equilibrium position. At this point the mass will stop momentarily, and then move **upwards** to the position of release. As the system is an idealised one, the mass will continue to move up and down – vibrate/oscillate – forever. Such a system is often called **Single Degree of Freedom,** or **SDOF** for short.

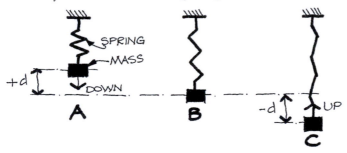

Fig. 15.3 – SDOF (Single degree of freedom) system

For the vibrating mass there are three important positions:

A – the point of release

B – the equilibrium position

C – the position where the mass stops momentarily, before changing direction

It should be noted that in describing dynamic behaviour many ordinary words are used as specific technical terms. The system of the mass endlessly going up and down is **vibrating**, or **oscillating**. The variable is **time**, usually denoted **t**. So the first thing of interest is how does the position of the mass vary with time? Here the position is **characterised** by the **value of the displacement**. Introducing **+** and **–** signs to indicate the mass is above or below the equilibrium position, the position **varies** from **+d** to **-d**. At the equilibrium position **d = 0**. If a graph is drawn that plots the position of the mass against time, **t**, a continuous **cosine curve** results – see **Fig. 15.4**.

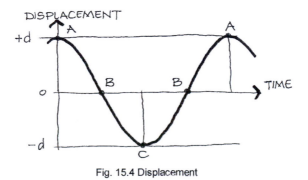

Fig. 15.4 Displacement

The curve given in **Fig. 15.4** shows a number of important things. The action of the mass moving from **A** to **C** and back to **A** is a **cycle**. The numerical value of the time taken for this is the **period**, and the **frequency** is the **number of cycles per second**. The frequency is usually measured in **Hertz** (named after the great physicist), or **Hz**, which is **one cycle/sec**. The height of the curve from the zero baseline gives the **amplitude** of the vibrations.

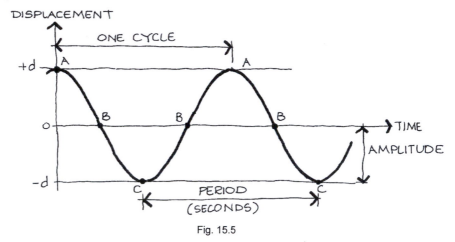

Fig. 15.5

There is an inverse relationship between frequency and period:

Period = 1/Frequency   **Frequency = 1/Period**

There are two things to notice about the frequency of this system:

- **The frequency is independent of the size of the initial displacement**
- **The frequency is entirely dependent on physical characteristics of the system: it is the NATURAL FREQUENCY**

The curve given in **Fig. 15.4** also shows that the displacement of the mass changes with time; it has a **velocity**. The curve of the velocity is basically the opposite of the **displacement/time curve**. At **A** and **C** the **velocity is zero**, whereas at **B** it attains its maximum value.

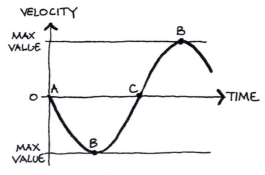

Fig. 15.6 Velocity

As **Fig. 15.6** shows, the velocity is not constant, but varies between zero and a maximum, so the **mass** must be **accelerating** and **decelerating**, during each cycle – a graph of the acceleration is shown in **Fig. 15.7**.

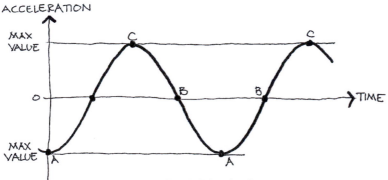

ACCELERATION

MAX VALUE

C

C

O

B

B

TIME

MAX VALUE

A

A

Fig. 15.7 Acceleration

Although only a simple system has been described here, a number of the quantities that have been identified are present in all vibrating systems that are **subject to an initial displacement**. These are:

- **There is an equilibrium position - B in Fig. 15.4**
- **The dynamic response of displacement is in the form of a cosine wave – see Fig. 15.4**
- **The system oscillates at a constant frequency – the natural frequency**
- **The amplitude is dependent on the initial displacement**

The fundamental property for any structure is its **natural frequency** denoted by **f** with a suffix **n**, so f_n is measured in **cycles/second** or **Hz**. The **circular natural frequency**, ω_n measured in **radians/second** is related to f_n by:

$$f_n = \frac{\omega_n}{2\pi}$$

Associated with the **natural frequency** f_n, is the **period T**, measured in **seconds**, and inversely related by:

$$T = \frac{1}{f_n}$$

To have a feel for the numerical values of frequencies is important for understanding dynamic behaviour, as the natural frequency of any system is so fundamental, but to relate numerical values to daily life is not easy. The musical note middle C has a frequency of 262Hz, with a musical string playing that note vibrating faster than the eye can see. However walking steadily, about two steps a second, has a frequency of 2Hz. So for the note of middle C, the period is 0.004 seconds, and for walking the period is ½ second, which is two steps a second. One can check the walking frequency by counting the number of steps taken in 30secs at normal walking speed.

15.2   More vibrating systems

The single mass bouncing on a single spring may seem to have little to do with building structures; but, by using the concepts obtained from examining this system, the dynamic behaviour of more complex building structures can be understood.

Consider a cantilever beam and a simply supported beam. Now instead of a single mass at a point, the mass is spread uniformly. If the tip of the cantilever and the centre of the beam are given initial vertical displacements that are then released they, due to their elastic stiffness, will vibrate – see **Fig.15.8**.

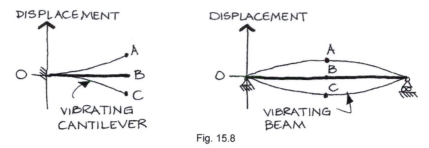

Fig. 15.8

The positions labelled **A**, **B** and **C** on the two structures can be related directly to those shown in **Fig. 15.3**. So everything in section **15.1** can be applied immediately to these two structures. However, there is one difference which is due to the fact that the mass is distributed along the structures, as is the elastic stiffness. To see what this difference makes, consider a system similar to the one shown in **Fig. 15.3**, but this time with a **second mass** suspended from the first mass by a **second spring**. Now there are **two ways** of giving the system an **initial displacement**. Either the masses can be displaced in **same direction**, or in the **opposite direction**. These will cause two different vibrating patterns or **modes of vibration** as they are usually called.

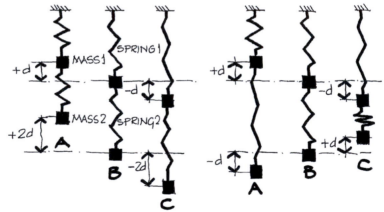

Fig. 15.9 First Mode (Left), Second Mode (Right)

The positions labelled **A**, **B** and **C** on **Fig. 15.9** can again be related to those shown in **Fig. 15.3**. There is one pattern where the two masses go up and down in the same direction – the **first mode**. The second pattern is where the two masses go up and down in opposite directions – the **second mode**. The **natural frequencies** of the higher modes in some simple case are integer products of the **fundamental frequency** f_n.

Returning to the cantilever and simple supported beam, what is shown in **Fig. 15.8** for each structure is only the **first mode of vibration**. Perhaps surprisingly, because the **mass** and **stiffness** is **distributed** – in mass and spring examples the masses are known as **lumped masses** – there are many modes of vibration. **Fig. 15.10** shows the **second mode** for each structure.

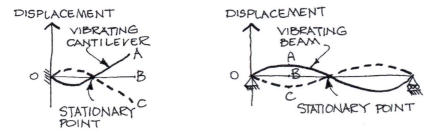

Fig. 15.10 Second modes for cantilever (Left) simply supported beam (Right)

The positions labelled **A**, **B** and **C** on **Fig. 15.10** can again be related to those shown in **Fig. 15.3** - but now the **C** position is shown dashed for clarity. There are two further points to notice about the **second mode**; now there is a **stationary point** during the vibration, and secondly, the **frequency** will be **higher** than the first mode. In other words the cantilever and the beam will be **vibrating faster** in terms of cycles/second. With each succeeding mode, there will be more stationary points, and increases in natural frequencies.

15.3   Energy and damping

The word energy is frequently used in everyday speech, and usually means the capacity to do something. In engineering it has the same meaning, but specific types of energy are identified. Returning to the vibrating system shown in **Fig. 15.1** two types of energy are present; **Potential Energy** and **Kinetic Energy**. As the names imply, **Potential Energy** means some form of stored energy. In this case it is stored in the spring, and it sometimes called **Strain Energy. Kinetic Energy** is related to energy in something that is moving. In physics, the **law of conservation of energy** states that the numerical sum of the total energy of an isolated system remains constant—it is said to be conserved over time. This gives the numerical equation:

Potential Energy + Kinetic Energy = PE + KE = TE (Total Energy) = a constant

For the system shown in **Fig.15.3**, the **Potential Energy is stored in the spring when the spring is compressed or stretched**, and the **Kinetic Energy is in the moving mass**. If the **Total Energy** is the number **TE**, then **Fig. 15.4** can be redrawn to show how the two different types of energy are related.

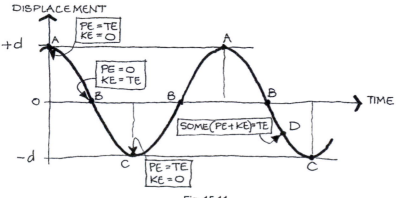

Fig. 15.11

Fig.15.11 shows three situations. At **A** and **C**, the spring is fully compressed or stretched, and the velocity is zero, so **PE + KE = PE + 0 = TE**. At **B**, the spring is neither stretched nor compressed, and the mass is moving at maximum speed, so **PE + KE = 0 + KE = TE**. And at an intermediate point **D**, the mass is moving so there is some kinetic energy, and the spring is partially compressed, or stretched, so there is some potential energy, so **Some PE + Some KE = TE**.

In a **real situation**, rather than an idealised one of weightless springs and vacuums, the vibrating mass will **NOT** vibrate forever but will vibrate with smaller and smaller amplitudes until it comes to rest. This is because there is another term in the total energy equation, and that is the **energy** being **dissipated**. In the real situation:

Potential Energy + Kinetic Energy + Dissipated Energy = PE + KE + DE = TE

Now **Fig. 15.4** is redrawn as **Fig. 15.12** to show a real situation.

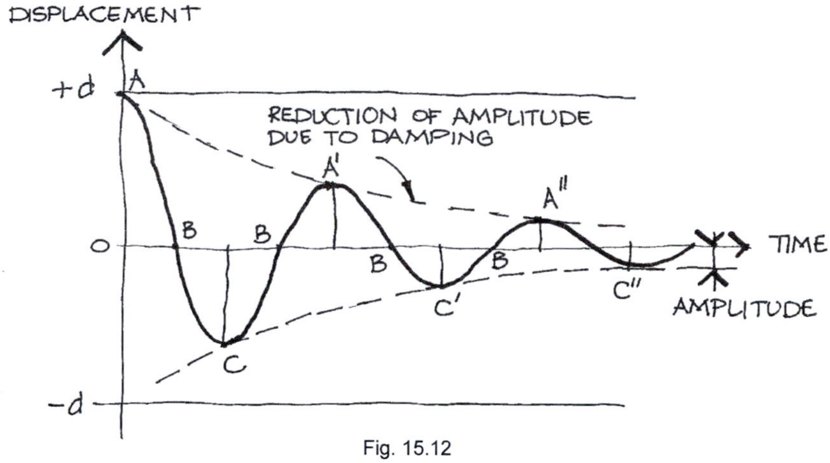

Fig. 15.12

Now the position labelled **A**, is relabelled, **A'** and **A"**, likewise with **C**, to indicate the vibrating system in not returning exactly to the points **A** and **C**, as they did in the idealised system. That is because the dissipated energy is **not recoverable**, so with each cycle the **strain** and **kinetic energies** are being reduced, meaning there is **less energy to vibrate the system**. As a consequence, the **amplitude reduces** with each cycle, but **not the frequency** which remains constant.

What is causing the vibrating system to lose energy and eventually come to rest? There can be many reasons, but in the case of the single lumped mass, the vibrating system will cause the air around it to be continuously disturbed and the spring may heat up. In other words, the vibrating system is **feeding kinetic energy into the surrounding air** by making it move, and **thermal energy into the spring** making it heat up. All these methods of taking energy away from a vibrating system are called **damping**. What is seen in this system are the two basic causes of damping: making something outside the system move, or making something heat up.

In any damped vibrating system, the amount of damping will affect how long it will take for the vibrations to stop. To assess how effective the amount of any damping is in stopping vibrations a technical quantity called the **damping ratio**, usually denoted by the Greek letter zeta, ζ, has been formulated. The value of ζ, a dimensionless quantity, divides dynamic systems into four types.

Undamped – ζ = 0 – Vibrations continue forever

Under-damped – 0 < ζ < 1 – Vibrations gradually reduce

Critically damped – ζ = 1 – System returns to its initial position during the period of the system, without vibrating

Over-damped – 1 < ζ < ∞ – System returns to its initial position eventually, without vibrating.

Fig. 15.13 shows graphically how different values of ζ affect the dynamic displacement behaviour of a **SDOF** system.

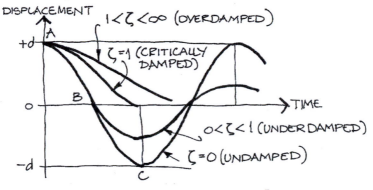

Fig. 15.13 The effect of the damping ratio ζ

The four types of damping can be clarified by thinking of the everyday situation of a double-swing door with a closing spring. The initial displacement is opening the door then letting the door spring close it. If ζ is zero then the door just swings backwards and forwards forever. If ζ is more than zero and less than one, then the door swings backwards and forwards gradually coming to the closed position. If ζ equals one, the door closes as quickly as possible without swinging, and if ζ is greater than one, then the door closes slowly, again without swinging. As a limiting case, the damping could be stronger than the restoring force of the spring, so the door would just remain stuck open.

In the case of building structures the damping factor ζ is rarely above 0.1 (10% of critical), and for welded steel structures ζ can be as low as 0.02. In other words building **structures will vibrate** if subjected to dynamic loads. This contrasts to the dampers – shock absorbers – of most cars, which do not allow any vibrations after an impact load – hitting a pothole, for example – as they have ζ = 1or ζ > 1.

15.4 Dynamic loading

So far, all the dynamic systems that have been considered have been given an initial displacement and then allowed to vibrate freely, however, this is an unusual cause of vibrations in building structures. There are numerous different causes for the vibration of building structures. These include vibrating machinery, dancing or marching people, various wind effects, blasts or collisions, and earthquakes.

The consequences of building vibrations are various. Human beings are highly sensitive to vibrations, especially when lying down, so even quite small vibrations can be detected and cause reactions from irritation to fatigue or even nausea. Vibrations can affect sensitive operations in laboratories, manufacturing and surgery. Reactions to dynamic loads from explosions, collisions or earthquakes often provoke building damage or even total collapse. How to quantify the effect of vibrations is a complex task.

Previous chapters in the book have only considered structures subjected to static loads; these loads are graphically illustrated by directed arrows – see **Chapter 1**. As dynamic loads change with time, such arrows are no longer adequate for graphical illustration; what is now needed is something that shows how the loads change with time, in other words a graph that plots the magnitude and direction of the load at a point may vary with time – see **Fig. 15.14**.

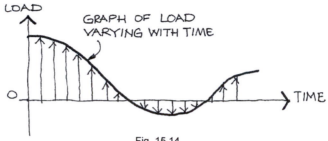

Fig. 15.14

There are three basic types of dynamic loading, which are **periodic loading, transient loading** and **random loading**. These are all characterised by graphs in the form of **Fig. 15.14**. As a graph is a representation of what is called in mathematics a **function**, and because these graphs show loads that are **forcing a structure to vibrate**, such graphs are often referred to as **forcing functions**.

Periodic loading has a graph, or **forcing function**, in which the same shape repeats with a **constant frequency**, called an **exciting frequency** or **forcing frequency**.

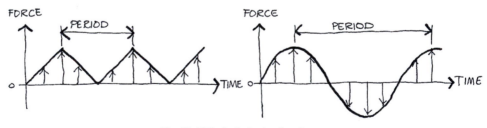

Fig. 15.15 Periodic forcing functions

There are many sources of **periodic loading** such as rotating or oscillating machines or effectively periodic like dancing or walking. Of particular interest for tall slender structures is a wind effect called **vortex shedding**. This happens when a steady wind of a critical speed blows on such a structure. As the wind flows around the structure, the flow may detach from the structure on the leeward side forming vortices. As these leave the structure, the release of pressure causes forces. At some wind speeds, the vortices leave the structure in symmetric pairs, causing periodic forces in the direction of the wind. At other wind speeds, the vortices leave asymmetrically causing periodic forces at right angles to the wind direction – see **Fig. 15.16**. Such vortices, or eddies, can often be seen in streams as the water flows past smooth boulders, and oscillations due to **vortex shedding** can be seen in tall slender lamp posts or flag poles on windy days.

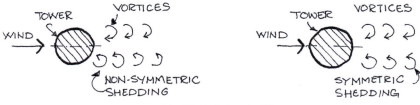

Fig. 15.16 Vortex shedding

Transient loading has a forcing function of short duration, no more than a few seconds at the most, and can have various shapes.

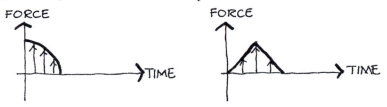

Fig. 15.17 Transient forcing functions

Transient loading is due to sudden events such as collisions, explosions or wind gusts. The structural design of some buildings needs to consider resistance to such events, and this subject forms part of the next chapter.

Random loading is caused by dynamic loads that are usually generated by natural phenomena such as wave action, wind action or seismic events (ground-borne vibrations).

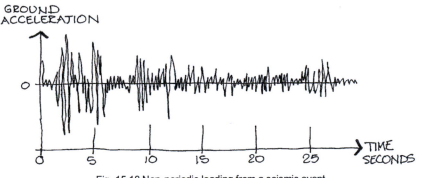

Fig. 15.18 Non-periodic loading from a seismic event

Seismic events rarely last for more than a minute, whereas dynamic loads from wind and wave action can be continuous.

15.5   Dynamic response

The main reason for dynamic analysis of structures is to see how they respond to dynamic loading. This allows important decisions to be made about a proposed structure which are based on the nature of the dynamic response. The basic question to be answered is:

- **Is the predicted dynamic response acceptable?**

Like many aspects of structural design, it is far easier to ask this question than answer it. To avoid difficult post-construction problems with dynamic effects, and before complex and lengthy dynamic analyses are embarked upon, it is helpful to identify how a problem could arise, and if it does, what is the solution? There are two situations which need to be identified before further work is done, these are:

- **Is there a clearly identifiable source of dynamic loading, and if so what is its frequency(s)?**
- **Is the proposed structure likely to be dynamically sensitive to the loading?**

Building structures are constantly subjected to dynamic loads in many normal situations. Daily or seasonal temperature or humidity changes cause varying loads, as do people by moving about buildings, or by moving objects. The wind is always a dynamic load, as are moving cars and trains. However, in most cases dynamic effects can be replaced by statically equivalent loads. In some cases regulations require that static loads are increased by a **dynamic load factor** in the form of a percentage increase. Dynamic sensitivity is traditionally dealt with by imposing strict deflection limits due to static loads. But there are cases where all this static equivalence does not remove a possible dynamic problem. A famous example, though for a bridge not a building, was the **Tacoma Narrows Bridge** which opened on July 1st 1940, and collapsed, due to unforeseen dynamic problems, on November 7th the same year. Before it collapsed, wind effects linked to **vortex shedding** – see **Fig. 15.16** – were clearly visible – see **Fig. 15.19**.

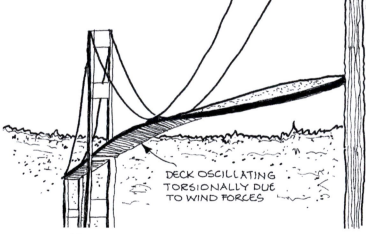

Fig. 15.19 Tacoma Narrows Bridge exhibiting dynamic behaviour

Whilst normal prescribed static loadings take into account dynamic effects, there are several circumstances where further consideration is required. These are:

- **Effect of heavy rotating or oscillating machinery or objects**
- **People involved in rhythmic activities: dancing, exercising, walking or marching**
- **The dynamic action of wind or waves**
- **Earthquakes and explosions – see sections 15.10 – 13**

The first three on the list above are **periodic loadings**, which will have a **fundamental circular frequency** – denoted by **ω** and measured in radians/second, and possibly higher frequencies. The effect dynamic loading has on a structure depends on a comparison of one or more of the frequencies of the periodic loading to the natural frequency of the structure. This is called the **frequency ratio – r = ω/ω$_n$**. The effect of the loading on the structure is measured by the **dynamic magnification factor, DMF,** which is the **ratio** of the **maximum displacement** due to the dynamic load to the **static displacement** caused a static load of the same magnitude. Once again this effect is best shown graphically – see **Fig. 15.20**. Each **damping factor ζ** – see **Fig. 15.13** – produces a different graph.

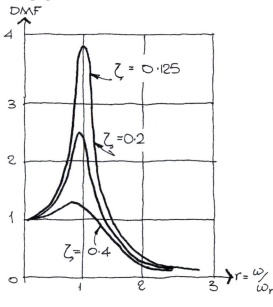

Fig. 15.20

Fig. 15.20 shows that when the **frequency ratio r** is near to **1**, the **dynamic magnification factor DMF** increases rapidly. As displacements increase, so do the associated bending moments, axial forces and consequent stresses. The lower the **damping ratio ζ,** the more marked is the increase in the **DMF**. As has been noted – page **409** – the **damping ratio** for buildings is rarely above **0.1** and often much lower. The dynamic behaviour when **r** is near to **1**, is called **resonance**, and has the effect of increasing the amplitude of the displacement with each cycle. **Fig. 15.21** shows the effect of resonance on an **undamped structure**; for damped structures the displacement is finite, but can be unacceptably large.

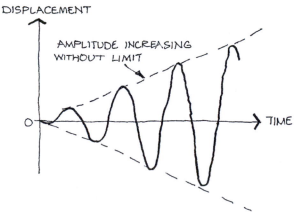

Fig. 15.21 – Resonance of an undamped system

The bulk of mathematics in books about structural dynamics shows how, for increasingly complex systems, the system moves (displaces) with respect to time. However, unlike in many engineering situations (for example the vibration from a ship's engines and propeller system where dynamic behaviour is unavoidable), in building structures the objective is to **prevent** or at least **limit vibration**. This is done in different ways, depending on the vibration source.

15.6   Vibration suppression

Where a source of vibration has not been identified during the design of a structure, especially if it has a frequency near to the natural frequency of the structure, which could cause resonance, the effect on the use of the structure varies from unfortunate to catastrophic.

When the **Millennium footbridge**, which crosses the Thames, opened on June 10th 2000, a large number of people crossing the bridge induced unacceptable almost periodic sideways movements, causing the bridge to be closed two days later on June 12th.[1] The reason for the sway was a complex interaction between the frequency of the lateral load caused by the walking crowd, and the **lateral natural frequency** of the bridge. Referred to as **synchronous lateral excitation**, two years later the bridge reopened after £5M had been spent and various types of dampers had been installed. This took as long as the initial construction period and at an extra 27% of the original cost. Apart from the extra money needed and the lack of use of the bridge, this dynamic problem was a public embarrassment for the designers. The bridge is now also known as the **Wobbly Bridge**.

The Tacoma Narrows Bridge – see **Fig. 15.19** – suffered a similar but worse fate. Under certain wind conditions a strange form of vortex shedding – see **Fig. 15.16** – took place, and was originally thought to be the cause of the failure. This assumed that increasing torsional displacements due to resonance – see **Fig. 15.21** – had destroyed the bridge deck.[2] So traumatic was the collapse that the causes were researched exhaustively, and it was eventually decided that the cause was a phenomenon called **single-degree-of-freedom torsional flutter due to complex separated flow;**[3] a complex behaviour whose description is beyond the scope of this book. Just five days before the collapse of the bridge deck, proposals had been made to alter the aerodynamic profile of the bridge.[4] All that could be re-used of the dynamically destroyed bridge were the tower foundations and the cable anchorages.[5]

What these two cautionary tales show is that dynamic effects have to be considered during the design process, even if in these two cases the designers might argue that the actual effects, **synchronous lateral excitation** and **aeroelastic flutter**, were not previously well-known. In fact, both designs were outside the normal limits of structural slenderness.

Dynamic behaviour of a structure subjected to dynamic loading depends on its **natural frequency** ω_n (or f_n) and its **damping factor** ζ. Mathematical analysis of the simplest dynamic system – that shown in **Fig. 15.3** – gives a simple relationship between ω_n the circular natural frequency, **M** the mass, and **k** the **stiffness** of the spring. **Stiffness** is defined as the force that produces a unit displacement.

$$\omega_n = \sqrt{\frac{k}{M}} \text{ radians/second}$$

Which gives the associated **natural frequency f_n** measured in **cycles/second** or **Hz** and the **period T** in **seconds** as:

$$f_n = \frac{\omega_n}{2\pi} \text{ Hz} \quad \text{and} \quad T = \frac{1}{f_n} \text{ seconds}$$

What can be seen is that the natural frequency of the simple structure depends on the numerical values of the stiffness of the structure – the spring – and the vibrating mass. If the spring is made stiffer, the period reduces and the system vibrates at a higher frequency; if the mass is increased, the period lengthens and the system vibrates at a lower frequency. And, as damping does not affect the natural frequency, the only way to alter the natural frequency of the system shown in **Fig. 15.3** is to alter **k** or **M**.

Although these statements are made about a very simple system, they can be generalised to more complex systems. In **Figs. 15.8** and **9** more complex systems are shown, and two modes of vibrations are shown for each one. It is no longer possible to define the natural frequencies of these systems by a simple expression; however the ideas that making the system or structure stiffer will reduce the period, and increasing the mass will lengthen it, apply in a general way. Making a beam stiffer by altering its cross-section or making it of a stiffer material will shorten the period, and the beam will vibrate faster.

The fact that the alteration of structural natural frequencies can only be made by changing the stiffness and/or the mass is the crux of the matter. As the cautionary tales show, if the natural frequency of the structure coincides with the frequency of an applied periodic loading, which then causes a resonance problem, putting it right can be extremely difficult. To avoid this, the following needs to be clear:

- **Is the building likely to be subjected to periodic dynamic loads?**
- **If so, what are the load frequencies?**
- **Do the natural frequencies of the building structure coincide with any load frequency?**

If the answer to the third question is yes, then a potential problem has been identified and needs to be addressed. This basically has two outcomes; the vibration of the building matters or it does not. Dynamic analysis is more complex and time-consuming than static analysis, so it should only be undertaken when strictly necessary.

Periodic dynamic loading of buildings mainly comes from these sources:

- **Rhythmic human activity: dancing, exercising or marching – see section 15.7**
- **Vibrating machinery or other objects such as swinging bells – see section 15.8**
- **Steady state wind effects such as vortex shedding, or more complex wind behaviour – see section 15.9**

15.7 Floor vibrations

The most common source of vibration that can cause nuisance in buildings is human activity, usually walking. Although the load is small, the walking-induced vibrations may not be, and can cause a annoyance to people working or living in the building, and especially for the use of sensitive equipment or to those engaged in motion-sensitive activities. The problem is more acute for more vigorous types of human activity such as dancing and jumping, and therefore designers of buildings featuring a gymnasium or dance studio, should take extra care to limit the vibrations in the rest of the building.

A person walking at a regular pace applies a periodically repeated forcing function to the floor at a frequency of between **1.6** to **2.2**Hz. Although dominated by the pacing frequency, the periodic loading caused by walking is made up of several frequencies superimposed on one another. When considering the possibility of resonance, account must also be taken of these higher excitation frequencies. For a walking frequency of **2**Hz, the higher frequencies are **4**Hz and **8**Hz. A typical force-time plot for walking is shown in **Fig. 15.22**.

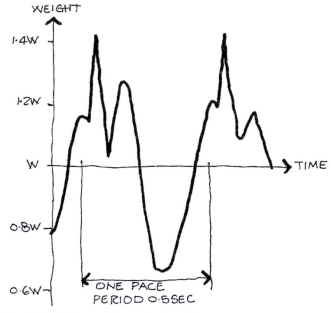

Fig. 15.22 – Measured forces due to walking

A first approximation for the natural frequency of a simply supported beam, f_n can be obtained from this simple expression:[6]

$$f_n = \frac{18}{\sqrt{\delta}} \text{ Hz}$$

Where δ is the static deflection due to the loads being considered. Given that static deflections are in the region of span/360 or so, then the range of natural frequencies can be calculated.

For a 10m span, $\delta = \dfrac{10 \times 10^3}{360} = 28$ mm, so $f_n = \dfrac{18}{\sqrt{28}} = 3.40$ Hz and for a 3m span, $\delta = \dfrac{3 \times 10^3}{360} = 8.33$ mm, so $f_n = \dfrac{18}{\sqrt{8.33}} = 6.24$ Hz

It must be remembered that calculation of the static deflection requires knowledge of Young's modulus of the material, and for some materials this is rarely available with any great accuracy, so very elaborate mathematical analysis aimed at establishing the natural frequency is often inappropriate.

Problems with resonance due to walking can be avoided if the fundamental natural frequency of the floor is **3Hz** or more, but for dancing or jumping the fundamental natural frequency should be at least **8.4Hz**.[7] These numbers can be substituted into the previous expression to give an idea of the effect these limitations have on structural dimensions.

For **3Hz** the allowable deflection $\delta_{all} = (18/3)^2 = 36$mm which for a deflection of **L/360** gives $L_{all} = $ **13m**. This shows that walking vibrations only affect relatively long span floors. However, for dancing or jumping, the situation is quite different. For **8.4Hz**, the allowable deflection $\delta_{all} = (18/8.4)^2 = 4.6$mm a deflection of **L/360** gives $L_{all} = $ **1.6m**, a very short span. So for spaces that are to be used for these activities, dynamic behaviour always needs to be considered.

More specific information is given in **Table 15.1**.

Activity	Forcing frequency f Hz (Harmonic)	Effective Live Load kN/m^2	Floor type	Minimum f_n Hz
Dancing and Dining	3.0 (1st)	0.6	Heavy floor	6.4
			Light floor	8.1
Concert or sports event	5.0 (2nd)	1.5	Heavy floor	5.9
			Light floor	6.4
Aerobics	8.25 (3rd)	0.2	Heavy floor	8.8
			Light floor	9.2

Table 15.1[8]

In **Table 15.1**, a **Heavy Floor** weighs **5 kN/m^2**, and a **Light Floor** weighs **2.5 kN/m^2**. As noted in the second column, the critical frequency is not necessarily the **1st Harmonic**. Where the minimum frequency depends on **2nd** or **3rd Harmonics** – see page **406-407** – these can be reduced if 'sufficient' damping is present to reduce resonance of these harmonics.

It should be noted that the guideline figures given above are just that – guidelines. Figures given in other documents may vary, but usually give broadly similar values.

15.8 Isolation of vibrations

Buildings frequently have to house machines that intermittently or continuously vibrate, and often the length and power of the vibrations make it necessary to reduce or, if possible, eliminate the transmissions of these vibrations to the rest of the building. There is a similar but opposite situation, where equipment is used or functions are carried out that are sensitive to vibrations being transmitted from the surrounding construction – see **Fig. 15.23**. In either situation, the solution is to use **specific isolating supports**. Whilst there are many types of **vibration isolators**, the most common use **springs** or **pads of material** like **cork**, **rubber** or **elastomeric materials**. The isolators may incorporate specific damping devices, usually by means of a hydraulic device similar to car shock absorbers – **viscous damping**.

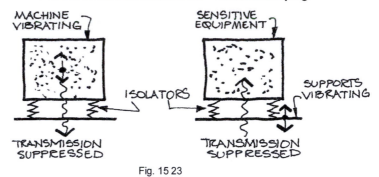

Fig. 15 23

The basic idea is to make the natural frequency of the object supported on the vibration isolators, f_n, different from the frequency of the vibrating source, **f**. Depending on the ratio, **r**, of these frequencies, various percentages of the vibrations will be transmitted; this is called the **transmissibility ratio T**. When comparing the effect of **r** on **T** for various **damping factors** ζ, curves not unlike **Fig. 15.20** are obtained – see **Fig. 15.24**.

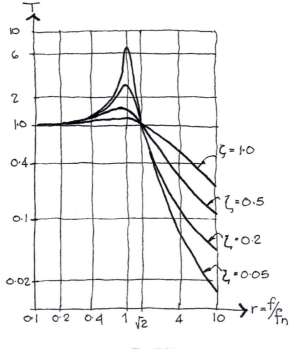

Fig. 15.24

As the graphs show, when **r = 1**, the introduction of such isolators causes **resonance**, and, depending on the damping factor, increases the transmissibility from **1.5** for ζ = **0.5** to a **very large number** if ζ = 0, i.e no damping at all. For **r** in the range **0.1 < r < √2**, the isolators of these frequencies cause a **dynamic magnification factor** as shown in

Fig. 15.20, the opposite of what is required. This is because these isolators have a high stiffness. For $r \geq \sqrt{2}$, transmissibility reduces dramatically, and perhaps counter-intuitively reduces faster with the reduction in damping factor. This is because the damping force adds to the transmissibility.

Where specific isolators are installed, provision must be made to maintain them, or change them if necessary.

15.9 Tall buildings

The basic questions are what is a tall building, and when does dynamic behaviour need to be considered? Codes of practice state that static analysis is normally appropriate for structures up to 50m in height, and dynamic analysis must be undertaken on any structure with height to breadth ratio greater than five, and a first mode frequency less than **1Hz**.[9] Approximate fundamental natural frequencies f_n can be estimated, where **h** is the height in metres, for concrete-framed buildings from: [10]

$$f_n = \frac{1}{0.075h^{0.75}} \; Hz$$

And for a steel-framed building from:

$$f_n = \frac{1}{0.085h^{0.75}} \; Hz$$

For other types of buildings, or framed buildings with masonry infill panels, the fundamental frequencies can be calculated, where **d** is the base dimension in the direction of the force in metres, from:

$$f_n = \frac{\sqrt{d}}{0.09h} \; Hz$$

For tall buildings the periodic dynamic loads are mainly due to vortex shedding – see **Fig. 15.16**. Whether this is likely to be problematic depends on the building's shape, cladding details, and location, and can only be decided definitively for a specific project. During the first phase of skyscraper building, between the late 19th century and the start of the Great Depression, exclusively in the United States, they were clad in masonry. Though not part of the design of the supporting iron and then steel structural frames, the heavyweight cladding added lateral stiffness. However, with the rise of Modern Movement architecture after WWII, and its desire to 'express the structure' starting with Lever House and the United Nations Secretariat in New York, both completed in 1952, skyscrapers became mostly glass-clad frameworks. This meant they were much more flexible laterally, and problems of discomfort due to sway started to appear.[11]

Two types of vortex shedding have already been shown in **Fig. 15.16**. However there can be up to six types of local airflow around an object. These are shown in **Fig. 15.25**.

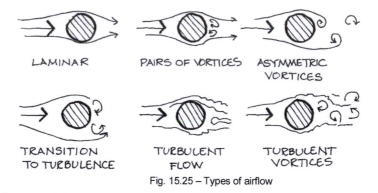

LAMINAR   PAIRS OF VORTICES   ASYMMETRIC VORTICES

TRANSITION TO TURBULENCE   TURBULENT FLOW   TURBULENT VORTICES

Fig. 15.25 – Types of airflow

Each type of flow is characterised by a dimensionless number called the **Reynolds number**, which is used to predict flow patterns in fluid flows,[12] and depends on a number of factors explained in specialised literature. For the smooth cylinder shown in **Fig. 15.25**, the Reynolds numbers are shown in **Table 15.2**.

Stage	Type of flow	Reynolds number
I	Smooth - laminar	R < 5
II	Symmetric Vortex shedding	5 < R < 40
III	Asymmetric vortex shedding	40 < R < 150
IV	Transition to turbulent flow	150 < R < 300,000
V	Turbulent flow	300,000 < R < 3,500,000
VI	Turbulent vortex shedding	3,500,000 < R

Table 15.2

The Reynolds number cannot be directly related to wind speed, but depends on the shape and smoothness of the object and the viscosity of the fluid medium. For example, airflow remains laminar around an airfoil section at high wind speeds, otherwise airplanes could not fly, whereas flow around a lumpy section becomes turbulent at a low wind speed – see **Fig. 15.26**.

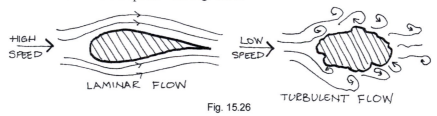

LAMINAR FLOW   TURBULENT FLOW

Fig. 15.26

Whilst Reynolds number defines the change of flow types, the frequency of vortex shedding f_v, is related to yet another number called the **Strouhal number S**. This number gives the frequency of vortex shedding with respect to the wind speed **V**, in metres/second, and the diameter of a tube **D**, in metres as:

$$f_v = \frac{SV}{D} \text{ Hz}$$

There is an empirical formula relating the Strouhal number to Reynolds number, but for a large range of Reynolds numbers the Strouhal number is about **0.2**. Furthermore, this number can be used for non-cylindrical shapes.[13] So, for a tall building with natural frequency f_n, and using **S = 0.2**, the above expression can be rearranged to given the critical wind speed, **V_crit** as:

$$V_{crit} = \frac{f_n D}{0.2} \text{ Hz}$$

Given that **D** for a typical skyscraper is about 50m, and a typical natural frequency is 0.15 Hz, the critical wind velocity would be 37.5m/s (83mph). This is not an unusual wind speed near the top of a skyscraper, and shows tall buildings are likely to be affected by vortex shedding. Whether these will cause significant dynamic forces and consequent significant stresses and deflections is a matter of detailed investigation. However, such dynamic excitation raises two issues, apart from the level of stresses, which are:

- **Will the horizontal vibrations cause human discomfort or worse?**
- **Is there sufficient damping for the dynamic magnification factor to be acceptable?**

As already noted, humans are very susceptible to vibrations of certain frequencies. With floors – see section **15.7** – the concern was with vertical vibrations, whereas for tall buildings it is horizontal vibrations that can cause discomfort. Again it is not only the frequency, but the accelerations that maybe troublesome.

When completed, in 1973, with 110 floors and a height above ground level of 417m, the twin towers of the World Trade Center, WTC, were the tallest buildings ever built. Each building was 63.14m square on plan with chamfered corners, and the storey height was 3.66m - see **Fig. 15.27**.

Fig. 15.27 – The original WTC towers

There were three basic structural elements:

- The external wall of closely-spaced steel columns and connecting beams. The columns were spaced at 1.02m and there were fifty-nine on each side: these walls formed a structural square tube carrying vertical and lateral loads.
- The central core was 41.8m by 26.52m, which housed the lifts and stairs. This had forty-seven steel columns and mainly carried vertical loads.
- The floors were insitu concrete cast onto permanent profiled steel formwork. The concrete was connected to steel formwork by shear connectors – see **Fig. 4.77**. In the core area the floor was carried on steel beams; between the core and the external wall, the floor was carried by long-span steel trusses. The floors also acted as horizontal diaphragms – see **Figs. 10.125** to **129** – to transfer lateral loads between the walls of the square tube.

The construction is shown in **Fig. 15.28**.

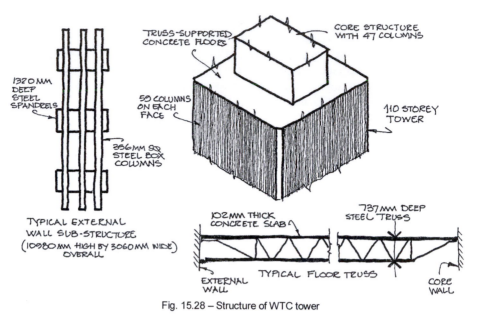

Fig. 15.28 – Structure of WTC tower

Aware that some smaller skyscrapers had caused human discomfort due to swaying the structural designers of the twin towers of the World Trade Center were to make pioneering advances in what became known as **wind engineering**. They made advances in three areas: human's susceptibility to swaying, wind tunnel testing of a structural models, and adding specific damping to modify dynamic behaviour.

Worried about negative publicity for this controversial building, sway tests on unsuspecting human guinea pigs were carried out by subterfuge as far away as possible from New York; in Eugene, Oregon. The designers had calculated the building would sway more than a metre. A room was built that could be moved horizontally inside what was labelled the Oregon Research Institute Vision Research Center, where free vision tests were offered. The Oregon Research Institute and the tests were genuine, but during them, unbeknown to the volunteers, the test room would be swayed by different amounts for different periods of time. The results were alarming, with patients feeling nauseous, groggy or rubber-legged; even the optometrist was sea-sick by the end of the day. This indicated humans were far more sensitive to horizontal movement than anyone had realised.

There are still no generally accepted international standards for comfort criteria in tall building design, but a considerable amount of research has been carried out into the parameters that cause human discomfort due to vibrations in the frequency range of 0-1 Hz commonly encountered in tall buildings. This discomfort is mainly caused by the acceleration – see **Fig. 15.7** – from 0.05 – 0.1 m/sec^2 being perceptible, up to 0.6 – 0.7 m/sec^2 being intolerable. These accelerations may seem low compared to that of gravity – 9.81 m/sec^2 – but for a bodyweight of 80 kg, and a frequency of 0.2 Hz, 0.7 m/sec^2 it would have the effect of being pushed horizontally with an alternating force of 5.7kg every 2½ seconds; clearly more than uncomfortable. It is because of this sensitivity, that it is commonplace nowadays for tall buildings to be fitted with damping devices to reduce the horizontal motion.

To understand the dynamic behaviour of the twin towers, models were tested in a wind tunnel at the Fluid Dynamics Laboratory at Colorado State University. Overseen by the 'father of wind engineering' Jack Cermak (1922-2012), they were the first comprehensive studies of wind loading of a structure in a wind tunnel.[14] The results were horrifying; the models in the wind tunnel indicated that under some wind conditions the top of the towers could sway 9 metres. Testing continued for two years, and the results showed that design changes were imperative.[15]

Changes were required to the basic structure to stiffen it, and as pioneer wind engineer Alan Davenport (1932-2009) put it, *'damping would be very helpful.'* The structural stiffening was achieved by altering the façade steelwork, by connecting the external steelwork to the cores at roof level by huge trusses, and by reorienting the core in one tower. An extra 503 tonnes of steelwork was needed.[16] Specific damping was introduced, the first time this had been used in a building for which engineer Leslie Robertson designed a visco-elastic damping device – see **Fig. 15.29**. Ten thousand of these devices were fitted between the ends of the floor trusses and the external walls; one hundred per floor from the 7th to the 107th floors. The natural frequency of the revised structure was 0.1Hz, which compares to 0.12Hz calculated from the approximate formula given on page **419**. But even with all these dampers, in windy conditions people at the top of the towers felt nauseous, and the water in toilets could be seen moving.

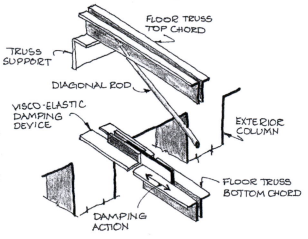

Fig. 15.29 – WTC Damping device

Since then it has become commonplace to test major structures in wind tunnels, and to add damping devices to tall buildings. There are many types of these, but the most common is called the **tuned mass damper**. This is an extra mass, m_d, added to the building that can move horizontally with respect to the building. It is joined to the building by a spring, k_d and a damping device, c_d – see **Fig. 15.30**.

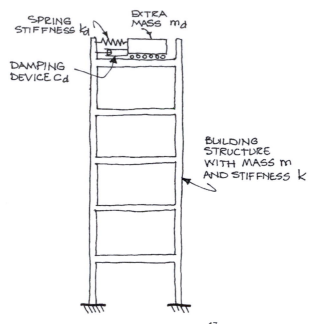

Fig. 15.30 – Tuned mass damper[17]

When the building tries to vibrate horizontally – for wind, tall buildings may be considered as vertical cantilevers, so the first vibration mode is as shown in **Fig. 15.8** – the damping mass m_d tries to move in the opposite direction due to its inertia. Whereas most buildings usually have **low damping factors** ζ, the introduction of a specific damping as part of the mass damper means it can have a higher damping factor ζ_d. The addition of the mass damper turns the single degree of freedom cantilever into a two degrees of freedom system – see **Fig. 15.9**. Because the damping mass is moving in the opposite direction to the building mass, the new system now vibrates similarly to the **second mode** of the system shown in **Fig. 15.9**.

By calculating the most effective damping mass m_d, and the damping coefficient ζ_d of the damping device c_d, the resonating vibration of the building caused by the coincidence of the natural frequency f_n with the frequency of the vortex shedding f_v can be modified. This means that the resonance – see **Fig. 15.20** – can be modified, as shown in **Fig. 15.31**.

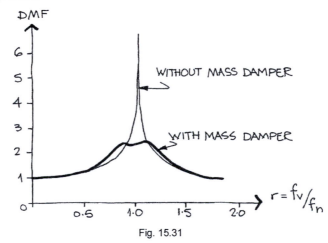

Fig. 15.31

Published figures for the natural frequency f_n of the 244m high steel-framed John Hancock Tower in Boston gives 0.14Hz, whereas the formula, on page **419** gives 0.19Hz. For the 278m high Citicorp Center in New York, also steel-framed, the published figure is 0.16HZ,[18] whereas the formula gives 0.17Hz. This means the period **T** for both buildings is in the order of 6 seconds, so that if the buildings were swaying in their first mode – see **Fig. 15.8** – it would take about 3 seconds for the buildings to sway from one side to the other; a time readily perceptible to a human.

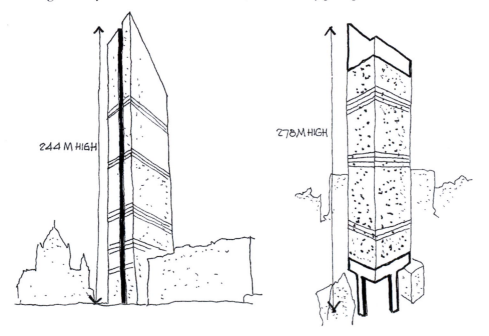

Fig. 15.32 – John Hancock Tower (left) and Citicorp Center (right)

By the time the Citicorp Center was constructed in 1977 – see **Fig. 15.32 (right)** – it was accepted that positive measures had to be taken to control sway due to wind effects, so the first tuned mass damper was installed. This was a 500 ton block of concrete installed at the top of the building that 'floated' on a bed of oil. It reduced lateral deflections by 50%.[19]

The John Hancock Tower in Boston – see **Fig. 15.32 (left)** – completed in 1976, also has a mass damper; in this case two 300 ton blocks of lead sliding on lubricated steel sheets. Unlike the Citicorp Center, it was only **after** the building was completed that it was realised that the damper was required – installing it cost $3,000,000.[20] Nowadays the installation of tuned mass dampers is common in tall buildings.

15.10 Earthquakes

As has already been noted, the planet Earth's outermost layer is a rocky **crust**, or **lithosphere** which is divided into eight main sections called **tectonic plates** – see page **184**. These plates are in constant movement, due to convection in the underlying mantle. Along the plate boundaries and within the plates are fault lines, and the plate movement means that there can be relative movement along these lines. There are three types of movement, **strike-slip** where the plates are sliding horizontally, **normal** where the plates are moving apart, and **thrust** where they are moving together. The surfaces at the faults are not smooth, which means neither are the relative movements. Instead, the movements are intermittent as forces build up along the fault line until there is a local failure of the crust, and this releases energy, about 10% of which causes **seismic waves**, in other words, an earthquake. Most of the energy is released as heat caused by friction.

The magnitude – the energy released – of an earthquake is measured on the well-known **Richter scale**, by numbers from less than 2 to more than 9. The felt magnitude is measured on the Mercalli intensity scale, measured in Roman numerals I to XII. This is not directly related to the Richter scale as it based on observed effects. **Table 15.3** shows the effects on earthquake resistant structures of earthquakes of magnitude 5 and above

Magnitude	Description	Mercalli Intensity	Average earthquake effects	Average global yearly frequency of occurrence (estimated)
5.0–5.9	**MODERATE**	VI to VIII	At most, none to slight damage except to poorly constructed buildings.	1,000 to 1,500
6.0–6.9	**STRONG**	VII to X	Earthquake-resistant structures survive with slight to moderate damage.	100 to 150
7.0–7.9	**MAJOR**	X to XII	Well-designed structures are likely to receive damage.	10 to 20
8.0–8.9	**GREAT**	More than XII	Will cause moderate to heavy damage to sturdy or earthquake-resistant buildings.	One
9.0– >9			Nearly total destruction - severe damage or collapse to all buildings.	One per 10 to 50 years

Table 15.3

It should be noted that the numbers on the Richter scale are logarithmic not linear. A Magnitude 2 earthquake has the same energy as the explosion of 15kg of TNT, whereas a Magnitude 8 has the energy of 15,000,000 tons of TNT exploding – or 1000 Hiroshima atomic bombs. The most powerful earthquake ever recorded was the 1960 Valdiva earthquake in Chile, which registered 9.5 on the Richter scale. But this does not make it the most destructive, as the Mercalli intensity was not recorded. Anyway, how destructive an earthquake is depends on many factors such as buildings collapsing, landslides and tsunamis, all of which can be fatal. Here, the concern is with the behaviour of buildings during an earthquake.

The exact location of an earthquake within the **crust** is called the **hypocentre**, and is at some depth below the surface of the Earth. The point vertically above this on the surface of the Earth is called the **epicentre**.

The non-heat energy causes **seismic waves**. Two types propagate from the **hypocentre** as body waves called **P(rimary)-waves** and **S(econdary)-waves**. The **P-waves** cause the surrounding material to **stretch** and **compress** in an axial direction, whereas the **S-waves** cause a **shearing deformation** – see **Fig. 15.33**.

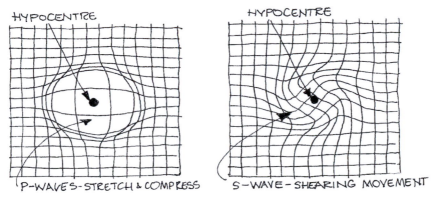

Fig. 15.33 – The effect of P-waves and S-waves shown two-dimensionally

When the **P-waves** and **S-waves** reach the surface of the Earth they cause **surface waves,** which are, again, of two types. They are named **Rayleigh waves** and **Love waves**, each named after a famous mathematical physicist, and they propagate from the **epicentre** – see **Fig. 15.34**.

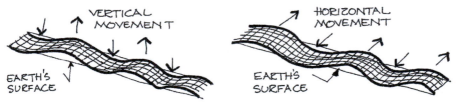

Fig. 15.34 – Rayleigh and Love waves

The Rayleigh waves are rather like the ripples on the surface of a pond into which a stone has been dropped, whereas the Love waves, also emanating from the epicentre, cause the surface to move backwards and forwards in a 'sideways' manner.

The **P-waves, S-waves, Love waves,** and **Rayleigh waves** all propagate at different speeds and these speeds are affected by the nature of the material through, or along which, they are passing. This means that, at any point, there is not one seismic wave but a series, which is why the **forcing function** for a **seismic event** – see **Fig. 15.18** – is not like that for an **impact** – see **Fig. 15.17**. For buildings, the most damaging are the **Love** and **Rayleigh waves**.

Earthquakes occur all the time all over the world, both along plate edges and along other faults. The questions where and when will an earthquake occur, and if it does what magnitude it will be, cannot be answered accurately.

To record earthquakes, the world is divided into 754 Flinn-Engdahl regions, grouped into 50 larger seismic regions. This allows areas of high and low seismicity to be identified. In many areas of high seismicity, seismic maps are made showing in which areas more serious earthquakes may be expected. The map shown in **Fig. 15.35**, divides India into four **zones of seismic intensity**, from **II – low –** to **V – very severe**.

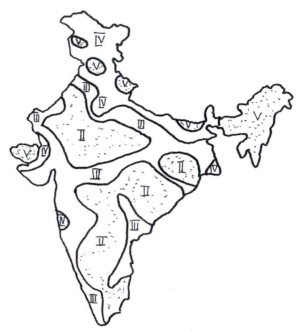

Fig. 15.35 – Seismic zone map of India

How building structures are designed to try and resist the effects of earthquakes is a huge subject, so only a brief outline can be given here. National building codes for countries that are considered to be in seismic zones give guidance for structural design to resist seismic effects. For instance, the map shown in **Fig. 15.35** appears in the Indian building code IS:1983 (Part 1):2002.

Table 15.3 implies there are three levels of earthquake magnitude to be considered. Earthquakes up to magnitude 5.9 should cause minimal or no damage, those up to magnitude 7.9 may cause damage but the building should not collapse, whereas those above magnitude 8 will cause damage and, if over 9, collapse may be difficult to avoid.

The main cause of dynamic loading of structures due to earthquakes is the horizontal ground movements, and this effect is modelled by considering the building to be subjected to equivalent horizontal loads that are a percentage of the **seismic load W_s** of the building. The seismic load is the total self-weight of the construction plus a percentage of the applied loads, usually in the range 25% to 50%. By applying factors that take into account variables like predicted intensity, building importance, type of underlying soil, the type of building structure, and the natural frequency, technical data allow a **design horizontal seismic coefficient A_s** to be calculated. Multiplying the seismic load by this coefficient gives the horizontal seismic base shear V_B; this is usually in the range of 5% to 20% of the seismic load. This load is then applied horizontally with a different percentage at each level, increasing with the height. **Fig. 15.36** gives a typical example for a three-storey concrete-framed structure.

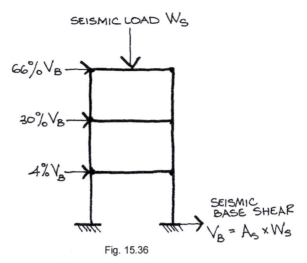

SEISMIC LOAD W_S

66% V_B

30% V_B

4% V_B

SEISMIC
BASE SHEAR
$V_B = A_s \times W_s$

Fig. 15.36

Whether these seismic loads should be applied as static loads or used for a dynamic analysis is not clear-cut, but national codes will often give guidance. In areas where **MODERATE** earthquakes could be expected, depending on the building layout, dynamic analysis should be considered for buildings more than about 70m high. In zones of higher seismicity, this height should be reduced to 30m.[21]

If buildings are not damaged by earthquake loading, and the structure remains in the elastic range, then the structure will vibrate in a relatively undamped manner. **Fig. 15.37** shows the dynamic behaviour of a 25-storey structure after an earthquake.

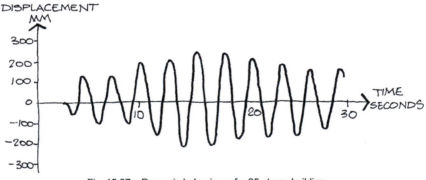

DISPLACEMENT
MM

300
200
100
0
−100
−200
−300

10   20   30

TIME
SECONDS

Fig. 15.37 – Dynamic behaviour of a 25-storey building

To improve the protection of building structures against seismic effects, it can be helpful to introduce specific damping like a tuned mass damper or base isolation – see **Figs. 15.23** and **15.30**.

There are a number of features of buildings and their structures that can reduce the effect of earthquakes. For instance buildings that have symmetric geometry and evenly distributed mass and stiffness, both on plan and elevation, suffer less damage than buildings that are geometrically or structurally irregular. In particular **soft storeys**, especially at ground level, should be avoided. A **soft storey** is one that has a much more horizontally flexible structure than the others; typically a soft storey will have columns where other storeys are stiffened by walls – see **Fig. 15. 38**.

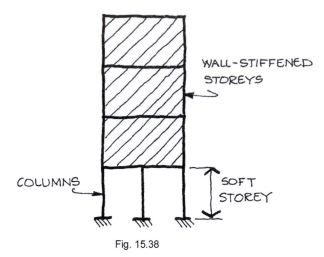

Fig. 15.38

Soft storeys tend to exacerbate the problem of **joint rotation** under dynamic load. Where frames are expected to absorb the energy by parts becoming plastic, the structural joints have to be detailed to ensure they have **sufficient ductility**. This requires extra reinforcement in concrete joints and more bolts in steel joints, but this depends on detailed technical design. Sometimes it is helpful to introduce **ductility** at predetermined positions to absorb energy and prevent sudden collapse.

Earthquakes can cause problems with the design of foundations and the bearing strata. During an earthquake separate foundations – see section **8.6** – may move relatively to one another in the vertical or horizontal directions. To reduce this effect, separate foundations should be tied together with ground beams. Tall buildings should be constructed on piles – again see section **8.6**.

By far the worst problem that earthquakes can cause foundations is **liquefaction** of the soil. This is a complex process, and happens when the water content of a soil is high; loose sands are especially susceptible. When the soil is shaken, it wants to compact, but if the water does not have time to drain then particles can go into suspension, turning the soil into a liquid, hence **liquefaction**. This can cause catastrophic foundation failure – see **Fig. 15.39**. Apart from avoiding such sub-soils, where necessary, it may be possible to alter the soil properties by various methods of ground compaction.

Fig. 15.39 – Effects of liquefaction on foundations

Around 30% of the world's population live or work in various types of buildings made from mud bricks, or adobe as it is often called, and many of these are in seismic areas. When an earthquake occurs, these tend to collapse causing great damage, often with numerous casualties. In 2003 an earthquake struck Bam, in Iran. Whilst the magnitude was 'only' 6.6 – i.e. a **STRONG** earthquake, see **Table 15.3** – the city, largely consisting of mud brick buildings, suffered enormous damage: over 26,000 people died and another 30,000 were injured.[22] Surprisingly perhaps, as earthquake engineering can seem a highly technical subject, such basic buildings can quite easily be made earthquake-resistant. This is done by tying together the tops of the walls with metal straps, or timber members that have nailed joints. A cheap tensile material, like the plastic meshes that are used for geotechnical projects, should be embedded in the surface of the walls.

It is interesting to compare the Bam earthquake with the 1994 Northridge earthquake in California. This earthquake shows how magnitude is **not** related to intensity. Although it had a magnitude minimally higher, 'only' 6.7, the recorded ground acceleration was 16.7m/sec². This can be compared to the 'intolerable' acceleration of 0.7 m/sec² quoted on page **422**. The **epicentre** was in a built-up area, Reseda, with the **hypocentre** 11 miles directly below, in a previously unknown fault. Fifty-seven people died, and more than 5,000 were injured, and it was one of the most expensive natural disasters the United States had ever experienced. This was in spite of the fact that California had a seismic building code. Many of the collapses were due to **soft storeys** at ground level, where houses were lifted up on slender columns to allow car parking underneath.[23]

Subsequent to the Northridge earthquake, the seismic code was altered and something called a **Special Moment Frame** was introduced. This was a normally-designed rigidly-jointed frame– see **Fig. 2.26** – in either concrete or steel, but the connections need extra bolts or reinforcement to ensure extra ductility to allow plastic hinges to form without failing rotationally – see **Fig. 6.38**.

15.11 Explosions and collisions

Explosions and collisions are very short-duration events, and they often take place during a fraction of a second, which is often not long enough to cause dynamic behaviour during the loading – see **Fig. 15.48**.

If a constant load – **Fig. 15.40 (left)** – is suddenly applied to a **SDOF** system, the **Dynamic Magnification Factor** is **2**, and the mass, in the absence of damping, vibrates forever.

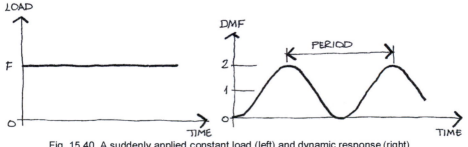

Fig. 15.40 A suddenly applied constant load (left) and dynamic response (right)

The steady state response to such a suddenly applied load is similar to a **SDOF** undamped system, given an initial displacement – see **Fig. 15.4**.

As **Fig. 15.40** shows, for a constant load suddenly applied and maintained infinitely, the **dynamic magnification factor** oscillates with the natural **frequency f_n**, about a value of **1**, taking the extreme values of **0** and **2**. If the load is applied gradually, then depending on how gradually, the **DMF** will revert to the **static load case**; that is the **DMF** becomes **1**. The time of application is called the **rise time** and is denoted here by τ. So the load function shown in **Fig. 15.40** is altered to the one shown in Fig. **15.41**.

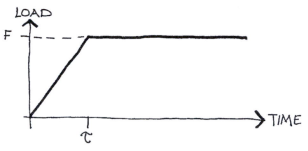

Fig.15.41 A gradually applied constant load

The effect of increasing the rise time τ with respect to the period **T** is to reduce the **DMF** to **1**, as might be expected – see **Fig. 15.42**. Strangely, the **DMF** does not reduce to **1** constantly, but has diminishing values **greater than 1** between **rise times** that are integer multiples of the period **T**.

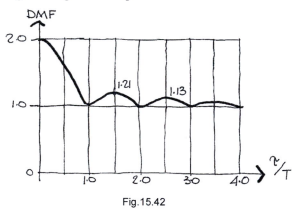

Fig.15.42

If, however, the constant load is only applied for a limited time t_d, it is called a **step load** – see **Fig. 15.43 (left)**. Then, depending on how t_d relates to the period **T** of the dynamic system, the **DMF** may be less than **2**. The limited time **step load**, and how **DMF** varies with t_d/**T**, is shown in **Fig. 15.43 (right)** – such graphs are often called **shock spectra**.

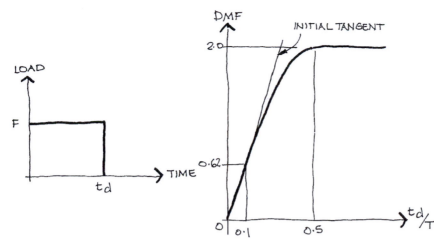

Fig. 15.43 Step load (left) and the resulting dynamic magnification factor variation (right)

The relationship between **DMF** and the variation in time duration of a **step load** – see **Fig. 15.43 (right)** – shows three distinct phases. Up to $t_d/T = 0.1$, the **DMF increases linearly**. After that, the increase follows a curved graph for $0.1 \le t_d/T \le 0.5$. For $t_d/T > 0.5$, the **DMF becomes 2**, which is the same as for the continuous constant function shown in **Fig. 15.40**.

This brief description of applying a constant load to a **SDOF** system in various ways – suddenly, gradually, or only for a short time – outlines the basis of the dynamic behaviour of structures subjected to **impact** and **blast loads,** as loads from collisions and explosions are usually called. Typical blast and impact load functions are shown in **Fig. 15.44**.

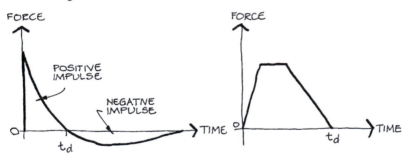

Fig. 15.44 Blast (left) and impact (right) idealised transient forcing functions

The behaviour of structures subjects to blast and impact loading, though similar, is not the same, so these are briefly described separately.

15.12 Blast loading

Explosions are normally seen as dramatic or extraordinary events, so to deal with them in a routine manner for the structural design of buildings is unusual. However, design against blast loading is required for various types of buildings. These could include 'bomb-proof' buildings for diplomatic or military uses; buildings for the manufacture or storage of explosive materials; buildings housing potentially explosive processes or buildings near them; or buildings in areas of controlled explosions like quarries. But designing for the effects of dynamic blast loads is complicated, and guidance is not included in general codes of practice – for instance it is not dealt with in Eurocodes – and so information has to be obtained from specialist publications. Designing the structures to be fully blast resistant is not usually a realistic and economical option, but the effects can be quantified and hence mitigated.

An explosion occurs when a gas, liquid or solid material goes through a rapid chemical reaction. When the explosion occurs, gas products of the reaction are formed at a very high temperature and pressure at the source. These high pressure gases expand rapidly into the surrounding area, and a **blast wave** is formed. The damage caused by explosions is due to the passage of compressed air in the blast wave. Blast waves propagate at supersonic speeds, and as they expand away from the source of the explosion, their intensity diminishes and the effect is reduced. The increase of the pressure above the ambient atmospheric pressure is called the **overpressure**.

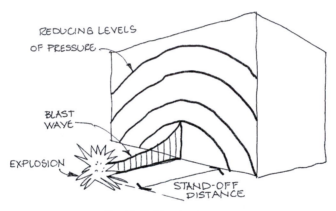

Fig. 15.45 Blast loading on a building

The **energy yield** of an explosion is usually quoted in terms of the **equivalent mass of TNT**. For instance, dynamite has only 60% of the energy yield of TNT, whereas Semtex is 25% more powerful. Knowing the distance of a structure from the explosion, and the TNT equivalent mass, the maximum overpressure and its duration can be calculated. The graph of the blast function shown in **Fig. 15.44** is curved, and shows a **positive overpressure**, followed by a much smaller **negative pressure**. This function is usually idealised as a **triangular load function**, and the negative pressure part is generally ignored. **Fig. 15.46** shows a typical idealised blast load function.

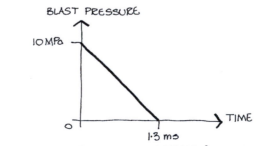

Typical idealised blast loading – 10MPa = 10,000 kN/m^2 – 1.3 millisec. = 1.3/1000 seconds

15

As has already been noted the graph shown in **Fig. 15.43 (right)** has three distinct phases. These phases are denoted as the **impulsive regime**, the **dynamic regime**, and the **quasi-static regime**, and are shown in **Fig. 15.47**.

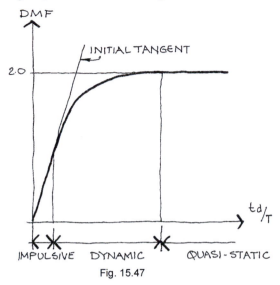

Fig. 15.47

The behaviour of the blast-loaded structure is different during each of these regimes. In the **impulsive regime** the duration of the load t_d is small when compared to the period of the structure **T**, so the structure only vibrates after the loading has stopped. In the **dynamic regime** when t_d is similar to **T**, the structure acts under a **transient load**. For the **quasi-static regime** when t_d is much longer than **T**, the structure acts similarly to one that has a suddenly applied constant load – see **Fig. 15.40 (left)**. **Fig. 15.48** compares the response of the structure during the **impulsive** and **quasi-static regimes**.

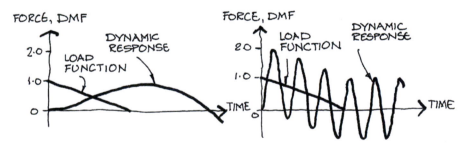

Fig. 15.48 Impulsive response (left) and quasi-static response (right)

Fast-acting forces like blast loading are often characterised by an **impulse**, which can be regarded as the change in **momentum** – defined as mass times velocity. The **numerical size of an impulse is equal to the area under the graph of the load function**, so its **measured units** are **pressure.time**. The graph shown in **Fig. 15.46** represents an impulse of **6.5 MPa.ms**. With this new parameter **impulse**, graphs like **Fig. 15.47** are redrawn as **Pressure-Impulse diagrams** or **P-I diagrams** as they are usually called – see **Fig. 15.49**.

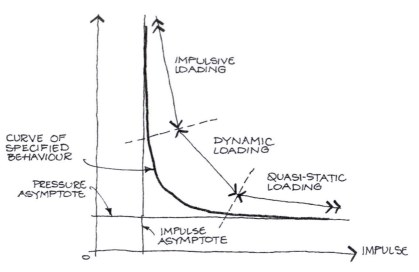

Fig. 15.49 Typical P-I diagram.

P-I diagrams are commonly used for the **preliminary design** of structures subjected to blast loading; these are usually based on a **SDOF system**. The damage criterion is usually defined in terms of deformation or displacement response. The reader should be warned that **P-I diagrams** are often drawn in the literature using various variations of the parameters **pressure** and **impulse**, and this can lead to confusion.

The curve on a **P-I diagram** shows what **combination** of **pressure** and **impulse** will produce a **specified behaviour** for a **particular structure**, commonly a column. The specified behaviour is often a **mid-height elastic deflection** or a **plastic moment of resistance** – see **Fig. 6.40**.

During the **impulsive regime**, the structure response is **sensitive** only to the **associated impulse** and not to the **peak pressure**. This forms a vertical line that defines the **minimum impulse** required to cause th**e specified behaviour**, which the curve approaches asymptotically at high pressures. Conversely, during the **quasi-static regime**, the response becomes **insensitive to impulse** but **very sensitive** to **peak pressure**. The horizontal asymptote thus represents the minimum level of peak pressure required to cause the specified behaviour. If the **specified behaviour** is for a **defined level of damage**, then **the curve defines two zones**, one where the combinations of pressure and impulse will cause **more damage**, and the other where **less damage is caused**.

Calculation of the curves shown on **P-I diagrams** can be complex for a number of reasons that include the fact that under rapid loading, as happens due to blasts, the mechanical properties of the structural materials can change dramatically. For instance, materials like steel and concrete can sustain stresses during such loading that can be up to six times higher than the stresses for static loading.

However, some standard methods have been developed to predict damage caused by blast loading. These produce a **family of curves** on the **P-I diagram**, each one indicating the degree of damage caused by combinations of pressure and impulse. **Fig. 15.50** shows a typical set of curves, each curve indicating the **percentage of damage** caused by various blast scenarios.

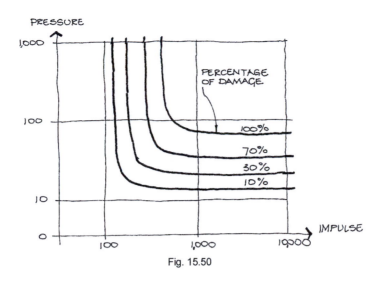

Fig. 15.50

15.13 Impact loading

Impact loading has much in common with blast loading in that it is sudden, unexpected and its magnitude is difficult to estimate. But there are differences as **Fig. 15.44** shows; the shapes of the forcing functions for blast and impact loading are quite different, and so is the duration of the loading. Earthquake loading usually lasts for several seconds, whereas blast loading is measured in milliseconds; impact loading is between the two, and usually lasts hundredths of a second – see **Fig. 15.56** at the end of the chapter.

There are basically two types of collisions between objects, **elastic collisions** and **inelastic collisions**. In elastic collisions, the **total momentum is conserved** as is the **total kinetic energy**. In inelastic collisions, however, whilst the total momentum is still conserved, the kinetic energy – see page **407** – is not. Elastic collisions can be characterised by two idealised rigid spheres each having mass, velocity and direction that collide head on. After the collision, depending on the numerical values, the two spheres will have changed velocity and possibly direction – see **Fig. 15.51**.

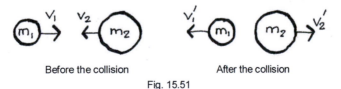

Before the collision   After the collision

Fig. 15.51

In the elastic collision shown in **Fig. 15.51**, the numerical value of the sum of the momentum of each spheres before the collision is equal to that after the collision; that is

$$m_1 \times v_1 - m_2 \times v_2 = -m_1 \times v_1' + m_2 \times v_2'$$

Where the minus signs are introduced they indicate velocities in different directions. The total kinetic energy is also conserved. But when the two objects do not separate after the collision, some kinetic energy is converted into other types of energy. The simplest case of impact on a structure is a **mass** dropped on a structure like a beam – see **Fig. 15.52**.

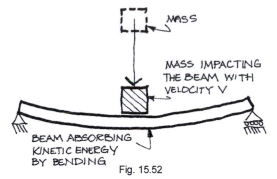

Fig. 15.52

This is a **SDOF system** - see **Fig. 15.3** – and when a load is suddenly applied, that is when **V=0**, the **dynamic magnification factor is 2** – see **Fig.15.40**. When the load is applied with a velocity **V**, the **DMF increases** – see **Fig. 15.53**.

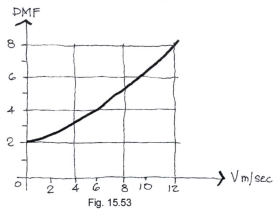

Fig. 15.53

If the beam remains elastic, then the **kinetic energy** of the load is converted into **strain energy** in the beam. Such a situation will arise if the beam is supporting a process that involves, for instance, the use of mechanical power hammers– see **Fig. 15.54**.

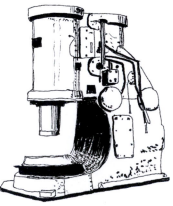

Fig.15.54 Large mechanical power hammer

But when an object collides with a structure accidentally, then it is common for the object and/or the structure to sustain some form of damage. In this, case the kinetic energy of the colliding object is converted into some form of dissipating energy that is absorbed by the object and/or the structure becoming damaged. The force can be estimated by using the **Work Energy Equation**:

Work = Kinetic Energy   or   **Force times distance = ½ Mass times (velocity)^2**

giving: $$F \times d = \frac{1}{2}MV^2$$

Where **F** is the **impact force**, **d** is the **length** over which the collision takes place, **M** is the **mass** of the **object** and **V** is the **speed at collision**. In most cases it is relatively easy to estimate the mass and velocity of the incoming object, however estimating the length of the collision is difficult. But this is crucial as the equation shows, and it determines the numerical value of the deceleration of the colliding object as it comes to rest.

By using the simple formula above, it is possible to calculate the impact force caused by a Boeing 707 jet airliner that weighs 90 tonnes and impacting at a speed of 360 km/hr. The length of the airliner is 47m, so suppose in crashing into a solid object the airliner is crushed to a length of 32m – 70% of the original length, the formula gives the force of impact as 3059 tonnes, nearly 34 times the aircraft's weight; and the time of impact would be 0.3 seconds. Usually, if an aeroplane does hit a building, the plane and part of the building disintegrates, so such a simple analysis is hardly realistic.

Large planes colliding with buildings are extremely rare events, but they have happened, with varying consequences. In 1945 a B-25 Mitchell bomber crashed into the Empire State Building between the 78th and 80th floors, making a 5.5m x 6m hole and killing fourteen people. Amazingly this impact load did not affect the structural integrity of the building, and the local damage was quickly repaired. In 1992, a large jet cargo aircraft nose-dived from the sky and into two high-rise residential buildings in an Amsterdam suburb. It exploded in a fireball, which caused the building to partially collapse inward, destroying dozens of apartments.

The best-know impact between a large aircraft and a building was the 2001 attack on the towers of the World Trade Center in New York, when high-jacked Boeing 767s were deliberately flown into the buildings. This appalling event was presaged not once but twice, but each time as an accident. During construction, part-owner of the Empire State building Lawrence A Wien, an implacable commercial enemy of the World Trade Center development, placed a large advertisement, complete with an eerily prescient photo montage, in the New York Times, on May 2nd 1968, predicting a large airliner would hit the WTC,[24] and in February 1981 one nearly did. Disaster was only averted by the rapid action of air-controller Donald Zimmerman.[25]

As is well-known, after the 2001 impact, both towers collapsed completely; this point will be returned to in the next chapter. But the towers did not collapse due to the impact; both remained standing for some time – one tower stood for 56 minutes and the other for 102 minutes. Clearly, when the aircraft hit each building there was not a simple impact; however, the kinetic energy can be calculated from the right-hand side of the equations given above. From one analysis the energy is dissipated as follows:[26]

E_{plane} = energy dissipated by the breakup of the aircraft

$E_{external\ columns}$ = energy to cut through the external columns

E_{floor} = energy dissipated by damage to the floors

E_{core} = energy absorbed by the structural core

The losses due to **friction** and the **elastic vibration** of the **building structure** were ignored in this analysis. Doing any post-attack analysis is hampered by the fact that both the towers suffered total collapse, so the evidence available is largely limited to videos of the aircraft hitting the towers, with little evidence obtainable from the debris. This means that an analysis has to make many assumptions, which is why there is no totally agreed report on the reasons for the total collapse of the towers. This analysis attributes the percentages of absorption of the kinetic energy, due to the incoming aircraft by destruction or plastic deformation of the different elements, to be:

$$E_{plane} = 23\% \quad E_{external\ columns} = 4\% \quad E_{floor} = 48\% \quad E_{core} = 25\%$$

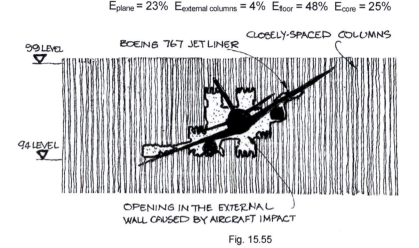

Fig. 15.55

Fig. 15.55 shows the damage that the aircraft did to the external structure of the North Tower. Thirty-three of the closely-spaced external columns were cut through, and at least three floors were impacted. The outer 9m of both 24m wings were assumed to be destroyed by the external structure and did not enter the building.

What did enter each building was the fuselage, the engines and those parts of the wings nearest the fuselage. How exactly these parts interacted with the floor and core structures has to be based on assumptions of the strength of each part. Clearly, the buildings' floor and core structures were not strong enough to act as rigid objects, and neither was the incoming aircraft. What happened was a form of mutual destruction, which is what the assessment of energy dissipation, given as a percentage of the total kinetic energy, shows.

15.14 Summary

Unlike many machines, where dynamic behaviour is part of their function, the dynamic behaviour of building structures is something that the design process aims to design out; in other words building structures should not vibrate. As **Fig. 15.20** shows, the fundamental requirement is that the natural frequency of the structure does not coincide with the frequency of the forcing function, in other words resonance must be avoided.

Where dynamic loads do occur they are basically of several types. There are dynamic loads that are numerically predictable, such as the operation of various types of machinery. There are those where a reasonable assessment can be made, such as dancing or vortex shedding. And those where prediction is difficult, such as earthquakes, explosions and collisions; however, even in these cases some form of assessment can be made.

For suddenly applied loads, as opposed to continuous periodic loading, the duration of the loading can characterise the type of loading, as is shown in **Fig. 15.56**.

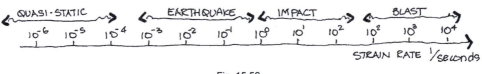

Fig. 15.56

Further reading

SR Damodarasamy and S Kavitha – **Basics of Structural Dynamics and Aseismic Design** – Prentice-Hall of India Pvt.Ltd – 2009

HM Irvine – **Structural Dynamics for the Practising Engineer** – Spon Press, 1966

James Glanz and Eric Lipton – **City in the Sky: the rise and fall of the World Trade Centre** – Times Books – 2003

S Graham Kelly – **Mechanical Vibrations** – Schaum's Outlines – 1996

Mario Paz – **Structural Dynamics; Theory and Computation** – Springer; 5th ed. – 2004

References – Chapter 15

1   Bground Millennium Bridge, London, https://en.wikipedia.org/wiki/Millennium_Bridge,_London
2   Tacoma Narrows Bridge (1940)
     https://en.wikipedia.org/wiki/Tacoma_Narrows_Bridge_%281940%29
3   ibid
4   Resonance Tacoma Bridge – http://www.ketchum.org/billah/Billah-Scanlan.pdf - p121
5   Tacoma Narrows Bridge (1940)
     https://en.wikipedia.org/wiki/Tacoma_Narrows_Bridge_%281940%29
6   Poul Beckmann and Robert Bowles – **Structural Aspects of Building Conservation** – Elsevier
     Butterworth-Heinemann – 2nd Edition 2004. p75
7   http://www.steelconstruction.info/Floor_vibrations p13, 14
8   Floor Vibrations. Due to Human Activity. *Thomas M. Murray, PhD, P.E.pdf - p38* –
     https://www.google.pt/?gfe_rd=cr&ei=UDMrV7jcPPKJ8QeZqY3YAg&gws_rd=ssl#q=Floor
     +Vibrations+Due+to+Human+Activity
9   Wind loads on tall buildings pdf - http://www.inti.gob.ar/cirsoc/pdf/accion_viento/200704.pdf –
     p44
10   Damodarasamy p248
11   RX FOR SWAYING SKYSCRAPERS By WILLIAM R. GREER –
     http://www.nytimes.com/1982/10/24/realestate/rx-for-swaying-skyscrapers.html
12   Reynolds number - https://en.wikipedia.org/wiki/Reynolds_number
13   Vortex shedding p12 - http://www.spartaengineering.com/vortex-shedding-and-tall-structures/
14   A Tribute to Jack E. Cermak p3 –
     https://www3.nd.edu/~nathaz/confs/%282003%29A_Tribute_to_Jack_E_Cermak.pdf
15   Glanz p157
16   Glanz p189
17   Tuned mass damper – https://en.wikipedia.org/wiki/Tuned_mass_damper
18   Structures Incorporating Tuned Mass Dampers, http://nisee.berkeley.edu/prosys/tuned.html
19   Citycorp Center https://en.wikipedia.org/wiki/Citigroup_Center
20   John Hancock Tower - https://en.wikipedia.org/wiki/200_Clarendon
21   Damodarasamy p248-9 . This reference does not give these figures but similar

22 https://en.wikipedia.org/wiki/2003_Bam_earthquake
23 https://en.wikipedia.org/wiki/1994_Northridge_earthquake
24 Glanz p174 & Photo
25 Glanz p224-5
26 Aircraft Impact Damage - Tomasz Wierzbicki et al – p53
  http://web.mit.edu/civenv/wtc/PDFfiles/Chapter%20IV%20Aircraft%20Impact.pdf

CHAPTER 16 *Progressive collapse and robustness*

A number of technical terms have been introduced to explain the behaviour of building structures, examples being bending moments, stresses, displacements and many others, all of which can given a numerical value – see **Chapters 14** and **15**. This allows comparisons to be made; for example it makes senses to say one beam, for the same span, is stiffer than another.

At the end of the 1960s, some new technical terms entered the formal vocabulary of building structures; these were **robustness**, **progressive** and **disproportionate collapse**. Unlike most previous terms, it is impossible to attach numerical values to these new terms so, their usefulness as engineering terms is questionable. The two collapses shown in **Fig. 16.1** can be used to illustrate these new terms.

Fig. 16.1

On the left of **Fig. 16.1** a modest four-storey building of standard construction is shown before and after an explosion in the semi-basement. The explosion blew out the flank wall, which triggered the total collapse of the four upper floors and the roof; they collapsed one after another, that is **progressively**. The building on the right of **Fig. 16.1** shows a multi-storey building that was subjected to a ground floor explosion, but here only the immediate area was destroyed, whilst the storeys above remained intact. It is unlikely that either building was designed to withstand the effects of an explosion.

The one on the left has **collapsed progressively**, whilst the one on the right, using the new term, was structurally **robust**. The essential question is: were these collapses, both triggered by unforeseen events – explosions – **disproportionate** to the events or not? This shows precisely why the question cannot be answered **quantitatively**, only **qualitatively**. The cost of making all modest four-storey buildings of standard construction **robust**, when subjected to the rare and unforeseen event of an explosion, may be deemed excessive compared to the cost of the repairing the collapse shown. Whereas if the ground and first floor damage caused to the multi-storey building had triggered a total collapse of the entire building, a different opinion might have been formed. How to decide which route to take is the problem, and can only be resolved by taking a view which could be consensual or divisive.

These new terms formally appeared after the partial collapse of a multi-storey residential block in 1968, which is described in the next section. The chapter goes on to describe the difficult birth of new regulations that apply to robustness, and what they currently demand. The chapter explores their worth, how they may be followed and to what extent they have they been effective. The conclusion outlines how **robustness** is currently approached.

16.1 The partial progressive collapse of Ronan Point

In the mid-1940s a number of firms in Scandinavia pioneered a new building systems based on pre-cast concrete panels – see **Fig. 16.2**. It became known as the **Large Panel System**, **LPS**, and it was used to build thousands of buildings all over the world, including many high-rise blocks of flats.

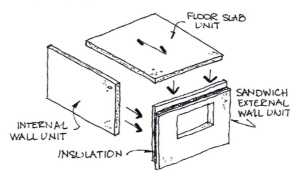

Fig. 16.2 – Pre-cast concrete LPS components

There was no structural framing, all the elements being two-dimensional – see **Fig. 3.3** – floor units and storey-height wall units. The buildings were erected storey-by-storey, with the joints between the wall panels and the floor slabs being filled with mortar or concrete as the work proceeded. The joints were strengthened with various arrangements of steel reinforcement, but reliance was essentially placed on gravity to hold the whole structure together.

The building called Ronan Point was the second of nine identical high-rise blocks of flats built in East London by Taylor Woodrow Anglian using the Larsen-Nielsen system. Construction started in 1966 and was complete by March 1968. The buildings had 22 floors of flats built on concrete-framed podiums. In each building there were 44 two-bedroom flats and 66 one-bedroom flats. The layout of a typical one-bedroom flat is in shown in **Fig. 16.3**. At 22 storeys, these blocks were the highest ever built using the Larsen-Nielsen system; in fact, the system was originally intended only for structures of **no more than six storeys**.

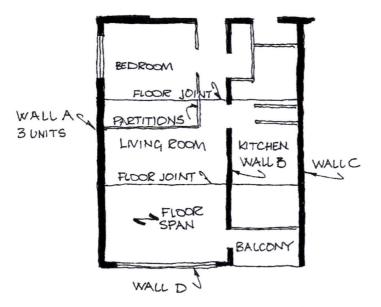

Fig. 16.3 – Typical plan of a one-bedroom flat

The floor slabs had longitudinal hollow cores, and toothed projections 32mm (1¼ inches) wide, to provide bearing. The whole width of the slab also bore onto the wall units for 19mm (¾ inch), giving a total bearing width of only 51mm (2 inches) – see **Fig. 16.4**. Taking into account a tolerance of ±¼ inches, as recommended by CP116.1965, this means the bearing width could be just 1¾ inches (44mm) wide, far short of CP116's requirement that bearings on concrete should be '*at least 3 inches*' (76mm).

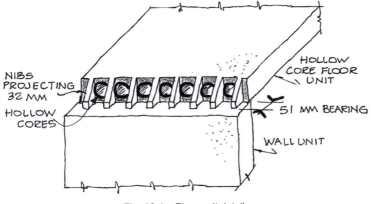

Fig. 16.4 – Floor unit details

Internal wall units were 178mm (7 inches) wide and supported two slabs, one on either side of the wall. The external wall units had a 152mm (6 inches) wide load-bearing inner leaf and a 105mm (4⅛ inches) non-load-bearing outer leaf. The inner leaf of the external wall units supported the floor units. What was to be crucial for the structural performance of the building was the way the floor units were joined horizontally to the load-bearing wall units; **Fig. 16.5** shows a typical joint.

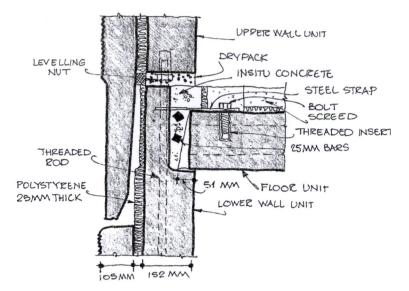

Fig. 16.5 – Joint between floor and external wall units

As the diagram shows the joint was complicated, leading to a construction process that required many separate operations. The floor units bore onto a recess in the lower wall unit. Thin metal straps protruded horizontally from the panel and were bolted to the slab via threaded insets that were cast into the floor unit. In the gap between the floor unit and the inner leaf of the lower wall unit were placed two 25mm (1 inch) square twisted steel bars that were concreted in during the floor screeding process. The upper wall unit was initially supported on nuts on 22mm (⅞ inch) diameter threaded rods that protruded from the top of the lower wall unit. In its final state, the joint between the upper and lower wall units was filled with dry-pack mortar – see **Fig. 13.12**.

It is not difficult to see that in the often harsh conditions of a construction site making these connections would be difficult, thus prejudicing something that was already not well engineered. It must be remembered that this joint is part of a primary load path for a 22-storey building. When the block was demolished in May 1986, just eighteen years after it was completed,* the demolition did not use explosives, but it was carefully taken apart so that the actual construction could be examined. What was revealed even shocked its many detractors, with a litany of defects being found, which confirmed the fact that it had been difficult to build.

At 5.45am on 16 May in 1968, Miss Ivy Hodge, who lived in a one-bedroom flat on the 18th floor, lit a match to light her gas stove to make a cup of tea. There was an explosion, as gas had leaked into flat from a faulty nut in the connection to her stove. Miss Hodge was knocked unconscious and left badly injured. The load-bearing **walls B** and **C** were slightly damaged, but the explosion blew out the external wall units – **walls A** and **D** – see **Fig. 16.3** – as well as the non-loadbearing internal walls of her flat. The removal of the external wall units in Miss Hodge's flat meant the walls and floors of the four floors above were left unsupported.

---

* By this date multiple social problems had arisen with 'towers-in-the-park' social housing, which were based Le Corbusier's ideas. After extensive surveys, *'Utopia on Trial'* by Alice Coleman was published in 1985, which called into question the entire basis of their design.

All their external wall units **A** then fell out, and their living room and bedroom floor units, that were supported by these walls, collapsed. However, the bedroom floor units on floors 18 to 22 remained hanging from the building, and the roof slab and the external wall units **D** of the top four floors remained in place until they were pulled down using a rope attached to a bulldozer.

The living room floor units above the 18th floor levels collapsed onto the slab of the 18th floor. This caused the floors of the living rooms, two of the three panels of external walls **A**, and all of wall **D** of all the flats below to **collapse progressively**. Parts of the living room slabs remained hanging from the building, as did the parts of the bedroom floor slabs from the 19th to the 22nd floors. The bedrooms below the 16th floor stayed partially intact due to fact that one panel of wall **A** remained, and the load-bearing role played by the non-loadbearing blockwork partitions. This saved a number of lives. The full extent of the damage is shown in **Fig. 16.6**. This failure following the explosion was given the term **progressive collapse**.

The explosion left four people dead, mainly those asleep in the bedrooms above level 18. Seventeen people were injured, including Miss Hodge. In spite of the relatively light casualties, this collapse not only horrified the occupants of Ronan Point, but it alarmed the nation. Naturally the structural engineering community was completely shocked. Whilst domestic gas explosions were rare, they were not unknown; but at worse they led to damage to single houses, not to the partial collapse of a 22-storey tower block. Clearly something was seriously wrong, but what exactly? That was the problem.

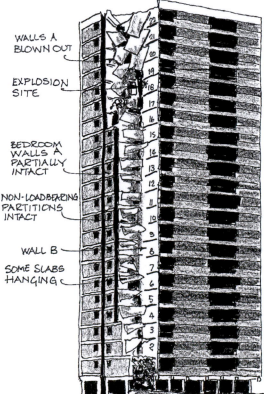

Fig. 16.6 – The Ronan Point collapse

16.2 The immediate aftermath

A public inquiry was immediately set up and reported on 14th October 1968, fewer than 5 months after the collapse. The report was prepared by the lawyer Hugh Griffiths (1923-2015) and the engineers Professor Sir Alfred Pugsley (1903-1998) and Professor Sir Owen Saunders (1903-1993), **neither of whom had any experience of designing building structures**. The report provided a great deal of descriptive information, but also contained a number of technical explanations, observations and recommendations, some of which were questionable. To understand the history of the approach to progressive collapse it is essential to identity the key points of the report, and note their validity.

The reason that the external wall units (**walls A** & **D** – **Fig. 16.3**) blew out was correctly identified as a failure of the joint between the wall and floor units at ceiling level in Miss Hodge's flat, which allowed the external wall units to *'move intact clear of the building.'* Some numerical values based on tests and technical assessments were given for loadings caused by the gas explosion. The most important pressure given was one of **about** 34 kN/m^2 (5 lbs/in^2), that was **estimated** to have been needed to crack the party wall unit – **wall C** – **Fig. 16.3**. It is important to remember that this loading was **estimated** to be **about 34kN/m^2**.

The report correctly noted that *'The jointing between walls and floor panels is fundamental to the integrity of the structure; without adequate connections it will be realised that the structure is essentially just like a tower built from a pack of stiff cards.'* The report goes on to state that *'...* **we do not consider that in its present form Ronan Point is an acceptable building**,'* but claimed it did *'comply with current building regulations.'* In fact, it did not comply with of the code of practice for precast concrete structures in force at the time **CP116:1965** with respect to bearing widths, as noted. Also, **Clause 346** required that *'**All members should be adequately tied together at all times**;'* whether the two metal straps shown in **Fig. 16.5** constitute 'adequate tying' is perhaps a moot point.

The report mentions that for framed buildings *'**it has long been known that there is little chance of local damage causing progressive collapse**.'* and that *'**High blocks built in frame construction are not likely to suffer progressive collapse**.'* This statement is supported by virtually all the available information, and is also a crucial point. The report considered that the event of a gas explosion was *'**unlikely to recur**,'* which is borne out by the fact that none of the hundreds of other similar blocks suffered a gas explosion.

In the introduction of the report, the authors note that *'we have not been referred to any English publication which draws attention to the need of ...* **structures requiring alternate paths** *to support the load in the event of the failure of a load bearing member,'* and goes on to say *'that there has been a blind spot ...* **with this type of construction**.'* Later in the report the concept of alternative load paths was generalised with the statement that *'It is the* **common aim of structural engineers to design their structures** *that if one or two component parts fail due to any cause, the remaining structure shall be able* **to provide alternative paths** *to resist the loads borne by the failed parts, even though with a reduced margin of safety.'* The statements probably reflect the opinion of one of the report's authors Sir Alfred Pugsley, whose career was mainly in the aircraft industry, and who had written two books on structural safety. However, at the time of the report it was not common practice to design building structures to have **alternative load paths**.

---

* **Note**: Text emphasis in this paragraph, and following two paragraphs by the author.

In spite of the traumatic events surrounding Ronan Point, hundreds of **LPS** built towers, in many different countries remained in use, without a single repetition of the Ronan Point collapse being reported. So before continuing with the complex history, it is useful to summarise the relevant points at this point:

- **The Ronan Point tower was badly engineered and badly built, and did not comply with the currently applicable code of practice.**

- **The idea of progressive collapse was considered only to apply to LPS structures, and NOT to framed structures.**

- **The gas explosion that triggered the collapse was thought unlikely to recur.**

- **The loading of 34 kN/m^2 was 'estimated' to be 'about that' which cracked a particular wall in the Ronan Point tower.**

- **Among the many hundreds of LPS blocks built in many countries, no other case of progressive collapse has been reported.**

- **At that time structural engineers did NOT provide alternative load paths in their designs.**

Those responsible for the production of authoritative guidance felt something had to be done, but what exactly was not entirely clear. Two documents were published in 1968 as something of a stopgap. Just nine days after the publication of the report, the Ministry of Housing issued Circular 62/68, which only dealt with **Flats constructed with pre-cast panels**, and only those **over six-storeys high**. A few weeks later, The Institution of Structural Engineers produced a document called Paper RP/68/01 – 1968, which only dealt with buildings which '**have no structural framework.**' In other words, the Inquiry Report's comments on framed structures had been heeded. It is clear that these documents were rushed out to calm the public, and to deal with, what at that time must have seemed a potentially dangerous situation; after all, it was not possible to know if the collapse at Ronan Point was just a one-off, or the first of many.

In February 1969, the Institution of Structural Engineers held an Open Discussion meeting in the presence of both Sir Alfred Pugsley and Mr Hugh Griffiths, two of the report's authors. The report of the meeting was entitled '*The Implications of the Report of the Inquiry into the Collapse of Flats at Ronan Point, Canning Town.*' This is probably **the most important document** in the whole history of the development of progressive collapse legislation, as it can be seen as reflection of the opinions of contemporary structural designers. It contained comments from forty-one contributors and a survey of their views on the Inquiry Report and its recommendations is telling. Only three of thee contributors were supportive, twenty-seven were critical and a further eleven contributions were largely peripheral to the central points – **essentially 90% were in disagreement**. In a highly critical contribution by the eminent engineer Peter Dunican (1918-1989), who had been involved in a successful industrialised building system, he noted that '*The structure of a building* **is not normally specifically designed so that the removal of any one of its primary load bearing members** *would not fundamentally impair its strength or create a state of potential collapse*'.[1] Perhaps the general mood of those critical to the Report of the Inquiry could be characterised by the contributor who stated that '*We have now burdened ourselves with incomprehensible and unnecessary legislation as a result of this muddled inquiry.*'[2]

Inexplicably, the contents of this important document have been forgotten and are almost never referred to in the extensive literature that this topic has spawned. For instance there is no reference to it in the copious 2007 document **Best Practices for Reducing the Potential for Collapse in Buildings**, nor is it referred to in the equally copious 2011 **Review of international research on structural robustness and disproportionate collapse** – see *Further Reading*.

16.3 The official response

Those responsible for drafting of building regulations in Great Britain chose to ignore what appeared to be the overwhelming opinion of those present at the 1969 Institution of Structural Engineers' meeting. An expanded version of the recommendations of Circular 62/68, that **now included all forms of structures**, was added to the UK Building Regulations in 1970 with the new **Fifth Amendment**; and these proposals became the basis of regulations that were to spread worldwide. When they were debated in the UK Parliament, one Member was moved to ask '*Was the Minister right to appoint a tribunal of this kind—three men, none of whom had ever been responsible for the design or construction of a building in his life, and* **whose conclusions were almost universally condemned by the engineering profession as a whole** *in vital respects as being unfair and harmful to the construction industry?*'[3] In spite of which, the new regulations passed into UK law, and the Hansard transcript of this parliamentary debate is **never referred** to in the literature.

The **new regulations now applied to ALL buildings that were over five storeys high whatever structural system was used**. The idea that alternative load paths were to be provided on the assumption that a load-bearing member was removed was maintained. Alternatively, supporting members of the structure should be able to carry a load of 34.5 kN/m² (5 lbs/in²). Essentially, these were the alternative methods – **Method A** and **Method B** – of the highly criticised Circular 62/68. A limit was put on the area of localised damage of 15% of the area of a storey or 70m² (750ft²).

The Institution of Structural Engineers' 1971 paper RP/68/05 suggested that framed structures designed in accordance with the then current structural codes of practice would automatically comply with the new regulations, and that tensile ties should be incorporated into floors at each level in approximately perpendicular directions. This reappeared in the Department of Environment circular 11/71 which recommended that the Fifth Amendment could be relaxed if structures complied with RP/68/05. In some ways, this confirmed the Inquiry Report's comments on framed structures, but the tying requirement was new. This requirement was not based on any rigorous analysis.

The aspects that dealt with **progressive collapse** were amended in many editions of the Building Regulations for England and Wales; specifically:

- **Building Regulations 1985 – Approved Document A: 1985 Edition**
- **Building Regulations 1991 – Approved Document A: 1992 Edition**
- **Building Regulations 2000 – Approved Document A: 2004 Edition**

- **Building Regulations 2010 – Approved Document A: 2004 Edition (no change in Document A)**

16.4 UK Building Regulations for disproportionate collapse

Section A3 of the 2010 edition of the Building Regulations for England and Wales, begins with: *'The building shall be constructed so that in the event of an accident the building will not suffer collapse to an extent disproportionate to the cause.'* The guidance for this follows in **Section 5: Reducing the sensitivity of the building to disproportionate collapse in the event of an accident**. This divides buildings into three classes – see **Table 16.1** – and there are different requirements to avoid disproportionate collapse for each class.

Where it is deemed necessary to provide measures against disproportionate collapse, there are three possible strategies:

- **To provide continuous horizontal and vertical structural ties throughout the building to tie the structure together.**

- **To check that after the removal of each supporting column, or beam supporting a column, the structure remains stable.**

- **To ensure that key structural elements are able to sustain a load of 34 kN/m^2, together with 1/3 of the wind and imposed loads.**

Class	Building Type and occupancy
1	Houses not exceeding 4 storeys Agricultural buildings Buildings into which people rarely go, provided no part of the building is closer to another building, or area where people go, than a distance of 1.5 times the building height
2A	5 storey single occupancy houses Hotels not exceeding 4 storeys Flats, apartments and other residential buildings not exceeding 4 storeys Offices not exceeding 4 storeys Industrial buildings not exceeding 3 storeys Retailing premises not exceeding 3 storeys of less than 2000m² floor area in each storey Single-storey educational buildings All buildings not exceeding 2 storeys to which members of the public are admitted and which contain floor areas not exceeding 2000m² at each storey
2B	Hotels, flats, apartments and other residential buildings greater than 4 storeys but not exceeding 15 storeys Educational buildings greater than 1 storey but not exceeding 15 storeys Retailing premises greater than 3 storeys but not exceeding 15 storeys Hospitals not exceeding 3 storeys Offices greater than 4 storeys but not exceeding 15 storeys All buildings to which members of the public are admitted which contain floor areas exceeding 2000m² but less than 5000m² at each storey Car parking not exceeding 6 storeys
3	All buildings defined above as Class 2A and 2B that exceed the limits on area and/or number of storeys Grandstands accommodating more than 5000 spectators Buildings containing hazardous substances and/or processes

Table 16.1 – Building types from 2010 UK Building Regulations

The guidance requires the following measures to be taken against disproportionate collapse for each Class of buildings as follows:

Class 1 - No additional measures against disproportionate collapse need be taken.

Class 2A - Provide effective horizontal structural ties, and effective anchorage of suspended floors to walls.

Class 2B - Provide effective horizontal and vertical structural ties in all supporting columns and walls. Alternatively, after the removal of a column, or a beam supporting a column, the structure remains stable. Furthermore, for any storey the risk of collapse does not exceed 15% of the floor area or 70m², whichever is smaller, and the collapse does not extend further than one adjacent storey – see **Fig. 16.7.**

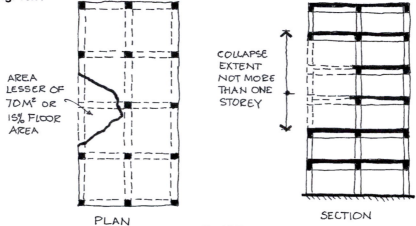

Fig. 16.7

Class 3 - A risk assessment should be made for all normal and any abnormal hazards. Critical situations for design should be selected for assessment due to the identified risks. Provision of effective horizontal and vertical ties, the effect of removal of vertical members and the design of key elements should comply with the relevant structural codes of practice.

By the time the 2010 edition of the Building Regulations came into force, all the structural codes of practice that were in use in the UK at the time of the Ronan Point collapse had been re-written. Now they all included clauses about robustness. For instance, the rewritten 1997 code for the structural use of concrete, **BS 8110**, includes various clauses about robustness, and gives some technical information for calculating forces in ties and anchorages. In the section **Basis of Design, clause 2.2.2.2 Robustness** starts with:

'Structures should be planned and designed so that they are not unreasonably susceptible to the effects of accidents. In particular, situations should be avoided where damage to small areas of a structure or failure of single elements may lead to collapse of major parts of the structure.'

By then, the need for buildings to be **robust** against **disproportionate collapse** had become an **accepted concept**, and engineering documentation in many countries included such requirements; for instance Eurocodes, the National Building Code of Canada, the Swedish Design Regulations and the New York City Building Code. Though there is general agreement on such a need, there is still some way to go to obtain universal acceptance. This fairly straightforward new requirement has generated a vast literature of articles, technical papers, reports and theses, some of 200 pages.

This extensive literature, perhaps surprisingly, is laced with negative comments about many aspects of the concept of the need to avoid progressive collapse; from 2007: *'The risk of progressive collapse to most buildings is very low. Without financial or regulatory incentives, progressive collapse-resistant design is not likely to be readily accepted.'* From the same source: *'"Normative" abnormal loads specified by an authority having jurisdiction for design (e.g., uniform pressure of 34 kN/m² (5 lbs/in²) that found its way into some standards following the Ronan Point collapse) are arbitrary.'* Or from 2008: *'A single column removal approach does not represent typical damage from an explosive attack on a building.'* And from 2009: *'To date, there is no unified theory of progressive collapse, nor is there agreement on terminology.'* And yet again in 2011 *'It is recommended that the terminology is standardised as a matter of urgency. Some such terms* **requiring clear definition** *are:* **progressive collapse, disproportionate collapse** *and* **structural robustness.**' So over 40 years after the triggering event, the engineering community still has some doubts about the meaning of the basic technical terms, and in some ways harks back to the initial dissatisfaction voiced so widely in 1969 – see pages **449-450**.

16.5 Practical results

Have the regulations that give guidance on how to make structures robust against disproportionate collapse brought tangible benefits? Of the two collapses shown in **Fig. 16.1**, the 2010 UK Building Regulations would put the 4-storey building into **Class 2A** and demand the floors were tied horizontally to the walls. As the end walls were of 350mm thick solid brickwork, with in situ reinforced concrete floor slabs built into them, it is possible, but not obvious, how these ties would have prevented the collapse. How the multi-storey building remained standing is unclear, or indeed how many storeys it has; the figure shows at least 10, so it would be at least **Class 2B**, requiring vertical and horizontal ties. Whether these were present is not known, however it is obvious alternative load paths were available and progressive collapse was prevented, mainly it appears by wall panels acting as bracing elements. In these cases it is not obvious how the regulations would have helped.

It is useful to look at two of the best-known progressive collapses since Ronan Point; the 1995 collapse of the Alfred P Murrah Federal Building in Oklahoma City, and the 2001 collapse of the North and South Towers of the World Trade Center in New York City. There is extensive literature on both these collapses – see *Further Reading* – so only the essentials are given here.

The Alfred P Murrah Building, Oklahoma City

The Alfred P Murrah Federal Building in Oklahoma City was a nine-storey office building that was completed in 1977. Its in situ reinforced concrete structure was well designed, detailed and built in accordance with the governing building codes. In spite of the fact that this was nine years after the Ronan Point collapse, the governing building code did not require any measures to be taken against accidental loads or progressive collapse.

The structure was straightforward. It was based on a column grid of 6.1m x 10.7m (20ft x 35 ft), with ten bays of 6.1m in the east-west direction, and two bays of 10.7m in the north-south direction. The typical floor structure was 150mm (6in) deep slabs spanning between 1220 mm wide by 509 mm deep (48in x 20in) beams that spanned 10.7m between columns in the east-west direction. At the second floor, on the northern face, there was a 1525mm deep by 914mm wide (5ft x 3ft) transfer beam that carried the more closely-spaced columns that went from second floor to the roof. Below the transfer beam were double-height ground-to-second-floor columns, spaced at 12.2m (40ft).

On 19th April 1995, Timothy McVeigh parked a truck containing a 3175 kg fertilizer bomb – equivalent to 1800 kg of TNT – on the north side of the building just as it opened for the day. He lit a two-minute fuse, and, at 09:02 am, a large explosion destroyed the north half of the building. It killed 168 people, including 19 children in the day care centre on the second floor, and injured 684 others. McVeigh was arrested tried, and convicted; he was executed on 11th June 2001.

The bomb had been placed 4.3m from the northern external building line, and 4.8m from the nearest structural column. After the explosion, half the occupiable space of the building had collapsed. On the northern face of the building all of the columns and edge beams collapsed over eight of the 6.1m bays from ground to roof levels. All the floors also collapsed over one 10.7m bay, but all the internal columns were left standing except one. The failure of this column caused the collapse of further floor areas. **Fig. 16.8** shows the extent of the structural damage. Around 90% of the injuries and fatalities were from the collapse of the building, rather than from the initial explosion.

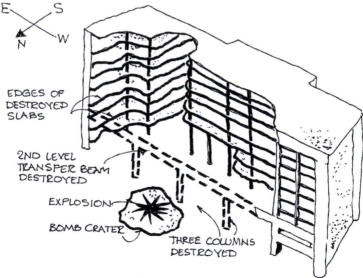

Fig. 16.8 – Structural damage

A report issued by a Building Performance Analysis Team (BPAT) explained that the nearest column to the explosion was shattered by the blast shock wave (brisance), and the adjacent columns failed due to shear forces caused by the blast. With the second floor transfer beam now spanning nearly 48.8 m instead of the 12.2m span it was designed for, this collapsed, causing the beams supporting the slabs above to collapse, taking the slabs with them. No explanation was offered for the collapse of the internal column. The calculated peak overpressures on the face of the building are shown in **Fig. 16.9**.

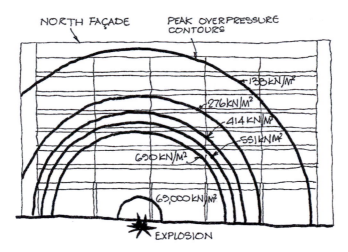

NORTH FAÇADE

PEAK OVERPRESSURE CONTOURS

138 KN/M²

276 KN/M²

414 KN/M²

551 KN M²

690 KN/M²

69,000 KN/M²

EXPLOSION

Fig. 16.9 – Blast loading on the north façade

The report notes that structure lost by direct effects of the blast was small, and most of the damage was caused by progressive collapse following the loss of the three ground level columns. The official report concludes that:[4]

Analysis of the Murrah Building shows that it would have been impossible to design the building to remain standing with one of its critical columns destroyed by the blast through the use of brute strength alone. However, if the additional amounts and locations of reinforcing steel called for in a Special (as opposed to an Ordinary) Moment Frame had been used, the Murrah Building would have had enough toughness and ductility that about half of the damage would have been prevented. That is, even though the individual columns and slabs would not have had enough strength to avoid being cracked, the reinforcing steel would have held many of the building elements in place, keeping large portions of the building erect (at least sufficiently erect to allow the occupants to escape after the blast).

Whilst the opinion that Special Moment Frames would have reduced the damage, and hence saved lives, may be correct, Oklahoma was not a seismic zone, so it was not incumbent on the structural designers to do this – see page **431** for Special Moment Frames.

The progressive collapse of the Alfred P Murrah Federal Building led to a requirement that progressive collapse needed to be examined for structures built in the USA. Code changes were enacted that were not unlike those introduced into the UK over twenty-six years earlier. However, would the UK regulations have prevented the progressive collapse? It seems unlikely. The building would be **Class 2B**, for which vertical and horizontal ties would have sufficed. As the structure was a reinforced concrete frame, adequate tying would come with the basic design. As **Fig. 16.9** shows, the calculated blast pressure in the area of the initial collapse, the transfer beam and three of its supporting columns were all subjected to loads far in excess of the 34 kN/m² the regulations required. In fact the average pressure over the whole of the façade was 965 kN/m² (140 lb/in²), over 28 times the required load. So it could be considered that the collapse was not disproportionate to the cause.

North and South Towers of the World Trade Center

When the World Trade Center, WTC, towers were built, the structure – see **Fig. 15.28** – was considered by the design engineers to be extremely strong and safe. Here are a few comments:

- According to calculations made by the engineers for the design of the Twin Towers, "*all the columns on one side of a tower could be cut, as well as the two corners and some of the columns on each adjacent side, and the building would still be strong enough to withstand a 100-mile-per-hour wind.*"
- One of the Trade Center's original structural engineers, Leslie Robertson said there is "*little likelihood of a collapse no matter how the building was attacked.*"
- The floor system design was not typical of open-web-joist floor systems. It was considerably more redundant and was well braced with transverse members.
- The building as designed is sixteen times stiffer than a conventional structure.

In 1993, the robustness of the WTC was partially put to the test when a large truck bomb was detonated on the second underground level, just outside the footprint of WTC Tower 1. Six people were killed, and more than one thousand injured. The explosion blew holes through five levels of 711 mm (28 inch) thick reinforced concrete slabs. As a result of the loss of several levels of concrete slab, some columns were left unsupported laterally over a number of levels thus considerably increasing the buckling length – see section **6.4**. In spite of this, the columns continued carrying their current loads, demonstrating the property of robustness of this part of the structure.

Naturally, this bomb attack prompted discussions about the structural safety of the WTC towers. One of the design engineers, John Skilling (1921-1998), was reassuring, stating that we "*looked at every possible thing we could think of that could happen to the buildings, even to the extent of an airplane hitting the side… A previous analysis carried out early in 1964, calculated that the towers would handle the impact of a 707 travelling at 600 mph without collapsing.*"

This was put to the test on September 11, 2001, when two large hijacked jetliners, Boeing 767s, were deliberately flown into each of the towers. At 8.46am, one jetliner hit the northern façade of WTC 1, the North Tower, between the 93rd and 99th floors, and at 9.03am, the other hit the southern façade of WTC 2, the South Tower, between the 77th and 85th floors. After being set on fire, WTC2 collapsed after 56 minutes and WTC1 after 102 minutes, killing 2830 people. While the towers remained standing, amazingly all the occupants below the impact zones were able to exit the buildings using the stairs.

An analysis of what happened on impact is also briefly described in **Chapter 15** – see pages **439- 440** and **Fig. 15.55**. But as already noted, this impact, though causing extensive local structural damage, did not cause the buildings to collapse, so what did? Whereas what happened to the structural façades after the impact was determined with accuracy from videos, what exactly happened to the structures within the impact zones can never be known with certainty.

At around 550°C steel begins to lose most of it structural strength – see page **121**. After the impact, fires took hold in the impact zones. Initially caused by the jet fuel, the fire was principally fed by the existing fire load in the offices – stationery, furniture and other combustible material. These fires rapidly reached temperatures of 550°C and above, so structural steel elements without adequate fire protection in these areas would quickly lose their load-carrying capacity. Fire protection for the building was provided by an automatic sprinkler system, and all the structural steelwork had steel protection in the form of sprayed-on material, or by being boxed-in with fireproof material – the floor system was rated at 2 hours for a continuous fire. The mechanical action of the impact of the aircraft destroyed the sprinkler system and *'the aircraft are believed to have dislodged fireproofing,'* as the FEMA report puts it. However, reports and photos taken before the attack speak of, and show, some areas of fireproofing missing from the floor trusses.

During the hour or so that the towers remained standing after the aircraft collisions, the structure in the impact zone – due to initial damage, loss of strength due to the lack of fire protection in the fire, and the progressive lack of lateral support to columns – gradually degraded until it was unable to support the weight of the undamaged floors above. What ensued was a sudden **collapse** of the **vertical structure** in the impact zone. This meant that the **potential energy** of the higher floors was converted into **kinetic energy** – see **Fig. 15.11** – as the upper floors fell through the impact zone. This caused an **impact load** on the intact structure below. However, this structure was not strong enough to convert the **kinetic energy** into **strain energy** and absorb the impact – see **Fig. 15.52**. In other words, the impact caused an unsupportable **dynamic magnification factor**– see **Fig.15.53**.

The upper floors, falling through the impact zone, provoked a progressive collapse of the intact floors below as the falling parts of the building gained more and more kinetic energy. What happened was that the whole building collapsed vertically at near to the rate of free-fall under gravity. The time for the collapse of the towers was roughly 10 seconds, compared to the free-fall time of 9 seconds.

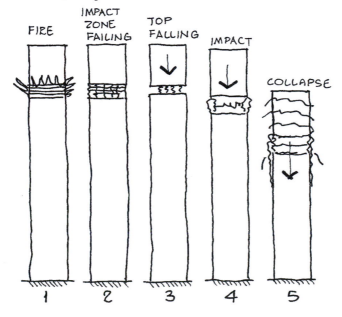

Fig. 16.10 – Stages in the WTC towers collapse

The UK Buildings Regulations would put this building into **Class 3**. It is clear from the claims of the design engineers and the actual performance of the building that there were adequate alternative load paths for not only one member to be removed. On the north face of the North Tower, no fewer than 33 of the 59 columns were cut on impact; well over half, and still the structure stood. But the regulations for Class 3 buildings require *'A risk assessment should be made for all normal and any abnormal hazards.'* Though not a structural matter as such, it is possible that such an assessment would have shown that the fire-proofing would not survive the impact, and the fire that followed would have led to the catastrophic collapses. However, it is not entirely clear whether the progressive collapses that followed the impacts were disproportionate or not, or that the UK Building Regulations would have saved the towers.

Other buildings

In writings about progressive collapse, scant evidence is presented to show that real buildings have been saved from disproportionate collapse by the application of the regulations, though one source claims that there is *'overwhelming evidence, including post-incident inspection of buildings damaged in past terrorist attacks, to support the view that tying is enormously beneficial,'* and the view of established experts Moore (2002) and Byfield (2007) is that *'tying makes a positive contribution to robustness.'*[5]

Though there may well be *'overwhelming evidence'*, it is not provided by the two published sources, Moore and Byfield. Moore provides two examples of bomb explosion survival.[6] These were Exchequer Court in London, bombed in 1992, and Kansallis House, also in London, that was bombed in 1993. Neither collapsed. As no complex post-explosion analyses were done, how progressive collapse was prevented is unclear.

Exchequer Court had a steel structure in the form of a braced frame. The bomb, whose force was much greater than and of a different type from that of a gas explosion, caused columns and floor beams to be severely bent, and connections were broken, however the building stood. Kansallis House had an in situ reinforced concrete frame. The explosion destroyed three ground floor columns, first floor beams and part of a ground-to-first-floor structural concrete wall. In spite of this, like many war-time similar bomb-damaged buildings, the structure stood, though according to a contemporary newspaper report it was damaged beyond repair.

In various papers, Byfield instances two further cases of buildings with ground floor columns removed due to Second World War bomb damage that did not collapse due to the shear strength of masonry walling. Two more cases are described. In one, the Hotel San Diego, two columns, including a corner one, were deliberately removed, but there was no progressive collapse as the building bridged over the damage through frame action and diagonal strutting by masonry walls. In another case, the 11-storey Crowne Plaza hotel, four ground level columns were removed; again there was no progressive collapse due to framing action and arching in the concrete floors.

In none of the six buildings cited above was there any evidence that specific tying had been introduced, or that even if it had been, how would it have played any part in preventing progressive collapse.

16.6 The role of cladding and internal partitions

Demolition engineers demolish tall buildings by using explosions to initiate a progressive collapse. To prepare for the demolition, all non-loadbearing walls are removed, as they stiffen the building. Then explosives are used to demolish the lowest two levels of columns. The idea is to cause a progressive collapse by turning the potential energy of the building above these levels into kinetic energy, which is why Ronan Point, the Alfred Murrah Building and the WTC Towers collapsed progressively.

In older buildings, non-loadbearing walls were often of masonry, which can provide considerable stiffening to framed structures when vertical structure is removed. Their presence explains why so many buildings bombed during the Second World War did not collapse, even after principal vertical elements had been removed. This is less likely with modern building as modern architecture eschews, in the main, masonry cladding preferring full glazing, or other forms of lightweight cladding. Also, modern office planning prefers open-plan offices rather than ones using a cellular plan. This has unwittingly made buildings less robust and more susceptible to progressive collapse, which could have been a factor in the collapse of the Alfred P Murrah building. At the Ronan Point tower, the presence of non-loadbearing blockwork internal partitions prevented the collapse of the lower bedroom slabs, thus saving a number of lives – see pages **446-447.**

16.7 Review of recommended prevention strategies

In the usual process of the design of building structures, numerical calculations are made by using accepted theory to calculate forces and stresses in the chosen structure. These are caused by loads calculated from data that is given in codes of practice and technical literature. In the case of prevention strategies required by the UK, and now other, building regulations, there is no way of calculating specific abnormal loads. So, except for special cases where the magnitude of exceptional loads can be calculated – such as buildings storing explosive materials – what is used is something called the **scenario-independent approach**. This means that **notional strengthening** is carried out to enhance the general level of robustness, without necessarily preventing failure.

By far the most common way of achieving robustness is to **provide horizontal ties** across a building in two opposite directions at every level. This idea does not seem to be based on any rigorous engineering analysis, but on the basis that such tying is bound to help. But what was it supposed to achieve? It has to be assumed the ties are added to increase the ability for a building to use **catenary action to carry a vertical load**. This is intimately related to **column removal**.

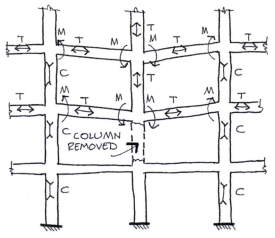

Fig. 16.11 – Catenary action after column removal

When discussing the idea that a notional element could be removed, a guide published in 2010 by the Institution of Structural Engineers called a *'Practical guide to structural robustness and disproportionate collapse in buildings'*, notes that the term 'notional' is used to emphasis it is an **imaginary scenario**. After providing some basic sketches to illustrate how structures might act after the removal of a column – see **Fig. 16.11** – it notes that *'because of the complexities of all this, calculations cannot be accurate; they can only be a crude approximations.'*

In **Fig, 16.11** the letters **C**, **T** and **M** indicate **compression forces**, **tensile forces** and **bending moments** that are a result of a column being removed. They are not all of the same magnitude and have to be added, or subtracted, to some of the forces and moments that existed when the column was in place. As can be seen, even crude approximations for this simple conceptualisation would be far from simple, and could quite likely involve assumptions that would invalidate any calculations. For example, it is far from obvious how far the unsupported columns would deflect, and this would influence the inclination of the beams above the removed column. This in turn would affect the magnitude of the tensile forces in these beams. Also the moment capacity of the beams could be affected by the tensile forces **T**.

But there are other factors to be taken into account when trying to use tying to achieve catenary action. The first is that, as the column is assumed to be removed suddenly then, if the reduced structure remains elastic, a **Dynamic Load Factor, DLF**, of **2** – see **Fig. 15.42** – should be applied to the load caused by the column removal. However if the **assumed catenary shape** results in some **plastic action** in the frame, as it is almost bound to do, then the **DLF** could be reduced to **1.3**. None of this is addressed in the UK Building Regulations.

However, to achieve anything like useful catenary action, the adjacent beam/column joints have to rotate in the order of 4°, which is unachievable for almost any normal structural connection either in steel or reinforced concrete. This led the 2011 CPNI report to state that *'**The mechanisms necessary to arrest progressive collapse cannot be developed by tying.**'*[7] So, complying with the Code requirements for tying forces does not appear to do anything specifically structurally useful.

In the case of the removal of a column, the **scenario-independent approach** only provides a **standard measure of robustness**. Any structural analysis for the removal of a single column, if an accurate result is required, is fraught with difficulty. The simplest is a **linear elastic static analysis** of the structure minus the column, but is hardly realistic. The most realistic analysis will be a **non-linear dynamic analysis** of the structure, with the column being removed as part of the dynamic analysis. This has the advantage of not requiring any assumptions to be made, however it is **highly complex**, and requires **qualified structural dynamics** experts to carry it out.

If for some reason the provision of ties, or the demonstration of robustness by single column removal cannot be achieved, then the third option is to **identify key elements** and design them to resist a loading of **34 kN/m²**. The origin of this load is an **estimate** of the load that was required to crack a wall in the Ronan Point tower – see page **448** – and was only **about 5 lbs/in²** in Imperial units. This load does not intend to represent any specific accidental loading, and it is dwarfed by loads caused by explosives – see **Fig. 16.9**. No guidance is given on how to identify key elements, or what area of the element should be designed for a static load of **34kN/m²**. For columns, it is assumed attached cladding is removed, and for slabs and walls, the 2010 ISE Guide suggests the area could be limited to **6m x 6m**.

The last requirement is that for some buildings, Class 3 buildings – see **Table 16.1** – for instance, a **risk assessment** be carried out; this is basically a **probabilistic approach**. The UK Building Regulations give no guidance on this, and neither do codes of practice. In fact, the usual procedure of structural design already has risk analysis built into it as was explained in **Chapter 6**. This introduced the **probability density function** of the **normal distribution** – see **Fig. 6.6**. This idea is used to show how a risk assessment is made for a normal hazard; that is the hazard of the design load being exceeded, or the load capacity of the structure being under strength. So two probability density functions are drawn on the same diagram, separated by a **Factor of Safety** – see **Fig. 16.12**.

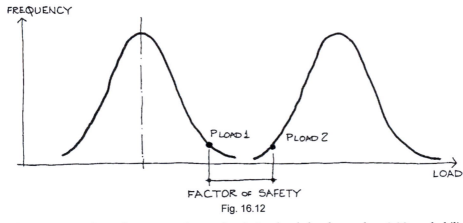

Fig. 16.12

In **Fig. 16.12** the point $P_{LOAD\ 1}$ shows the design load that has only a 0.02 probability of being exceeded during the use of the building, and point $P_{LOAD\ 2}$ shows there is a 0.98 probability of the structure supporting it. The diagrams are moved apart to provide a **Factor of Safety**. **Chapter 6** has already described this in detail. So basically, normal risk assessment is buried in the standard procedures. However, it is unclear whether overloading of a structure is the normal hazard referred to in the Building Regulations.

Buildings are normally given a design life of **50 years**, so if there is a set of statistical data, like wind speed, or snowfall kept over a long period of time, the probability of a maximum event occurring during the design life can be calculated from a formula derived from a **binominal distribution**. The **probability**, which is a **number p, 0 < p < 1**, and, can be calculated from:

$$p = 1 - \left(1 - \frac{1}{T}\right)^N$$

The number **1/T** is the **frequency**. So if **T = 50yrs**, then the frequency of **once in 50 years** is the **number 1/50 = 0.02**. This does not mean that such an event will occur, or that it will be the same event as occurred in the last 50 years. The equation for the probability can be re-arranged to give the frequency for a given probability, **p**, and lifetime **N**, as:

$$\frac{1}{T} = 1 - (1 - p)^{\frac{1}{N}}$$

The Building Regulations require that risk assessment should take into account '*all the normal hazards that may reasonably be foreseen, together with any abnormal hazards,*' without giving any indication what are normal and/or abnormal hazards.

In 2013, the ISE published a document with the title '*Manual for the systematic assessment of high-risk structures against disproportionate collapse.*' It recommends that '*the structural engineer should start from the 'position of a robust, safe structural form*' – see section **16.8** below for **inherent robustness** – going on to note that '*a risk-based approach has no prescriptively codified requirements*' which means that '*risk-based decisions can be successfully navigated using sound engineering judgement.*' From these statements it is obvious that clear guidance will not be forthcoming, as the term **robust** is still yet to be clarified, and it is hard to imagine why anyone would not use **sound engineering judgement**; a term that is woolly at best. One author on the subject thought that '*It is clear that a probabilistic risk assessment of low-risk high-consequence events is almost impossible and is unlikely to be meaningful*;'[8] but the terms low-risk and high-consequence are not defined.

The 2013 ISE Guide has a table which tabulates **Likelihood**, **Frequency** and **Approximate Return Period**. Though '**likelihood**' and '**probability**' are colloquially synonymous, in statistics they are not; as probability attaches to possible results and likelihood attaches to hypotheses – it is unclear here which definition is being used. **Table 16.2** is an amended version of that found in the Guide. Here the **Likelihood** column is as the original, the **Frequency** column gives the same values in the more usual form, and the values in **Return** period have been calculated from the algebraic expressions. The ISE table gives an **Approximate Return period**. Columns for **Probability in 50 years**, and **Exponential Frequency** have been added, as has line for **Serviceability**.

Likelihood	Probability in 50 years	Frequency	Exponential frequency	Return period
Frequent		Once in 5 years		6 years
Serviceability	0.63	Once in 50 years	2×10^{-2}	50 years
Likely	0.40	Once in 100 years	10^{-2}	75 years
Unlikely	0.095	Once in 500 years	2×10^{-3}	475 years
Rare	0.02	Once in 2500 years	4×10^{-4}	2500 years
Improbably	10^{-3}	Once in 50,000 years	2×10^{-5}	50,000 years
Negligible	2×10^{-4}	Once in 250,000 years	4×10^{-6}	250,000 years

Table 16.2

In the 2013 ISE Guide, the written descriptions equated to the frequencies or the return periods are not given any basis, so must be opinions, and even with that, no specific events are linked to these frequencies. It may seem odd, because it is odd, that structural designers now are expected to provide resistance, for a building that has a design life of 50 years, for an event that is statistically expected only to occur during a much longer period.

In 2003 a paper was published[9] which gives the following frequencies **per year** for some abnormal events:

- **Gas explosions (per dwelling): 2×10^{-5}**
- **Bomb explosions (per dwelling): 2×10^{-6}**
- **Vehicular collisions (per building): 6×10^{-4}**
- **Fully developed fires (per m² per building): 5×10^{-8}**

These values are not substantiated, and are only used as illustrations. So, with no reliable data, no universally agreed list of hazards, and no prescriptively codified requirements, it is hard to see how this approach can yield useful results in terms of actual, rather than notional structural design, to prevent disproportionate collapse.

There is now a new approach that uses advanced statistics to calculate something called a **Reliability Index**. This is set out in **Handbook 2** of the **Implementation of Eurocodes – Basis of structural reliability and risk engineering**. Early in this document it is noted that *'The vagueness caused by inaccurate definitions (in particular serviceability and other performance requirements) may be described by the means of fuzzy sets.* ** *However, these methods have a little practical significance, as suitable experimental data is rarely available.'*[10]

16.8 Inherent robustness and omissions

The 2010 ISE Guide notes that *'**Well detailed in situ reinforced concrete is inherently robust**'*, and that *'**Well detailed steel frames should be inherently robust**,'* which agrees with the Ronan Point Inquiry Report which noted that for structural steelwork or reinforced concrete frames, *'it has long been known that there is little chance of local damage causing progressive collapse'* – see page **448**.

The same Guide also notes that *'**timber trussed rafter roofs have inherent robustness**'* and *'**platform timber frame construction on a cellular plan...is inherently robust**.'* Also *'**the traditional cellular plan form of masonry structures offers inherent robustness**.'* **This means that ALL of the usual types of structures used in buildings are inherently robust**. It is only with precast concrete structures that the ghost of Ronan Point is evoked, noting that *'for precast construction the provision of robustness requires more direct engineering intervention,'*[11] going on to provide a number of typical details of provided adequate tying between elements. Of course, when Ronan Point was being built CP116 was available, which required that *'**All members should be adequately tied together at all times**'* – see page **448**.

However, there are a large number of situations that are not covered by the present legislation, and it is not clear whether this is because they do not have to comply, or they just got left behind. Many of these are highlighted in the 2011 CPNI report. There is little information on the robustness of lightweight steel construction, modular construction, or large span structures used for warehouses and superstores. Research is needed on the robustness of Slimdek floors, voided slabs, waffle slabs and slabs using pre-cast permanent formwork with in situ concrete topping. The role of transfer beams still seems problematic.

How any of the methods of providing robustness against disproportionate collapse apply to existing buildings receives scant attention. The CPNI report notes that 'For alterations and extensions, the general principle is the limited objective of the building being made only marginally less satisfactory than it was before, irrespective of the scale of the alteration or extension.'[12] The 2010 ISE Guide says

---

** Fuzzy sets generalize classical sets, since the indicator functions of classical sets are special cases of the membership functions of fuzzy sets.

that *'Whilst the prescriptive rules applicable to buildings may be suitable for some alterations, the difficulties associated with retrofitting ties can be formidable.'*[13]

What this short section indicates is that **usual structures**, are, more or less automatically, **inherently robust**, and for less usual ones, the guidance is scant or even absent.

16.9 Conclusions

There are numerous unknowns in the present approach for providing structural robustness, however a few things can gleaned from the now enormous quantity of literature on the subject; these are:

- Most structures, properly designed against normal design loads will be **inherently robust** – see section **16.8**.

- Except for exceptional cases, it is not possible to derive specific 'abnormal' loads, so any attempts to carry out structural analysis for these cases has to be done by using the **scenario-independent approach**, which provides **notional strengthening** – see section **16.7.**

- There are a number of structural concepts, forms and situations where there is no guidance on how progressive collapse is to be avoided, if indeed it needs to be considered – see section **16.8**.

- If some form of rigid cladding or internal partitioning can be guaranteed, then this will enhance a building's robustness – see section **16.6**.

- The basic codes of practice for the various structural materials have risk assessment built into them for overloading due to normal loads, and/or the reduced strength of the built structure – see **Section 16.7**.

However, it seems clear that if the structure for Ronan Point had been conceived, designed and built to a professional standard it would, in all likelihood, have withstood a domestic gas explosion with nothing more than local damage. Consequently the concept of robustness against disproportionate collapse probably would not have appeared.

Further reading

Arup – **Review of international research on structural robustness and disproportionate collapse** – CPNI – October 2011
https://www.gov.uk/government/uploads/system/uploads/attachment_data/file/6328
MN Bussell and AEK Jones – **Robustness and the relevance of Ronan Point today** – The Structural Engineer – 7 December 2010
Zdeněk P Bažant, Yong Zhou – **Why Did the World Trade Center Collapse? – Simple Analysis** – Journal of Engineering Mechanics January & March 2002
Building Performance Analysis Team – **The Oklahoma City bombing: improving building performance through multi-hazard mitigation (FEMA 277)** – August 1996 – http://www.fema.gov/media-library-data/20130726-1453-20490-7474/fema_277_ok_city.pd

BR Ellingwood, R Smilowitz, DO Dusenberry, D Duthinh, HS Lew, NJ Carino – **Best Practices for Reducing the Potential for Reducing Progressive Collapse in Buildings (NISTIR 7396)** – February 2007

http://www.nist.gov/customcf/get_pdf.cfm?pub_id=860696

James Glanz and Eric Lipton – **City in the Sky: the rise and fall of the World Trade Centre** – Times Books – 2003

Hugh Griffiths, Professor Sir Alfred Pugsley, Professor Sir Owen Saunders – **Collapse of Flats at Ronan Point, Canning Town** – Her Majesty's Stationary Office – 1968

Institution of Structural Engineers – **The Implications of the Report of the Inquiry into the Collapse of Flats at Ronan Point, Canning Town** – The Structural Engineer, July 1969, N° 7 Vol 47 – p255-284

Institution of Structural Engineers – **Practical guide to structural robustness and disproportionate collapse in buildings** – October 2010

Institution of Structural Engineers – **Manual for the systematic risk assessment of high-risk structures against disproportionate collapse** – October 2013

Kausel, Eduardo ed – **The Towers Lost and Beyond** – Massachusetts Institute of Technology – 2002 - especially see Oral Buyukozturk, Franz-Josef Ulm – **Chapter 6**

Leonardo da Vinci Pilot Project – **Basis of structural reliability and risk engineering** – 2005

http://www.eurocodes.fi/1990/paasivu1990/sahkoinen1990/handbook2%5B1%5D.pdf

Theodor Krauthammer – **Modern Protective Structures (Chapter 9)** – CRC Press – 2008

Uwe Starossek – **Progressive collapse of structures** – Thomas Telford Ltd – 2009

References – Chapter 16

1   Institution of Structural Engineers – **The Implications of the Report of the Inquiry into the Collapse of Flats at Ronan Point, Canning Town** – The Structural Engineer, July 1969, N° 7 Vol 47p259
2   ibid – p282
3   HANSARD 1803–2005→ 1970s → 1970 → March 1970 → 9 March 1970 → Commons Sitting → ORDER OF THE DAY – BUILDING REGULATIONS
4   **The Oklahoma City bombing: improving building performance through multi-hazard mitigation (FEMA 277)** – August 1996 -P5-2
5   Arup – **Review of international research on structural robustness and disproportionate collapse** – CPNI – October 2011- p76
6   DB Moore - **The UK and European Regulations for Accidental Actions** - BRE - p5-8
7   Arup - **Review of international research on structural robustness and disproportionate collapse** – CPNI – October 2011- P76
8   Stuart Alexander -**The Structural Engineer – 7 December 2004**– see box p16
9   **Ellingwood BR**. *Load and Resistance Factor Criteria for Progressive Collapse Design*. Prevention of progressive collapse: national workshop of the Multihazard Mitigation Council of the National Institute of Building Sciences. Washington, D.C., July 2002
10   Leonardo da Vinci Pilot Project – **Basis of structural reliability and risk engineering** – 2005 – P I – 2
11   ISE Guide 2010 p36
12   Arup - **Review of international research on structural robustness and disproportionate collapse** – CPNI – October 2011- P40
13   ISE GUIDE 2010, p67

CHAPTER 17 *The mathematical basis*

For a complete picture of structural behaviour, as this book wants to give, the use of mathematics for the understanding of structures has to be included. Whilst research into the applications of mathematics for the description of structural behaviour continues, the basis was laid at the beginning of the 19th century which led to three things:

- **methods of carrying out predictive calculations became available**
- **the separation of structural concepts from architectural concepts began**
- **the excessive interest in theory by engineers reduced their design capacity**

This is not to say that there is anything wrong, as such, with the use of mathematics as a tool for predicting structural behaviour, in fact it is essential. The ever increasing use of mathematics as a tool is part of technological advancement. However it should be generally available, and not restricted to a small group. The reasons for this are buried deep in societies' view of mathematics in general. As mathematics is a demanding subject there is a predominant idea that only a chosen few are capable of using mathematics for anything; nothing could be less true. In mathematics, as with structural behaviour, it is the concepts that have to be grasped, after which calculations become arithmetic.

To understand the mathematical basis of the behaviour of structures, no new structural concepts are required. But this mathematical world can only be entered through the **differential calculus**. This was developed independently in the 17th century by Isaac Newton and Gottfried Leibniz, and remains the single most important tool for the mathematical description of the physical world.

In this chapter only skeletal structures will be considered but mathematical analysis carried out for building structures often uses this idealisation – see **Chapter 18**. Only the rudiments of the differential calculus are required for this analysis, and they are explained in this chapter. Apart from this, simple algebraic manipulation and the basic arithmetic operations are also used.

17.1 Functions and differentiation

The new mathematics required is to make possible the differentiation of ordinary functions with respect to one of the variables. This may sound technical but a clear physical picture of the process can be had by imagining how it feels to ride a bicycle along a smooth straight but undulating road that runs beside a lake. The journey has a start point, an **origin**, and a **reference axis**, the water level of the lake. As the road undulates the slope, the **gradient**, is changing continuously and how this varies is the information that the process of differentiation provides.

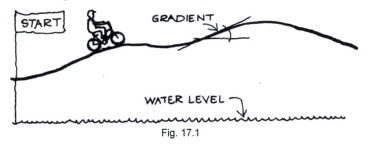
Fig. 17.1

This picture is converted to a mathematical description. The line representing the water level is renamed the **x-axis.** The distance travelled from the start point is called the **x-coordinate** and the height of the road above the water is called the **y-coordinate**. The profile of the road itself is called the **graphical representation** of the function. The **gradient of the function**, the slope of the road, is given by how a line drawn tangential to the function meets the x-axis. **Fig. 17.2** shows this.

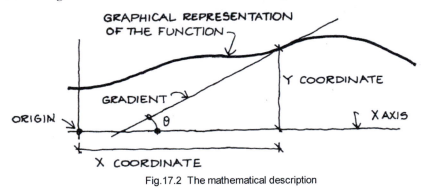
Fig.17.2 The mathematical description

For each point on the function there is an **x** and a **y** coordinate and these are related by the function. This can be written as a mathematical relationship as

$$y = f(x)$$

This means that **y is a function of x**, and for any given value of **x** the function **f** gives the value for **y**. The function could take many forms, like 'add 3', or 'multiply x by 17 and take away 2.5'. In this way the graphical representation of the function, or **graph** for short, can be drawn. Values of **x** are chosen allowing the values of **y** to be calculated from the function. For each value of **x** the 'height' of **y** is drawn from the x-axis; joining the tops of these lines by a smooth line gives the graph of the function.

Example 17.1   Draw the graph of the function **y = 0.25 x²**, a parabolic function.

when x = 2, **y** = 0.25 × 2² = **1**.
when x = 3, **y** = 0.25 × 3² = **2.25** etc

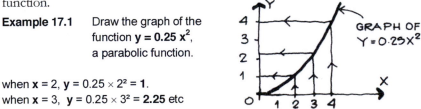

The question is: what is the gradient of the graph of the function for any value of **x**? For a first approximation of the gradient, values near to **x** can be chosen and the straight lines joining the points will give the approximate gradient.

Example 17.2 Find the approximate gradient of the function **y = 0.25x²**, at **x = 2**, by considering values below of, **x = 1.5** and 1.75 then above of **x = 2.25** and 2.5. Compare the results and draw diagrams.

For **x** = 2, **y** = 0.25 × 2² = 1,

using values of **x** less than 2

x = 1.5, **y** = 0.5625
∴ **gradient** = (1 − 0.5625) ÷ (2 − 1.5) = **0.875**
x = 1.75, **y** = 0.7656
∴ **gradient** = (1 − 0.7656) ÷ (2 − 1.75) = **0.9376**

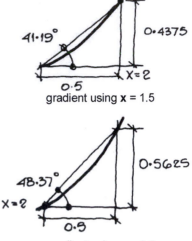

gradient using **x** = 1.5

using values of **x** more than 2

x = 2.25, **y** = 1.2656
∴ **gradient** = (1.2656 - 1) ÷ (2.25 − 2) = **1.0675**
x = 2.5, **y** = 1.5625
∴ **gradient** = (1.5625 - 1) ÷ (2.5 − 2) = **1.125**

the angles of the gradient lines can be calculated
from **tan θ = gradient, gradient** = 0.875, θ = **41.19°**
and **gradient** = 1.125, θ = **48.37°**

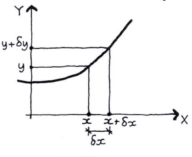

gradient using **x** = 2.5

Four approximate values have been obtained and, as can be seen, the nearer the adjacent value chosen is to x = 2, the nearer the gradient seems to be to the correct value. The reader should experiment with other near values.

This method of finding the gradient by using points that are near can give a good approximation, but it is time consuming. A mathematically based method is needed. This is done by considering a small interval on the x-axis called 'delta x' and denoted by δ**x**. Suppose the function gives a value **y** for a value **x**, then it will give a value **y** + δ**y** for a value **x** + δ**x**. It should be noted that δ**x** and δ**y** are not necessarily equal.

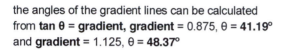

Fig.17.3

Now, by using the function to calculate the values at **x** and **x** + δ**x**, the same geometric triangular construction can be made to find the value of the gradient at **x**.

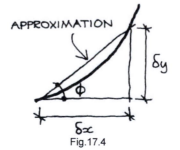

Fig.17.4

The approximate gradient of the graph of the function at **x** is written as:

$$\text{gradient} = \frac{\delta y}{\delta x} = \tan \phi$$

Example 17.3 For the function $y = x^2$ obtain an expression for δy in terms of **x** and δx and another expression for the gradient.

$$y = f(x) = x^2$$

and

$$(y + \delta y) = f(x + \delta x) = (x + \delta x)^2 = x^2 + (2x\delta x) + \delta x^2$$

and as

$$\delta y = (y + \delta y) - y = f(x + \delta x) - f(x)$$

then the expression for δy is

$$\delta y = (x^2 + (2x\delta x) + \delta x^2) - x^2 = (2x\delta x) + \delta x^2$$

to obtain the expression for the gradient each side is divided by δx giving

$$\frac{\delta y}{\delta x} = \frac{2x\delta x}{\delta x} + \frac{(\delta x)^2}{\delta x} = 2x + \delta x$$

In **Example 17.2** it was shown how, as the interval between **x** and the near point reduces, that is as δx gets smaller and smaller, so the approximation for the gradient becomes more accurate.. In **Example 17.3**, as δx gets smaller, the gradient gets nearer to **2x**.

This approximate gradient at **x** has to be made into the actual gradient at **x**, that is the **differential**. This is done by making δx so small that it is as near to zero as possible without actually being zero and so can be ignored in the part **2x** + δx. This process of δx approaching the limiting value zero is written as:

$$\frac{dy}{dx} = \text{limit}_{\delta x \to 0} \frac{\delta y}{\delta x}$$

The symbol on the left of the equals sign is the differential called '**dee y by dee x**'. Now the differential **dy/dx**, of the function $y = f(x) = x^2$ with respect to the **x-axis** can be written:

$$\frac{dy}{dx} = \frac{df(x)}{dx} = 2x$$

This process of obtaining a differential of a function, called **differentiation,** is the basic operation of the differential calculus. It depends on the concept of $\delta x \to 0$. This poses some intellectual problems because how can a number be so small, infinitely small, that is as close to zero as possible but at the same time be a number? When the differential calculus was discovered simultaneously by Leibniz and Newton in the late 17th century, see page **8**, it was subjected to a devastating critique by Bishop Berkley who noted that "...*if something is neglected, no matter how small, we can no longer claim to have the exact result but only an approximation*".[1] The intellectual problem persisted for nearly 200 years and was only clarified in 1872 by Karl Weierstrass (1815-1897). However. the process of differentiation, using the intellectually suspect infinitesimally small numbers, yielded useful results so research using the new mathematics progressed rapidly.

So far only the function $y = f(x) = x^2$ has been differentiated. Clearly a process is needed to differentiate any function having terms like x^n; this is given by the **general rule for differentiation:**

$$\frac{dy}{dx} = nx^{n-1}$$

This is the **central relationship** used for differentiating functions.

Example 17.4   Differentiate the function $y = x^3 - 0.2x^5$ with respect to x and evaluate the gradient at $x = 1.2$. Draw the graph and the gradient line at $x = 1.2$.

using the general expression for differentiation

$$\frac{dy}{dx} = 3x^{3-1} - 0.2 \times 5x^{5-1} = 3x^2 - x^4$$

and at $x = 1.2$, the gradient is

$$\text{gradient} = \frac{dy}{dx} = 3 \times 1.2^2 - 1.2^4$$

$$= 4.32 - 2.0736 = 2.24$$

and as **gradient = tan θ** then

$$\tan θ = 2.246 \quad \text{so} \quad θ = 66°$$

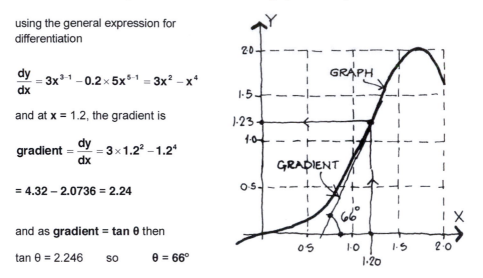

Any function $y = f(x)$ that contains any number of powers of x, that is, x^n, can be differentiated piecewise using the general rule. More complex functions can also be differentiated, but as they are not required here these need not be explained. There are two important points to be noted about the expression for the general rule of differentiation which are:

- **it defines a new function, the derived function**
- **it is a differential equation**

Why the process of differentiation defines a new function is shown in **Example 17.4**. Here the derivative, **dy/dx**, was given in terms of **x**; hence it is a function of **x** and can have a graphical representation.

Example 17.5   Draw the graph of the derived function of

$$y = x^3 - 0.2x^5$$

that is

$$\frac{dy}{dx} = 3x^2 - x^4$$

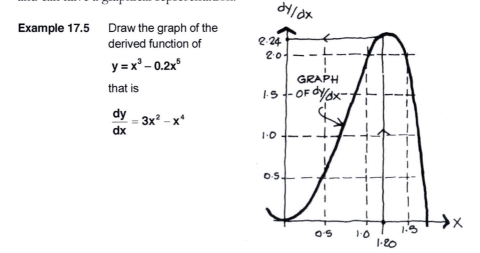

As **dy/dx** is a function of **x**, it seems reasonable to ask whether this derived function can be differentiated, and it can be by using the general rule.

Example 17.5 contd. Differentiate, with respect to **x**, the derived function $\dfrac{dy}{dx} = 3x^2 - x^4$

$$\frac{d}{dx}\left(\frac{dy}{dx}\right) = \frac{d^2y}{dx^2} = 2 \times 3x^{2-1} - 4x^{4-1} = 6x - 4x^3$$

The second derivative, or the derived function of the derived function, is called **'dee two y by dee x squared'**. This process can be continued until there are no more **x**s to be differentiated. And **dy/dx** = $3x^2 - x^4$ is a **differential equation** because it contains **dy/dx**, a differential.

Physical phenomena, which include the behaviour of structures, can often be described by differential equations. In the following sections, differential equations are developed that describe the behaviour of a column and of a beam. These equations are developed for the general case, and then solutions are sought for particular cases, a cantilever with a uniformly distributed load for example. The solution will be in the form of a function, or functions, and these will represent bending moments, shear forces, displacements and curvatures. So 'solving' the differential equation means finding a function.

Example 17.6   What is the 'solution' to the differential equation **dy/dx** = $3x^2 - x^4$?

from **Example 17.4** the solution is $y = x^3 - 0.2x^5$

because if it is differentiated it will equal the right-hand of the differential equation.

The answer in **Example 17.6** has been obtained by 'undifferentiating' the differential equation. How can this be done in general, and is it the only 'solution'? To answer this in a general way, the process of **integration** must be explained.

17.2 Integration

What is needed is, given derived function **dy/dx** = **f(x)**, a general rule for finding another function, **y** = **f(x)**, that gives the derived function when differentiated. The derived function is assumed to be of the type **y** = x^n. This rule can be stated directly, from the general rule for differentiation given on page **469**, as the **general rule for integration**:

$$\int y\,dx = \int x^n dx = \frac{x^{n+1}}{n+1} + C$$

The sign $\int$ means 'the integral of' and the **dx** means that the integration is being carried out with respect to **x**. The letter **C** is the **constant of integration** and is explained later.

Example 17.7   Given the derived function   **dy/dx** = $3x^2 - x^4$, find, by using the general rule of integration, a suitable function in the form **y** = x^n

$$\int\left(\frac{dy}{dx}\right)dx = y = \int(3x^2 - x^4)dx = \int 3x^2 dx - \int x^4 dx = \frac{3x^{2+1}}{2+1} - \frac{x^{4+1}}{4+1} + C = x^3 - 0.2x^5 + C$$

The derived function has been integrated piecewise, that is, each part individually. As can be seen the original function, **y** = $x^3 - 0.2x^5$, has been recovered, but with the addition of **C** the constant of integration. Why has this constant of integration appeared? The reason is that the recovered function is not unique, because if there were two functions $y = f_1(x) = x^3 - 0.2x^5 + 0.5$, and $y = f_2(x) = x^3 - 0.2x^5 - 0.5$, when differentiated, using the general rule, both would give $dy/dx = 3x^2 - x^4$. Here C takes the value $+0.5$ in $f_1(x)$ and -0.5 in $f_2(x)$. If the graphs of the two functions are drawn it can be seen that the gradients, which are what the derived functions give, are the same.

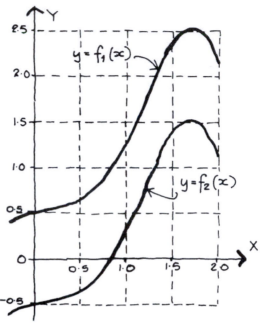

Fig.17.5 Graphs with different constants of integration

To return to the cycling analogy shown in **Fig. 17.1**; given a profile of a road, the same road can be placed at any height above the level of the water level. The cyclist will experience the same gradients. Therefore to find the unique function, $y = f(x)$, the unique road, one more piece of information is required. This a specific value of y for some x. So to obtain the graph shown for **Example 17.4**, the values at $x = 0$, $y = 0$, would be sufficient, in other words $C = 0$.

What has been achieved is the solution of a **first order differential equation** by **direct integration**. A general solution was obtained and, with extra information, a unique solution was obtained. The solutions are in the form of functions. In this example the first order differential equation is $dy/dx = 3x^2 - x^4$ and the general solution is $y = f(x) = x^3 - 0.2x^5 + C$. As C can take any value, there is an infinite number of these equations. With one piece of extra information C can be evaluated and a unique solution obtained.

The term **first order** was used to denote that only dy/dx was involved. But if the derived equation involves d^2y/dx^2, a **second order differential** equation, can a solution, in the form of $y = f(x)$ be obtained by direct integration? It can be, by proceeding as before, but now the integration has to be carried out twice.

Example 17.8   Given the derived function $d^2y/dx^2 = 6x - 4x^3$, find, by using the general rule of integration, a general solution in the form $y = x^n$

First application of the general rule of integration

$$\int \left(\frac{d^2y}{dx^2}\right)dx = \frac{dy}{dx} = \int (6x - 4x^3)dx = \int 6xdx - \int 4x^3dx = \frac{6x^{1+1}}{1+1} - \frac{4x^{3+1}}{3+1} + C = 3x^2 - x^4 + C$$

Second application of the general rule of integration

$$\int\left(\frac{dy}{dx}\right)dx = y = \int(3x^2 - x^4 + C)dx = x^3 - 0.2x^5 + Cx + D$$

So the general solution is: $\qquad$ $y = x^3 - 0.2x^3 + Cx + D$

Each time the integration rule is used another constant of integration appears. As it has been used twice in this example, there are two; **C** and **D**. But because **C** appeared due to the first application of the integration rule, it is subject to the rule for the second integration. That is **C**, when integrated with respect to **x**, becomes **Cx**. This can be seen formally as:

$$\int Cdx = \int Cx^0 dx = \frac{Cx^{0+1}}{0+1} = Cx$$

where the convention $x^0 = 1$, has been used. Now to obtain a unique solution, two additional pieces of information are needed to evaluate **C** and **D**.

Example 17.8 cont. Suppose the additional information is that at **x = 0, y = –0.5**

Then, substituting these values into the general solution gives:

$$-0.5 = 0^3 - 0.2 \times 0^5 + C \times 0 + D = D$$

allowing the constant of integration **D** to be evaluated as –0.5

the second piece of information is obtained from:

$$y = 0 \text{ which gives } x = 0.835$$

substituting these values into the general solution, and using the value for **D** gives:

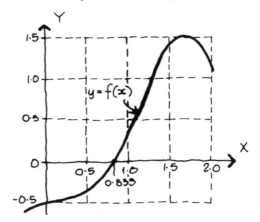

$0 = 0.835^3 - 0.2 \times 0.835^5 + C \times 0.835 - 0.5$
$\quad = 0.582 - 0.082 + C \times 0.835 - 0.5$

giving **C = 0** so the unique solution is

$y = x^3 - 0.2x^5 - 0.5$

giving the lower graph of **Fig. 17.5**

Differential equations of this type of any order can be solved by this method of direct integration. Every time the order of a differential equation increases, so the integration has to be carried out one more time, giving more constants of integration. For a fourth order equation, $d^4y/dx^4 = f(x)$, the integration has to be carried out four times, and each time a constant of integration will be needed. So the final function **y = f(x)**, the solution, will need four extra pieces of information for a unique solution. The differential equation of the beam, see section **17.4**, is of this type.

With these two mathematical processes, **differentiation** and **integration**, and the **solution** of the consequent differential equations by **direct integration**, the mathematical world of structures can be entered.

17.3 The axially loaded element

In this section the mathematical description of an axially loaded element is derived. This will be in the form of a second order differential equation. First the structural element has to be considered as an **interval** on the x-axis.

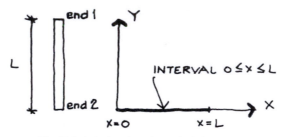

Fig.17.6 Actual and mathematical elements

Now all the required information about the axially loaded element is given in the form of functions of **x**. So the applied load of **p** kN/m becomes **p(x)**, the axial force in the element **N** kN becomes **N(x)** and the axial displacement **u** mm becomes **u(x)**. The functions may have values outside the interval $0 \le x \le L$, but these are of no interest. As far as signs are concerned, values of the functions are considered positive in the direction from **end1**, that is **x = 0**, to **end2**, that is **x = L**. For axial forces this means tensile forces **N** are positive with corresponding positive axial displacements **u**.

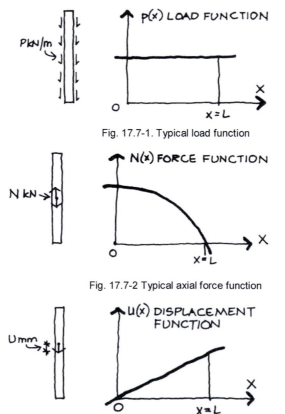

Fig. 17.7-1. Typical load function

Fig. 17.7-2 Typical axial force function

Fig. 17.7-3 Typical displacement function

These functions are obtained by solving the governing differential equation of the axially loaded element. This is derived by applying concepts of equilibrium and stress and strain that have already been used to a thin 'slice' of the element. It is assumed that the force applied to the element, **N**, increases across it by **δN**, but that the load along the element, **p**, is sensibly constant over the thickness of the 'thin' slice **δx**.

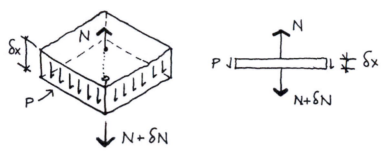

Fig. 17.8 Forces on a slice

For equilibrium of the slice in the axial direction, that is in the direction of the **x** axis:

$$N = p\delta x + (N + \delta N)$$

so cancelling the **N**s, rearranging and dividing by **δx** and assuming **δx** and **δN → 0** the equilibrium equation can be written as the following **differential** equation:

$$p(x) = -\frac{dN}{dx}$$

In a similar way the **axial displacement** of the slice can be related to the **strain**, that is the displacement divided by the original length, see page **385**:

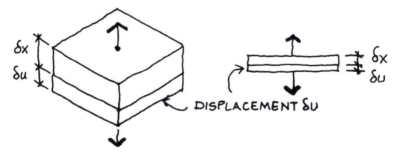

Fig. 17.9 Displacement of a slice

From the definition of strain, and letting **δx** and **δu → 0** the following **differential** equation can be written:

$$\varepsilon = \frac{du}{dx}$$

Using the assumption that the axial stress **f$_{ax}$** is constant over the cross-section of area **A**, it can be related to the axial force **N**, see page **66**, as:

$$f_{ax} = \frac{N}{A}$$

Using **Hooke's Law** to relate stress to strain by the modulus of elasticity **E**, see page **385**, then:

$$E = \frac{f_{ax}}{\varepsilon} = \frac{N}{A\varepsilon}$$

To express the relationship between strain ε and internal force **N**, this is rearranged as:

$$N = EA\varepsilon$$

Now three equations have been derived that express the following relationships:

- **external load** to **internal force** or p(x) = –dN/dx

- **internal force** to **strain** or N = EAε

- **strain** to **displacement** or ε = du/dx

These are the same as the relationships listed on page **399**, but now two of the relationships are expressed by differential equations. It is now possible to combine these relationships into one equation as follows:

$$p(x) = -\frac{dN}{dx} = -\frac{d}{dx}(EA\varepsilon) = -\frac{d}{dx}\left(EA\frac{du}{dx}\right) = -EA\frac{d}{dx}\left(\frac{du}{dx}\right) = -EA\frac{d^2u}{dx^2}$$

It is assumed that **E** and **A** are constant throughout the length of the element, so they are not functions of **x**. The complete behaviour of an axially loaded (one-dimensional) element can now be described by the **second order governing differential equation**:

$$\frac{d^2u}{dx^2} = -\frac{p(x)}{EA}$$

This differential equation relates the applied load function **p(x)**, to the axial displacement function **u(x)** of the element. The solution will be in the form of a displacement function **u(x)** that satisfies this equation, this can be obtained by integrating twice with respect to **x**. Proceeding as **Example 17.8**, the solution u = f(x) is:

$$u(x) = \int\left(\int\frac{d\,u}{dx^2}dx\right)dx = \int\left(\int\frac{-p(x)}{EA}\,dx\right)dx = -\int\left(\frac{p(x)x}{EA} + C\right)dx = -\frac{p(x)x^2}{2EA} + Cx + D$$

This is the **general solution** for the displacement function **u(x)** in terms of the load function **p(x)**, and the constants of integration **C** and **D**. It should be noted that if the load function varies along the length, see load function of **Exercise 17.1**, then theses terms have to be integrated as part of the solution process. For a particular element, the constants of integration can be evaluated from given information.

Example 17.9   An element of length **L** is restrained against axial displacement top and bottom and is loaded axially with a constant load **p** kN/m. Find the displacement and force functions **u(x)** and **N(x)**, from the governing differential equation. Draw graphs of these functions.

As the load is constant it does not vary with **x** so the displacement function **u** is:

$$u(x) = -\frac{px^2}{2EA} + Cx + D$$

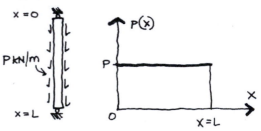

What information is available to allow the evaluation of the constants of integration, **C** and **D**? The support conditions are known, giving the following information: at **x = 0**, the axial displacement **u** is **0** and likewise at the other end, that is at **x = L**. First use the information that **u = 0** at **x = 0**. So:

$$u(0) = 0 = -\frac{p \times 0^2}{2EA} + C \times 0 + D \qquad \text{giving} \qquad D = 0$$

using **u = 0** at **x = L**

$$u(L) = 0 = -\frac{pL^2}{2EA} + CL \qquad \text{giving} \qquad C = \frac{pL}{2EA}$$

Substituting the values for **C** and **D** into the displacement function the unique solution for this element is obtained, with some algebraic rearrangement, as:

$$u(x) = \frac{p}{2EA}\left(Lx - x^2\right) \qquad \text{thus at } \mathbf{x = L/2}$$

$$u\left(\frac{L}{2}\right) = \frac{p}{2EA}\left(\frac{L^2}{2} - \frac{L^2}{4}\right) = \frac{1}{4}\left(\frac{pL^2}{2EA}\right)$$

substituting other values of **x** into the displacement function gives the information required to draw the graph of the function **u(x)**, for **0 ≤ x ≤ L**, which has the parabolic shape shown.

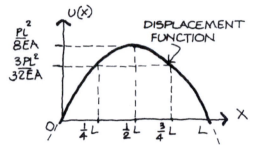

To obtain the force function **N(x)**, the equations for **internal force/strain**, **strain/displacement** and the expression for the displacement function are used as follows:

$$N(x) = EA\varepsilon = EA\frac{du}{dx} = EA\frac{d}{dx}\left(\frac{p}{2EA}\left(Lx - x^2\right)\right) = \left(\frac{p}{2}\right)\frac{d}{dx}\left(Lx - x^2\right) = \frac{pL}{2} - px$$

thus substituting the value **x = L/2** into the force function $N(x) = \frac{pL}{2} - px$ gives
N(L/2) = 0

substituting other values of **x** into the force function gives the information required to draw the graph of the function **N(x)**, for **0 ≤ x ≤ L**, which has the linear shape shown.

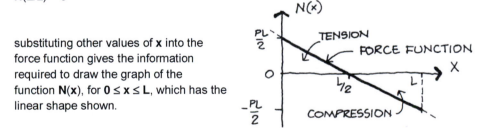

The functions **u(x)** and **N(x)** have values for all values of **x**, but for values outside the interval **0 ≤ x ≤ L** they do not relate to the structural element and so are of no interest. The results of this analysis in the interval **0 ≤ x ≤ L** show that the maximum axial displacement will be at the mid-point, that is **x = L/2.** The top half of the element will be in tension and the bottom half in compression which makes physical sense.

The constants of integration were evaluated using information that depended on the way the element was restrained at its ends. In the example, the condition that the axial displacement was zero, **u = 0**, at each end, **x = 0** and **x = L**, was used.

Because these values were at the ends of the element, in effect the boundary of the element with the 'rest of the world', these are often called the **boundary conditions**. As it is usually at the boundary something definite is known, the use of boundary conditions is common for the solution of these differential equations.

Exercise 17.1 An element of length **L** is supported top only, at **x = 0**, and is loaded axially with a linearly varying load (**p** × **x/L**)kN/m. Show that the displacement and force functions **u(x)** and **N(x)** are as follows:

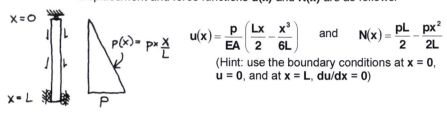

$$u(x) = \frac{p}{EA}\left(\frac{Lx}{2} - \frac{x^3}{6L}\right) \quad \text{and} \quad N(x) = \frac{pL}{2} - \frac{px^2}{2L}$$

(Hint: use the boundary conditions at x = 0, u = 0, and at x = L, du/dx = 0)

Draw graphs of these functions and obtain the values shown below.

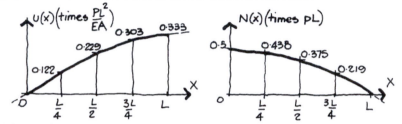

Note: The reader may find it easier to first do the exercise using a constant value for **p** rather than the varying one shown.

17.4 The laterally loaded beam

The process for developing the mathematical description of a laterally loaded beam is the same as that used for the axially loaded element in the previous section. Once again the beam is considered to be an interval **0 ≤ x ≤ L** on the x-axis.

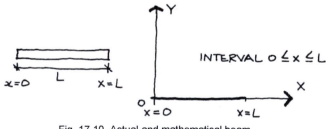

Fig. 17.10 Actual and mathematical beam

As with the axially loaded element, the load on the beam is a function of **x**.

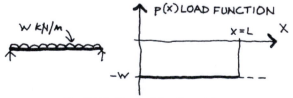

Fig. 17.11 The load function p(x)

Unlike the axially loaded element there are two force functions, the shear force function **S(x)** and the bending moment function **M(x)**.

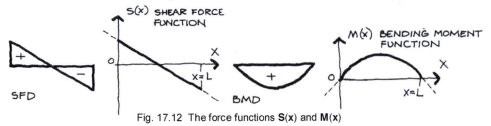

Fig. 17.12 The force functions **S(x)** and **M(x)**

And again there are two displacement functions, the slope function **θ(x)** and the lateral displacement function **u(x)**.

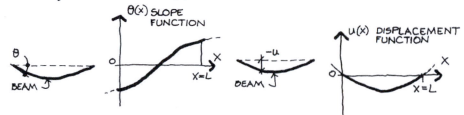

Fig. 17.13 The geometric functions **θ(x)** and **u(x)**

As with the axially loaded element, the equilibrium of a thin slice is examined to establish relationships between the applied load **w**, the shear force **S** and the bending moment **M**. Again the forces are assumed to be increasing along the beam, that is in the **x** direction, whilst the load is sensibly constant along the slice.

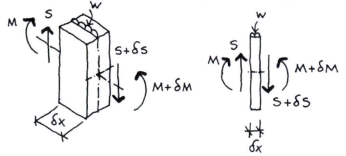

Fig. 17.14 Forces on a slice

As with the axially loaded element, the beam slice has to be in equilibrium in the direction of the shear forces **S** so:

$$S = w\delta x + (S + \delta S)$$

So cancelling the **S**s, rearranging and dividing by δ**x** and assuming δ**x** and δ**S** → **0** the equilibrium equation can be written as the following **differential** equation:

$$w = -\frac{dS}{dx}$$

But the beam slice also has to be in moment equilibrium. So that the load **w** does not enter the equation, moment equilibrium is considered about the centre of the slice, so the shear forces **S** and (**S** + δ**S**) act at distances δ**x**/2 from the faces of the slice. The moment equilibrium is given by:

$$M + \left(S \times \frac{\delta x}{2}\right) + \left((S + \delta S) \times \frac{\delta x}{2}\right) = M + \delta M$$

Now cancelling the **M**s, ignoring the product of the 'small' quantities δ**S**×δ**x**/2, rearranging and dividing by δ**x** and assuming δ**x** and δ**M** → **0**, the moment equilibrium equation can be written as the following **differential** equation

$$\mathbf{S} = \frac{\mathbf{dM}}{\mathbf{dx}}$$

Now there are two differential equations, one relating the shear force to the applied load and the other relating the bending moment to the shear force. These can be combined to give a differential equation that relates the bending moment to the applied load as follows:

$$\frac{\mathbf{dS}}{\mathbf{dx}} = \frac{\mathbf{d}}{\mathbf{dx}}\left(\frac{\mathbf{dM}}{\mathbf{dx}}\right) = \frac{\mathbf{d^2M}}{\mathbf{dx^2}} = -\mathbf{w(x)}$$

Here the equilibrium between bending moment **M** and the load function **w(x)** is given by a second order differential equation. The relationship between the displacement of the beam **u(x)** and the slope θ**(x)** is given directly by the fact that the slope is the **gradient** of the graph of the displacement function, see section **17.1**.

$$\theta(\mathbf{x}) = \frac{\mathbf{du}}{\mathbf{dx}}$$

The relationship between the bending moment and the deflected shape of the beam is given in terms of **E** the modulus of elasticity, **I** the moment of inertia, and **K** the curvature of the deflected beam.

$$\mathbf{M(x) = E \times I \times K(x)}$$

This relationship was derived from the geometry shown in **Fig. 14.41** and work done on page **387**. But there is no relationship between the displacement function **u(x)** and the curvature function **K(x)**. In section **14.9** a beam with constant curvature was used, but in most beams the curvature will vary along the beam and so will be a function of **x**.

In section **17.1** the idea of a function was explained, this is a formal mathematical relationship expressed by **y = f(x)**. 'Pictures' of functions were then drawn using the idea of a graphical representation, see **Example 17.1**. From this the mathematical operation of differentiation was defined by considering the gradient of the graph of the function, that is, the graph became a **geometric object**. In this way the line of the beam that deflects under lateral loading is both a curved geometric object, and the graph of the displacement function **u = f(x)**. Not only does this curved geometric object have a slope (gradient) at each point, it also has a radius of curvature **R**, and hence the curvature **K = 1/R**.

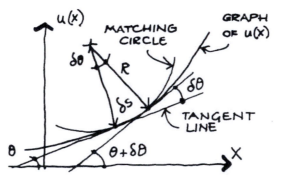

Fig. 17.15 Graph of function **u(x)** and matching circle

A relationship is required between $u(x)$ and $K(x)$, this is derived from geometric considerations. A small part of the graph of the function $u = f(x)$ is matched to a circle of radius R. This is shown in **Fig. 17.15**. It is assumed that the part of the graph δs is so small that it matches exactly the arc of the matching circle of radius R. So this gives the relationship:

$$\delta s = R\delta\theta$$

and the curvature is given as:
$$K = \frac{1}{R} = \frac{\delta\theta}{\delta s}$$

as δs and $\delta\theta \rightarrow 0$ the curvature is given by the differential equation:

$$K = \frac{d\theta}{ds}$$

That is, the curvature is the gradient, the rate of change, of the angle that the tangent line makes with the x-axis with respect to the length of the graph. What is required however, is the curvature in terms of the function $u = f(x)$ with respect to x. The derivation of this requires more differential calculus and quite a lot of algebraic manipulation. This adds nothing to the understanding of structures and the derivation is widely available in elementary books on the calculus.[2] Therefore the relationship is simply stated as the following rather complicated differential equation:

$$K(x) = \frac{\dfrac{d^2y}{dx^2}}{\left(1+\left(\dfrac{dy}{dx}\right)^2\right)^{3/2}}$$

Example 17.10 Obtain the expression for the curvature function $K(x)$ for the parabolic function $y = x^2$. Calculate the curvature at $x = 1$. Draw the graph and show the matching circle for $x = 1$.

Using the general rule for differentiation given on page **469**

$$\frac{dy}{dx} = 2x \qquad \text{and} \qquad \frac{d^2y}{dx^2} = 2$$

substituting these values in the general expression for the curvature $K(x)$ gives:

$$K(x) = \frac{\dfrac{d^2y}{dx^2}}{\left(1+\left(\dfrac{dy}{dx}\right)^2\right)^{3/2}} = \frac{2}{\left(1+(2x)^2\right)^{3/2}} = \frac{2}{\left(1+4x^2\right)^{3/2}}$$

Substituting $x = 1$ into the curvature function $K(x)$ gives:

$$K(1) = \frac{2}{\left(1+4\times1^2\right)^{3/2}} = \frac{2}{5^{3/2}} = \frac{2}{11.18} = 0.179$$

which gives the radius of the matching circle as:

$$R(1) = \frac{1}{K(1)} = \frac{1}{0.179} = 5.59$$

The position of the centre of the matching circle can obtained from the fact that the radius is at 90° to the tangent line to the graph of $y = f(x)$

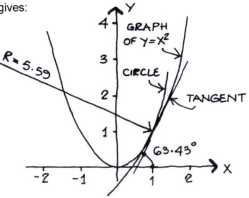

The equation for the curvature of a beam was first given by James Bernoulli (1654-1705), at the end of the 17th century. Clearly the expression is complicated due to the presence of the differential in the denominator. James' nephew Daniel Bernoulli (1700-1782) proposed an important simplification for real beams; this was that the differential $(dy/dx)^2$ in the denominator could be neglected without loss of accuracy. This gives the far simpler differential equation for curvature as:

$$K(x) = \frac{d^2y}{dx^2}$$

In the mathematical treatment of beams, the function $u = f(x)$ is the actual geometry of the beam deflected under load. For beams used in real building structures the gives the ratio of deflection to the span of about **300** (see **Table 14.8**). So if a parabola was to represent the geometry of the beam, it would be much 'flatter' than the parabola used in **Example 17.10**.

Example 17.11   A beam spans 6m. Derive a parabolic expression for the deflected shape assuming a central deflection of span/300. Calculate the radius of curvature for mid-span and 1.5m from the centre.

$6 \div 300 = 0.02$ so at $x = 3$, $y = 0.02$ $\therefore 0.02 = C \times 3^2$ so $C = 0.02 \div 9 = 1/450$

$\therefore$ the equation of the deflected beam is $u = \dfrac{x^2}{450}$

GRAPH OF
$v = \dfrac{x^2}{450}$ $u(x)$

giving $\dfrac{du}{dx} = \dfrac{2x}{450}$ and $\dfrac{d^2u}{dx^2} = \dfrac{1}{225}$

substitution in the expression for curvature at $x = 0$ gives

$$K(0) = \frac{\left(\dfrac{1}{225}\right)}{\left(1 + (0)^2\right)^{3/2}} = \frac{1}{225}$$ so   **R = 225m** and for **x = 1.5**

$$K(1.5) = \frac{\left(\dfrac{1}{225}\right)}{\left(1 + \left(\dfrac{2 \times 1.5}{450}\right)^2\right)^{3/2}} = \frac{1}{225.015}$$ so   **R = 225.015m**

This example shows that for the deflected shapes of real beam, Daniel Bernoulli's approximation is valid. This allows the mathematical description of the beam to be given in the form of ordinary differential equations.

Now three equations have been derived, similar to those for the axially loaded element, see page **476**, that express the following relationships:

- **external load** to **internal bending moment** or $d^2M/dx^2 = -p(x)$

- **bending moment** to **curvature** or $M(x) = E \times I \times K(x)$
- **curvature** to **displacement** or $K(x) = d^2u/dx^2$

Again these are the same relationships listed on page **371**, but two of the relationships are expressed by differential equations. It is possible to combine these relationships into one equation as follows:

$$-p(x) = \frac{d^2M}{dx^2} = \frac{d^2}{dx^2}\left(E \times I \times K(x)\right) = \frac{d^2}{dx^2}\left(E \times I \times \frac{d^2u}{dx^2}\right) = EI\frac{d^4u}{dx^4}$$

where it is assumed that **E** and **I** are constant throughout the length of the beam. Now the complete behaviour of a laterally loaded beam is described by the **fourth order governing differential equation**:

$$EI\frac{d^4u}{dx^4} = -p(x)$$

This differential equation relates the applied load function **p(x)**, to the lateral displacement function **u(x)** of the beam. The solution will be in the form of a displacement function **u(x)** that satisfies this equation and can be obtained by integrating it four times with respect to **x**. Basically this is the same as for the axially loaded element shown on page **476**, but as the integration is done **four times** there will be four constants of integration with the attached powers of **x**. As with the axially loaded element, see page **477**, if the load varies along the beam then the integration will have to take account of this, see **Exercise 17.1**. The steps of the integration are as follows:

1st integration

$$EI\int\left(\frac{d^4u}{dx^4}\right)dx = EI\frac{d^3u}{dx^3} = \int -p(x)dx = -p(x)x + A$$

2nd integration

$$EI\int\left(\frac{d^3u}{dx^3}\right)dx = EI\frac{d^2u}{dx^2} = \int(-p(x)x + A)dx = -p(x)\frac{x^2}{2} + Ax + B$$

3rd integration

$$EI\int\left(\frac{d^2u}{dx^2}\right)dx = EI\frac{du}{dx} = \int\left(-p(x)\frac{x^2}{2} + Ax + B\right)dx = -p(x)\frac{x^3}{6} + A\frac{x^2}{2} + Bx + C$$

4th integration

$$EI\int\left(\frac{du}{dx}\right)dx = EIu(x) = \int\left(-p(x)\frac{x^3}{6} + A\frac{x^2}{2} + Bx + C\right)dx = -p(x)\frac{x^4}{24} + A\frac{x^3}{6} + B\frac{x^2}{2} + Cx + D$$

There are now five equations, one algebraic equation and four differential equations. These equations have the following physical meanings:

1   The lateral displacement u(x): $u(x) = \frac{1}{EI}\left(-p(x)\frac{x^4}{24} + A\frac{x^3}{6} + B\frac{x^2}{2} + Cx + D\right)$

2   The slope θ(x): $\theta(x) = \frac{du}{dx} = \frac{1}{EI}\left(-p(x)\frac{x^3}{6} + A\frac{x^2}{2} + Bx + C\right)$

3   The bending moment M(x): $M(x) = EI\frac{d^2u}{dx^2} = -p(x)\frac{x^2}{2} + Ax + B$

4   The shear force S(x): $S(x) = EI\frac{d^3u}{dx^3} = -p(x)x + A$

5   The lateral load p(x): $p(x) = -EI\frac{d^4u}{dx^4}$

As with the axially loaded element, the constants of integration are evaluated from the boundary conditions. For a laterally loaded beam there are three idealised support conditions and each one defines two boundary conditions, these are:

1   **Pinned support**

the beam is fixed against vertical movement so the vertical displacement is zero:

$$u(x) = \frac{1}{EI}\left(-p(x)\frac{x^4}{24} + A\frac{x^3}{6} + B\frac{x^2}{2} + Cx + D\right) = 0$$

the beam is free to rotate so the bending moment is zero:

$$M(x) = EI\frac{d^2u}{dx^2} = -p(x)\frac{x^2}{2} + Ax + B = 0$$

2   **Fixed support**

the beam is fixed against vertical movement so the vertical displacement is zero:

$$u(x) = \frac{1}{EI}\left(-p(x)\frac{x^4}{24} + A\frac{x^3}{6} + B\frac{x^2}{2} + Cx + D\right) = 0$$

the beam is fixed against rotation so the slope is zero:

$$\theta(x) = EI\frac{du}{dx} = -p(x)\frac{x^3}{6} + A\frac{x^2}{2} + Bx + C = 0$$

3   **Free 'support'**

the beam is free to displace vertically so the shear force is zero:

$$S(x) = EI\frac{d^3u}{dx^3} = -p(x)x + A = 0$$

the beam is free to rotate so the bending moment is zero:

$$M(x) = EI\frac{d^2u}{dx^2} = -p(x)\frac{x^2}{2} + Ax + B = 0$$

So finally, after all this mathematical derivation applying the differential calculus to the concepts of beam behaviour, it is possible to obtain all the information about a laterally loaded beam. This information gives the distribution of the shear forces and bending moments, as well as information about the slope of the deflected beam and the lateral displacement.

In practical terms the maximum lateral displacement of a beam is required to check that it is within acceptable limits, see **Table 14.8**, and occasionally the end rotations of a beam are required.

With this new description of the behaviour of a beam, the '**basic building block**' of structural engineering, the laterally loaded, simply supported beam is now analysed.

Example 17.12   Use the mathematical description of the beam to derive expressions for the shear force, $S(x)$, the bending moment, $M(x)$, the slope, $\theta(x)$ and the lateral displacement $u(x)$ for a simply supported beam of span L, loaded laterally with a constant load of w kN/m.

The general expressions given on page **483** are used. For them to apply to the beam shown, the constants of integration, **A**, **B**, **C** and **D** have to be evaluated using the boundary conditions at **x = 0** and **x = L** for a pinned support.

These boundary conditions are shown diagrammatically.

$$u(0) = 0 \qquad\qquad\qquad v(L) = 0$$
$$M(0) = 0 \qquad\qquad\qquad M(L) = 0$$

First use the boundary conditions **M(0) = 0** at **x = 0** and **L** to evaluate **A** and **B**.

at $x = 0$ $M(0) = -w\dfrac{0^2}{2} + A \times 0 + B = 0$ $\quad \therefore \; B = 0$

at $x = L$ $M(L) = -w\dfrac{L^2}{2} + AL = 0$ $\qquad \therefore \; A = wL/2$

Now use the boundary conditions **u(0) = 0** at **x = 0** and **L** to evaluate **C** and **D**.

at $x = 0$ $EIu(0) = -w\dfrac{x^4}{24} + A\dfrac{x^3}{6} + B\dfrac{x^2}{2} + Cx + D = -w\dfrac{0^4}{24} + \dfrac{wL}{2}\times 0 + C\times 0 + D = 0$

$\therefore \; D = 0$

at $x = L$ $EIu(L) = -w\dfrac{L^4}{24} + A\dfrac{L^3}{6} + B\dfrac{L^2}{2} + CL + D = -w\dfrac{L^4}{24} + \dfrac{wL}{2}\dfrac{L^3}{6} + CL = 0$

$\therefore \; C = -wL^3/24$

Now all the constants of integration have been evaluated using the boundary conditions, and are summarised as follows:

A = wL/2   **B = 0**   **C = -wL³/24**   **D = 0**

To obtain the expressions for the various functions for this specific beam, the values of the constants, noting that **B** and **D = 0**, are substituted into the expressions as follows:

For the shear force function S(x): $\qquad S(x) = EI\dfrac{d^3u}{dx^3} = -wx + A = -wx + \dfrac{wL}{2}$

For the bending moment function M(x): $M(x) = EI\dfrac{d^2u}{dx^2} = -w\dfrac{x^2}{2} + Ax = -w\dfrac{x^2}{2} + \dfrac{wL}{2}x$

The graphs of shear force and bending moment functions are:

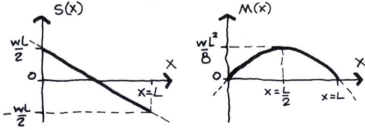

For the slope function θ(x):

$$\theta(x) = \dfrac{du}{dx} = -w\dfrac{x^3}{6EI} + A\dfrac{x^2}{2EI} + C\dfrac{1}{EI} = -w\dfrac{x^3}{6EI} + wL\dfrac{x^2}{4EI} - wL^3\dfrac{1}{24EI}$$

For the displacement function $u(x)$:

$$u(x) = \frac{1}{EI}\left(-w\frac{x^4}{24} + A\frac{x^3}{6} + Cx\right) = -w\frac{x^4}{24EI} + wL\frac{x^3}{12EI} - wL^3\frac{x}{24EI}$$

The graphs of slope and displacement functions are:

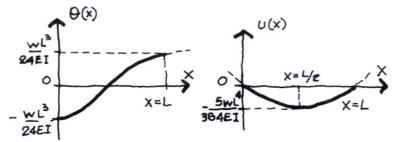

The results for the shear force and bending moment functions were derived, using equilibrium considerations alone, on page **365**, for this beam. A method was given in section **14.9** for calculating the deflection of a beam bent to a circular shape, but now it is possible to calculate the deflection for any beam and load function.

Example 17.13 Calculate the central deflection of a simply supported beam spanning 4m loaded laterally by 10kN/m. The beam is an **IPE 180** so I = 1317 E4 mm^4 and **E** = 210 E3 N/mm^2.

Working in millimetres and Newtons the central deflection is

$$u_{central} = \frac{-5wL^4}{384EI} = \frac{-5 \times 10 \times 4000^4}{384 \times 210E3 \times 1317E4} = \frac{-1.28E16}{1.062E15} = -12mm$$

which is the value given in **Fig. 12.43**.

In **Chapter 14** a not altogether successful attempt, see pages **371-372**, was made to find the shear forces and the bending moments in a beam that had a fixed support at one end and a pinned one at the other end. This type of beam is sometimes called a **propped cantilever**.

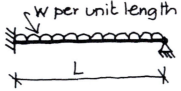

Fig. 17.16 A propped cantilever

The reason that it was 'not altogether successful' was that only the equilibrium conditions could be used, and these did not yield enough equations. To overcome this, a 'pin' was 'inserted' in the guessed position of the point of contraflexure. Now, with the geometrical information available, the mathematically 'correct' distribution of shear forces and bending moments can be found by using the right boundary conditions.

Example 17.14 Use the mathematical description of the beam to derive expressions for the shear force, **S(x)**, the bending moment, **M(x)**, the slope, θ**(x)** and the lateral displacement **u(x)** for the 'propped cantilever' shown in **Fig. 17.16**.

As before the constants of integration, **A**, **B**, **C** and **D** have to be evaluated using the boundary conditions at **x = 0** and **x = L**.

These boundary conditions are shown diagrammatically.

$u(o)=0$
$\theta(o)=0$
$u(L)=0$
$M(L)=0$

First use the boundary conditions **M(L) = 0** at **x = L** to obtain a relationship between **A** and **B**.

$$M(L) = -w\frac{L^2}{2} + AL + B = 0 \qquad \therefore \quad B = w\frac{L^2}{2} - AL$$

Now use the boundary conditions θ(0) = 0 at **x = 0** and **L** to evaluate **C**

$$\theta(0) = \frac{1}{EI}\left(-w\frac{0^3}{6} + A\frac{0^2}{2} + B\times 0 + C\right) = 0 \qquad \therefore \ C = 0$$

Now use the boundary conditions u(0) = 0 at **x = 0** to evaluate **D**

$$EIu(0) = -w\frac{0^4}{24} + A\frac{0^3}{6} + B\frac{0^2}{2} + D = 0 \qquad \therefore \ D = 0$$

Now use the boundary conditions u(L) = 0 at **x = L** to evaluate **A**

$$EIu(L) = -w\frac{L^4}{24} + A\frac{L^3}{6} + \left(w\frac{L^2}{2} - AL\right)\frac{L^2}{2} = 0 \ \text{giving} \quad AL^3\left(\frac{1}{2} - \frac{1}{6}\right) = wL^4\left(\frac{1}{4} - \frac{1}{24}\right)$$

which gives $\quad A = \frac{5}{8}wL \quad$ and hence $\quad B = \frac{wL^2}{2} - \left(\frac{5wL}{8}\right)L = -\frac{wL^2}{8}$

Now all the constants of integration have been evaluated using the boundary conditions, and are summarised as follows:

$$A = \frac{5}{8}wL \qquad B = -\frac{wL^2}{8} \qquad C = 0 \qquad D = 0$$

To obtain the expressions for the various functions for this specific beam the values of the constants are substituted into the expressions as follows:

For the shear force function **S(x)**: $\quad S(x) = EI\frac{d^3u}{dx^3} = -wx + A = -wx + \frac{5wL}{8}$

For the bending moment function **M(x)**:

$$M(x) = EI\frac{d^2u}{dx^2} = -w\frac{x^2}{2} + Ax + B = -w\frac{x^2}{2} + \frac{5wL}{8}x - \frac{wL^2}{8}$$

The graphs of shear force and bending moment functions are:

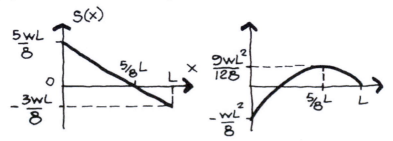

For the slope function $\theta(x)$, noting C and $D = 0$:

$$\theta(x) = \frac{du}{dx} = -w\frac{x^3}{6EI} + A\frac{x^2}{2EI} + B\frac{x}{EI} = -w\frac{x^3}{6EI} + \left(\frac{5}{8}wL\right)\frac{x^2}{2EI} + \left(-\frac{wL^2}{8}\right)\frac{x}{EI}$$

For the displacement function $u(x)$, noting C and $D = 0$:

$$u(x) = \frac{1}{EI}\left(-w\frac{x^4}{24} + A\frac{x^3}{6} + B\frac{x^2}{2}\right) = -w\frac{x^4}{24EI} + \left(\frac{5}{8}wL\right)\frac{x^3}{6EI} + \left(-\frac{wL^2}{8}\right)\frac{x^2}{2EI}$$

The graphs of slope and displacement functions are:

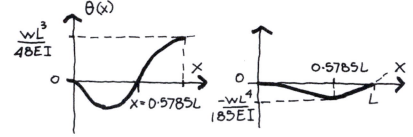

Exercise 17.2 Evaluate the displacement **u** at **0.5785 L** and plot the functions for slope $\theta(x)$ and displacement **u(x)** to scale.

With this new analysis it is now possible to calculate the mathematically 'correct' moments at the support and at mid-span shown in **Fig.14.15**. This is left as an **exercise**.

In **Chapter 14**, beams are loaded with point loads, as they often are in real structures. How can these be dealt with using the mathematical approach? The short answer is not very easily. Implicit in the **Fig. 17.1** cycle ride was a smooth and continuous undulating road. There were no gaps in the road – it was continuous, and no steps or similar obstacles – it was smooth. For a point load on a beam to become a mathematical function it will only have a value at a point, the point of load application, and will not exist elsewhere.

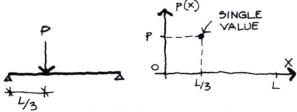

Fig. 17.17 Point load as a function

Without the comforts of continuity and smoothness, the limit process, $\delta x \rightarrow 0$, explained on pages **469**, does not work. There are basically two ways to resolve this firstly, use more complex functions to give the point load function the required properties of continuity and smoothness.[3] Secondly, can be considered to be several beams joining the parts of the original beam between the non-continuous loads. Then considerations of continuity of the beam at the load positions can be used to formulate simultaneous equations. Both these approaches are outside the scope of this brief introduction.

17.5 The general beam element

The treatment of a single beam, with various different boundary conditions, given in the previous section is useful from a practical point of view, but limited. Because in skeletal frames the beams are joined to other beams, what is wanted is an analysis that allows for this. The first step is to derive what are known as the **slope deflection equations**. These relate the bending moments and shear forces in a beam to end rotations and displacements. From a historical point of view the mathematical analysis of beams given in the previous system had been given by Navier in his 1826 book, and the extension to the slope deflection equations by Emile Clapeyron (1799-1864) in 1857. Until the wide availability of programmable computers in the late 1970s, engineers and mathematicians struggled to find methods of general analysis, many of which were based on these equations.

However, before the derivation of these equations it is important to be clear about signs, that is + and − , so far these have been used in a rather casual manner. Signs are important in the derivation of the slope deflection equations so first the signs used for the beam equation are clarified. The idea of positive and negative gradient, slope, must be clear, this is really like going uphill, positive, and downhill, negative, on the **Fig. 17.1** cycle ride from the start point.

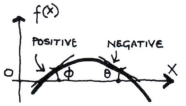

Fig. 17.18 Positive and negative slopes

To see how this applies to the analysis of the simply supported beam given in **Example 17.12**, the results are examined with respect to signs. As has been seen the functions given by the analysis are sequential derived functions, so the derived function of the load function **w(x)** is the shear function **S(x)**. This means the slope of the shear function is constant and negative with a value of **−w**.

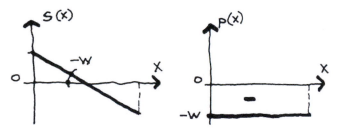

Fig. 17.19 The load function as the derived function of **S(x)**

Similarly the shear force function **S(x)** is the derived function of the bending moment function **M(x)**. So the values of the shear function give the gradient of the bending moment function.

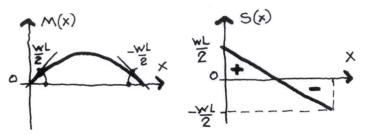

Fig.17.20 The shear function as the derived function of **M(x)**

This can be continued with the curvature function **K**, (= **M/EI**), which is the derived function of the slope function θ(**x**).

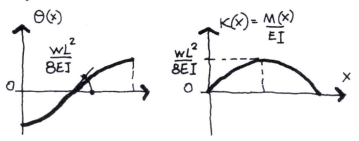

Fig. 17.21 The curvature function as the derived function of θ(**x**)

And finally the slope function θ(**x**) gives the gradient of the displacement function **u(x)** and is the actual slope of the real beam.

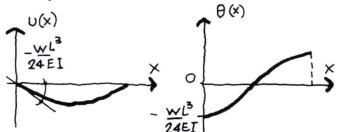

Fig. 17.22 The slope function as the derived function of u(x)

The sign convention shown also agrees with that shown in **Figs. 2.30** and **31**. An exception is drawing the positive bending moment above the x-axis. This still means tension on the bottom of the beam, but has to be drawn like this to agree with the vertical positive axis.

The **general beam element** does not have a lateral load applied, but has displacements and rotations imposed at the ends; these are called **prescribed boundary conditions**. To aid clarity, the rotations and displacements are treated separately and then the results added. First the end rotations:

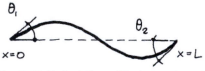

Fig. 17.23 End rotations of the beam element

To obtain a beam of this shape bending moments have to be applied to the ends which cause bending throughout the beam element.

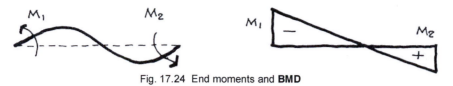

Fig. 17.24 End moments and **BMD**

It should be noted the **BMD** has been drawn not the bending moment function. Associated with this bending moment distribution are end reactions and a constant shear force.

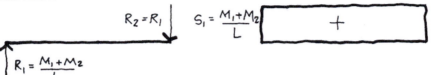

Fig. 17.25 Reactions and **SFD**

The reactions are obtained by considering moment and vertical equilibrium as follows.

Consider moment equilibrium about the right-hand end: $R_1 \times L = M_1 + M_2$ $\therefore$ $R_1 = \dfrac{M_1 + M_2}{L}$

and from vertical equilibrium: $R_1 = -R_2 = -\left(\dfrac{M_1 + M_2}{L}\right)$

The differential equation of the beam is now used to obtain relationships between the end rotations θ_1 and θ_2 and the end moments M_1 and M_2. There is no lateral load and the bending moment function can be written directly from the **BMD** as:

$$M(x) = -M_1 + (R_1 \times x) = -M_1 + \left(\frac{M_1 + M_2}{L}\right)x$$

Giving directly the second order differential equation:

$$EI\frac{d^2u}{dx^2} = -M_1 + \left(\frac{M_1 + M_2}{L}\right)x$$

Now integrating the equation with respect to **x** gives:

$$\int EI\left(\frac{d^2u}{dx^2}\right) = EI\frac{du}{dx} = -M_1 x + \left(\frac{M_1 + M_2}{L}\right)\frac{x^2}{2} + A$$

From the prescribed boundary condition **du/dx** = θ_1 at **x** = **0** the constant of integration **A** can be evaluated as follows:

$$EI\frac{du}{dx} = EI\theta_1 = -M_1 \times 0 + \left(\frac{M_1 + M_2}{L}\right)\frac{0^2}{2} + A \qquad \text{giving} \quad A = EI\theta_1$$

so the differential equation for the slope is: $EI\dfrac{du}{dx} = -M_1 x + \left(\dfrac{M_1 + M_2}{L}\right)\dfrac{x^2}{2} + EI\theta_1$

As before the differential equation for the lateral displacement function **u(x)** is obtained by integrating the slope function and this gives:

$$\int EI\left(\frac{du}{dx}\right)dx = EIu(x) + B = -M_1\frac{x^2}{2} + \left(\frac{M_1 + M_2}{L}\right)\frac{x^3}{6} + EI\theta_1 x + B$$

The mathematical basis 491

as at $x = 0$, $u = 0$ then $B = 0$, so the differential equation for the displacement is:

$$EIu(x) = -M_1 \frac{x^2}{2} + \left(\frac{M_1 + M_2}{L} \right) \frac{x^3}{6} + EI\theta_1 x$$

What is required are equations that relate the end moments M_1 and M_2 to the end rotations θ_1 and θ_2. This is done by rewriting the equations for slope and displacement at $x = L$. Using the slope equation and noting that at $x = L$, $du/dx = \theta_2$:

$$EI\theta_2 = -M_1 L + \left(\frac{M_1 + M_2}{L} \right) \frac{L^2}{2} + EI\theta_1$$

which can be rearranged as

$$M_1 = M_2 + \frac{2EI}{L} (\theta_1 - \theta_2)$$

and using the displacement equation and noting that at $x = L$, $u = 0$:

$$0 = -M_1 \frac{L^2}{2} + \left(\frac{M_1 + M_2}{L} \right) \frac{L^3}{6} + EI\theta_1 L$$

which dividing by L^2 and multiplying by 6 and rearranging gives:

$$M_2 = 2M_1 - \frac{6EI\theta_1}{L}$$

now this value for M_2 can be substituted into the equation for M_1, giving an expression for M_1 in terms of E, I, L, θ_1 and θ_2:

$$M_1 = \left(2M_1 - \frac{6EI\theta_1}{L} \right) + \frac{2EI}{L} (\theta_1 - \theta_2)$$

which can be rearranged to give the first slope deflection equation for rotations:

$$M_1 = \frac{4EI\theta_1}{L} + \frac{2EI\theta_2}{L}$$

substituting this value into the expression for M_2 and rearranging, the second slope deflection equation for rotations is obtained as:

$$M_2 = \frac{4EI\theta_2}{L} + \frac{2EI\theta_1}{L}$$

This gives the first part of the derivation of the **slope deflection equations**. It should be noted that E and I have been assumed to be constant throughout the length of the beam, which means that the structural material and the cross-section do not vary. Also these equations assume that the end rotations, θ_1 and θ_2, are in the directions shown in **Fig. 17.23**. The reader should carry out all the rearranging of the various equations in detail.

Before moving to the derivation for the equations for an end lateral displacement an example is given.

Example 17.15 Assuming that the prescribed end rotations of a beam element are in the sense shown in **Fig. 17.23** and are both **equal** to θ, derive expressions for the slope function $\theta(x)$ and the lateral displacement function $u(x)$. Draw the graphs of these functions.

Substitute $\theta_1 = \theta_2 = \theta$ into the slope deflection equations to obtain values for M_1 and M_2 in terms of the rotation θ.

$$M_1 = M_2 = \frac{4EI\theta}{L} + \frac{2EI\theta}{L} = \frac{6EI\theta}{L}$$

Substituting these values in the differential equation of the slope function, see page **491**, gives:

$$EI\frac{du}{dx} = -M_1x + \left(\frac{M_1 + M_2}{L}\right)\frac{x^2}{2} + EI\theta_1 = -\frac{6EI\theta}{L}x + \left(\frac{12EI\theta}{L^2}\right)\frac{x^2}{2} + EI\theta$$

dividing by **EI** and rearranging, the following expression for the slope function is obtained:

$$\frac{du}{dx} = \theta\left(1 - \frac{6}{L}x + \frac{6x^2}{L^2}\right)$$

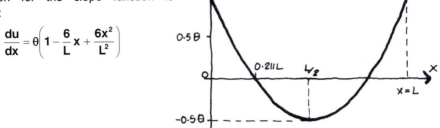

and substituting the values for **M₁** and **M₂** in the differential equation of the displacement function, see page **492**, gives:

$$EIu(x) = -M_1\frac{x^2}{2} + \left(\frac{M_1 + M_2}{L}\right)\frac{x^3}{6} + EI\theta_1 x = -\frac{6EI\theta}{l}\frac{x^2}{2} + \left(\frac{12EI\theta}{l^2}\right)\frac{x^3}{6} + EI\theta x$$

dividing by **EI** and simplifying and rearranging, the following expression for the displacement function is obtained:

$$u(x) = \theta\left(x - \frac{3x^2}{L} + \frac{2x^3}{L^2}\right)$$

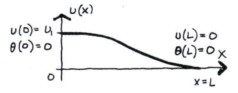

Note: The vertical scales used in the graphs are NOT the same as the horizontal ones.

Now the other part of the slope deflection equation can be derived, that is, the effect of a prescribed displacement, in a similar way.

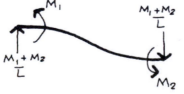

Fig. 17.26 End displacement of the beam element

The bending moments and the end reactions take exactly the same form as those for the end rotations.

Fig. 17.27 End moments and reactions

The second order differential equation relating the curvature to the bending moment function is exactly as before, see page **491**.

$$EI\frac{d^2u}{dx^2} = -M_1 + \left(\frac{M_1 + M_2}{L}\right)x$$

And again the equation for the slope is of the same form as that given on page **491**.

$$EI\frac{du}{dx} = -M_1x + \left(\frac{M_1 + M_2}{L}\right)\frac{x^2}{2} + A \quad \text{as at } x = 0, \ du/dx = 0 \quad \text{then} \quad A = 0$$

The equation for the lateral displacement also has the same form, see page **491**, except **A = 0**, so:

$$EIu(x) = -M_1\frac{x^2}{2} + \left(\frac{M_1 + M_2}{L}\right)\frac{x^3}{6} + B \quad \text{at } x = 0, \ u = u_1 \ \text{so} \ B = EIu_1$$

As before, what is required are expressions that relate the end moments **M₁** and **M₂** to the prescribed displacement **u₁**, this is done by using the other boundary conditions. At **x = L, du/dx = 0**, gives:

$$0 = -M_1L + \left(\frac{M_1 + M_2}{L}\right)\frac{L^2}{2} = -M_1L + \frac{M_1L}{2} + \frac{M_2L}{2} \quad \text{giving} \quad M_1 = M_2 = M$$

and at **x = L, u = 0** giving

$$0 = -M_1\frac{L^2}{2} + \left(\frac{M_1 + M_2}{L}\right)\frac{L^3}{6} + EIu_1 = -M\frac{L^2}{2} + \left(\frac{2M}{L}\right)\frac{L^3}{6} + EIu_1 = \left(-3M + 2M + \frac{6EIu_1}{L^2}\right)\frac{L^2}{6}$$

which gives, after some cancelling and rearranging the other part of the slope deflection equation as:

$$M_1 = \frac{6EIu_1}{L^2} = M_2$$

Before assembling the **complete slope deflection equations**, the slope and displacement functions for a prescribed end displacement are derived in the following example:

Example 17.16 Assuming that at **x = 0** the lateral displacement is **u₁**, derive expressions for the slope function **θ(x)** and the lateral displacement function **u(x)**. Draw the graphs of these functions.

Substitute the values for **M₁** and **M₂** given by the slope deflection equation into the equation of the slope function to obtain the slope in terms of the displacement **u₁**.

$$EI\frac{du}{dx} = -M_1x + \left(\frac{M_1 + M_2}{L}\right)\frac{x^2}{2} = -\left(\frac{6EIu_1}{L^2}\right)x + \left(\frac{6EIu_1 + 6EIu_1}{L^3}\right)\frac{x^2}{2}$$

Dividing by **EI** and rearranging this gives:

$$\frac{du}{dx} = \left(\frac{6u_1}{L^2}\right)\left(\frac{x^2}{L} - x\right)$$

Now substitute the values for **M₁** and **M₂** given by the slope deflection equation into the equation of the displacement function to obtain the displacement in terms of **u₁**.

$$EIu(x) = -M_1\frac{x^2}{2} + \left(\frac{M_1 + M_2}{L}\right)\frac{x^3}{6} + EIu_1 = -\left(\frac{6EIu_1}{L^2}\right)\frac{x^2}{2} + \left(\frac{6EIu_1 + 6EIu_1}{L^3}\right)\frac{x^3}{6} + EIu_1$$

dividing by **EI** and rearranging, the following expression for the displacement function is obtained:

$$u(x) = \left(\frac{6u_1}{L^2}\right)\left(-\frac{x^2}{2} + \frac{x^3}{3L}\right) + u_1$$

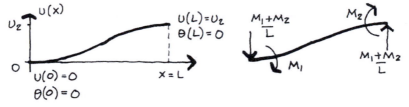

If there is a prescribed displacement at $x = L$, that is $u(L) = u_2$ then the boundary conditions and forces are as shown in **Fig.17.28**.

Fig. 17.28 Boundary conditions and forces for $u(L) = u_2$

As all the forces are opposite to the case for the prescribed boundary condition $u(0) = u_1$ then the slope deflection equation for this prescribed displacement can be written immediately, by inserting a minus sign, as follows:

$$M_2 = -\frac{6EIu_2}{L^2} = M_1$$

Now a diagram can be drawn for a beam element with all the prescribed boundary conditions occurring simultaneously.

Fig. 17.29 Prescribed boundary conditions for the general beam element

Now the partial **slope deflection equations**, given on pages **492** and **494**, can be added together to give the complete equations as follows:

$$M_1 = \frac{4EI\theta_1}{L} + \frac{2EI\theta_2}{L} + \frac{6EIu_1}{L^2} - \frac{6EIu_2}{L^2}$$

and

$$M_2 = \frac{4EI\theta_2}{L} + \frac{2EI\theta_1}{L} + \frac{6EIu_1}{L^2} - \frac{6EIu_2}{L^2}$$

and the end forces S_1 and S_2 are given directly from $\pm(M_1 + M_2)/L$ as

$$S_1 = \frac{6EI(\theta_1 + \theta_2)}{L^2} + \frac{12EI(u_1 - u_2)}{L^3} = -S_2$$

On page **385** stiffness was defined by the relation:

Force = Stiffness × Deflection

The **slope deflection equations** give exactly this relationship. M_1, M_2, S_1 and S_2 are **forces** applied to the end of the beam element, the rotations θ_1 and θ_2 and the displacements u_1 and u_2 are **deflections**. Terms like **4EI/L** and **6EI/L²** are the **stiffness** and are sometimes called **stiffness coefficients**.

The slope deflection equations were first written by Clapeyron in 1857, in 1914 George A Maney (1888-1947) presented the **slope deflection method**. In 1930 Hardy Cross (1885-1959), presented the method of **moment distribution** – see pages **511-2** – which again uses the slope deflection equations. His method became the most widely used for structural analysis before programmable computers became available. Yet again these equations were used to develop computer programs for structural analysis. The basis for this is explained in the next section.

17.6 Joint stiffness

The slope deflection equations are not much good on their own, as real beams rarely have prescribed boundary conditions. The value of the equations is that, having described the structural behaviour of a **general beam element**, in terms of end rotations and displacements, frames can be analysed as assemblies of elements.

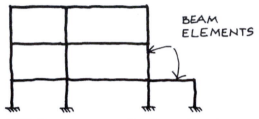

Fig.17.30 Frame as an assembly of beam elements

The method of analysis is to derive equations for the joints that relate the forces on the joint to the displacement of the joint. This is done through the stiffness coefficients of the elements that meet at a joint to give the **joint stiffness**. Consider a simple structure of two vertical axially loaded elements loaded where they are joined.

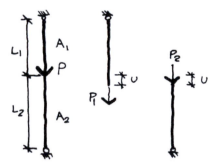

Fig. 17.31 Axial elements

The vertical displacement at the joint is **u**, so the upper member has to stretch by **u** and the lower member has to compress by **u**. So the force in each member is calculated for the displacement **u** from the stiffness, see page **385** for axial stiffness.

For the upper member $u = \dfrac{P_1 L_1}{EA_1}$ and for the lower member $u = \dfrac{P_2 L_2}{EA_2}$

So $P_1 = \left(\dfrac{EA_1}{L_1}\right)u$ and $P_2 = \left(\dfrac{EA_2}{L_2}\right)u$

Giving $P = P_1 + P_2 = \left(\dfrac{EA_1}{L_1} + \dfrac{EA_2}{L_2}\right)u$ and the stiffness of the joint is $k_{joint} = \left(\dfrac{EA_1}{L_1} + \dfrac{EA_2}{L_2}\right)$

Now consider another simple structure consisting of two vertical and two horizontal beam elements meeting at a joint. The remote ends of all the elements are totally fixed.

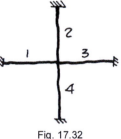

Fig. 17.32

The joint can now move in three ways, it can displace vertically u_V, horizontally u_H and it can rotate by θ.

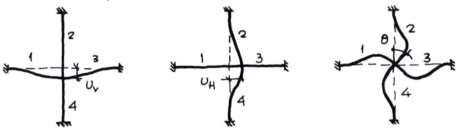

Fig.17.33 Joint movements

And associated with these movements are three joint forces, a vertical force P_V, a horizontal force P_H and a moment M.

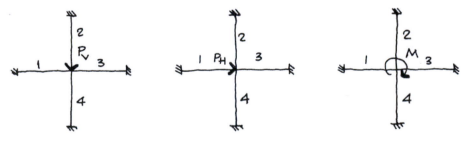

Fig.17.34 Joint forces

The joint stiffness k_{JOINT}, that links the movements to the forces, now consists of three parts; a vertical stiffness k_V, a horizontal stiffness k_H and a rotational stiffness k_θ. The equilibrium of the joint, vertical, horizontal and rotational, is given by three equations:

$$P_V = k_V \times u_V \qquad\qquad P_H = k_H \times u_H \qquad\qquad M = k_\theta \times \theta$$

Assume, for simplicity, that all the elements have the same length, cross-section and are made of the same material. The joint equilibrium equations now have the following form:

$$P_V = (k_{1\text{- LATERAL}} + k_{2\text{- AXIAL}} + k_{3\text{- LATERAL}} + k_{4\text{- AXIAL}}) \times u_V$$

$$P_H = (k_{1\text{-AXIAL}} + k_{2\text{-LATERAL}} + k_{3\text{-AXIAL}} + k_{4\text{-LATERAL}}) \times u_H$$

$$M = (k_{1\text{-ROTATIONAL}} + k_{2\text{-ROTATIONAL}} + k_{3\text{-ROTATIONAL}} + k_{4\text{-ROTATIONAL}}) \times \theta$$

Then using the axial stiffness and the slope deflection equations the **three equilibrium equations** can be written using the **stiffness coefficients** as follows

$$P_v = \left(\left(\frac{12EI}{L^3}\right)_1 + \left(\frac{EA}{L}\right)_2 + \left(\frac{12EI}{L^3}\right)_3 + \left(\frac{EA}{L}\right)_4 \right) \times u_v$$

$$P_H = \left(\left(\frac{EA}{L}\right)_1 + \left(\frac{12EI}{L^3}\right)_2 + \left(\frac{EA}{L}\right)_3 + \left(\frac{12EI}{L^3}\right)_4 \right) \times u_H$$

$$M = \left(\left(\frac{4EI}{L}\right)_1 + \left(\frac{4EI}{L}\right)_2 + \left(\frac{4EI}{L}\right)_3 + \left(\frac{4EI}{L}\right)_4 \right) \times \theta$$

Example 17.17 Calculate the stiffness coefficients for the structures shown. Calculate the vertical displacement u_V and the rotation θ for the loads shown. Calculate the bending moments in member **3** and draw the **BMD**. For all the members $A = 0.09m^2$, $I = 6.75E\text{-}4m^4$ and $E = 1E6 \text{ kN/m}^2$

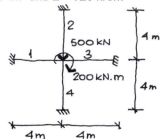

Directly from the above equations

$$k_v = \left(\left(\frac{12EI}{L^3}\right)_1 + \left(\frac{EA}{L}\right)_2 + \left(\frac{12EI}{L^3}\right)_3 + \left(\frac{EA}{L}\right)_4 \right)$$

and as $EI = 675kN/m^2$ and $EA = 90000kN$

$$k_v = \left(\left(\frac{12 \times 675}{4^3}\right)_1 + \left(\frac{90000}{4}\right)_2 + (= 1)_3 + (= 2)_4 \right)$$

giving:

$k_V = ((127)_1 + (22500)_2 + (127)_3 + (22500)_4) = 45\ 254kN/m$ and $k_H = k_V = 45\ 254kN/m$

$$k_\theta = \left(\left(\frac{4EI}{L}\right)_1 + \left(\frac{4EI}{L}\right)_2 + \left(\frac{4EI}{L}\right)_3 + \left(\frac{4EI}{L}\right)_4 \right) = \left(\left(\frac{4 \times 675}{4}\right)_1 + (= 1)_2 + (= 1)_3 + (= 1)_4 \right)$$

giving $k_\theta = ((675)_1 + (675)_2 + (675)_3 + (675)_4) = 2700kN.m/radian$

substituting these values into the equilibrium equations gives

$P_V = 500 = 45\ 254 \times u_V$ so $u_V = 500 \div 45\ 254 = 0.011 \text{ m} \equiv 11mm$

$P_H = 0 = 45\ 254 \times u_H$ so $u_H = 0$ and

$M = 200 = 2700 \times \theta$ so $\theta = 200 \div 2700 = 0.074$ radians $\equiv 4.24°$

To obtain the bending moments in beam element **3**, the values for u_V and θ are entered into the slope deflection equations.

$$M_1 = \frac{4EI\theta}{L} + \frac{6EIu_v}{L^2} = \frac{4 \times 675 \times 0.074}{4} + \frac{6 \times 675 \times 0.011}{4^2} = 49.95 + 2.78 = 52.73kN.m$$

$$M_2 = \frac{2EI\theta}{L} + \frac{6EIu_v}{L^2} = \frac{2 \times 675 \times 0.074}{4} + \frac{6 \times 675 \times 0.011}{4^2} = 24.98 + 2.78 = 27.767kN.m$$

BMD for beam element **3**

Exercise 17.3   Calculate the axial forces, bending moments and shear forces in all the beam elements for the structures shown in **Example 17.17**. Draw the **AFD**, **BMD** and **SFD** for all the beam elements.

The structure shown in   **Fig. 17.32** has only one joint that is able to have displacements, so the three equilibrium equations given on page **498** could be solved directly, as was shown in **Example 17.17**. But real structures tend to have far more than one joint that can have displacements. To see what happens when more than one joint can have displacements, consider a three-span beam with the extreme ends completely fixed in position.

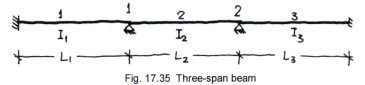

Fig. 17.35 Three-span beam

Here each beam element has a different span and moment of inertia. The only possible joint deformations are rotations at joints **1** and **2**, θ_1 and θ_2. At these joints there will be moments M_1 and M_2.

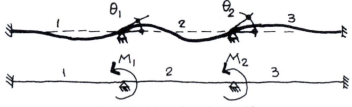

Fig. 17.36 Joint deformations and forces

Using the slope deflection equations, the equilibrium equations can be written for each joint. At joint **1** the total moment, M_1 is the sum of the end moments of beam elements **1** and **2**, so:

$M_1 = m_2$ (of beam element 1) + m_1 (of beam element 2)

giving:
$$M_1 = \left(\frac{4EI_1\theta_1}{L_1}\right)_{beam1} + \left(\frac{4EI_2\theta_1}{L_2} + \frac{2EI_2\theta_2}{L_2}\right)_{beam2}$$

And similarly, M_2 is the sum of the end moments of beam elements **2** and **3**, so:

$M_2 = m_2$ (of beam element 2) + m_1 (of beam element 3)

giving:
$$M_2 = \left(\frac{4EI_2\theta_2}{L_2} + \frac{2EI_2\theta_1}{L_2}\right)_{beam2} + \left(\frac{4EI_3\theta_2}{L_3}\right)_{beam3}$$

Now the two equations are linked as θ_1 and θ_2 appear in both. So the actual value of θ_1 and θ_2 must satisfy each equation at the same time, that is simultaneously, so there are **two simultaneous equations**. Each time there is a joint in a structure, if it is not restrained in any way, it will be able to have the three movements shown in **Fig.17.33**. Also at the joint will be the three forces shown in **Fig.17.34**. The equilibrium equations at each joint will give a set of **simultaneous equations** in terms of the joint forces, the joint movements and the stiffness coefficients. Usually the joint forces are known from the loading on the structure, and the stiffness coefficients are known from the geometry and material of the structure, so the **unknowns are the joint deformations**. What has been achieved is to turn the 'problem' of structural analysis into the problem of **solving a set of simultaneous equations.**

17.7 The stiffness method

The stiffness method, as it is generally called, is now the predominant method of structural analysis and uses the equilibrium relationship already given as:

Force = Stiffness × **Deflection**

Using the concept of stiffness coefficients, the structural analysis of any structure is turned into a set of simultaneous equations, which are based on the known loads and structural properties. The solution of these equations gives the values of the deformations at the joints. From these values it is then possible to calculate the forces, axial and shear forces and bending moments, in the individual elements. Thus all the required information about the structural behaviour is obtained.

The fact that structural behaviour could be described by a set of simultaneous equations has been known at least since the end of the 19th century. The difficulty facing the analyst was their solution. With hand methods of calculation it is extremely difficult to solve more than very few equations, six would be quite a lot. Throughout the 20th century engineers and mathematicians battled, with limited success, to find methods to do this. However, with the arrival of the programmable computer, programs could be written to solve large numbers of simultaneous equations. With current computers thousands of simultaneous equations can be solved which permits the numerical analysis of huge structures. This penultimate section shows how these equations are obtained and organised.

To set up and solve the simultaneous equations, a high level of organisation is needed, this has two parts. The first is to rationalise the symbols used for a beam element. Firstly, a joint axes system is chosen.

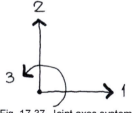

Fig. 17.37 Joint axes system

Thus the horizontal direction has suffix **1**, the vertical **2** and rotations **3**. Now all deformations at a joint are called **u**, with the joint number and a suffix, so **u2₂** is the vertical displacement at joint number **2**.

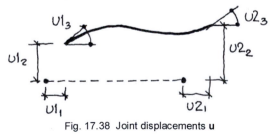

Fig. 17.38 Joint displacements **u**

And all forces at a joint are called **p**, with the joint number and a suffix, so **p1₃** is the moment at joint number **1**.

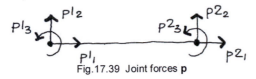

Fig.17.39 Joint forces p

Using these new 'organised names' for M_1 and M_2 in the equilibrium equations given on page **499** for the three span-beam are rewritten as:

$$p1_3 = \frac{4EI_1 u1_3}{L_1} + \frac{4EI_2 u1_3}{L_2} + \frac{2EI_2 u2_3}{L_2} \qquad \text{and} \qquad p2_3 = \frac{4EI_2 u2_3}{L_2} + \frac{2EI_2 u1_3}{L_2} + \frac{4EI_3 u2_3}{L_3}$$

The second part of the organisation of the equations is to write them in **matrix form**. Matrices and matrix algebra are described in many books,[4] but little of that is needed here. Essentially a matrix is a mathematical object that has lists of numbers, or other mathematical 'things', inside square brackets. The two equations above can be written in matrix form as follows:

$$\begin{bmatrix} p1_3 \\ p2_3 \end{bmatrix} = \begin{bmatrix} 4EI_1/L_1 + 4EI_2/L_2 & 2EI_2/L_2 \\ 2EI_2/L_2 & 4EI_2/L_2 + 4EI_3/L_3 \end{bmatrix} \begin{bmatrix} u1_3 \\ u2_3 \end{bmatrix}$$

On the left-hand side of the equals sign is a vertical list of the forces, the **force matrix p**. On the right-hand side there are two matrices. One has two rows each of two elements, the stiffness coefficients, and is the **stiffness matrix K**. The other has a vertical list of the displacements, the **displacement matrix u**. Now the two equations can be written as a **matrix equation**.

$$[p] = [K][u]$$

On the right-hand side of the matrix equation, two matrices, **K** and **u**, are multiplied together. The rule for matrix multiplication is that a row of the first matrix multiplies a column of the second matrix by multiplying the individual elements and adding them together. So for two matrices **A** and **B**, each with three rows and three columns, multiplication gives:

$$\begin{bmatrix} a_{11} & a_{12} & a_{13} \\ a_{21} & a_{22} & a_{23} \\ a_{31} & a_{32} & a_{33} \end{bmatrix} \times \begin{bmatrix} b_{11} & b_{12} & b_{13} \\ b_{21} & b_{22} & b_{23} \\ b_{31} & b_{32} & b_{33} \end{bmatrix} = \begin{bmatrix} (a \times b)_{11} & (a \times b)_{12} & (a \times b)_{13} \\ (a \times b)_{21} & (a_{21} \times b_{12} + a_{22} \times b_{22} + a_{23} \times b_{32})_{22} & (a \times b)_{23} \\ (a \times b)_{31} & (a \times b)_{32} & (a \times b)_{33} \end{bmatrix}$$

Here only the (a×b)₂₂ element is shown in detail. As the matrix **u** only has one column, the multiplication of **K** and **u** results in a new matrix of only one column.

$$\begin{bmatrix} 4EI_1/L_1 + 4EI_2/L_2 & 2EI_2/L_2 \\ 2EI_2/L_2 & 4EI_2/L_2 + 4EI_3/L_3 \end{bmatrix} \times \begin{bmatrix} u1_3 \\ u2_3 \end{bmatrix} = \begin{bmatrix} (4EI_1/L_1 + 4EI_2/L_2) \times u1_3 + (2EI_2/L_2) \times u2_3 \\ (2EI_2/L_2) \times u1_3 + (4EI_2/L_2 + 4EI_3/L_3) \times u2_3 \end{bmatrix}$$

The result of the matrix multiplication is a matrix of one column with two elements. These elements are the expressions of the right-hand side of the two equilibrium equations given above. To save the constant writing of elements like **4EI₁/L₁ + 4EI₂/L₂** the matrix equation can be rewritten as:

$$\begin{bmatrix} p1_3 \\ p2_3 \end{bmatrix} = \begin{bmatrix} k_{11} & k_{12} \\ k_{21} & k_{22} \end{bmatrix} \begin{bmatrix} u1_3 \\ u2_3 \end{bmatrix}$$

Using this matrix way of writing equations, it is now possible to write all the equations for the beam element using the new organised notation of **u**, **p** as:

$$
\begin{bmatrix} p1_1 \\ p1_2 \\ p1_3 \\ \cdots \\ p2_1 \\ p2_2 \\ p2_3 \end{bmatrix}
=
\begin{bmatrix}
EA/L & \circ & \circ & \vdots & -EA/L & \circ & \circ \\
\circ & 12EI/L^3 & 6EI/L^2 & \vdots & \circ & -12EI/L^3 & 6EI/L^2 \\
\circ & 6EI/L^2 & 4EI/L & \vdots & \circ & -6EI/L^2 & 2EI/L \\
\cdots & \cdots & \cdots & \vdots & \cdots & \cdots & \cdots \\
-EA/L & \circ & \circ & \vdots & EA/L & \circ & \circ \\
\circ & -12EI/L^3 & -6EI/L^2 & \vdots & \circ & 12EI/L^3 & -6EI/L^2 \\
\circ & 6EI/L^2 & 2EI/L & \vdots & \circ & -6EI/L^2 & 4EI/L
\end{bmatrix}
\begin{bmatrix} u1_1 \\ u1_2 \\ u1_3 \\ \cdots \\ u2_1 \\ u2_2 \\ u2_3 \end{bmatrix}
$$

The dotted lines show how the matrices can be divided into sub-matrices so this equation can now be written in an even more compact form as:

$$
\begin{bmatrix} P_1 \\ \cdots \\ P_2 \end{bmatrix}
=
\begin{bmatrix} K_{11} & \vdots & K_{12} \\ \cdots & \vdots & \cdots \\ K_{21} & \vdots & K_{22} \end{bmatrix}
\begin{bmatrix} U_1 \\ \cdots \\ U_2 \end{bmatrix}
$$

Where P_1 represents all the forces at **end 1**, U_1 all the displacements at **end 1** and K_{11} the sub-matrix of stiffness coefficients that give **forces at end 1** due to **displacements at end 1**, and similarly for **end 2**. As can be seen from **Fig. 17.38** the general beam element is not joined to the 'rest of the world'. This is like the beam equation before it had any boundary conditions, see section **17.4**. Now suppose that the beam element is completely supported at **end 1**, and unsupported at **end 2**, in other words a cantilever. Furthermore let there be a downwards load of **P** at **end 2**.

Fig. 17.40 Beam element as a cantilever

Now all the joint loads, except for $p2_2$, are zero as are all the displacements at **end 1**. And because there are no axial forces, the axial displacement $u2_1$ is also zero. This means there now only two unknowns, the displacements $u2_2$ and $u2_3$. This makes the equilibrium matrix equation look quite different:

$$
\begin{bmatrix} \circ \\ \circ \\ \circ \\ \cdots \\ \circ \\ -P \\ \circ \end{bmatrix}
=
\begin{bmatrix}
\circ & \circ & \circ & \vdots & \circ & \circ & \circ \\
\circ & \circ & \circ & \vdots & \circ & \circ & \circ \\
\circ & \circ & \circ & \vdots & \circ & \circ & \circ \\
\cdots & \cdots & \cdots & \vdots & \cdots & \cdots & \cdots \\
\circ & \circ & \circ & \vdots & \circ & \circ & \circ \\
\circ & \circ & \circ & \vdots & \circ & 12EI/L^3 & -6EI/L^2 \\
\circ & \circ & \circ & \vdots & \circ & -6EI/L^2 & 4EI/L
\end{bmatrix}
\begin{bmatrix} \circ \\ \circ \\ \circ \\ \cdots \\ \circ \\ u2_2 \\ u2_3 \end{bmatrix}
$$

Where a stiffness coefficient, k_{11} for example, is multiplied by zero it is ineffective so it has been set to zero in the stiffness matrix. For this particular beam element the stiffness matrix has been **reduced** from 6 columns and 6 rows to 2 columns and 2 rows. In 'matrix language' the **6×6** matrix is reduced to a **2×2** matrix. So for the cantilever with a point load the equations are:

$$\begin{bmatrix} -P \\ 0 \end{bmatrix} = \begin{bmatrix} 12EI/L^3 & -6EI/L^2 \\ -6EI/L^2 & 4EI/L \end{bmatrix} \begin{bmatrix} u2_2 \\ u2_3 \end{bmatrix}$$

Example 17.18 For the cantilever shown, with $I = 3m^4$ and $E = 1E6$ kN/m^2, write the equilibrium equations in matrix form.

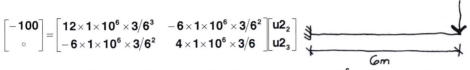

$$\begin{bmatrix} -100 \\ 0 \end{bmatrix} = \begin{bmatrix} 12 \times 1 \times 10^6 \times 3/6^3 & -6 \times 1 \times 10^6 \times 3/6^2 \\ -6 \times 1 \times 10^6 \times 3/6^2 & 4 \times 1 \times 10^6 \times 3/6 \end{bmatrix} \begin{bmatrix} u2_2 \\ u2_3 \end{bmatrix}$$

evaluating the stiffness coefficients, and putting a factor of 1×10^6 outside the stiffness matrix, the equilibrium equations in matrix form are:

$$\begin{bmatrix} -100 \\ 0 \end{bmatrix} = 1 \times 10^6 \begin{bmatrix} 0.167 & -0.5 \\ -0.5 & 2 \end{bmatrix} \begin{bmatrix} u2_2 \\ u2_3 \end{bmatrix}$$

Putting the equilibrium equations into matrix form, as in the example, does not provide the 'answer' because what are required are the values of the displacements **u2₂** and **u2₃**, in other words the solution to the two simultaneous equations. This is done by using the **inverse matrix** of **K**, which is the matrix **K⁻¹**. To explain this a small amount of matrix algebra is required.

For an ordinary algebraic equation like **y = 4x** for any value of **y** the unknown **x** is found by dividing each side of the equation by **4**. That is, multiplying each side by the inverse of **4** which is ¼. So:

$$\frac{1}{4} \times y = (4)^{-1} \times y = \left(\frac{1}{4}\right) \times (4) \times x = (4)^{-1} \times (4) \times x = 1 \times x = x$$

This lengthy derivation for the solution of the simple equation has been done to show the similarities between ordinary algebra and matrix algebra. Matrix algebra is very, but not completely, similar to ordinary algebra, so, using a similar derivation the solution to the matrix equation **[p] = [K][u]** can be written as:

$$[K]^{-1}[p] = [K]^{-1}[K][u] = [I][u] = [u]$$

Here the matrix **[I]** is the **unit matrix** and functions in matrix multiplication as the number **1** does in ordinary multiplication, that is it does not change the matrix it multiplies. The unit matrix has **1** for the diagonal elements and **0** elsewhere so:

$$\begin{bmatrix} 1 & 0 \\ 0 & 1 \end{bmatrix} \times \begin{bmatrix} a_{11} & a_{12} \\ a_{21} & a_{22} \end{bmatrix} = \begin{bmatrix} 1 \times a_{11} + 0 \times a_{21} & 1 \times a_{12} + 0 \times a_{22} \\ 0 \times a_{11} + 1 \times a_{21} & 0 \times a_{12} + 0 \times a_{22} \end{bmatrix} = \begin{bmatrix} a_{11} & a_{12} \\ a_{21} & a_{22} \end{bmatrix}$$

Or, as matrix algebra: $[I][A] = [A]$ if $[K]^{-1}[K] = [I]$ then $[K]^{-1}$ is the inverse matrix of $[K]$

So all that is required for any **[K]** is its inverse **[K]⁻¹**, unfortunately this is not a simple matter. Methods for finding inverse matrices were devised a long time ago, but the actual computation by hand calculations, except for quite small matrices, is almost impossible. The computer has changed all this. Now computers automatically assemble the matrices and then find their inverse. So the problem of inverting matrices, providing a computer is available, is a thing of the past. To see how it all works, but without explaining how they were obtained,[5] inverse matrices are used here.

Example 17.19   For the cantilever in **Example 17.18** using the given inverse matrix K^{-1} calculate the unknown displacements and draw a diagram of the cantilever showing the deflected shape.

The inverse matrix is given as $[K]^{-1} = \dfrac{1}{10^6}\begin{bmatrix} 24 & 6 \\ 6 & 2 \end{bmatrix}$

As $[u] = [K]^{-1}[p]$ then $\begin{bmatrix} u2_2 \\ u2_3 \end{bmatrix} = \dfrac{1}{10^6}\begin{bmatrix} 24 & 6 \\ 6 & 2 \end{bmatrix}\begin{bmatrix} -100 \\ 0 \end{bmatrix} = \dfrac{1}{10^6}\begin{bmatrix} -2400 \\ -600 \end{bmatrix}$

Giving the vertical displacement

$u2_2 = -2\,400 \div 10^6$ m $\equiv -2.4$ mm

and the rotation

$u2_3 = -600 \div 10^6$ radians $\equiv -0.034°$

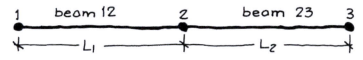

Exercise 17.4   Carry out the matrix multiplication for $K^{-1} \times K$ to get the unit matrix **I**.

Exercise 17.5   Enter the values for $u2_2$ and $u2_3$ obtained in **Example 17.19** into the slope deflection equations to obtain the bending moments and shear forces in the cantilever. Draw the **BMD** and the **SFD**.

To end this section a slightly more complicated structure, a two-span beam, is examined. The procedure follows that used for the single beam.

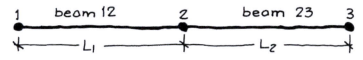

Fig. 17.41 General two-span 'beam'

Now the equilibrium matrix equation can be written in partition form, using sub-matrices as

$$\begin{bmatrix} P_1 \\ \cdots \\ P_2 \\ \cdots \\ P_3 \end{bmatrix} = \begin{bmatrix} K_{11} & \vdots & K_{12} & \vdots & K_{13} \\ \cdots & \cdots & \cdots & \cdots & \cdots \\ K_{21} & \vdots & K_{22} & \vdots & K_{23} \\ \cdots & \cdots & \cdots & \cdots & \cdots \\ K_{31} & \vdots & K_{32} & \vdots & K_{33} \end{bmatrix}\begin{bmatrix} U_1 \\ \cdots \\ U_2 \\ \cdots \\ U_3 \end{bmatrix}$$

The meaning of the sub-matrices is as before. The elements of the column matrices are sets of three forces and displacements at each joint. So for example P_1 is the sub-matrix of the forces $p1_1$, $p1_2$ and $p1_3$ at joint 1, and U_3 is the sub-matrix of the displacements $u3_1$, $u3_2$ and $u3_3$ at joint 3. The sub-matrices of the stiffness matrix are not quite so straightforward. The sub-matrices K_{11}, K_{12} and K_{21} are as before, see page **502**, but K_{22} now has to include the effect of both **beam 12 and beam 23**. This is because the force required to displace joint 2 is related to the stiffness of **all** the beam elements that are connected to the joint, see **Figs. 17.32** to **34**. By the same logic because 'end2' of **beam 23** is **not** joined by the beam to joint 1 the sub-matrix K_{13} will be zero, as will K_{31}. The equilibrium matrix equation is now written in detail:

$$\begin{bmatrix} p1_1 \\ p1_2 \\ p1_3 \\ \cdots \\ p2_1 \\ p2_2 \\ p2_3 \\ \cdots \\ p3_1 \\ p3_2 \\ p3_3 \end{bmatrix} = \begin{bmatrix} \frac{EA_1}{L_1} & o & o & \vdots & -\frac{EA_1}{L_1} & o & o & \vdots & o & o & o \\ o & \frac{12EI_1}{L_1^3} & \frac{6EI_1}{L_1^2} & \vdots & o & -\frac{12EI_1}{L_1^3} & \frac{6EI_1}{L_1^2} & \vdots & o & o & o \\ o & \frac{6EI_1}{L_1^2} & \frac{4EI_1}{L_1} & \vdots & o & -\frac{6EI_1}{L_1^2} & \frac{2EI_1}{L_1} & \vdots & o & o & o \\ \cdots & \cdots & \cdots & & \cdots & \cdots & \cdots & \vdots & \cdots & \cdots & \cdots \\ -\frac{EA_1}{L_1} & o & o & \vdots & \frac{EA_1}{L_1}+\frac{EA_2}{L_2} & o & o & \vdots & -\frac{EA_2}{L_2} & o & o \\ o & -\frac{12EI_1}{L_1^3} & -\frac{6EI_1}{L_1^2} & \vdots & o & \frac{12EI_1}{L_1^3}+\frac{12EI_2}{L_2^3} & -\frac{6EI_1}{L_1^2}+\frac{6EI_2}{L_2^2} & \vdots & o & -\frac{12EI_2}{L_2^3} & \frac{6EI_2}{L_2^2} \\ o & \frac{6EI_2}{L_1^2} & \frac{2EI_1}{L_1} & \vdots & o & -\frac{6EI_1}{L_1^2}+\frac{6EI_2}{L_2^2} & \frac{4EI_1}{L_1}+\frac{4EI_2}{L_2} & \vdots & o & -\frac{6EI_2}{L_2^2} & \frac{2EI_2}{L_2} \\ \cdots & \cdots & \cdots & & \cdots & \cdots & \cdots & \vdots & \cdots & \cdots & \cdots \\ o & o & o & \vdots & -\frac{EA_2}{L_2} & o & o & \vdots & \frac{EA_2}{L_2} & o & o \\ o & o & o & \vdots & o & -\frac{12EI_2}{L_2^3} & \frac{6EI_2}{L_2^2} & \vdots & o & \frac{12EI_2}{L_2^3} & \frac{6EI_2}{L_2^2} \\ o & o & o & \vdots & o & \frac{6EI_2}{L_2^2} & \frac{2EI_2}{L_2} & \vdots & o & \frac{6EI_2}{L_2^2} & \frac{4EI_2}{L_2} \end{bmatrix} \begin{bmatrix} u1_1 \\ u1_2 \\ u1_3 \\ \cdots \\ u2_1 \\ u2_2 \\ u2_3 \\ \cdots \\ u3_1 \\ u3_2 \\ u3_3 \end{bmatrix}$$

As with the single beam element these two beam elements are not joined to the rest of the world, so they need supports, boundary conditions. Suppose at joints **1** and **2** the elements are pinned and there is a downward load of **P** at joint **3**.

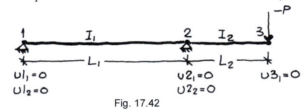

Fig. 17.42

Now five of the displacements are zero so the matrices are reduced in size by five to give:

$$\begin{bmatrix} p1_3 \\ p2_3 \\ p3_2 \\ p3_3 \end{bmatrix} = \begin{bmatrix} 0 \\ 0 \\ -P \\ 0 \end{bmatrix} = \begin{bmatrix} 4EI_1/L_1 & 2EI_1/L_1 & o & o \\ 2EI_1/L_1 & 4EI_1/L_1+4EI_2/L_2 & -6EI_2/L_2^2 & 2EI_2/L_2 \\ o & -6EI_2/L_2^2 & 12EI_2/L_2^3 & -6EI_2/L_2^2 \\ o & 2EI_2/L_2 & -6EI_2/L_2^2 & 4EI_2/L_2 \end{bmatrix}\begin{bmatrix} u1_3 \\ u2_3 \\ u3_2 \\ u3_3 \end{bmatrix}$$

Exercise 17.6   Carry out the matrix multiplication in the detail for the above equation to get the four slope deflection equations. (Hint: take great care with signs etc.)

Example 17.20   For the two-span beam shown, with $I = 3m^4$ and $E = 1E6$ kN/m², write the equilibrium equations in matrix form. Using the given inverse matrix K^{-1} calculate the unknown displacements and draw a diagram showing them.

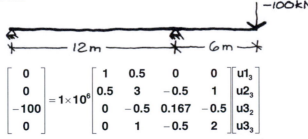

$$\begin{bmatrix} 0 \\ 0 \\ -100 \\ 0 \end{bmatrix} = 1\times10^6 \begin{bmatrix} 1 & 0.5 & 0 & 0 \\ 0.5 & 3 & -0.5 & 1 \\ 0 & -0.5 & 0.167 & -0.5 \\ 0 & 1 & -0.5 & 2 \end{bmatrix}\begin{bmatrix} u1_3 \\ u2_3 \\ u3_2 \\ u3_3 \end{bmatrix}$$

the inverse matrix $\mathbf{K}^{-1}$ is 'given' as:

$$[\mathbf{K}]^{-1} = \frac{1}{10^6} \begin{bmatrix} 1.33 & -0.67 & -4 & -0.67 \\ -0.67 & 1.33 & 8 & 1.33 \\ -4 & 8 & 72 & 14 \\ -0.67 & 1.33 & 14 & 3.33 \end{bmatrix}$$

so now the unknown displacements are evaluated as:

$$\begin{bmatrix} u1_3 \\ u2_3 \\ u3_2 \\ u3_3 \end{bmatrix} = \frac{1}{10^6} \begin{bmatrix} 1.33 & -0.67 & -4 & -0.67 \\ -0.67 & 1.33 & 8 & 1.33 \\ -4 & 8 & 72 & 14 \\ -0.67 & 1.33 & 14 & 3.33 \end{bmatrix} \begin{bmatrix} 0 \\ 0 \\ -100 \\ 0 \end{bmatrix} = \frac{1}{10^6} \begin{bmatrix} 400 \\ -800 \\ -7200 \\ -1400 \end{bmatrix}$$

Giving the vertical displacement at joint 3 as $u3_2 = -7200 \div 10^6$ m $\equiv -7.2$mm

and the rotations at the joints 1, 2 and 3 as $u1_3 = -400 \div 10^6$ radians $\equiv -0.024°$

$u2_3 = -800 \div 10^6$ radians $\equiv -0.046°$ and $u3_3 = -1400 \div 10^6$ radians $\equiv -0.08°$

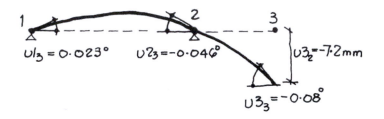

Exercise 17.7   Carry out the matrix multiplication for $\mathbf{K}^{-1} \times \mathbf{K}$ to get the unit matrix **I**.
(Note: A more accurate result will be obtained by using the values as fractions rather than decimals.)

Exercise 17.8   Enter the values for the displacements obtained in **Example 17.20** into the slope deflection equations to obtain the bending moments and shear forces in the beams. Draw the **BMD** and the **SFD**.

The procedure for the stiffness method, for any given structure, can now be summarised as follows:

- Calculate the stiffness matrices of the individual elements

- Assemble the structure stiffness matrix using the individual matrices

- Reduce the overall matrices by introducing the support conditions

- Obtain the inverse $\mathbf{K}^{-1}$ of the structure stiffness matrix

- Calculate the unknown joint displacements

- Use the calculated displacements to evaluate the forces in the beam elements

Nowadays this analysis is almost always carried out by a computer. The structure geometry and loading are entered as data and the computer, by setting up and solving the matrix equation, calculates and outputs the displacements and member forces.

17.8 Summary

The inclusion of this chapter in what is in many ways an elementary book may seem strange so why is it here? Reading and understanding this chapter will demand a considerable effort on the part of most readers, and it is not necessary for getting the all important conceptual understanding of structural behaviour. It is included however for several reasons, which are:

- **It allows the dedicated reader to move into the mathematical world of engineering**

- **It shows how the mathematical approach has become fundamental for the analysis of structures**

- **It shows how the mathematical approach uses the basic structural concepts**

- **It gives a deeper understanding of structural behaviour**

What is presented shows the essential points which are:

- **Derivation of governing differential equations**

- **Obtaining solutions to these equations where possible**

- **Developing programmable routines to deal with a variety of similar structures**

As complications are introduced such as two-dimensional elements, three-dimensional structures, the effect of buckling, dynamic loads, tapered elements, non-linear materials or large displacements, the mathematical description can become extremely complex. In **Chapter 18** – *The basis for computer calculations*, some of these more advanced topics are outlined. But when dealing with these complexities it is essential that the concepts are always clear.

References – Chapter 17

1   PJ Davis & R Hersh – **The mathematical experience** – Penguin Books 1983 – ISBN 0-14-2456-p 244
2   AJ Sherlock et al - **Calculus** – Arnold 1982 – ISBN 0-7131-3446-1 – p 482-483
3   JT Oden & EA Ripperger – **Mechanics of elastic structures** – Hemisphere Pub. Co. 1967 ISBN 007-047507-5 – p 171
4   FGJ Norton – **Advanced mathematics** – Pan Books 1982 – ISBN 0-330-29429-6, Ch. 19
5   ibid.

CHAPTER 18   *The basis for computer calculations*

Chapter 17 – *The Mathematical Basis* is an introduction to how forces in structures made of beams and columns can be found by applying the **differential calculus** – see sections **17.1** and **2**. The chapter is self-contained and mathematically complete, and the last section – **The Stiffness Method** – shows how the **slope deflection equations** – see page **495** – can be written in matrix form – see page **501**. **Examples 17.19** and **20** use this method to calculate the displacements of simple beam structures. To do this the **stiffness matrix K** was inverted to find $\mathbf{K}^{-1}$, which for matrices larger than **5 x 5** is a challenge using hand calculations. For this reason the **stiffness method** only became possible when computers could be programmed to carry out matrix inversion. However, before the advent of the programmable computer, these equations formed the basis of the most successful method of the analysis of framed structures; the **Moment Distribution Method**, which was used widely up to the late 1970s.

This chapter is **not** mathematically complete, and only serves as a guide to the more complex methods of structural analysis that the programmable computer has made feasible. To put it into context the chapter returns to the slope deflection equations, and how they can be used to find the forces in simple beam structures using hand calculations.

The chapter then moves on to outline the basis of structural analysis that computers now use; in particular the **Finite Element Method** – see section **18.5**.

18.1 Background

On page **495** the **slope deflection equations** for a simple beam were given as follows:

$$M_1 = \frac{4EI\theta_1}{L} + \frac{2EI\theta_2}{L} + \frac{6EIu_1}{L^2} - \frac{6EIu_2}{L^2}$$

and

$$M_2 = \frac{4EI\theta_2}{L} + \frac{2EI\theta_1}{L} + \frac{6EIu_1}{L^2} - \frac{6EIu_2}{L^2}$$

Fig. 18.1 End moments and the **BMD**

and the end forces S_1 and S_2 are given directly from $\pm(M_1 + M_2)/L$ as

$$S_1 = \frac{6EI(\theta_1 + \theta_2)}{L^2} + \frac{12EI(u_1 - u_2)}{L^3} = -S_2$$

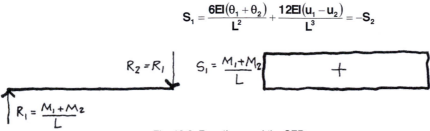

Fig. 18.2 Reactions and the **SFD**

These are special solutions to the **fourth order governing differential equation** for a beam, given on page **483** as:

$$EI\frac{d^4u}{dx^4} = -p(x)$$

The Sheerness Boat Store built in 1859 – see page **304** – is usually considered the first rigid frame structure, and afterwards, with reinforced framed structures – see page **306** – rigidly jointed frames, formed of beam and column elements, became a standard structural form – see **Fig. 18.3**.

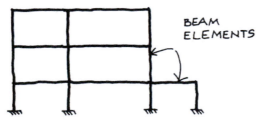

Fig. 18.3 – Rigidly framed 2-dimensoinal structure

Using the **slope deflection equations**, the idea of **joint stiffness** could be formulated – see section **17.6**. Now the challenge was to find the forces in these frames when they were loaded, and this is where the slope deflection equations helped. First proposed by George A Manley in 1914, he used the equations to find forces in rigidly-joined structures by setting up a number of simultaneous equations, which were solved to find the unknown joint rotations. A simple example illustrates the ideas.

The structure shown in **Fig. 18.4**, has three 10m spans, span **AB** with a point load of 10kN, the central span **BC** is loaded with a uniform load of 1kN/m and the span **CD** is centrally loaded with a point load of 10kN. The support at **A** is **pinned**, and the support at **D** is **fixed**. The beam is continuous over the supports **B** and **C**. The central span has a stiffness of **2EI**, whereas the side spans have one of **EI**.

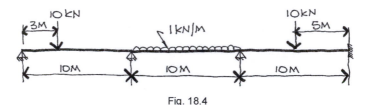

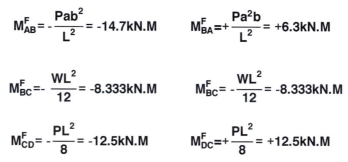

Fig. 18.4

Initially it is assumed all the joints are fixed against rotation, so the **fixed end moments, FEM**, can be calculated from standard expressions as follows:

$$M^F_{AB}= -\frac{Pab^2}{L^2} = -14.7kN.M \qquad M^F_{BA}=+\frac{Pa^2b}{L^2} = +6.3kN.M$$

$$M^F_{BC}=-\frac{WL^2}{12} = -8.333kN.M \qquad M^F_{BC}= -\frac{WL^2}{12} = -8.333kN.M$$

$$M^F_{CD}= -\frac{PL^2}{8} = -12.5kN.M \qquad M^F_{DC}=+\frac{PL^2}{8} = +12.5kN.M$$

Anti-clockwise **FEMs** are given a negative sign, and clockwise a positive sign. The **BMD** is shown in **Fig. 18.5**.

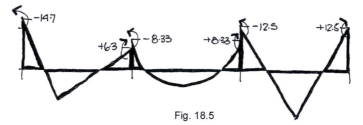

Fig. 18.5

Notice that with the rotations fixed at supports **A**, **B** and **C**, the **FEMs** are not in **rotational equilibrium**. As support **A** is **pinned**, M^F_{AB} should be zero.

As **L = 10**, and the only movements at the supports are rotations, the moment deflection equations give the **end moments** as:

$$M_{AB}=0.4EI\theta_A+0.2EI\theta_B \qquad M_{BA}=0.2EI\theta_A+0.4EI\theta_B$$

$$M_{BC}=0.8EI\theta_B+0.4EI\theta_C \qquad M_{CB}=0.4EI\theta_B+0.8EI\theta_C$$

$$M_{CD}=0.4EI\theta_C \qquad M_{DC}=0.2EI\theta_C$$

As support **D** does not rotate, there is only a lack of rotational equilibrium at joints **A**, **B** and **C**. So, by writing equilibrium equations for these joints **three simultaneous equations** are obtained in θ_A, θ_B and θ_C as follows:

$$\sum M_A=M_{AB} +M^F_{AB}=0.4EI\theta_A+0.2EI\theta_B-14.7=0$$

$$\sum M_B=M_{BA} +M^F_{BA}+M_{BC}+M^F_{BC}=0.2EI\theta_A+1.2EI\theta_B+ 0.4EI\theta_C+(+6.3-8.333)=0$$

$$\sum M_C = M_{CB} + M_{CB}^F + M_{CD} + M_{CD}^F = 0.4EI\theta_B + 1.2EI\theta_C + (+8.333 - 12.5) = 0$$

These three simultaneous equations can be solved to give:

$$\theta_A = \frac{40.219}{EI} \qquad \theta_B = \frac{-6.937}{EI} \qquad \theta_C = \frac{5.785}{EI}$$

Substituting these values into the **slope deflection equations** and adding in the **FEMs**, the **final bending moments** at the joints are:

$$M_{AB} = 0.4 \times 40.219 + 0.2 \times (-6.937) - 14.7 = 0 \text{ Kn.M}$$

$$M_{BA} = 0.2 \times 40.219 + 0.4 \times (-6.937) + 6.3 = +11.57 \text{ Kn.M}$$

$$M_{BC} = 0.8 \times (-6.937) + 0.4 \times 5.785 - 8.333 = -11.57 \text{ Kn.M}$$

$$M_{CB} = 0.4 \times (-6.937) + 0.8 \times 5.785 + 8.333 = +10.19 \text{ Kn.M}$$

$$M_{CD} = 0.4 \times 5.785 - 12.5 = -10.19 \text{ Kn.M}$$

$$M_{DC} = 0.2 \times 5.785 + 12.5 = +13.66 \text{ Kn.M}$$

The final **BMD** is shown in **Fig. 18.6**, where the **simply supported BMDs** have been added to each span.

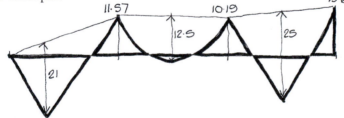

Fig. 18.6 – The final BMD in kN/M

Even though sets of simultaneous equations could be set up using the slope deflection equations for any size of structure the task of solving more than three simultaneous equations by hand calculation becomes rather impractical. This impracticality was solved in 1930 by Hardy Cross when he published an iterative method for solving these equations. It became known as the **Hardy Cross Method** or the **Moment Distribution Method, MDM**. It was used widely from the 1930s to the late 1960s, or even later, when it started to be superseded by computer methods.

The **MDM** starts as the slope deflection method does by calculating all the **FEMs**. Then the relative stiffnesses of each member joining a joint are calculated. This is done by using the expressions for the moment required to for unit rotation when the far end is 1) fixed and 2) pinned. The values are given in **Fig. 18.7**.

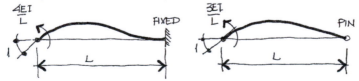

Fig. 18.7 – Bending moments for unit rotation

The other important fact is that for a beam element of constant cross-section, and one end fixed, if a moment **M** is applied at the end that can rotate, it will cause a moment of one half the magnitude at the fixed end, **M/2** – see **Fig. 18.8**.

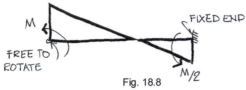

Fig. 18.8

Using the information given in **Figs. 18.7** and **8**, two important quantities can be identified; the **Distribution Factor, DF**, and the **Carry over Factor, CoF**. Using these, it is possible to solve the slope deflection equations semi-automatically using an iterative method. The **DF**s are calculated by attributing the stiffness of each beam elements meeting at a joint as a proportion of the total **1**, and the **CoF** for constant section beam elements is **½**.

Redo the previous example using the **MDM**. First calculate the **DF**s at joints **B** and **C**.

At joint **B** the proportions are $D_{BA} = \dfrac{\frac{3EI}{L}}{\frac{3EI}{L} + \frac{4 \times 2EI}{L}} = \dfrac{3}{3+8} = 0.273$ so $D_{BC} = 1 - D_{BA} = 0.727$

At joint **C** similar calculations give $D_{CB} = 0.667$ and $D_{CD} = 0.333$

Now the method can be used by writing it in a tabular form:

	Joint A			Joint B		Joint C		Joint D	
DFs	0	1		0.273	0.727	0.667	0.333	0	0
FEMs		-14.7		+6.3	-8.333	+8.333	-12.5	+12.5	
Balance Jt A		+14.7							
Carry over to Jt B				+7.35					
Balance Jt B				-1.45	-3.865				
Carry over to Jt C						-1.933			
Balance Jt C						+4.069	+2.031		
Carry over to Jts B & D				+2.035				+1.016	
Balance Jt B				-0.556	-1.479				
Carry over to Jt C						-0.740			
Balance Jt C						+0.494	+0.246		
Carry over to Jt D								+0.123	
Final Moments kN.M		0		+11.644	-11.642	+10.223	-10.223	13.639	

Table 18.1 – Moment Distribution calculation

As can be seen from **Table 18.1**, the final moments are virtually the same as those obtained by solving the simultaneous equations, and shown in **Fig. 18.6**. For practical purposes, it is sufficient to work to only two decimal places.

Whilst nowadays mainly of historical interest, the **Moment Distribution Method** was the mainstay for the structural analysis of framed structures before computers were widely used. With further refinements, the method could be used for a variety of framework geometries.

18.2 Matrix formulation for skeletal structures

Whilst structural designers were using the **Moment Distribution Method**, and other methods, engineering mathematics was, from the early 1930s, being written using matrices – see section **17.7** – mainly by researchers working on aircraft structures. Over the next decades, the use of matrices proliferated, giving rise to such descriptions as **matrix methods** or **matrix analysis**. It also gave rise to a great deal of confusion as two methods were used, usually called the **stiffness method** (also known as the **displacement method**), and the **flexibility method** (also known as the **force method**); each with their adherents. The **stiffness method** has already been described in some detail in section **17.7** but it is helpful to briefly explain the essential differences between the two methods.

A simply supported 3-span beam is used, loaded as shown in **Fig. 18.9**.

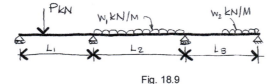

Fig. 18.9

For the **stiffness method**, all the **joints of the beam are rigidly connected to the supports**, in other words, the **real structure** is made stiffer, whereas for the **flexibility method**, pins are introduced into the beam to make it **statically determinate**. This new structure is sometimes known as the **reduced structure**, and devices, in this case pins, that are introduced to make the original structure statically determinate are called **releases** – see page **373**. The two altered beams are shown in **Fig. 18.10**.

Fig. 18.10 – Stiff beam R, statically determinate beam L (the reduced structure)

With these modified beams it is now possible to calculate all the bending moments. For the stiff beam, from known solutions for fixed-end beams, and for the statically determinate beam, from statics; these are shown in **Fig. 18.11**. The left-hand diagram shows what is called a **kinematically admissible solution**, and the right-hand one shows a **statically admissible solution** – see page **372**.

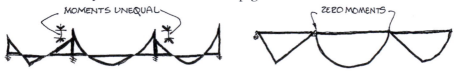

Fig. 18.11 – Kinematically L and statically R admissible solutions

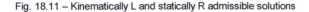

Neither the bending moment diagrams shown in **Fig. 18.11** are correct for the real beam shown in **Fig. 18.9**, because both violate certain conditions.

The **kinematically admissible solution**, shown in **Fig. 18.11L**, violates the equilibrium condition at the supports, because at the end supports, where the moment should be zero, there is the fixed end moment. At the inner supports, the moments at the ends of the beams meeting at the supports which should be equal, are unequal; they are **not in equilibrium**. However, the beam itself is still continuous, so it meets a **compatibility condition**. For the beam that is shown in **Fig. 18.4**, the initial fixed end moments that give a **kinematically admissible solution** – these are **not in equilibrium**. The stiffness method for skeletal structures can be expressed by the matrix equation:

$$Ku = p$$

Here **K** is the **stiffness matrix** of the structure; **u** is the **displacement matrix**, that is, a list of the unknown displacements of the structure at the places where it has been fixed. The **force matrix p**, is a list of the loads applied to the structure. The equation is a statement of equilibrium, where **Ku** are the forces in the structure that have to be in equilibrium with the applied forces **p**.

The **statically admissible solution**, shown in **Fig. 18.11 R**, violates the **compatibility condition**, because at the inner supports, the slopes at the ends of the beams meeting at the support will be different, in other words a **rotational gap** has opened up. However, the **beam bending moments** are in **equilibrium** with the loads.

The unknowns in flexibility method are **forces**, often called **bi-actions**, that are required to close the openings in the structure that have occurred where **releases** have been introduced to make the real structure statically determinate. In the case of the beam shown in **Fig. 18.10R**, moments, **M₁** and **M₂**, have to be applied at each **release** (pin), as shown in **Fig. 18.12**.

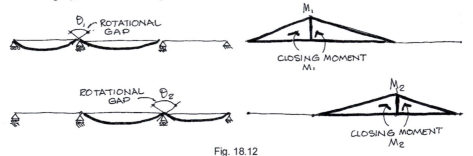

Fig. 18.12

The **bi-actions** are **self-equilibrating**, that is, they do not impose any loads on the structure. The forces caused by bending moment **M₁** are shown in **Fig. 18.13**. As can be seen, the sum on these forces is zero.

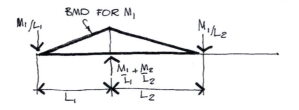

Fig. 18.13 – Self-equilibrating forces for M_1

Compatibility is restored, that is the 'gaps' shown in **Fig. 18.12** are closed, with the solution of the following matrix equation:

$$Fx = r$$

Where **F** is the **structure flexibility matrix**, **x** is the unknown **bi-action (force) matrix**, which is a list of the **bi-actions** applied at the releases, and **r** is the **release displacement matrix**, which is a list of the displacements at the **releases** caused by the **real loads** on the **reduced structure**. In the case of the example, the elements of **x** are the bending moments M_1 and M_2 and the elements of **r** are the rotations θ_1 and θ_2. Solution of the matrix equation gives numerical values for the bending moments M_1 and M_2.

The details of the flexibility method are beyond the scope of this book, and can be found in numerous technical publications. The two methods are summarised in **Table 18.2**.

Name	Stiffness method	Flexibility method
Alternative name	Displacement method	Force method
Altered structure	All joints fixed	Releases introduced
Initial conditions	Kinematically admissible solution	Statically admissible solution
Results from initial condition	Forces at joints: matrix **p**	Movements at releases: matrix **r**
From structure details	Stiffness matrix **K**	Flexibility matrix **F**
Governing matrix equation	**Ku = p**	**Fx = r**
Solution	Gives displacements: matrix **u**	Gives bi-actions: matrix **x**
Solution restores	**Equilibrium**	**Compatibility**

Table 18.2 – Comparison of Stiffness and Flexibility Methods

So far it has been assumed that the structures used are **linear elastic** – see page **129** – with **static loads**. It should be noted that using either method it is possible to introduce various modifications such as the effect of **buckling** – see section **6.4**, **dynamic behaviour** – see **Chapter 15**, or **plastic behaviour** – see section **6.3**. These modifications are beyond the scope of this book and are explained in technical literature.

Which method is better has not been resolved, and is discussed briefly in section **18.7**.

18.3   Continuum mechanics

In **Chapter 3** the idea of structures being **assemblies of elements** was introduced, with a **basic element** being seen as a rectangular block with dimensions **A**, **B** and **C** see **Fig. 18.14**.

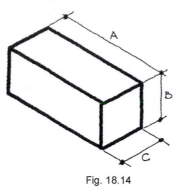

Fig. 18.14

If the dimension **B** is considered small compared to **A** and **C** then the element becomes **two-dimensional**. If two of the dimensions, say **B** and **C**, are considered small compared to dimension **A**, then the element can be considered a **one-dimensional element** – see **Fig. 18.15**.

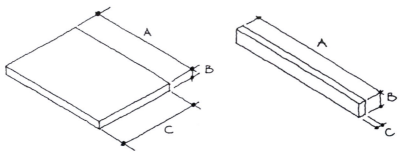

Fig. 18.15

In the descriptive part of the book – **Chapters 1** to **13** – the behaviour of structures made of one, two and three dimensional elements, or combinations of these elements, has been explained. But when the **numerical approach** was introduced in **Chapter 14** and the **mathematical basis** was explained in **Chapter 17**, only structures made of one-dimensional elements, beams and columns were considered.

In **Chapter 17**, governing differential equations were derived for axially loaded – see section **17.3** – and laterally loaded – see section **17.4** – one-dimensional elements. By considering forces on thin slices of these elements, **governing differential equations** were derived. For the **axially loaded element** – a column – this is a second order ordinary differential equation – see page **476** – given as:

$$\frac{d^2u}{dx^2} = -\frac{p(x)}{EA}$$

And for the **laterally loaded element** – a beam – the equation is a fourth order ordinary differential equation – see page **483** – given as:

$$EI\frac{d^4u}{dx^4} = -p(x)$$

Solutions to these equations were obtained by simple integration; however these solutions had to be modified depending on how the elements were supported at their ends – their **boundaries**. Different **end supports - boundary conditions** – are shown on page **477** for a column, and page **484** for a beam.

Even though many building structures are made from one-dimensional elements, in many cases two-dimensional elements, in the forms of slabs, deep beams and walls are used. Sometimes the slabs are curved in one or two directions to form shells – see page **93**. Sometimes structures in buildings can be considered to be three-dimension elements; pile caps – see **Fig. 8.30** – are an example.

Describing the structural behaviour of beams and columns by using differential equations are simple examples of a vast subject called **mathematical physics**. The first person to effectively apply mathematics to physical phenomena was Isaac Newton (1642-1726), who in his famous book *Philosphiæ Naturalis Principia Mathematica* ("Mathematical Principles of Natural Philosophy"), first published in 1687, laid the foundations for **classical mechanics**, often called **Newtonian Mechanics**.

In the following centuries, systems of differential equations were developed which found applications to celestial mechanics, magnetism, aerodynamics and much more. The mathematical modelling of structures is part of **continuum mechanics**. This is the part of **mathematical physics** that deals with the mechanical behaviour of materials that can be modelled as a continuous mass rather than as discrete particles. The differential equations given above are examples of the continuum mechanics approach to one-dimensional elements. Now, similar equations are required for two and three dimensional elements. These will be partial differential equations.

They are described as partial because the equations are functions of more than one independent variable, and they include terms that are differentiated with respect to only one or more of the variables; hence, these terms are partially differentiated. To indicate this, the symbol ∂ is used to indicate **partial differentiation** rather than **d**, which is used to indicate **ordinary differentiation**.

The derivation of the partial differential equations for two and three dimensional elements is complex and is normally part of advanced topics in engineering science. Some results are given here to give an idea of what is involved. For a two dimensional element, normally called a **plate**, loaded axially, the loads, forces and displacements are shown in **Fig. 18.16**.

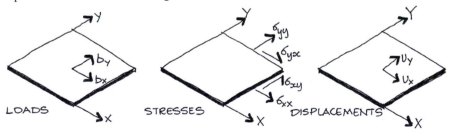

Fig. 18.16 – Axially loaded plate

The governing equations can be written as three matrix equations as follows:

$$\begin{bmatrix} \partial/\partial x & 0 & \partial/\partial y \\ 0 & \partial/\partial y & \partial/\partial x \end{bmatrix} \begin{bmatrix} \sigma_{xx} \\ \sigma_{yy} \\ \sigma_{xy} \end{bmatrix} = \begin{bmatrix} b_x \\ b_y \end{bmatrix}$$

$$\begin{bmatrix} \sigma_{xx} \\ \sigma_{yy} \\ \sigma_{xy} \end{bmatrix} = \begin{bmatrix} \dfrac{E}{(1-v^2)} & \dfrac{Ev}{(1-v^2)} & 0 \\ \dfrac{Ev}{(1-v^2)} & \dfrac{E}{(1-v^2)} & 0 \\ 0 & 0 & \dfrac{E}{2(1+v)} \end{bmatrix} \begin{bmatrix} e_{xx} \\ e_{yy} \\ 2e_{xy} \end{bmatrix}$$

$$\begin{bmatrix} e_{xx} \\ e_{yy} \\ 2e_{xy} \end{bmatrix} = \begin{bmatrix} \partial/\partial x & 0 \\ 0 & \partial/\partial y \\ \partial/\partial y & \partial/\partial x \end{bmatrix} \begin{bmatrix} u_x \\ u_y \end{bmatrix}$$

Where **E** is **Young's Modulus** and **v** is the **Poisson's ratio**, σ is the axial stress and **e** is the axial strain. These three matrix equations can be compared to the three equations listed with bullet points on page **476** for the axially loaded one-dimensional element

These matrix equations can be combined to give two governing equations, one each for the loads **b$_x$** and **b$_y$**. For brevity only the one for **b$_x$** is given here as follows:

$$\frac{E}{(1-v^2)}\left(\frac{\partial^2 u_x}{\partial x^2} + v\frac{\partial^2 u_y}{\partial x\partial y}\right) + \frac{E}{2(1+v)}\left(\frac{\partial^2 u_x}{\partial y^2} + \frac{\partial^2 u_y}{\partial x\partial y}\right) = b_x$$

As can be seen this **second order partial differential** equation bears some relationship to the second order ordinary differential equation for the **axially loaded element** – a column – given on page **516**.

For the case of the laterally loaded **plate**, there is only one vertical load, **p(x,y)** and one vertical deflection, **u(x,y)** – see **Fig. 18.17**.

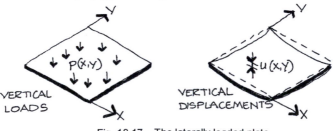

VERTICAL LOADS

VERTICAL DISPLACEMENTS

Fig. 18.17 – The laterally loaded plate

In this case the governing equation, a **fourth order partial differential equation**, is:

$$\frac{\partial^4 u}{\partial x^4} + 2\frac{\partial^4 u}{\partial x^2 \partial y^2} + \frac{\partial^4 u}{\partial y^4} = \frac{p(x,y)}{D}$$

This equation is called the **plate equation**, and similarities can be seen between this equation and the beam equation given on page **516**. The plate equation was first derived at the beginning of the nineteenth century. Its history shows the difficulties of mathematical physics.

Towards the end of the eighteenth century Ernst Chladni (1756-1827) did a number of experiments to show how plates vibrated. At the beginning of the nineteenth century the French Academy for Science offered a prize for a mathematical explanation of Chladni's experiments. There was only one contestant, Sophie Germain (1776-1831). Starting work in 1809 she submitted her answer in 1811; it did not win the prize as the judging commission felt that "*the true equations of the movement were not established*." The contest was extended and Germain re-submitted her answer in 1813; although given an honourable mention "*the fundamental base of the theory [of elastic surfaces] was not established*." Still she persisted, and submitted again in 1816 and this time received a *prix extraordinaire*, but with the caveat that her method did not predict experimental results with great accuracy. Obviously, as a woman in the country of *égalité*, she was not allowed into Academy's building to receive her prize. It was only in 1820 that the engineer and physicist Claude-Louis Navier (1785-1836) presented the first satisfactory theory for the bending of plates.

Throughout the 19th and 20th centuries work proceeded on deriving governing differential for three-dimensional elasticity, singly and doubly curved shells, the effects of buckling, dynamic behaviour, plastic behaviour and various other refinements. Unsurprisingly, these resulted in evermore complicated equations.

It is one difficult thing to derive the equations, but it is quite another to use them to provide answers in terms of stresses, displacements, bending moments etc. for real structures. Although functions could often be found that satisfied the general equation, the problem was to satisfy boundary conditions. The boundary of a geometric object is one dimension less than that of the object. So for a one dimensional object like a beam, the boundary is zero dimensional, that is, just the end points. For a plate, a two dimensional object, the boundary is one dimensional, a line or curve. Using the example of a rectangular plate with fixed supports on two sides, and free and simple supports on the others, and following the results given on page **484** for the beam element, the boundary conditions are those shown in **Fig. 18.18**.

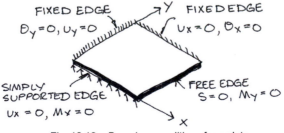

Fig. 18.18 – Boundary conditions for a plate

For the boundary conditions shown in **Fig. 18.18** for a rectangular shaped plate, theoretical solutions can be found. However, for slabs and walls in real buildings it is rare to find such simple shapes and boundary conditions. Usually slabs – plates – are supported on beams, and often have openings or other changes in shape – see **Fig. 18.19**.

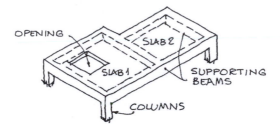

Fig. 18.19 – Typical slabs in a building structure

Irregular shapes mean that it is difficult, or impossible, to find functions to satisfy the governing equations, and the boundary condition are also complicated. A supporting beam, for example providing a spring support of variable stiffness, is difficult to model mathematically in a way that can yield useful results, likewise the presence of openings in a slab means more boundary conditions have to be imposed, adding to the theoretical difficulties.

It is for this reason that the derivation and solution of these governing differential equations mainly remained in the realm of research and academia, and rarely were used in the design of building structures. A rare case where they were, was the work of the mathematically gifted engineers Franz Dischinger and Ulrich Finsterwalder, who, using mathematical shell theory, were able to build millions of square metres of economically viable shell roofs – see page **317**. Engineer Ronald Jenkins had also successfully used complex mathematical shell theory to design a number of shell roofs in the 1950s. But it was his inability to solve the equations for the complex shapes and boundary conditions for the Sydney Opera House roof that led to his resignation from the project – see pages **326** and **327**.

18.4 An axially loaded triangular plate

In this section, the equations for an **axially loaded triangular plate** are derived in terms of the **corner displacements** – here the **plate** will be called **an element**. The corners of the triangles are called **nodes**. The **objective** is to derive an equation that relates the **nodal displacements** to **nodal forces** through a **stiffness matrix**. Only an outline derivation is given here, for a full exposition the reader should consult the large number of available publications.

The geometry of the triangle can be described by **Cartesian coordinates**– these are shown in **Fig. 18.20**.

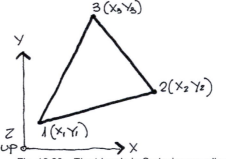

Fig. 18.20 – The triangle in Cartesian coordinates

or by **triangular coordinates** – these are shown in **Fig. 18.21**.

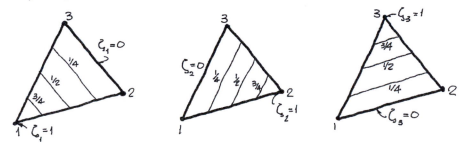

Fig. 18.21 – The triangle in triangular coordinates

The **area of the triangle A** is given by $2A = (x_2 y_3 - x_3 y_2) + (x_3 y_1 - x_1 y_3) + (x_1 y_2 - x_2 y_1)$

The **triangular coordinates** are an example of a **parametric representation** of functions. The **triangular coordinates** are **not independent** as:

$$\zeta_1 + \zeta_2 + \zeta_3 = 1$$

The **Cartesian** and the **triangular coordinate systems** are connected as follows:

$$\begin{bmatrix} 1 \\ x \\ y \end{bmatrix} = \begin{bmatrix} 1 & 1 & 1 \\ x_1 & x_2 & x_3 \\ y_1 & y_2 & y_3 \end{bmatrix} \begin{bmatrix} \zeta_1 \\ \zeta_2 \\ \zeta_3 \end{bmatrix}$$

By using standard techniques to invert the **3x3 matrix**, a more complex expression can be found that relates the **triangular coordinates** ζ to the **Cartesian coordinates** **x** and **y**, as follows:

$$\begin{bmatrix} \zeta_1 \\ \zeta_2 \\ \zeta_3 \end{bmatrix} = \frac{1}{2A} \begin{bmatrix} x_2y_3-x_3y_2 & y_2-y_3 & x_3-x_2 \\ x_3y_1-x_1y_3 & y_3-y_1 & x_1-x_3 \\ x_1y_2-x_2y_1 & y_1-y_2 & x_2-x_1 \end{bmatrix} \begin{bmatrix} 1 \\ x \\ y \end{bmatrix} = \frac{1}{2A} \begin{bmatrix} 2A_{23} & y_{23} & x_{32} \\ 2A_{31} & y_{31} & x_{13} \\ 2A_{12} & y_{12} & x_{21} \end{bmatrix} \begin{bmatrix} 1 \\ x \\ y \end{bmatrix}$$

Where $y_{23} = y_2 - y_3$ etc., and A_{23} is the area of the triangle formed by apexes 2 and 3 of the element and the origin of the Cartesian coordinate system. From this equation the partial derivatives of the ζs can be obtained with respect to **x** and **y**, are given typically as follows:

$$\frac{\partial \zeta_1}{\partial x} = \frac{1}{2A} y_{23}$$

$$\frac{\partial \zeta_1}{\partial y} = \frac{1}{2A} x_{32}$$

If a **function f(x,y)** varies linearly over the triangle then $f(x,y) = a_0 + a_{1x} + a_{2y}$. Here the conditions that determine the **coefficients** are the **nodal values** of **f** which at the corners are f_1, f_2 and f_3. The expression of the function with respect to the triangular coordinates can be written:

$$f(\zeta_1, \zeta_2, \zeta_3) = f_1\zeta_1 + f_2\zeta_2 + f_3\zeta_3 = [f_1 \quad f_2 \quad f_3] \begin{bmatrix} \zeta_1 \\ \zeta_2 \\ \zeta_3 \end{bmatrix}$$

From this, the **partial derivatives** of the **function f**, are found using the chain rule of differentiation[*] as follows (only $\partial f/\partial x$ is shown):

$$\frac{\partial f}{\partial x} = \frac{\partial f}{\partial \zeta_1} \cdot \frac{\partial \zeta_1}{\partial x} + \frac{\partial f}{\partial \zeta_2} \cdot \frac{\partial \zeta_2}{\partial x} + \frac{\partial f}{\partial \zeta_3} \cdot \frac{\partial \zeta_3}{\partial x}$$

The partial derivatives of the function **f** with respect to **x** and **y** can be given in matrix form as

$$\begin{bmatrix} \dfrac{\partial f}{\partial x} \\[2mm] \dfrac{\partial f}{\partial y} \end{bmatrix} = \frac{1}{2A} \begin{bmatrix} \dfrac{\partial f}{\partial \zeta_1} & \dfrac{\partial f}{\partial \zeta_2} & \dfrac{\partial f}{\partial \zeta_3} \end{bmatrix} \begin{bmatrix} y_{23} & x_{32} \\ y_{31} & x_{13} \\ y_{12} & x_{21} \end{bmatrix}$$

The **displacements** of the **element** with respect to the **x** and **y** coordinates are u_x and u_y at an arbitrary point $P(\zeta_1, \zeta_2, \zeta_3)$. These are given by the matrix equation:

$$\begin{bmatrix} u_x \\ u_y \end{bmatrix} = \begin{bmatrix} \zeta_1 & 0 & \zeta_2 & 0 & \zeta_3 & 0 \\ 0 & \zeta_1 & 0 & \zeta_2 & 0 & \zeta_3 \end{bmatrix} \begin{bmatrix} u_{x1} \\ u_{y1} \\ u_{x2} \\ u_{y2} \\ u_{x3} \\ u_{y3} \end{bmatrix} = N\, u^e$$

Where **N** is the **shape function matrix**, which in this case are just the **triangular coordinates** and u^e is the **matrix of element nodal displacements** that are shown in **Fig. 18.22**.

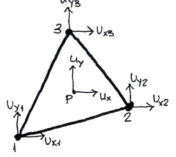

Fig. 18.22 – Element displacements

The objective of all this algebraic manipulation is to arrive at an expression for the **displacements u** that can be differentiated to obtain expressions for the **strain e**, that is similar to the **third matrix equation** of the governing differential equations for an axially loaded elastic plate given on page **518**. This is done by differentiating the **shape function N**, which in this case are the triangular coordinates, with respect to **x** and **y** to give the **strains** as follows:

$$e = \begin{bmatrix} e_{xx} \\ e_{yy} \\ e_{xy} \end{bmatrix} = \begin{bmatrix} \dfrac{\partial \zeta_1}{\partial x} & 0 & \dfrac{\partial \zeta_2}{\partial x} & 0 & \dfrac{\partial \zeta_3}{\partial x} & 0 \\[2mm] 0 & \dfrac{\partial \zeta_1}{\partial y} & 0 & \dfrac{\partial \zeta_2}{\partial y} & 0 & \dfrac{\partial \zeta_2}{\partial y} \\[2mm] \dfrac{\partial \zeta_1}{\partial y} & \dfrac{\partial \zeta_1}{\partial x} & \dfrac{\partial \zeta_2}{\partial y} & \dfrac{\partial \zeta_2}{\partial x} & \dfrac{\partial \zeta_2}{\partial y} & \dfrac{\partial \zeta_3}{\partial x} \end{bmatrix} \begin{bmatrix} u_{x1} \\ u_{y1} \\ u_{x2} \\ u_{y2} \\ u_{x3} \\ u_{y3} \end{bmatrix} = B\, u^e$$

---

[*] see https://en.wikipedia.org/wiki/Chain_rule, for instance

Where **B** is called the **strain-displacement matrix**. In this case typical elements are $y_{23}/2A$ – see page **521** – which are just numerical values. That shows that for this element, with the shape functions that are just the triangular coordinates, the strains are constant over the triangle. Because of this, this element is often called a **constant strain triangle**.

The **stiffness matrix of the triangular element** is:

$$K^e = \frac{t}{4A} \begin{bmatrix} y_{23} & 0 & x_{32} \\ 0 & x_{32} & y_{23} \\ y_{31} & 0 & x_{13} \\ 0 & x_{13} & y_{31} \\ y_{12} & 0 & x_{21} \\ 0 & x_{21} & y_{12} \end{bmatrix} \begin{bmatrix} \dfrac{E}{(1-v^2)} & \dfrac{Ev}{(1-v^2)} & 0 \\ \dfrac{Ev}{(1-v^2)} & \dfrac{E}{(1-v^2)} & 0 \\ 0 & 0 & \dfrac{E}{2(1+v)} \end{bmatrix} \begin{bmatrix} y_{23} & 0 & y_{31} & 0 & y_{12} & 0 \\ 0 & x_{32} & 0 & x_{13} & 0 & x_{21} \\ x_{32} & y_{23} & x_{13} & y_{31} & x_{21} & y_{12} \end{bmatrix} = At\, \mathbf{B}^T \mathbf{E}\, \mathbf{B}$$

Where **t** is the **thickness** of the element, and **E** is the **elasticity matrix** already given on page **518**.

The element has **body forces** b_x and b_y that are **constant** throughout the element, so the **nodal forces** p^e are **equal** to **one third** of the **total body force in each direction at each node**, so:

$$p^e = \frac{At}{3}[b_x \quad b_y \quad b_x \quad b_y \quad b_x \quad b_y]^T = [P_{x1} \quad P_{y1} \quad P_{x2} \quad P_{y2} \quad P_{x3} \quad P_{y2}]^T$$

The **body** and **nodal forces** are shown in **Fig. 18.23**.

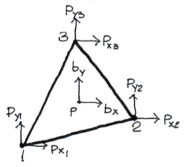

Fig. 18.23 – Body and nodal forces

Now an **equilibrium equation** can be written for the element using the **stiffness K^e**, **displacement u^e** and **load matrices p^e** as:

$$p^e = K^e u^e$$

This is similar to the equation written for the **beam element** on page 501. However, unlike the beam element – see section **17.5** – which can form part of a building structure in an obvious way, this **axially loaded triangular plate element is not obviously part of any structure**. How it can become part of a structure is explained in the next section.

18.5 The Finite Element Method

Whereas, in general, designers of building structures were able, by making various approximations and simplifications, to avoid the difficulties of continuum mechanics, aircraft designers needed to be able to design structures of complex shapes. Early aircraft had a structural frame of wood or aluminium, covered with fabric to provide the aerodynamic surfaces. But from the end of WWI, instead of fabric, the frames were often covered with plywood or a thin metal sheet. It was quickly realised that covering the wings and fuselage with wood or metal sheets made them part of the structure, making the structure of the aeroplane stiffer and stronger – the term monocoque was coined for such structures. As weight reduction is paramount for aircraft structures, aircraft designers had strong incentives to find practical methods for structurally analysing structures of complex shapes that included two-dimensional elements.

Starting in the 1920s, aircraft structural analysts tried a whole range of techniques to try and obtain useful results from continuum mechanics. These frequently used various forms of numerical approximations, with lengthy calculations being carried out using various types of mechanical calculators. One technique was something called relaxation methods of which the **Moment Distribution Method** – see pages **511-512** – is an example. Most of the types of analysis used were based on the **Force** (or **Flexibility**) **Method** – see **Table 18.2**. But in 1956, a team working at Boeing Aircraft Corporation led by MJ 'Jon' Turner, published a seminal paper entitled '*Stiffness and Deflection Analysis of Complex Structures*' - see **Fig. 18.24**.

JOURNAL OF THE AERONAUTICAL SCIENCES

VOLUME 23	SEPTEMBER, 1956	NUMBER 9

Stiffness and Deflection Analysis of Complex Structures

M. J. TURNER,* R. W. CLOUGH,† H. C. MARTIN,‡ AND L. J. TOPP**

Fig. 18.24 – Title of the seminal paper by MJ Turner et al

During 1953, Turner and his team worked on the idea on arbitrary sized triangular and rectangular plates, being assembled into larger structures. These **elements** were the basis of what became known as the **Finite Element Method**, though the name was only coined in 1960. Luckily for the team, Boeing had the resources to purchase a main frame computer, which at the time was enormously expensive. Luckily, because their pioneering work would have been impossible to implement without a computer being available to carry out the large number of numerical calculations their method needed, though it was only in 1957 that a high level computer language (Fortran I) appeared that allowed engineers and scientists to write their own programs.

The paper by Turner et al introduced rectangular and triangular plate elements, noting that the triangular element '*will be used as the basic "building block" for calculating stiffness matrices for plates of arbitrary shape.*' The triangular element that was described has since been named the **Turner triangle**. The geometry of the triangle can be described by **Cartesian coordinates**, or by **triangular coordinates** – these are shown in **Figs. 18.18 and 19**. The **triangular coordinates** are an example of a **parametric representation** of functions, and is crucial to the **Finite Element Method** – henceforth denoted **FEM** (not to be confused with **FEM ≡ fixed end moment**).

It can now be seen that the derivation of the **stiffness K^e**, **displacement u^e** and **load matrices p^e** for the axially loaded triangular plate in the previous section are for the **Turner triangle**. To relate these to a real structure, any number of these triangular elements can be joined together, as shown in **Fig. 18.25**.

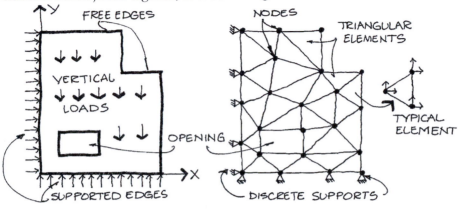

Fig. 18.25 – Finite element model

In **Fig. 18.25 R** the real plate is shown made from an assembly of triangular finite elements. There are several points to be noted about this model:

- A plate of any shape can be modelled using finite elements.
- The number and arrangement of the finite elements used to model the real plate is arbitrary.
- Similar to that for the beam shown on page **505**, the element stiffness matrixes can be combined to form a **structure stiffness matrix K**. This is then used to solve the **equilibrium equation Ku = p**. The **u** and **p** are the **displacement** and **load matrices** for all the **nodes** in the **structure**.
- Because the edge displacements of each element are straight lines between the nodes, there are no 'gaps' between the elements.
- Because each element has constant stress, the stresses in each element will be different, so along the edges of the elements the stresses will be different on either side.

Because of the last point, the solution to the equilibrium equation is not exact in the way it is for the beam shown in **Example 17.20**.

There are various ways this could be improved. As something 'smooth', the real plate, is being modelled by an 'unsmooth' finite number of triangles, the more triangles that are used, the 'smoother' the finite elements model will become, and the more accurate will be the results given by the solution of **Ku = p**. This is called **refining** the **mesh**.

In the 1950s, this obvious improvement presented various difficulties. As the size of the **matrix K**, for any real structure of interest, would be too large to invert by hand – see **502-504** – a computer has to be used. As noted, high level languages were only developed in 1957, and all the assemblies of elements had to be done by hand, with all the coordinates being entered into the computer; a slow and laborious task.

But both computer technology and the theory and development of the **Finite Element Method** advanced with extraordinary rapidity. This allowed an amazing advancement in the analysis of structures, but it was all linked to the use of computers, as the **FEM matrix sizes** that were generated could never be inverted by hand calculations.

So apart from increasing the number of elements, how did the **FEM** develop? One way is to use more complicated shape functions, than the simple one used for the **Turner triangle**. This means that the finite element needed more nodes, as shown in **Fig. 18.25**.

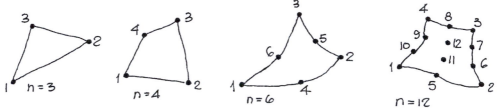

Fig. 18.26 – Finite elements with different numbers of nodes

Now the **shape function matrix N** - see page **522** – has dimensions **2 x 2n**. Naturally these elements with more nodes generate more complicated theoretical and numerical computations, but all follow the pattern already outlined. So the individual element stiffness matrices K^e increase in size, from **6 x 6** for the **basic triangle**, to **24 x 24** for the **12-node element**. So with more refined meshes and higher order elements the size of the structure matrix **K** can quickly attain dimensions of hundreds, or more. Equations with stiffness matrices sizes of **10,000 x 10,000** are routinely solved by commercial software.

The enormous amount of research generated by the **FEM** has developed a huge number of different elements. In **Fig. 18.27**, a **nine-node bi-quadratic quadrilateral element** is shown, together with the lines used for the shape function N_9^e and a plot of shape function $N_9^e = (1 - \xi^2)(1 - \eta^2)$.

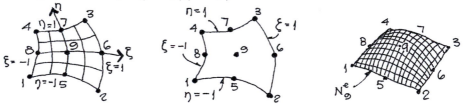

Fig. 18.27 – Details for the shape function N_9^e

Elements for **plate bending, three-dimensional elasticity** and **shells** have also been developed, all with complicated shape **functions** and derivations of the **element stiffness matrices.**

The development of the **FEM** means that now it is possible to have elements that simulate cracking, buckling, plastic behaviour, dynamic behaviour or non-linear materials; in fact almost any engineering phenomena that can be imagined can be modelled using the **FEM**. Rather like **continuum mechanics** – see section **18.3** – the **FEM** has become so sophisticated and complex that its details are now the realm of the specialist rather than the structural designer.

This development in the **FEM** has been mirrored by the advances made in computing, both for the software and for the hardware. Gone are the days when hours had to be spent preparing sheets of numerical data, and then interpreting results that were output as reams of paper covered in numbers. Geometric data can be generated directly from computerised drawings. Programs now output technical information in a graphical form. Computer programs also generate finite element meshes, and output results as three-dimension images, as shown in **Fig. 18.28**. This shows the post-bucked shape of a vertically loaded thin-gauge metal member, where the side flanges have opened.

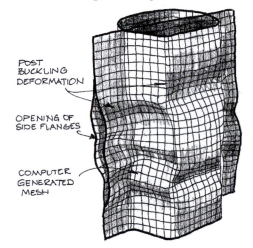

POST
BUCKLING
DEFORMATION

OPENING OF
SIDE FLANGES

COMPUTER
GENERATED
MESH

Fig. 18.28 – Graphical computer output

And not only do computer programs generate graphic output, but post-processing programs can use the computer results to produce reinforcement and steel fabrication drawings.

18.6   The magic wand, how good is it?

It now could appear that designers of structures for buildings, or for anything else for that matter, have been given a magic wand. Any structure, no matter how little technical understanding has informed its conception, can now be fed, semi-automatically, into a computer, and within a short interval, graphic output pours out giving deflected shapes, colour coded diagrams of levels of stress, bending moment diagrams, post-buckling behaviour, crack prediction and more. What are the advantages, what are the dangers?

The advantages when designing what might be called straight-forward structures, is that, unlike with calculations done by hand, computers give more information. This 'extra' information can include bending moment, shear force and axial force diagrams. But also numerical and graphic information on displacements can be obtained, something that is hard to produce by hand; for example the **Moment Distribution Method**, gives no direct information about displacements.

But where the structural conception is, in one way or another, architect-led, (see section **12.8** for more on this) the appearance of these sophisticated computer programs is a boon, because structural designers can feel reasonably secure that indeed **anything can be made to stand up**. It is well to remember the problems that beset engineers when they were confronted with architect-led structural conceptions before the advent of computer programs. Faced with the geometric 'solution' of the Phillips Pavilion, engineer Hoyte Duyster had to have structural models tested to provide design information – see page **323**. The analytical struggles of the Sydney Opera House are legend – see pages **324** to **327**. Interestingly, for the final scheme, in 1962, the Arup engineers were pioneer users of computers for a building structure. But a **flexibility solution** was programmed not a **stiffness** one.

However, even the availability of advanced computer programs does not always ensure that an engineer finds it easy to make a 'non-structural' proposal stand up. When Hanif Kara (b1982), who is Professor in Practice of Architectural Technology at Harvard Graduate School of Design, was confronted with the Phæno Science Center – see **Fig. 12.65** – he needed to work with software companies for nearly 18 months before he had a computer model that revealed that indeed it would stand up – see **Fig. 18.29**. During that period he '*never admitted [to the architect Zaha Hadid (1950-2016)] that the building did not stand up.*' Without these advanced computer programs, no doubt the project would have gone the way of the Phillips Pavilion, or the Sydney Opera House.

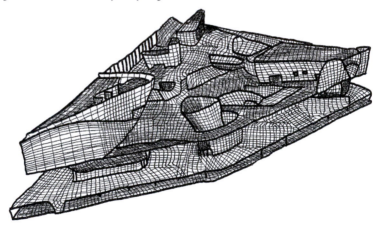

Fig. 18.29 – The finite element model of the Phæno Science Center

If those are the advantages, is there a downside? Well that is rather a matter of opinion.

The basic question is one of dependency. That is, should structural design be done that is entirely dependent on computers? For the calculations for Sydney Opera House, the technical paper presented states that '*The method of analysis relied very heavily on the use of computers. It is difficult to visualize how the necessary calculations could have been made without them.*' This project was a turning point for the conception and design of building structures from many points of view, and was perhaps the first project where this dependency was exhibited. In the case of the Phæno Science Center the dependency appears to have been total.

Such dependency has drawbacks for two important principles of building structure conception. The first of these, and perhaps the most important, is that when a designer proposes a structural system, at that point, it should be clear what are the load paths, and what structural actions are required in each load path to carry the loads. This is fundamental, and any other approach is courting danger. The second is that there should be confidence that numerical calculations that are carried out to verify the strength and stiffness of the various load paths are reliable.

Computer output looks so technically convincing it can be quite difficult to imagine it could be wrong. Wrong how? Because computers, unlike humans, do not make numerical errors, that cannot be a source of error. So what can be? Assuming of course that correct loads, geometry and material properties have been entered, there are two sources of error. If finite elements are being used, they are by definition approximations, so they will diverge in some way from a correct continuum mechanics solution; but by how much? Those responsible for formulating finite elements and writing programs using them are aware of this, and so perform a **patch test**. In this a few elements are assembled, and the results of the analysis are compared with known continuum mechanics solutions. Even if patch tests are passed, results using **ill-conditioned** elements will not give good results. These often occur in areas of rapidly changing stress, like sharp corners. Different arrangements of finite elements will give quite different answers, and probably none will give the correct one – see **Fig. 18.30**.

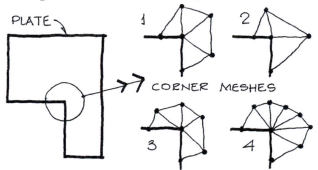

Fig. 18.30 Corner finite element configurations

It would be unusual if the four different finite element configurations shown in **Fig. 18.30** gave the same result, or, for that matter any of them gave the correct one. Configuration 4, shows very pointed triangles which do not obey the 'rules of thumb' that require all corner angles should be equal, or at least not be less than 15°. Poor automatic meshing is shown in **Fig. 18.31**.

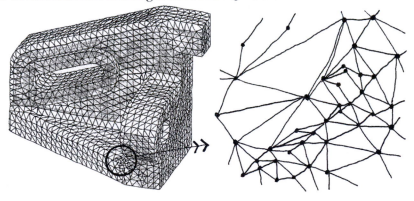

Fig. 18.31 – Poor automatic meshing

Again software engineers are aware of these problems and many programs have methods of either highlighting such problems, or correcting them automatically.

But it is not just programs with finite elements that can give 'incorrect' answers, so can programs using one-dimensional beam and axial elements. The cable supported roof structure shown in **Fig. 18.32** was analysed using three different commercial programs and the results compared.

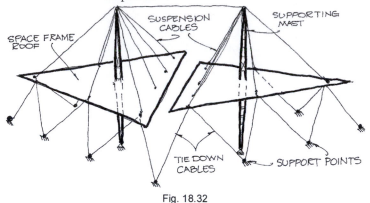

Fig. 18.32

The axial forces calculated from the three different programs varied considerably, for some cables the values from one program was up to 10 times more than given by the other programs. Clearly they cannot all be correct, yet all the programs used were successful commercially. In this case it was because some of the elements were prestressed cables which could not be treated as simple axial elements. This is because **all software is NOT created equal.**

Nowadays the idea of doing the numerical structural analysis of a building structure without recourse to a computer program seems almost eccentric. But it needs to be remembered that when a computer was used for the Sydney Opera House in 1962, all building structures before that date, and many after were calculated by hand. This of course means buildings like the Eiffel Tower, the Crystal Palace, the market hall in Basel, the Zarzuela Hippodrome, the CNIT Exposition Palace and all of Candela's shells – see the *Index* for page references – and many more were calculated by hand. So are computer programs essential for the designers of building structures? The answer is obviously not, but they can help, and that is how they should be seen.

To quote Professor Leroy Emkin, '*Real structural engineers can create simplified models of complex structural systems, perform appropriate analyses on such simplified models, and create designs that can be constructed that are safe, reasonably economical and functional.*' Before a designer resorts to the computer program, such simplified models should have been created so that basic numerical information is available to check against subsequent computer calculations

18.7   Stiffness or flexibility?

The **stiffness** and **flexibility methods** are compared in **Table 18.2**. When the Arup engineers pioneered the use of a computer for a building structure they used the **flexibility method** – the **reduced structure** is shown in **Fig. 18.33**. According to the technical paper, the structures '*were analysed initially by hand and later by a specially written flexibility matrix program.*'

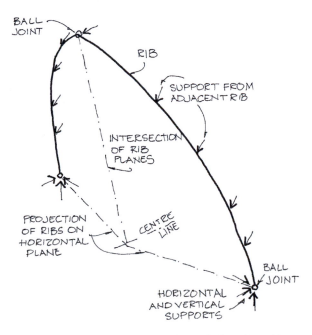

Fig. 18.33 – Reduced structure for the Sydney Opera House

The **flexibility method** has the advantage that the **primary unknowns** are **forces**, which is the essential information required for the numerical analysis of structures, whereas for the **stiffness method** the **primary unknowns** are **displacements**. This may seem irrelevant, but in the complex procedures used in computer programs to solve hundreds or thousands of simultaneous equations, numerical errors can result. Here's a simple example that shows what can happen:

If $f(x) = \frac{1}{(x-1)}$ then near $x = 1$ the expression is **ill-conditioned** as $x = 1.1$ returns $f(x)$ = 10 whereas $x = 1.01$ returns $f(x) = 100$, so a variation of 8% in x results in a variation of 90% in $f(x)$. Near $x = 10$, the expression is **well-conditioned** as $x = 10.1$ returns $f(x) = 0.10989$ and $x = 10.8$ returns $x = 0.10204$, a difference of 7% in x results in a variation of only 7% in $f(x)$.

In the **stiffness method**, as the **forces** are recovered via the **displacements**, any numerical errors will be exaggerated when the calculated displacements are used to calculate the forces. Of course the elimination of numerical errors is of prime concern to those involved in writing these solution procedures and is a specialist subject called **numerical analysis**.

Before the advent of useful computers for engineers, around 1957, flexibility methods were favoured over stiffness methods for many reasons. But the advent of the programmable computer meant ease of programming was a key factor. In this the stiffness method had huge advantages over the flexibility method, principally because of difficulty in automatically generating a reduced structure – see **Fig. 18.8**. When the **FEM** was presented in 1956, it was in the form of a **stiffness method**, and this sounded the death knell for the **flexibility method**.

During the 1960s and 1970s an enormous amount of work went into trying to find methods for frameworks that could automatically generate **reduced structures** and **bi-actions**, but nothing commercially viable resulted.

In 1965 NASA signed two contracts to build the NASTRAN finite element system; one contract was based on the **stiffness method** and the other on the **flexibility method**; in 1969 the contract for a flexibility method based system was cancelled. However, research into the use of the flexibility method continues in academia, and maybe one day it will bear fruit.

It is apparent that the matrix stiffness method is easier to implement for automatic computation. It is also easier to extend it for advanced applications such as non-linear analysis, stability, vibrations, etc. For these reasons, **the matrix stiffness method is the method of choice for use in general purpose structural analysis software packages**.

The main redeeming factor in learning the flexibility method nowadays is its educational value in imparting the concepts of equilibrium and compatibility. **In contrast, the procedure of the direct stiffness method is so mechanical that it risks being used without much understanding of structural behaviour.**

18.8 Closing caveat

In 1990, RW Clough, a member of MJ 'Jon' Turner's ground-breaking Boeing team wrote: *'In closing this paper, I will reiterate some concerns that I expressed in a paper written over ten years ago, in which I deplored the excessive confidence that some engineers had in the results of computer analyses of complex structures. The major point of those comments was that the results of a finite element analysis cannot be better than the data and the judgment used in formulating the mathematical model, regardless of the refinement of the computer program that performs the analysis of complex structures'* Quite.

Further reading

K.J. Bathe – **Finite Element Procedures** – 1st Edition, Prentice Hall, 1996; 2nd Edition, Watertown, MA: Klaus-Jürgen Bathe – from internet 2014 – https://www.google.pt/#q=K.J.+Bathe%2C+%22Finite+Element+Procedures%22%2C+1st+Edition%2C+Prentice+Hall%2C+1996%3B+2nd+Edition%2C+Watertown%2C+MA:+Klaus-J%C3%BCrgen+Bathe%2C+2014.

D Johnson – **Advanced Structural Mechanics** – Collins – 1986

Lawrence Malvern – **Introduction to the Mechanics of a Continuous Medium** – Prentice-Hall – 1969

George E Mase – **Continuum Mechanics** – Schaum's Outlines – 1970

J.S Przemieniecki – **Theory of Matrix Structural Analysis** – Dover – 2012

SP Timoshenko and JN Goodier – **Theory of Elasticity** – McGraw-Hill International Editions – 1970

Olek C Zienkiewicz – **The Finite Element Method: Its Basis and Fundamentals** – Butterworth-Heinemann; 7th edition – 2013

CHAPTER 19 *The successful structural project*

The main objective of this book is to provide accessible explanations for the technical behaviour of structures, and how these structures work as a part of a building. Later chapters provide information on various aspects of more advanced topics, including the role numerical calculations and mathematics take in the design of structures. This final chapter deals with the many different, mainly non-technical matters that influence the conception, design and construction of real structures, and in particular what is required to make a structural design project a success.

To carry out a project for a structure that is part of a building is a serious undertaking. This means conceiving a suitable structural form and preparing all the project documentation that typically consists of calculations, drawings, specifications, material quantities and an estimate of the cost. The chosen structure needs several qualities of which being an integral part of the overall design is central. Additional requirements include that the structure is buildable, is durable and is easy to alter for future changes of use. To achieve all this in a successful manner is no mean feat.

19.1 Work scenarios

To design and build a building normally requires many different people, and who they are and what role they play inevitably has an effect on the work of those responsible for the conception and design of a building structure. Usually, there are people that fulfil the following roles:

- **The client**
- **The architectural designer**
- **The interior designer**
- **The structural designer**
- **Designers of other technical specialities, such as drainage, electrical supply and so on**
- **Those responsible for quantities, cost control, contract documentation and project management**
- **Technical surveying and testing experts**
- **Checking and approving authorities**
- **General building contractors**

- **Specialist sub-contractors**

- **Building users committees**

Not every building contract has all of these, but on larger contracts most will be present. Many of these may have some influence on, or interest in the structural aspects of a project, and the structural designer should be aware that many may only have a rudimentary understanding of structural behaviour. This means that the structural designer often has to fulfil an unofficial role of a teacher, a role that should be carried out with patience and humility.

How these possible players relate officially can take many forms, and though not altering the **basic role of the structural designer**, this can influence their overall role. Frequently, the people involved will be meeting for the first time, so while crucial design decisions are being made, important working relationships are being established. Possible project organisations may be any of the following:

- **An entirely self-contained organisation, to which all the roles listed above belong**

- **A design and build contractor, who fulfils all the above roles except the client, and maybe the checking and approving authorities**

- **A government department that fulfils all the roles except that of the general contractor**

- **A client, and an architect who is responsible for all the other roles except that of the general contractor**

- **A project where all the roles listed above are completely separate entities**

- **Other permutations of the listed roles**

The way the project is organised may influence the work of the structural designer in a number of ways. For instance, there may be a preference for a structural material; pre-cast concrete rather than insitu concrete for example. There may be time constraints that are rigidly imposed. The structural designer may be responsible for only part of the structure, for instance the choice and design of the foundations could be the responsibility of specialists or nominated sub-contractors. It is not hard to imagine many other scenarios, and for each the structural designer's 'authority' may be quite different; from having a completely free hand, to having to comply with various imposed constraints and conditions. Though none of these influence the **basic role**, they can have important effects on how the people fulfilling the various roles relate to each other.

19.2   Structural integration

What is regarded as the primary structure of a building is not a separate entity but is an integral part, and indeed it may fulfil other roles. Until the advent of industrialisation and the introduction of specific elements in buildings whose sole function was to carry loads, such as iron columns or beams, whose performance was predicted by numerical calculations done by people called engineers, the division of buildings into structure, services, construction, cladding and all the rest was less clear. A vertical load-bearing element could be a column, and at the same time a sculpture – a caryatid.

Fig. 19.1 Greek and Baroque caryatids

The Greek caryatids are clearly vertical load-bearing elements, whereas the load-carrying function of the Baroque ones is less clear. Neither element would result from a ruthlessly logical process of structural design that follows the famous dictum that 'an engineer can do for sixpence (10p) what anyone else can do for half a crown (50p)'.

Up until the 19th century buildings were conceived by two groups of people. The majority of buildings were conceived by the builders themselves using local traditional methods which did not have the idea of a separate structural form; such buildings are usually designated vernacular buildings and several examples have appeared in the book – see **Figs. 0.1-0.5**, **13.1-13.2**, and **13.6-13.8**. Far fewer in number, but more important culturally, were buildings conceived by an aesthetic elite. These buildings tended to demonstrate power in various forms – cathedrals, palaces, government buildings – and they often had important structural elements that were the result of some form of structural conception – St Paul's Cathedral for example - see section **12.1**.

With the introduction, in the 19th century of mathematically-based methods of structural conception, a new group of builders appeared – the engineers. These three groups tended to operate independently, as they worked in mutually exclusive areas, each with a different approach to structural conception. The situation can be summarised as follows:

- **Vernacular builders used implicit structural conception as part of local tradition.**

- **Aesthetic builders (called architects or surveyors) often used explicit structural concepts not based on technical understanding.**

- **Engineering builders who used mathematically-based explicit structural concepts.**

These independent methods of building lasted right up to the period immediately after the Second World War; then things changed with a fundamental alteration within the architectural profession as the ideas of the Modern Movement were adopted on a global scale – now called modern architecture.

This gave rise to an awkward situation, as those responsible for the technical detailed design, the engineering builders, were not always responsible for basic structural ideas, which were often conceived by architects or others. Nowadays, even though every item of a building is a structure to which all the concepts apply, structural conception is usually limited to the main load-carrying elements. So a stair structure will be part of the structural part of the building, whereas the stair's handrail is not usually seen in that way.

Throughout the book the approach to providing successful structures has been to ensure that two basic criteria are met:

- **Every load has a complete load path**
- **Each load path is strong enough and stiff enough**

At the same time it has been shown that there is **no correct structure**, there are always choices to be made. Each choice has to be tested against various criteria, not just the two basic ones. The structure of a building has to form part of the whole building in a way that satisfies many different parties: the client, the checking authority, the architect, service engineers and eventually the contractor, and maybe others. Each of these parties will have their own criteria for the structure. Non-structural criteria include:

- **Client preferences and economic constraints**
- **Aesthetic considerations – see Chapter 12 and section 19.8**
- **Integration with building construction – see Figs, 11.65 to 72**
- **Accommodation of building services – see Figs. 11.68 to 73**
- **Cost control**
- **Contractor preferences**

What this list shows is that designing a building structure is not straightforward, so the design process is not a linear one that proceeds smoothly from perfect initial choices to project completion. In fact, it can degenerate into utter chaos with consequent financial and emotional burdens for all concerned. And this can result in various types of failure, so it is better to be realistic. As Alan Holgate put it 'It would be better for everyone if we did not delude ourselves and others that the application of technology is an entirely objective and rational undertaking.'[1]

19.3 The KISS principle

KISS is an acronym for **Keep It Simple Stupid**, the stupid is added to emphasise that it would be stupid not to keep it simple. The principle states that most systems work best if they are kept simple rather than made complicated. The phrase was coined by the brilliant aeronautical engineer Clarence 'Kelly' Johnson (1910–1990); the principle is best exemplified by the story of Johnson handing a team of design engineers a few tools, and challenging them to make the jet aircraft they were designing repairable by an average mechanic in the field under combat conditions, with only those tools.

Associated with this principle is **practicality**; the point Johnson was trying to make with his 'few tools challenge.' However, **practicality** and the **KISS principle** are not quite the same thing, as a simple example shows. Suppose a structure requires a 3-span beam; a simple structural concept is shown in **Fig. 19.2** with its associated **bending moment diagram**, BMD – see **Fig. 2.15** and **Fig. 14.15** for examples of bending moment diagrams.

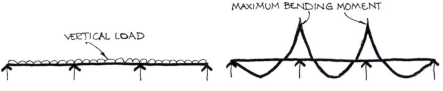

Fig. 19.2 Structural and bending moment diagrams for a 3-span beam

This simple structural concept may, or may not be practical depending on the material chosen for the beam. Suppose that the 3-span beam is made from three individual beam elements joined at the supports. Noting that the maximum bending moment is at the supports, it is practical to make the joint between the separate beam elements bending-resistant using reinforced concrete, but far less practical using structural steel.

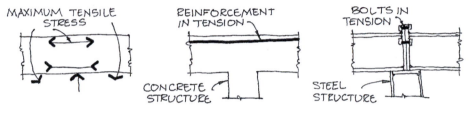

Fig. 19.3 3-span beams support joints

As **Fig. 19.3** shows, the maximum tensile force from the support bending moment has to be carried through the joint between adjacent beam elements. For reinforced concrete, this a simple part of the construction process, with reinforcement being placed over the joint. For structural steel this is far less practical, as the forces have to be transmitted by bolts and end plates, or similar devices – see pages **286-288** for a detailed description of such connections. So more practical options could be to use three simply-supported beams, or move the joint away from the support and make is near the point of contraflexure, where a simple pin joint could be used (see **Fig. 2.24**) – see **Fig. 19.4**.

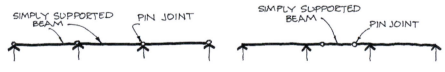

Fig.19.4 More practical structural concepts

If other structural materials such as pre-cast concrete or timber were to be chosen for the 3-span beam, it would also be difficult to make moment-resisting joints at the supports.

This elementary example illustrates what can be a subtle difference between a KISS principle structural concept and the practical realities of construction. What this also illustrates is the necessity for a structural designer not only to have a thorough knowledge of all the practical facets of structures, but to take an active interest in them. In parts of this book various aspects of how structures are built have been touched upon, but to get a real understanding time has to be spent in factories and on building sites.

19.4 Being organised

Few people would see any advantage in being badly organised, but avoiding this for the total process of structural design needs advance planning and, above all, discipline from everyone working on the project. But there are usually many different people and organisations involved who may not be well-organised, so the overall organisation needs to be sufficiently robust to cope with this.

In the days before computers were used, organisation was easier in some ways, as all information was on paper. Nowadays, when much information is stored and transmitted as computer files, the challenge is greater. An essential part of being organised requires that every piece of information has a unique name and location, and furthermore the scheme for the naming and storing of information is in place **before** anything is produced. For any group – business, consultancy, department etc. – that is responsible for structural projects, there are **organisational golden rules** which are:

- **There should be a standard way of organising all projects from small to large.**
- **The standard way should be clearly documented and everyone working in the group should be briefed.**
- **No deviation from the organisation standard can be tolerated.**

This may seem dictatorial and it is, because the way group members may show their individuality is by the quality of their work, not how they reference it or where they keep it.

The **standard way** must be decided by people within the organisation, not by a consultant who is unlikely to understand in detail how projects are done. Ideally, the **standard way** will be in the form of a **standard job kit**, which starts with **a unique project number** that is the first part of the identification of every document produced. The **project list** is an essential management tool. Centrally located it should contain information about the project; value, project team, stage, etc. A project number should be allocated before any information is produced, which means there can be no unreferenced information.

All project information should be stored in an open filing system, which keeps all the information, ideally, in one location. This means that all members of the group know where to find things and put things; this is easily said but not so easily done.

Each project should have a way of locating geometric positions. This is usually done by **placing a grid on the plan**, usually orthogonal, with grid lines generally spaced between 4 and 8 metres apart. Often grid lines mimic a column grid, which can be advantageous, but it is not essential; the existence of the grid is the main point. Standard levels usually follow the agreed floor levels, but it is helpful for them to have numbers like **level 2**.

Using a grid and level numbering generates automatic referencing for both drawn and written information, whether on paper or as a computer file, and is also helpful for written and verbal communication. The earlier this is agreed the better, and obviously it is ideal if it is used by everyone involved, but where this does not happen, the structural designers can create their own. A basic grid system is shown on **Fig. 19.5**.

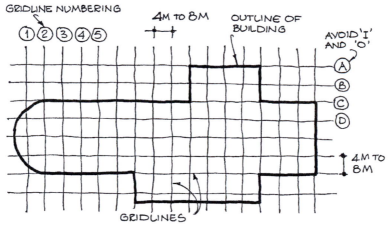

Fig. 19.5 A basic grid system

Where a building plan needs more than one drawing sheet at a chosen scale, **(1/50 is often appropriate)**, the building should be divided into numbered areas – **zones**. The most common size for drawings is **A1** which is **594 x 841mm (23.4 x 33.1inches)**. Using different size drawing sheets on the same project leads to storage and location difficulties, so the same size should be maintained, even if on some drawings it might seem wasteful. It can be useful to designate a **Zone 0**, which contains basic general information. It can explain the zones, grid and level information, standard details, or information about the materials and codes of practice used for calculations. A typical **zoning scheme** is shown on **Fig. 19.6**.

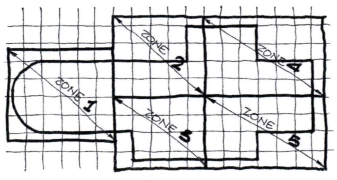

Fig. 19.6 Typical zoning scheme

As the drawing sheet for each zone will cover more of the building than just one zone, some parts of the building plan will appear on more than one drawing; there will been an **overlap area**. Drawing sheets for **Zone 3** and **Zone 5** are shown on **Fig. 19.7**, together with the **overlap area**. Although parts of the structure that appear in the overlap area should be drawn, it is essential that technical information should only appear in the relevant zone. So, for instance if a column appears in the overlap area, technical information about the column – dimensions etc. – **should only appear once**, on the drawing of the zone to which the column actually belongs.

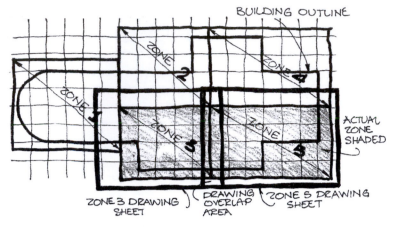

Fig. 19.7 A1 drawings for Zones 3 and 5

Keeping track of drawings, both those produced by the design team and those received from other parties, is crucial. Once again it requires strict discipline from all members of the team. When drawings existed as negatives on tracing paper there were some advantages as only one definitive drawing existed – the negative, which could be stored in a central location. Each and every alteration was recorded on the negative. However, with the advent of drawings as computer files there is no definitive drawing as such, and as files can be readily copied and stored in different electronic locations this means that the concept of a definitive version stored in a designated file location can easily be lost. So a **strict protocol for drawing alterations** must be established. The concept of drawing uniqueness must be grasped and adhered to by every team member.

Drawings, during the design, and often during the construction phases, will be altered or revised, to use the more common term. These revisions must be given unique references; letters are often used, so drawing **1243/3/28** becomes **1243/3/28 A**. What **revision A** is, should be clearly noted on the drawing. It can be helpful to ring the revised area on the drawing and mark it clearly with the revision letter. This saves recipients wasting their time looking for an alteration that has been denoted as '**A – minor revisions**'. Again, how all this is organised depends on the '**the standard way**', but team members must grasp the conceptual importance.

Given the central importance of calculations, it is strange that they are often treated casually. This has given rise to expressions like '*we just jotted down a few numbers on a back of an envelope.*' In fact, in 1986, a conference was held with the title '*How good is the 'Back of the Envelope' solution.*'[2] The conference had a serious objective which was to '*show that the semi intuitive short calculation still has a role to play in the age of very large readily available computers.*'

This is a very important point, and the enduring role of hand calculations must be maintained to provide basic information about preliminary ideas; however, the idea they should be done on the back of an envelope betrays a casual attitude to the whole subject of satisfactory calculation documentation.

An instance of casualness occurred during the design of the Sydney Opera House, reinforces this point. Crucial calculations could not be located:

> '*The engineers asked London for the calculations*'... '*if they are not in this file, I am sorry to say that we have lost them.*' ... '*I am pleased to say we have found* **your** *calculations.*

Eureka! They were with a miscellaneous batch found at the back of a correspondence filing cabinet' ... 'After a purge which has made de-Stalinization look like spring cleaning we found – **quite by chance** *– Joe Huang's calculations on the canopies.'*[3]

There are four absolutely basic points to be made about calculations, which are:

- **The calculations are the project calculations, they do not belong to any individual**

- **Every calculation must be done on a proper calculation sheet, prepared and numbered as if it was to be checked by someone else.**

- **Every sheet of the calculations must be given a complete and unique reference before any calculations are done on the sheet.**

- **All calculations must be subjected to a numerical check**

Check lists can be a great help in preparing project documentation. Compulsory use of check lists was a practice initiated in the airline industry for essential cockpit tests; surgical check lists are now mandatory in several countries and have cut deaths by half, so it is easy to see their value. So far, there are no mandatory or even recommended check lists for structural design projects. Such a checklist would ensure that the basic requirements of any structural design have been met, and they should be used before a project is submitted for review. This will check that all aspects have been addressed.

Design reviews should be undertaken at various points in the design process, the crucial one being at the end of the preliminary design stage, by which time all the critical decisions have been taken. There are many way of doing these reviews, but the best way is to submit the technical information to an independent designer, without any verbal discussions or presentations. In this way, the independent reviewer can not only verify basic design decisions and crucial numerical results, but the ease of doing the review from documents is a good test of their quality. Here again check lists are invaluable. If such a preliminary review is successful from all aspects, a final review is unlikely to reveal serious shortcomings.

The successful production of design information requires that the following questions are clearly answered as an ongoing process:

- **Does the design documentation have a clear organisation?**

- **Is every item of the documantation referenced uniquely?**

- **Can an independent authority readily answer questions about the project?**

This should not be difficult to achieve if the designing organisation follows the **organisational golden rules** listed on page **538**. If this is not seen as an ongoing process it is difficult to manage the inevitable changes of personnel, deal with questions when team members are absent, and end up with a professionally documented project.

19.5 Building Information Model

With the advent of three-dimensional computer draughting programs it is now possible to draw a projected building in three dimensions. This can usually only be done at the later stages of the design of a project when most of the design decisions have been made. With modern computing technology, the separate designs of each team, providing, they are using compatible software, can be brought together into what is called a **Building Information Model** or **BIM** for short.

Fig. 19.8 Part of a building information model - BIM

Who assembles the **BIM** and at what stage of the project is a matter for how any particular project is organised. Clearly, such a model can show huge advantages, because basically it builds the building digitally before it is built physically, which ought to ensure that there are no constructional anomalies. What is absolutely essential with the **BIM** is control over who is permitted to alter it. Before the **BIM** is created an **alteration protocol** has to be established and strictly adhered to, otherwise it is easy for various versions of the **BIM** to be stored in different electronic locations, each version being tinkered with independently and, in so doing, undermining the enormous value of the **BIM**.

19.6 A successful structural project

It could be argued that any design for a building structure that provides strength and stiffness for all the load paths is a successful project, which, in a way, it is. Here, the definition of **successful** is narrowed to mean a structural project that not only fulfils the basic engineering requirement, but one where the design and building processes are carried out efficiently and within time and monetary constraints by following the **KISS principle** and exhibiting **practicality**.

Several such projects have already been mentioned that can be considered successful using this restricted definition. The building for the 1851 Great Exhibition, better known as the **Crystal Palace**, was completed in just eleven months, with Joseph Paxton's design drawings taking only nine days – see section

12.2. Though no details of cost or building programmes are available, both the **CNIT Exposition Palace** – see section **10.4**, and the **Bank of China** – see section **10.6**, exhibit clear structural concepts that were turned into real buildings, each one exceptional in its own way.

However, the 1930s **Empire State Building** broke not just records for height but also for efficiency of both design and construction. The building was the brainchild of businessman John J Raskob (1879-1950), who wanted something taller than the projected-to-be tallest building in the world, the Chrysler Building. He achieved this with the Empire State Building becoming the tallest building in the world, which it remained for over four decades.

Raskob chose William Lamb (1883-1952) to be the architect. At their first meeting, Lamb asked about Raskob's vision for his building. Raskob, in reply, pulled a thick pencil out of his drawer and held it up and asked William Lamb, *"How high can you make it so that it won't fall down?"* Lamb understood his gesture. To achieve this, Lamb went to Homer G. Balcom (1870–1938), the most prominent consulting structural engineer in America after the First World War.

Lamb, who had studied architecture at the Neo-classically based Ecole des Beaux Arts in Paris, wrote in 1930, *"The day that he [an architect] could sit before his drawing board and make pretty sketches of decidedly uneconomic monuments to himself has gone. His scorn of things "practical" has been replaced by an intense earnestness to make practical necessities ..."* Which was just as well, as the client who had bought the 13-storey Waldorf-Astoria hotel in September 1929 wanted the new building to be ready for business on 31st May 1931, just 20 months later.

The hotel was torn down, piece by piece. Even before the demolition of the Waldorf-Astoria was complete, on 22nd January 1930 excavation for the new building started. Two shifts of 300 men worked day and night to dig through the hard rock in order to make the foundations. On March 17th steel frame construction began. Two hundred and ten steel columns made up the vertical frame. Twelve of these ran the entire height of the building.

The construction of the Empire State Building was a model of efficiency. The builders created various innovations that saved time, money, and man-power. While the outside of the building was being constructed, electricians and plumbers began installing the internal necessities of the building. Timing for each trade to start working was finely tuned. It was like an assembly line of a factory, the only difference being that the assembly line did the moving; the finished product stayed in place.

The project was completed ahead of schedule and under budget. Instead of taking 18 months as anticipated, the construction took just under fifteen. Due to reduced costs during the Depression, the final costs totalled only $24.7 million instead of the estimated $43 million. In September of 1930, only partially finished, the Empire State Building officially became the world's tallest skyscraper. The 1046-foot Chrysler Building, which was completed in May 1930, had held the title for only a few months. When the 85th floor of the Empire State Building was completed, it officially eclipsed its rival. Construction was completed on April 11, 1931, one year and 45 days after it had begun.

JUNE 26   JULY 7   JULY 24   AUGUST 18   SEPTEMBER 7   NOVEMBER 10

Fig. 19.9 Construction of the Empire State Building between June and November 1930

Due the speed of design and construction and economic factors, the Empire State building remains an outstanding example of both the KISS principle and of practicality. However, as most of the office space remained unlet until after the Second World War, only becoming profitable in 1950; it became known as the "Empty State Building". On the other hand, it has become an icon, and a random poll of Americans found it to be their favourite piece of American architecture.

19.7   An unsuccessful structural project

Having defined a successful structural project as one where the design and building processes are carried out efficiently and within time and monetary constraints, clearly an **unsuccessful structural project** is the opposite. A number of such projects have already been described in **Chapter 12**. These include the **Crown Hall** at IIT – see **Fig. 12.27** – The **Phillips Pavilion** – see pages **322** to **324** – the **Sydney Opera House** – see pages **324** to **327** – and the **Pompidou Centre** – see pages **328** to **332**. It could be argued that **Wren's dome** for **St. Paul's Cathedral** came into this category, as his complex design led to various serious problems over the years – see pages **298** to **302**.

But a building that served as a paradigm for modern architecture ignores both the **KISS principle** and **practicality** in almost every aspect of its structural conception, design and construction. It is known as **the Unité d'Habitation** and was designed between 1945 and 1947 and built, in Marseilles, between 1947 and 1952. Its full name is the **unité d'habitation de grandeur conforme**, which translates as 'standard large housing unit.' Basically a 17-storey block of flats, it was designed by Swiss-French architect Le Corbusier, as a prototype for blocks that were to be built all over the world.

The building is 134m long, just over 24m wide and nearly 55m high. There are seventeen storeys, with levels seven and eight used for shops and a hotel. The roof has a running track, a kindergarten and other social facilities. Full length corridors at seven levels give access to apartments and shops. Standardised split-level, L-shaped apartments lie right across the building, with a balcony at either end. Apartments are arranged in opposing pairs, with the entrance at the lower level in one, and at the upper level in the other, with an access corridor at every third level. The whole superstructure sits on a first-floor transfer structure (christened the 'artificial ground'), which served no useful purpose other than to allow the building to be supported on pilotis – these were one of Le Corbusier's *'Five Points of a New Architecture,'* but pilotis are just columns – see page **311**. The basic arrangement of the building is shown in **Fig. 19.10**.

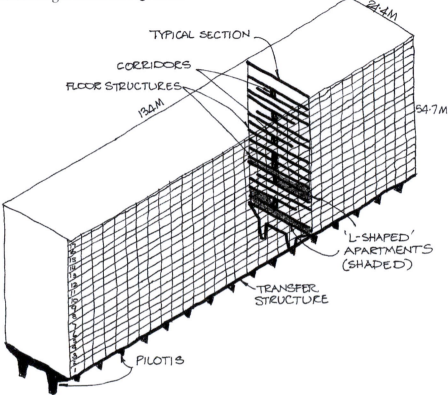

Fig. 19.10 Basic arrangement of the Unité d'Habitation

Above the transfer structure a standard reinforced concrete or a steel frame might be expected, since both were common by 1947. However, there is a confusing arrangement of concrete columns, walls, slabs and beams, together with structural steel and timber floors, block walls, plasterboard-faced timber walls, and over fifty different types of pre-cast concrete units, all with a very low rate of repetition.

The 'L-shaped' apartments are arranged in pairs interlocked around a central corridor. As the apartments have one and half floors, each pair covers three floors, with the central corridor on the middle floor. This three-floor pattern is repeated, more or less, up the building forming a type of **geometric module**. Shown in **Fig. 19.11** is a cross-section through a typical geometric module is shown, together with the floor structures.

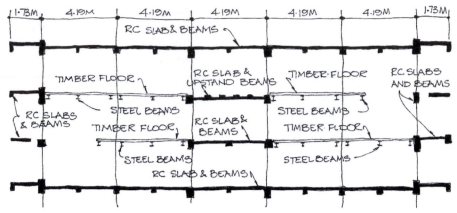

Fig. 19.11 Section through the geometric module

As can been seen, there is little repetition. Each section of reinforced concrete has different size beams and different levels. In several areas, a timber floor is supported on steel beams that are supported on concrete beams that span between columns on the grid lines. In these areas the formwork for the concrete structure had to be supported through two, or three levels, meaning standard equipment could not be used. The steelwork below already constructed concrete floors could not be craned in from above, but had to be manhandled into position. This was made worse by the fact that the steel beams were not connected positively to the concrete beams, but was supposed to sit on lead pads due to a misguided attempt to provide sound insulation.

But there was a lot worse. Above the lines of the pilotis, the vertical structure included two concrete walls, always slow and expensive to build, made more difficult in this case as banks of vertical hot-air heating ducts were cast into the walls. These connected, in a complicated way, to ducts and fans housed inside the transfer structure. The housing of the fans was also complicated – see **Fig. 19.12**.

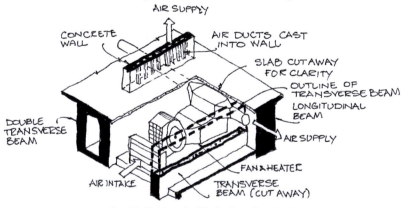

Fig. 19.12 Fans inside the transfer structure

There were many more constructional problems which are explained in detail elsewhere.[4]

As the Unité was supposed to be a prototype it should have been quick to build at a low cost. It failed monumentally at this fundamental level, as the predicted construction period of one year had to be extended to five years, and the initial estimate of 353 million French Francs rose nearly eight times to an estimated 2800 million; no final cost was ever published. Le Corbusier did schemes which included no fewer than sixty-eight Unités, but only five were built; the original, and four heavily-modified copies. Virtually all the 'good ideas' incorporated in the original were abandoned, as none of them turned out to be any good.

The reason that this project was unsuccessful, from almost any constructional point of view, was the **KISS principle** was absent and there was a persistent lack of **practicality**. Nevertheless the building remains an icon for many in the architectural community.

19.8   The architectural/structural conundrum

The architectectural/structural conundrum is explored in some depth in **Chapter 12**, especially in sections **12.3** to **12.8**. In section **12.7 – Engineering fantasy becomes reality**, the problems caused by ill-conceived, architect-led structural concepts are outlined for several high profile projects, and the structural problems encountered in the design of the **Phæno Science Center** show that the conundrum is still unresolved – see **Figs. 12.65** and **18.29**.

The conundrum originated with the two dominant figures of modern architecture; Le Corbusier and Mies van der Rohe, each promoting the architect as a structural designer in slightly different ways. Although Le Corbusier wrote copiously, he wrote little or nothing about structures; he promoted his prowess as a structural designer via his **Dom-ino House project** – see **Fig. 19.13**.

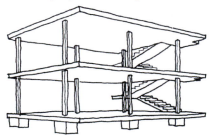

Fig. 19.13 Structure for the Dom-ino House

Le Corbusier was under the impression that he had conceived a radical structure, writing in 1960 that *"Invention of the Domino houses, and a most unexpected invention at the time ... This type of building never found acceptance, either in reconstruction schemes after 1918 or since 1945. It was too new!"*[5] But it was not new, even in 1915, as art historian Eleanor Gregh pointed out in 1979, writing *"The principle of hollow tile and concrete joist construction for producing smooth floor slabs was perfectly orthodox in 1914."*[6]

But the architectural establishment could not get the point, so 99 years later a full-size wooden version of the Domino House structure appeared at the 2014 Architectural Biennale and, according to Brett Steele, the director of the influential AA school of architecture, *"As a project Domino distils modern architecture to a set of guiding, abstract and idealised principles. This is a key reason why the 'afterlife' of Domino can still be seen and felt today, a hundred years later on."*[7]

Mies did it differently. When Mies became a professor of architecture at ITT in 1938, one of the things the students were to learn was '*the advanced expression of structure*', whatever that could mean. This was done by the students making models of structures, which teaches nothing about the behaviour of structures, just how to make models of structures; a completely pointless exercise. Mies van der Rohe also designed buildings that used poorly-conceived steel structures as a major design features, but often they were merely decoration. This can be seen in **Fig. 19.14** where the real structure, the primary structure, is steel encased in concrete, and oversized external I-beam mullions act as a decorative 'structure;' but not according to Mies who, talking about these I-beams claimed rather enigmatically that '*To me structure is something like logic. It is the best way to do things and express them.*'[8]

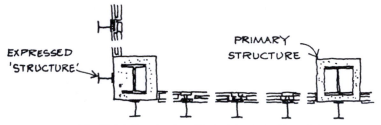

Fig. 19.14 The structure 'like logic' at Lake Shore Drive

Structure was so important to Mies' architecture that Peter Blake (1920-2006) entitled his 1963 paean **Mies van der Rohe: Architecture and Structure**.

In the 1950s, this concern with structures was given new impetus, ironically, **by** structural engineers like Eduardo Torrja who wrote *Philosophy of Structures (1958)* and Pier Luigi Nervi who wrote *Aesthetics and Technology in Building* (1965). These books were not technical in the text-book sense, but were full of written explanations, drawings and of course seductive photos of their structures. Other similar books followed **about** outstanding engineers, like *Candela the Shell Builder (1963)* by Colin Faber, and *Robert Maillart (1969)* by Max Bill. The type of structures that these new engineer-heroes designed, and built, is typified by Nervi's hangar at Oriveto – see **Fig. 19.15.**

Fig. 19.15 A typical engineer-hero structure

Architects' love affair with structures was consummated when Jørn Utzon won the competition for the Sydney Opera House in 1956, with a structurally audacious entry – see **Fig. 12.49**. The saga of the design and construction has been told many times. Most accounts dwell on the many technical difficulties the structural engineers had to overcome, but few note that they were caused by the fact that Utzon had conceived the structure without engineering advice or any basic understanding of structural behaviour. It was like trying to make a square-wheeled bike rideable, a considerable achievement but more suitable for a circus than normal life, with an almost endless succession of square-wheeled-bike structures being designed and built up to the present day.

This is all very strange, as in parallel with this almost wilful refusal by architects to understand basic structural behaviour, there haves been some attempts to reverse this situation. In 1991, a book was published called '*Bridging the Gap*' with the sub-title '*Rethinking the Relationship of Architect and Engineer.*'

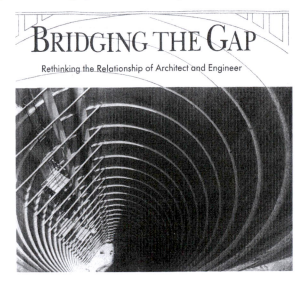

Fig. 19.16 1991 Book cover

The book is based on the proceedings of a symposium held in New York in 1989, where ten engineers and three architects, as the sub-title suggests, tried to rethink the relationship between architects and engineers. Naturally the book is full of platitudes about '*need for greater mutual understanding*', a lot about collaboration and so on, but a number of frank and revealing statements about the problem are sprinkled throughout the text. Statements such as '*students of architecture and of engineering belong to different breeds of the human species,*'[9] or the '*existential differences between the architect and the engineer,*'[10] or '*we try to have architecture and engineering students collaborate. It doesn't work.*'[11] In the end no rethinking was achieved.

In spite of the apparent impossibility of finding common ground, over the years numerous books have appeared with the words **architecture**, **structure** and **art** combined in various ways to produce titles like '**Structure and Architecture**' or '**Structure as Architecture.**' These books are mostly written by engineers, who are often staff members at schools of architecture, and most follow a similar pattern. They are visually attractive, often full of photos of modern architecture which are used as examples to illustrate basic structural principles, though few go as far as explaining how calculations are actually made. The second edition of one written in 2015 still hopes that '*this book will bridge the gap between the two professions*'[12] – which, given it uses the same words as were used twenty-six years previously, is hardly encouraging. This is because the real reasons are never stated. There are basically two. The first is:

- **Architectural education leads architects to think that the understanding of structural behaviour can be gained by looking at photos and drawings of structures.**

This training is not intent on teaching architectural students how structures carry loads, but teaching them to make *'architectural readings of the structures of existing buildings,'* in other words architectural designers see structures in buildings not as something that has a technical function, but something that is merely visible. The superficiality of this approach is demonstrated by the quotations from acclaimed architects Oscar Niemeyer (1907-2012) and Sarah Wigglesworth. In 1988 Niemeyer was asked *'Is your priority the shapes or engineering solutions?'* he replied, perfectly seriously, that *'If shapes are beautiful they will have a function,'*[13] thus showing a complete lack of basic understanding. Architect Sarah Wigglesworth, in 2003, was more straightforward, admitting that *'I am absolutely useless with structures...my approach is totally intuitive,'*[14] as though intuition would work for something that is not understood.

An important subdivision of modern architecture was High-Tech architecture, which flourished in the 1970s and 80s (and still lingers on) mainly in Great Britain, with Richard Rogers and Norman Foster being its leading exponents. This was really a continuation of Mies' concentration on the importance of structure to architecture, but added a penchant for rods, and cables and especially the expression of aesthetically-conceived structural connections. One of the most influential buildings in this style was the Pompidou Centre. With this building it is possible to see the conundrum at work, as its architect, Richard Rogers, at the 1989 *'Bridging the Gap'* symposium claimed that the *'process of construction'* was *'legible to the viewer'* which meant that *'if someone wishes to read the building, he can read the beam and column, the cables, the expression of the forces'.*[15] As the description of the structural behaviour shows – see pages **328 to 331** – the system of forces was, due to its flawed conception, contorted, and reminds once again of engineer Frank Newby's quote; *"I don't think high-tech has made any contribution to the development of structures at all...architects just started using structure as decoration..."*[16] However, Otl Acher (1922 – 1991) who was a graphic designer, clearly agreed with Rogers' assessment of the Pompidou structure, writing *'At the Centre Pompidou, it is a similarly intelligent interplay between the elements of tension and support that makes it the fascinating work it is'.*[17]

And the second point is:

- **Most structural designers, like the population in general, are unsympathetic to modern architecture.**

This may seem contentious, and merely an opinion, but apart from various polls, one of the most interesting validations of this statement was a test carried out in 1987. Architectural students and other students, including engineering students, were shown photos of unfamiliar people and buildings and were asked to rate their attractiveness. The correlation of all student's ratings for the attractiveness of people was very high, but not for the buildings. Amongst the non-architectural students the most-disliked building was the architectural students' second favourite building.

Having used quotations about the Pompidou Centre to support the 'first real reason', it can also be used to support the second. Members of the public who are not enamoured with the Pompidou Centre have nicknamed it the **'Cruise Liner.'** But buried in the May 1977 edition of the prestigious magazine the *Architectural*

Review, which was largely an eulogy to the icon, is the extraordinary statement; *'contemplate what the centres of our cities would be like if they were chiefly composed of buildings of this kind and you would see* **what a repellent fix we would be in**.'[18] (author's emphasis).

So the conundrum produces a new and rather strange definition of the successful project; it is one where the previously used criteria are put into abeyance. No longer is a clear structural concept, that can be built rapidly and economically, valued, but instead, the success of the structural project means that it has the symbolic virtue of 'structural readability' for those with little or no understanding of basic structural behaviour. In many cases, the readable structure is central to building becoming a photogenic modern architectural icon. As any form of technical efficiency or clarity is eschewed, the structural designer, whether sympathetic to the architectural concept or not, seeks solace in overcoming technical difficulties similar to that of making a square-wheeled-bike rideable. This section can be summed up by the CCTV building in Beijing; completed in 2012, the local population have dubbed it '**Big underpants**' or the '**Haemorrhoids**', due to its silhouette being reminiscent of someone caught in a private act – see **Fig. 19.17**.

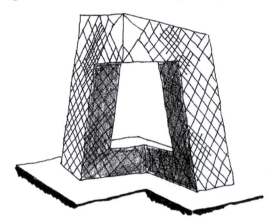

Fig. 19.17 The CCTV building Beijing aka Big Underpants

The lines on the external faces of the building follow the lines of the structure. The structural designer for this building is quoted as saying that '*the structural gymnastics have a purely aesthetic justification*', whereas the architectural designer casually wonders "*Was it merely a landmark, one more alien proposal of meaningless boldness? Was its structural complexity simply irresponsible?*"[19]

Due to the general dissatisfaction with the present situation, and keeping in mind that such master-builders as Nervi and Torroja were engineers, it has been suggested that a new type of master-builder should be found in the engineering community, but there is no obvious answer. As Alan Holgate noted way back in 1986 '*there is little chance that a master builder of the future would be the direct descendant either of engineers or architects,*'[20] and without a cataclysmic event that dislodges the present entrenched positions the arrival of such master-builders seems as far off as ever.

19.9 An ethical structure

Ethics are a human concept concerned with morality and are unlike things like gravity or temperature that are physical entities. So whilst structures are subjected to gravity and temperature how could it be possible to apply the idea of ethics to a structural concept? It could seem far-fetched; however the term ethical is often linked to exploitation, especially with respect to human interaction, so is it unreasonable to consider non-inter-human activities like destroying rain forests or hunting tigers to extinction unethical? Surely not? It is in this context one may seek an ethical dimension in structural concepts. Consider the two ways that the columns shown in **Fig. 19.18** meet the ground; the **column-ground interface**.

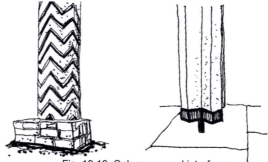

Fig. 19.18 Column ground interface

The column-ground interface of the column shown in **Fig. 19.18L**, which is in Durham Cathedral, follows what one might expect from an understanding of column and ground structural behaviour; that is the ground is unlikely to be as strong as the stone of the column, so as with a pad foundation – see **Figs. 8.23** and **24** – the cross-sectional area required to support the column load is being increased. The column-ground interaction of the column shown on the right, which is in Coventry Cathedral, is the exact opposite. Here, at the column-ground interface, the column cross-section is abruptly reduced to a very small proportion of its original size, wilfully contradicting structural logic. Here, one could posit, structural logic and materials are being exploited for non-structural reasons, maybe even unethically. The column-ground interface was taken to its (il)logical and possibly unethical conclusion by Peter Eisenman (b1932) where in House VI one column in the kitchen hovers over the kitchen table, not even touching the ground.

Whilst Eisenman's column is interior decoration and not a column, as it does not carry any vertical load (except its own weight), the question becomes just because it can be done, is it structurally ethical to do so? Apparently '*many architects profess a longstanding love for the drama of cantilevers*' so buildings frequently cantilever, often unnecessarily it could seem – and - maybe unethically? Zaha Hadid does quite a bit of cantilevering at Issam Fares Institute in Beirut – see **Fig. 19.19**.

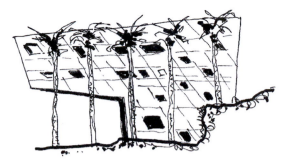
Fig. 19.19 Hadid cantilevering in Beirut

This cantilevering is necessary so that, according to the architect's description, the reading room, conference workshops and research rooms can 'float' above the exterior courtyard.[21] It is clear from the figure that such a building form would not comply with structural conceptual logic, so clearly, like John Stillman, the structural designer was not saying no; but when should a structural designer say no? If it can be done, then should not the answer always be yes? Well, only if the client also wants yes; if the yes is public-funded then the public's view should matter.

Returning yet again to that seminal project the Sydney Opera House, towards the end of the prolonged design period the structural designers presented the architect with two schemes. One was a steel space frame supporting concrete skins top and bottom, and the other was a ribbed arch scheme. The ribbed scheme was thought to be more expensive. That is the one the architect chose, ad he considered it was structurally more 'honest,' a concept that particularly annoyed Ove Arup.[22] On choosing the more expensive scheme, the architect Jørn Utzon is reported to have said '*I don't care what it costs, I don't care what scandal it causes, I don't care how long it takes, but that's what I want*;'[23] and that was the one that got built using public money. Taking into account that Arup thought that it was the '*duty of the engineer to point out that the beautiful structure is rarely the same as the economic structure*,'[24] it is not difficult to see this episode raises some ethical questions.

This is really just another facet of the architectural/structural divide which obviously should not, and should never have existed. It must be unethical for someone to insist on, or actually even contemplate a design of a technical object that is usually far from cheap, in this case the structure of a building, that does not fulfil its function in the most efficient manner. This is not what happens to most technical objects. For instance, styles of cars may come and go, but their technical efficiency increases over time and is not compromised for aesthetic reasons. This is not what happens with building structures which, as has been seen, often have their efficiency compromised for aesthetic reasons. And if this is unethical but is excused by the fact the designer is ignorant of basic concepts, then surely the technically qualified people who aid and abet this behaviour can only be seen as acting in their own interests. This is hardly laudable or hardly environmentally friendly; another unethical dimension.

The irony in all this is that a strong impetus for the new modern architecture, around or just after the First World War, was to take on the aesthetics of technical objects – machines – to adopt a **machine aesthetic**, causing respected architectural writer Reyner Banham (1922-1988) to write of architects in 1920s and 30s that '*they were for allowing technology to run its course...even without having bothered to acquaint themselves* *with it very closely.*[25] So when the architectural community began to champion structural designers such as Nervi and Maillart, who worked without architectural input and produced structures that were all based on engineering and economic efficiency, they could only be seen as visual objects that were to be copied using Niemeyer's maximum *'If shapes are beautiful they will have a function.'* Hence a series of, often disastrous, building structures were built that were unethical from any point of view. A situation that one can only hope will be rectified one day.

19.10 Emotional effects

Most writing about structural design revolves around what are basically technical issues. Little space is given to the emotional effect it has on the people involved. Naturally, for such a responsible task, those involved are often under a lot of pressure, not just to meet deadlines for information, but especially when doubts are raised about the correctness of technical decisions. Because it is not an exact science, something called engineering judgement is often relied upon, and like most judgements these can be good or bad.

When things go catastrophically wrong, the effect on those involved can be extreme. For example Sir Thomas Bouch (1822–80), a British railway engineer, was knighted in 1879 after the successful completion of the first Tay Railway Bridge in 1878. But on 28th December 1879 the bridge collapsed in a storm taking with it a whole train, causing the deaths of 75 people. He died within 18 months of being knighted as his health, already not good, gave way under the shock and distress of mind caused by the disaster.

But some engineers are able to cope with extreme pressures; William LeMessurier (1926 – 2007) who was the engineer for the Citicorp headquarters tower – see **Fig. 15.32 (right)** – when things went horribly wrong. As a result of a question from a student Diane Hartley, LeMessurier realised that the tower had not been designed for the maximum wind-load. During construction, several changes had been made that reduced the strength of the wind-carrying load path. LeMessurier agonized over how to deal with the problem. He approached Citicorp, and persuaded it to repair the building without informing the public. During the night, over a period of three months, 50mm thick steel plates were secretly welded over each of the skyscraper's 200 bolted joints. And this remained a secret for almost 20 years until it was revealed in an article in *The New Yorker* magazine in 1995. After that there was much discussion as to how ethically LeMessurier had acted, but by the time of his death he had been laden with engineering honours.

Engineers who were associated with flawed structural schemes, such as Ove Arup, Peter Rice and Ted Happold, also ended up being widely acclaimed and heaped with honours by the time of their deaths, mainly from the world of architecture rather than that of engineering. There are awards for engineers, but these tend attract little publicity, so if this is what is wanted then the role of a designer of structures is unlikely to be gratifying. But, in general, designing building structures is not a route to fame and acclaim, usually quite the reverse, so satisfaction is gained by rarely acknowledged achievements that bring to the designers of successful structures a private reward. This doesn't suit everyone...

Further reading

Gans, D – **Bridging the Gap** – Van Nostrand Rheinhold – 1991
Alan Holgate – **The Art in Structural Design** – Clarendon Press – 1986

References – Chapter 19

1   Holgate, p27
2   **How good is the 'Back of the Envelope' solution in Stress Analysis**, Institute of Physics, April
     1986.
3   David Messent - **Opera House Act One** – 1997, p386-7
4   Millais, Malcolm – **A critical appraisal of the Unité d'Habitation** – Journal of Architecture
     and Urbanism - Vol 39, Nº2, June 2015.
5   Le Corbusier (1960) – **Creation is a Patient Search** – Praeger - p43
6   Eleanor Gregh – **The Dom-ino Idea** – Oppositions 15/16 1979 – p66
7   http://www.dezeen.com/2014/06/09/le-corbusiers-maison-dom-ino-realised-at-venice-
     architecture-biennale/
8   Puente, Moises – '**Conversations With Mies**'. New York, Princeton Architectural Press –
     2008 - p31
9   Gans – p xiii
10   ibid – p xi
11   ibid – p161
12   Andrew Charleson – **Structure as Architecture** – Routledge – 2015 – p230
13   Building Design 24 June 1988 p22.
14   Larsen, Olga & Tyas, Andy– **Conceptual structural design** – Thomas Telford – 2003 – Case
     Study 1
15   Gans – p148.
16   M Pawley – **The secret life of the engineers** – Blueprint March 1989 – p 36
17   Ackermann, Kurt – **Building for Industry** – Watermark Publications – 1991 – p211
18   Architectural Review, May 1977, p272. No author was given for the article, but the editor
     at the time was Lance Wright.
19   http://designobserver.com/feature/koolhaas-and-his-omnipotent-masters/5337/
20   Holgate – p92.
21   http://www.dezeen.com/2014/06/10/issam-fares-institute-beirut-zaha-hadid/ – project
     description from Zaha Hadid Architects
22   Jones, Peter– **Ove Arup** – Yale University Press – 2006 – p165
23   Murray, Peter – T**he saga of the Sydney Opera House** – Spon Press – 2004 – p31.
24   Jones – p165
25   Banham, Reyner– **Theory and Design in the First Machine Age** – Architectural Press –
     1960 – p329.

Index